# Forgotten Armies

# CHRISTOPHER BAYLY
## AND
## TIM HARPER

# Forgotten Armies
*The Fall of British Asia, 1941–1945*

THE BELKNAP PRESS OF
HARVARD UNIVERSITY PRESS
Cambridge, Massachusetts
2005

First United Kingdom publication in 2004 by Penguin Books Ltd.

Copyright © Christopher Bayly and Tim Harper, 2004

The moral right of the authors has been asserted

Library of Congress Cataloging-in-Publication Data

Bayly, C. A. (Christopher Alan)
Forgotten Armies : the fall of British Asia, 1941–1945 / Christopher Bayly and Tim Harper
p. cm.
Includes bibliographical references and index.
ISBN 0-674-01748-X (cloth)
1. World War, 1939–1945—Asia, Southeastern. 2. Great Britain—Colonies—Asia,
Southeastern—Defenses. 3. Asia, Southeastern—History—20th century. 4. Asia,
Southeastern—Relations—Japan. 5. Japan—Relations—Asia, Southeastern. I. Harper, T. N.
(Timothy Norman), 1965– II. Title

D767.B39 2005
940.54'25—dc22     2004054300

# Contents

# List of Illustrations

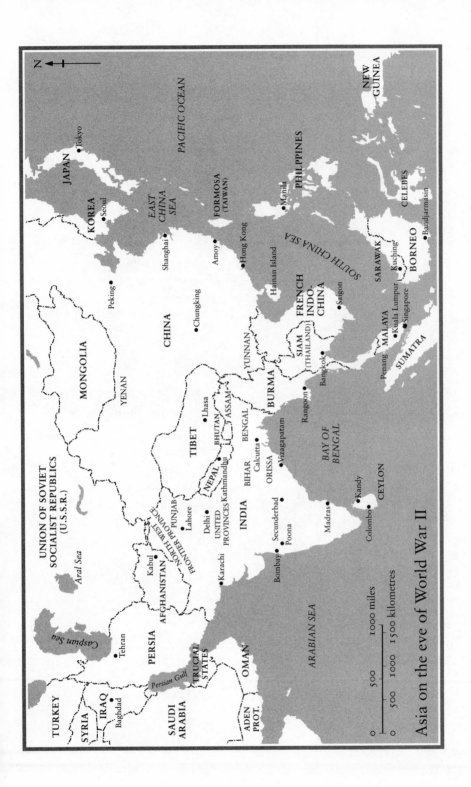

Asia on the eve of World War II

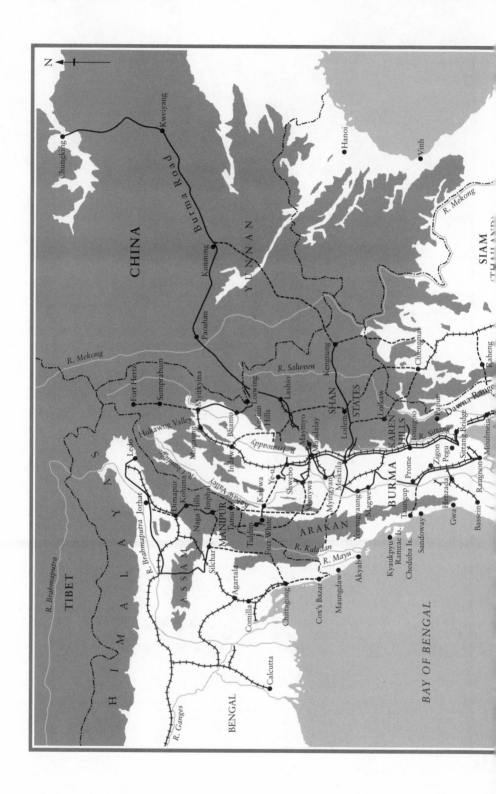

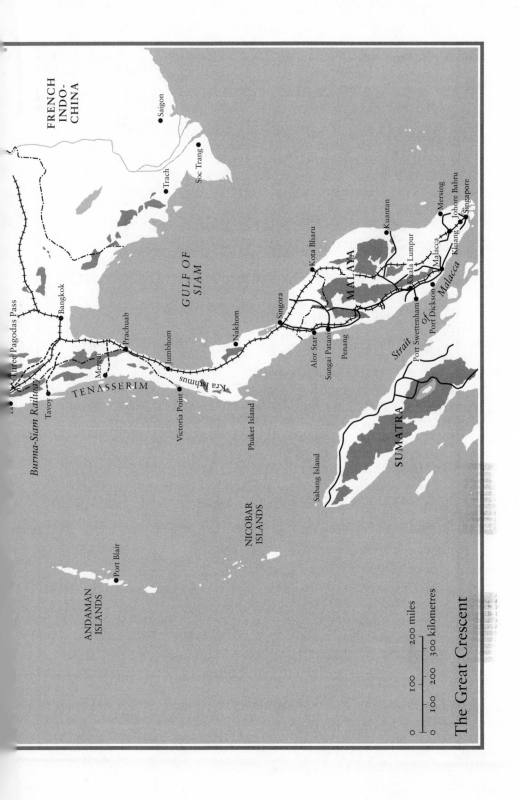

The Great Crescent

FRENCH INDO-CHINA

Saigon

Soc Trang

Trach

GULF OF SIAM

Three Pagodas Pass

Burma-Siam Railway

Bangkok

Prachuab

Tavoy

Mergui

TENASSERIM

Chumbhom

Kra Isthmus

Victoria Point

Phuket Island

Nakhom

Singora

Kota Bharu

Kuantan

MALAYA

Alor Star

Sungai Patani

Penang

Kuala Lumpur

Mersing

Johore Bahru

Singapore

Kluang

Malacca

Port Dickson

Port Swettenham

Strait of Malacca

SUMATRA

Sabang Island

NICOBAR ISLANDS

ANDAMAN ISLANDS

Port Blair

0    100    200 miles

0    100    200    300 kilometres

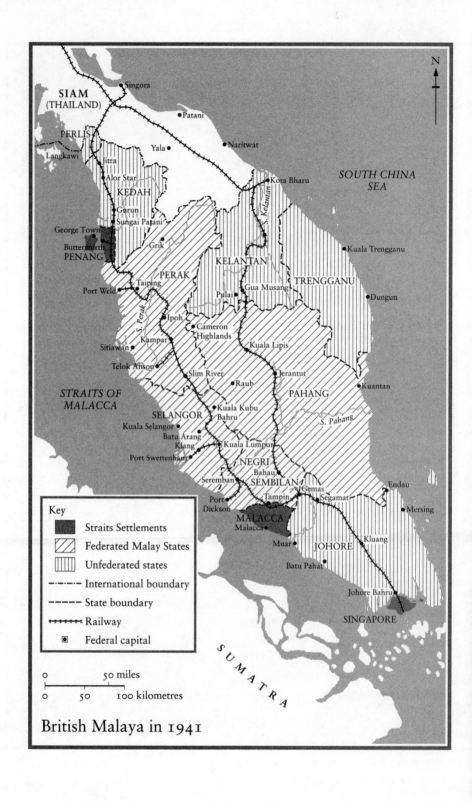

N

SIAM
(THAILAND)

● Singora

● Patani

PERLIS
Langkawi ●
Jitra ●
● Alor Star
KEDAH
● Gurun
Sungai Patani ●

● Yala

● Naritwat

● Kota Bharu

SOUTH CHINA
SEA

George Town
Butterworth
PENANG

● Grik

KELANTAN

S. Kelantan

● Kuala Trengganu

PERAK

Port Weld ● ● Taiping
S. Perak
● Ipoh
● Kampar
Sitiawan ●
Telok Anson ●

● Pulai

● Gua Musang

TRENGGANU

● Dungun

Cameron
Highlands

● Kuala Lipis

STRAITS OF
MALACCA

Slim River ●
● Raub
● Jerantut

● Kuantan

SELANGOR
Kuala Selangor ●
Batu Arang ●
Klang ●
Port Swettenham ●

● Kuala Kubu
Bahru

PAHANG

S. Pahang

● Kuala Lumpur

NEGRI
Bahau ●
SEMBILAN
Seremban ●
Port
Dickson ●
● Tampin

● Endau

● Gemas
● Segamat

● Mersing

MALACCA
Malacca ●

● Muar

JOHORE
● Kluang

● Batu Pahat

● Johore Bahru

SINGAPORE

S U M A T R A

**Key**

| | |
|---|---|
| ▨ | Straits Settlements |
| ▨ | Federated Malay States |
| ▥ | Unfederated states |
| —·—·— | International boundary |
| — — — | State boundary |
| ┼┼┼┼┼ | Railway |
| ◉ | Federal capital |

0      50 miles

0   50    100 kilometres

## British Malaya in 1941

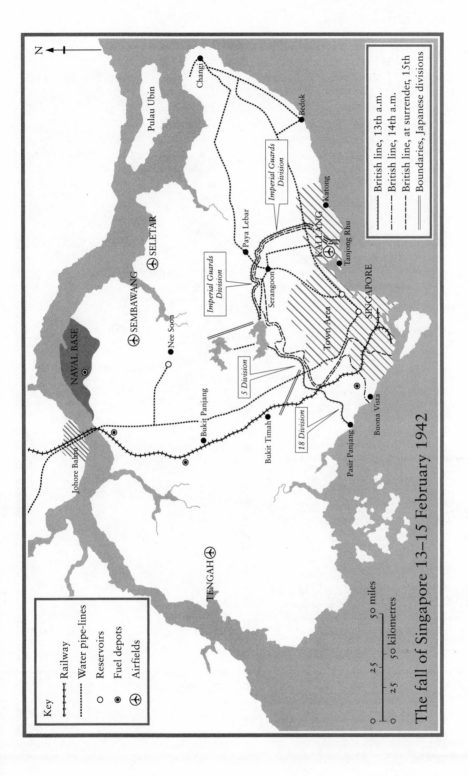

The fall of Singapore 13–15 February 1942

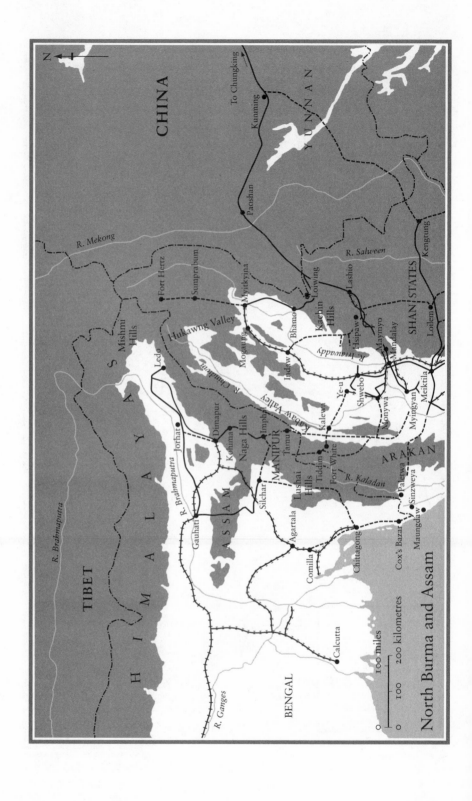

North Burma and Assam

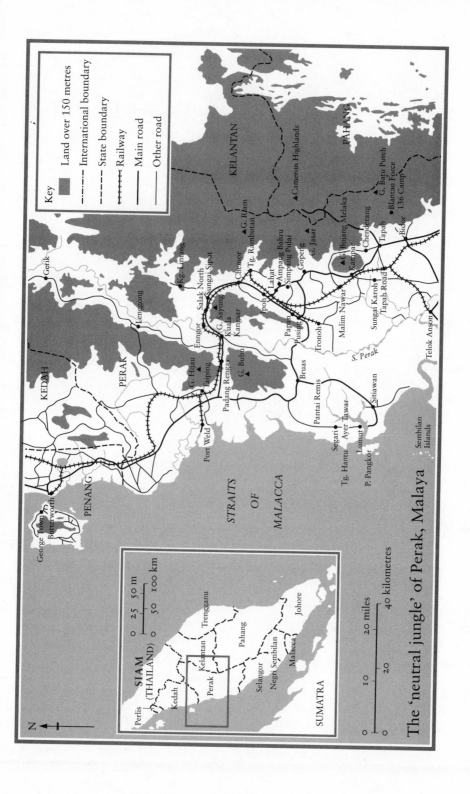

The 'neutral jungle' of Perak, Malaya

# Some Key Characters

**Abdul Razak bin Hussein** (b. 1922). A student at the elite Raffles College in Singapore on eve of fall of Malaya; then worked as an official in his native Pahang, where he secretly aided resistance. Second Prime Minister of Malaysia, 1970–76.

**Amery, Rt Hon., Leopold, MP** (b. 1873). Conservative politician and Secretary of State for India and Burma, 1940–45.

**Auchinleck, General Sir Claude** (b. 1884). Commander North African Front, 1940–42; Commander in Chief India, 1943–7; co-ordinated India base for the Burma campaign.

**Aung San, Thakin or 'Bogyoke' (General)** (b. 1916). Leading Burmese revolutionary; commander of Burma Independence Army, 1942; Minister of Defence under Ba Maw, 1943–5. President of Anti-Fascist People's Front Freedom League. Assassinated 1947.

**Ayer, S. A.** Propaganda and Information Minister in Subhas Bose's Government of Free India; accompanied him on the 1945 campaigns in Burma and wrote *Unto him a witness* after the war.

**Ba Maw** (b. 1893). Lawyer, politician and Prime Minister of Burma, 1937–9. Emerged as main collaborator with Japanese 1942 and became 'Adipadi' (First Man) of independent Burma 1943. Fled to Tokyo, imprisoned by Allies 1945.

**Bennett, Major-General Henry Gordon** (b. 1887). Gallipoli veteran and successful businessman. Commander of Australian Imperial Force in Malaya, 1941–2. Escaped Singapore in controversial circumstances.

**Bose, Rash Behari** (b. 1880 or 1886). Indian radical anti-colonialist; escaped to Japan following 1905–10 radical movement in Bengal; leader of Indian Independence leagues, East and Southeast Asia. Died 1945.

**Bose, Subhas Chandra, or 'Netaji' ('leader')** (b. 1897). Bengali politician and radical leader within Forward Bloc of Congress. Arrested by British 1940, fled to Berlin 1941; took over leadership of Indian National Army and Free India Government 1943. Retreated from Imphal with Japanese 1944; presumed dead in plane crash September 1945.

**Bower, Ursula Graham** (b. 1914). British anthropologist working among the Naga hill people of eastern Assam; helped co-ordinate local resistance; known as 'the Naga Queen'.

**Brooke-Popham, Air Chief Marshal Sir Robert** (b. 1878). Brought from retirement after Governorship of Kenya, 1937–9, to become Commander in Chief, Far East, 1940–41. Replaced by Wavell in January 1942.

**Chapman, F. Spencer** (b. 1907). Well-known author; surveying and film-making in Arctic and Tibet. Appointed to 101 Special Training School in Singapore, and senior 'stay-behind' officer in Malaya until arrival of Force 136. After the war, worked for the Outward Bound Trust and as a schoolmaster. He shot himself in 1973.

**Chennault, Claire** (b. 1890). Commander of American Air Volunteer Group (the 'Flying Tigers') fighting with Chiang Kai Shek against Japanese; leader of the air defence of Burma, 1942.

**Chiang Kai Shek** (b. 1887). Chinese nationalist leader and 'Generalissimo' of Chinese armies fighting Japan since 1936; drawn into fighting in Burma 1942 to keep Burma Road open. Pressed for Allied campaign against Burma 1943–4.

**Chin Peng** (b. 1924). Nom de guerre of Ong Boon Hua. Communist liaison officer with Force 136 in Perak, Malaya. Secretary-general of the Malayan Communist Party, 1947–. Led rebellion against the colonial government in 1948 and became 'the most wanted man in the British Empire'.

**Cocteau, Jean** (b. 1889). French writer and playwright. Visited Malaya and Singapore in 1937. Representative of the many literary travellers who passed through Southeast Asia in the 1930s.

**Cooper, Alfred Duff** (b. 1890). Conservative politician. Secretary of State for War (1935–7) and First Lord of the Admiralty in 1938, when he resigned in protest against the Munich Pact. Chancellor of the Duchy of Lancaster and 'Resident Minister' in Singapore, December 1941–January 1942. Married to socialite Diana Manners (b. 1892).

**Cripps, Sir Richard Stafford** (b. 1889). Labour politician, Leader of House of Commons 1942; visited India to treat with Indian National Congress (the Cripps' mission) 1942; visited India with Labour Government's Cabinet Mission 1946.

**Davis, John** (b. 1910). A policeman in Perak before the war; senior Force 136 officer in Malaya, 1943–5. Afterwards a district officer in Malaya; escorted old comrade Chin Peng to the abortive Baling peace talks in 1955.

**Donnison, Colonel Frank S. V.** (b. 1898). Burmese civil servant, Secretary to Government, 1939–41. Burma Government representative in Delhi, 1942–3. Commissioned, joined Civil Administration Secretariat (Burma) during reconquest, 1944–5, later wrote official history of the war and military administration.

**Dorman-Smith, Sir Reginald** (b. 1899). Governor of Burma 1941–6; escaped from Myitkyina 1942, exiled in Simla, returned as civil Governor of Burma, autumn 1945.

**Fujiwara, Iwaichi** (b. 1908). Japanese intelligence officer; instrumental in formation of the Indian National Army and in liaison with Malay nationalists.

**Furnivall, J. S.** (b. 1878). Retired Burma civil servant and Fabian Socialist, well connected with radical Burmese Thakins; advised on reconstruction of Burma in Simla, 1943–4; returned to Burma after independence as an economic adviser.

**Gandhi, Mohandas Karamchand** (b. 1869). Symbolic head of Indian National Congress; apostle of non-violence. Headed the anti-British

Quit India movement of 1942. Jailed by the British for much of the rest of the war, during which time he staged a hunger strike.

**Haq, Fazlul** (b. 1873). Bengali Muslim political leader. Chief minister Bengal, 1937–43. Blamed by many for inaction as Bengal famine began.

**Hirohito, Showa Emperor of Japan** (b. 1901). Implicated in aggressive Japanese policies in China and Southeast Asia. Remained on throne in 1945, under American tutelage.

**Ho Thean Fook** (b. 1921?). A schoolteacher in Papan, Perak. Recruited to communist underground and the jungle army. After the war he abandoned politics and worked as a bank clerk.

**Ibrahim, Sultan of Johore** (b. 1873). Independently minded sultan of southernmost state of peninsular Malaya; ruled from 1895 until 1959. Friendly to Japan before the war, but stayed aloof from politics during the occupation.

**Ibrahim Yaacob** (b. 1911). Leader of pre-war Kesatuan Melayu Muda who worked with Japanese regime to further Malay independence. Fled to Indonesia in August 1945 and died in Jakarta 1979.

**Iida, Lieutenant-General Shojiro** (b. 1888). Commander of Japanese armies in Burma 1941–3.

**Khin Myo Chit.** Socialist radical, Buddhist and literary figure. Women's official in Ba Maw's government 1943–5; teacher in Rangoon University after war.

**Konoe, Prince Fumimaro** (b. 1891). Right-wing Japanese politician and foreign minister 1940–41, replaced by Tojo. Came to doubt wisdom of assault on Britain and USA. Died 1945.

**Lai Teck** (b. 1900?). The best-known alias of the Vietnamese-born secretary-general of the Malayan Communist Party. Exposed as a British and Japanese agent in 1947; fled to Bangkok, where he was assassinated later the same year.

**Lakshmi Swaminathan** (b. 1914). Madras-born doctor. Settled in Singapore. Led the women's regiment of the Indian National Army, the 'Rani of Jhansi Regiment'.

**Lee Kuan Yew** (b. 1923). A student at Raffles College in Singapore in 1942. Worked as a translator for the Japanese during the war. Prime Minister (1959–90) and later Senior Minister (1990–) of Singapore.

**Lim Bo Seng** (b. 1909). Singapore Kuomintang leader. Recruited agents for SOE in Nationalist China, after the fall of Singapore, and returns undercover with Force 136 to Malaya in late 1943. Died in a Japanese prison in 1944. Canonized as a national martyr in Singapore.

**Lim Boon Keng** (b. 1869). Straits Chinese leader, educator and social reformer. Forced by the Japanese to head an 'Overseas Chinese Association'. Returned to China where he died in 1957.

**Lim Kean Siew** (b. 1922). Son of leading Penang Straits Chinese Lim Chean Ean. A student at Raffles College in Singapore on the eve of the war. Memoirist of the Japanese occupation of Penang. A prominent socialist politician in the 1960s.

**Leyden, John L.** (b. 1904). Burma Frontier Service from 1927. Well connected with Kachins and Chins; involved in covert operations 1942–3. Returned to Frontier Areas Administration 1946.

**Linlithgow, Lord Victor Alexander John Hope** (b. 1887). Viceroy of India, 1936–43, declared war on behalf of India 1939, directed suppression of 1942 Quit India movement.

**Maung Maung, Bo** (b. 1920). Young recruit to Aung San's Burma Independence Army who takes part in the anti-Japanese revolt in 1945 and later career in Burmese military.

**McCall, A. G.** British civil officer working among the Lushai of the eastern Bengal hills; organized the Lushai Total Defence scheme, 1942–3.

**Mountbatten, Admiral Lord Louis** (b. 1900). Supreme Allied Commander, South East Asia Command, 1943–6; rebuilt army morale 1943; assumed overall direction Imphal-Kohima campaign 1944; cultivated relations with Aung San's Burma Defence Army, 1945 and aided its rebellion against the Japanese March 1945. Viceroy of India 1947.

**Mustapha Hussain** (b. 1910). A schoolteacher on the eve of occupation and vice-president of the Kesatuan Melayu Muda; accompanied the Japanese advance to Singapore, but rapidly became disillusioned with them. Wrote a vivid memoir in defence of his reputation.

**Ne Win** (b. 1911). One of 'Thirty Comrades' of Burma Independence Army; military commander of Burmese Defence Forces 1943–5; AFPFL. Later dictator of Burma.

**Nehru, Jawaharlal** (b. 1889). Congress Socialist leader, he favoured the Allies over the Axis, but went to jail following the Quit India movement, 1942; later first Prime Minister of independent India.

**Ng Yeh Lu** (b. 1913). Leading public face of the Malayan Communist Party in 1937–41. Arrested by Japanese 1942–5. Turned away from left-wing politics after 1945.

**Nu, Thakin** (b. 1907). Burmese student activist and devout Buddhist. Minister in Ba Maw's government 1943–5; AFPFL, 1945–6. Became Prime Minister to lead Burmese independence on assassination of Aung San, 1947.

**Onn bin Jaafar, Dato** (b. 1895). Leading Malay of Johore. Worked as a food controller and district officer during the war. In 1946, headed the United Malays National Organization: the first national leader of Malay opinion. Knighted 1953.

**Paw Tun, Sir** (b. 1883). Conservative Arakanese politician. Prime Minister of Burma 1942; exiled to Simla in India with Dorman-Smith. Member of Governor's Executive Council from 1945.

**Pearce, Major-General Sir Charles Frederick** (b. 1892). Governor's Secretary, Burma, 1939. Commissioned into army, became a key figure in Civil Administration Secretariat (Burma) during reconquest, 1943–5. Counsellor to Governor 1946.

**Percival, Lieutenant-General Arthur Ernest** (b. 1897). GOC Malaya Command, 1941. Interned as a prisoner of war and later active in ex-POW associations.

**Purcell, Victor** (b. 1896). Malayan civil servant, and a key figure in planning for post-war Malaya. Returned as adviser on Chinese affairs in 1945. Later critic of post-war policy; historian of the Chinese in Southeast Asia.

**Rudra, Ajit 'Jick'.** Leading soldier in the British Indian army, one of few who held a King's Commission, a key staff officer of Auchinleck, he helped sustain Indian army morale.

**Saw, U** (b. 1900). Minister of Forests, later prime minister of Burma; flew to London 1941 on goodwill mission; imprisoned in Uganda during war for contacting Japanese. Returned Burma 1946; implicated in assassination of Aung San 1947; hanged 1948.

**Shahnawaz Khan.** Punjabi Muslim soldier, from an old military family. Stayed aloof from Mohan Singh's INA, but joined when Subhas Bose took the helm. Fought in Burma. A defendant at the Red Fort Trials; later Congress MP for Meerut.

**Shinozaki, Mamoru** (b. 1910). Pre-war Japanese press attaché in Singapore, convicted of espionage; a leading Japanese civil affairs officer in Singapore, 1942–5. Emerged as a 'protector' of the Chinese and Eurasian communities.

**Singh, Mohan** (b. 1909). Sikh soldier. Recruited by the Fujiwara Kikan to lead the first Indian National Army, but his independent stance led to his removal by the Japanese in December 1942. Detained for the duration of the war. He surrendered to the British in Java in 1945. He joined Congress and was elected to the Rajya Sabha (upper house of Indian parliament).

**Slim, General (later Field Marshal) Sir William** (b. 1891). Commander 1st Burma Corps, 1942, during retreat with Gen. Harold Alexander. Main figure in rebuilding 14th Army and success of its Burma campaigns 1944–5. Commander Allied Land Forces South East Asia, 1945.

**Smith Dun** (b. 1906). Karen military officer who fought with 14th Army in Burma campaign; became commander in chief of Burma's armed forces 1948, but was speedily dismissed.

**Soe, Thakin** (b. 1905). Communist leader, set up 'base area' in Burma

Delta, 1942–5; broke with Anti-Fascist People's Front government and led Red Flag Communists, 1946.

**Suhrawardy, H. S.** (b. 1892). Bengali Muslim politician. Minister of Labour 1937. Minister of Supplies in Bengal Government during 1943 famine.

**Suzuki, Colonel Keiji** (Burmese name Bo Mogyo). Founding member of Minami Kikan organization planning Burmese rising against the British. A leader of the Burma Independence Army, 1942.

**Tan Cheng Lock** (b. 1883). Straits Chinese leader, businessman and legislator. Fled to India on Japanese invasion of Malaya. Figure-head leader of left-wing united front in 1947; founding president of the Malayan Chinese Association in 1949. Knighted 1952.

**Tan Kah Kee** (b. 1874). Leader of the Overseas Chinese; headed the China Relief Fund (1937–41). As Japanese invaded Malaya, British turned to him to organize last-ditch Chinese resistance. Before capitulation, fled to Java, where he spent the rest of the war.

**Tan Malaka** (b. 1897). Sumatra-born Comintern leader. Hiding in Singapore on outbreak of war, and later escaped to Indonesia. Died during the Indonesian revolution in 1949.

**Thein Pe, Myint** (b. 1914). Burmese Communist who escaped to India in 1942; wrote *What Happened in Burma*, an attack on Japanese occupation. Sent to Chungking, China, but maintained links with Burmese resistance to Japanese. Secretary, Burma Communist Party 1945.

**Thomas, Sir T. Shenton** (b. 1879). Governor of Singapore and High Commissioner of the Malay States 1934–42. Detained in Singapore and interned in Taiwan.

**Tin Tut** (b. 1905). Barrister and Burmese member of Indian Civil Service, accompanied U Saw to London, 1941; joined Dorman-Smith in Simla 1942; left ICS and became financial spokesman for AFPFL government. Assassinated 1948.

**Tojo, Hideki** (b. 1884). Japanese military commander and Prime

Minister and Minister of War from 1941–4. Masterminded Greater East Asia plan. Hanged for war crimes 1947.

**Tokugawa, Marquis** (b. 1886). Last of Tokugawa dynasty. Political advisor to Japanese occupying forces in Malaya.

**Tsuji, Masanobu** (b. 1902). Influential Japanese strategist of invasion of Malaya. Leading force behind *sook ching* massacres. Went to ground in Bangkok in August 1945. Escaped war-crimes trials to forge career in politics.

**Tunku Abdul Rahman** (b. 1903). Malay prince of Kedah. Served as a district officer during war. As head of the United Malays National Organization led Malaya to independence in 1957; Prime Minister until 1970.

**Wang Ching Wei** (b. 1883). Japanese puppet ruler in China.

**Wavell, General Sir Archibald** (b. 1883). Supreme Allied Commander South West Pacific. Viceroy of India (1943–6).

**Yamashita, Tomoyuki** (b. 1885). Commander Japanese 25th Army; the 'Tiger of Malaya'. Later served in China and the Philippines. Hanged for war crimes in 1946.

# Preface: The Many 'Forgotten Armies'

'It seemed like the end of everything.' So thought many of the British administrators and civilians who fled precipitately in the face of the stunning Japanese thrust into Malaya and Burma during the 'cold weather' of 1941 and 1942. To the people of Asia the world had been turned upside down. There were few parallels in history to this sudden and dramatic humiliation of an old and complacent supremacy – the British Empire in Asia – by an underrated and even despised enemy. One might have to look as far back as Alexander the Great's lightning destruction of the Persian Empire of Darius to find anything like it. The memory of what Asians saw as abandonment and betrayal by their fleeing white masters in those terrible days of 1942 still lingers amongst the old generation of the former Indian, Malayan and Burmese servants of the British Raj. The ultimate victors forged heroic legends around the later successes of British arms in the Eastern War: Wingate's Chindits, Force 136 in Malaya, Sir William Slim's great victories over the Japanese at Imphal and Kohima in 1944. Yet these events never quite eradicated the bitter sense of humiliation felt by those who witnessed the surrender of the Singapore garrison and the flight of the 'heaven born' civil servants from Malaya and Burma in 1942.

The revolution which took place in the minds of Asians and some, though not all, Europeans was greater even than the political and economic revolutions on the ground. For in reality the British in Asia struggled back from the abyss after that year dependent on the temporary sufferance of Asians. Above all, it was Indian soldiers, civilian labourers and businessmen who made possible the victory of 1945. Their price was the rapid independence of India. Equally, an independent Burmese army controlled much of the countryside into which the British 14th Army stormed in 1944 and '45 after the dramatic rebirth of its military prowess. Its prize, too, was a rapid transition to Burmese self-rule. Even in Malaya where British rule struggled on after 1945 for twelve years, it did so to a significant extent because conservative Chinese and Malays wished to use the British connection as a shield against communist insurgency.

These events are now passing from the memory of the living, and need reassessment for a new generation. This book tells the stories of many soldiers and recounts the great battles and guerrilla campaigns in which they took part. Yet it is not a conventional military history. Innumerable fine histories have been written of the fall of Singapore and the Burma campaign of 1942–5. Dozens of memoirs and web sites tell poignant tales of the sufferings of Allied troops on the Burma–Thailand railway and of conditions inside Changi prison on Singapore island. Instead of retelling these stories, this book is intended to create a panoramic picture of one of the world's most important and populous regions as it was ravaged by the consequences of warfare, nationalist insurgency, disease and famine. The 'forgotten armies' of the title certainly include Britain's 14th, which finally triumphed over neglect in London and Washington, and malaria, monsoon rain and poor morale in the field. They also include the Indian National Army which fought alongside the Japanese to liberate India, but found itself to be the ghost at the feast in Prime Minister Nehru's independent and non-aligned India. The book's forgotten armies also include the Burma Independence Army of Aung San, father of today's Burmese democracy activist, Aung San Suu Kyi, Chin Peng's communist guerrilla army in Malaya and even the huge forces thrown by the Japanese against India in 1942. All deserve this title, though the opening of archives and people's desire to memorialize the history of their nations have begun to renew the historical record.

This book also considers the vast 'armies' of Asian workers who laboured and died in the terrible wartime conditions prevailing in the 'great crescent' of former British territory. For these armies are still forgotten even today. Huge bodies of Indian refugees poured out of Burma into India in 1942. Thousands died in the mud and 'green hell' of the high, forested passes of Manipur and Assam. The Asian labourers who worked and died on the Burma–Thailand railway – men, women and children – perhaps outnumbered the Allied prisoners by more than ten to one. They, too, are largely forgotten. Hundreds of thousands of Indian coolies, tea estate workers and tribal people were thrust by want or the hope of reward into supporting and supplying the Japanese and British armies and associated bodies of guerrilla fighters. These men, women and children also laboured and perished along the high passes of Assam to the north and in the dense jungles of central Malaya to the south. Armies of nurses and doctors – Indian, Chinese, Anglo-Indian and Anglo-Burmese – provided aid and compassion in the midst of fighting which brought the brutalities of the Middle Ages face-to-face with modern mechanized killing. Across the whole region as many as 100,000 women and girls were pressed into service as sex slaves, some by direct compulsion, as with Japan's 'comfort women', and many more by the insidious operation of famine and the 'free market' in the British territories.

This book spans a huge territory from India to Malaya: the heart of the British empire in the East. Of course, 'British Asia' was larger than this. It encompassed Hong Kong and the Treaty Ports of China; there were possessions east of Singapore: the territories of the 'White Rajah' of Sarawak and the British North Borneo Company. The experiences of Hong Kong and Shanghai are central episodes of the war in China; and the fate of British Borneo became interwoven with that of the Netherlands East Indies. But these campaigns lie somewhat outside our story. We focus instead on the connected crescent of land between Calcutta and Singapore: the pivot of the fighting of the Far Eastern war. We do so because this was the territory spanned by the people of these forgotten armies themselves, whose experiences give a unity to our story. Since the immediate post-war years, the historical study of South and Southeast Asia has collapsed into a series of academic specialities and public memory has also fragmented. Burmese history, in particular, has been almost forgotten following the country's retreat into virtual isolation after 1960. The story of India at war from 1939 to 1945 has been pushed to the margins by the telling and retelling of the story of independence and the partition of British India into the republics of India and Pakistan. The memory of war in Malaysia and Singapore is troubled by many events that later national histories have tried to forget, and the full story of the resistance to the Japanese has been obscured by the shadow of the communist insurgency of 1948–60. Above all, it has been forgotten that the histories of these different regions were firmly intertwined, and above all during the Second World War. Japanese commercial communities across the whole region provided an unofficial fifth column for their army's invasion of 1942, for instance. Indian lawyers, businessmen and plantation workers scattered throughout Southeast Asia by decades of migration became recruits to the Japanese sponsored Indian Independence League and the pro-Japanese Indian National Army. Punjabis and Baluchis from the far northwest of Britain's Indian Empire fought in Burma and Malaya under the British flag. The Overseas Chinese too fought Japan in Malaya and, with their financial muscle, in China itself. Japanese armies and their camp followers thrust together into one unit the British, French and Dutch colonies in 1941 and 1942. For some months in 1945, the whole area from the borders of Bengal and Assam almost as far as the Australian Sea was united by the Allies for the first and only time in a single, interconnected administration. The very term 'Southeast Asia' was coined to describe this huge crescent of land. The aim of this book, therefore, is to reassemble and reunite the different, often unfamiliar but connected narratives of these epic events and to put the stories of the great men and the great battles of the period into the context of the histories of ordinary Asian men and women.

In doing so we are conscious of our debt to the many hundreds of powerful memoirs and histories that have been written of the war years in the East. We also recognize the debt we owe to the many people who have carefully written and preserved their memories or have given their papers and their oral testimony to the great public collections in Britain and Asia. These include those in London (the British Library and National Archives; Liddell Hart Centre for War Studies at King's College London; the Imperial War Museum); Cambridge (the Centre of South Asian Studies, Royal Commonwealth Society Collection); Oxford (Rhodes House Library); Southampton University; Singapore (the Singapore National Archives and National Library of Singapore); Malaysia (the Arkib Negara Malaysia and Perpustakaan Universiti Malaya, Kuala Lumpur); and the Netaji

Research Bureau, Calcutta. We are particularly grateful to Dr Kevin Greenbank, Ms Rachel Rowe, Professor Sugata Bose, Dr Susan Bayly, Dr Thant Myint-U, Ms Chua Ai Lin, Dr Katherine Prior, Dr Paul Kratoska, Professor Jomo K. S., Dr Ronald Hyam, Dr Lizzie Collingham, Ms Yeo Seok Lian and to Norman and Collette Harper. Many people in Britain, India, Myanmar, Malaysia and Singapore have helped us elucidate points of detail and while we cannot name them all we are grateful to all of them. This book has its origins in a document-based 'special subject' we taught in the Cambridge History Faculty between 1997 and 2002. We are grateful to the several generations of students who made this an enlightening and enlivening experience.

# Prologue, Part I: Escaping Colonialism

## JAPAN'S ASIAN VISION AND THE COMING OF WAR

Two events in Japan towards the close of 1940 signalled the gathering of the typhoon across Asia. On 4 October the Japanese government announced a three-way military alliance with Nazi Germany and fascist Italy as Hitler's and Mussolini's armies rampaged across Europe and North Africa. Then November witnessed a climax of Japanese nationalistic fervour as the people celebrated what the authorities claimed was the 2,600th anniversary of the foundation of the Japanese Empire. The country was festooned with flags and pictures of Emperor Hirohito. Millions feasted in the streets. Some 50,000 representatives from Japan and all over the world, including members of the Hitler Youth, shouted in unison 'Banzai!', 'a thousand years!' or 'long life!', while 'warships anchored in Tokyo Bay fired salutes; and radio coverage of the joyous event continued throughout the day'.[1] The festivities were repeated across Asia. The 3,000-strong Japanese community in Singapore celebrated with a sports festival, sumo wrestling and an archery tournament. The local Japanese Boy Scout troop turned out on parade.[2] One of the messages promoted in these celebrations was that Japan was leader of the 'Asiatic peoples'. Many Vietnamese, Burmese and Indians resident in Tokyo eagerly participated. Indian organizations, founded to press for India's immediate freedom from British rule, congratulated the emperor. Almost unnoticed, Aung San, a young, taciturn Burmese radical, slipped into Tokyo airport from China the day the festivities drew to a close. The shape of the future great Southeast Asian war was already outlined.

Since their country's spectacular leap forward during the Victorian age, the Japanese devoutly believed that being modern meant being imperialist and Japan's zone of conquest would be the former Chinese Empire. The Japanese regarded China in rather the same way that the previous generation of Britons had regarded France, as a cultural reference point, but a contemptible nation-state. One young nationalist explained it like this: 'America and Britain had been colonizing China for many years. China was a backward nation . . . we felt Japan should go there and use Japanese technology and leadership to make China a better country.'[3] The Great Depression of the 1930s added further economic justifications for aggressive nationalism. Japan needed an easily plundered store of raw materials and already had a client kingdom in Manchukuo, the former Chinese province of Manchuria.[4] But now nationalist China itself was stirring under the leadership of the mercurial Chiang Kai Shek and began to reassert its sovereignty in the north.

In 1937 skirmishes between China and Japan had turned to bloody, all-out war. Japan conquered most of the eastern seaboard of China and brutally suppressed its civilian population. The Japanese military, with Emperor Hirohito firmly at its head, regarded international law as a Western fabrication. Thousands of prisoners of war were summarily executed. The Japanese armies experimented with chemical and biological weapons and carried out what they routinely called 'annihilation campaigns'.[5] The nature of the coming war in Southeast Asia was now clearly signalled, too. Yet the imperial army somehow could not seem to finish the fight. The Chinese forces fell back on the city of Chungking, far inland up the Yangtze river. Chungking sustained continuous aerial bombardment. The British and Americans, who opposed Japanese policies in China, kept the embattled nationalists going with financial support and provisions. Americans saw China as a great future trade partner and President Franklin Roosevelt himself had family business connections in China. Americans applauded the advances that American Christian missions seemed to be making in the country. China would one day be the United States of Asia: prosperous, Christian and free.

Relations between Japan and the USA soon soured further.[6] The USA began to re-equip Chiang's armies. The German invasion of

France in 1940 worsened the outlook further for the Chinese, with Japan seizing French Indo-China and cutting off one major route to Chungking. Yet the British and Americans still managed to supply Chiang along a road which snaked up from Rangoon through the hills into southern China.[7] Day and night, huge quantities of goods and war supplies poured northward as lorries, tail to bumper, strained up through the boom town of Lashio to the Chinese border. This was the famous Burma Road.[8] It remained a lifeline for the Chinese, except for a few months in 1940, when the British authorities panicked and closed it, afraid to antagonize the Japanese while an invasion of mainland Britain seemed imminent. Then came the announcement of the Japanese military pact with Germany and Italy, provoking the British into opening the Burma Road again, to the ill-concealed rage of the Japanese.[9] The British Empire was now firmly in Japanese sights and the Japanese military and foreign office began to cultivate Britain's enemies in Asia with a new vigour.

In the eyes of the outside world Japan seemed secure and powerful. It was allied with the victorious Nazis. Its most dangerous enemy, Soviet Russia, seemed to be reconciled with Germany. Yet Japan's rulers were plagued by anxiety. They believed that their nation had always suffered from diplomatic and political isolation. With American embargoes now being applied to oil and other essential war materials, and with 70 per cent of its budget going on the China war, Japan 'would have to do something or collapse'.[10] By the summer of 1941, when both Britain and Russia were distracted by the war against Germany, Japan's course of action seemed inevitable: the Japanese would have to break out of what they called the 'ABCD encirclement'.[11] The initials referred to America, Britain, China and the Dutch East Indies. By building up a yet bigger empire in Asia, Japan hoped to reinforce its own security. It would finish off the Nationalist Chinese and seize the oil of the Dutch East Indies, the mineral resources and rubber of French Indo-China and British Malaya. It would create a Greater East Asian Co-Prosperity Sphere in which grateful Asian nations would live under the tutelage of Japan and contribute in turn to its material needs. The bluntly named Total War Research Institute in Tokyo buzzed with grandiose plans for conquest.

Japan was not really particularly well placed to fight a war in

Southeast Asia. The army was preoccupied with China and Russia and paid little attention to the region. The powerful Pacific fleet which was soon to strike such a devastating blow against the Americans saw Pearl Harbor as its primary target. But the Foreign Office and some major Japanese firms with overseas interests had been keeping an eye on Southeast Asia for a long time, if only because Chiang and the Chinese nationalists had many wealthy backers in the region. By the mid 1930s there were scores of 'language' and 'foreign affairs' schools throughout Japan specializing in Malay, Burmese, Thai and Indian languages. These schools were really mini military academies. They maintained punishing regimes of sumo wrestling and martial arts along with language instruction.[12] Their ideal was a kind of muscular Buddhism mixed with emperor worship. Right-wing politicians with contacts in the imperial cabinet loved to tour them and make speeches about Japan's manifest destiny as the dominant state in Asia.

One further advantage lay in Japan's pan-Asian diplomacy. Since the 1870s when it began to catch up with the West, other Asian nations had regarded Japan with admiration. In 1904–5, Japan destroyed attacking Russian armies and sunk the Russian imperial navy. It became the first Asian country to defeat a European power for more than a century. Newly born babies in India and Burma were named after the Japanese admirals. Asians 'looked to the east'. In Thailand, which was never a colony of the West, the Japanese imperial revival of the Meiji era had captivated the reforming kings of the Chakri dynasty. King Vajiravudh had expatiated on its example in the Thai press under a pseudonym. Warming to the contemporary racist language, he also denounced the Chinese as 'the Jews of the Orient'. By the 1930s, a significant element within the Thai military elite had embraced the pan-Asian dream. They saw in alliance with Japan the prospect of realizing the goal of a greater Thailand, particularly the recapture of territories which had been lost to the French in Indo-China and to the British in Malaya. Even to Muslims in Britain's Southeast Asian colonies, understanding the Japanese achievement was seen as essential to being modern. One of the earliest Malay descriptions of a 'nation' came from a translation of the Egyptian reformer Mustafa Kamil's travels in Meiji Japan. In 1906, the Singapore journal *Al-Imam* – 'The Preacher' – praised Sultan Abu Bakar of Johore for visiting Japan: 'his heart was filled with the intention to work and to uplift the Malay People to the highest standard possible as . . . the Japanese had done for their people'.[13] His successors kept the connection alive: his son, Sultan Ibrahim, visited Tokyo in 1934, where he was fêted by the aristocracy, and given imperial honours for his protection of Japanese interests in his state.

As anti-colonial movements burgeoned in India and Southeast Asia, radical nationalists flocked to Tokyo. Students from Asian countries eagerly attended courses in the new Japanese universities. They joined anti-colonial debating societies and kept in touch with businessmen from their homelands. Japanese travellers, meanwhile, visited the Buddhist holy places in India, Nepal and Southeast Asia. On the side, some of them were working for Japanese intelligence agencies, relying on contacts made for them by radical young Burmese, Indians or Vietnamese. In the 1930s, as secret societies and paramilitary organizations pushed Japanese politics to the right, they too turned their gaze southwards. The leader of the extreme nationalist Black Dragon Society lent protection to the Indian revolutionary-in-exile Rash Behari Bose, who took a wife with family connections to the Society. The British, French and Dutch colonial intelligence services were aware that something was going on, but by the time they found out what, it was too late.

There was underway no less than a creeping Japanese colonization of Southeast Asia. It is striking in the years before 1941 how much of the region's trade had fallen, almost by stealth, to the Japanese. After the First World War, business strategists toured the region in 'sight-seeing' parties. Spurred on by communities of long-term migrants, enflamed with patriotic purpose, the Japanese colonial government of Taiwan sought to extend its development schemes southwards. Japanese trade and investment in this period is a crucial link in the history of the modern economic dynamism of Southeast Asia. Japanese goods were at the heart of the consumer boom in Malaya in the later 1930s. The closure of American markets in the Depression led Japanese manufacturers to focus their attention on the emerging markets to the south. In 1941, Japanese investments in British Malaya totalled 85 million yen. Japanese firms attempted to corner the market in goods from matchboxes to condensed milk; they imported over half of Malaya's everyday goods. The people of Singapore marvelled at the new technology in a 'Japanese Commercial Museum'. Children in Malaya grew up with toys from the 'ten-cent' stalls on Middle Road in Singapore and elsewhere; the small army of Asian clerks depended on Japanese stores such as Echigoya for the cheap white shirts and ties they were required to wear in European offices.[14] The Japanese were responsible for what was perhaps the most revolutionary innovation within the rural economy of Southeast Asia at this time: the bicycles with which country people could get their own goods to market. In the Blitzkrieg in Malaya in 1941, this technology would be used to devastating effect by General Yamashita's shock troops in a highly mobile form of warfare.

The Japanese had been a prominent feature of the urban landscape of Southeast Asia for many decades. Japanese ships routinely visited the ports; Japanese sailors drank in the bars and cafés, many of which catered especially to their needs. In the early period of Japanese southward enterprise, some of the earliest economic pioneers were the *karayuki-san*, the Japanese prostitutes. The rationale for this was, in the words of one pimp: 'Put a whorehouse anywhere in the wilds of the South Pacific and pretty soon you've a general store to go there with it.'[15] In the face of the 1915 boycott of Japanese businesses by the Chinese in Southeast Asia, it was largely the *karayuki-san* that kept Japanese commerce afloat. After the First World War, Japanese expatriate communities became respectable. But the linkage between sexual servitude and imperial expansion was revived in the 1930s and 1940s. In every small town on the Malay peninsula there were Japanese photographic studios, chemists and taxidermists. Japanese hotels serviced the growing tourist trade. In Singapore, a fleet of 100-odd motorized fishing boats and 1,500 fishermen supplied the larger proportion of the colony's needs. Up until December 1941 Japanese barbers – such as Yamashita Hairdressing, Bishop Street, Penang – were cutting the hair of British and Australian troops. The community had its own schools and newspapers, and its own golf club in Singapore. It came together to fête the Japanese royals who regularly passed through on their way to Europe; it also celebrated British royal coronations and jubilees. Some Japanese men and women married locals, such as Indians resident in Malaya. They also felt the full force of

European racism and the social exclusion of colonial societies.[16] Redress became a key war aim. The strategist Masanobu Tsuji produced a pamphlet to be distributed to the troops on the eve of the greater East Asian war. It was called *Read This Alone – and the War Can Be Won*: 'These white people may expect, from the moment they issue from their mothers' wombs, to be allotted a score or so of natives as their personal slaves. Is this really God's will?'[17]

British intelligence became increasingly alarmed. The leisure outings of photographers, the tours of commercial agents and journalists, all came under close scrutiny. A special Japanese unit of the Singapore Special Branch was set up in the mid-1930s. Was it possible that a co-ordinated espionage network had been laid down? Or were the British merely witnessing the legitimate collection of commercial information: the geologist surveying for minerals; the trawler captain charting dangerous reefs; the cultural attaché fostering international understanding? Yet it was noted that the Japanese were particularly adept in cultivating interests in niches that were neglected by British rule, or where control was weak. The most important Japanese assets were iron mines: by 1928, one mine in the Malay state of Johore produced 40 per cent of Japan's needs of ferrous raw materials. By 1934, it was supplemented by new sources in the backwater east-coast states of Kelantan and Trengganu, and new seams of manganese and bauxite were opening up. The largest mine, at Dungun in Trengganu, employed over 3,000 people: it was practically a state within a state. These mines were tolerated for the wealth they brought in to Malaya: they supplied up to 17 per cent of Kelantan's wealth.[18] The Special Branch began to see sinister designs in the location of these businesses. Many of them were to be found at nodal features of the countryside, such as crossroads, by the railway line and on major promontories. At Pengarang Point, at the southeastern tip of the Malay peninsula, the British had built a large gun emplacement to protect the new naval base on the northeast side of the island of Singapore. Access to the guns, on a short railway line, was through a Japanese rubber estate. The manager, and most of the Japanese staff, had been officers in the Japanese navy.[19] Yet the synergy between patriotism and trade, the often spontaneous information-gathering by Japanese individuals and societies, made any underlying conspiracy hard to expose.

Colonel Suzuki Keiji was one of the men responsible for developing contacts with the graduates of the foreign language schools and radical young Asian expatriates in Tokyo. Officially, he was chief of the Shipping Section of the General Staff Headquarters. This mundane title concealed his real task. This was to develop an offensive strategy in British Asia and ultimately to close the Burma Road.[20] Suzuki was a hard-driving and dynamic officer who was passionate about covert operations. He wanted to enlist the support of radical young nationalists in Burma, Thailand and Vietnam to fight the British. Later described as a Japanese Lawrence of Arabia, Suzuki seems to have been genuinely concerned to help what his countrymen called the 'racial movements' of colonial peoples against their European overlords. The Japanese were heartened that after two centuries of British colonial rule in India and fifty years or more in Burma, a younger generation was clamouring for complete independence. Even in Malaya, politics was heating up.

In the late 1930s Suzuki and a handful of other Japanese with business and diplomatic experience in Southeast Asia established what was effectively a freelance intelligence and subversion service. Working from Bangkok in supposedly neutral Thailand, they developed contacts with radical Indian and Burmese émigrés who were resident there. In May 1940 Suzuki and a colleague slipped incognito into Rangoon where they already had an agent posing as a Buddhist monk. They opened a secret office in Judah Ezekiel Street, Rangoon, in June 1940. The networks they created were to form the basis of the Minami Kikan, the Japanese secret subversion organization, established to advance the cause of Asian independence from colonialism.[21] Ironically, the comparison between Suzuki and Lawrence of Arabia went beyond their common penchant for wearing native clothes and working behind enemy lines. Like Lawrence and his Arab protégés, Suzuki was ultimately to be sidelined by military realists who found that true Burmese independence was incompatible with Japan's strategic aims.

# AUNG SAN'S FAR EASTERN ODYSSEY

For some time, Suzuki and his comrades had been interested in the young radical nationalist party in Burma, the Thakins. The Thakins were mainly recruited from students of Rangoon University and young labour organizers in the docks and oil installations. Their name was an ironic reference to the way the British rulers of Burma insisted on being called 'master' or *thakin*. It was as if Indian nationalists had called themselves *sahibs*. Younger Burmese became more active and more resentful of British rule after 1936. In this year, the British rulers introduced a limited form of local self-government to the country as part of a package to buy off discontent in imperial India, Burma having remained an administrative unit of India until that year. Behind the scenes, the British still tightly controlled Burmese politics. What passed for Burmese 'self-government' was seen by younger nationalists as an orgy of patronage and profiteering, with lawyers-turned-politicians, such as the pre-war premiers, U Saw and Dr Ba Maw, feathering their own nests. European and Indian schoolmasters and university dons controlled the studies of young Burmese as if they were in an infants' school. Though the British later denounced them as 'quislings' and 'fascists', there was no real ideological link between the Thakins and the Japanese imperialists. These young Burmese men and women had grown up on a heady diet of Left Book Club tracts and Sinn Fein propaganda. Much of this they read in the small bookshop set up in Scott Market, Rangoon, with the help of a retired left-wing British official, J. S. Furnivall. There was an electric atmosphere among Burmese youth in Rangoon during the last years before the outbreak of war. A prolonged student strike took place in 1936. Activists camped for two and a half months around the great Shwedagon pagoda, the glittering, gold-leafed temple which dominates Rangoon. Industrial trouble also rumbled on throughout the immediate pre-war years. In 1938 Thakins took a prominent role in a wave of anti-Indian rioting which convulsed Rangoon. Many Burmese regarded the Indians who had settled among them as unscrupulous opportunists looting their country on the coat tails of the British.

For their part, the British authorities detested the Thakins. They regarded them as a bunch of bazaar toughs, rickshaw pullers and student agitators. Their response to demonstrations was the well-tried Indian Empire tactic of multiple *lathi*-charges on unarmed demonstrating crowds. The *lathi* was a heavy, metal-shod bamboo cane capable of causing crippling injuries and occasionally death. From time to time when the crowds got really out of hand, the police fired live rounds at them. As the European war broke out in 1939 the Thakin radicals were put under heavy surveillance. The older nationalist politician and former prime minister, Dr Ba Maw, who had long been making clandestine overtures to the Japanese, was eventually jailed. Initially, though, the Thakins were regarded as too young and inexperienced to cause serious trouble.

Domestic and religious life was hardly better in the eyes of young people. To them, the Buddhist priesthood was hidebound and obsessed with its rituals of bells and incense. Parents told their children to be patient. Khin Myo Chit, a young intellectual who later wrote a moving memoir of the war, remembered her irritation. Girls should stay at home, she was told. Boys should be dutiful. If the British still ruled, it was because of the bad karma of the Burmese.[22] They deserved their enslavement and would simply have to wait until the colonialists granted independence from the goodness of their hearts. An alternative, or in many places a complement, to joining the Thakins was religious fervour. Some joined 'protestant' Buddhist movements. Khin Myo Chit remembered one pre-war Buddhist puritan who advised young women to give up their colourful jackets and dress in plain brown garb to signal their renunciation of worldly pleasures. This attack on 'luxurious' clothes did not last very long. Brown satin and silk jackets and blouses soon became fashionable items of dress to be worn at parties and *pwes* or dramatic performances, she noted wryly.[23] Others were more resolute. Thakin Tun, later leader of one of Burma's communist parties, became a steely enemy both of the monks and of British and Indian businessmen. By contrast, Thakin Nu, who was to become Burma's first independent prime minister ten years later, struggled to keep the Buddha's precepts in the midst of a raunchy student life.[24] A lot of students boycotted British produce, along the lines of contemporary Indian nationalists. Some went as far as giving up cheroots which were produced by British companies. These experiences of frustration and political activism were to be critical to the formation of the minds of independent Burma's first leaders.

There was also a harder, more military edge to all of this. As war drew nearer, some young people became convinced that only revolutionary resistance to the British would resolve Burma's problems. The Burmese needed to form a subterranean resistance movement. They needed to train secretly and regain their long-lost military tradition. Even if the British army in Burma was a poor thing with almost no connection to the ordinary Burmese, the radicals knew that any Burmese independence army would need outside help. But from where would this come? Most Thakins were just as hostile to what they saw as Japanese imperialism as the China war escalated. Thakin Nu published *Secret Agent of Japan*, an account of Japanese atrocities in Korea and China. In reality, Thakins had more in common with Chinese nationalists or Chinese communists than with Japanese militarists.

Yet England's difficulty was Burma's opportunity, as many glibly repeated. The violent suppression of the agitations of 1938 and an anti-war movement in 1939 further embittered young Burmese. They would now accept help from any quarter, even one as suspect as the Japanese Empire. Their Indian communist mentors warned the young Burmese against Japanese 'fascism'. But Burmese communists and socialist Thakins together with members of Ba Maw's group founded a clandestine National Revolutionary Party. This shadowy organization began to plan for a Burmese army of independence on the model of the Irish Republican Army of the 1910s. Its leadership aimed to build a force in the inaccessible parts of Thailand close to the Burmese border, finding recruits amongst the many local Burmese expatriates and Shan or Thai people, who maintained contact with their kinsmen inside Burma. This force was then to invade the long southern peninsular area of Burma called Tenasserim. Significantly, the plan quite closely resembled the one Suzuki and his agents were hatching in Bangkok and Tokyo.

Aung San was the most distinctive and in some ways the oddest of the young Burmese nationalists.[25] He was the son of a small-town lawyer from the Magwe district on the Irrawaddy river, south of Mandalay. Aung San was a much rougher diamond than his sophisticated college contemporaries from Rangoon and Mandalay. He had none of their fluency in spoken or written English and often appeared taciturn and shy, though he was capable of breaking into long, rambling political speeches. Educated in a local school run by a nationalist foundation rather than a posh Rangoon establishment, he thought of himself as a countryman. Though he sometimes quoted chunks of Karl Marx, his real heroes were Abraham Lincoln and Benito Juarez, the nineteenth-century Mexican revolutionary. He learned a lot about them from Hollywood films. Booed in the Rangoon student union debates for his execrable English and propensity to rant, Aung San spent hours memorizing and reciting the speeches to parliament of British orators such as Edmund Burke. Despite his small size, moodiness and various obsessions, he impressed all his contemporaries with his intensity and directness. He was exactly what he seemed, a passionate nationalist with little concern for his own appearance, future career or even security. Like so many Indian nationalist leaders, he withdrew from the civil-service examinations. This allowed him to spend yet more time on student politics as political tension grew with the approach of war. In 1939 and 1940 Aung San played an increasingly dangerous game with the British authorities. He toured Burma and India, speaking to students, nationalist associations and farmers. His speeches became more and more radical. In June 1940 he finally irritated the British censors once too often and an arrest warrant was issued against him. Rather than joining his colleagues and Ba Maw in jail, he went underground. His resentment of the British intensified when they placed a mere Rs5 reward on his head. He remarked that this was 'about the price of a fair sized chicken'.[26]

Still uncertain of his destination or of the identity of his future allies, Aung San was smuggled out of Rangoon by his associates on a tramp steamer bound for the Chinese port of Amoy. He left at the time when the Luftwaffe intensified the Battle of Britain.[27] Aung San spent fruitless weeks waiting for word from the Chinese communists.[28] Then, in November, an emissary of Suzuki contacted him. By now Suzuki's plan of creating a Burmese nationalist fighting force was taking shape. The Japanese flew Aung San to Tokyo. On 12 November 1940, Suzuki and Aung San met for the first time on the tarmac of Tokyo airport. The young Burmese was just in time to attend the imperial anniversary celebrations. Like his Japanese hosts, he bowed to the imperial palace on that auspicious day. But he already had nagging doubts about Japanese commitment to Burmese freedom and their methods of war. As a socialist, he instinctively distrusted monarchies.[29]

As 1941 approached, events moved quickly. War in the Pacific and Southeast Asia seemed imminent. Aung San along with other young nationalists and their Japanese collaborators planned to enter Burma and smuggle out a small group of young radicals. These were to be trained by the Japanese to become the core of the Burma Independence Army. A Tokyo dentist fitted Aung San with a set of false teeth to conceal his identity for his clandestine return to Burma. A photograph of him has survived from this period. He looks like a chipmunk, but is still recognizably Aung San.[30] This disguise was enough, however, to put British intelligence off the scent. He reached Rangoon on 3 March 1941. Over the next three months the Minami Kikan organization smuggled out thirty young men from Burma. These were to be the famous Thirty Comrades, the Knights of the Round Table of Burmese independence and its evergreen heroes. They passed through Bangkok and arrived at a naval base on the Japanese-occupied island of Hainan.

During the second half of 1941, as the international situation reached crisis point, the young Burmese were put through a rigorous regime of military training by the Japanese, first in Hainan and later in Taiwan. Then they returned to Bangkok at the very point when the Japanese air force assaulted Pearl Harbor. On 31 December, as Rangoon was itself recovering from ferocious Japanese bombing, the Thirty Comrades enacted a ritual of loyalty at Aung San's lodgings in Bangkok. They mixed their blood in a silver bowl and took it in turns to drink.[31] By now Aung San had given Suzuki Keiji a Burmese name: Bo Mogyo, or 'Thunderbolt'. This was a reference to an old prophecy that was believed to mean that British rule in Burma would one day be destroyed by a bolt of lightning.

Whatever the military record of the Burma Independence Army, its symbolic significance was incalculable. The once proud Burmese military tradition, battered by defeat at British hands in 1824 and 1852, had finally been snuffed out in 1886 when the remainder of the country was occupied. Under British rule, the Burmese forces were predominantly drawn from the peoples of the northern hills or from resident Indians, Gurkhas and Anglo-Burmans. Yet, at a stroke, Suzuki, Aung San, Ne Win and the others had recreated Burma's military lineage. In both Europe and Asia in the 1930s and '40s, parade-ground nationalism was in the ascendant. Being a nation meant having an army. Yet there were unresolved questions. The Japanese army had taken over control of this operation from the navy. Its track record in China and Manchukuo hardly inspired confidence. How much independence would be given to local peoples in the event of a land war in Southeast Asia? Would Suzuki remain in control on the Japanese side? What precisely did Japanese commanders mean when they promised to fight for Burma's independence?

To have any hope of success against the British in what was expected to be a long war, the Burmese now knew that Japanese help was essential. The Japanese had long planned to guarantee air cover during the invasion of Tenasserim by Burmese patriotic forces and provide an auxiliary land force. The Japanese expected to concentrate their own attack on the Burma Road, which they were desperate to close. Though the Burma Independence Army was to be initially under Japanese command, as soon as Tenasserim was occupied the Japanese government would recognize the independence of the new Burmese state. There was a good deal of vagueness and wishful thinking on the part of both parties to this agreement and the Burmese were aware that Japanese policy-making was haphazard and faction ridden.

For the time being, though, the Burmese stifled their doubts and played along. Thein Pe, a communist, wrote of the 'political naiveté and amateurishness' of the Burmese leadership, but he also recognized that what he called 'fascist race theory' was having its effect in his country. People were dreaming of the old Burmese kings and dynasty founders. They warmed to the Japanese slogans of 'We Burmans', 'We Buddhists', 'Asia for the Asiatics' and 'Co-Prosperity', forgetting that the Japanese Buddhist Asiastics had been ruthlessly carrying out a sanguinary and predatory war of extermination on the Asiatic soil of China.[32] A covert wave of pro-Japanese sentiment in Mandalay and Rangoon gave the Minami Kikan organization a green light to go ahead and build up a branch within Burma. This ensured an ecstatic reception for the BIA when it finally entered the country.

# 'SIGNOR MAZZOTTA' FLEES
# TO BERLIN

Japanese propaganda and intelligence activities in India, Nepal and Ceylon could hardly be said to have been vigorous or co-ordinated. Yet the subversion of British India, as part of a Japanese effort to drive colonial power from Asia, had become a more and more plausible aim to their policy-makers as Indian troops were drafted into the European and Middle Eastern war after 1939. So unpopular was the Raj in many quarters in the subcontinent that Japan's operatives did occasionally hit lucky. The Japanese consulate in Calcutta had been a centre of espionage and clandestine contacts since 1936. The record suggests that both Japanese espionage and British counter-measures were pretty amateurish. They involved night-time sleuthing and the kind of surveillance of sinister Japanese doctors and German landladies reminiscent of *The Thirty-nine Steps*. Appropriately, the German vice consul at the centre of this web was Baron von Richthofen, a nephew of the First World War air ace. On one occasion British intelligence noted that the Japanese consul was seen visiting an all-Japanese brothel while his wife waited patiently outside in an official car.[33] One good subterfuge in India, as in Burma, was to use international Buddhism as a cover. Large numbers of monks came from Japan every year to visit the sites of the Buddha's life in northern India and the holy cities of Benares and Gaya, where the Buddha had found enlightenment. In this guise, Japanese agents made contact with Indian radicals.

Particular targets of the Japanese intelligence agencies were the recruiting areas for the Indian army.[34] They could not expect to do much among the fiercely monotheistic Muslim military families of the North West Frontier, but there were many links between Nepali Buddhists and the Hindu Gurkha soldiers who were such a critical element of the British Indian army. In the late 1930s a Bengali religious radical, Swami Satyanand Puri of the Hindu Mission in Calcutta, had helped a member of the Japanese legation to visit Kathmandu, the Nepalese capital, on a religious pretext. Besides being a political radical, Satyanand was a trustee of nearly all of the Japanese Buddhist temples in India. Japanese interests in Nepal's cobalt mines provided another cover. At this point there was much dissatisfaction in Nepal with the rule of the hereditary prime ministers of the state, the Ranas, who seemed to be milking the country for their own profit. This worried the British because it was the Ranas, above all, who had an interest in keeping recruits flowing to the British forces. Military pay provided the impoverished families of the high valleys with some income with which they could pay their taxes to Kathmandu.

Japanese attempts to muscle in on the Great Game in the Himalayas do not seem to have borne a great deal of fruit. Rather more promising as targets of their persuasion were India's angry nationalists, especially Bengalis. Indians had been particularly struck by the rise of Japan. At the time of her defeat of Russia in 1905, Indian nationalists in Bengal, the political bellwether of the country, launched a campaign of resistance and terrorism against the British authorities. Some of the first generation of Indian revolutionary nationalists, such as Rash Behari Bose, had fled to Tokyo and had helped spread anti-British propaganda amongst the Indian students who went to Japan's technical universities. Like the Burmese, though, the Indians had their doubts about Japan.

Subhas Chandra Bose was the Cambridge-educated leader of the most radical nationalist group outside the Indian Communist Party, the Forward Bloc. This was a pressure group within the Indian National Congress, which remained the only credible nationalist organization. Subhas Bose was a powerful speaker and a charismatic political leader. Stung by racism, he had cast aside a career in British service for national politics and long terms in jail. For all that, he was something of a misfit in the circles of more cautious politicians in the Congress. Japanese agents in Calcutta, the capital of Bengal, had contacted him a few years earlier. He admired the Japanese for their rejection of Western tutelage and their hostility to the British Empire. Yet he also deplored Japan's aggressive and militaristic policy in China. Bose asked why Japan's renaissance could not have been achieved 'without Imperialism, without dismembering the Chinese republic, without humiliating another proud, cultured and ancient race'.[35] When he was not in British prisons, Bose had spent much time in Europe during the 1930s, meeting opponents of British policy. He visited Eamon de Valera and the radical Irish nationalists. He professed admiration for Mussolini and had met

Nazi leaders, though he harboured some reservations about the latter regime in particular.

The Calcutta in which Bose lived in 1940 was not yet a city at war. The press carried stories about 'Life in the Indian navy'. There were endless, officially inspired features on Britain's gallant mobilization. *The Battle of the River Plate* was playing at the Lighthouse Cinema. Indians were more interested in the music festival at 'Ganesh talkies' and Ranjit's forthcoming movie melodrama, *Holi*. In 1940, though, Indian politics was on a knife-edge. As in Burma after 1936, where limited self government had led to political paralysis, nationalist unity was submerged in a tide of patronage and intercommunal antipathy. The heady days of Gandhi's great campaigns of the Depression era appeared to be over but, as usual, British policy was calculated to stir everything up again. In 1939 the viceroy declared war on India's behalf without consulting Indian politicians. Outrage at this decision did not immediately spark a new civil disobedience movement. Mahatma Gandhi and Jawaharlal Nehru, the two dominant leaders of the Congress, counselled caution. Even in India's most volatile and politically sophisticated province, Bengal, many nationalists seemed inclined to give the British time. They insisted that India 'should be regarded as an independent nation' with a universal franchise. Only then would it successfully mobilize for war as Britain's partner.[36] Peaceful persuasion, individual resistance, rather than confrontation seemed the best course. Bose, however, demanded an immediate civil disobedience movement against the British, even though it was a time of war. Gandhi was horrified by the prospect of a major campaign. It would lead to 'anarchy and red ruin', he said.[37] Bose, who had been elected president of the Congress against Gandhi's wishes, was forced to resign.

As Indian protest was stifled by wartime regulations, Bose decided to polarize the situation. He began by rallying discontented students and farmers across the country into his Forward Bloc of radical politicians. He needed to build opposition around a symbolic issue of the sort that Gandhi was able to spot so brilliantly. The one he chose says a lot about Bengali politics at the end of the 1930s. In the summer of 1940 Bose began a movement to demolish the so-called Holwell Monument in Calcutta.[38] This unprepossessing obelisk had been erected to commemorate the British garrison and residents who died

17

in the infamous Black Hole of Calcutta in 1756. Indian nationalists found the monument offensive because the villain of the piece was Siraj-ud Daulah. This prince, who had incarcerated the British in the Black Hole, had been the last independent ruler of Bengal. Nationalists asked why there was no memorial to the thousands who had died at the hands of the British over the years.

Muslims dominated the Bengal ministry, which was elected on a limited franchise under the terms of the 1935 Reforms. The chief minister of the province, Fazlul Haq, was a wheeler-dealer sort of politician who made much of his Bengali Muslim patriotism. At a stroke, Bose was able to outflank the conservatives of the ruling party by lauding the long-dead Siraj-ud Daulah as a great Muslim Bengali patriot. The ministers shamefacedly agreed to demolish the monument, but local British opinion was outraged and the governor exerted pressure behind the scenes. On 1 July 1940 Subhas Bose decided to force the issue. He organized a huge demonstration for the next day. Fearing wider disturbances, the authorities arrested him under the Defence of India Act and carted him off to the Presidency Gaol.[39] By this time, the prison had become virtually a home from home for Bengali political leaders.

There followed an avalanche of protest. Non-violent demonstrators courted arrest and were clubbed by the police. Huge crowds gathered at the town hall for a commemoration meeting in honour of Siraj-ud Daulah. The Bengal Legislative Assembly went into spasm, with congressmen arguing that the Black Hole story was invented by the colonialists. Fazlul Haq shed crocodile tears about his 'great grief and sorrow over the arrest of Bose'.[40] Meanwhile, the permanently inflamed British Calcutta press accused Bose of being a stooge of Hitler, a serious charge in the very weeks when Nazi troops were marching into Paris.

As he whiled away his days in jail, Bose formed a new plan. France had fallen. Japan was poised to strike. Finally, the conditions for India's freedom seemed to be beginning to take shape. He needed to make contact with Britain's enemies quickly and obviously could not do this in the Presidency Gaol. In late November 1940 Bose began a hunger strike. As his health weakened, the British, who were still playing by 'gentleman's rules', allowed him to return to his home on

Elgin Road. On the night of 16 January 1941 Subhas and his young nephew, Sisir Kumar Bose, quietly left the family house under the noses of a dozen dozey CID snoopers.[41] Uncle and nephew drove north in the family car.

A few weeks later, Bose surfaced in Kabul, where he made contact with the German legation. Using the alias Orlando Mazzotta, Bose passed through Moscow, now allied with Hitler. He arrived in Berlin during the first week of April 1941. Initially, the German establishment was unsure of what to do with the Indian nationalist who had suddenly arrived at their door. Bose, however, made contact with the Foreign Ministry through a German aristocrat, Adam von Trott, who had been educated at Balliol College Oxford. In due course the Germans decided to give Bose charge of a unit called Hitler's Indian Legion. This was a group of anti-colonial Indian prisoners of war captured by German forces in the western desert. Subhas Bose now had his army. Yet he remained restless and apprehensive. He was on the wrong side of the world. In that hot Berlin summer of 1941, there was one other looming event that was ultimately to unravel the whole of his plan for Indian independence. Hitler was on the point of invading the Soviet Union, the decision that was ultimately to ensure the defeat of the Axis powers.

## MR TAN KAH KEE VISITS MAO

For over three years before these events a large section of Southeast Asian society had already been at war with Japan. China, ever since Japan's first extortionate '21 Demands' in 1915, had looked to its communities in the south, in the Nanyang ('southern seas') for moral and financial support. Leaders of clan associations in Southeast Asia organized boycotts of Japanese goods and shops. This introduced a new turbulence to the politics of colonies such as Malaya and Singapore, where the largest concentration of Overseas Chinese was to be found: over 2.3 million in 1941. 'Anti-enemy backing-up societies' mobilized the strong arm of the Triads to enforce the campaigns. As Japan swept across China in July 1937, it was clear to the Chinese in Malaya that responsibility for national salvation rested upon them. Trishaw riders, stevedores and shopkeepers formed spontaneous 'mosquito' relief-fund committees. The new campaign was on an unprecedented scale.

At the centre of this whirl of activity was the unlikely figure of Tan Kah Kee, a sixty-seven-year-old tycoon and philanthropist. The 'Henry Ford of Malaya' was born in Fukien province in China, near Amoy. He had made his fortune from rubber plantations and his interests extended right across the region to Thailand, Indonesia and the Philippines. His business empire had collapsed in 1934, but his prestige survived this embarrassment. He was the only private individual in China to found a university: in his home region at Amoy. He was a leading member of the Singapore Chinese Chamber of Commerce, of dialect and clan associations, and he used as his base of operations a 'millionaires' club' in Singapore, the Ee Hoe Hean Club. Tan Kah Kee was the Nanyang dream incarnate: the hard toil of the pioneer had been rewarded with wealth, respectability and even a measure of acceptance by the British. Like many leading men of the *towkay*, or business, class, Tan Kah Kee exercised power through a matrix of traditional associations. But he did so on a uniquely grand scale, and his vision reached beyond this, to the creation of a unified Overseas Chinese community, that transcended clan and regional loyalties. In 1937 he headed the China Relief Fund, which became the greatest political undertaking of the Overseas Chinese and the only mass political movement in pre-war Malaya. For a brief period, it brought together the largest political organization in Malaya, the Kuomintang, with the most radical, the Malayan Communist Party. This was a mirror of the fragile alliance that had been formed between right and left on the Chinese mainland.

Tan Kah Kee's view of the world was transformed by his own return visit to China in December 1939, his first since 1919. He flew over the 'hump' from Rangoon to Chungking. He found the new capital of China to be a brash, decadent and corrupt place. He was appalled by the cultural chaos he found. The survival of Manchu dress amongst the men contrasted with the painted faces, the clinging *cheongsams* and high heels of the women. He deplored the fact that, at a time of national emergency, $80,000 had been allocated for the entertainment of his mission. He was received by Generalissimo Chiang Kai Shek at a lavish, European-style banquet. He grilled a journalist from a

Singapore newspaper on conditions at the front and was told that 'the front-line was tense in battle, the back-line was tense in pleasure-seeking'. In the face of obstruction by Kuomintang officials, he determined to leave Nationalist-held territory and make the arduous overland journey to visit the communist redoubt of Yenan in the north. There he spent nine days in a spartan guest house in a converted cave. Southeast Asian Chinese who had made their way to Yenan to serve the patriotic resistance welcomed him. Mao Zedong received him on equal terms, in a simple room. They dined together informally in the guest house, and Tan noted that none of the other guests bowed to Mao. 'I then realized that this was the new system of equality with no class distinction'. Like many travellers from Chungking to Yenan, Tan Kah Kee was deeply affected by the contrast between the two Chinas. By now he saw the Kuomintang leaders as 'wild adventurers with wild ambitions'.[42] He admired the austerity and social commitment of the Yenan experiment and was moved by Mao's personal modesty. He came to the conclusion that Chiang Kai Shek was a leader who was incapable of uniting the Chinese nation. In the final reckoning, Mao would prevail.

Tan Kah Kee made his return journey in March 1940, this time overland across the Yunnan border, through Burma and down the Malay peninsula. He then threw himself into a speaking tour to explain to the Overseas Chinese that the communists were not savages or sexual libertines, as they had been portrayed in Kuomintang propaganda. They were the future of China. Kuomintang hatchet men arrived in Malaya to launch a smear campaign against him. He was accused of being a communist himself, of 'hanging the head of a goat but selling dog's meat'. But these bitter exchanges only seemed to highlight the bankruptcy of the Chungking regime. Tan Kah Kee's stature grew. He encouraged a flurry of other travellers between Malaya and China. Young Chinese volunteered to fight in China, and many died there. Some 3,200 drivers and mechanics were recruited, many of whom worked the Burma Road in appalling conditions. Others received training in Yenan and were to return to Malaya on the eve of the great Asian war. Between 1937 and 1942 vast funds were remitted home by the Southeast Asian Chinese, perhaps $360 million in Chinese currency; one estimate in Chungking put it at one third of the war expenditure of the regime. To the Japanese Tan Kah Kee was 'Public Enemy Number One'.[43]

There was also a flow in the opposite direction, of political refugees escaping the brutal Japanese occupation of the Chinese seaboard. Some were seasoned international revolutionaries. One such was the legendary Comintern leader, Tan Malaka. He was the prophet of a socialist dream of a co-prosperity sphere in the East, which he called 'Aslia'. 'The Scarlet Pimpernel of Asia', he fled Amoy in 1937 with a fake Chinese passport and some *chiak-tek*, or bribe money, to Rangoon, to Penang, and then to ground in Singapore.[44] Here there was a large influx of Chinese literati who transformed a migrant community composed for the most part of labourers and traders. Schoolmasters on the run took jobs in small-town schools and breathed life – and politics – into Chinese education in Southeast Asia. They were paid less than their English-educated counterparts and admired for their dedication. An unprecedented wealth of artistic and literary talent surfaced in Singapore. For many Shanghai- and Paris-trained artists Malaya provided a safe haven and artistic utopia. One such, Xu Bei Hong, was commissioned to paint the governor of Singapore, Sir Thomas Shenton Thomas.[45] Under the influence of the Nanyang Academy of Fine Arts from 1938, these painters explored local meanings and new styles. The Chinese poet Yu Dafu, one of the most effective literary voices of the resistance movement, announced on arrival in Malaya that 'there should be no dividing line between politicians, the military and the intellectuals.'[46] If art and writing did not reflect war themes it was dismissed as 'against the spirit of the age'. The journalist and critic Hu Yuzhi, soon after his arrival in 1940, became editor of the influential Singapore newspaper *Nanyang Siang Pau* and a close associate of Tan Kah Kee. He was a Paris-educated lawyer, well known for his role in translating into Chinese Edgar Snow's *Red Star over China*, a eulogy of the Chinese Communist Party's Long March published in 1938. Snow introduced Asian communism to the English-speaking world, and Hu Yuzhi did the same for the Overseas Chinese, inspiring not least Tan Kah Kee's visit to Yenan. It was only shortly before his death in 1986 that Hu Yuzhi admitted that he had been a secret member of the Chinese Communist Party, sent to Singapore by its leadership in 1940 to breathe new life into anti-Japanese propaganda.[47]

The principal beneficiary of all this activity was the Malayan Communist Party. It had been founded in 1930 as a multi-ethnic organization, but its membership was pre-eminently Chinese, and it threw itself into the cause of national salvation. It had spent the years after 1934 in the wilderness, plagued by the British Special Branch and compromised by arrests and deportations. In the urgent patriotic mood the party widened its support within the Chinese community, particularly in schools and cultural circles. An array of organizations under its influence – from trades unions to amateur theatrical troupes – transformed themselves into anti-enemy backing-up societies. By 1939, perhaps as many as 700 associations, with over 40,000 members and ten times as many sympathizers, came together under the slogan 'Anti-Japanese is paramount: all for anti-Japanese'. The struggle against British imperialism and capitalism was put aside. A semi-underground force, the anti-enemy backing-up societies provided propaganda and muscle to enforce the boycott. Its travelling theatre shows reached labourers in remote mines and plantations. Plays such as Yeh Ni's *The Military Hospital* had a tremendous impact on local audiences. A students' anti-enemy backing-up society thrived in the Chinese middle schools across the peninsula. Money was collected door to door, street to street. At the instigation of the Cantonese songstress Xin Qin Qin, Chinese prostitutes took to the streets to sell red flowers. They were known as the 'fragrance of the chrysanthemum sisters'.[48] Fish caught by Japanese trawlers were doused with kerosene. 'Traitors' faced intimidation and violence: their shop-boards were tarred, their goods seized and, this failing, their ears sliced off. In July 1938 there were three days of riots in Penang in protest against the arrival of a large consignment of soya beans from Japan. The Japanese consulate evacuated its women and children. In January 1941 a Chinese in Singapore was charged with trying to murder a Japanese by poisoning his curry.[49] The 500 Japanese iron miners at Dungun lived in terror of their Chinese workforce. In 1938, at the instigation of the young Kuomintang leader Lim Bo Seng, 2,000 Chinese walked out *en masse*, to be replaced by a makeshift crew of Japanese fishermen. Amazingly, production did not fall off. The new workforce dug on through the monsoon season, and Japanese firms bought up Malaya's stocks of scrap iron. Nevertheless, the campaign hit hard: between

1937 and 1939, Japanese exports to Malaya dropped by 75 per cent.[50]

In the anti-enemy backing-up societies, the best and brightest cadres of the Malayan Communist Party emerged from the shadows of the secret world. Foremost among a new wave of activists was Ng Yeh Lu, a graduate of Tan Kah Kee's Amoy University and a teacher at another Tan Kah Kee foundation, the Chinese High School in Singapore. His outspoken anti-Japanese stance in the classroom brought him to the attention of the party leadership, and from 1938 he orchestrated the anti-Japanese effort in the north of the peninsula to great effect. It introduced a new generation of recruits to the Malayan Communist Party. One such recruit was a schoolboy, Ong Boon Hua, from Sitiawan in the state of Perak. He was to become one of the dominant and most feared figures across the whole of Southeast Asia over the next two generations. Ong Boon Hua was enthralled by the news of the war; too young to enlist for China, he joined the anti-enemy backing-up society at his Chinese school. He devoured the Chinese translations of both *Red Star over China* and the works of another American sympathizer, Anna Louise Strong. This led him to Mao Zedong's *On Protracted War* and a course of self-indoctrination, which he undertook whilst ostensibly running a branch of his family's bicycle shop. By January 1940 he had been recruited as a probationary member of the Malayan Communist Party; by July, aged only fifteen, he had gone underground to avoid arrest.[51] Like his contemporaries, many of whom were, like him, born or educated in Malaya, Ong Boon Hua's world-view was shaped by this 'war of resistance culture'. He engaged in a struggle for China, but one fought in Malaya and increasingly shaped by its local conditions. Ong was later to lead the guerrilla armies of the Malayan Communist Party against both the Japanese and the British. He took a nom de guerre: Chin Peng.

Ng Yeh Lu, for his part, would return to Singapore and become a leading public face of communism (he was dubbed 'Malaya's Chou En Lai', after the leading intellectual star of the Chinese party). He advocated making common cause with other anti-fascist forces in an 'All Communities United Front'. In May 1941 he was arrested and imprisoned by the British for membership of the proscribed Malayan Communist Party. When his sentence was served the British planned to banish him to China; however, he was to play a further, pivotal role in the story of communism in Malaya. Like many of his fellow-travellers, his journey was to be a long one with many strange twists and ironies. His career ended in the 1970s, under a different name, as the Republic of Singapore's ambassador to Japan, doyen of a new capitalist ruling group.[52]

The National Salvation alliance between the Kuomintang and the communists reached its peak of influence in late 1938, but it did not endure. It became clear, in the words of one Kuomintang leader in Malaya, that the two parties 'were having different dreams in the same bed'.[53] They were divided in their attitude to the British government in Malaya, and the British in turn played the major role in the disintegration of the United Front. The colonial regime had initially permitted the anti-Japanese demonstrations a degree of latitude. The governor of Singapore, Sir Shenton Thomas, who recognized the need to canalize such an outburst of feeling, had personally sanctioned Tan Kah Kee's leadership of the China Relief Fund. But after the 'soya beans affair' in Penang, he became increasingly alarmed by the prospect that the British were facing 'an anti-Japanese *cum* anti-British movement'. The outbreak of the war in Europe created the opportunity for a clampdown. Across the colonial world, the left was thrown into confusion by the Molotov–Ribbentrop Pact, and the Comintern's opposition to the 'imperialist' war. The anti-fascist movement in Malaya was deeply divided. Tan Kah Kee threw his weight behind the British war effort. During the Blitz on London, he raised Chinese money for the Lord Mayor's Air Raid Distress Fund. 'Malaya is our second home,' he argued. 'It is our bounden duty to assist in the fight against aggression, for by helping Britain win the war, we are making our homes safer.'[54] However, the Malayan Communist Party followed the Comintern line and launched a series of strikes in key industrial sectors. Rising prices and disrupted trade created fertile ground for disorder. The British reacted ruthlessly. After mass protests on May Day 1940, police swoops crippled the Malayan Communist Party leadership. By October there were 1,000 communists in custody, awaiting banishment to China. In July 1940, in the face of this and of a sudden haemorrhaging of Chinese support, the Malayan Communist Party reversed its policy and announced a suspension of its struggle against

British colonialism. The British, however, were not listening, and the arrests continued.[55]

The Japanese became obsessed with the problem of the Overseas Chinese. This would be taken to a tragic conclusion during the war, when the entire community was seen as a security threat. Japanese agents tried to drive a wedge between the communists and other Chinese. They promoted their puppet regime in occupied China under the warlord Wang Ching Wei, and exploited his commercial fronts in Hong Kong and Malaya to collect information. They forged links with unscrupulous businessmen and gangsters, which were to endure during the occupation, and they infiltrated their own Chinese agents from the Japanese colony of Taiwan.[56] These creatures were to reappear in the baggage train of the Imperial Army. They became notorious for their opportunism, corruption and brutality. Japanese agents jotted down from the columns of the local newspapers the names of those who had donated to the China Relief Fund.

The main thrust of Japanese espionage was directed at other communities, who had remained outside the National Salvation struggle for China. Suzuki was active amongst the Indian community in Bangkok, and other agents fomented rebellion in the Indian garrisons of Singapore. This awoke for the British memories of the Sepoy mutiny in Singapore in 1915, which had left a dark imprint on the psyche of Europeans in the colony. Then, humiliatingly, the British had needed to borrow a militia of Japanese sailors to restore control. There was a cat-and-mouse game between the colonial police and Japanese agents throughout the 1930s: there were at least two Japanese suicides in police custody. The Singapore Special Branch set up a Japanese section in 1938 to track the threat more closely. It had some successes. Soji Saito, a Japanese sailor, was put on trial for sketching near the famous 'big guns' of Blakang Mati. A gregarious Japanese press attaché, Mamoru Shinozaki, was also arrested in September 1940. This man denied that he was a spy, claiming his collection of press clippings and meetings with British servicemen were a routine part of his work. So too was his taking two Japanese soldiers on a sightseeing tour of southern Malaya, one of whom happened to be Colonel T. Tanikawa, the planning chief of the Imperial Army. After a two-week trial, Shinozaki was sentenced to three years' hard labour in the new showpiece Changi jail, which had opened two years previously, built on the model of Sing Sing in New York State. He was placed in a cell with European prisoners: some deserting soldiers and a corrupt official. On his first morning in Changi, he composed a bad poem in Chinese:

> Alone in Singapore
> No merit, yet in jail
> Look for northeast in dawn light
> Bow my head in heartbreak!

His imprisonment caused a minor diplomatic row and, as Anglo-Japanese relations deteriorated further, Shinozaki was moved in with the Asian prisoners. He buried himself in Vicky Baum's novel of the resistance war in China, *Nanking Road*, and made himself agreeable to his new cellmates.[57]

Yet for all this, the Japanese found the building of credible fifth-column support profoundly difficult in such a multi-ethnic society. It was very late in the day that Japanese agents turned to the Malay community. Barely a majority population in Malaya itself, the Malays had not figured largely in the political arithmetic of the Greater East Asian Co-Prosperity Sphere. In a sense, the Japanese had accepted the governing assumption of British rule that the Malays were politically backward and quiescent. Yet, added to long-standing Japanese connections with the Malay royal courts, there was among Malays at a popular level a general fascination with things Japanese. Intelligence officers looked to Tani Yutaka, a Japanese from a family who ran a barber shop in Trengganu, who, after his young sister was kidnapped and killed by Chinese protesters, took to the hills with a Malay bandit gang, it was said to be 3,000 strong. He was a legend along the east coast, known as 'Raja Harimau' – 'King Tiger'. The Japanese portrayed him as a Malayan Robin Hood.[58] By the late 1930s a small group of Malay radicals were hunting for allies. The leading figure was Ibrahim Yaacob. He was a commoner, a junior civil servant turned journalist, who founded in 1937 the Kesatuan Melayu Muda, Union of Malay Youth. It was anti-colonial and anti-feudal in outlook. Ibrahim and his associates eagerly embraced the atmosphere of intrigue that descended on Malayan politics in these years. They met clandestinely, often in the cabarets of the towns. There was undoubtedly some secret diplomacy between Ibrahim Yaacob and the Japanese in Singapore. Yet, at the same time, the British regarded him as their own secret agent. At one point Ibrahim claimed that he had royal backing from Malay courts for his contacts with the Japanese. At another, that he had approached the British – in meetings with the head of the Singapore Special Branch and with Governor Shenton Thomas himself – and offered to provide intelligence on Japanese plans. He was also implicated in a quixotic scheme to create an independent Malay kingdom in the old courtly centre of Riau, in the islands south of Singapore.[59]

Ibrahim's true intentions are lost in a fog of ambiguity and cloak-and-dagger fantasy. This reflected the deepening complexity of the secret world of Singapore. All too conscious of this, the British, after the fall of Singapore, would agonize over the scale of the deception practised on them. However, their subterfuges did little for the Japanese military at the time. They also did little for Ibrahim Yaacob. The schemes for a Malay fifth column had not gone far and, like many prospective fellow-travellers, Ibrahim found his later relations with the Japanese very uneasy. When imperial forces later landed on the peninsula, Ibrahim Yaacob and 112 followers were to be picked up and jailed by the British. The Japanese of British Asia also seemed to vanish overnight. The fishermen-turned-miners of Trengganu took to the sea. Those left behind were swiftly detained. They were 'treated like convicts'; the men were arrested at dawn, taken to the infamous Pudu jail in Kuala Lumpur and shipped in secret to Changi, about to become even more infamous, where some 1,700 in all were incarcerated. Another thousand or so Japanese women and children were rounded up and sent to St John's Island, previously a place of quarantine. Malayan radio, in a broadcast that infuriated its Chinese listeners, billed the camp as a paradise island, but conditions were squalid, the Japanese were fed rotten salt fish, and in the words of one internee, Miss H. Katano, 'the food was barely sufficient to sustain life'. Many had made their entire lives in Malaya. One internee, a wicker-furniture dealer named Tomizi Harada, had been resident since 1927. He was taken from hospital, against the advice of doctors, and eventually lost his sight. In January 1942 the men were bundled out in two groups to India; the women joined them there, complaining that they had been kicked and bullied in transit. Many were to die there.[60] They were the first civilian casualties of a long and terrible war.

These Asian journeys of 1939 and 1940 foreshadowed the nature of the conflict to come. It was to be much more than a war between the British, Americans and Japanese. It would also be a series of bloody civil wars amongst Indians, Burmese and Malayans, the consequences of which would reverberate far into the future and would inspire and scar the memories of these peoples down to the present day. The army that Aung San and the Thakins created in those troubled months of 1940 and 1941 fought first with and then against the Japanese invaders of their homeland. The story of Aung San and his Thirty Comrades became in time the founding myth of modern Burma, conjured up by Burma's military rulers and democratic activists from the 1940s until today. Subhas Chandra Bose's Indian National Army, the eastern successor to Hitler's Indian Legion, left a more mixed legacy. Its story did not fit well with the non-violent national movement inspired by Bose's political opponents Mahatma Gandhi and Jawaharlal Nehru. In 1944 and 1945 Bose's army clashed with the huge Indian army unleashed by the British against the Japanese invaders of Malaya and Burma. Only now, fifty years on, has Subhas Chandra Bose begun to claim his still deeply controversial legacy as the greatest military hero of India's modern history. Finally, in Malaya, Chin Peng and the men inspired by Mao Zedong's communist legacy first aided the British in a guerrilla war against the Japanese and conservative Malays and then staged an attempted red revolution against the returning British. These journeys out of colonialism did not simply spell the beginning of the end of generations of British dominion in the East. They also sowed the seeds of today's Asian world. Yet in those last twilight days the might of the Raj and the privilege of its white subjects seemed as immutable as ever. The next chapter ventures into that vanished world, a world of bridge parties, pink gins and pliant servants, founded on the rigorous control of plantation and mining labour the length of the Malay peninsula.

# Prologue, Part II: Journeys through Empire

## THE GREAT CRESCENT

The historian Jack Gallagher once compared the British Empire to a gouty old man who shrieked with pain each time anyone came near his swollen extremities. Immediately before the Second World War, the Empire felt itself to be afflicted with serious internal diseases, too. Policemen, growing ever more obsessive in the tropical heat, saw anti-colonial politics as an insidious infection; they cloaked their acts of repression in medical metaphors of 'quarantine' and 'containment'. By the outbreak of war they were particularly worried that communists would rise to power by harnessing and directing local social unrest. They believed this even though doctrinaire communist parties seemed to be making little headway in India and Burma, and in Malaya were paralysed by arrests and deportations. The security services were wary of the Japanese after their invasion of Manchuria, but policemen and politicians remained fixated on the 'red menace'. As a Malay fifth-columnist observed of one of the Japanese residents of Malaya, now working as an intelligence officer in 1941: 'He was a mere barber who could play tennis . . . Why weren't the British cautious of people like him?'[1]

Besides Hong Kong, the part of Britain's eastern empire which was most vulnerable to the Japanese was the 'great crescent' which stretched from Bengal and Assam in eastern India through Burma to the Malay States and Singapore, interrupted only by independent Thailand. It was part of a greater strategic arc that linked Cairo to Sydney and Auckland. Even after the coming of the railway and steamship, communications down the crescent remained partial and spasmodic. Trade connections were certainly increasing. Burma's rice exports made up for any shortfall in that staple for Bengal's huge population. Malaya's tin and rubber went in quantities to industrial plants in Burma and India; Malaya too was dependent on some 53,000 tons a month of rice from Burma and Thailand. Over several generations, Indian and Chinese merchants had woven a network of branch agencies for their firms all the way from Calcutta to Singapore and north again to Canton and Shanghai. The poor also linked the region together in their ceaseless search for a livelihood. Muslims from what is now Bangladesh drifted south into Burma. Indians from the eastern and southern parts of the subcontinent migrated as workmen to the rubber estates of the Malay peninsula. By 1941 there were nearly three-quarters of a million Indians resident there. Telok Ayer Street in the heart of Singapore's Chinatown represented this world in motion. It contained an Indian Muslim shrine to a saint, a mosque, a Chinese Methodist Church and a Chinese temple dedicated to the sea goddess Kwan Yin dating from the foundation of the British settlement in 1819.

Yet even in 1939 the great crescent was still fragmented by political and ecological diversity. Like everything British, starting with the British Isles themselves, the crescent was an administrative jumble inhabited by populations of vastly differing size which had been accumulated in fits and starts. No Napoleon had tried to impose order on its constitutive elements. For example, the English East India Company had seized Bengal from its Muslim rulers as early as 1765. Its population had reached nearly 80 million by 1939. Assam, with a population of about 25 million, had been acquired in the early nineteenth century. It was finally hived off from Bengal in 1919. The Indian authorities had bitten off Burma by chunks in 1826, 1852 and 1886. Its population was about 15 million at the beginning of the Second World War. Malaya was the ultimate administrative patchwork, even though its population of 5 million was only slightly bigger than that of some of the largest Bengal districts. The colony of the Straits Settlements had brought together, from 1826, the trading posts of Penang, Malacca and – what had become the 'Clapham Junction' of empire in the East – Singapore. The rest of the peninsula had been acquired by treaties of 'protection' with Malay kingdoms between

1874 and 1914. Thailand remained an independent kingdom, a crucial divide in the crescent of British power between Burma and Malaya, though the Bank of England and British financiers ruled its economy.

The 'red on the map' spilling down the crescent and denoting British rule concealed a variety of administrative anomalies. Away from the plains of the Ganges, Brahmaputra and Irrawaddy, and especially in the upland areas, the British ruled not directly through members of the elite and largely white civil services, but through a variety of local magnates. These were called rajas or nawabs in India, sawbwas in the Shan states of Burma and sultans in Malaya. Many outlying areas scarcely saw a British civil servant from month to month. Even in Bengal, where the British had done a deal with groups of important magnates in the eighteenth century, the Indian Civil Service had not developed the paternalistic form of local government that was famous in the Punjab. The Bengal government was both hands-off and laissez-faire. In Malaya, again, there were sharp contrasts in practice: the Straits Settlements were subject to elaborate municipal management while the Malay States were a classical example of Britain's vogue for 'indirect rule' through local dignitaries. The states of Perak, Selangor, Negri Sembilan and Pahang, where the larger part of British investment was concentrated, had been drawn together as the Federated Malay States in 1895. Here, at every level, British officers shadowed the Malay regime, and most of the district officers were British. The other states were 'unfederated'. British acquisition of them was more recent. The northern states had been ceded from the nominal sovereignty of Thailand in the 1900s. The large southern state of Johore, despite its wealth and proximity to Singapore, had come under full British protection only in 1914. Here the touch of British power was lighter: Johore had no British district officers. A full understanding of these bureaucratic mysteries was possessed by very few, such as the 'high born' of the Malayan Civil Service, and they guarded their secrets jealously.

The continuation of government by the seat-of-the-pants in many small units was partly a deliberate British policy. After the First World War and again in 1935 with the Government of India Act, Britain tried to mollify nationalists by giving them some small share of power in the imperial provinces. In 1936 Burma became an independent entity under the crown, but a very curious one. It was now neither part of the Indian Empire nor a crown colony. The constitutional lawyers simply shuffled this anomaly under the table. 'British Malaya' was merely a geographical expression. In part, though, the jumble of jurisdictions simply reflected the enormous variety of landscape, economy and culture which characterized the great crescent. The flat plains of Bengal were made up of a huge patchwork of small peasant plots growing rice for local consumption or cash crops such as the jute used in the mills of Calcutta and Dundee. Lower Burma was also a flat rice-growing land, though much of its produce was exported. Some of the river plains of Malaya also supported peasant rice agriculture, especially in Kedah and Kelantan in the north which produced half of Malaya's home-grown rice. Away from the river plains, there was great variety. The British had colonized the hills of Assam with their tea plantations. British timber companies operated across the Indian and Burmese hills. Oil was pumped from installations along the Irrawaddy. Some local people and many emigrant labourers or coolies worked these bigger enterprises. The profits, however, went mainly to the City of London.

If India was the jewel in the imperial crown, Malaya was the industrial diamond. In 1940, the governor of Singapore estimated, Malaya was 'worth' an estimated £227.5 million to the British Empire. Its exports were £131.25 million, of which £93 million were to foreign countries, especially to the United States, to which it sold more than any other territory of the British Empire except Canada. From 1895 until the Japanese war, at no point did British Malaya need financial help from outside. Its status as a model colony was achieved from its own resources, and its accumulated budget surpluses saw it through the Great Depression. The key to the great public works and civic conceits of the Straits Settlements was opium. Duty on opium accounted for between 40 and 60 per cent of its annual revenue. Its production was monopolized by the government 'Chandu factory' on Pepys Road in Singapore which turned out 100 million tubes a year. Much of the revenue burden of Malaya therefore fell upon the Asian, particularly Chinese, labourers who were the greatest consumers of opium.[2] The British crescent in Asia was supported by narco-colonialism on a colossal scale.

One of the most dramatic effects of the coming war was the way it forged the crescent into a bloodstained unity. First, the Japanese unified the peninsula from Singapore through Thailand to the borders of Assam by armed invasion. In response the British punched a land route from north India through the nearly impassable ranges of Assam and north Burma into the Irrawaddy valley. Reoccupying the Malay peninsula, they reclaimed their Southeast Asian patrimony. In fact, the designation 'Southeast Asia' was itself the brainchild of the military strategists who created South East Asia Command in 1943. Yet, as jazz-age imperialism drew to its end in 1939, there seemed little enough as yet, besides their rock-solid belief in British superiority, to draw together the white settler societies of the crescent.

There were tensions and divisions at the heart of these settler societies. These focused on people of 'mixed race' – those descended from Europeans who had children by Indian, Burmese, Malay and Chinese partners. Their status was open to doubt and raises some difficulties of terminology. Generally speaking, these people themselves wanted to emphasize their part-British origins, calling themselves 'Anglo-Indians' or 'Anglo-Burmans', etc. By this period British expatriates generally referred to them as 'Eurasians'. Occasionally and confusingly, though, the term 'Anglo-Indian' was also used of British expatriates who had spent a large portion of their lives in the East. These issues of identity affected all communities. A similar problem arises, for example, with the term 'Burman'. Sometimes this word was used to mean any indigenous inhabitant of Burma, but more often in the 1930s and '40s, it was used to mean people of ethnic Burmese Buddhist stock, so distinguishing them from the Karen, Shan, Kachin and other minorities who spoke different languages, had different customs and their own sense of history.

Yet, after the war, the long imperial summer of the 1930s would be remembered by the British in Asia as a lost idyll: a time of peace, prosperity and tropical chic. It climaxed in the literary voyages and celebrity tourism of that decade. Expatriate travellers moved by sea from luxury hotel to luxury hotel down the crescent. They disported themselves in the Great Eastern in Calcutta, The Strand in Rangoon, the Eastern and Oriental in Penang, and came to rest alongside the characters at the Long Bar of Raffles Hotel in Singapore. The days of Conrad's Eastern World had dimmed, but colourful relics of it lingered on in colonial clubhouses and quiet backwater out-stations. Aldous Huxley, W. Somerset Maugham, W. H. Auden and Christopher Isherwood all passed east and had the east leave a deep imprint on their writing. Their pen-portraits of colonial society in Asia were often cruelly satirical. Yet the remoter outposts of this world were suddenly accessible in a way they had not been a generation earlier. In the 1930s this tropical paradise became a playground for wealthy European tourists; the rich cultures of the region fascinated European artists. This was a world in which a Scottish-American hotelier could reinvent herself as the 'K'tut Tantri' of Balinese legend, and as the radio voice of a national revolution 'Surabaya Sue'.[3]

Actors and film stars came east to visit some of their most enthusiastic audiences. Noël Coward was cornered by expatriate Mrs Worthingtons, who wished to put their daughters on the stage, and took his revenge in scandalizing planters' wives by awarding the top prizes in a beauty competition on his ship to two Eurasian girls. When, in 1936, Charlie Chaplin was fêted through Singapore and on to China, Japan and the Pacific, it was one of the last moments at which such a grand tour would be possible. As the long day of empire waned, British Asia had a filmic quality. Chinese entrepreneurs marketed Singapore as a location for Hollywood producers. Dorothy Lamour 'sexed-up' the new fascination with the tropics with her famous sarong. She was the most popular sex symbol in Malaya too, although locals observed that she sported her sarong 'in a style no Malayan, Indonesian, or Polynesian ever wore'.[4] In 1940 she starred in the first of the 'Road' movies with Bob Hope and Bing Crosby: *The Road to Singapore*. It could have been the road to anywhere: its working title was 'The Road to Mandalay' and it was shot in California. Yet it lodged Singapore in the world's imagination. With bleak irony, British and Australian troops adopted its theme tune as a marching song when they retreated down the Malay peninsula in the face of the Japanese advance in December 1941.[5]

One of the most distinctive of the travelogues of this time records the insight of the outsider. In March 1936, in a parody of Phileas Fogg's famous wager, Jean Cocteau set out to travel around the world in eighty days. He followed almost immediately in the footsteps of

35

Charlie Chaplin and met up with him on the boat to Japan. To follow Phileas Fogg over sixty years on was still to journey around the British Empire through its trans-Asian bastions.[6] This was a crossing many soldiers soon would make in less comfortable conditions. It was the close of the era of these leisurely passages in which the different castes of colonial society, from proconsul to coolie, travelled in strange proximity. Cocteau went on the same ship as the incoming viceroy of India, Lord Linlithgow. The two men do not seem to have been introduced and they would not have found that they had a great deal in common if they had been. Cocteau arrived in Bombay, where the new and the departing viceroy crossed paths at the Gateway of India. 'A city of cleanliness and squalor', this too would be the first encounter with Asia for the British troops as the military build-up began a few months later.

Cocteau took the *Imperial Mail* – 'Kim's *te-rain*' – across the furnace of central India to Calcutta. For the European heading east, Calcutta was a centre of banking and supply, rarely a place to linger. Here Cocteau re-embarked with white-capped pilgrims returning from Mecca and red-faced rubber planters in shorts. As he moved further down the crescent he began to experience a subtle shift in sensations. In Rangoon he was met by 'an amalgam of India, Burma and China'; he had his first experience of a Chinatown and of an authentic opium den. Cocteau had little time to do more than visit the great Shwedagon pagoda: 'it was in the same class as the Acropolis, the Castel Sant' Angelo and the Pyramids'. A place of pilgrimage for all visitors, it was to be a central stage for the great political theatre that would be set in motion in Burma by the war. The Shwedagon had always been deeply symbolic to national struggle in a land where Burmese had to appear barefoot before European officials whilst white men defiled Burmese temples in their shoes, spats and topis. When Lady Diana Cooper visited it in late 1941, as the wife of the resident cabinet minister in Asia, she took off her shoes to enter. She gleefully claimed that the governor, Sir Reginald Dorman-Smith, reprimanded her for this, saying that she had dealt such a blow to white prestige that the British might lose Burma.[7]

## A MALAYAN PASTORALE

Cocteau crossed the eastern Indian Ocean into new landscape tones. The island of Penang, approached from the sea, was a fantasy of the tropical picturesque. The voyager from India was confronted by a densely forested hill of over 2,500 feet reaching down to the western shoreline of the island, which was skirted by Malay fishing villages on stilts. Then, rounding the island's northern coast, there came a sudden vision of the tiled roofs and clock towers of colonial George Town, where the liners swam in to berth almost on the main street. Across the narrow strait from the waterfront lay the hazy palm-dressed lowlands and the distant limestone peaks of the Malay peninsula. Penang was the oldest British settlement in Malaya, founded in 1786. It was chosen for its fecundity, as a natural crossroads for the junk trade, and for the mildness of the climate of Penang Hill. This was the first of the imperial belvederes, where the Europeans took their ease away from the enervating effects of the heat and humidity. Penang set the pattern for future European colonization in the east. There was a chain of hill stations down the central range of the peninsula, where resorts and golf courses had been carved out of the jungle, at an atrocious physical cost to the Asian labourers who built them. They bore the names of European pioneers: Maxwell Hill, Frazer's Hill and the Cameron Highlands, where the ova of trout were carted up on ice to supply its streams.

It was in Penang that the traveller encountered another social universe. On leaving the Eastern and Oriental by rickshaw at night, Cocteau felt that 'China was everywhere'. But he was plunged into a Chinatown in the heart of the Malay world. Until 1867 the Straits Settlements had been governed from British India, and with its Tamil stevedores, Sikh policemen, Chettiar moneylenders and Indian penal code, George Town still bore the imprint of the Raj. The civic splendour of the waterfront around the Esplanade and King Edward Place reproduced that of Calcutta or Madras on only a slightly smaller scale. Penang was the original, classic form of the colonial port city in Southeast Asia: the creation of migrants from every corner of the world. It was a city of all nations, where it was misleading to speak even of one 'Chinese' or 'Indian' or 'Malay' community.

The classical lines of the imperial city gave way within yards to baroque Chinese street architecture. Cocteau marvelled at the rows of shophouses with their narrow, ornate facades, which enclosed the 'five-foot way' which sheltered pedestrians from the sun and the traffic. These buildings were ubiquitous in the Straits; they reached far back from the street, enclosing internal courtyards. To European residents, the Chinese town was an unsanitary warren which defied control. Shophouses were often sub-let into infinite fractions: simultaneously lodging houses for unmarried migrants, industrial workshops, barber-shops, dentists and medical halls, shops of every description. They were a riot of signboards in many languages. The street names recorded the complexity of Penang's migrant pasts, in which Hokkien Chinese, Jaffna Tamils and Scotsmen fought for civic recognition. Armenian Street had been the Penang residence of the founding father of modern China, Sun Yat Sen, during his long years in exile. Next to it, Acheen Street possessed one of the oldest mosques in Malaya, of Sumatran design, and ran alongside the wealthiest Chinese clan house in South-east Asia. Leith Street had the grandest Chinese mansions. Love Lane was a place for anything but.

Beyond Chinatown lay the Palladian mansions of the Straits Chinese merchant princes. These exceeded in magnificence even the sprawling bungalows of the Europeans. The Straits Chinese were local-born, permanent residents of several generations. They placed themselves at a distance from the *hwa qiao*, or China-born, whom they saw as coarse country cousins. They had got rich in the rice trade or as pioneers of plantation agriculture. They sought respectability and were quick to adopt European manners and business practice. They wove proud family networks. Uniquely as a community in Malaya, the Straits Chinese enjoyed the privilege of British citizenship. Younger generations had taken to the English Bar and the Scottish medical colleges. The Straits Chinese had adopted the lingua franca of the archipelago, Malay, to various degrees. Most were not literate in Chinese. The Cambridge-educated magistrate Lim Cheng Ean wondered in his youth why anyone would wish to be so. Yet the Straits Chinese retained their Chinese heritage in other ways. Lim Cheng Ean in later years would turn to the study of Chinese literature. He and his brother Lim Cheng Teik were the first Asians to be co-opted by the British as municipal commissioners. With their other brothers they were stalwarts of the Straits Chinese British Association and, being loyal 'King's Chinese', joined the Straits Settlements Volunteer Corps. They spent their evenings in a colonial-style mess, drinking whisky *stengahs* – half-and-half with water in the planter fashion – and playing poker.[8]

'The city reeks of pious institutions, swarms with schools,' complained Cocteau. 'Everywhere we saw schoolboys on bicycles and bespectacled Chinese girls with gold crosses and sanctimonious airs.' Yet communities of overseas Indians, Ceylonese burghers and Eurasians also had grasped the opportunities presented by English language education, government service and Christianity. An inter-racial elite had emerged in the Straits around a rich nexus of civic institutions: from sports clubs, social clubs and automobile clubs to the Red Cross, the racecourse and the Rotary Club. But the Straits Chinese, through their wealth, long residence and the ability to inhabit many cultural worlds, held a special standing with the British as the voice for the larger Chinese community, and as the prototype 'Malayans'. This was not mere sycophancy: the Straits Chinese saw in the British Empire the fulfilment of a cosmopolitan ideal. In his 1917 book *The Great War from a Confucian Point of View*, the Singaporean Lim Boon Keng saw in the British Empire 'the prelude to the federation of the world'.[9] On this basis, the community donated cash for troops and aeroplanes for imperial defence. Lim was a medical doctor and man of letters; he was also, at various periods, a Christian apostate, a Confucian revivalist and a founder of the Kuomintang in Malaya. He spent long periods in China, teaching at the 'Malayan Henry Ford' Tan Kah Kee's Amoy University. In his absence the Malacca Straits Chinese Tan Cheng Lock had emerged as a champion of the 'Malayan' interest on the legislative council, where he was fond of lacing his pronouncements with Plato, Schopenhauer, Nietzsche and Confucius. These men did not speak for the masses. In 1935, Tan Cheng Lock had retired from public office in disillusion to Switzerland. He returned to Malaya quietly in late 1939 on the heels of the German invasion of Poland. Like Lim Boon Keng, who had himself come back from China two years earlier, he was by this time an elderly tribune without a following.[10] However, in 1942 both men would be propelled into new leadership roles.

From Penang, Cocteau moved down the Straits of Malacca to Port

Swettenham, the principal gateway and railhead of the Federated Malay States. It was at this point that the rice paddy and coconut groves of the coastal plains gave way inland to a scarred landscape of mining pools and plantations. The frontier economy cut deeply into some of the oldest rainforest on earth, which still accounted for 40 per cent of the land cover of the peninsula. At its foothills lay Malaya's Ruhr, the Kinta valley in Perak. This was to become the front line of the peninsular wars. Here, Chinese *towkays* had created the tin-mining industry by risking their money in places where the City of London had feared to tread. In 1905 Malaya had produced over 50 per cent of the world's tin, and the Chinese controlled three-quarters of the output. But by 1937 this share had shrunk to less than a third. Chinese open-cast mines became unproductive after 1912, when European firms began to introduce large mechanical dredges. The Chinese miners struggled on as marginal producers, their vast labour forces at the mercy of shifts in the global market for tin, which was increasingly controlled by European cartels. The issuing of mining licences favoured the Europeans and was scandalously corrupt at every level: the Japanese spy, Mamoru Shinozaki, shared a cell in Changi with Captain Robert Loveday, a senior surveyor in the office of the chief engineer of Malaya who had been convicted in August 1940 on eight counts of fraud. Rubber was controlled by similar methods. In 1938, there were over 2 million acres of rubber in Malaya; three-quarters of it owned by Europeans. Falling prices and decreasing production in the Depression had hit this industry hard, but it hit hardest the production of smaller plantations owned by Asians which, through official discrimination in the allocation of export coupons, fell at a rate nearly four times that of the European estates.[11] To Malay peasants, who had seen rubber smallholding as a way out of poverty, this was a historic injustice.

The great *towkays* or business leaders had survived by diversifying their economic empires. Before its collapse, Tan Kah Kee's had been extremely wide-ranging; his son-in-law, Lee Kong Chian, was still the undisputed 'rubber king of Malaya' and a prime mover in the establishment of the Overseas Chinese Banking Corporation. He led the way in the National Salvation movement with a personal donation of $300,000. Tan Kah Kee's main political rival, Aw Boon Haw, came originally out of Burma, and owed his fortune to a patented herbal salve that was perhaps the first Chinese medicinal brand to secure a global market. 'The Tiger Balm King' also owned Chinese and English newspapers. Each of the Malay states had its own local bosses. In Perak, one of the emerging forces was from the pioneering Hakka community, Lau Pak Khuan. He arrived in Malaya at the age of twelve and worked as a miner; by the 1930s he had become a founding director of another of the larger Chinese banks in Malaya and was a Kuomintang stalwart. He organized Malaya's first lottery sweep. In Selangor, the coming man was the Cambridge-educated Cantonese H. S. Lee. He had served as a customs officer in Hainan island in China and a banker in Hong Kong; after a visit to Malaya in 1924 he bought a tin mine that laid the foundations of his fortune.[12] These men were the heirs to the old 'Kapitan China' through which the British had controlled the frontier in earlier times. But they were no longer back-woodsmen. The inter-war years were the zenith of their prestige and power.

Labourers' lives were a world apart from those of the wealthy *towkays* and townsmen and were lived in isolated industrial enclaves. There were perhaps 724,000 industrial workers in Malaya in 1931; this was about 16 per cent of the total population. It was a unique concentration of workers: only perhaps 0.7 per cent of the population of India could be classified in this way.[13] They were often recently arrived migrants and were overwhelmingly male. In the case of the Chinese, there were just over two men to every woman. From the moment of their arrival in Penang or Singapore, Chinese were locked into a chain of bondage: to shippers of the 'coolie trade' who brought them to Malaya or to the lodging-house keeper who advanced them food and other necessities. Early pioneers had fought hard to retain a measure of control over their lives and work. They had banded together in *kongsi*, self-governing communities of *towkays* and their men, often sharing a common dwelling hut. This practice survived in some pockets, but as larger businesses moved in the relative independence of the *kongsi* had been lost. With their traditions of self-help they were demonized as criminal 'secret societies' by the British. By the 1930s most Chinese worked under labour contractors, who tendered mines and estates for work and docked commissions from labourers' wages for goods and services. In the Depression government and business had tried to stem the flow of labour and force down costs. The tin-mining labour force more than halved and, in 1930–32, over 75,000 labourers were repatriated to China. This was an insecure world in which gambling and opium were the principal means of escape for the worker. British doctors justified the government monopoly in opium by arguing that Chinese workers could not tolerate the conditions without it.[14]

Yet, below the surface, the rule of the bosses was being challenged. The labouring world of Kuala Lumpur was a hotbed for the first Chinese anarchists who came to Malaya in the wake of the May 4th movement of national awakening in China. On 23 January 1925 a woman anarchist exploded a bomb in a briefcase in the Chinese Protectorate, injuring herself and two British officers. For days she had been shadowing the governor. The bomb was retribution for those who had banished her lover to China and caused his early death. It was Malaya's first act of political terrorism. Anarchism appealed to groups of labourers whose traditions of self-help were already strong. By the late 1930s trades unions and the Malayan Communist Party had made inroads in the small industrial towns of the west coast. The vast domain of Malayan Collieries at Batu Arang in Selangor was a state within a state. Here the management saw its elaborate controls over a 6,000-strong workforce as modern and enlightened. But it was also a place where workers' indebtedness under the contract system was most severe. In March 1937 a soviet was established, and Malaya's principal source of power was paralysed by strikes. It was part of a wave of protest that enveloped the mines and rubber estates along the west coast, involving as many as 100,000 workers. The Batu Arang Soviet was crushed ruthlessly by 250 police and 200 Malay troops. They shot one worker and injured four more. Lacking citizenship, hundreds were banished to China. It was harsh, summary justice. The men banished after a Johore pineapple workers' strike in 1940 had an average age of thirty-three years and an average residence in Malaya of nine years.[15] Labourers found other ways of breaking their bonds. In the Depression, there was a flow of people into the forest behind the industrial areas, where they grew food in small market gardens. In the eyes of colonial law they were illegal 'squatters'. Their numbers would swell to nearly half a million in the war; their settlements became fortresses for the forgotten armies.

Indian labour was concentrated on rubber estates, living in what were virtually closed societies. The 'tappers' were mainly Tamil Hindus from south India. Before the First World War, a system of indenture had operated across the British Empire. The dire working conditions and systemic sexual abuse of the labourers had become a global scandal. It was on this issue that the young M. K. Gandhi had cut his teeth. But after its abolition in 1917, the rubber plantations of Malaya still remained perhaps the most strictly regimented workplace in the British Empire. Whole families, including children as young as ten, were put to work. The 'General Instructions of the Company' acted as a kind of King's Regulations for the workforce. Asian clerks – the *kirani* – were the NCOs of the estate, responsible for the parade and roll-call each morning. They were the often unbending enforcers of the rules that a labourer must dismount from his bicycle on passing a planter's bungalow, and only wear his hair parted in the traditional way. The *kirani* lived apart from the labourer. They were usually of a different community – Ceylonese or Malayalam-speakers from Kerala, for instance – and were often Christians. Below them stood the recruiter and overseer, the *kangany*, by turn the oppressor and the leader of the tappers.[16] The war unleashed an ugly struggle for power within these insular communities. Meanwhile, European planters superintended the whole from large bungalows at elevated points in the estate. Old methods of control died hard. After the war, a columnist in their trade magazine reminisced fondly: 'in the good old feudal times the planter was always metaphorically and occasionally (bad luck, Sir!) literally the father of his flock'.[17]

The Indian soldiers posted to Malaya after 1939 were horrified at the conditions endured by their countrymen, particularly the discrimination in their rates of pay relative to Chinese workers. The social scourge of estates was *toddy*, the alcoholic sap of the palm tree. It was the opium of the tapper, on which the government levied a tax and the estate made $25 per thousand bottles. It was a target for movements of religious renewal, such as the Dravidians. Action spread. Untouchables demanded entry to the temples on estates; there were parades on Gandhi's birthday and younger labourers wore homespun cloth in the

Congress fashion. The president of the newly formed Central Indian Association of Malaya might state that 'there is absolutely nothing in common between the politics of India and the politics of Malaya',[18] but any campaign to bolster the position of the Indians in Malaya needed links with the mother country and above all recognition and inspiration from the Indian National Congress. These links were strengthened by the triumphal progress of Jawaharlal Nehru through Malaya in 1937. The war was to catapult Malayan Indians to the front line of the subcontinent's struggle for freedom.

Passing from the port to the federal capital at night, Cocteau travelled through an endless semi-urban landscape, a 'big city' with 'a name that sounded vaguely French, ending "l'impure"'. Unlike Penang or Singapore, the capital of the Federated Malay States, Kuala Lumpur, was a frontier town. It was a new city, which numbered amongst its residents some of its first Asian and European pioneers. Notwithstanding the growing presence of the colonial bureaucracy, 'KL' retained an improvised feel that was characteristic of many other up-country towns that were emerging in this period. Cocteau waxed prophetic:

By night the 'impure' city seems floating in the darkness, levitated on the pinions of its innumerable fans. Shop fronts glitter with diamonds, with silken fabrics, with fruits and scent bottles. The big city proliferates further than the eye can reach, wears out the wanderer in its midst, defeats our last naïve belief in the supremacy of things European . . . We dared not so much as think of Paris.

He passed the shadowy verandas of the European hotels, built on a hillside near the minarets of the railway station. 'For whom?' he asked. 'Monkeys climb into the bedrooms, pilfer, and slit their throats with razors snatched from dressing tables. Not a white man was to be seen.'

The absence of Europeans was a central conceit of imperial power. The British saw the world in terms of immutable racial difference and governed it accordingly and at a distance. The Tamil was childlike and needed discipline, and was left largely to the authoritarian paternalism of the planters and a small labour department. The Chinese governed themselves through what one Chinese-speaking official called 'the ineradicable secret-society complex'.[19] Specialist European 'Protectors of Chinese' kept the peace with minimal interference. As one of the last of them, Victor Purcell, explained, they liked to see themselves as the local equivalent of the Mandarins in China.[20] The Malay was happy with his farming and fishing, in his *kampong*, or village, shy of towns, shy of work, under the feudal sway of his sultan. British district officers treated them as 'parishioners'.[21] European business encouraged ethnic specialization in the economy. To some extent migrants themselves chose to specialize, or to seek the security of others of their community concentrated in certain kinds of work. At other times they fought against this ethnic division of labour. But their ability to do so was lessened in the face of tightening controls over land and labour. A retired ICS officer from Burma, J. S. Furnivall, described this in the 1930s as 'the plural society': ethnic groups lived side by side, but separately from one another. They met only in the marketplace. It was a pessimistic picture of deepening communal antagonism.[22]

British rule over the Malay States was government by smoke and mirrors. The sprawling Moorish fantasy of the Federal Secretariat in Kuala Lumpur was run, it was said, by two men and a girl. The Malay rulers remained sovereign. They were cultivated through a mixture of bribery and flattery, and indulged with elaborate pantomimes of state. The Sultan of Johore received more guns in a salute than any Indian prince. Their very titles, 'sultan' for instance, were in many cases gifts of the British crown. Malay rulers and British Residents cultivated shared tastes, such as for the turf. The Kuala Lumpur and Singapore polo clubs were inner sanctums of rule: one of the final acts of imperial retreat in 1941 was to shoot the horses. Members of the Malayan Civil Service were avid consumers of Malay honours and pageantry. They were often *plus royalistes que le Roi*. The legendary architects of 'British Malaya' such as Sir Frank Swettenham and Sir George Maxwell defended Malay supremacy in retirement from the Travellers' Club in London's Pall Mall. Just as in the past nominal Chinese or Thai overlordship had been acknowledged with the ritual annual tribute of the white elephant kind, Protection did not necessarily affect the substance of local power. Malay rulers were required to act on the advice of the British Resident in all matters, except those relating to 'Malay custom and religion'. Yet for the Malays 'custom and religion' constituted the lifeblood of the states where the rulers added to their names the honorific 'Allah's Shadow on Earth'. The charismatic aura that went with this gave service to one's raja, proximity to his person, a powerful meaning. When, in December 1941, British Residents evacuated their posts, their Malay colleagues rallied round their rulers.

Al'Sultan Sir Ibrahim ibni Al'Marhum Al'Sultan Abu Bakar DK, SPMG, GCMG, KBE (Mil), the ruler of Johore, more than any monarch, illustrates the fragility of Britain's grip on the Malay world. His father, the first maharaja, Abu Bakar, had built Johore out of very little into one of the wealthiest and most independent of the Malay States. After his death in 1895, Ibrahim maintained this tradition. He was a big man in every sense. He could trace Malay princes, Bugis seafarers and 'pirates', Balinese and Danish in his ancestry. He had little formal education, and spoke English and Malay, it was said, equally well and equally badly. Although under closer British tutelage by a treaty of 1914, Johore had retained its own civil service, its own constitution and, uniquely in the British Empire, its own military forces, which outnumbered the British-raised Malay Regiment. The sultan even had his own Masonic lodge, the 'Lodge Royal of Johore', in which Masonic formulae were incanted in tandem with injunctions from the Holy Quran and the Hadith.[23] Ibrahim conducted independent diplomacy, visiting Japan in 1934 and befriending the Marquis of Tokugawa and a prince of the imperial family. They came to Johore to shoot big game. He was adept at playing off Singapore against London. Indeed, Ibrahim had a large personal fortune and spent much of his time in Europe, where he was an object of fascination to the popular press. A martyr to his gout, he went for periodic treatments to spas on the continent. In 1939, on one such visit, he was received secretly by Reichschancellor Adolf Hitler. The French police detained him briefly as a spy. The governor Shenton Thomas, like his predecessors, unsuccessfully tried to get the Colonial Office to block the return of Sultan Ibrahim to Johore. Yet Ibrahim had shrewdly given a gift of £250,000 to the British government, on top of an earlier £500,000 for the defence of Singapore. On his return to Johore he tried to expel a Jewish doctor and dressed his military forces in fascist-style armbands. In this fixation with military display, Sir George Maxwell likened him to Göring. Yet there is little evidence of serious duplicity on the part of Ibrahim or of any other Malay ruler. Ibrahim vigorously defended his interests, and his shrewdness in this inspired grudging respect from Europeans. The *kampong* Malays gave deference to his office, and admired his bravado. As a senior man in the Colonial Office conceded, he was 'in many ways a more able and energetic Ruler than is to be found amongst the princely houses of the other Malay States'.[24] During his rule, Johore became the prototype of crony capitalism with a European veneer.

There were other centres of power within Malay society. In the villages, individual *ulama*, or religious teachers, exercised great sway through networks of *madrasahs*, or religious schools, and increasingly, books and newspapers. They often possessed wider international connections than the Malay courts. The northeastern state of Kelantan was often portrayed as an isolated and introverted society, yet its *madrasahs* and village Quran schools attracted teachers from beyond its borders, from the Thai-ruled state of Patani to the Arab world, central Asia and Afghanistan. There were nearly 1,200 peninsular Malays in Mecca in 1942. They were Malaya's first refugees of war.[25] From the 1920s, in the newspapers and schools, Muslim scholars engaged in polemics between the 'Old' school of Islam and the 'New', which sought to modernize and purify local practice. In some *kampongs*, partisans of different camps took to praying in different mosques on a Friday. The religious feelings of the Malays were also expressed through the *tarekat*, or mystic orders, whose shaykhs commanded large followings of adherents. The holy man Haji Fadil of Johore, a favourite of the sultan, was said to have 4,000 followers. Some shaykhs were believed to have miraculous powers.[26] This tradition of leadership would resurface when things fell apart during the war.

There was also a challenge to the rulers from within their own courts. In 1928 a Johore notable, Onn bin Jaafar, attacked Sultan Ibrahim in an English-language newspaper with a sensational series of articles entitled 'Tyranny in Johore'. Both Onn's father and brother had been long-serving chief ministers of the state. The latter had recently been dismissed and banished to Singapore, where Onn himself lived in self-imposed exile, scraping a living editing the Malay newspaper *Warta Malaya*. A stormy petrel of a man with an air of scandal about him, Onn had fallen foul of the sultan on many occasions. Most of his allegations against the ruler, from nepotism to an early form of 'road rage' to which the sultan was unfortunately prone, rang pretty well true. Timorous Malay observers likened Onn's attack to the regicide of 1699 that had disabled the state of Johore for over a century. Eventually, though, the Sultan had to accept Onn back into favour, sending him in 1939 to run the Johore pavilion at the San Francisco World's Fair. This was a crucial admission of the growing power of letters.[27] The British had tried to find a role for such men in a second echelon 'Malay Administrative Service'. After preparatory school in England, Onn bin Jaafar had briefly attended the school founded for this purpose, the Malay College, Kuala Kangsar. At 'the Eton of the East', high-born young Malays were drilled in rugby and taught to eat with knives and forks. Some of the most vocal graduates established a series of State Malay associations in the late 1930s. They did not, however, seek to overthrow the system that still privileged them. Onn bin Jaafar was an altogether rarer and more dangerous creature: a republican. He was to resign from royal service in 1940 and re-emerge in 1945 as the first undisputed national leader of the Malays.

A new generation of Malay commoners was also finding a voice. An important source for this was the Sultan Idris Training College for Malay schoolteachers in Tanjong Malim, just north of Kuala Lumpur. The college was an unlikely site for innovation because it was founded to provide teachers for vernacular schools, the stated role of which was to educate Malays only to become better fishermen and farmers. Yet the Malay staff of the college generated a new enthusiasm for Malay literature and history, particularly the vanished golden age of the fifteenth-century empire of Melaka. They developed the Malay language in a new, standard Romanized script. The Japanese ally Ibrahim Yaacob was a graduate, and it was from amongst his co-students that many of the members of his Kesatuan Melayu Muda – the Union of Malay Youth – were drawn. To Ibrahim Yaacob, the rulers had left the Malays like 'a boat without a steersman'. His writings were a call to awareness of the Malay nation, the 'Bangsa Melayu', which was to take precedence over old loyalties. In this, the young had a special role. A Penang magazine called *Saudara* ('Friend') had created a revolutionary league of pen-friends modelled on the 'Teddy Tail League' of the *Daily Mail*. It allowed young Malays to address each other as strangers, as equals and across gender lines.

Conservatives panicked that it would encourage girls to write love letters. What began as a society for juveniles had become, by 1937, a body of 12,000 young adult Malays. It held the first peninsula-wide congress of Malays around the slogan 'Hidup Bahasa! Hidup-lah Bangsa!' – 'Long live the language! Long live the nation!' Malay fiction – much of it published by Sultan Idris Training College graduates – embraced new social and national themes. Amateur writers found a ready outlet in the eighty-one new newspapers or magazines that appeared in the 1930s, many in up-country towns. All of the newspapers were owned by non-Malays, particularly by the small but wealthy Arab community. The Kuala Lumpur daily Majlis, initially under the inspirational editorship of Abdul Rahim Kajai, carved out a reputation for the articulate defence of Malay interests. After 1939 it was edited by Ibrahim Yaacob, and he used his position, and Japanese money, to acquire the Warta Malaya. But a landmark event was the foundation in Singapore in 1939 of a Malay newspaper with both a Malay editorship and a Malay ownership: Utusan Melayu – 'The Malay Herald'. Its founders toured the mosques of Singapore and southern Malaya to raise capital: some 400 Malays responded, including taxi-drivers, hawkers and farmers. Among its founding editors were Abdul Rahim Kajai and Yusof bin Ishak, who was to become the first head of state of independent Singapore.[28]

Much of the received imperial wisdom about the 'the real Malay' was wrong, and the more perceptive British observers of Malay life began to point this out. The timeless lassitude of the kampong was a myth. Even in the Malay heartland of the northern states, rice growing and fishing co-existed alongside forms of waged employment and petty trade. The village community had a symbolic place in the life of all Malays, and was still the principal focus of life for most of them. However, Malays were becoming urbanized at a faster rate than any other community on the peninsula. The kampong was invaded by religious controversy and by a new generation of Malay entrepreneurs and opinion-makers. A central question was: 'Who are the Malays?' By taking on Arab and Indian Muslim business interests, Malay writers had sharpened their sense of ethnic identity. Through searching examinations of the Malay condition, they had argued for the strengthening of the Malays' position in Malaya. They were aware that by 1931 the

Malays had become a minority in their own country. Yet many 'Malay' areas of the peninsula were themselves sites of new settlement from Indonesia, particularly on the west coast and in the major cities. In a tea stall in Kuala Lumpur the Indonesian political exile, Sutan Jenain, would introduce local youths to the vocabulary of its revolution, particularly the word *merdeka* (independence). 'A nation is like a fish. If we are *merdeka*, we can enjoy the whole fish head, body and tail. At the moment, we are only getting its head and bones.'[29] The political imagination of the 'Malay world' stretched across territorial boundaries in dreams of a 'Greater Indonesia', which Ibrahim Yaacob himself voiced. But the central question was left unresolved: what was the Bangsa Melayu ultimately founded upon? If not the ruler, was it based on race, language, or religion? And what stake in it was there for the non-Malay peoples of the peninsula? What did the members of Malaya's kaleidoscopic society have in common?

## THE 'NEW WORLD' OF SINGAPORE

These questions were asked with greatest urgency in Singapore. Here all roads east crossed. Jean Cocteau stopped off on his voyage of 'leaps and bounds' and lingered there for six of his eighty days. Like most visitors, he was struck by the city's cleanliness, its 'elegant modernity'; its domestication of the jungle into parks, golf courses and a surfeit of playing fields. 'It is an axiom of British policy,' he reflected, 'that, if you keep young folk amused, they do not conspire against you.' Singapore was by the 1930s outwardly one of the most prosperous cities in the British Empire. Its civic and monumental heart expanded dramatically in the 1930s. It was centred on the hallowed ground of the Padang, a sports field surrounded by the Singapore Cricket Club, St Andrew's Cathedral, the Municipal Building and a magnificent new neo-classical Supreme Court. 'It's like Liverpool,' remarked one old hand returning in 1935 after a long absence, 'except that Liverpool has more Chinese.'[30] Across the narrow river lay Raffles Square, 'Singapore's Bund', and clustered around it were other wonders: modern offices and departmental stores. These too were sources of civic pride. Singapore was a triumph of telephony, refrigeration and air-conditioning. Emblematic of this was its first skyscraper, the Cathay Building and cinema, opened in 1939, the accompanying festivities including a special screening of *The Four Feathers*. It was to be a seat of government for a succession of regimes during and after the war. It was owned by the Chinese film magnate Loke Wan Tho. Loke and his rivals the Shaw brothers, Run Run and Run Me, served one of the most enthusiastic film audiences on earth. Shaw Brothers alone had 139 cinemas across the region.[31] After the fall, in an assault on Western cultural imperialism, the Japanese seized 50,000 reels of British and American films.

Singapore offered to celebrity travellers an instant glimpse of Asia: a tamed tropicality and luxury that had become legendary. Its havens were Raffles and the Adelphi Hotel where Cocteau stayed, but also the clubs around which Singapore's social world pirouetted. From here, literary visitors recycled old legends of the colonial frontier beyond the two-kilometre causeway that was the island's umbilical cord to the Malay peninsula. But what gave Singapore its special glamour was the breadth of its cosmopolitanism. More than Calcutta, London, or even New York, it was perhaps the first truly global city of the twentieth century. It was a hub of communications, and a city of infinite ethnic fractions. Arabs, Armenians, Jews, Parsis, White Russians and, not least, the 3,000-odd Japanese residents all contributed in their way to Singapore's general obsession with technology and consumption. Built not only for trade, but also for pleasure, Singapore was obsessed with modernity. 'Its god was money', recalled a newly married, newly arrived doctor from Madras, Dr Lakshmi Swaminathan, mourning the absence of the intellectual circles in which she had lived in India. As she ordered the latest in furniture for her home, she reflected that prosperity came at a price. Apart from a very privileged few, Asians in Singapore experienced a colour bar far higher than that of Madras, but most seemed indifferent to it.[32]

Ignoring expatriate advice, Cocteau fled the colonial town by night to another city, to a place known as the 'New World'. 'No white men come here. There is a medley of eastern races which, however, sort themselves out for the theatre. The Chinese, Mahometan, Malay and Japanese theatres are so close together that words and music mingle from stage to stage.' Cocteau walked from theatre to theatre – he saw identical crowds intent on Malay courtly pageants, Chinese domestic melodramas, fights and seductions, 'interminable monologues . . . no signs to a beginning or an end to the performances . . . a cacophony of squeals of nasal voices shifting from key to key, and several orchestras assailed our ears'. Cocteau paid the 'New World' nightly visits, and through it glimpsed Singapore's Asian underside.

To understand this part of Singapore's life, one needs to look away from the municipal heart of the city; away even from the older Chinatown and other ethnic enclaves, to newer Asian towns on its fringes. A Malay poet was to call them the 'now becoming towns/ with yellow electricity and greyish pipe-water/ here some of the characteristics of the jungle are intact.'[33] Yet they were as energized, cosmopolitan and intricately connected as the colonial city. They were a floating world of clerks and servants, of sailors and peddlers, of itinerant teachers and dancing girls; a place for the newly arrived and transient. One such area was Kampong Melayu, founded in 1927 on the eastern outskirts of the city. It was neither a *kampong* nor solely Malay. It was distinctly urban with no traditional village housing; it was in a place like this that growing numbers of Javanese or other peoples from the Indonesian archipelago were to be found. Many residents had come in through the pilgrimage brokers, who serviced Singapore's position as a transit point to Mecca. However, they came not only as pilgrims, they came to work. Kampong Melayu, and other such centres, were places for young people without family ties: men seeking adventure, or consumer goods and a new lifestyle, divorced women wanting anonymity and waged work as a domestic.[34] Such areas were a source of alternative services outside the colonial town, yet vital to the workings of Singapore society. To the Europeans, Kampong Melayu was an invisible city. When colonial society collapsed in 1942, it was to come into its own.

Cocteau had sensed something of this in the 'village-cities' of Penang and Kuala Lumpur. In Penang, Balik Pulau, literally the area behind the island, was a complex and turbulent mix of Chinese, Malay and Indonesian settlers. In Kuala Lumpur, there was a Malay 'new village' in the heart of the city, Kampong Bahru, and other similar enclaves that linked town and country. They brought different communities into day-to-day contact as never before. New arrivals had to form new ties quickly. These could, of course, be based on ethnicity. The Chinese had their clan associations; migrants from Indonesia had shared houses of people from the same place of origin, which were villages in miniature. Many jobs in the informal economy – rickshaw pullers, for example – were notoriously clan-based. Yet the expansion of the service economy, for the home, the office and the municipality, had created a more mixed labouring world. A wealthy European or Asian home would bring together a Chinese *amah*, or maid, a Malay *syce*, or chauffeur, and an Indian *kebun*, or gardener, operating through a Malay lingua franca. On a larger scale, in the invisible city, ethnic communities were pushed closer together, often for the first time. Individual men and women had to deal constantly with new encounters, in a wide variety of new situations. They had to improvise a way of speaking to each other. They had to undertake delicate negotiations, not least in crowded cities, over the sharing of space. Above all they had to forge a degree of trust. Life in this environment was a constant adventure, not without its risks and misunderstandings, but one in which many innovations in life and thought could occur.

Town life demanded new types of organization. Trade unionism was spearheaded by people in trades which were dispersed in small workforces and had looser conditions of employment, such as stevedores, barbers, shopkeepers, artisans and domestic servants. They were the first to realize the importance of forming larger collectives to bargain with employers. The early organization of the Malayan Communist Party was dominated by Hainanese, a Chinese community legendary for its clannishness and traditions of self-help and concentrated in these types of work. When the Special Branch raided a European home at 24 Nassim Road in April 1930 they succeeded in arresting most of the Party's leadership. Whilst the master and mem were away, the house had been used by servants for a political meeting. This was not untypical: many recent Indonesian migrants, for example, went into domestic service and took with them the more radical politics that flourished in their homeland. Malay trade unionism was pioneered among Malay *syces*. The Malayan revolution was a revolution of the houseboys.

The invisible city was a haven for exiles. When Tan Malaka fled China and settled in Singapore in 1937 he taught English in a Chinese school and moved constantly between different parts of the Asian city. When British surveillance of the Kampong Melayu became intense, he would decamp to the Chinese town. At this level, a certain neighbourliness resisted colonial policing. Tan Malaka was struck by how multiethnic the old community enclaves had become. At this level, too, people could lose some of their ethnic identity. Names themselves became ambiguous. Tan Malaka's memoirs, *From Jail to Jail*, make great play with the different passports he used and the various ethnic identities he assumed. They are written in an unusual, experimental kind of Malay, which is interwoven with English and other terms.[35] Malay writers adopted a bewildering style of shifting pseudonyms and acronyms. Their Chinese counterparts began to inject 'local colour' into their work, such as using equivalent Chinese phonemes for Malay words, to show how the various languages mixed in everyday speech. This style was to become characteristic of the left. One of the leading figures of the Malayan Communist Party at this time was a man known to posterity as Lai Teck. His ethnicity was at the time entirely ambiguous. He spoke English, French and Malay as well as Vietnamese and Chinese dialects. He used Vietnamese, Chinese and English noms de guerre – Chang Hong, Soh King, Lighter. After the war the newspapers would demand of him: 'Who is Mr Wright?' – his Special Branch codename.

Every detail of Lai Teck's life was shrouded in mystery, even his real name and place of birth. One of the few personal recollections of him that has survived comes from another senior party man in Singapore, Ng Yeh Lu. He believed Lai Teck's original name to have been Hoang A Nhac, born in the Nghe Tinh region of Vietnam, it seems, of Chinese or Chinese-Annamese parents. Lai Teck was, at any rate, around forty years of age in 1941; a dark-skinned, stocky man of around 5 feet 3 inches. The few extant photographs show a lean face, thin-lipped, with dark penetrating eyes. Ng Yeh Lu was to reflect on his physiognomy many years later: 'these are the features of a cruel, heartless and dangerous face, like the treacherous villain in a Chinese opera'.[36] Lai Teck cultivated his mystique. His early career seems to have included a period in the French navy, and activism with the Communist Party of Indo-China, in Vietnam, and also in Canton, Hong Kong and Shanghai, where he served on the town committee of the Chinese

Communist Party. Sometime in 1930 he was sent to Moscow for training, but seems to have been arrested at the border by the Chinese police and jailed in Mukden. Ironically, it was the Japanese invasion of Manchuria that saved him; the Chinese authorities opened the jails and Lai Teck spent time moving between revolutionary circles in the French concessions in Tientsin and Shanghai.

It was at this point that an extraordinary sequence of events began. Lai Teck fell into the hands of the French colonial police, the Sûreté. Yet rather than jailing him, they fed him back into Annam as their agent. He was blown in 1934, and useless to the French. However, he passed into the care of the British Special Branch in Hong Kong. He was then reintroduced into Singapore. His true identity was known to only a few senior intelligence men in Singapore. It was for them a massive coup, and upon it much of their illusion of security rested. Lai Teck's success must have exceeded expectations. He posed as a Comintern troubleshooter, sent to heal the divisions in the movement that had opened up after the aborted soviets of 1937. He worked on the wharves, and was active among labourers there. The mystique of his outside connections made a tremendous impact on the rank and file in Malaya; it is said that much of his support came from 'illiterate Hainanese'. He himself was illiterate in Chinese. He was, however, a vocal advocate of the united front for China, and in 1939 he emerged as secretary general of the party.[37] That Lai Teck remained undetected as a British spy for so long defies easy explanation. But it begins to make sense in the context of the fluidity of the social world he inhabited, a world where most people were strangers. There were many like Lai Teck who were disguising their past, living multiple lives, and many who were playing complex double games. There were other Comintern visitors. The founding meeting of the party in Johore in April 1930 had been attended by a Vietnamese, then called Nguyen Ai Quoc but better known by his alias Ho Chi Minh. Lai Teck was nearly unmasked as a fraud when he failed to recognize the veteran Comintern agent, Alimin, who visited Kuala Lumpur under a Chinese pseudonym.[38] The Frenchman Joseph Ducroux, alias Serge Leclerc, was arrested and jailed on a similar Comintern mission in 1931. The Malay radical Shamsuddin Salleh, working as a British agent, was involved in the affair and wrote a series of novels about it including *Hidup yang derhaka*: 'A revolutionary life'. The way in which Ibrahim Yaacob simultaneously courted the British, the Japanese and the Malayans could have been a plotline from any of these.[39] Lai Teck was a fan of spy movies, and was reported to have seen one film ten times in the occupation years. He thrived in the invisible city and its new trans-ethnic popular culture.

The New World, the amusement park at Kitchener Road that Cocteau repeatedly visited, captures this moment. It was opened in 1923 by two Straits Chinese merchants, offering cabaret boxing contests, wrestling matches, variety shows and operas. It was followed by Great World, which later was taken over by the film entrepreneurs the Shaw Brothers.[40] From the late 1920s, the Worlds emerged as a dramatic new feature of popular culture along with the radio and cinema, but enjoyed a much wider popularity than either on the Malayan scene. There was Hollywood Park, Great Eastern Park, Fairyland and Bukit Bintang in Kuala Lumpur; Fun and Frolic and Wembley Park in Penang; others in smaller towns. They provided accessible entertainment for all budgets. They featured prominently in the fiction and film of later eras; they were places for new styles and attitudes. Cocteau was deceiving himself that no Europeans visited the Worlds. For the colonial elite they had an exotic allure as 'the international stomping-grounds ... Here the colour of skins is, for a few short hours, not important: white and black unselfconsciously dance with yellow and tawny and enjoy it.'[41] There were Filipino jazz-bands and Chinese torch singers; the 'taxi-dancers' came from every conceivable background. Many of the Chinese girls had been displaced by the Sino-Japanese war and positioned themselves at the forefront of the patriotic struggle for China in Singapore.

Amongst all these attractions, the one that captures best the mood of the invisible city was the *commedia dell'arte* of the region, the Malay opera. Known as 'opera' chiefly because of its borrowings from Western vaudeville and its hybrid style and language, it brought a cosmopolitan palimpsest of stories – from *Don Quixote* to *Hamlet*, *The Thousand and One Nights* to *The Mask of Zorro* – to large urban and rural audiences. It was perhaps the most democratic art form in pre-war Malaya. It was fiercely secular: unlike Chinese opera it had no function in appeasing the gods. It was commercial: it attracted heavy investment and advertising. It popularized both the lilting sound of the *keroncong*, which became the mainstay of the local record industry, and the use of the Malay language. The Malay opera was multi-ethnic at every level, bringing together Straits Chinese owners and Malay writers and performers. Chinese artists of the new *Nanyang* school earned money as scenery painters. It outstripped the cinema in popularity, because it offered what the cinema did not: plays were broken up with special turns and improvised dialogue with the audience.[42] By the 1930s it adopted a more scripted form that addressed local issues more directly. Above all, opera gave a stage to the new politics. The China Relief Fund used theatre and the amusement parks for fund-raising, not least as a way of escaping a blanket ban on political meetings. Ibrahim Yaacob held political court in the cabarets of Bukit Bintang in Kuala Lumpur. There the new elite gathered. Some were seduced away from politics by the jazz age of imperialism. 'Was this not the thirties?' wrote Mustapha Hussain, then a young lecturer in an agricultural college. But he would also remember the haunting quatrains of a Malay songstress as a call to political action:

> Indian boys pray in their temple,
> Each carrying a candle,
> We are like the grass on the ground,
> Stamped upon by others day and night.[43]

Onn bin Jaafar was an aficionado of the *bangsawan*, and horrified his family by briefly marrying an actress.[44] Lai Teck himself part-owned, with one of his two wives, a coffee shop on Orchard Road, and was well known for his high living. These men and women were all part of what was known in the Dutch East Indies as 'the billiard generation'.[45]

There was a dark underside to this world. The urban population was still disportionately male and prostitution was ubiquitous. The Japanese *karayuki-san* had departed, but traffic in women was endemic to the British Empire in Asia. It was only in 1940 that the trade was ended in *mui tsai*, the so-called 'little sisters', impoverished children imported into Malaya from China as relatives and forced to become concubines. The cities were a place of moral panic: the plight of fallen women in the towns was a staple of Malay fiction. Tan Kah Kee raised the issue personally with Chiang Kai Shek: the Kuomintang businessmen behind the Worlds had placed a slur on China's prestige: 'in earlier times it was actually quite difficult for an Englishman to associate with a Chinese woman'.[46] As fighting men poured into Singapore there was a growing concern with commercial sex: it was 'nasty, brutish and in shorts'.[47] Venereal disease rates were high: in 1940 the infection rate for troops in Malaya was 115 per 1,000.[48] A report on the mental health of Singapore just after the war found suicide rates to be particularly high amongst taxi-dancers.[49] Taxi-dancers went on strike at Great World in September 1941. There was little help for these women. The charitable Po Leung Kuk Homes attempted to find fallen Chinese women a respectable husband. Some prostitutes formed sororities which provided for their members in old age. However, this was a young population that did not have strong arrangements for care of the old and vulnerable. The European citizens of the towns were reminded of this in the plain chant of the urban poor: 'no father, no mother, no *makan* [food], no whisky, no soda'. In the city there was a very thin line between often spectacular success and abject failure. This would be central to the collective memory of the war, and working women would be amongst its first and most defenceless victims.

Beneath the veneer of the model colony lay a volatile urban world. The British built up a formidable armoury to keep the peace. They had Chinese-speaking expatriate officers, local Chinese detectives, a small army of translators to pore through the vernacular press. They created a sub-culture of informants eager to give tittle-tattle at a piece rate. By the late 1930s colonial policemen flattered themselves that they had Malaya under control. But there was a more insidious threat. The theatre and cinema inflamed sensitivities and were a nightmare to control. What law could possibly govern what was improvised on stage? Hollywood too was seen as the villain. Movies showed, for the price of a few cents, 'the superior race at play, or at war with itself'.[50] Above all, it displayed white women as lascivious and sexually access- ible. When the planter turned secret agent Bruce Lockhart returned to Malaya in 1935 after an absence of twenty-five years, having been ejected after a tempestuous affair with a Malay woman, he discovered that the film version of his earlier escapades had been banned.[51] Singa- pore was a place for pleasure, but its prissiness exasperated visitors. The governor's wife was serenaded by Noël Coward:

Oh, Lady Clementi, you've read a lot of G. A. Henty.
You've not read Bertrand Russell and you've not read Dr Freud.
Which perhaps is the reason you look so unenjoyed.
You're anti-sex in every form, or so I've heard it said,
You're just the sort who would prefer a cup of tea instead.
You must have been a riot in the matrimonial bed.
Whoops – Lady Clementi.[52]

Lady Clementi's crime was her campaign to make the bars and clubs close by midnight. For his part, Jean Cocteau was glad to leave the European world of Singapore. He was worried that 'if, in an island where Kodaks are confiscated ... if here the Intelligence Service had an eye on us, they may well have wondered what we were after in the slums'. He had no regrets about his time spent there. As he sailed for Hong Kong, on a Japanese ship, the *Kashima Maru*, Cocteau was reassured by the thought that 'despite its lawns and tennis courts, shops and banks, Singapore is still a creature of the wild'.

## MALAISE

Britain's Malayan pastorale was at an end. Europeans in Malaya would remember the late 1930s with frangipani-fringed nostalgia. The personal horrors that were to follow ensured this. The Europeans in Malaya were a small but distinctive settler community, some 31,000 strong. Some families had served over several generations: the Maxwells, the Braddells and the Braddons. The British liked Malaya and liked the Malays. They admired their aristocratic ease and their good-natured placidity: 'Nature's gentlemen', Sir Frank Swettenham called them. To read memoirs and letters of these years, the British in Malaya lived absorbed in a pageant. They spoke a patois of Malay interspersed with outmoded English slang. They did not lack refinement; every official had to know a language to achieve promotion. The accumulation of local knowledge over several generations was reflected in an impressive tradition of scholar administrators that led back to the founder of Singapore, Thomas Stamford Raffles himself. It reached its apogee with figures such as Sir Richard Winstedt, of whom it was said

'God gave the Malays a language; Winstedt gave them a grammar'.[53] In the 1930s there was growing work on the early history and archaeology of the region by men such as the gargantuan Pieter von Stein Callenfels, whom Conan Doyle took as a model for Professor Challenger in *The Lost World*. But there was also a transience about the life of the British in Malaya. This was brought home by an influx of new people by the 1930s, who, old hands felt, were not quite the thing and did not know the country. This was the imperialists' nostalgia for what they had themselves destroyed. Old hands held on to a vision of what Winstedt called 'the real Malaya, shy and reserved to all but her lovers'.[54]

The media declared war on the British in Malaya long before the Japanese ever did. The phrase 'whisky-swilling planters' was coined by *The Times*' correspondent Ian Morrison in his despatches from Batavia after the fall. It was to stick. A few years before Cocteau visited Malaya, another Frenchman, Henri Falconnier, won the Prix Goncourt with a biting satire of planter life. It began: 'The anniversary of the armistice was celebrated in Kuala Paya by two minutes' silence and two days' orgy.'[55] To be sure, the flood of new arrivals after 1940 found Malaya a curious place. Many were shocked by its social excesses, outraged that Malaya partied while London burned. Other visitors were rather disappointed. The newly wed Australian wife of the district officer of Klang, Jean Falconer, complained in a letter home: 'I imagined a more Somerset Maugham atmosphere, more "jungly" and enclosed and somewhat redolent of mystery'. Instead she chafed at the endless tea parties.[56] Up-country, arcane rituals survived, such as 'calling', leaving one's card at the houses of the wives of one's seniors; not to be received, but to acknowledge the hierarchy and to hope to be invited in the future. Many called; not all were chosen. There was much to parody: the cloying ennui and 'muck sweat' of the up-country club; the slow alcoholism of *stengahs* and *pahits* [bitters] punctuated with sudden, guilty physical excesses, such as the Hash House Harriers run, which had its origins in the 'Spotted Dog' of Kuala Lumpur, the Royal Selangor Club. Expatriates 'who would vote conservative in Moscow' were a soft target for the journalists who swept into Malaya on the eve of the war.[57]

Old Malayan hands resented this bitterly.[58] British administration had its material and intellectual achievements: great works and a deep pool of local knowledge. A deputy municipal engineer argued the case for the defence in a memoir published in 1943: the standard of living was 'just and necessary' given the hardships and sacrifices of tropical life. For example, 'cars could not be considered a luxury in Singapore', to walk was a physical impossibility.[59] 'They have but to shave themselves and to eat, everything else is done for them', wrote the editor of the Penang *Straits Echo*, George Bilainkin. Yet, that done, he argued, life for a young man in the tropics was a tragic condition of 'fighting loneliness everywhere'.[60] There was a bitter price for living an idyll. Aside from amateur theatricals, what was there for a European to do? As Katherine Sim, the artist wife of a customs officer, put it: 'For the European sojourner in Malaya, the lifelines back to his intellectual sources are too long.' Given this, the Anglo-Malayans could be excused their whisky *stengahs*. At the root of it all was a recurring image of the jungle landscape which seemed to reclaim all human endeavour. Malaya was rich in civilizations which had left little material residue. 'Masterpieces can't be risked out here – at the mercy of white ants and mildew.'[61] This was the inescapable sadness of the tropics, the mocking melancholy of empire in the East.

Even to the privileged residents of the Malay states, Singapore was an altogether brasher world. Here, to be European was not merely to transplant a British identity and lifestyle to the tropics, it was to take it to a new plane altogether. The rituals of suburban life were played out in grotesque. When Bruce Lockhart returned to Malaya, 'the most fundamental change' he observed was 'the huge increase in the number of white women and the passing of the directing force of social life into their hands'.[62] To Lockhart, as to many others, this was not altogether a good thing. Women of 'English or Scottish suburban class' were 'pampered and admired out of all proportion to their deserts'.[63] But this was not a situation created solely by the women themselves. To the men, women were charged with reinforcing a febrile obsession with white prestige and purity, whether out in society or in the ordering of the home. A guide to this, *Malay for Mems*, was published in 1927 and was still being reprinted after the war. It was written entirely in the language of command: 'Put up the tennis net'; 'You must follow the Mem', 'Shoot that man'.[64] Yet there were intrinsic tensions to this:

even in the home, domestic service brought an inescapable intimacy with and dependency upon Asians. Some women rebelled against their role, but there were intense pressures to maintain 'form'. The high cost of living was not the least of the white man's burdens. Prestige increasingly demanded a diet of imported foodstuffs from the Cold Storage emporium: 'Horror!', one correspondent to the *Straits Times* exclaimed in 1933. 'Dogs must be licensed. Why not servants? . . . If they ask such high wages as $30 a month, muzzle 'em.'[65] The Depression widened the gap between European officials and the Malayan Civil Service, whose ability to maintain 'form' was supported by cost-of-living increases. Destitute Europeans who could not sustain this were deported. It was a world where Europeans did not carry money. Everything went on a 'chit'. In every sense, colonial society lived on credit.

The definition of 'European', the boundaries of who was 'in' and who was 'out', were tightened in these years. There was pressure from the inner core of colonial society to maintain social distance and to keep in line any Europeans who threatened to blur the margin. At that margin lay the Eurasians, a prominent and diverse community. The subtle screen that divided Singapore society was symbolized at Singapore's ceremonial core. At one end of the Padang stood the exclusive Singapore Cricket Club; at the other the Eurasian club, the Singapore Recreation Club. When cricket matches were played European and other spectators stood at different sides of the field. Distinctions were upheld in salary scales for the same work. At this racial boundary, mere suspicion of Eurasian blood was enough to set the limits of ambition to a young man's career or to a woman's marriage prospects. It was not so much dalliance that was frowned upon as its legitimation in marriage, when the inheritance of property became an issue. 'There is no place for the individual who rebels against Singapore's strictest convention.'[66] Racial boundaries were manipulated to define who had access to wealth and power and who did not. They were not enshrined in law, but in social convention and through the subtleties of salaries and employment and a range of municipal fiats that were rarely couched in terms of race at all. British Malaya was built on a viciously insidious form of apartheid.

Only the most powerful of subjects could challenge this. Johore was one place where social exclusion was impossible: the International Club was in the grounds of one of Sultan Ibrahim's palaces. In 1930 the sultan married Mrs Helen Wilson, widow of a Scotsman from Singapore, who had been employed as governess to his grandchildren. This put sensitivities on edge. Could this woman be recognized as sultana, a point upon which Ibrahim insisted? Even more vitally, could she be received at Buckingham Palace? The issue was fudged. The following year she was received with an 'ordinary entrée' presentation; she did not take her place with her husband on the dais at the more formal state ceremonial. The question re-emerged with the coronation of 1937. There it was agreed on 'the undesirability of anything being done which tends to glorify a mixed marriage'. 'It is', a courtier argued, 'one of the few subjects upon which East and West are in agreement.'[67] Notwithstanding his own exotic parentage, Ibrahim himself had expelled subjects who had married Europeans. The British consoled themselves that at least the marriage kept the sultan out of Johore, and that the sultana was beyond child-bearing age. Yet they agonized over the succession. The secretary of state ordered an investigation. It revealed that the ultimate taboo had been broken: in Perak, a European woman had become the mistress of a Malay.[68] After the Sultan of Johore's marriage was dissolved, he set the nerves of the Colonial Office jangling again with a highly publicized friendship with a cabaret dancer. When she died tragically in the Blitz, the sultan, now in his late sixties, married again in November 1940, after a whirlwind romance, Marcella Mendl, a Romanian émigré. They had met at Grosvenor House, London, where she had taken shelter during an air raid, after he had bought a Red Cross flag from her.[69] The sultan and 'Lady Ibrahim' returned at the beginning of January 1941 to a 21-gun salute and public holiday. He grumbled to the press that his favourite Lucky Strike cigarettes were unavailable and, with great prescience, urged his people to grow tapioca and potatoes.[70]

The local obsessions of race were taken to grotesque extremes with the arrival in 1941 of tens of thousands of white proletarians. Soldiers' journeys into colonial Asia were fraught with tension. Troopships had to follow the longer route via Freetown in Sierra Leone – still the unhealthiest port in the entire Empire – with brief stops at the Cape and Mombasa. By late 1940 they were making the voyage in large numbers. Bombardier Harry Innes of the 122nd Field Regiment sailed from Glasgow to India in early January 1941 on, of all vessels, the *Empress of Japan*. In a letter home he wondered at it: 'a real grand ship, a luxury ship. I bet it would cost me over a £100 for a trip in her in peace time to where we are going.'[71] Of course, he was unable to tell his family where that was. Harry Innes wrote home of the sight of 'black men' and monkeys and of watching Chaplin in *The Great Dictator* in a Bombay picture palace. From here, the troops would move on to be acclimatized at camps in Bombay Presidency such as Deolali, the traditional preventive against going 'doolally' in the heat. Or they would push on further east: Innes sailed in a convoy of twenty-one troopships, guarded by the state-of-the-art battleship *Prince of Wales*, three cruisers and eleven destroyers, one of the troopships being, incognito, the *Queen Mary*.

Bombardier Innes's letters home from Malaya speak of isolation and frustration. British soldiers were bored; bored of shows, bored with the routine of morning drill, and with constantly changing their clothes in the heat. They were bitter that they alone of the troops in Malaya had to wear tunics. In the afternoons they played sport. 'If it weren't for the match every night I am sure we would go barmy.'[72] On the whole conditions were poor. Most of the military rations were imported. Soldiers went hungry in comparative abundance. If food was in short supply, drink was not. Duty-free liquor and cigarettes cost the government 1 million Straits dollars in 1940. The Australians, who arrived from early 1941, were humiliated by the treatment meted out to 'poor whites' in Singapore. They were not permitted to enter the sacred European clubs and hotels; the people they were sent to defend did not wish to know them socially. Even former residents whose membership dated from before the war were denied their clubs in Australian uniform. They took to the bars of Lavender Street and were despised for it. In the Worlds, the troops of the Dominions met with the Argylls who were already established on the island: 'great and bloody were the battles'. Society women were instructed to 'adopt' and entertain troops. This was not a success.[73] However, the ANZAC clubs established by Australian expatriates became very popular by throwing their doors open to British troops.

As the Australians moved up the peninsula they fraternized more readily with the local communities than did the British. As a Ceylonese lawyer in Batu Pahat observed, 'it was our first contact with a citizen army'. He discovered thirty lawyers in the brigade stationed there. A dinner was organized. Remembrance Day 1941 was 'commemorated with gay abandon. Thousands flocked to witness the fete on the town *padang*. The gayest of all were the Australians, who delighted the crowds by dancing the *ronggeng*', a sensual Malay rhythm.[74] In nearby Malacca, officers were given sumptuous European dinners with turkey and champagne by Tan Cheng Lock.

The egalitarian ethos of the citizen army was anathema to British professional soldiers.[75] The global publicity of the fighting record of ANZACs was a matter for resentment by British officers, and may explain in part the scapegoating of the Australian troops and their commanders after the fall of Singapore. It was resented by Malaya's Indians too, who heard little news of the seventeen Indian battalions sent to defend them.[76] The Australians felt that they were innocent victims of Singapore's reputation. They grew violently disgusted with their own press, which suggested they were enjoying a tropical holiday. There were pictures of them taking their ease with taxi-dancers; some were sent white feathers from home. The journalist Gilbert Mant had been in Malaya in late 1941 as an enlisted man in the Australian Imperial Force. He was recalled home, only to return a few months later as a Reuters correspondent. He found his old comrades to be 'mentally sick . . . They had a hatred of Malaya almost amounting to a phobia.'[77]

For Indian troops, contacts with the local population were less cordial. The Punjabis of 8th Indian Brigade who were stationed at Malaya's first line of defence were remembered for the suppression of the Malay rebellion of Tok Janggut in 1915, an event which was a living memory of some, part of the folk memory of all. But there was a deeper problem. Indian officers were subject to the colonial exclusion of Malaya. This was an unforeseen and shocking humiliation. G. S. Dhillon of the 1/14 Punjab Regiment had worked his way up from a sepoy mule driver to a captain. In Malaya he was confronted not only with racial slights, but with the promotion of planters above the rank of Indian officers. European officers were increasingly at odds with Indian officers; Indian officers were not allowed to join the local club or ride in the same railway carriage as Europeans. However, Hindu and Muslim officers did begin to sit together at the same table to eat, against all army traditions and reflecting both an increasing antagonism towards the British and an increasing sense of national solidarity. One of the most disenchanted was Major Mohan Singh, who would later lead the Indian National Army; he was no longer on speaking terms with his commanding officer.[78] Some troops were already close to mutiny: in May 1941 the 4/19th Hyderabad Regiment at Tyersall Park in Singapore rebelled when an Indian officer was ordered home, ostensibly for living with a white woman. His nationalist views were well known amongst his troops. The regiment was disarmed by the Argyll and Sutherland Highlanders, the officer reinstated, and the whole business hushed up.[79] The British hastily recruited Chinese agents to report on the loyalty of the Sikhs in Penang.[80]

Despite these tensions, colonial society approached the last days of peace in a strange illusion of security. The Malayan Civil Service, the plantocracy and their mems, began to prepare slowly for war. The men organized themselves into volunteer reserves. This was an extension of the Malayan Civil Service maxim that the right sort of chap could turn his hand to anything. In Negri Sembilan they spent ten days in the Jelebu jungle with the chief game warden. A jungle fighting unit was trained in the north at Kroh; it recruited Malays, chiefly from the forestry service.[81] Only one in ten Europeans were exempt in reserved occupations. In one firm of eighty-eight European staff, fifty-nine were mobilized. Perhaps, it was later argued, they would have been more use at their posts, or as liaison officers for the regulars who did not know the country or its languages. British Malayans resented professional soldiers taking their ease. They were at pains to point out that they were doing two jobs, the soldiers only one. Many women involved themselves in paid work for the first time. Certainly there was something of what one diarist called a 'musical comedy setting' to the war effort. The preparations for war reflected the Singapore obsession with neatness and order. When the blackouts were introduced, a neat white line was placed down the middle of each street and the trunks of the trees bordering them were lime-washed; immense energy was diverted to removing posts and that uniquely British road fixture, the traffic island, of which Singapore had many.

The lack of civil preparation, the general 'Malaise', was to be a persistent charge against the British in Malaya. But, by the outbreak of war, the people of Malaya had experienced more intrusive government than at any time in its history, especially in the form of food controls and price fixing. Mindful of Malaya's dependence on imported rice, the authorities had by 1940 built up reserves for 180 days. The state also took on new functions such as surveillance and propaganda. By April 1940 there were 312 officers involved in censorship in Singapore and 58 in Penang, plus a number of part-time workers, many of them European wives reading each other's mail.[82] Much of the propaganda was recycled material from the BBC and the Ministry of Information, who were convinced that Chinese, Indians and Malays would be most persuaded by pictures of the English countryside, Buckingham Palace and the changing of the guard. However, the Ministry of Information in Singapore soon had a staff of over 100 and issued Chinese newspapers and illustrated propaganda in four languages at a rate of a million pieces a month. Before December 1941 the Japanese could not be mentioned. Instead was broadcast – in the style of Orson Welles's adaptation of *War of the Worlds* – a 'nightmare' of conquest by the fascists. The dire situation was disguised by over-confident propaganda which encouraged complacency about the scale of the threat.[83] When the war began, the need to maintain this posture immobilized the British regime. The Japanese-owned daily the *Singapore Herald* fought against the mood by applauding Chinese cabaret girls for dancing with Japanese men and with such headlines as 'Down with alarmism' and 'Prepare for peace'.[84] In October, around 600 Japanese and their families were evacuated, and the consul-general was recalled at the end of the month. But many remained.

The cost of Malaya's war by the beginning of 1941 was in the region of £3 per head, most of it falling on Asians whose average income was between £4 and £5 a month. The lotteries to pay for the war effort enflamed civic morality by targeting the poor. Much of the work was being done by Asians too. In the early days there was opposition to this, particularly to demands for labour and the harsh wartime conditions of its employment: in 1941 there were new curbs on trades unions. When Indian rubber workers in Selangor launched a fresh wave of strikes from early March for a minimum wage, they met with violent suppression. After an incident on 15 May at a French-owned plantation in Klang, when four Indians died by army bullet or bayonet, a state of emergency was declared there. Yet there was also a quiet revolution underway, a mobilization of civic life that was an important seizure of initiative by Malayans going beyond gestures of loyalty to the imperial regime. Asians from all communities came forward as night watchmen, volunteer firemen and air-raid wardens. There were 4,300 wardens in Singapore and 1,340 in Penang. Boy Scouts worked as spotters; 2,100 enlisted in the St John Ambulance Brigade.[85]

The British attempted to revive the martial tradition of the Malays, which they had spent nearly seventy years of colonial rule trying to subdue. The Malay Regiment founded in 1933 was expanded to nearly 1,500 men, including those of the Johore military forces. So too were the local Volunteer Forces. The motives for joining these units in days of peace varied. At least some of the Volunteers were attracted to a diversion from the monotony of small-town life: recruits pocketed a transportation allowance of 20 cents a mile, which gave money for the weekend's entertainment, and gained access to a European-style clubhouse and swimming pool. This was perhaps more of a draw than any abstract empire-loyalty. Few thought they would ever have to fight. 'We are only meant [to be] something like boys scouts and all', as one Malacca Volunteer put it.[86] Yet by the outbreak of war volunteer armed forces numbered over 10,000, with around 33,495 civil defence volunteers of one kind or another coming forward. Although the militias were staffed with more European officers in wartime, the head of the voluntary civil defence in Selangor was the businessman H. S. Lee. He controlled 6,000 men, an unprecedented level of authority for an Asian. Independently of the British, politicized young Indians enlisted in the Indian Passive Defence Force; it was over 900 strong, running five relief camps and a community hospital along Buffalo Road. These centres provided Chinese porridge to the displaced in the absence of community leaders, who, one activist noted, had 'gone back [to India] to save their own skins'.[87] The leaders of these groups would continue to mobilize their communities after the fall of Singapore. Civil society did not collapse in Malaya, even if the British component of it did.

Meanwhile, the last days of peace saw a final flurry of arrivals and departures across the crescent. The celebrities continued to drop in. The journalist Martha Gellhorn – then Mrs Ernest Hemingway – came, and immediately left, disappointed to find no war in progress. American reporters such as Cecil Brown of Columbia Broadcasting were particularly scathing about British colonialism and fell foul of its censorship. The former Soviet foreign minister, Maxim Litvinov, was put up at Government House in Singapore, en route to the United States, and sank into a deep Slavic depression. British officers, on the other hand, embraced the gaiety of Singapore wholeheartedly. As one civilian grumbled, they could be accused 'amongst other things, of raising market prices, spoiling servants, and being a little too obvious in bars and restaurants'.[88] One pilot's wife spoke of 'living on Pink Gin Pahits and Benzedrine tablets'.[89] There was a sudden influx of European women, service wives and nurses to reinforce the military hospitals. They too were swept up in the social whirl. An Australian girl stranded on holiday in Kuala Lumpur, Caroline Reid, worked with the volunteer forces there. She recorded her weekend of 29 and 30 November 1941, the last of peacetime. Saturday began with a call on the military emergency line, a demand for tips for the races. In the evening, dinner at the chief secretary's hill top mansion Carcosa, the band playing in the Sultan of Selangor to the tune of 'Pop Goes the Weasel'. Then there was the inevitable amateur dramatics for the War Fund (*No Time For Comedy*), and back to Carcosa for drinks. She went to bed at 3 a.m., only to rise early to attend an elephant round-up. It all brought to mind 'the old story of the Eve of Waterloo'.[90]

# I

# 1941: Last of the Indian and Burmese Days

When Cocteau made his journey down the great crescent to Singapore it was still possible to ignore the sounds of war. But the journeys of 1940 and 1941 took place in an atmosphere of high tension. In the autumn of 1941, a few weeks after Subhas Chandra Bose reached Berlin, and ten thousand miles away in Tokyo, the cautious Prince Konoe was abruptly replaced as prime minister by General Tojo Hideki, a tough, fifty-seven-year-old soldier and leader of the war party. After the war, Konoe revealed how Emperor Hirohito had come to see eye to eye with the militarists: 'gradually he began to lean towards war. And the next time I met him he leaned even more towards war ... as a prime minister who lacked authority over the high command, I had no way of making any further effort because the emperor, who was the last resort, was this way.'[1] During the months of October and November Japan's dizzying war plan rapidly took shape. Far from vacillating as last-ditch negotiations in Washington to avoid conflict ran into the sand, the high command were already planning how to end triumphantly a war they had not yet even started. Their 'Working Plan for Ending the War with the U.S., Britain, the Netherlands and Chiang kai-shek' recommended: 'wait for a good opportunity in the European war situation, particularly collapse of mainland England, ending of German–Soviet war and the success of our policies towards India'.[2] The day originally planned for the Pearl Harbor attack, 8 December, was only a stepping stone on this long advance. By early November Hirohito had already approved the forward strategy. Visions of conquest danced before his eyes: 'I understand you are going to do Hong Kong after Malaya starts. Well, what about the foreign concessions in China?'[3]

# INDIA ON THE BRINK

While the Japanese gave no thought to how they would defend the perimeter of the huge area they were intending to conquer, the British appeared equally unprepared. India was the only significant source of British military power in the East and Indian armies were to play a disproportionate role in the fighting in Burma and Malaya. Yet young British and American officers who came to India later in the war often claimed they were astonished by the lethargy of the government of India and India Command. Eric Stokes, later historian of the Raj, served with a mountain artillery regiment. He wrote that, even at the end of the war, his commanding officer was 'a horsey fellow' who disliked 'stinking mechanical vehicles'.[4] Throughout the war India Command's fortnightly situation appreciations conventionally began with an account of operations on the North West Frontier in which British officers pursued shadowy mullahs over the hills and frustrated the plots of obscure tribal insurgents. Stokes felt that the Faqir of Ipi, a Muslim rebel and long-time thorn in the imperial flesh, seemed to loom as large in their minds as Tojo and Hitler even when the Japanese stood at the gates of India. By then, bashing the 'gin-swillin' pukka sahibs' in the East had become a British national pastime.

The Indian top brass, however, were not necessarily as short sighted as they seemed. The North West Frontier was menaced by sporadic revolts over the border and inside by the sustained resistance of the pro-Congress Red Shirt movement of Abdul Ghaffar Khan. It also remained critical to Britain's war effort because many of the best Indian army troops who fought in North Africa and later Italy and Burma were recruited here. The Indian army, while still starved of money and poorly equipped, was not as staid as it appeared either. As a force of Indians recruited from the so-called martial races with one third British other ranks, but officered mainly by Britons, it was beginning to adjust to Indians' national aspirations as well as to the need for modern weapons. It had changed out of all recognition in the first two years of the war. During the Depression years there was still a large pool of British public-school boys waiting for a life of service under the tropical sun. That pool drained away abruptly in 1939 and

1940. Young British servicemen were still being drafted into the Indian army as officers but, according to Sydney Bolt, not all of them were the 'right type', that is public-school men from old Indian families who regarded politics with disdain. Bolt, who arrived in India as a subaltern, certainly knew that he was 'the wrong type'. A Cambridge-educated member of the Communist Party, his aim was to 'bore into the Raj from within.'[5] Scarcely had he arrived in the subcontinent than he made contact with Indian communists across the country. While few were as politically committed as Bolt, many of the new British officer class in India had no natural allegiance to the Empire.

The biggest change was on the Indian side. The process of Indianizing the officer corps, which had proceeded very slowly in the 1920s and '30s, was gathering pace. Now hundreds of young Indian men were being commissioned as Viceroy's Commissioned Officers. A few Indians even achieved a King's Commission and stood on equal terms with their British brother officers, at least in theory.[6] The fledgling Royal Indian Air Force and Royal Indian Navy were expanding, too. Indian fighter pilots flew in the Battle of Britain. Most of these new officer cadet recruits were from old landed families in the Punjab and North West Frontier Province, home of the 'martial races', but increasing numbers now came from middle-class families in the towns and from areas such as Madras and the United Provinces. These populations had long been classed as effeminate or politically suspect by the old army 'wallahs'. Why did Indians enlist? The honour of military service and a relatively secure income in an impoverished country certainly attracted these young men. A sense of adventure and a chance to learn new skills were difficult to pass up. K. K. Tewari, later major-general, a Punjabi Brahmin educated at Foreman Christian College, Lahore, and his brother were typical.[7] While the two brothers were sitting for the Indian State Railways entrance examination in 1940 they got to know a certain Lieutenant-Colonel Kilroy, a local recruiting officer. Tewari believed that Kilroy had used his influence to get them failed in the examination so that he could recruit them into the army. Tewari went on to a distinguished military career in signals in the British and independent Indian armies.

Yet many of these officer recruits still insist today, when their views are regarded with suspicion by their countrymen, that they joined up with British colours because they genuinely believed that the Allies were fighting against fascist barbarism. Lieutenant A. M. Bose, nephew of Sir J. C. Bose, India's most famous contemporary scientist, was a case in point. He had spent some time in Britain, Germany and Austria. He wrote to Ian Stephens, the radical British journalist, in 1943: 'I am now in the Army since three years as I wanted to do my bit to fight the Nazis.'[8] Yet even after taking the king's shilling, many recruits still counted themselves as nationalists and made clear to their British officers early in the war that the writing was on the wall for imperial rule. This was to be a source of underlying anxiety in the army. Another characteristic recruit of this type was a young nationalist, T. B. Dadachanji. He was in Britain at the beginning of the war and also identified with the struggle against Hitler. As Gandhi's Quit India movement exploded in the summer of 1942, he was to face an acute clash of allegiance.[9]

That these tensions did not generally lead to mutiny was the result of the tact of a small group of senior officers, British and Indian. One of them was the craggy Anglo-Irishman and last British commander-in-chief of the Indian army, General Claude Auchinleck.[10] Auchinleck served long in India, quietly identified with Indian aspirations and was one of the originators of the Indianization policy of the 1930s. He had personally seen to it that Indians were put in command positions whenever their British officers were on leave or out of station. Ironically, for a man whom Churchill identified with the hidebound traditions of the Indian army, he was viewed askance by the real military conservatives.

A typical lynchpin of the army put in place by Auchinleck was Ajit 'Jick' Rudra, later major-general and a commander of independent India's armed forces. Rudra was from a Bengali family of teachers who had first been influenced by the reformist Brahmo Samaj (Divine Society) and had then converted to Christianity. The family's allegiances were complex. Rudra's father was responsible for bringing Gandhi from South Africa to India during the First World War and Gandhi remained a family friend. Rudra himself was not a very political man. In 1915 he had gone up to Cambridge University, hoping for an undergraduate sporting life but finding the place even duller than usual because all the young men were away in the trenches. He joined the

British army in search of manly adventure. At this time the India Office in London was still trying to stop Indians getting a King's Commission. For obscure reasons, Rudra held a Ceylonese passport and got round this restriction. He had a 'good war' and returned to India to staff college and a career among the skirmishes of the North West Frontier. Rudra was appalled by the repressive British actions against nationalist demonstrations in 1919. Was it right to remain in the British army? He went to Gandhi to seek advice. According to Rudra's account, the Mahatma refused to pass judgement, saying that Rudra was a mature man and knew his own mind. Irritated, he snapped at Gandhi, who replied mildly that India would one day be given its freedom by the British and India would then need its own army.[11] Reconciled to his career, Rudra went on to play a key role in bolstering the morale of Indian officers and men during the last days of the Raj, from time to time smoothing over incidents when British personnel treated their Indian equals and subordinates with racial prejudice and contempt.

One other key figure beginning his career in the Indian army in the 1930s was a Burmese Karen, Smith Dun, who was to become the first head of the army of independent Burma.[12] The majority of the Karen people who lived in lowland Burma were Christians and directly or indirectly British officials favoured them. To distinguish themselves from Burmese Buddhists, it was the fashion of young Karens to give themselves an English name, often that of the local pastor or schoolmaster. Smith Dun acquired his name from a film he saw in a cinema in the town of Bassein in the late 1930s. The lead character was a 'strong man', possibly James Stewart in *Mr Smith Goes to Washington*. Dun's elder brother had been a corporal in the First World War and had risen to the rank of VCO subadar major in the Indian army. Dun was determined to emulate him even though he was only four feet tall. He was a humorous, athletic young man who could jump his own height from a standing position and his British officers liked him. Between 1939 and 1941 he was posted with the Burma Military Police in the south of his own country, far from the war – or so it seemed.

Men like this were ultimately to form the core of a truly national army. Or rather they would form the basis of the four national armies which were to emerge under the surface of British rule in India and

Burma. These were the Indian army, the Pakistan army, the Indian National Army, which fought with the Japanese, and the Burmese army, which fought on both sides. The speed of change this involved cannot be exaggerated. The British Raj, in its extremity, was forced to adopt just the sort of state plan of industrialization that it had avoided for generations. It was a distorted, military-based modernization, of course, but it was better than nothing. Many recruits were put through a crash course in modern mechanics. The Ordnance Training Centre at Jubbulpore alone was planned to train as many as 5,000 mechanics by 1943.[13] The Motor Transport Corps turned out skilled drivers from people 'previously totally ignorant of the workings of mechanical vehicles'. For the first time India manufactured armour plating, vehicle chassis and bodies, aircraft parts and many other industrial products. Once the war with Japan had broken out, the East India Railway, one of the world's largest civilian organizations, was also put under military discipline. Railway workshops began to turn out tanks and guns while air-raid precautions in Calcutta were co-ordinated by the superintendent, headquarters division, East India Railway. Margaret Stavridi, an English woman married to a railway engineer, remembered that the chief Indian officers of the railway were all staunch nationalists. But they believed that India would be worse off under the Japanese and took seriously their oaths of allegiance to the crown.[14]

Commercial and civilian bodies played an active role, though officials often railed against Indians' failure to support the patriotic war. British outfits responded quite effectively, though British society in India remained frozen in its bubble of class and race-consciousness. One of the biggest businesses in Asia, the Assam tea industry, provided large quantities of Indian labour for military work. Seeing the possibility of expanding its market, it shrewdly provided a number of 'tea cars' for the North West Frontier, Middle East and other war fronts. 'Each car,' a propaganda booklet declared, 'is fitted with canteen facilities, a radiogram, loudspeakers and records in English, Urdu, Punjabi, Nepalese and Pushtu. They can serve 10,000 cups of tea in 12 hours.'[15] India was indeed mobilizing more rapidly than might have been predicted a few years before when fierce battles had arisen between the governments of India and Britain about which of them should pay for the upgrading of the army.

Yet it was at the level of grand strategy more than manpower and logistics that the British in the East were not prepared for the nature and the intensity of the threat that faced them. Neither the Indian government, nor the British government nor General Headquarters, India, had the slightest inkling of their vulnerability. One former official, Victor Bayley, produced in early 1941 a book entitled *Is India Impregnable?* This must surely be counted among the most poorly timed books in the English language, but it was a symptomatic rather than simply a stupid production. Bayley wrote in the aftermath of the German–Soviet non-aggression pact of 1939. His book was designed to show that the real threat to the British east was likely to come from a fresh Russian round in the 'Great Game' of diplomacy and war in central Asia. The Russian Horde would mobilize northwards seeking alliances with the Afghan Pathan, 'sitting alone in his mountain fast-nesses staring out over the rich plains'. Here Bayley, true to form, invoked the spectre of the shadowy Pathan mullahs. Together, he speculated, the Russians and Afghan rebels would try to invade the 'treasure house of the world', as the Great Mughals had called India. Nevertheless, India was ready, Bayley insisted. Food supplies were plentiful. The defenders of India would 'never again have to face famine'. Strengthened with good strategic railways and fortified by her martial races, India would see off any threat from beyond the Khyber Pass.

By the time Bayley's book was published it was already out of date. By the end of 1943 events had falsified more or less every statement. Even before publication, the Soviets had become gallant allies of Britain, an embarrassment that Bayley turned to his advantage. He advised the reader in a hastily appended introduction that all he needed to do was to change the word 'Russian' to 'German' and everything in the book still held true. Among these verities was the fact that only an unlikely alliance between the Russian and Japanese fleets could shake the Anglo-American dominance in Far Eastern waters. Singapore, he went on, 'cannot be attacked from the land for no army can march down the thousand miles of tropical jungle which covers the Peninsula – it is a sheer impossibility.'[16] In the month when this book was published, the Japanese high command finalized their plan to do just that. Shortly afterwards, they began to consider invading Burma through wooded passes over the Thai border, another 'impossibility' according to the military planners in Whitehall and Simla.

The summer of 1941 saw a brief glimmer of light before disaster struck. Archibald Wavell, soon to be commander-in-chief, India, and the British army in the Western Desert were scoring successes against the Italians. At the battle of Sidi Barani in December 1940 the Indian army had celebrated one of the greatest victories in its history. The whole of North Africa seemed to be opening up as a second front with British, Indian and Gurkha troops capturing hundreds of thousands of the enemy. Many Italians were shipped back to prison camps in India because the U-boat threat made it too hazardous to send them by sea to Britain.

A select group of Indian and Anglo-Indian pilots were fighting in the continuing air war over the British Isles and north Germany. A typical example was the young man from Punjab University who had notched up a hundred hours of flying time with the University Air Training Corps and joined up in 1939. By late 1941, he was flying with the Hurricane Squadron of Fighter Command with several kills to his credit. Out of twenty-four Indian pilots so far selected for service in England eighteen came from the 'fighting Punjab'. Provinces and communities vied with each other for military glory. The visibly ageing viceroy, Lord Linlithgow, now in his fifth year of office, took pride from the rapid build-up of India's war effort: 'India is awake, she is mighty, she is formidable', he intoned in a speech which tried distantly to echo Churchill's stirring rhetoric.[17]

## INDIAN POLITICS AS USUAL?

In 1941 Indian politics spluttered on with its characteristic vigour, passion and hatreds, despite the constraints of war. Martial themes abounded. The country's natural conservatives outbid each other with pledges of support for the empire. That ever-loyal prince, the Maharaja of Dumraon, for instance, put out a statement claiming that an unlikely group, which he called the 'Rajputs of Bengal', was wholeheartedly in support of the war effort.[18] In Calcutta, by contrast, the embattled members of Subhas Bose's Forward Bloc continued their defiance of

the Raj. Every member of the Bose family remained under surveillance following Subhas's spectacular escape from confinement the
previous year. In early September 1941, one of Subhas's brothers,
Satish Chandra, and his son were convicted by the Alipore district
magistrate of kidnapping a police watcher who had presumably
bugged them once too often.

Although Bose's supporters were quite clear of their direction, most
nationalists were still uncertain of what stance to take. They continued
to pledge their loyalty to the Allies while demanding self-rule from the
British government. Mrs Sarojini Naidu, 'the nightingale of India',
expressed her admiration for the British people 'from Mr Winston
Churchill down to the youngest child of Britain', going on to insist
that Indians would achieve more from non-violence than all the armies
in the world.[19] M. R. Jayakar, from the Hindu right, said that India, a
poor country, should not have been drawn into the war, but now, with
the Japanese in Thailand and the Italians in the Western Desert, it had
no choice but to play its full part. The long-established pattern of
Hindu–Muslim political rivalry seethed just beneath the surface. Both
sides could see that there was something to be gained by being sup-
portive of the war effort. The main Hindu organization, the Hindu
Mahasabha, contemplated setting up a volunteer force to place at the
service of the viceroy as a symbol of the resolution of the 'Hindu
nation'. Muslim India meanwhile gloried in its renewed status as the
breeding ground of martial heroes.

The Atlantic Charter, announced by Churchill and Roosevelt on
14 August, galvanized the nationalist imagination in India as it did in
many parts of the world. The Charter proclaimed the right of all
peoples to political liberty. But if the Allies were fighting for the
self-determination of peoples in Europe, why was it that the right
of self-determination was not extended to Europe's Asian colonies?
Despite wartime controls, the Indian press began to pose this question once Labour MPs in Britain had asked it. Why, asked the Indian
press, were more Indian officers not being enlisted? It was quite obvious that Indians were essential to the war effort. One need only
compare the stout defence of the Soviets against Nazi invasion with
the feeble incompetence of all those public-school-educated British
officers in the field. The floodgates of competitive claims were opened

up. Representatives of the Sikhs pointed to the fact that hundreds of thousands of Sikhs were gallantly serving with the British armies. Why did they not have a reserved seat on the viceroy's Executive Council?[20] B. R. Ambedkar, leader of the 'untouchables' or Harijans, argued that India's untouchables were doubly victims, once for their race and again for their caste.[21] The viceroy should concede the right of unrestricted enlistment in the Indian army to untouchables, if the democratic pretensions of the Atlantic Charter were to mean anything. These, the poorest of the poor, were discriminated against in the army as in civilian life and were usually consigned to menial tasks as camp or hospital orderlies. Harijans, the 'children of God', were endowed with fighting qualities like any other group, Ambedkar insisted.

The government of India needed to strike a rapid propaganda counterblow. To do this it chose the unlikely figure of Dr Percival Spear, the scholarly and bespectacled historian who after the war wrote the very popular *Penguin History of India*. Spear was an Anglican Christian who had worked in St Stephen's College, Delhi. Through his mentor, C. F. Andrews, an intimate associate of the Mahatma, Spear was in close touch with many moderate nationalists. He was now working for the information and propaganda branch of the government of India. In September, Spear published a series of articles in the *Leader* titled 'Development of New Ideas through Danger and Suffering'. He warmed to his theme that Hitler was a blessing in disguise. The world, including India, would be redeemed through suffering. The Atlantic Charter was less important, he said, than the solemn promises made by the British on India's future. Those promises would be honoured, but only after India, that 'deeply religious country', had joined the Allies to fight evil.[22] This can have done little more than irritate Indian nationalists.

As the monsoon of 1941 slackened and petered out, India stood uneasily perched between peace and war. The Calcutta races went ahead with particular splendour that year. The Aga Khan had a fine stable of racehorses and the betting was fierce, almost in defiance of the threat of war. New films like *Holiday in Bombay* played at the picture houses alongside *Gone with the Wind*. European high society went on as ever with whist and bridge at the hotels and a fine new chef at the Bengal Club. Soothing words were heard from high places. Duff

Cooper, a senior British minister, toured the region. In Singapore he stated that the Allies were 'overwhelmingly superior' in the Pacific.[23] The Japanese would never attack the Fortress City and bring down the wrath of the rest of the world on her head. He added, with rather greater prescience, that the East and the Pacific were soon destined to play a larger role in world affairs than the West and the Atlantic.

All the same, the Indian newspapers ruminated uneasily as the Japanese moved deeper into Indo-China and Thailand. Their concern was fed by stories and letters received from Indian communities stretched across the whole of Southeast and East Asia. 'Japan is coming nearer', said a headline in the *Leader*. There were other straws in the wind. Indians looked with dismay on the politics of Burma. The ministry there had introduced a strict rice-control policy and Bengal in particular was dangerously dependent on Burmese rice imports. That same ministry was also moving to limit Indian immigration. Indians were outraged. They were ready to fight to defend Burma. They had 'developed' Burma and now they were to be excluded. Yet much public comment continued to focus on the death of Rabindranath Tagore, the great novelist, poet, nationalist and first Asian winner of the Nobel prize for literature. There was a palpable sense that an era was coming to its end.

## BURMA UNREADY

Further down the great crescent of Britain's Asian territories in Burma, military preparations remained sluggish. The Burmese ministers saw the war effort as none of their business. They had nothing in particular against the Japanese. Instead, they were historically suspicious of their huge northern neighbour, China. They were unwilling to commit themselves resolutely for the Chinese and against the Japanese, despite numerous Chinese good-will missions. They insisted on taxing free American lend–lease goods going over to Chungking via Yunnan, the Chinese border province, to help the Chinese war effort.[24] The British government eventually had to pay back this money to the Chinese. Both Burmese ministers and the British officials, who in reality still controlled the country, contributed to the fiction that the Japanese would be antagonized by vigorous civil preparations for war, such as the construction of air-raid shelters. Burmese ministers made anodyne speeches about loyalty to the crown and support for the Allies. Their real interest was in an immediate declaration by the British government of complete home rule and a watering down of the powers of the governor.

One reason for the lack of military preparedness was that the Burmese had been effectively excluded from the military, as Aung San and the young radicals, the Thakins argued. In the seventeenth and eighteenth centuries, the Burmese had built a reputation as one of the most militaristic of the peoples of southern Asia. They had sacked the Thai capital, caused grief to the Indian Mughals and had seen off the Chinese. In 1824, their great commander, Mahabandula, had sworn to bring the governor general of India back to Mandalay in silver fetters. Lord Amherst had not made that journey, however, and the Burmese had been sharply defeated in three major wars. The final one, in 1886, had seen the end of Burma's independence and its last monarch packed off into exile near Bombay. After 1886, the British did not recruit ethnic Burmese into their forces, as they had the Sikhs of the Punjab when they were conquered a generation earlier. At first, this was because the Burmese continued fiercely to resist British occupation for much longer than the Sikhs. Later, all sorts of pseudo-anthropological arguments were used about their unfitness. Burmese Buddhists, the British said, regarded soldiers as beings 'not very high on the human scale' because they took life. They, like the Bengalis, were supposedly 'effeminate' and could not take extremes of heat and cold.

This was all nonsense, as some British officials realized. A small company of Burmese sappers had done exceptionally well in the Meso-potamian campaign during the First World War where it had been 125 degrees in the shade.[25] They also took the cold of the North West Frontier uncomplainingly. The basic reason that the British did not maintain the slightly increased percentage of Burmese recruits after 1918 was that Indians and recruits from the Burmese minorities were cheaper. All this meant that the vast majority of 'Burmese' in outfits such as the Burma Rifles and the Burma Frontier Force were Kachins, Shans, Karens like Smith Dun, or else locally resident Indians and

Gurkhas. There were hardly a thousand ethnic Burmese officers or NCOs under arms in 1940. This stored up huge problems for the British in the Second World War. When the Japanese offered young Burmese military training, they leapt at the opportunity. It was a matter of pride as well as politics. How could the Burmese be a people if they did not have an army?

## THE WORLD OF THE HILLS AND THE 'TRIBES'

The British, then, had not fostered a strong Burmese army to defend the country and the Indian army was not all that it seemed. In 1942 and 1943, Indian and British troops performed poorly, unused to jungle conditions and Japanese tactics. The war was to become bogged down in the frontier and hill lands between India and Burma. It is worth considering these regions for a time because it was the stubborn resistance of their inhabitants and the aid they gave the Allied armies that were to be crucial in blocking the further advance of the Japanese. For here there was another Asia, the Asia of the minority groups. Some of these were inhabitants of upland and wooded areas, including the Malayan Orang Asli (original people) and the Kachins, Nagas and Lushai of Burma and India. Others were plains dwellers, such as the Karens of Burma, who wore different dress from their Burmese neighbours and prized a separate history. From the period of the Burmese kings and the Mughal rulers onward, peoples such as these had developed varied relationships with the majority population. Sometimes they fought for them, sometimes they sent looting parties against them. Much of the time they traded with them. The coming of British rule had put wholly new pressures on the tribals and minorities. The Raj demanded peace and an end to local warfare. Vigorous punitive expeditions had been sent into the hills. In the aftermath of the First World War, for example, a British force had invaded the Naga hills, punishing dissident tribes by burning villages and crops. The memory of this savage local conflict was to colour attitudes even in the 1940s.

With the coming of more direct British rule, the hill-dwellers found themselves in a novel economic environment. Forest officers were assigned to create woodland reserves and stop their customary practice of slash-and-burn agriculture. Indian, Chinese and Gurkha settlers and merchants penetrated the hills and forest lands, exploiting the local people's ignorance of commerce but also giving some of them, especially the chiefs and others with local power, the chance to make money. Missionaries also found the hills to be a paradise for conversion since they were not faced with an established priesthood, doctors of law or an intelligentsia who would argue back against them, as was the case in the plains. By 1940 up to 30 per cent of the Naga, Karen, Shan, Chin and Kachin population of the hills of north Burma and eastern India had formally become Christian. European missionaries were much thicker on the ground among these scattered populations than were British officials.

Despite their desire to tax, settle, trade with and convert these hill populations, the British also wished, paradoxically, to 'preserve' them. That aim became more pressing in the 1920s and '30s when Indian and Burmese nationalists from the plains began to make themselves known in the hills and forests, preaching a common alliance of all ethnic peoples against imperialism. The British had long been solicitous of the local chiefs: the hill rajas of Assam, the Naga chiefs, the Chin princes or *sawbwas* and the lords of the Kachin hills. They often gave them powers and privileges which they had never held in the looser organization of the old order.[26] Now the British moved more resolutely to establish protected areas, excluded areas and frontier jurisdictions which, they hoped, would preserve what they saw as the political innocence and conservatism of these peoples against nationalist 'agitators'. Sometimes they gave these ethnic groups and their leaders special political representation on councils and committees which they convened in the hope of holding the demand for freedom at bay. As the international situation worsened, the British began to establish militia levies amongst all the tribal and minority peoples. The need for some basic defence and intelligence system outweighed the danger of arming these independent-minded hill men. Karen, Kachin and Shan levies were organized by Frontier Service officers. The middle and northern sections of the Burma–Thailand border gave most cause for concern. Here in the eastern part of the Karenni states amongst the teak forests, old Mauser rifles and other weapons left over from the last big local rebellion in 1931 were brought out of cupboards in the rural police stations. Each levy was issued with 'one pair khaki shorts, one khaki shirt with badge marked K.L. [Karen Levies], one pair rubber soled shoes and one locally made bamboo hat'.[27]

Amongst the Kachin of the northwest hills of Burma modern political radicalism had made little headway. The Kachins seemed to regard the Burmese as a 'traditional enemy' and, in general, saw the British as protectors against the incoming Burmese settlers and traders.[28] They, too, had a substantial Christian population by the 1930s. In one version, the word Kachin was a Burmese corruption of the Chinese 'yei jein' or 'jungle man'. They actually called themselves Jinghpaw and were organized into clans which moved slowly in a pattern of shifting cultivation through the hills. Hunters adept at using poisoned arrows against their prey, the Kachin were also noted for their rice-wine drinking bouts and elaborate rituals to keep the dangerous spirits of the forest at bay. They gave their allegiance to powerful chieftains, but also reserved the right to revolt against them and bring them to heel. This tension between despotism and egalitarianism amongst the Kachins struck many observers, including the London School of Economics anthropologist Edmund Leach, who was carrying out research amongst them when the European war broke out in 1939. News of the war puzzled the Kachin according to J. L. Leyden, an officer who had worked among them for many years. They wondered why the Germans in 1918 had 'not been disarmed and enslaved in the manner in which Kachin custom demands that Kachins deal with their enemies'.[29] Under their chiefs, Kachins flocked into the new territorial levies.

## DORMAN-SMITH REACHES HIS 'BACKWATER'

The British governor of Burma as the Japanese approached was Sir Reginald 'Reggie' Dorman-Smith. He was to remain a key figure in the politics of the country through to 1949. As a career politician turned colonial governor, Dorman-Smith was a relatively unusual figure in the later British Empire where civil servants usually headed colonial administrations. An old boy of Harrow School, he was an Irishman with family lands on both sides of the border and he remained a citizen of Eire. He once startled British Cabinet colleagues who were casually discussing the internment of Irish citizens at the beginning of the war by revealing his citizenship.[30] His nationality did give him an interestingly ambivalent view of empire and nationalism. He claimed to sympathize with nationalist aspirations though his political conservatism meant that it was only pukka, old-style Burmese and Indian politicians that he could really tolerate. He was armed with a mordant wit and considerable literary talent, though it is clear that many of his colleagues regarded him as 'a bit of a phoney'. Dorman-Smith had been a member of the pre-war Conservative administration as minister of agriculture. As the war began in earnest, he fell out with Churchill and his powerful scientific adviser Frederick Lindemann, Lord Cherwell. Ejected from the Cabinet to make room for Socialists and Liberals as the wartime coalition was formed, he joined the army and found himself made a civil-military liaison officer in the Home Defence Executive.

One day in the depths of the Cabinet Office canteen drinking tea, Dorman-Smith had the following conversation with a senior official:

'Reggie, would you like to go out to be governor of Burma?'

'Don't be silly!'

'Don't you be silly! That is not for you to decide. If I were asked to be Archbishop of Canterbury, I'd say yes because and only because other people clearly thought I could do that job . . . Not that you were our first choice. Don't flatter yourself.'[31]

Dorman-Smith hesitated: Burma was so far from anywhere where there was likely to be trouble that it might seem like ratting, running out on the nation during the Blitz. He also hesitated because 'my knowledge of Burma was precisely nil. I knew approximately where it is on the map, that its capital was Rangoon and that the Irrawaddy flowed through it, but my knowledge did not extend beyond this.'[32] This was despite fancying himself as an 'Empire man' in parliamentary speeches. Then again, Dorman-Smith thought, Irishmen should always take up challenges of this sort even though they seldom led anywhere.

Dorman-Smith arrived to take up his brief and dramatic period of office in May 1941. The usual round of official receptions and parties at Rangoon went ahead despite Japan's moves in Indo-China. Though he later wrote of it as 'a great cosmopolitan city' the new governor really found his capital stiff, socially unpleasant and provincial.[33] His wife disliked their 'enormous monstrosity' of a government house, nicknamed St Pancras Station,[34] preferring the 'toy town' prettiness of the government's summer retreat at Maymyo near Mandalay. The couple had good reason for their disappointment. Despite the myth of the cheerful, friendly Burman and the old stories of happy inter-racial marriage and sex, race relations were poor and had become poorer during the Depression when a widespread peasant rebellion in the rice-growing areas had been harshly suppressed by the British. It was almost as if the Burmanization of the civil service underway in the 1930s had made European non-officials even more determined to play the race card.

Rangoon prided itself on its difference, but it had a lot in common with the other colonial port cities of the region. As a resident told a journalist: 'they are all much the same – Bombay, Calcutta, Singapore, Shanghai – a garish show on top and a pretty stinking world underneath. But you can't blame Burma for this. Rangoon isn't Burma really. It's much more an Indian city, with a bit of China thrown in, run by Scots and Irishmen.'[35] In Rangoon, the Burmese were not allowed into the main metropolitan haunts, the Pegu, Gymkhana and Yacht clubs, though few of them would probably have wished to join. Only the Gold and Turf clubs had Asian members. The main Asian club was the Orient Club; this still had a few European members but no new ones were admitted in retaliation for the colour bar operated by the Europeans.[36] This aloofness affected the whole society. G. H. Luce, the most important British scholar of classical Burma and a professor in Rangoon University, had a Burmese wife who was herself an academic. In consequence he was ostracized by a large part of the 8,000-strong white population of the city.[37]

Even out in the districts, relations were no closer. Many of those Europeans born and brought up in Burma had golden memories of the country and its inhabitants. People working among the minorities or in agricultural, forest and technical departments felt that they were doing a worthwhile job. But it is striking how many of the letters and memoirs of civil servants in Burma and India during this period give a sense of disillusionment and regret at odds with the romantic picture of the young Briton dispensing justice and good order to 'the natives'.[38] At Maymyo, according to Frank Donnison, the financial secretary to government, the British sought 'at all costs to forget they were in Burma'.[39] They attended Debussy concerts in spacious parks and had picnics at the incongruously named Hampshire Falls. John Clague, another civil servant, reminisced: 'strange it is to look back and feel that we Europeans lived in a world where very often the people hardly counted in our human or intimate thoughts. No Burman belonged to the Moulmein Gymkhana. No Burman came to dinner and breakfast.' Clague's days were spent in hot and smelly courtrooms 'listening to lies being interpreted', overwhelmed by a 'sense of injustice and illegality'.

British society in Burma was not a wholly aloof or hedonistic one, of course. The expatriates engaged in a certain amount of 'do-goodism', for this was the era of moral rearmament. In the capital, the ladies of the Vigilance Society made occasional raids into the native quarters to 'save' women from brothels. Other women were expected to join sewing parties. They could 'work for the Blind Deaf School or sell flags for causes that neither they nor the Burmese had any interest in'. Yet this high moral tone stood in sharp contrast to the pervasive mean spiritedness.

The European war and the advance of the Japanese did little to change attitudes. True, there were a few air-raid drills and collections for the Lord Mayor of London's Relief Fund. Mostly it was still bridge and whist, though there was a new game of 'military whist' which was said by the *Rangoon Times* to be ideal for entertaining a large party. This half-hearted mobilization was scarcely designed to catch the Burmese imagination and even moderate Burmese nationalism was ambivalent about the unfolding struggle in Asia. Burmese women organized the Rangoon civil evacuation scheme. Official voices and ministers made less-than-stirring calls to aid the Allies. Local festivals began to include stilted anti-Nazi sketches.[40] The Japanese penetration of Thailand to the south was watched with anticipation as well as concern among Burmese. As Burma's leading literary figure Daw Mya Sein said, Burmese had much in common with Thais. The Shans in Burma were Siamese, according to national mythology, and those of the south were probably the best-adjusted minority in Burmese society. Burma's version of the great Indian epic, the Mahabharata, was an import from Thailand.[41] Since the fall of the Burmese kingdom in 1886, the Thai king had been regarded as 'defender of the Buddhist faith' in Burma. Many asked themselves quietly whether a Japanese-led Buddhist and Asian national solidarity was possible and whether this was Burma's future. Unaware that Aung San and other young radicals were already building a secret national army over the Thai frontier, most Burmese watched and waited, untroubled by the small flurries of activity among Europeans.

One very distinctive group among the whites in the city was the Americans, who were to provide one of the few heroic stories in the defence of Burma some months later. They had been there from before the European war, helping to co-ordinate US government aid to the embattled Chinese nationalist government at Chungking, 900 miles to the northeast. Once the war started this turned into an American lend–lease operation. Some Americans were already fighting. Men of the American Volunteer Group, the famous 'Flying Tigers', were also based at Rangoon's airport under the command of Claire Chennault. They flew missions to protect the Burma Road against the depredations of Japanese fighters. Though it had American government support, the AVG was a voluntary organization, its pilots hard-living and hard-drinking. They got a large bonus from Chiang Kai Shek for every Japanese plane they shot down. One grouse they had when stationed in Burma was that they did not get bonuses while there. They were reputed to hold the best parties in town and to have a talent for sniffing out the most available girls. The parties regularly got out of hand. The airmen 'thought little of using one of their smaller servants as a volley ball'.[42]

## BURMESE AND OTHERS

Though much of the Asian elite of Rangoon, Mandalay and Maymyo resented the attitude of the British, especially some of the pushy commercial expatriates connected with oil and timber, it was deeply divided amongst itself. These divisions were to open up like festering wounds when the first Japanese troops thrust into Burma. Burmese nationalists were already in a heightened state of excitement in the later 1930s, particularly in Rangoon. It was a nationalist fervour that was increasingly anti-foreign, turned against Indians, Chinese and minorities. As the Far Eastern war approached the country, the different Burmese political parties did their best to outdo each other. On the last day of March 1941, Burma's new flag was hoisted for the first time. This was an attempt by the British to capture Burmese enthusiasm for the war effort. The flag was a blue ensign emblazoned with a peacock, symbol of the old Burmese Buddhist empire. But all things Burmese were in vogue. The exploits of the 'Burmese Sherlock Holmes', Maung San Shar, were particularly popular. The radio was careful to broadcast Burmese music and popular songs along with Judy Garland and *Operetta Selection*, introduced by Noël Coward. *Sun Magazine* printed stories about the doings of an idealized Burmese family. Unfortunately, though, not all manifestations of Burmese nationalism were so harmless. Much of its energy was directed outward against the Indians.

Burmese resentment of Indians had been heightened by Buddhist–Muslim riots in 1938, when a Muslim publication had allegedly insulted the Buddha. In 1940 and 1941 the major issue in Burmese politics was Indian immigration. Since 1937 successive Burmese administrations had tried to stem the influx. Finally succumbing to this pressure, the British agreed in 1940 to enact legislation severely limiting the number of Indians allowed into the country. They also created a class of expatriate Indian subjects with the right to work and in some cases to vote in Burma. Naturally, Indian commercial people and even poor labourers rushed to bring their families and dependants into the country in order to secure this right of abode. The new intake raised resentment amongst Burmese politicians who asserted that their country was being taken away from them. Major Indian employers in the country took on very few of the large numbers of Burmese jobless. In turn, Burmese began to say: 'You must either be Indians or Burmans, you cannot be both.'[43]

How had this antagonism arisen? Indians had always regarded Burma as a land of opportunity, a kind of 'Wild East' in which fortunes were to be made and where the ordinary conventions of Indian life did not hold good. Amongst Indian men there was a strong folk opinion that Burmese women were beautiful and available, but extremely difficult to handle and a match even for the white expatriates. More important was that India had a vast pool of impoverished labour and a go-ahead and entrepreneurial business class which had settled all over Southeast Asia, the Middle East and East Africa during the years of British rule. The Great Depression of the 1930s had made the attraction of emigration even greater by bringing down wages in the huge subcontinent and creating new pockets of poverty there. Indians saw Burma as a foreign land, but, equally, moving there was just an extension of their own internal migration patterns. A few regions sent a disproportionate number of labourers to what after all had been just another administrative province of British India until its partition in 1936. Many Indians, especially Muslims, drifted down through the border province of Arakan into north Burma, where they dominated the seaport of Akyab and its hinterland.[44] There were a quarter of a million Chittagonians alone in Burma when the last census had been taken in 1931. Serious tensions between Bengali Muslims and Arakanese Buddhists had already arisen in the 1930s.

Many of the poorest coolies came from Orissa, a backward province adjoining Bengal and just across the Bay of Bengal from Rangoon. Orissa and nearby Chota Nagpur had long provided an impoverished but disciplined labour force for the rich tea estates of Assam. Yet other Indians in Burma were, as in Malaya, Tamil plantation workers from Madras who worked in the rice paddies of the delta districts. On the other side, there were also large numbers of commercial people. These ranged from the rich Madras Chettiar merchants who had bought up much of Tenasserim from impoverished Burmese peasants in the 1930s through to humble Punjabi Muslim traders and urban moneylenders. Between the rich merchant and professional elite of Akyab, Mandalay, Rangoon or Bassein and the poor coolies there was a large middling group of Indians, clerks in government and private offices, doctors, drivers, lower management in the oil wells and the teak sawmills. Most of the lower officials who ran the Irrawaddy Flotilla Company's paddle steamers on the great river were from Chittagong, just over the Arakan border. Most of the skilled labour in the oilfields was also Indian. Indians tended to recruit their countrymen for the skilled and managerial jobs.

While Indians became increasingly the targets of Burmese resentment, many were to be found amongst the poorest of the poor. About half the coolies or labourers who crossed the sea paid their own fares from minimal savings for passage on the ships of the British India Steamship Corporation or the Scindia SSC. A quarter borrowed from moneylenders. About 12 per cent were brought over to man the mines, oilfields and Rangoon docks by labour contractors – *maistrees* – who advanced them the cost of their transport and kept them in debt bondage for ever afterwards.[45] The British hardly bothered to regulate the system at all before the later 1930s, so it was systematically abused. Conditions on the transport ships were horrifying. They lacked sanitation, proper food and medical supplies and were often unsafe. Gandhi, who was used to the bad conditions of Indian indentured labour in South Africa, was appalled by what he saw on the Rangoon ferries when he ventured across the Bay of Bengal. A British police inspector wrote that the 'conditions of labour in Rangoon were a disgrace to any civilized and allegedly democratic country'. Thousands of slaves had been freed in the tribal north of Burma a mere ten years earlier, but nothing was done in the city for the 'thousands of slaves to the dividends of the steamship companies'.[46]

Even worse conditions awaited the labourers when they got to Burma. They were housed in dilapidated barns and hostels, subject to outbreaks of disease and fires. They were fed by corrupt contractors in filthy canteens. As the British assistant protector of immigrants was forced to admit, the coolies got 'a bare minimum of nutrition'.[47] The coal and salt stevedore workers in the ports generally got only ten days' work per month. As in India, most of the labouring was casual and uncertain. The 12,000 Indian rickshaw pullers worked night and day without a break. Many of them suffered from heart disease. The filthiest jobs of all were almost all filled by low-caste Indians. These were the conservancy sweepers who removed human waste from houses in the major cities, few of which yet had modern sanitation. Ironically, the whole urban society rested on the poor, abused sweepers. When they fled in numbers in 1942 urban life soon collapsed in a stinking disease-ridden morass. Conditions for these labourers were dreadful but still they came and numbers built up again in the later '30s because conditions in India were even worse.

Employers in Burma liked Indian labour. Indian employers always hired other Indians. But among Chinese, Europeans and even Burmese bosses and landowners the myth was rife that the Burmese were lazy and fractious. They were certainly too proud to put up with what the Indians tolerated. As a British ICS officer put it, the Burmese had generally 'not yet succumbed to living in slum conditions' in their own country.[48]

Some Burmese, however, had no choice in the matter. It was the Depression that brought matters to boiling point. In 1930 and 1931 many Burmese peasants, artisans and small traders lost their livelihoods. They were forced on to the labour market to compete for jobs with low-paid Indian labour. Many had had their lands bought up by the rich *kala* or foreigners. Others resented the way in which Indians were marrying Burmese women. There was a song, 'Do Bama' ('We the Burmese'), which said, 'The Chinese and Indians are fortune hunters; not content with our money and lands, they have gone off with our mothers and sisters, too.' The law protected Burmese women's property, but if they married Indian Muslims, male members of the husband's family inherited under Indian law. This led to savage inter-community hostility.[49] W. S. Desai, an Indian government officer, candidly noted that hundreds of thousands of rupees were transferred by money order alone to India every year from Burma. Indians had complained for a hundred years of the 'drain of wealth' from India to Britain.[50] In Burma, the Indians proved quite as adept as the British. Most Burmese were not economists, but they could see the large and rising proportion of prized jobs in the oilfields which were going to Indians. In 1941, Indians held about 40 per cent of such positions.

Tension had gradually developed in the 1930s. There were fierce anti-Indian riots in 1930 and scuffles and outbreaks throughout the decade. There is strong evidence, too, that the Buddhist priesthood and the sleazy Burmese politicians who held office in the later 1930s encouraged their supporters to attack Indians.[51] It was a popular cause. There were now large numbers of young unemployed men around who needed work and by convention could not marry until they had a job. These were rather different from contemporary Hindu–Muslim riots in India because their aim was to frighten the foreigners away and get their jobs in the mines, docks and rice fields. Despite the hostile atmosphere Indian numbers reached an all-time peak in 1941 and early 1942. The Burmese ministry was bent on setting a limit to immigration, having once registered all Indian workers who had lived in Burma for some years. Consequently, as H. Mukherji, a clerk, noted: 'Indians from all parts, those who never knew the name of Burma, rushed there on some plea or other, got a permit and swelled the Indian population.'[52] Those already there did not venture to send their families away, fearing they would not be able to bring them back if the bill were enacted. As the Japanese marched closer to Burma's border, Burmese relations with the Indian minority worsened.

Relations between Chinese and Burmese were a bit better. The Census of 1931 counted about 200,000 Chinese in Burma. About 40,000 of these were Yunnanese from the far southern province which bordered northern Burma. Itinerant Chinese coolies and traders had for many years simply drifted over the border from Yunnan.[53] The rest were Cantonese and Fukienese, like the majority of Chinese trading communities in Southeast Asia. The connections had often been made by Chinese overseas traders who exchanged China silk or tea for Burmese jade, which was greatly prized in the Middle Kingdom. The Chinese were very strongly represented among petty traders, money-lenders and in the carpentry business. Relations between China and Burma were ancient, but wary. By tradition the Chinese emperors had viewed Burma as a tributary kingdom. A Chinese army had invaded the country in 1796, but it had retreated in disarray when it ran out of food. In order to pacify the Chinese, the British had recognized some Chinese rights in north Burma when they conquered it after 1886, even sending present-bearing delegations to Peking, symbolizing Burma's fealty. Some parts of the northern Kachin areas were technically leased from China and the Shan state of Kengtung was ruled by a Sino-Burmese dynasty. Chinese school atlases coloured much of north Burma as Chinese. Oddly, China also retained the right of free passage along the Irrawaddy river, something that suddenly became contentious in 1942 when Chinese armies began to operate there alongside the British against the Japanese.

There was also a large Sino-Burmese community, much of which dated to the days of the Burmese kings. As for Indians, Burma had been a land of opportunity for the Chinese. Chinese men had married Burmese women, learning Burmese and adopting the prevailing style of Theravada Buddhism. The Burmese called the Chinese 'next of kin', or 'guest friends' – *pauk hpaw*. They thought of them more as they did the Arakanese and Kachens, Karens and Shans, than like the Indians.[54] There was a bit of trouble in 1930 in Rangoon when Chinese shops were burned following the anti-Indian riots and the anti-British Tharawaddy rebellion, but this seems to have been a consequence of general Burmese xenophobia during the Great Depression. In general, Chinese and Burmese were not competing for the same jobs.

By the end of the 1930s strains were growing in both Rangoon and the north. Dependent on the Burma Road for supplies, the Chinese nationalist government sent good-will missions to Rangoon and Mandalay. Japanese influences worked to stir up the radical young Burmese against Chinese 'capitalists' plundering their country. The massive graft and corruption surrounding the Burma Road to China had swelled Chinese business in Burma and made it fat. Chinese merchants began to buy up land and houses and to flaunt their wealth. They invested heavily in Chinese war bonds and factories making parts for the lorries that would travel down the Burma Road. After 1936 the influx of Americans and Chinese strained to breaking point the accommodation provided by the three 'miserable' European hotels in Rangoon. Back roads were packed with trucks about to make the Rangoon–China run and observers wrote of an endless 'line of headlights and roaring engines going north'. Thirty thousand tons of goods per day were hauled up the road. The Chinese and Indian drivers walked cockily around the city picking up Burmese girls. Chinese-related crime increased and there was a shift from internecine 'tong'-type crime to crimes involving Burmese goods and businesses, further raising tension. The American lend–lease aid to China seeped out into Chinese hands. Much of the vast quantity of goods supposedly bound for Chungking was clearly destined for elsewhere. One inquisitive official noted a huge consignment of lifebelts in one of the lorries. This raised his suspicions because Chungking was so clearly landlocked. Further north, the Chinese were even more strongly entrenched. Lashio, a village near the border, swelled to an enormous size. In its streets, 'the new aristocracy of China, the Burma Road truck drivers, swaggered about with pistols and revolvers of every description bulging out of their hip pockets'. Among them swarmed

Sikh tailors, Kachin tribesmen carrying bundles, Chinese and Burmese prostitutes and Chinese nationalist soldiers.[55]

## ENDGAME: THE GOVERNOR AND THE POLITICIANS

When Dorman-Smith arrived in Rangoon in 1941 he found it an odd place, part boom town and part slum. As the summer advanced, nerves jangled when British setbacks in the Middle East mounted and the Japanese made increasingly bellicose noises about the Burma Road and the neutrality of neighbouring Thailand. Practically the only thing that kept Rangoon happy was alcohol. British supplies had been cut off after 1939 but the city was awash with beer from Shanghai, Singapore brandy and South African crème de menthe. Much of the booze continued to find its way to the parties hosted by the American Volunteer Group.

Even though he was not a career civil servant, Dorman-Smith was reasonably well received on his arrival. Burmese politicians and British civil servants alike had grown tired of his predecessor, Sir Archibald Cochrane, a crack First World War submariner who was thought to have 'no interest in or sympathy for the civil service'. A. C. Potter, his aide, found the new governor charming, 'a nice looking fellow too, but he looks older than his 42 years'. Dorman-Smith was given to using terms like 'swizz' and Potter concluded that 'in many ways he is a complete boy, and a very likeable one'.[56] Dorman-Smith bustled around the country with his ministers, giving advice 'in case we should be at war with Japan'. He was making up policy on the hoof and had received little advice on his departure. An exception was that tendered by R. A. Butler, the wily Conservative politician, who warned him not to accept the post unless he could be satisfied that the country was properly defended.[57]

In early 1941 that advice seemed more or less academic. Apart from the huge fortress of Singapore, which guarded the whole of Southeast Asia, Burma seemed secure behind its massive natural defences of mountain and forest. Dorman-Smith remembered that one military officer alone had been worried that there was no effective land link between India and Burma. When he wrote his memoirs in the late 1940s, Dorman-Smith pondered again on this conversation. It was true that if there had been a land link then thousands of the Indian refugees who had died in the great flight of early 1942 might have been saved.[58] On the other hand, the Japanese might have been able to invade the subcontinent more easily from a conquered Burma. Even when the British began hesitantly to take war preparations seriously, they were of two minds. How could Rangoon be defended from air attack? It was impossible to build underground air-raid shelters in the marshy land on which the city stood. Maybe people should be advised to decamp to the jungle. But how then could essential services be maintained? One serious constraint was that there was still a desperate desire not to offend the Japanese and so bring them into the war inadvertently. This meant that any film, radio broadcast or press article that was deemed even faintly anti-Japanese was vigorously censored. If people could not be roused to face a real enemy all that war propaganda could do was to issue 'mouse-stirring appeals for loyalty and law and order', as Jack Belden, a particularly mordant journalist, described them.[59]

British complacency about the colony's defences was matched by the attitude of Burmese politicians. Dorman-Smith's prime minister at this time was U Saw, leader of the Myochit Party, a man whose shadow was to fall over Burma for the next decade.[60] Born in 1900, the son of a well-to-do landowner, Saw had become a member of the legislative assembly at the age of twenty-eight. He built up his nationalist credentials by speaking up for the 1931 rebels, trying to get their sentences commuted. In the early thirties he formed a private army, the Galon League, mainly from young unemployed men. This put him in a strong position when the first elections were called under the new Burma Act in 1937.

Saw was a 'Vicar of Bray-like figure', in other words a consummate trimmer. He tacked to the Japanese in 1936 and 1937 and their Rangoon consulate was pleased to present him with a motor car. He gushed that the Japanese 'were the only Asiatic people to become a great world power'.[61] Saw's exaggerated respect for Buddhism also went down well with the young monks of Mandalay, many of whom were pro-Japanese themselves. He set up a university to teach the classical language of the Buddhist scriptures, Pali, but later, when the Japanese failed to come up with the private aircraft they had promised him, the relationship cooled. Now he began to bemoan Japanese atrocities in Manchuria and made pleasant noises to the Chinese. All the while Saw kept in with the British, not least because his house hosted more or less continuous parties, notable for the presence of attractive women. Convivial drinking bouts with the more relaxed British officials did not stop U Saw sniffing the new scent in the wind after Munich. In 1939 he got hold of a copy of *Mein Kampf* and was heard praising Hitler and the political theory of dictatorship. It was rumoured that he had become head of the Burma branch of the nationalistic Black Dragon Society, indicating a tilt back towards Japan. It was this sort of vacillation by the ministers, combined with their blatant corruption, which nauseated young radicals such as Aung San and Nu. Saw's Galon League was so called after the mythical bird, Garuda, which carried the god Vishnu in the Hindu myths. Young Thakins would turn up at Saw's party meetings shouting 'Vulture! Vulture!' from the back row, signalling that this was the bird they really associated with him.[62]

U Saw and his ministry became more than usually slippery as the situation worsened in the summer and autumn of 1941. U Saw wanted to use his Galon army as a kind of home guard, so guaranteeing him a powerful national armed force should the war go badly. The British were suspicious because, in so far as U Saw had a policy at all, it was less to prepare the country for war than to hold at bay his long-time enemy among the nationalist politicians who had built their careers out of the 1935 Act, Dr Ba Maw. This former prime minister, who had been ousted by Saw in 1938, was of Burman-Portuguese, or some said Armenian, descent. He was the son of a former courtier of the Mandalay court, U Shwe, who had continued with covert anti-British activities after 1886. Ba Maw himself had helped in the defence of the 1931 rebels, as had many of his nationalist colleagues.[63] In 1935 he had founded the Sinyetha Party. This professed socialist aims and had some support among Burmese port and oilfield workers, but in the countryside, like most other political parties, it was a loose coalition of conservative landowners, local strongmen and others who had benefited from Ba Maw's patronage.

If U Saw was the likeable rogue of Burmese politics, Ba Maw was, in the parlance of the day, the consummate 'lounge lizard'. Inordinately impressed by his own good looks and charm, Ba Maw had an account of himself prepared for propaganda purposes in 1942 when he became chief collaborator with the invading Japanese. At school, this effusion recorded, Ba Maw's 'extreme fairness and girlish beauty embarrassed the other school boys and himself'.[64] Later this 'debonair' and 'strikingly handsome' young man become 'a brilliant debater, scholar and nationalist'. He feasted on the glories of English literature, but soon found that the English themselves east of Suez were 'disgusting'. Falling out with his English schoolteacher and becoming the scourge of the Rangoon expatriates, he went briefly to Cambridge and left rapidly in unexplained circumstances. He ended up doing a doctorate in religious studies in the University of Bordeaux, having found France 'more favourable to his Burmese temperament'.[65]

During the later 1930s Ba Maw and U Saw fought a long political duel. Within the boundaries of British censorship, each sought to be more nationalist than the other. Both called for a restriction on Indian immigration and both vied for support amongst the increasingly political and anti-British monasteries of Rangoon and Mandalay. In the summer of 1940 Ba Maw overstepped the mark. He declared himself dictator of his party and said that he refused to help the war effort. Resigning his seat in the legislative council he announced that he would form another legislature which would oppose the British. Only just staying out of jail under the Defence of Burma rules, he spent the next twelve months trying to undermine U Saw from outside government. Ba Maw was closer to the young student nationalists, the Thakins, than U Saw, but many of them secretly despised him. These tensions were to become politically explosive during the Japanese occupation. For his part, U Saw was constantly discovering anti-British plots on the part of Ba Maw and his other enemies in the hope that he could get them interned for the duration of what was intended to be an election season. The stalemate between the two held until war actually broke out and they both found themselves interned in different parts of the world for their pro-Japanese sympathies.

If the British and the Burmese were unprepared, their Chinese allies had problems too. The Chinese tended at this time to treat the British in the East with condescension. They had been fighting the Japanese for the better part of six years. The British had no idea what they might be up against soon and were suspicious of Chinese designs on north Burma, but, given the way that the British Empire forces were so stretched, help from the Chinese and their American advisers would be essential in the event of a Japanese attack. The Chinese command at this point was in serious disarray. Technically, the rough old China hand, General Joseph 'Vinegar Joe' Stilwell was in command, lent by the US to command China's forces. But as General Du, who also claimed command, put it, 'Ah, Your Excellency, American general only thinks he is commanding.' When war broke out, the situation became even murkier, with the British general commanding the Burma front, Harold Alexander, staking his own claim.[66] Dorman-Smith's staff later wrote a poem to describe this imbroglio.[67]

> Alexander, Stilwell and Du,
> met in GH in Maymyo,
> They were somewhat perplexed,
> And equally vexed
> when trying to sort out who's who.
> Then Stilwell (whose name sounds like 'Stool'),
> Said 'Let's stop playing the fool.
> By the great Chiang kai Shek,
> who's a marshal by heck,
> I've got orders the armies to rule.'
> Then up spoke the great general Du,
> 'I really think nothing of you,'
> But, said Alexander,
> 'I'm the commander,'
> Joe Stilwell said,
> 'How do you do?'

Some observers failed to see the joke. Major Edwin 'Tommy' Cook, Dorman-Smith's son-in-law and ADC, travelled around Burma and up to Chungking in the summer and autumn of 1941. He realized how precarious British rule was. 'Basically the cultivator is the most important man in the country. He is consequently always considered last. The Civil Service comes first. It is a vast service, unbelievably top-heavy.'[68] He also understood the direction of Japanese moves more quickly than many of his senior officers. In July, as the Japanese occupation of French Indo-China was imminent, he noted 'presumably this would indicate preparations against Singapore and Malaya to include an attack against the Netherlands East Indies'.[69] Burma would inevitably be drawn in because the Japanese needed to cut the Burma Road. Even if a Japanese attack on Burma did not initially succeed, 'the disorganisation of Burmese defences and China supplies would certainly be stupendous'. A. C. Potter similarly reported in August that 'the situation is pretty tense in this part of the world. Few could have imagined that a Jap threat to Burma would develop in the way it has done.'[70]

In September, the public mood also began to change for the worse, at least in Rangoon and Mandalay. Bing Crosby and Dorothy Lamour were still playing in *The Road to Zanzibar* at the New Excelsior Cinema, Rangoon, and Swami Kavishwar, an Indian 'political seer' with powers of foresight, announced that Burma would be safe from the havoc of war. But on 4 September the press announced the 'death of appeasement' in the East. Prince Konoe, the Japanese prime minister, who was already on the skids, declared that Japan was facing the greatest crisis in its history. He wrote to Roosevelt demanding that the US stop aiding Japan's enemies, China and Russia.[71] In Singapore the Burmese minister of health said that the international situation was 'very grave' and that the country was still unprepared for the sort of air bombardment that China had suffered. A small change that registered the country's near-war status was that informal Burmese dress had been introduced in all government offices. Burmese no longer had to wear silk turbans and Europeans could sport open-necked shirts.[72] Here too the Atlantic Charter had stirred the political pot. 'When was Burma to receive self-determination?' demanded the politicians. The *Rangoon Times* carried advertisements for natty ladies' 'evacuation slacks', available for Rs4–8 at Watson and Son Ltd.[73] Everyone anticipated some kind of attempt by the Japanese to close the Burma Road once again. This was now carrying astonishing quantities of war materiel and oil to the Chungking troops. What really hit home, however, was the shift of the ground to the south, in Thailand. Burmese in Rangoon and Moulmein had good connections to Bangkok-based Burmese and Shan. Growing Japanese influence there was quickly registered. Rumours were heard that after some kind of commercial dispute an enraged Japanese representative had told Thai contacts that 'You will soon be saluting me!' A spate of rumours of Japanese residents and companies buying up strategic land trickled out of the country.

A. T. Steele, a reporter for the *Chicago Daily News*, presciently compared British Burma to Iraq, an oil-rich state facing an external Axis threat with a strong anti-British youth movement in its cities. He realized that 'no more appeasement in the East' meant that the British would not cave in to Japanese pressure to close the Burma Road again.[74] That meant war, since the Japanese were unlikely to be able to mount a naval blockade of Burma. There were two jungle roads into Burma from Thailand, but Steele and almost everyone else still believed them to be impassable. A recent intelligence report had described how difficult was the 'Three Pagodas Route' from Thailand into Burma, but after all it *had* been used by Burmese royal troops invading Thailand in the old days. The report concluded that 'the odds would definitely be in favour of Burma in the present well prepared state of defences'.[75] The author of this report went on to record one unfavourable feature, apparently without the slightest trace of irony: 'It cannot be denied that the Burmans are one of those peoples who do not fully appreciate the benefits of British rule.' John Clague, an intelligent civil servant, took a different view. In 1938 he had minuted that it would be easy to invade Burma through those passes. Burmese elephant thieves drove stolen animals into Thailand this way on a regular basis.[76]

As the tension built in the early winter of 1941, one important figure in the Burmese imbroglio left the stage. In order to bolster Burma's fighting spirit, Dorman-Smith had agreed that Prime Minister U Saw should be allowed to go to London to talk to Leo Amery, the secretary of state for India and Burma, and Winston Churchill about Burma's constitutional future. The idea was to convey, through him, to other Burmese politicians the message that the government was serious about giving Burma independence once the war was over. U Saw himself probably hoped that he might use British weakness to extract further concessions, perhaps even getting a fixed timetable for a rapid move to dominion status – the same constitutional footing as Canada or Australia. This would buttress his position on the political stage against Ba Maw and the Thakins, both of whom had made steady gains since the anti-Indian riots and labour disputes of 1938 which they had helped to instigate.

The governor was impressed by Saw. He saw him as a 'true patriot', a 'likeable rogue', one of the few politicians he actually got on with at a personal level. He also regarded his Galon army, a private party militia, as a major political force. If properly handled, it might be possible to use it to bolster the colony's turgid war effort. Amery was less impressed with the idea of a visit by Saw, and Churchill not at all. The British prime minister really did not want Burmese politicians floating around London at this critical point and had even less time for them than he had for Indians. He agreed to the visit only on condition that it was Amery who took care of Saw and that he was not bothered more than once.

Saw duly left for the UK in October, proclaiming that he 'was not going to London simply to kiss Mr Churchill'.[77] Tommy Cook, Dorman-Smith's ADC and son-in-law, fixed him up with a letter to the Duke of Devonshire. In it he noted that his protégé should enjoy a little private visit to Pratts Club and 'Whiskey Corner' at Brooks's, 'if the old meeting places are still standing' after the Blitz.[78] At a final dinner with Dorman-Smith, the governor expressed his hope that when U Saw returned he would not have to lock him up for subversion immediately after his welcome-home dinner.[79] Saw replied professing profound esteem for the governor. The next day he flew out of Rangoon accompanied by U Tin Tut, ICS, the leading Burmese civil servant who was also to play a major part in his country's history over the next seven years. True to form, Saw had the plane in which they were flying make a triumphal pass round the gleaming spire of the Shwedagon pagoda as it took off, offending the less politically minded monks.

To no one's surprise, very little came out of the London meetings. After all, the government was not to be panicked even into winning over Indian opinion until Sir Stafford Cripps's mission to Delhi early in 1942. In late 1941, Burma was so far down the list of political priorities as to be invisible. U Saw, wined and dined in style but disappointed in his mission, left London in early December on his tortuous route back to Burma via the United States, Canada, Hawaii and Lisbon. He had decided to see American officials and harp on the promises of freedom in the Atlantic Charter. Then all hell broke loose. The Pearl Harbor and Hong Kong debacles suddenly revealed the hollowness of Allied power to Saw. In San Francisco he witnessed a city terrified by stories of attacking Japanese submarines off its coast. He formed the view that US public opinion was irresolute and defeatist. Impulsively, he sought out again Japanese contacts which he had made during the mid 1930s when their diplomats in Rangoon had befriended him. In Honolulu he ran off to the Japanese consulate, which amazingly was still functioning, and offered his services if the Japanese invaded Burma. Later, re-routed away from the new conflict zone via Lisbon, he also visited the Japanese consul in Portugal.

At this point the British intelligence record becomes sparse and guarded. Amery let Dorman-Smith know that Saw had performed a 'treacherous act'. The information was 'conclusive, but most secret'.[80] He was informed that a British official had confronted Saw and told him that his treachery was known, and in detail. Even Dorman-Smith was never told the full story and it was not until many years after the end of the war that more details became available. What had happened was that Saw had become a victim of British cypher success. Early in the war the British had broken the Japanese naval and diplomatic codes and had a full transcript of what Saw had said to the Japanese in Lisbon. This fact could never be revealed for fear of compromising the code-breakers' secret. Churchill was initially determined to have U Saw tried for treason on the grounds that it was important to 'bring traitors to justice'. Linlithgow, the viceroy, knew what had happened and was interested to know if there was any chance of 'trying him and Tin Tut on capital charges and of shooting both or either of them'.[81] He clearly had the demonstration's effect on India in mind.

In the event, the Cabinet was sensible enough not to try Saw for treason and have him executed. That would have raised too many questions amongst journalists around the world. Instead he was sent off to cool his heels in British East Africa for the duration of the war. If Saw had been in Burma in 1942, he would probably have occupied the position that Ba Maw came to hold as chief collaborator with the

Japanese. As it was, four years of intense frustration and his burning desire to make up time and get back quickly into Burmese politics at the end of the war was to prove momentous enough for the future of independent Burma. Meanwhile, for the time being, Saw's old rival was also in jail. The British had picked up Ba Maw and carted him off to Mogok prison in the ruby-bearing hills north of Mandalay. The authorities now trusted neither the Thakins nor their elders amongst the nationalist politicians of the 1930s. The elderly conservative Sir Paw Tun, a bitter enemy of most of the other politicians and the Thakins in particular, became prime minister of Burma. Within a few days Japanese Zero aircraft swooped in over Rangoon, carpeting the docks area with bombs. The enfeebled structure of British rule in Burma was quickly smashed beyond repair and the political and ethnic tensions which had built up over the previous decade were released in a frenzy of murder and destruction.

# 2

# 1942: A Very British Disaster

## THE FORTRESS THAT NEVER WAS

The defence of the British crescent in Asia, as every schoolboy knew, rested on the 'fortress' at Singapore. Yet it was not clear where this fortress actually was. There was the naval base at Sembawang on the north of the island, with its huge dry dock built by Swan Hunter of Tyneside. The Japanese iron mines of Johore had provided the ballast to sink it. The huge artillery installations that covered its sea approaches to the south made it one of the most heavily defended pieces of territory in the British Empire. It was also one of its most valuable pieces of real estate. The base had cost over £25 million since its inception in 1922. It was a vital political symbol; a statement of Britain's imperial intent in Asia, and of a larger arc of commitment that reached down to her southern dominions. By 1930, 23 per cent of all the empire's trade passed through the Indian Ocean, and hence through Singapore. In the case of Australia, the figure was 60 per cent.[1] For the Australians, 'Fortress Singapore' was an article of faith, for without it they faced economic strangulation.

In early 1941, however, Sembawang was still more of a building site than a base, and it housed no large warships. The 'Singapore strategy' has become a classic study of strategic delusion.[2] The central weakness of the fortress was that its outer defences stretched so far beyond the island as to make the concept meaningless. The Japanese officers who visited Singapore in 1940 had told Masanobu Tsuji and his planners that 'it is impossible to attack Singapore from the sea, that is from the east, south or west. Attack is possible only from the Johore Strait north of Singapore.'[3] That same year an appreciation by the army commander in Malaya, Lieutenant-General Lionel Bond, conceded that the defence of Singapore demanded the defence of the entire Malay peninsula. But this meant securing an area the size of England itself, with few natural barriers to stall a determined and well-prepared adversary. British soldiers tended to think of the peninsula as an impenetrable jungle: it was not. Bond also realized that a naval presence alone would be insufficient to deter a Japanese invasion. Nor were the fabled big guns effective in land warfare. They could be rotated landwards, but they only had armour-piercing shells for use against ships; the heaviest, 15-inch guns had no high-explosive rounds for use against artillery or infantry.

To hold the peninsula, Bond estimated that he needed between thirty-nine and forty-two infantry battalions. With sufficient air support, that might be reduced to twenty-five, but some 336 first-line aircraft were required. An elaborate network of airbases was constructed to house them. But, noted one engineer, there were 'nearly as many landing grounds as first class bombers'.[4] In September 1940 there were only ninety first-line aircraft in Malaya, mostly ageing Brewster Buffaloes, the 'flying beer barrels' that had been rejected for service in Europe. In Indo-China, the Japanese had concentrated 600 combat-ready planes. In London, the Sea Lords stood unwilling to commit valuable ships to a naval base that could not be defended from the air. Yet Churchill insisted that the visible presence of the Royal Navy would be enough to deter any aggressor. A further symbolic gesture was therefore made: in late October 1941 a small flotilla, 'Force Z', was assembled under Vice-Admiral Tom Phillips. It included the navy's most modern battleship, the *Prince of Wales*, the vessel that had carried Churchill to the Atlantic conference with Roosevelt, and one of its oldest battle cruisers, *Repulse*, together with four destroyers. There were no aircraft carriers.

The fate of Singapore was sealed by the fall of France. In the wake of further losses in the Mediterranean, for the 'Singapore strategy' to have any realistic chance of success two articles of faith had to hold: first, that there would be sufficient warning of any Japanese attack on Malaya to allow for reinforcement; second, that if the attack came, American help would be on hand. By late 1941 it was clear that neither of these assumptions had substance. At a War Cabinet meeting on

12 November 1941 Churchill outlined his strategy of moving forces from theatre to theatre when the need arose. The meeting was attended by an Australian special representative to Britain, Sir Earle Page. Churchill broke the news to him that large-scale reinforcements would not be available for Malaya, and that the Middle East must have first call on resources. In the stormy days that followed Churchill clung to this position; it determined all his other actions, and much of the issue of the war. As for Japan: 'The answer was to maintain a stiff attitude towards her, but not to become involved in war with her unless we had the assurance of the United States' participation.'[5] Yet Churchill also warned that it was dangerous to push President Roosevelt too far ahead of American public opinion. The cautious attitude of the United States was a serious constraint on British strategic planning in Southeast Asia.

The 'back door' to British Malaya was Thailand. Its military government, under Field Marshal Pibunsongkhram, confronted with growing Japanese influence within Thailand, and its military build-up in northern Indo-China, had adopted a stance of 'watchful waiting'. This was an obstacle to a British pre-emptive strike into southern Thailand to secure the borders of Malaya. The codename given to this contingency was 'Matador': a sweep to occupy key air and sea bases around Singora that would, in theory, allow air cover of the northern approaches to the Malay peninsula. There was a further default plan, 'Krohcol', to hold a defensive position known as The Ledge, south of Patani. The lead formation in Malaya – the 11th Indian Division – was locked into 'Matador'. It was a good plan.[6] Yet it violated Thai neutrality and there were fears of provoking not only Thai resistance, but the ire of the United States. Britain's man in Bangkok, Sir Josiah Crosby, was a long-term resident and a fluent Thai speaker. He was sympathetic to the Thai dilemma. As he put it in August 1940: the Thais 'have a very full conviction of the power of Japan to do them harm, but, alas!, they have no faith at all in our power to assist them'.[7] Crosby frustrated British subterfuge operations against Japanese sympathizers within the Thai elite. By this time Bangkok was a nest of cloak-and-dagger intrigue, as Britain and Japan each sought to provoke a pre-emptive move from the other. The Thais had good reason to mistrust British motives: there had been imperial grand designs for uniting British

Burma and Malaya at the Kra Isthmus, and to build there a new Suez canal to link the eastern Indian Ocean with the South China Sea. This clashed with both Thai irredentism and Muslim separatism in the Malay lands of Thailand's southern marches. British and Japanese agents took sight-seeing tours to the area, and on occasion found themselves staying in the same hotels. After months of uncertainty, the United States gave its approval for British defensive action in Thailand on 1 December 1941. After some weeks of lobbying in London, the British commander-in-chief in the Far East, Air Chief Marshal Sir Robert Brooke-Popham, was finally signalled on 5 December that he was authorized to 'Matador' if the Japanese invaded Thailand, or were seen to be approaching it. But when Japanese hostile intent was this far advanced, they were likely to get to the vital bases first. Brooke-Popham's chief of staff handed the cable to him with the dry comment: 'They've now made you responsible for declaring war.'[8]

This said, it was unclear in Singapore as to where the ultimate responsibility for the defence of Malaya lay. Brooke-Popham had been in post from only October 1940; he was sixty-three years old, roused from retirement after a period as governor of Kenya. He had no authority over the civil administration or the navy. The governor of Singapore and high commissioner of the Federated Malay States, Sir Shenton Thomas, was a nominal 'commander-in-chief', an honorific that dated back to the swashbuckling days of war against Malay pirates and Chinese secret societies. Thomas was noted for his minute-writing qualities, but not for his charisma. He was seen as something of an interloper by what was, quite literally, the freemasonry of the Malayan Civil Service establishment. His long service in the African bush earned him the disdainful nickname 'Tom-Tom'.[9] His decision in April 1940 to take long home leave gave ammunition to his many critics. He used it to push the case for the reinforcement of Malaya personally in Whitehall, but did not return until early December. His amanuensis was Malaya's civilian defence secretary, a veteran of the 'high born' Malayan Civil Service establishment, C. A. Vlieland. He argued throughout 1940, with remarkable prescience, that the army was deluded by 'the invention of the imaginary fortress of Singapore'. He campaigned for a fuller mobilization of civilian expertise and local knowledge to meet an attack in the north of the peninsula.[10] Military commanders resented his advice, and were quick to criticize the complacency of civil defence preparations. In May 1941, Brooke-Popham installed his protégé Lieutenant-General Arthur Percival as GOC Malaya Command. Percival's main instrument of war was III Indian Corps in the north of the peninsula, under Lieutenant General Sir Lewis 'Piggy' Heath. This was reinforced by the 8th Australian Division, under Major-General Gordon Bennett, to which was assigned the defence of southern Malaya.

These men embodied very different aspects of the imperial experience. Percival had pioneered counter-insurgency war against Sinn Fein in Ireland, but had spent much of his subsequent career on the staff. He had, however, the advantage of a twenty-month tour in Malaya in 1936–7, and had warned then of the dangers of Japan trying to 'burgle Malaya by the back door'.[11] Heath possessed the élan of a border soldier of the North West Frontier of the Raj, and arrived in Malaya after defeating Mussolini's imperial ambitions in Eritrea, with a young pregnant wife in tow. He had not attended staff college. The fiery red-haired Bennett, after distinguished service at Gallipoli, had made his fortune in business, chairing chambers of commerce and ending up as sole municipal commissioner for the city of Sydney. He was an irascible individual, rather aloof from his troops, but very clubbable with newsmen. He disdained modern methods, trusting instead to the innate fighting qualities of a citizen army. The British, Australian and Indian units remained locked in separate worlds. The Australians, encouraged by Bennett, cultivated an air of being hardier than British troops. Their officers bivouacked in the open, whereas, for their British counterparts, 'His utility was unpacked and an efficient batman erected a comfortable bed covered by a mosquito net, under which its owner retired between clean sheets, as though he were on some well-arranged hunting trip.'[12] In turn, British officers continued to sneer at Australian indiscipline and lack of professionalism. But the underlying reality was that all the imperial forces were ill equipped, ill trained and ill conditioned to the tropics. By November 1941 Percival had ten infantry brigades. But he had no tanks, and Indian troops in the front line who had never seen one. For all units there was little preparation for fighting across the Malayan terrain. Priorities were confused at all levels. The public works department was still employed not on military fortifications but in providing amenities for the camps, such as electric lighting. Military commanders, witnesses would recall, conducted the war 'like at OTC [Officer Training Corps] field day on Salisbury Plain'.[13] Tensions within the officer corps remained strongest in the Indian contingent. After an incipient mutiny in May 1941, the commanding officer of the 19th Hyderabad Regiment had to be given an escort to protect him from his own men.

A flurry of late arrivals intensified these quarrels, in particular that of Alfred Duff Cooper, Chancellor of the Duchy of Lancaster, and his society wife Lady Diana Cooper, who – in the words of one agency house clerk – 'descended on Singapore like some rare and exotic species, birds of a different paradise'.[14] Duff Cooper was having a bad war. The general impression was that his career was rapidly on the wane after a dismal period as minister of information during which, after a boozy lunch with journalists, he had been made to look ridiculous by attacking P. G. Wodehouse's broadcasts from Nazi Germany. Lady Diana spent much of her time in Singapore writing letters to get him back home. Cooper had taken seven weeks to reach Malaya, and had prepared himself by reading *War and Peace*, immersing himself in the last glittering days before the fall of Moscow. Certainly, on arrival Lady Diana revelled in Singapore's 'Sino-Monte-Carlo' atmosphere:

Most frail, tarty and peasant-pompous – there is the working life of the chinks going on before your eyes down every street – coffin-making, lantern-painting, and a tremendous lot of shaving. I never tire of strolling and peering and savouring.[15]

Shenton Thomas saw Diana's presence as evidence of a lack of seriousness on Duff Cooper's part. There was even controversy over the number of suitcases she had brought with her – over one hundred according to some reports. Before December 1941 the Coopers spent little time in Singapore. They embarked instead on a frantic tour of the crescent, to Burma, Batavia, Bali and the Antipodes. Their period in Singapore was one of the final clashes of metropolitan sophistication with local stuffiness. The resident minister launched into impersonations of Shenton Thomas at private dinner parties at the 'Duff Coopery', their residence in Jervois Road. After a month in the region Cooper wrote a damning report to Churchill on British administration.

He spared no one. Brooke-Popham was 'damned near gaga'. The administration of Malaya had 'undergone no important change since the days of Queen Victoria'. Cooper argued for a war council with a minister for the Far East, or at least a military governor as its chair. He told Churchill that he did not want the job and suggested the former Australian prime minister Sir Robert Menzies. Churchill disagreed: Duff Cooper should stay and do the job himself. This was not acted upon until the Japanese attacked Malaya. The immediate upshot was that Brooke-Popham ('Old Pop-off' to the Coopers) was to be shuffled off the scene with a baronetcy. By November 1941 most of Singapore knew this.[16] Shenton Thomas never forgave Cooper for his disloyalty. The presence of Admiral Phillips, another warrior whose campaigns had been mainly conducted behind a desk, with naval Force Z added to the gridlock at the top. Its arrival on 2 December was recorded by Lady Diana Cooper. 'Today a little fleet arrived to help', she recorded. It was 'a lovely sight but on the petty side'. The next evening Lady Diana attended a party hosted by Tom Phillips. She danced on the wide deck of his flagship under a red and white awning: 'Brussels ball once again'.[17]

By the autumn of 1941 the front line of British Asia lay in the northeastern Malay State of Kelantan and its Thai borderlands across the Golok river. In imperial terms, Kelantan was a quiet outpost of the islands; its economy was dominated by the Malay fishing fleets that trawled the South China Sea. They continued to sail from the river shore opposite its crucial airbase. Nearby, towards the beachhead, a Japanese, known to the Malays as Ayah [Father] Kawa, had recently been putting in a pipeline to supply water to the surrounding paddy fields. The sole land route to Singapore was the bridge over the Kelantan river, the longest in Malaya. Yet even here the old world was passing away. In the inter-war years the Malay courtly capital of Kota Bahru had expanded dramatically. Modern shophouses now stood side by side with Malay *kampong* dwellings. By 1937, the town had 338 coffee shops and licensed premises; its steamy environment was to be immortalized in Anthony Burgess's chronicle of late imperial ennui, *The Enemy in the Blanket*. The military had brought a minor revolution to Kelantan, a sudden wave of industry as lorries streamed in, bridges were strengthened and earth tracks became metalled roads. But by early December the excitement and expectation had subsided. The monsoon rains had set in, swelling the rivers, 'flooding everywhere and filling everyone with a mild depression'.[18] The frontiersmen of British Malaya had been put on a vigil for several weeks. A planter on a French-owned estate, Bill Bangs, like many of his kind, enlisted in the Frontier Patrol. In early December he went to Yala in southern Thailand, disguised as a Seventh Day Adventist. He stayed in the Green Hotel there, only to have to get out of town when the real local Adventist representative called upon him. He fled to Patani, assuming the more plausible identity of a rubber manager inspecting estates. Here his 'boy' overheard Japanese from the old Bukit Lanchap mine in Kelantan boasting drunkenly in a bar in Naratiwat about an invasion happening the next day. He raced to the border where he was detained by the Thais on 7 December, but eventually escaped across the river by sampan. He passed on his information that night to the British commander in Kota Bahru. It was too late: as he retired to bed, Bangs heard the first gunshots.[19]

## THE ARROW LEAVES THE BOW

As the Japanese war machine was embarked for the Malay peninsula on 4 December in an armada of twenty-seven transport ships, its commander, Yamashita Tomoyuki, penned a poem:

> On the day the sun shines with the moon
> The arrow leaves the bow
> It carries my spirit towards the enemy
> With me are a hundred million souls
> My people of the East
> On this day when the moon shines
> And the sun both shine.[20]

Yamashita was the son of a country physician, but groomed by his father to be a career soldier from an early age. He had risen fast. He was an imposing physical presence; when on a peacetime posting to Korea he had taken up calligraphy and used the nom de plume 'Daisen', or 'Giant Cedar'. He was a political general in whom many had seen a rival to Tojo, a man with whom, in his early career, Yamashita had been close. They became estranged when radical, reformist young officers of the 'Imperial Way' clique looked to Yamashita for leadership. When some of them were involved in a failed coup d'état in February 1936, Yamashita had interceded for them by insisting that an imperial representative should witness their suicides. This impertinence incurred the wrath of the emperor. In many ways, Yamashita saw his subsequent career as an act of expiation for this transgression. Thereafter, even on campaign, he would always place his desk to face the imperial palace in Tokyo. He fought in North China and was entrusted with a mission to Nazi Germany in June 1941, where Hitler and Göring had briefed him on Operation Barbarossa, the invasion of the Soviet Union. On his return from Europe, he was posted by Tojo out of sight to Manchukuo, but such were his abilities that he was suddenly recalled to Tokyo when the government took the decision to go to war with the West. Only on 8 November 1941 was he given command of the 25th Army: three divisions of 60,000 men. On joining his command at its great muster in Hainan island, Yamashita announced he would be in Singapore by New Year's Day.[21]

There was hard calculation behind Yamashita's optimism. Japanese planners were by now well briefed on British weaknesses. In November 1940, a British ship, SS *Automedon*, had been sunk in the Indian Ocean by a German raider. It was carrying to Singapore the pessimistic defence appreciations of the Imperial General Staff and, with them, a clear indication that Britain was unable adequately to reinforce Malaya. This golden trove of documents had been passed on to Tokyo.[22] But Yamashita also knew that, should he fail, his career would be at an end. His officers were experienced, but most were unknown to him. Many key commanders, such as the sinister planning chief Masanobu Tsuji, were closely identified with his rival Tojo. The men of two of his divisions, the 5th and 18th, were hardened veterans of the war in China. They were supported by the elite Imperial Guard. Yamashita's first order in assuming command in the field was 'no looting, no rape, no arson'. To Yamashita, the war was not only one of liberation of subject peoples of Asia, but a sacred task undertaken beneath the full gaze of world opinion. On board the ship, each soldier was given a copy of Masanobu Tsuji's booklet: *Read This Alone and the War Can Be Won*. It described war in 'a world of everlasting summer': the jungle and mangrove terrain, the food and hygiene, even etiquette in a mosque and local toilet habits ('the left hand is regarded as unclean'). Soldiers were ordered to 'show compassion to those who have no guilt'. But, ominously, they were also warned of the 'Overseas Chinese': they were extortionists and beyond the pale of any appeal to 'Asian brotherhood'.[23]

The armada soon ran into cloud. As it broke, around 3 p.m. on 6 December, 300 miles out from the coast of Malaya, the pilot of an Australian Hudson flying out of Kota Bahru sighted the ships. The message was radioed back to British commanders. Both Heath in Kuala Lumpur and Percival, en route from there to Singapore, expected Brooke-Popham to launch Operation Matador. He did not do so. He felt he had insufficient evidence of Japan's hostile intent. Although Ultra intercepts made it clear that Japan was planning a strike against both Thailand and Malaya, they also left open the possibility that a feint was underway to provoke a British breach of Thai sovereignty, which – as Crosby in Bangkok kept impressing upon Brooke-Popham – might have disastrous diplomatic consequences.[24] Further aircraft were scrambled, and a Catalina flying-boat approaching the fleet on the morning of 7 December was shot down by a Japanese naval Zero. The Japanese task force fanned out towards its landing sites along the coast. Still Brooke-Popham hesitated, to the fury of his subordinates. Proof positive of hostile intent came only with a sighting of warships and transports off Patani and Kota Bahru on the evening of 7 December. By this time Matador became, as it has remained, an academic exercise: it was never launched. Percival declared that it was now 'unsound' as it was too late to deny the Japanese the key landing grounds in Thailand. By 1.35 a.m. on 8 December Japanese landings had begun at Kota Bahru. It was the first land battle of the great Asian war: the attack on Pearl Harbor was still several hours away. The battle for Kota Bahru centred on its aerodrome; the Japanese rained fire on its defences. In one day sixty Allied planes in northern Malaya were put out of action. There was a shocked mood of paralysis in the town. As British officials gathered in the residency on the night of 8 December, there was 'an eerie quietness' in the air. 'There was absolutely nothing to do,' one recalled. It was never intended to defend Kota Bahru. The British commander took the view that once the European women and children were evacuated and the Sultan of

Kelantan and his wives had withdrawn to his private residence inland, there was nothing there to defend. The Indian garrison fought back to the railhead at Kuala Krai. In the chaos of the retreat, the 1st Hydera-bads who guarded the aerodrome killed their British senior officer. After the aerodrome fell, largely intact, the remaining civilians were ordered out. They told their Malay colleagues to stay at their posts and hope for the best.[25] Kota Bahru would set a pattern to be repeated across the entire peninsula.

Shenton Thomas's initial reaction to the landings would later haunt his memory: 'I suppose you'll shove the little men off', he is said to have commented.[26] The British had been blinded by racial assumptions: that the Japanese were small, myopic and with a level of military achievement below that even of the Italians. But Allied commanders were soon to concede that the Japanese were far tougher than their own troops. Many of the men of the 18th Division were hardy Kyushu coalminers. Wavell himself called them 'an army of highly trained gangsters'.[27] Most of the British soldiers had not seen combat before. Their steel helmets and respirators were superfluous; the Japanese went to war in shorts, a light shirt and plimsolls. This was inelegant but effective. The assumption that the Japanese could not tolerate jungle conditions was an irrelevance. 'Malaya had the best roads in the British Empire', wrote one engineer shortly afterwards, 'with the poss-ible exception of Great Britain.'[28] The Japanese hurtled down them, bypassing British prepared positions. Each Japanese division had been issued with 6,000 bicycles. Years of Japanese imports had left a pro-fusion of spare parts in the towns and villages of Malaya. The 'bicycle Blitzkrieg' was strikingly effective; Allied troops mistook the sound of it for the rumble of tanks. One Japanese officer noted that those who had made the long journey down the peninsula, often cycling twenty hours a day, afterwards 'had a lot of trouble in walking'.[29]

Shenton Thomas had assumed, as did most of Malaya, that a British counterblow would come swiftly. One potential response was a rapid response from the Royal Navy. Yet on 8 December Admiral Phillips was in Manila, and there was no agreement in London as to Force Z's role. Phillips initially planned to make for Darwin and then, in a symbolic gesture of Anglo-Saxon solidarity, to support the remnants of the US Pacific Fleet. Given the failure to repel the landings in the northeast of the peninsula, Phillips steamed north, leaving Singapore on the late afternoon of 8 December, to engage and destroy the Japanese landing flotilla. It was a bold, risky undertaking. Phillips demanded air cover off the Malayan coast at daylight on 10 December. He was told as he sailed that 'Fighter protection on Wednesday 10th will not be possible'. Phillips had to rely on surprise. But late on 8 December he was sighted by Japanese aircraft, and decided to turn back to Singapore. He had almost come within sight of the Japanese strike force. Then, just before midnight, came reports of further Japanese landings at Kuantan. Force Z turned to meet them. Phillips did not ask for air cover, probably because he believed none was available, and that he was out of range of Japanese strike aircraft. He also believed in maintaining radio silence at sea. In the event, the Air Force did not know where he was. Neither, initially, did the Japanese. From Indo-China thirty bombers and fifty torpedo bombers had been despatched early on 10 December to find Force Z; they had flown far to the south, and, low on fuel, were returning home, when, just after 11 a.m., the cloud broke and the ships were sighted and attacked. *Repulse* and *Prince of Wales* were sunk. Phillips went down with his flagship and 840 men. Fighters had been scrambled from Singapore on the news of the attack. They arrived in time to see the destroyers picking up survivors.[30] The sea lanes to Ceylon, India and Darwin lay open and unprotected.

On the same night as the Kota Bahru landings, the first air raids struck Singapore. They hit the shopping arcades of Raffles Place, blew out the windows of the department stores and threw up the turf of the Padang. But Chinatown bore the worst of it: around sixty people were killed. There was no blackout. The head of air-raid precautions was at the cinema at the time. Lim Kean Siew, son of the Penang Straits Chinese notable Lim Cheng Ean, witnessed the event with his student friends from the elite Raffles College. Its Class of '41 included men who would dominate the government and politics of Singapore and Malaya for two generations, including two future prime ministers and one future king. 'The heavens have opened', commented one student. 'The heavens had indeed opened for us', Lim Kean Siew wrote. 'From a languid, lazy and lackadaisical world, we were catapulted into a world of somersaults and frenzy from which we would never recover.'

Like many of his friends, Lim left Singapore and headed up-country for Penang to be met on arrival with word of the sinking of *Prince of Wales* and *Repulse*.[31] This event stunned Britain's Asian empire more deeply than any of the worse news that was later to come. The relentless demonstration of Japanese technological prowess did more to break civilian and military resistance than any other factor. Few people knew the fleet had even put to sea. The kingpin of the China Relief Fund, Tan Kah Kee, was called at his millionaires' club on the night of 12 December with the 'terrible news. I could not sleep a wink all night ... the enemy had already landed on mainland Malaya, and since the enemy bombers were this effective, it seemed unlikely that Singapore could be defended'. When he was told the next day that the British treasurer had removed government bonds worth $8 million from the Overseas Chinese Banking Corporation, ready for them to be burnt, he concluded that the British had no intention of defending the island.[32]

The main thrust of the Japanese advance shifted to the west coast. The British default defence of the borderlands, Krohcol, failed, and Heath's III Corps fell back into northern Malaya. Yamashita had ordered *kiromomi sakusen*, a 'driving charge'. His 5th Division and Imperial Guards competed against each other in the advance. The first of a series of theoretical lines of defence for the British was at Jitra in Kedah. Tsuji commented later that it should have held out for three months, but it collapsed in fifteen hours when Japanese tanks threw its defenders into demoralized confusion. Yamashita celebrated this at his forward HQ in the state capital of Alor Star whilst his troops foraged for 'Churchill supplies' of abandoned tinned food and fuel for their vehicles. Yamashita had now captured four 'Churchill aerodromes'. The tactical retreat and piecemeal British defence of the north created chaos within Heath's forces. For the remainder of the campaign they were unable to fall back to properly prepared positions. He told Percival that the only practical recourse was to draw back further and form a more robust line of defence in Perak. Vast military stores were abandoned. Within a month of hostilities 3,000 vehicles were crammed into northern Malaya. But within another month they had changed direction. Their Asian drivers were the principal targets of Japanese war planes.[33] In Perak planters were recalled from their soldiery to get their labourers to work on defence projects in the state; they too were attacked from the air. Many of them fled, as people began to abandon the towns of northern Malaya.

The moral collapse of British rule in Southeast Asia came not at Singapore, but at Penang. The retreat through Perak had left Britain's oldest possession in Malaya stranded. It too was a fortress with a designated 'fortress commander'. But the decision was taken not to defend it. This gave the Japanese assault when it came, on 9 and 10 December, a terrible surreal quality. For the first two days Japanese planes flew reconnaissance missions, unchallenged. To E. A. Davis, an employee of the Eastern Smelting Company working as a volunteer fireman, it was 'just like an aeronautical display'. The whole of George Town turned out to watch. However, on Thursday 11 December the planes attacked with bombs and almost continuous machine-gun fire. The spectators were hit in their hundreds. 'They watched with fascination', wrote Lim Kean Siew, 'not knowing what was coming as a shoal of fish would stay to watch in silence as a fisherman surrounds them with a net.' A downtown market was a principal target. Parked handcarts with their handles pointing skywards had been mistaken for ack-ack guns.[34]

An English doctor, Oscar Fisher, recorded in his diary that the scene was like H. G. Wells's *War of the Worlds* come to life. Refugees fled George Town to the suburbs and villages around Penang Hill. The centre of the metropolis had moved overnight. By evening of the first day traffic control, food distribution and policing were largely maintained by Asian and Eurasian ARP wardens and auxiliary firemen. The general hospital was overwhelmed by around 700 casualties: of these 126 died in the first twenty-four hours. There was no anaesthetist available and amputations were carried out in the conditions of a nineteenth-century battlefield. There were fourteen operating tables being worked at once. 'Everybody that could hold a knife was doing all sorts of operations'. The stench of gangrene was appalling. The full extent of the butchery was impossible to assess; it was two to three days before the fallen could be buried.[35] Bodies still lay on the streets after the city's capitulation. The resident commissioner estimated the number of dead and injured at 3,000; some 1,000 lay under the rubble. Army disposal units were overcome by the stench even wearing gas masks. Then came cholera and typhoid.[36]

Japanese radio broadcasts taunted the British: 'you English gentlemen: "How do you like our bombing? Isn't it a better tonic than your
whisky soda?" '[37] In the crisis, the politics of racial segregation within
colonial society were taken to their brutish extreme. According to
one British volunteer fireman who managed to escape, the resident
commissioner of Penang, L. Forbes, forbade fire crews to take pumps
past a line drawn along Penang Road, a commercial thoroughfare
that divided the main area of European settlement from the Asian
shophouses of George Town. Efforts were to be concentrated on residential property. The rest could burn. When the blazes later spread,
he refused to have European homes destroyed as a firebreak. Firemen
believed the Japanese planes were targeting them: of the 200 on duty,
around sixty perished.[38] The European evacuation was surreptitious
and ignominious. The order to leave came quietly in the night on
16 December. Europeans gathered at the Eastern and Oriental Hotel,
many of them under strict orders, disgusted at leaving their local staff
and servants. Dr Fisher was told abruptly that it was 'total war' and
he was needed elsewhere. Europeans crowded to the docks on every
conceivable form of transport: six people to a rickshaw. At the quay-
side, the one senior Asian civil servant who had been served the order,
the Chinese judge and Volunteer Force officer Lim Khoon Teik, was
turned out of the boat, yet the fortress commander still managed to
get his car on board. The quay was cordoned off by armed volunteers.
Survivors from the *Prince of Wales* manned the ferries that evacuated
the women. J. A. Quitzow, like many single women, had demanded to
stay but was ordered out. The manner of the British withdrawal, she
wrote a few weeks later, was 'a thing which I am sure will never be
forgotten or forgiven'.[39]

There was no British officer to surrender the island to its new
masters. It was M. Saravanamuttu, the Indian editor of the English
language newspaper, the *Straits Echo*, who lowered the Union flag at
Fort Cornwallis the next morning. Only one European stayed on the
island, a doctor in the general hospital. The news of the surrender of
the town was delivered to the Japanese by a Eurasian racehorse trainer,
who cycled twenty-one miles to the command at Sungei Patani to tell
them and to request that the bombing cease. Thus, over a century and
a half of British rule came to an end.[40]

The outrage at the desertion of Penang was inflamed by Duff Cooper's statement, in a radio broadcast from Singapore on 22 December, that 'the majority of the population had been evacuated', and by accompanying images of Europeans disembarking from the ferries to tea and sympathy on the dockside at Singapore. Shenton Thomas had assured the Legislative Council of the Straits Settlements a few days earlier that there would be 'no distinction of race'. But this was already contradicted by the military's offer of free passages out for service wives.[41] By the end of December the work of European women was on such a scale, with several hundreds in 'essential war services', that Thomas continued to resist the compulsory evacuation of married women without children and wondered if any compulsion should be placed on unmarried women to leave. And, as Percival too recognized, they worked side by side with Asian women.[42] Duff Cooper and the governor were at loggerheads on the issue. The War Cabinet discussed it on the same day as Duff Cooper's speech and Churchill affirmed the earlier principle of non-discrimination. 'But', the Cabinet noted, 'this might not be so easy, since Chinese and Malayans would not be permitted to land in many countries.' At this point only fifty Chinese and fifty Europeans had been given entry to the Commonwealth of 'white' Australia. Ceylon would only take 500 refugees and wanted preference given to the Ceylonese of Malaya. One solution was to take a token few non-European civilians out, land them in the Dutch East Indies and turn round the ships as quickly as possible. The application of this policy was left to the discretion of Duff Cooper.[43] But he believed that it was scandalous to evacuate British troops first 'and to leave the women and children to the tender mercies of a cruel Asiatic foe'.[44]

Yamashita was enraged by reports of indiscipline in the wake of the capture of Penang. He had offenders from the Kobaysahi Battalion court-martialled and executed. Their battalion and regimental commanders – who were still in the front line – were placed under close arrest for thirty days. The rumour of war created terror and disorder ahead of the Japanese vanguard. Horror stories reached Malaya from the fall of Hong Kong on Christmas Day 1941. There had been a horrendous slaughter of civilians, over 2,000, as drunken Japanese soldiers ran amok in the flush of victory. European nurses had been raped and killed. Their patients had been bayoneted. British propaganda had played not only on the impregnability of Malaya's defences, but on Japanese atrocities in China, particularly against women. It had striking success. So much so that when the British ceased to have faith in their ability to defend their own womenfolk, colonial rule shed much of its threadbare legitimacy. The loyalty of key servants of the eastern Raj was severely shaken. In Singapore, Sikh policemen were read a statement by the inspector general of police to explain the abandonment of many of their colleagues in Penang; they were told to accept it as 'the fortune of war'. Reading it to them, their immediate senior officer added his personal assurance that he would stick by them in Singapore. He was later to escape the island.[45] Japanese propaganda played on these betrayals. 'Malayan and Indian soldiers!' it proclaimed, 'Pack up your troubles in your old kit bag and cooperate with the Nippon Army!'

The leader of the Indian Independence League in Bangkok, Pritam Singh, called on overseas Indians 'to eliminate the Anglo-Saxon from the whole of Asia'.[46] Major Fujiwara Iwaichi, another Japanese intelligence officer who saw himself in the T. E. Lawrence mould, flew down from Bangkok with Pritam Singh to establish a branch of the IIL at Alor Star in Kedah. Fujiwara approached a disaffected Sikh captain of the 1/14 Punjab named Mohan Singh, who had been stranded in the retreat and surrendered near Jitra on 15 December. Fujiwara was impressed by the authoritative bearing and sense of discipline of the Indian army officer. He was enlisted to control Indian stragglers in the north, and persuaded to organize them into a new fighting force. It was to be an Indian National Army. From the outset, Mohan Singh impressed on the Japanese that the soldiers were 'a very strange mixture' and were dispirited by the fighting. It would take time to build and prepare a force. At a meeting in Alor Star on New Year's Eve, the Indian officers involved insisted they would not fight in Malaya, but only in India, and then on equal terms with the Japanese. The name of Subhas Chandra Bose, still in Berlin, was mentioned. 'In most cases', Mohan Singh wrote to Fujiwara, 'people worship him like a god.'[47] Mohan Singh came south with the advance, to Ipoh, Kuala Lumpur and finally Singapore. The POWs who came forward were given white armbands with the letter 'F' on them, to show they worked for Fujiwara's organization. There were only 229 of them, but they added to the atmosphere of rumour and the disillusionment of Indian troops.[48] Mohan Singh had brought into being, by this simple act, one of the great legends of the war in the East and a healing balm for India's sense of self-respect. In Berlin, Subhas Bose learned of it almost immediately.

As European society rolled back down the peninsula it became entirely detached from the society it governed. The fall of Malaya was not only a military failure but a complete collapse of British administration. Alien artefact that it was, the Malayan Raj was very dependent on its technocratic achievements for legitimacy. The scorched-earth policy destroyed much of this and had a devastating psychological effect on the people of Malaya. Some questioned the policy; Percival himself was very conscious of the dangers of destroying Asian businesses. Many Europeans mourned a life's work gone up in smoke. In Pahang, the British hastened to abandon not only the port of Kuantan but also the great lode tin mine, the largest in the empire, and the Raub gold mine.[49] Everywhere the story was similar. Officials spent the last days of rule burning their papers, settling wages and dumping stores of rice. All useable transport, tanks, guns, agricultural and engineering plant, and even domestic animals, then joined the stampede south. In Trengganu, with the river bridges blown up and rumours of further Japanese landings at Kuantan, Europeans found themselves stranded, with no order to evacuate. The only way out was over the central range to Kuala Lipis. Fourteen Europeans, including two women, made a 120-mile forced march through the forest to the railhead, accompanied by two Malay policemen.[50] The two European residents on Langkawi island north of Penang only heard about the fall of the north in a Japanese proclamation setting out the new arrangements of government. They fled by sampan and were picked up hundreds of miles south near Port Swettenham. Elsewhere, others took to the jungle.

By this time the industrial heartland of Perak and Selangor was no sanctuary. The casualties from air-raids on up-country towns were heavy; the first raid on Taiping claimed around sixty civilian lives. There was no alert and, again, the market and its surroundings were targeted. The army insisted on a curfew, with a shoot-on-sight policy, just as people began to take to the roads, especially along the coasts where more Japanese landings were expected. The British Resident in Perak was himself shot at as he evacuated, because there were several Malays in his car, who at this stage were all seen as suspect fifth columnists or looters.[51] On 22 December the hotels and golf-courses of the Cameron Highlands were abandoned. The manager of the Cameron Highlands Hotel, Felix Inggold, described morosely to his client the Rajah of Sarawak how he destroyed his Christmas stock of liquor, all $14,000 worth. As the British pulled out an emotional appeal was made to the Asian members of the local defence force to show their loyalty by remaining with their units. 'After lengthy discussions amongst themselves, they settled the matter by resigning as a body'.[52] This was repeated elsewhere. Communities had to take responsibility for their own defence. For Ho Thean Fook, a young primary school teacher in Papan in Perak, the first sign of the British rout came with the arrival of a Chinese propaganda theatre troupe from the mining centre of Ipoh. A young actor announced to the townspeople: 'the British are treating their empire as property and handling the whole thing as if it were a business transaction'. The civic-minded had already taken basic services into their own hands. They had the presence of mind to lay on a tea party for the vanguard of the Imperial Army. As Japanese troops rolled in they demanded women. But in this, too, the townspeople were prepared: all the young women were in hiding. One local recognized the Japanese interpreter as the owner of a photography shop in nearby Ipoh.[53]

On 20 December Port Swettenham was bombed, and on 26 December Klang and Kuala Lumpur. In Klang, Japanese planes came in low over the rubber estates and machine-gunned everything they saw. It was, the British ARP warden, wrote, 'Klang's Waterloo, for from that day it ceased to exist as an organised community'. The bombing had lasted less than a minute. Businesses closed, the streets cleared.[54] In Kuala Lumpur, government buildings were demolished and the local watering place, the Spotted Dog, was hit. Kuala Lumpur was the scene of some of the most drastic scorched earth, with the destruction of railway stock and the great marshalling yards at Sentul. British soldiers resented the hard labour this involved. One subaltern saw a sign affixed to an army truck: 'We are the wogs'.[55] As many as 51 million cigarettes, $50,000 worth of whisky and 800 tons of meat in Cold Storage's stockroom were destroyed. There was general looting, less for profit than for food from shuttered provision stores. On the night of 9 January the final clearance occurred. The general hospital was abandoned by the military, who had occupied it, and its patients consigned to the care of Asian doctors. Bangsar power station was blown up and the police disbanded. The residency was cleared in five cars and three lorries. The stokers for the trains south from Kuala Lumpur were again recruited from survivors of the *Prince of Wales*. The government veterinary officer at Banting, on the coast, with Tamil labour drove 2,300 head of government Bali cattle nearly fifty miles down the coast; this stampede was eventually to arrive in Singapore.[56] It was estimated that three-quarters of the Asian population had left the town. One European, the medical officer of the leper settlement at Sungei Buloh, refused to leave. The patients were left with a little food and with 60,000 *hoons* of opium; 2,000 sufferers of a population of 3,000 were to die within two years. They were also to become a centre of support for guerrilla resistance to the Japanese.[57]

For the Japanese, the principal obstacle on the road to Kuala Lumpur was a 'rocky bastion' at Kampar, a 4,000-feet high crag some ten miles south of the mining centre of Ipoh, which was evacuated by 26 December. The last to leave here were the Chinese and Eurasian girls who had manned the telephone exchanges for the military. The position was caught by a dramatic Japanese flank attack, using a flotilla of forty motor boats brought overland from the beachhead at Singora in Thailand and reassembled at the mouth of the Perak river. There were no Royal Navy ships to intercept them. Faced with the landings of Imperial Guards, the British were forced to fall back from Kampar to the Slim river, where Japanese medium tanks cut through the battered and exhausted troops of 11th Indian Division and all but broke it as a fighting force. There were few anti-tank rifles; key bridges were not blown up; stranded units fell into the hands of the Japanese. The road to Kuala Lumpur was open. The first Japanese troops entered the capital of what had been the Federated Malay States on the evening of 11 January. Lieutenant-Colonel Tsuji was among them: 'This metropolis', he recorded, 'presented a dignified and imposing modern appearance.' Passing through streets lined with Chinese shophouses,

'We felt as though we had entered the crossroads of the central province of China.'[58]

## THE BATTLE OF MALAYA

In Singapore, as the reports of up-country reverses came in, British and Australian commanders had gone to war with each other. Heath urged a rapid withdrawal to Johore; Percival was reluctant to surrender the airbases in the west. In the event, the Indian troops of III Corps were condemned to a demoralizing fighting retreat of ten miles a day over nearly two months.[59] On 9 December Duff Cooper had been ordered by Churchill to preside over a 'war council'. Yet its responsibilities were unclear. At its first meeting Brooke-Popham reminded Duff Cooper that he reported to the chiefs of staff in London and Shenton Thomas to the Colonial Office. In frustration, Cooper launched another biting attack on the Malayan establishment. Brooke-Popham was 'on the edge of nervous collapse'. Percival, he said, had been a schoolmaster once (which was quite untrue), and perhaps should have remained one. Shenton Thomas, Cooper told Churchill, was 'one of those people who find it impossible to adjust their minds to war conditions'.[60] The governor saw it as his duty to preserve the prestige of the eastern Raj to the end. As much as possible of local life should continue undisturbed. He fought Cooper's attempts to seize control of the civil defences of Malaya. Diana Cooper wrote of the governor and his entourage on 28 December, they 'grow daily in black, obstructive defeatism, plus foxy eelishness'.[61]

Percival's orders were to fight a holding action in northern Malaya, to buy time for reinforcements, but he was given the authority to fall back at his discretion. On 5 January Percival made the decision to abandon the central portion of the peninsula and retreat to a further notional line of defence across the heart of Johore. This would relieve III Corps and bring into play the Australian Imperial Force, under Gordon Bennett. Bennett, for his part, was exuding confidence in his command. Brooke-Popham was shipped out on New Year's Eve and was replaced, briefly, by General Henry Pownall. But on the morning of 7 January, as the battle at Slim river came to its humiliating con-

1. 'Great World' amusement park, Singapore, 1930s

2. Flower girls supporting the China Relief Fund, c. 1940

3. Reginald Dorman-Smith
touring the Shan States, 1941

4. U Saw and Leo Amery
in London, 1941

5. Claire Chennault, Stilwell and the Flying Tigers

6. Special Branch portrait
of Lai Teck

7. Chin Peng

8. Chiang Kai Shek, Madame Chiang and General Joseph Stilwell

9. Yamashita: 'The Tiger of Malaya'

10. Percival in May 1941

11. Straits Settlements Volunteers Force, c. May 1941

12. The sinking of HMS *Prince of Wales*

13. Japanese war artist's painting of the Singapore surrender

14. Sketch of *sook ching* massacres of Chinese by Liu Kang

15. Japanese troops marching into Rangoon

16. A bombed-out
Buddhist temple in
Rangoon, 1942

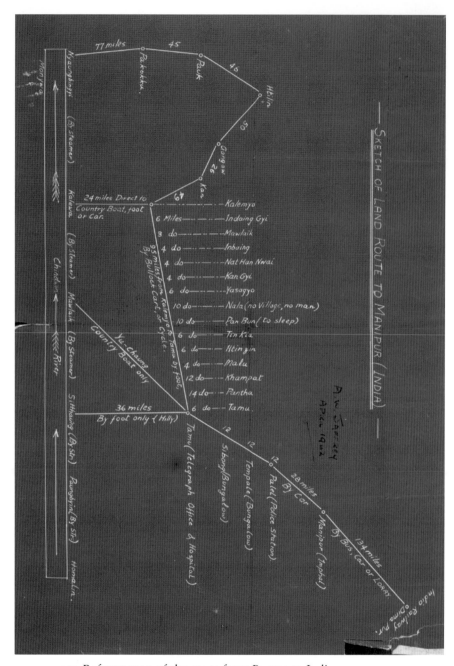

17. Refugee map of the route from Burma to India, 1942

clusion, he was superseded by the new ABDA commander Sir Archibald Wavell. Wavell was charged with holding the 'Malay barrier' of the central part of the great crescent, but he knew that the window for reinforcement and counter-attack in Malaya was closing the nearer the Japanese got to Singapore. He rushed up to the front to interview the exhausted field commanders and then he made his own decision to fall back to what was now known as the 'Johore line'. He cabled London that the situation was 'becoming critical' and flew to Java to review his command centre there. Diana Cooper was not convinced by his energy. 'The impression he gives is not brightened by his being very deaf and by having one wall-eye dropping and sightless. I suppose he can smell and feel still.'[62] But the Coopers were also on the way out. Duff Cooper told Churchill that he felt himself to be 'a tourist' and begged to be recalled. By the time this complaint was received, on 9 January 1942, Churchill had come to the same conclusion. The event was hailed by Shenton Thomas in his diary 'with shouts of joy! . . . A rotten judge of men, arrogant obstinate and vain; how he could have crept into Office is beyond me, and indeed beyond us all. Lady Diana has not appeared in public since the war began, and we gather has complete jitters! Their God is publicity.'[63] As Cooper travelled home, his former adversaries began to prepare for the end; by the time he reached London, the siege of Singapore was over.

In the disorder and acrimony of the British retreat, fears of fifth-columnist activity went into overdrive. The British faced treachery in their own ranks: an Irish-Burmese intelligence officer, Patrick Heenan, was radioing information about air deployments to the Japanese. He had been recruited after spending a long leave in 1939 in Japan. It seems that he met with summary execution by the harbour wall in Singapore, shortly before its fall.[64] The legendary Japanese bandit hero 'Harimau' had materialized to harass British lines, but could not keep up with the pace of Yamashita's divisions. Seriously ill with malaria, he collapsed in late January and died shortly after the fall of Singapore. After the mass arrests of Ibrahim Yaacob and other Malay activists, the only radical leaders at large were Ibrahim's brother-in-law Onan Siraj, whom Ibrahim had passed off to the British as his driver, and Mustapha Hussain, the vice-president of the Kesatuan Melayu Muda, who had been released from the prison where he had been interned on the eve of war. The number of Malay radicals riding in the baggage train of the Japanese was rather small. Their main work was in protecting Malay policemen from Japanese reprisals. Japanese officers of the Fujiwara Kikan lacked faith in them.[65] When, after the fall of Kuala Lumpur, more KMM members began to come together, assembling in the Spotted Dog, Mustapha Hussain demanded the Japanese support a declaration of independence under the red and white banner of Indonesia. He was brushed aside with the patronizing words: 'Let the Japanese be the father. Malays, Chinese and Indians live like a family. However, if the Malay child is thin, and needs more milk, we will give him more milk.' The Indian Independence League leader Pritam Singh, who was also travelling with the Japanese, warned Mustapha not to trust their promises. Thereafter, Mustapha realized that independence would not come from the hands of the Japanese. As they moved south, he warned his friends: 'This victory is not our victory!'[66]

Reports that Malays were acting as scouts and guides for the Japanese in large numbers lacked substance. They were fostered by Japanese propaganda. But more often they were the result of confusion on the ground. Jumpy and inexperienced Allied military intelligence officers exaggerated stories of Japanese dressing up as locals. 'The way they worked this theme one began to wonder when the rubber trees would be cited as 5th columnists.'[67] Few European soldiers could tell the difference between a Malay, a Chinese and a Japanese. They lacked the liaison officers who might have taught them how to do so. In the Segamat area an order was issued that all natives approaching any unit HQ or bicycling down a main road should be shot on sight. The Malays in the area did not hear of the order. It was rescinded only at the pleading of a forestry officer in the Volunteer Force.[68]

This was a society that did not know what war was. There had been no significant violent conflict for several generations. The people of Malaya had to make urgent reassessments as to where their security best lay. For Malay elites, colonial rule rested on treaties of 'protection'. The British had failed to meet their obligations under them. The mandate that underwrote Britain's Malay empire was broken. As one British official noted, the Malays fought 'so long as the front line was above their homes'.[69] The British tried to bundle some of the key sultans out of the country to India. They refused to leave. When the

Regent of Kedah, acting for his ailing father, looked like complying, his brother, a Cambridge-educated district officer, Tunku Abdul Rahman, kidnapped their father, and took him to a *kampong*, where the villagers gathered to protect him. One of the few Malays in the Malayan Civil Service was Mahmud bin Mat, from a leading Pahang family. The Sultan of Pahang had evacuated to Temerloh by river with around 200 retainers in a large convoy made up of his speedboat and many humble river craft. There Mahmud and other men formerly in British service joined him.[70] The British watched the Sultan of Johore closely. After all, this was a man who had presented Lady Diana Cooper with a parrot that spoke only Japanese. Yet British and United States intelligence reports were to exonerate him from acting as a one-man fifth column. His business dealings with the Japanese, observed a pre-war intimate, were 'opportunistic'. His main concern was the future of his state.[71] With this in mind, the sultan refused to allow the destruction or denial of anything within a twelve-mile radius of his capital Johore Bahru.[72] British gunners were ordered not to fire on the Moorish Johore administration building. It was used by Japanese spotters. Yamashita himself made the tower of the sultan's palace at Bukit Serene his tactical headquarters. At this point Sultan Ibrahim, like most leaders of the Malay community, lay low and awaited the issue of the battle of Singapore.

For the battle of Malaya was all but over. Australian and Indian troops along the Johore line fighting hard, and at great cost in lives, slowed the Japanese advance but did not stop it. At Parit Sulong in Johore, Japanese soldiers took bitter retribution by butchering over 150 Australian and Indian prisoners of war who had been left behind in the retreat.[73] Yamashita's Imperial Guards Division broke resistance in the west after barely a week: what had been billed as the 'main battle' for Malaya was lost. Wavell returned to Singapore and afterwards, on 14 January broke the news to Churchill that there was no 'fortress' at Singapore, the fixed defences of the island were virtually non-existent. Churchill was horrified: this was, he told the chiefs of staff, 'one of the greatest possible scandals that could possibly be exposed'.[74]

The final retreat was paralysed by a colossal traffic jam through south Johore to the causeway as European society retreated in a collective hysteria into a Bastille, within the fortress that never was. 'I saw military lorries streaming south through J[ohore] B[ahru] carrying personal effects such as carpets, rattan chairs, golf clubs, tennis rackets and even canaries in cages'.[75] Behind them, the rearguard of the stragglers saw some of the bitterest fighting of the campaign. Only sixty-three men from 22 Indian Brigade made it out of the jungle of Johore. The final order to retreat came on 27 January, and the final rearguard by the Argylls on the 31st, the Argylls' bagpipes playing 'Jenny's Black E'en' and 'Hieland Laddie' as they crossed the causeway before it was blown up. Only a thirty-yard stretch of a total length of 1,250 yards was destroyed; the stragglers easily crossed over. The explosion, however, resounded across the island. In the heart of the city, at Raffles College, the British principal W. E. Dyer demanded of some passing boys what it was. 'That is the end of the British Empire', a young Chinese swiftly replied. His name was Lee Kuan Yew, future first citizen of the Republic of Singapore.[76]

The Japanese advance was an epic achievement. Tsuji proudly recorded the statistics in his memoir: in fifty-five days Japanese troops had conducted a fighting advance of twenty kilometres a day, in the midst of which they had fought ninety-five engagements and repaired over 250 bridges. This was, he wrote, 'unparalleled in the history of war'.[77] A journal of quite another kind survives, written by a Japanese civilian in uniform. It is unsigned but entitled 'My Diary 1942'. It is written in a page-a-day journal bought from an Indian shop in Singapore. It seems to be a crude translation into English of an original written in Japanese. The probable name of the author, preserved on a bill for cod liver oil within its pages, is 'Mr Nakane'. It opens with an entry for New Year's Day, headed: 'Near Kampar'. Nakane was lodged in a Chinese house, with a garden and a pool. 'We had a happy beginning of the year. Yes it is.' The next days record a journey through a landscape of scorched earth and abandoned military transport. On 3 January: 'last night and early this morning, the enemy retreated. In the morning we heard nothing dangerous. So quick it was we felt a little funny.' Nakane entered the house of the Chinese owner of a tin mine: he marvelled at the 'luxurious fixtures and decorating'. Kampar was deserted, its houses looted: 'They fled in the hills.' Nakane helped himself to a razor and moved on. The next day, the same scene greeted him in Tronoh. He was delighted to find some English magazines. 'I could not find such a magazine in Japan.' By 9 January he had reached the Slim river: 'The scene was beyond description, everywhere was full of arms left by the enemy. It was the first time they had . . . seen such a thing.'[78]

On 12 January Nakane's party had reached the outskirts of Kuala Lumpur. They were given strict briefings to maintain discipline. He stayed at the residence of a Dr Soo, on Circular Road. 'The room we stayed in was of women, lady, scent of clothes, perfumes and others belonged to its owner. Could not help, it's female power overwhelmed me.' He took down the owner's full name and address in his diary. Nakane practised his golf swing on the front lawn. Soon his surroundings palled: it was a 'too-much-beautiful residence I did not like such taste, too much furnishings about'. As he headed further south, the warnings about conduct and strict discipline became ever sterner. Nakane himself was greatly angered when an officer took away some books from the Soo house. He contented himself with back issues of *Sphere* and *Reader's Digest* to occupy him through the more isolated landscape of Johore. He was greatly struck by its beauty, but also, staying on 25 January in the manager's bungalow on a rubber estate at Ulu Paloh, he reflected: 'I cannot help but admire the courage of the English men who live in such a remote place by themselves.' By 4 February, Nakane's advance came to a halt outside Johore Bahru. There was nothing to do but 'talking, eating and sleeping' whilst boats were prepared for the final assault on Singapore. 'How is the British army in the Singapore Front? They would not give up the fighting so easily not after the succession of defeats.'[79]

## 'THE MODERN POMPEIIANS'

For weeks before the causeway was blown, as European refugees had flooded into Singapore, thousands more Asians streamed in the opposite direction, heading up-country, away from the terror bombing, into the lines of the advancing Japanese. But the island was still crowded with over 85,000 Allied troops and the stock of war, all of it looking for a resting place. The herds of Bali cattle from the north were driven onto the links of the Royal Singapore Golf Course. Most of the human refugees were rather helpless. Some had lost everything. They lodged with friends and acquaintances and haunted the hotels and bars. The glittering social world of Singapore had become suddenly squalid. As the hotelier Felix Inggold complained, 'It was almost impossible to get a taxi . . . It was difficult to get a cup of tea unless you went to the Adelphi or Raffles.'[80] The urbane broadcaster Giles Playfair had sailed into Singapore for the first time just as the first bombs fell. The exotic East did not live up to its billing. Raffles itself was looking like 'a second rate station hotel', with a dance floor where couples swayed in evening dress 'trying to forget that Singapore is no longer what it was'. He threw himself into producing morale-boosting plays about Florence Nightingale 'to rouse the courage of the women of Malaya', and wrote features on 'Hints to motorists' and the early works of Noël Coward.[81] About the war itself, there was a relentlessly upbeat tone. This made capitulation, when it came, all the more traumatic. This propaganda disgusted many Asians. The future prime minister of Malaya, Abdul Razak bin Hussein, was a student at Raffles College: 'Although the Malays had two battalions of regular troops and a large number of volunteers actively served with the British Army, there was no mention of our community.' He set out for home, in Pahang, up beyond the British lines.[82]

The mood was bitter within the garrison. One volunteer summarized the situation in Churchillian cadences:

> Never before have so many
> Been****** about by so few
> And neither the few nor the many
> Have**** all idea what to do.[83]

Up to two days before the surrender still more Indian, Australian and British troops poured in. Many of the Englishmen were territorials from the East Anglian fens. The Cambridgeshires had embarked at Gronrock on 29 October for Halifax, on the USS *Mount Vernon*, the first time a US ship had been used to transport British troops, and thence to Trinidad and Cape Town, where they were allowed three days' shore leave. On arriving on Singapore on 13 January, they were immediately posted to the fury of the front at Batu Pahat. Their commander, Major-General M. B. Beckwith-Smith, had already faced one Dunkirk. He was soon to face another. The Australians who arrived on 24 January were a far inferior levy to that which had fought so doggedly in Johore; some said they were the sweepings of jails. 'They spend two or three weeks in a recruiting depot, pushed over to Singapore. They knew nothing; they were hardly soldiers.'[84] Others went further: 'daffodils', they said – 'pretty to look at, but yellow all through'.[85] It was rapidly apparent that they were not ready for war. The ebullience of their commander, Gordon Bennett, had given way to a mood of dark pessimism after his failure to halt the Japanese in southern Malaya. Some British troops arrived as late as 13 February; one of the final troopships was sunk. The rankers were still seasick, their officers disorientated. They were bewildered not to have entered a fortress. One reported opening his map case to find only a map of the Isle of Wight. The new arrivals were sent directly into the front line to cover the losses in the final stages of the battle of Malaya, or ordered to dig in around the city centre. Their morale was hit further by the destruction of the naval base, the very thing they had been sent to defend. In the words of one soldier, the plume of black smoke was 'a constant reminder that things were not as they should be'.[86]

The British had laid no plans for last-ditch guerrilla action against the Japanese. Percival, a man who had fought Sinn Fein in Ireland, was antipathetic to this kind of war, and loath to drain valuable manpower. Shenton Thomas felt that it would be fatal to morale. But after the Kota Bahru landings, Percival authorized the formation of parties behind enemy lines. This was organized by the Oriental Mission of Special Operations Executive. The main figure involved was Major Freddy Spencer Chapman, a mountaineer of some celebrity. He headed up the peninsula to conduct a reconnaissance along the Perak river. The whole scheme was hastily improvised and envisaged separate European and Chinese parties. The plan was to divide Malaya into zones and sub-areas, each with a European agent with local knowledge. The British parties were, for the most part, settlers in arms: rubber planters, mining engineers, surveyors, game wardens. They were hurriedly indoctrinated in the black arts of sabotage at 101 Special Training School in Singapore. Only eight could be trained at a time, but it was difficult to find this many recruits. The first parties were infiltrated from 6 January, beginning with a group led by Spencer Chapman himself, which went to ground at the European playground above Kuala Lumpur, Frazer's Hill. The mission did not go well: the party lost its stores and wireless set and had to find its way out via Sumatra. Chapman himself missed the rendezvous. He was not heard from again for nearly two years.

A later damning criticism of Malaya's war effort concerned the British refusal to countenance an alliance with the anti-Japanese movement of the Overseas Chinese. The formation of Chinese irregulars had been mooted in July, but the commissioner of police had vetoed the idea on the bizarre grounds that they 'could not tell on which side the Chinese would fight'.[87] But after the fall of Penang, Britain turned to the military resources of the Kuomintang and the Malayan Communist Party. On 19 December, the Malayan Communist Party offered its services; a few days earlier some communist prisoners had been released as a gesture of good faith. A rendezvous with the party's secretary general, Lai Teck, was held the same day in Geylang, above a charcoal dispensary that was used as a party safe house. The colonial government was represented by Spencer Chapman, Lai Teck's controller Captain Innes Tremlett of the Special Branch, and a representative of the Secret Intelligence Service.[88] The negotiations were hampered by the extreme secrecy of the party's organization: all discussions, even of minutiae, were conducted through Lai Teck, who was hooded at the meetings. Two Chinese-speaking Malayan civil officers, Richard Broome and John Davis, were appointed to lead the training of Chinese guerrillas. Volunteers came forward in large numbers. The only constraint on recruitment was the lack of arms.

The Malayan Communist Party had a vision of large guerrilla bands, in the 'Yenan way' of Mao Zedong's movement in China. The first batch of MCP cadres entered 101 Special Training School on 21 December. Some were from Singapore, but soon more appeared from up-country: in all 165 of them. A branch of the school was opened in Kuala Lumpur, at the Chunjun Chinese School. Tan Chen King, chairman of the town committee of the party in Kuala Lumpur, provided 100 recruits and hung up pictures of Stalin and Churchill. Tan himself and thirty more went to Singapore. They were, SOE reported, the finest men the school had handled: 'They were all young – mostly 17 to 20 years old – physically fit, intelligent and inspired with an almost fanatical eagerness to fight the Japanese.' Broome and Davis surveyed sites for caches of arms and supplies, and personally escorted them into the field. The 101 Special Training School graduates were merely the nuclei of the forces the party itself planned. A first group, self-styled the Perak Patrol, infiltrated Japanese lines, and became the core of a much larger force. Another fifteen trained men were introduced on 5 January at Serendah, near Kuala Lumpur: there they inducted 150 more. Six other parties were infiltrated into southern Malaya, up until 30 January 1942. The Kuomintang recruits received no such training: they may have been formally allied to the MCP, but tensions were such that they could not be housed together with them at 101 Special Training School. Chinese officers from Chungking, who had come to Singapore to observe and set up an office there, were alarmed that the communists had been armed but not the KMT men. Around a thousand KMT fighters were raised, but it was too late for them to be infiltrated back onto the peninsula; they were not issued with weapons until 1 February. SOE defended this decision. It was far less impressed with the KMT men; they were 'the town-living type'.[89]

At the same time as plans for secret armies were launched, Shenton Thomas asked the industrialist and admirer of Mao Zedong, Tan Kah Kee, for labour for civil defence. Although Tan Kah Kee was received on equal terms by the likes of Chiang and Mao, it says much about the way the British viewed the Chinese community at this time that the go-between linking Tan and the governor of Singapore was the chief of police. Tan Kah Kee, depressed by the Japanese seizure of his rubber factories in Perak, was in no mood to take on the responsibility. He was only persuaded to do so after a week of pressure, when told that no other man could. On Christmas Eve, a Chinese Mobilization Council was formed with Tan Kah Kee at its head. With the inclusion of groups from the Chinese Chamber of Commerce, cultural representatives and the Malayan Communist Party it was the largest and most representative body of Chinese, or for that matter any community, hitherto formed in Malaya. At the first meeting, the 'open' representative of the MCP, Ng Yeh Lu, freshly released from jail, pressed a motion for 'arming the people'. Tan Kah Kee opposed him. There was a British army to do the fighting, he argued. It would be folly to send in Chinese civilians. However, Tan observed that Shenton Thomas went out of his way to shake the hand of each of the released communist members of the council. As he did so, Thomas declared that he was willing to give them guns.[90]

This was a heroic episode, which is barely mentioned in the official histories. To the British, the Chinese irregulars were known as 'Dalforce', after the Special Branch Officer John Dalley who commanded it from a Chinese teacher training college. To its members, it was the 'Singapore Overseas Chinese Volunteer Army', around 2,000 strong. It was the first of the forgotten armies of the great Asian war. It was dressed in blue uniforms, hastily run up by women from Tan Kah Kee's council. Their insignia was a triangle of red cloth on the arm and yellow cloth around their heads. The British had no helmets to give them. The volunteers elected their own sergeants and went to war with sporting guns. The force was a mixture of labourers, clerks, students and dance-hall hostesses.[91] Many women and girls arrived to enlist and 'they wanted to fight'. One of them, Cheng Shang How, would become known as *La Pasionaria* of Malaya, after the famous woman fighter of the Spanish Civil War. She and her husband had experience of fighting in China. The Indonesian communist Tan Malaka was working incognito, teaching English in the Nanyang Chinese Normal School. It too became a centre of recruitment for the army. Tan was asked to brief students on the political situation. 'Did it not look as though the British were trying to wipe out both their enemies, domestic and foreign, by sacrificing the Communist Party and the radical Chinese youth to the Japanese Army?'[92] The volunteers tackled fires in the docks, and fought hard in the Kranji area of the island, where of the five officers and 150 men who went in, only three officers and fifty men came out.[93] Tan Kah Kee was deeply distressed at British issuing of guns to the volunteers. He too felt that to arm the Chinese in these circumstances was 'ruthless and cunning'. 'Not only were these thousand men being sent to their deaths, when the Japanese entered Singapore, they would kill many more Overseas Chinese because of the actions of the first thousand.' To register his dissent he decided to leave Singapore.[94]

By this time the battle for the island had been joined with terrible ferocity. Bombing resumed from high altitudes after 29 January. Many of the Allied pilots sent out to stop this were veterans of the Battle of

Britain, and they included Americans seconded to the RAF. They lodged with wealthy refugees in the luxury Sea View Hotel: it was, one noted, 'a strange lair from which to go forth to battle'. A Chinese businessman made a standing offer of a bottle of champagne for every Japanese plane destroyed.[95] But they were too few, and there was pressure to move the small number of valuable Hurricanes which had arrived to shore up the air defences to Sumatra, the last eight planes leaving on the night of 9 February. Civilians and soldiers alike viewed the failure of the air defence with particular bitterness. Despite the individual heroism, the RAF were nicknamed 'penguins', 'because only one in a thousand flew'.[96] But by this time the reputations of all the fighting forces were in shreds. The final defence of the island was chaotic. There was a last-ditch scramble to create the defences of 'Singraltar'. But before the siege there was barely a shred of barbed wire along 120 kilometres of coastline.

The Japanese assault on 8 February was preceded by a barrage of shelling that recalled to veterans the first bombardments of the Battle of the Somme.[97] For the British and their allies it was vital to hold the beaches. But by the early hours of morning on 9 February, units had begun to fall back to a final, desperate perimeter, the so-called Jurong–Kranji line, beyond which there was no room to fall back and launch a counter-attack. Crucial opportunities to throw back the Japanese before they got a secure foothold on the island were lost. Communications broke down to such an extent that any plans for a more concerted rallying thrust could not have been implemented. When Wavell, in Singapore for the last time, ordered it on 10 February, it was too late. At this point the bitterly divided high command could make little impact on the fighting. The Japanese had Singapore by the throat. They controlled the reservoirs and the oil reserves had been fired. The two armies faced each other across the suburbs around the city centre, into which the last reserves of troops defending the beaches of the east and south were withdrawn on 12 February. There was a counter-attack at Bukit Timah, and on 14 February the Malay Regiment made a stand in Bukit Panjang on the west coast of the island, near where some of the Malay princes of the islands were buried. In these last encounters the Malay Regiment and the Volunteers took heavy casualties. The plantocracy, too, at the end, fought hard for

Malaya: many fell, including the founder of the Hash House Harriers, A. S. Gilbert, who perished in the battle for Bukit Timah.[98]

It was clear that this was the end. The hospitals were charnel houses. On 8 February an Australian surgeon, a veteran of the Somme, noted that he had performed sixty-five operations in the last thirty hours in blanketed rooms, devoid of air.[99] The women of the St John Ambulance in the last three days had no fresh water and 'kept washing wounds in bloody water'.[100] The FMS Volunteers could not find ammunition. In a diary that survived him, H. R. Oppenheim, a chartered accountant from Ipoh and an FMS Volunteer, described how he went by turns to Alexandra depot, where he found the magazine locked and the keys lost, then to the HQ at Fort Canning, to find the clerks in charge were out to lunch. There was a strange and dangerous mood in the city just before the fall. News of the landings spread through the streets very slowly: the word employed in official communications was 'infiltration'. At the same time the city was also infiltrated by many Allied troops separated from their units. Along Orchard Road troops broke into the pawn shops and Cold Storage looking for liquor, which 'they were drinking . . . straight off the bottle and smashing the bottles all over the road.'[101] The night before the Japanese landing in Changi, Staff Sergeant Edward Burrey, with 8 Division of the AIF, recorded in his own diary: 'Had marvellous night with boys. Drinks of every description. Craven A smokes laid on . . . half shot most of the day.'[102] There were strange moments of calm. Oppenheim recorded in his diary how he spent 7 February: 'PT – reading – arguing – drinking – bathing in the well and bed'. On 9 February he was granted a day's leave in Singapore; 'have a hair cut at Robinson's where all is normal. The place is full of folk having elevenses.'[103]

In the mass of British narratives of the fall, with the final advance of the Japanese, the Asian city vanishes. Or rather, it appears as pathos, in a series of cameos of departure. Giles Playfair marvelled, without irony, that his 'admirable and remarkable Chinese servant' continued to lay his slippers at the foot of his bed at the Goodwood Park Hotel, up until the time he vacated it on 10 February. 'I wish I knew his name', he added. On 12 February Shenton Thomas mourned the passing of his manservant in a direct hit on the back veranda of

Government House. 'Terribly sad about my boy. He was such a faithful soul.'[104] Behind the anonymity of these farewells, another great drama was being played out. The final phase of the attack on Singapore saw daylight terror raids in which perhaps 150 to 200 people a day perished. British engineers reported that high explosives were filled with scrap metal: oil bombs, sulphur bombs and other anti-personnel bombs were used to terrorize the civilian population. There were stories of pens and dolls filled with explosives on the streets. Rumours of gas spread through the town. There was ammonia on the wind from the Cold Storage plant. The well-to-do built their own air-raid shelters. There was a run on hardware goods for construction. If families had relatives who worked in the hospitals, they took refuge there. For many the only refuge was to huddle in the monsoon drains that lined the roads. In the final week of the attack, perhaps 7,000 civilians died. A resident of Chinatown described the scene. 'There was no time to bury the dead. Some of the dead people, the poor people, the beggars, those who died, were left at the roadside and the five-foot ways.'[105] The bombing did most damage in the 'invisible city' on the outskirts of the main city. The Malays were particularly hard hit.[106] The Cathay Cinema was a haven: it was the sturdiest and safest building in Singapore, and the cinema screened continually. Its restaurant was the last air-conditioned nightspot for the elite. Its large basement resembled an East End tube station during the Blitz, packed with the urban poor.

As the colonial regime retired to its bridgehead around the Padang and the river, it was dependent as never before on the municipal workforce, the volunteer civil defence and the armies of clerks and peons to maintain basic services. Water, electricity and gas supplies never completely vanished. As a Eurasian accountant in the water department, P. C. Marcus, reported, the water supply was never cut off during the campaign. The causeway main was blown but 'there was still water to go around'. Only when the Japanese invaded Serangoon in the fringes of the city was the water supply turned off there. By 7 February the pall of acrid grime from the burning naval base had turned the water grey. Residents used the plentiful wells instead. Marcus was told by the Europeans that, as the most senior non-European, 'your job is not to be detained'. He was promoted on the spot to an 'engineer'.[107] Out of the collapse of colonial society, phoenix-like, new centres of power were rising.

The European civilians were helpless at the end. In a society in which Europeans did not carry money, and were used to having their signatures accepted everywhere, in the last weeks their ability to buy goods had tellingly dissolved with the general collapse of credit. With the departure of the houseboys and *amahs* at the suburban front line of siege, Europeans were unable to find food. They gravitated to luxury hotels and clubs around the Padang, where there was still some service and supplies to be had. They shopped out John Little and Cold Storage; finally they burned the currency reserves. Those who chose, or were compelled, to remain spent the last days of the short siege crowded in a small ethnic enclave that encompassed the symbolic buildings around the Padang, Raffles Place and Collyer's Quay: the Bund of Singapore, 'nail on the big toe of Asia'. The chief surveyor of Singapore surveyed three generations of British Malaya hunched around the bar of the Singapore Club in the monolith-like Fullerton Building. 'Washed out of hearth and home by the ever-advancing waves of the hordes of Nippon: the fossils of Malaya are all there, paleozoic . . . mesozoic . . . and cainozic (me).' In the last days, even the governor moved into the Singapore Club. Its first floor was a hospital, where Shenton Thomas's wife was warded, stricken with dysentery but refusing to leave the island. A hospital was also set up in the cathedral; the men's vestry became an operating theatre. Even here the situation could not be sustained. Mindful of stories of Japanese atrocities in Hong Kong, in a final act of scorched earth the Europeans were instructed to dispose of all alcohol by midnight on 12 February. They gathered to drink as much as possible before the deadline. This lay behind many of the stories – most of them true – of the parties in Raffles, and on the holy ground of the Cricket Club where 200 cases of whisky were dispensed. 'Such *stengahs*', wrote the chief surveyor that night in his diary, 'it matters not one, two, three, four fingers, the rest will be down the drains and into the Singapore River'. Nevertheless those present still went through the formality of signing chits for them.[108]

There was, at the end, not much else to do, and drink was about the only thing that was not in short supply. One of the last to leave was Val Kabouky, a Czech motor engineer, who had escaped the Nazi advance in 1939 by walking to Italy, shipping to Shanghai, then fleeing through Indo-China to Singapore, where he seems to have won his passage out by working as an agent for British intelligence in Thailand. In his interrogation he described the people of Singapore as the 'Modern Pompeiians'. As for the scenes of debauchery of the end, Kabouky reflected: 'he did not blame them on the military, as on the Singapore tradition. He was only a garage manager but he ran two cars of his own, and had a fine house and servants, and would probably never live at such a high standard again'.[109]

Yamashita had vowed to secure Singapore by 11 February, as a gift-offering for the emperor on National Foundation Day. In the event the advance was halted to allow for regroupment and preparation in secrecy. Despite this, Yamashita's troops took heavy casualties: about 40 per cent of the 1,713 Japanese killed and 3,378 wounded in the battle for Singapore fell in the landings. Soldiers later recalled how they would pause to hack off the finger or burn off the flesh of a fallen comrade, so his bone could be taken back to his hometown in an urn.[110] 'Mr Nakane' crossed the straits to Singapore on the night of 9 February. The firing was intense and he noted that many Chinese civilians had been caught up in it. He bivouacked and awoke the next morning to find 'everything in sight covered by the black rain. All was black, water, forest and everything. The sea was black and could not wash face . . . The black smoke was just reaching to the sky. The sight was beyond description.' He headed towards the dairy farm on Upper Bukit Timah Road, where he picked up some more magazines. It was, he wrote, 'very dangerous'. On 12 February, 'The enemy against us did not retreat, and resisted our offensive. The division sent its main power in this direction . . . but there were many casualties in our army.' For three days Nakane dug in. 'I sometimes stayed in the trench and sometimes went out. But I did not feel safe. Read the magazines *Parade* and *Men Only*.' On 14 February he emerged: 'I was awoke by the firing between the enemy and us. It was dawn, the sun was still glittering in the sky. The heads rose from every hole . . . The whole-scale attack will be made today.'[111]

The garrison of Singapore was ordered to hold on, whatever the human cost. On 10 February Churchill sent an extraordinary signal to Wavell:

There must be at this stage no thought of saving the troops or sparing the population. The battle must be fought to the bitter end and at all costs . . . Commanders and senior officers should die with their troops. The honour of the British Empire and the British Army is at stake.

Wavell read it without comment, and passed it to Percival. He dictated his own slightly softened version as his order of the day. He then left for his new headquarters in Java. The order was not well received. As H. R. Oppenheim recorded in his diary: 'the OC reads it and hands it to one or two near by then changes his mind and destroys all the Battery Copies. The gist of the Order is: Everywhere else in the World everyone is fighting superbly. The Russians in Russia, Rommel in Libya and McArthur in Corregidor while in Singapore the whole army with a few exceptions is a disgrace to the Allied cause.'[112]

There were clear indications across the city that the will of the garrison to resist was broken. This fatalism reached to the highest levels of command. On the evening of 9 February Percival had been cornered by an Australian brigade commander. 'In civil life I am a doctor. If the patient's arm is bad I cut it off, but if the whole body goes bad then no operation can save the patient – he must die. So it is with Singapore – there is no use fighting to prolong its life.'[113] By 11 February the Japanese invasion force heading for Sumatra had effectively encircled the island. On 'Black Friday', 13 February, the last officially sanctioned evacuations of key personnel occurred: they were to sail into the heart of the Japanese Imperial Navy. At a staff conference on that day, Percival argued that honour demanded they continue to fight. 'You need not bother about your honour', came Heath's acerbic response. 'You lost that a long time ago up in the North.' The governor too pressed for surrender. Bennett told his government that he would surrender the AIF independently if need be. Percival informed Wavell that he could hold out for only two days. The next day, Churchill and the chiefs of staff gave Wavell permission to surrender 'when no further result can be gained'. Just as the responsibility for beginning the war had been left to commanders on the spot, so too was the responsibility for ending it. Percival was reluctant to shoulder this burden, but a final conference on the morning of 15 February came to the unanimous conclusion that there was no alternative. Yet he was still under instructions to fight to the last.[114]

Relief came later in the day, in the shape of a signal from Wavell giving Percival the discretion to cease resistance. A brigadier and the colonial secretary, Hugh Fraser, were sent with an interpreter to negotiate with the Japanese. They were turned back three times because of the bomb damage and held up at revolver point by a British outpost. In the end, Fraser walked through the minefield along Bukit Timah Road. He met the Japanese officers at 2 p.m. The ceasefire was to begin at 4 p.m., but was delayed, because the Japanese refused to give the order until the high command had signed. On the way back he was stopped again at gunpoint by a drunken British soldier.[115] The garrison's acceptance of the ceasefire was signalled with a white flag on top of the Cathay Building. A meeting was proposed, initially at City Hall, but Yamashita, fearing a trap, insisted on a face-to-face confrontation with Percival at the Ford motor factory in the lee of Bukit Timah hill. The meeting, at 5.15 p.m., lasted fifty-five minutes. The official Japanese war artist's view of the event portrayed Yamashita's angry impatience at Percival's vacillation. In truth, Yamashita's ire was reserved for his interpreter. The discussions focused on securing agreement on the need to maintain 1,000 British troops in arms to prevent rioting and to keep the Japanese out of the town area. That evening a major Japanese assault was planned to push through to the sea. There was relief on both sides that it could be countermanded. The people of Singapore were spared the advance of Japanese fighting forces into the city centre, and Yamashita was spared the necessity of using the last of his dwindling stocks of ammunition.[116] His staff retired to a table laid with cuttlefish, chestnuts and *sake*, gifts of the emperor. They faced northeast and toasted him, but few had any stomach for the feast. The losses had been heavy; the artillery had barely 100 rounds of ammunition apiece.[117] The Japanese invasion of Singapore island was a gigantic and wholly successful piece of bluff.

The news had been passed down the line: 'We are packing in at four'.[118] Oppenheim and his Volunteers were in a Catholic priest's house in Queen Street. There had been rumours from Friday 13th that the garrison had surrendered. When more rumours came that Singapore had capitulated at 4.30 p.m. they were not believed as the fighting continued. 'Some say the capitulation has been cancelled',

Oppenheim wrote. When a written order came, still no one knew if it was authentic or not. Oppenheim and some fellow officers tried to escape. His CO gave them his blessing, 'tells us officially we are asleep'. They found a Malay sampan. In it was Major-General Gordon Bennett and his ADC Gordon Walker. A debate ensued as to whether to row to Malacca or head for Sumatra. They chose the latter. 'After 13 years in Malaya, I leave it with one pair of trousers, a pair of shorts, a shirt, pair of socks, boots and my life.'[119] His Asian comrades had to confront the problem of Japanese reprisals. In some places these had already begun. Some of the captured survivors of the Malay Regiment's stand in Bukit Panjang were massacred, including their Malay officer, Lieutenant Adnan bin Saidi, who was hung upside down from a tree and bayoneted. The interventions of the Malays who had crossed with the Japanese army saved some of them. The Malacca Volunteers had no protectors. They were mobilized for only two weeks. Of their strength of 500–600 over a hundred were killed. The survivors were left high and dry by the capitulation. As the Volunteers gathered at Fort Canning they were each given $50 and told to 'destroy everything – throw away your uniform, throw away your identification, everything. And don't disclose that you are a Volunteer.'[120] The troops of Dalforce had to settle for $10. They too shed their improvised uniforms and faded away.

## FLOTSAM AND JETSAM

Nakane's diary entry for Sunday 15 February reads: 'It was a lovely morning with the bright sun and the cool breeze'. At 4 p.m. the news came through that the white flag had been flown over the Cathay Building. Nakane and his comrades were 'standing and looking at each other', unsure of what to do. They were ordered to stay where they were. 'We ate dinner in the dark. No fire we heard. It was so quiet.' Next morning, the quiet continued, 'only the breeze in rubber trees was heard with its chirping of birds. So quiet that we felt a little strange.' There were many British and Indian bodies around them. His unit occupied the clubhouse of the Royal Singapore Golf Club. Soldiers practised their drives on the lawn outside it. 'That evening I was outside and recollected what the British day was in its height.'[121]

The streets of the colonial town were empty. The great bungalows and mansions were abandoned, many looted by retreating troops. Gay Wan Guay, an evacuation officer, later described the end: 'When the looting started it just happened that we knew. No special announcement that was in words and so on. But we just knew that it was the end.' He reported for work: 'there was nobody. The place was empty. Everything, just bits of paper.'[122] The day of the fall was the first day of the Chinese New Year. The previous evening some families opted to continue with the traditional family reunion dinner. But the outlying settlements of the city were now devastated. Families began to take refuge in the rural areas of the island. These were the people who would lose most in the looting of homes. There were grand pianos abandoned by the roadside; antique furniture trashed for firewood. Across the city people began to help themselves to the flotsam of war. Looters appeared with vans, station wagons or just long poles to carry goods. Rickshaw men were particularly well-placed to profit. The opium warehouse was a principal target. There were some extraordinary scenes on the roads. Some saw men handing their daughters over in marriage. 'This is your son. I give my daughter away. Let them get married . . . Let them both be happy. It's better [than falling] in the hands of the invading forces.'[123] In the city, Japanese flags appeared out of nowhere. The lunatics were released from the asylum. The Japanese internees who had not been shipped to India – a press attaché from the Japan consulate, some Okinawa fishermen and some old women – took over Changi prison and released some 500 inmates.[124] The population waited anxiously to see how the new order would declare itself.

After the surrender, there was a surreal lull for the British and Australian servicemen. Many of the European civilians and officers had gravitated to the area around Raffles Place. Even at the end, distinctions of status were maintained. The officers went into Robinson's Departmental Store, the other ranks into a building to the west of the notorious Change Alley. Denis Russell-Roberts, who was one of the few of the 5/11 Sikh Regiment to survive the desperate fighting in Johore, put into action his foraging skills. 'Some of the officers were playing billiards in the games department, some were selecting suitable footwear from the shoe department, but most of them were just sitting in silence, a confused and rather sad expression on their faces. It seemed extraordinary that none of them should have ventured up onto the top floor. Maybe it was because the lift was no longer working.' There Russell-Roberts made himself comfortable in the furniture department.[125] The full enormity of what had happened was only slowly becoming apparent: a garrison of over 85,000 men had surrendered to an assault force of around 30,000 Japanese troops.

British officers who served with Indian troops, such as Russell-Roberts, would defend their fighting reputation to the end. They were 'lost and bewildered rather than broken'. Troops generally were 'disappointed and dispirited and were struggling about not knowing what to do or where to go'.[126] Japanese orders were that Indians were to be identified with the challenge 'Gandhi?' – to which a nod and a sign of recognition was the signifier. Captain Prem K. Saghal had watched his English second in command beheaded in front of him. Saghal himself escaped when he told the officer that his father knew Gandhi. A colonel offered him cognac. It was then that the full reality of what had happened dawned on him.[127] 'The Fall of Singapore finally convinced me of the degeneration of the British people and I thought the last days of the British empire had come.' He felt too that the British had renounced all claim on India's allegiance, that the defences of India were light and would be exposed to the full fury of the Japanese.[128] The abandonment of these troops had a traumatic effect on some men who had behind them several generations of military service to the Raj. As one officer, Shahnawaz Khan, the best cadet of his year at the RIMC, put it: 'I was brought up to see India through the eyes of a British officer, and all that I was interested in was soldiering and sport . . . at the back of my mind was the traditional urge of loyalty to the King. I owed all my education to him. My family and my tribe were one of the privileged classes in India. They were all prosperous and contented. This too we owed to the British Government and I knew that no change in India would bring them any more prosperity.' Yet at Singapore he saw British officers fall back to the right and the left with their units. To be called to the front and not to fight was 'a crime and an injustice to my honour'. His commanding officer, Major MacAdam, had final words with him on the morning of 16 February: 'I suppose, this is the parting of our ways.'[129]

The next day, some 40,000 Indian troops were concentrated at Farrer Park, a small stadium near the Indian centre of Singapore, Serangoon Road. There is considerable debate about what occurred here, and its significance. There was a perfunctory speech from a British officer, Colonel Hunt, who told the assembled that they were prisoners of war and had been turned over to the Japanese. Some Indian officers recollected that he had said: 'now you belong to the Japanese army'. This was to be a critical point for those who claimed that the Indian National Army, which fought alongside the Japanese, was a legitimate force. Rumours of Hunt's alleged speech were also heard in India and spread the conviction that the Raj was tumbling towards its end. Hunt then left. Fujiwara spoke, in Japanese, which was translated into English then Hindustani. He told the troops that they would not be treated as prisoners, but as brothers. This sequence seemed like a formal British abdication of responsibility. Fujiwara then gave the microphone to Mohan Singh. Mohan Singh spoke in Hindustani and announced the formation of an 'Indian National Army'. There was a mixed reaction to this: some men shouted, some wept. Many Indian officers present were deeply disturbed. One of them, Shahnawaz Khan, felt he and his men had been 'handed over like cattle by the British to the Japs'. But he also believed Mohan Singh to be an 'average' officer, 'not *politically* competent enough to undertake a task of such magnitude'.[130] The Indians divided into two groups. Most went to large POW camps at Neesoon, Bidadari and other, smaller sites. Others went with Mohan Singh to a new 'Supreme Command' in the northern suburbs of the city.

The European civilians too were herded together. They were ordered to assemble on the Padang on the morning of 17 February with clothes for ten days. Many European civilians believed that, as residents of Malaya, they would not be interned as enemy aliens. In his first pronouncement after the surrender, Yamashita made it clear that by their flight they had forfeited any such right. Then they began the long march down East Coast Road, past crowds of Asians. 'They looked at us half-drugged with disillusionment', wrote Denis Russell-Roberts.[131] The civilians were housed in a police station and a house and compound built by a Sultan of Kedah on Joo Chiat Road. There the Japanese announced that although the Japanese internees had received only rice and salt, the British would be given more than this. But there would be no communication with home, because the Japanese internees had none. It would be many months before news of who had perished and who had survived would begin to filter back to Britain, India and Australia. Around 13,000 British imperial soldiers fell in the battle of Malaya; over 8,000 in the battle of Singapore Island. The Japanese lost 3,500 men in the entire campaign. Over 130,000 prisoners fell to the Japanese, more than half of them Indian.[132] Over 45,000 British and Australian soldiers were marched to Changi in the far east of the island, into an area of six square miles, bounded by the sea on three sides.

The Europeans who had managed to escape Singapore were dispersed across the crescent and far beyond. The fortunate ones got to India, Australia or the Cape. After the fall of Hong Kong, among the last of the big ships to sail was by a bitter irony the former *Empress of Japan*. There was an air of unreality about these departures. The *Ile de Paris*, it was claimed, had only 300 people on board as stately mems refused to share cabins. 'They were behaving like de luxe tourists choosing a summer cruise.'[133] In the last days before the fall, a flotilla of small ships was mustered for British Asia's Dunkirk: coast steamers, Chinese freighters, even the White Rajah of Sarawak's yacht the *Vyner Brooke*. European nurses were given priority berths. The first nurses left on 11 February, on the *Empire Star*. It had only twenty-four cabins but carried 2,500 passengers to Batavia. Most travelled through the Riau islands of the Dutch East Indies, then by the island of Bangka, towards Java, or via the river ports of Sumatra and overland to Java, the designated fallback position for ABDA. It is unclear how many small ships were sunk, perhaps as many as ninety.[134] The *Vyner Brooke* was attacked and sunk. Many of the survivors of these sinkings who made it to Bangka island were lined up and shot on the beach.[135] The last to leave was the *Kuala*. It sailed with a Chinese ship, the *Tien Kwang*, on the evening of 13 February. It carried around 400 women and children, 300 Public Works Department officers and around fifty nursing sisters. It was attacked off Pompong island. Japanese planes machine-gunned the survivors in the water. Those who made it to land fell into the hands of the Japanese. Some survivors were picked up by the navy, some by a small cargo steamer, the *Tanjong Penang*, which was itself hit. Of the Queen Alexandra's nurses on board, only one survived.[136] The women interned in these remote areas experienced some of the worst conditions of the war, and it was many months before their fate was known.

In the weeks and months after the fall the British MI2, the specialist division of military intelligence responsible for Asia, interrogated escapees in Ceylon and London and intercepted their mail. These transcripts are a terrible testimony to the collapse of an army. One officer reported that the Argylls 'shot any officers who refused to lead them'.[137] The last-ditch defence of the west of the island was left to Australian troops who some said pushed Indian soldiers in front of them at bayonet point.[138] These British accounts, the first to reach Whitehall, tended to scapegoat the Australian forces for the confusion of the last days of the defence of Singapore. One reported that 'their conduct was bestial.' On the night of 11/12 February they massed on the waterfront and tried to storm the boats; 200 men forced their way onto the *Empire Star* with tommy guns. They were arrested in Batavia. Forty more men were evicted from the *Matahari*. The intelligence report on this event stated that a sense of the futility of defending the island had percolated down from the divisional command. Australian officers were said to be scared of their men.[139] Another British observer put it slightly differently: the men streaming into town were on unofficial strike, 'not for more cash, but for a few more years on earth'.[140] In these stories it is easy to see the playing out of the bitter social resentments that had arisen between British and Australian officers before the campaign. They must be read in the context of a much wider failure. Shortly before the fall, the Australian representative in Singapore reported home Gordon Bennett's own assessment of his men: '95 per cent of his men are magnificent, but they have been repeatedly let down by other troops on their flanks, and ... these experiences and resulting continual withdrawals have broken the spirit of the remaining 5 per cent. They are all moreover dead tired.'[141]

These narratives also provide disturbing evidence of the anguished discussions on whether to stay or to leave that were often conducted between those who possessed departure passes and those who did not. Many of the so-called desertions fell somewhere between official sanction and private initiative. At a military conference, a staff officer liaising with the civilian government had been given leave to issue 300 evacuation passes to civilians. He called the head of the Public Works Department who took seventy-five for his own staff (ignoring all the other technical departments) and one F. D. Bissecker, a businessman from Penang whom Duff Cooper had appointed to the war council, who undertook to distribute 100 more to persons 'of his delection'. Only 125 were handed over to the committee responsible for selecting who was to be evacuated. In the case of the police, on 11 February they were ordered to remain at their posts. On 13 February they were told that once the surrender was announced they were free agents, and 'owe loyalty only to the Empire'. Some, believing Singapore had fallen, or was about to fall, jumped the gun. In internment, the policemen who had stayed took down bitter statements from each other about those they felt had deserted their posts. This would be a canker at the heart of British administration in Asia after the war. There was a story that during the departure of one police boat, a Malay boatman was pushed overboard.[142] The officer in charge had been ordered to take leading Chinese from Tan Kah Kee's resistance army, including the young Kuomintang leader Lim Bo Seng. He left without them, and also left behind a secret list of Chinese to be protected. Lim Bo Seng was furious: he vowed, 'I will never help the British again.'[143]

In fact, Lim Bo Seng was one of the few Asians to get out. His diary betrays no anger at the British, but only his agony at having to leave behind his wife and children as there was no room for them in the boat. Lim made the decision that they would be safer from reprisals if he was not with them.[144] A few lucky ones had got out much earlier. The British had issued an order preventing Asian males from leaving the country, but some made it to Chungking, others to India, where a community of Malayans in exile emerged, including the Selangor tycoon H. S. Lee and the Straits Chinese leader Tan Cheng Lock. Tan's hospitality to the Australians in Malacca had been repaid by an offer of asylum in Australia. But on 8 January he used his position as director of a shipping company to get a passage for his family to India, where some Persian friends had offered him support, despatching all his liquid funds ahead of him by telegraph. He was well advised. On the Japanese entry into Malacca, Tan Cheng Lock's name was at the top of the list of those they sought. His country house was ransacked, but luckily his library survived.[145] Aw Boon Haw fled to China. He left two of his four wives behind and lost his youngest son in the bombing. They were treated cordially by the Japanese in the family mansion, and his valuable jade collection was left intact. A struggle began for control of his company.[146] When British personnel began to withdraw from Singapore, Tan Kah Kee and a number of his most prominent supporters called on Shenton Thomas. They were told that the British could not evacuate them. Two privately owned motor launches were prepared and, when it appeared that the British were about to requisition these, Tan Kah Kee and his party left for Sumatra. They were perhaps the most wanted men in Malaya. The cultural struggle had not diminished: Chinese street plays and alley speeches had rallied the defenders; street choirs continued to sing 'The Volunteer Army March' and 'Traitors Are Fools'. As one writer remarked: 'Such great poems could only be produced in a tumultuous era such as this.' But these brilliant propagandists were told, through Tan Kah Kee, that they could expect no succour from the British. They discussed with Ng Yeh Lu the possibility of joining the guerrilla resistance: he dissuaded them. The intellectuals would lack the stamina for jungle life and, as speakers of the Shanghai dialect, they would not be able to gain the trust and support of the peasants. The journalist Hu Yuzhi, the poet Yu Dafu and twenty-eight others joined the nerve-wrenching exodus to Sumatra by boat.[147]

There were many dramatic individual escapes, but of the British and Australian departures it was Gordon Bennett's that was the subject of most controversy. He informed his fellow escapees that he had 'told Percival to surrender and on him refusing to do so said they would withdraw'. They were unimpressed. Oppenheim was in the party: 'The General screams like a young girl and curses Gordon Walker who is standing up in the nude for doing so saying it would be scandalous if the Japs saw him like that.' As they floated in the sampan, tempers frayed to such an extent that 'it was touch and go whether there was to be a general shoot out on board'. They made it to Sumatra, however, where the British and the Australians parted company, Bennett to Sydney, where, unhelpfully, his wife had made a statement insisting that he would never quit his post without orders. There was an enquiry at which he was cleared of desertion, but not of loss of judgement.

Oppenheim eventually reached Sawah Loento, just above Padang. Padang had been designated 'The HQ of the British Army in Sumatra'. Colonial life rapidly reconstituted itself. 'Here we met all and sundry and the atmosphere was like that of Saturday morning in any club in peace time. Drinking, gossip and quarrels.'[148] The flotsam and jetsam of war gathered there to await the last shipping. Hundreds of soldiers and civilians had made the difficult journey across Sumatra, many on their own initiative. The atmosphere in the town was drunken and volatile. Most of the European women were in rags, some sold their jewellery in the marketplace for food and cloth. There were ugly scenes as they demanded precedence, at meals, in the bathroom, for transport, over the Asian nurses who had survived with them the bombing and shipwrecks in the seas south of Singapore.[149]

Two days before the fall of Singapore, the secretary general of the MCP, Lai Teck, asked the British for instructions in the event of capitulation. He was told to order his cadres to go underground and build up their organization 'on a more secret basis'. The British, he was told, would not re-conquer Malaya for at least eighteen months. The communists were to await future attempts to contact them; meanwhile funds were forwarded to the MCP through the Special Branch; each recruit was to receive a fixed sum. Lieutenant-Colonel Alan Warren of the Oriental Mission tried to establish a forward base for the underground war with exiles from Singapore at the small fishing town of Bagan Si-Api-Api in Sumatra. This was short lived, they being forced back to Padang and surrendering with the Dutch garrison there in March. Broome and Davis of 101 Special Training School crossed the Straits of Malacca from there back to Sapan on the southern coast and tried to contact the communist resistance. They learned of the movements of bands of guerrillas into the forest interior of central Malaya, and heard talk of larger formations in the north; beyond this, nothing. They spent only twenty-four hours in Malaya and Davis, Broome and his 'boy' Ah Choon managed to bail out of Sumatra, making a forty-two-day crossing to Ceylon in a Malay *prahu* from Padang. They were among the last of the British to escape.[150]

While the British fought and lost the battle of Malaya, another battle had begun. Chinese gangsters took to the streets to defend at least some parts of the community. There was a settling of scores in some places. In Kuala Lumpur a guerrilla resistance seems to have begun spontaneously from below. Young Chinese would snipe at Japanese soldiers. The retributions here, as everywhere, were brutal, but a rebel tradition was being forged that drew in patriotic young Chinese, and not only committed communists. There were two aspects to the Malayan Communist Party's mobilization. The communist fighters who had been to the jungle training schools in Singapore and Kuala Lumpur were only its core. They were to withdraw to the deep jungle and, avoiding confrontation with the Japanese advance, build camps and store the materials of war. They were equipped with rifles and pistols, some tommy guns and grenades. The British had been generous with explosives. Beyond this there was a need to build up a network of recruitment and supply. In the confusion of retreat, party cadres looted abandoned stores and weapons including Bren guns. Peasant farmers helped them cache these goods. The English-educated teacher in Papan, Ho Thean Fook, although not a communist, joined a raid by old schoolfriends on an abandoned arms truck and moved its contents by bicycle to a secluded cave.[151] By such acts was the guerrilla organization built up. In Perak this occurred independently of the central committee, with which the leaders on the ground had lost touch. Working underground, Chin Peng had emerged as political commissar to one of its companies; they were, he later admitted, 'all very raw, very inexperienced'. His leader had proved his steel by knifing a collaborator, a Chinese traditional medicine man, in broad daylight. His deputy was a tinsmith, the political officer a barber from Telok Anson. This band was later designated the 4th Company of Fifth Independent Regiment of the Malayan Peoples' Anti-Japanese Army.[152]

The news of the fall of Singapore reverberated around the world. It was felt in the inhospitable landscape of Purana Qila, the medieval fort on the outskirts of New Delhi. There in tropical clothes in the cold north Indian winter, the Japanese of Malaya and Singapore were encamped behind barbed wire. They slept on charpoys and fed themselves on rice, meat and a sprinkling of local vegetables. There was little milk. Yet they marked the news from Singapore with a feast: 'fishermen from the Andamans, the shopkeeper from Singapore and the dentist from Kuala Lumpur all joined in the festivities'.[153] The news came to London at the nadir of Churchill's premiership, in the face of mounting frustration at the progress of the war. The fall of Singapore provoked public outcry and bitter introspection by politicians in London. There were two levels to this debate. The first focused on military error. This aspect was pushed to one side. Churchill received the reports on the controversy over the Australian desertions and did no more than pass them to the Australian high commissioner in London. He opposed to the end of his days any commission of inquiry into the fall of Malaya. But the damage was done. The most influential account was that of the *Times* journalist Ian Morrison, who posted damning indictments of colonial rule from Batavia. Few of the key figures were able to argue back but those who could, Gordon Bennett amongst them, gave a spirited defence of their own actions. The military controversies were to sour and ruin many of the survivors' lives.

But there was a deeper level to the debate. The entire legitimacy of the Asian empire had been shaken. Harold Nicolson witnessed Churchill's sombre mood. As he confided to his diary, drawing a parallel with the fall of the first British Empire to the American colonists:

The Singapore surrender has been a terrific blow to all of us. It is not merely the immediate dangers which threaten the Indian Ocean and the menace to our communications with the Middle East. It is dread that we are only half-hearted in fighting the whole-hearted. It is even more than that. We intellectuals must feel that in all these years we have derided the principles of force upon which our Empire is built. We undermined confidence in our own formula . . . The intellectuals of 1780 did the same.[154]

Yamashita's first address to the people of Malaya said something similar, using a rather unusual metaphor: without Singapore, British power in Asia was 'a fan without a rivet or an umbrella without a handle'. For the British, it was the end of a world that was never to be recreated, despite a second occupation after 1945 of nearly twenty years. Colonial Singapore had possessed a modernity that was in many ways in advance of London's. This blow at modernity struck hardest in the Asian communities, who also had invested their fortunes in it and its fetishes: the cars, refrigerators, air-conditioning. The image of the bright lights blazing through the air raids is an enduring one. There was a sense in which the fall of Singapore, seen as a glittering outpost of European civilization, had challenged its universality. This sense was shared both by those who acquiesced in Japanese rule and also by those who were to fight against it.

# 3

# 1942: Debacle in Burma

Despite its megalomaniac character, the Japanese war plan drawn up the previous autumn had not mentioned seizing central and upper Burma. Malaya was the objective and, as for Burma, the Japanese merely intended to take Tenasserim, the southernmost point of the Burmese section of the great crescent of Britain's imperial possessions. This was to prevent a British counter-attack with forces from India on Japan's now-exposed flank in western Malaya.[1] Intoxicated with their success, the Japanese army and air force now contemplated a full-scale assault on Burma and India. After the most glorious months in Japanese military history, the high command restated their objectives in more bullish terms. 'In order to force Britain to submit and the United States to lose its will to fight, we shall continue expanding from the areas we have already gained, and . . . working long-term to establish an impregnable strategic position, we shall actively seize whatever opportunities for attack may occur.'[2]

## THE ROAD TO RANGOON

Burma was one such opportunity and the campaign was a replay of the Malayan one. The Japanese ruthlessly signalled their intentions, initiating hostilities by blitzing Rangoon over the Christmas holiday of 1941. They attacked the docks area where thousands of curious Indian labourers gathered to watch what they thought was a harmless air display. Then sticks of anti-personnel bombs rained down on them. One raid alone took 2,000 lives. Thousands more were horribly maimed by jagged, exploding fragments.[3] A large part of the Burmese population fled to out-of-town monasteries. Indians simply scattered in terror. It was weeks before anything like the normal life of the city resumed. By then a full scale Japanese land invasion from Thailand was underway, supported by the new Burmese Independence Army.

The British were wrong-footed time and time again. The Japanese struck through 'neutral' Thailand by those same jungle pathways which almost everyone had regarded as impenetrable a few months before. They first established themselves on the southernmost tip of Burma's long southern appendage, at Victoria Point. Then they moved rapidly up the peninsula supported by up to 600 fighter planes. Japanese air command quickly switched aircraft from Malaya and the Philippines, where their forces had already made staggering gains against the Americans. According to Dorman-Smith, enemy troops simply 'walked around' the defending British and were already in Tavoy, half-way up the 'tail' of Tenasserim, by 19 January.[4] 'Bitterly disappointed by the scale of reinforcements', the governor complained that Tavoy might have been another Tobruk, the North African strong-point which temporarily held the Axis forces. But in Tavoy there were no air or naval defences.

By early February the retreat had begun to look like a rout. The Japanese had committed themselves to the conquest of the whole of Burma and were thrusting north up the three great river valleys, the Salween, the Sittang and the Irrawaddy, infiltrating through the jungle and surrounding British forces wherever they encountered resistance. Some British and Indian units fought well but others were so poor that General Archibald Wavell became 'a bit disturbed' about their quality.[5] Some British troops gave up easily just as they had done in Malaya. The Indians, far from strengthening the resolve of the Burma Rifles and other local units, had the opposite effect. The small Burmese units had the added disadvantage that the language of command was generally Hindustani, which neither the officers nor the men understood well.[6] Nevertheless, they gave a good account of themselves because this was, after all, their home. Conflicts quickly arose between the civil and military authorities. The governor complained of 'quite unnecessary withdrawals' as the Japanese quickly seized Moulmein, a town at the northern end of the peninsula and less than a hundred miles across the Gulf of Martaban from Rangoon itself. His complaints against the military were undermined because they knew that several key civil officers had also deserted their posts without being ordered to leave. The district commissioner of Mergui, whose officers had fled, doubted 'whether we will ever be able to hold our heads very high there again'.[7] Thus began a long and unseemly wrangle between the civil and military authorities about who was to blame for the ignominious scuttle.

The Americans kept up a barrage of criticism against the British. Stilwell, commander of the Chinese and American forces, deeply distrusted them, as he also distrusted Chiang Kai Shek. American commanders burnt lend–lease vehicles destined for China rather than letting the British get their hands on them. Stilwell complained that the British officers were still playing golf while the Japanese advanced, but, as Dorman-Smith pointed out, he should really have begun to worry when the British left off playing games. There were growing concerns about morale, though. Some soldiers had decided that there was little point in facing a ferocious enemy to defend a pointless backwater of the British Empire. Others were naively bullish. The 'morose and taciturn' American war correspondent Jack Belden put this down to 'a Kipling like belief in the ability of a British square to lick any fuzzy-wuzzies who might come along'.[8] Yet the problem was as much training and tactics as morale. Even those 'splendidly offensive' troops the Gurkhas did not do as well as they had done in the Middle East because they had never been properly trained in jungle warfare. The British units easily became bogged down because their heavy artillery and armour were not suitable for jungle fighting. One observer noted that, straight out of the Western Desert, they remained basically 'desert minded'.[9] The Japanese simply surrounded them and pounded them with their light trench mortars. Again and again the British forces withdrew in order to regroup further north.

After the initial terror caused by the bombing raids over Rangoon in December, the city had briefly returned to a semblance of normality. By early February panic was setting in again.[10] Morale deteriorated rapidly among the Indians when the army withdrew well to the north of Moulmein and European and Anglo-Burman women and children were rather hurriedly evacuated from the capital. The exodus of refugees from the city made it increasingly untenable as the base for any counter-offensive. Already by 11 February the governor was wiring the secretary of state in London with plans for the establishment of a new headquarters in Upper Burma. The writing was on the wall: 'I doubt whether we could ever recapture [Rangoon] except from the sea. We certainly have no means of maintaining and equipping a force which might operate from Upper Burma.'[11] Communications with India were exceptionally poor and north Burma's airfields would be open to continuous attack once Rangoon and its airport had fallen.

The dismal situation within Burma was made gloomier by the fall of Singapore on 15 February. Businessmen in Rangoon began to press the governor to help evacuate essential personnel. Within a short time Indian National Airlines and the Dutch airline KLM were flying out 400 women and children, the families of oil workers at nearby Yenan-gyaung, from Mandalay's Magwe airport. Dorman-Smith sent his own daughters to the hill station of Maymyo, hoping that this would not further dent morale. Getting in a dig at his allies, the governor wrote: 'Our American cousins are ratting rapidly.' The US consul general left for Chungking without paying his respects and the Burma China Mission was rapidly clearing out: 'Yanks . . . difficult people!'[12]

Meanwhile, the Japanese had established 'a complete moral ascendancy' on the battlefield. By late February, after constant retreats and further encirclement, the 17th Indian Division was broken. It became 'almost a pathological case'. On 21 February, the crossing point between lower and central Burma at the Sittang river was lost. Hundreds of British and Indian troops were caught on the wrong side of the river when the bridge was blown prematurely. The survivors had to swim across under enemy fire. A bitter dispute over who was responsible broke out and rumbled on for years after the end of the war. Despite the pleas of the Burma government few British reinforcements arrived, but another large force, a Chinese army under Stilwell, entered the country to support the Allies. Chiang Kai Shek was persuaded that defence of the Burma Road was vital to the survival of his regime. The Chinese fought well, according to British observers.[13] Yet they had been called in too late because of political concerns about Chiang's designs on north Burma. Wavell was later severely criticized for this. He played down the political issue, claiming instead that the Chinese were too dependent on exiguous British air support and administrative back-up to play a full part in the campaign. One recent account also accuses Stilwell of forcing the Chinese troops on to the offensive when the defensive strategy advocated by Chiang would have been more successful.[14] The Chinese blamed the British for 'defeatism' and there was a good deal of truth in this. Some troops from India did arrive in the days before the fall of Rangoon. But the home authorities were already determined not to waste more reserves in a fruitless attempt to hold Burma, and so imperil the defence of India and the battle in the Middle East.

The only bright side of the first Burma campaign for the Allies was the war in the air. Chennault's American Volunteer Group, whose parties had been such a feature of pre-war Rangoon, fought splendidly. They were supported by a small number of RAF planes.[15] At first the British were suspicious of Chennault, a man they thought of as 'inscrutable' and 'a mercenary', expecting him to pull out and disappear back to Chungking at any moment. But Rangoon was too important as a supply point for nationalist China to the north. The US government was itself alarmed by the prospect of the loss of Burma and urged Chennault to fight on. The Allies were determined that they would not allow their air force to be destroyed on the ground as it had been in Malaya. A small number of AVG and RAF pilots inflicted such heavy casualties on the Japanese that they were forced to halt daytime sorties against Rangoon and the north. Japanese planes laden with bombs were shot down in large numbers or were forced to return to base, harmlessly dropping their bombs in the countryside. Soon, the 'paddy fields at Mingaladon were dotted with the wrecks of Japanese bombers and fighters, but still they came'.[16] Many observers compared the defence of Rangoon and Mandalay to the Battle of Britain. Yet this success could not be maintained indefinitely. The civil telephone system was in disarray, which made it difficult to give early warning of impending attacks. The only radar unit in Burma was sent back to India before the end of February in order that Assam should not be left undefended.

More important, the battle was already lost on the ground. W. E. Abraham, a liaison officer from the Middle East theatre, visited the front on a fact-finding mission. He found the British commanders 'dead tired'. 'The general atmosphere of gloom was almost impossible to describe,' he wrote; 'GHQ at Athens when getting out of Greece was almost light hearted by comparison.'[17] Withdrawal was no easier than defeat. By early March only two trains a day were being loaded at Rangoon for the journey north. The Indian staff was 'neutral or unfriendly', according to Abraham. It was very difficult to keep employees working at the oilfields which fuelled the army and civilian evacuation. A few bombs had them running. At one installation, skilled labour agreed to keep on working only when the authorities agreed to have a train in waiting, making steam in a nearby siding. In this way the staff could make their escape at a moment's notice. The roads were completely clogged with vehicles backed up to each other, often struggling across broken bridges.

As the Japanese crept closer 'gradually the life of the great cosmo-politan city came to a standstill'[18] and the enemy were to occupy it without a single shot being fired, except at looters. Markets ceased to function because no one in the interior was prepared to risk requisition and non-payment to bring food and supplies in.[19] The Burmese fled the city for their villages and monasteries, returned and fled again. Suddenly the fragility of British power was brought home to them. Old prophecies about the fall of the Raj were resurrected. How would the Japanese behave? As always, there was concern about foreigners violating the pagodas: 'Do you think that the Japanese would remem-ber to take off their shoes when they walk through our pagodas?' a Burmese asked.[20] The British veered between defeatism and stoicism. Dorman-Smith recorded that the expatriates sometimes played a game in which they pretended Rangoon was London and the Japanese the invading Nazis. Would the Germans be at Esher now or at Guildford? By 21 February fires were raging on a large scale and looting was going on day and night. Only seventy police remained at their posts and most of the conservancy staff had deserted once again.

The problems of disease and an appalling lack of sanitation fore-shadowed in December now became overwhelming. The poor Indian low-caste sweepers who had kept the city clean, emptying the pails under the sahibs' 'thunder boxes' and quietly cleansing the Indian and Burmese quarters, all fled in terror. As the governor came to realize: 'life begins with the sweeper. That lowest of all human beings, who holds in his hands the difference between health and disease, cleanliness and filth.'[21] Most other essential workers were soon deserting their posts. Here the British were truly hoist with their own petard. The ruthless system of free enterprise which they had allowed to flourish in the labour market left no room for any form of workers' rights, so, wrote the governor, 'there were no representatives of labour I can call into consultation. There are no responsible trade unions.'[22] The city stank. Bloated rats scurried in the deserted streets. There were glorious ochre sunsets as the setting sun peered through the smoke of fires set by arsonists. The general collapse of civil and military communications meant that orders were sometimes passed prematurely. Someone released all the inmates of the prison and the lunatic asylum.[23] Many of the asylum's patients were mistaken for looters and shot as they were trying to make their way to what they thought was home. Odd rumours were afoot: the black panthers from the zoo were said to be roaming the streets.

The governor himself sometimes went out with the night patrols vainly trying to stop the looting. One night Dorman-Smith and his military liaison officer heard noises coming from a jewellery shop. They waited in the shadows sweating, their guns cocked. 'At last a figure appeared silhouetted in a doorway. We relaxed. It was an American AVG lad loaded with goods of all descriptions, as were his pals who followed him.'[24] They bid them good night and clambered back into their jeep, with the liaison officer's words 'Discretion, H.E! Discretion!' ringing in his ears. The fires got worse and worse as all available fire engines had been sent to the north. The official report read: 'The docks during the night [of 21 February 1942] were in a state which it is hardly believable could have existed in any British possession. Apart from our small party, I do not think that there was a single sober man anywhere. The crews of the boats alongside and the troops had looted liquor and were rolling about the place in the last stages of drunkenness.'[25] A riot on one of the boats resulted in its crews using bottles of tear gas as missiles.

All the while visitors kept passing through from those other embattled cities, Chungking and Singapore, and were put up in Government House, the only functioning hotel left in town. Among them was Wavell, trying to boost failing morale and symbolize order amongst the chaos. He dropped in to Rangoon on a regular basis 'like a Harley Street specialist, complete with a black bag, coming to see a very sick patient'. Dorman-Smith remembered that once he was nearly shot down while flying in from Chungking: 'there was not a tremor in his hand when he took his well-earned gimlet. He might have come in from a pleasant game of golf.'[26] This was ironic indeed in view of Churchill's denunciation of Wavell as a man competent to run a country golf club and little else. The rock-solid quality of Wavell's nerve was further demonstrated when, according to Dorman-Smith, he began to have a passionate love affair with a young woman who was staying with the governor. The future viceroy of India attempted to gain the lady's affection with bananas, but the outcome of this tryst is not known.

Less welcome visitors were the many British and American war correspondents who alighted on the city like vultures, as Dorman-Smith put it. By now they had really scented dying flesh. The headlines screamed that the civil administration in Burma had collapsed. After all, was it surprising that the complacent 'gin-swillin' pucca sahibs' out East had let the military and the empire down? And Dorman-Smith was at their head. When one of the journalists visited the exiled governor in Simla months later, he greeted him with the words: 'I have come to see the most unpopular man in India.'[27] The civil administration did break down and some civilian officers scuttled out of their postings with unbecoming speed. The military did just as badly, however. Their often precipitate withdrawal left the civil authorities with a dilemma. Should they get their men out in order to fight another day, or should they hang on to preserve their prestige and protect the stunned civilian population? The authorities were later hounded for not destroying transport, especially boats, in order to deny them to the advancing Japanese. But how could a few men destroy hundreds and thousands of craft when their terrified Burmese assistants had fled into the jungle? Anyway, this lesson was learned too well. Thousands of river craft were destroyed prematurely on the coasts of eastern India in the following months. Peasants were unable to get their goods to market, contributing significantly to the devastating Bengal famine of 1943.

There were other politically resonant rumours that sprang up like the bloated rats from the dying city, most significantly that the Burmese were all traitors. This coloured the attitude of many people in authority to the country and made later accommodation with the Burmese nationalist forces yet more difficult. Dorman-Smith himself wondered rather naively why it was that, after a century of rule, the British had not managed to cultivate active loyalty amongst the population of lower Burma as he thought they had done 'among other subject nations'.[28] In fact, outside the ranks of the invading Thakins themselves, few Burmese set out to harass or attack the retreating British. These rumours stemmed from attempts by the army to justify and explain its failure in a way which would not damage fragile domestic morale. Frank Donnison, who was not at all well disposed to Dorman-Smith, later met Brigadier Jehu, the army's public relations officer, in a bar in India. Over a drink, Jehu confirmed 'that he had been told to use Dorman-Smith as a scapegoat and to pin all the blame for the collapse of Burma in 1942 on him, so as to divert attention from the Army's failures'.[29] Jehu did his work very well.

Despite these dirty tricks, senior soldiers were well aware that, whatever the failings of civil administration, the army was also to blame. Wavell continued to express his doubts about the fighting qualities of some of the troops in Burma. This usually equable soldier revealed his anxiety when he gave several of his senior commanders in Burma a severe dressing down for dither and delay. In London, Alan Brooke was hardly warming to his new job as Chief of the Imperial General Staff either. He wondered why the army was not putting up a better defence of Singapore and Burma. He mused, 'I have during the last ten years had an unpleasant feeling that the British Empire was decaying and that we were on a slippery slope to decline! I wonder if I was right. I certainly never expected that we should fall to pieces as fast as we are and let Hong Kong and Singapore go in less than three months.'[30]

Privately, Brooke was forthright enough in blaming the Australians for the imminent collapse in Burma. Their 'parochial' attitude to the war led Dr H. V. Evatt, the Australian Labor politician and minister for external affairs, to advise his government to refuse to divert an Australian division from the Middle East to Rangoon at the critical point. Brooke complained that they seemed not to realize that Allied defeat in Asia would expose Australia itself even more grievously.

Later, in a more penitent mood, Brooke acknowledged that he himself had been partly at fault. The decision to continue to reinforce Singapore in its dire extremity had divided the Commonwealth forces, which should have been sent straight to Burma. As early as 17 December Brooke had already admitted that Singapore could probably not be saved. If in mid-December, or even in early January, troops had been sent straight to Burma rather than to Singapore it might have been possible to hold Rangoon and so protect India and the route to China more effectively. The only thing that maintained Brooke's morale at this desperate time was Churchill's ebullience. The prime minister seemed to flourish in adversity. He was wont to receive the CIGS in his bedroom clad 'like a Chinese mandarin',[31] in his red and gold dressing gown, with a large cigar in his mouth and his bed scattered with despatches, ringing his bell continuously for secretaries, typists and stenographers.

In Rangoon there was no such ebullience. The British authorities had planned that, once non-essential personnel had been evacuated, the final withdrawal from the city would be accompanied by a 'policy of denial'. This involved the destruction of all installations and particularly oil storage tanks which would be vital to the enemy. The plan was postponed when General Alexander, now commanding land forces, Burma, attempted on Wavell's orders one last counter-attack against the Japanese forces advancing up the river valley. Alexander was nearly trapped in the environs of the city and barely managed to extricate his forces northward. Wavell, who had countermanded an earlier order to withdraw given by the local commander General T. J. Hutton, was clearly in error and more or less admitted so later.[32]

Finally, the red signal for evacuation went up. Dorman-Smith paced the empty St Pancras Station-like barn of Government House. As disaster approached his tone became more and more ironic. Wiring Amery on 29 February, he noted 'I appreciate fact that any decision I make will probably be wrong.'[33] He bade farewell to his personal possessions and especially his prized top hats, hoping that the Burmese would loot them and that they would not end up as prizes in Tokyo. He had a nasty sense that the paintings and photographs of his bewhiskered and bemedalled predecessors as governors were eyeing him contemptuously. He imagined them exclaiming: 'Young man, *we* did not lose Rangoon in our time!'[34] As part of the policy of 'denial' of essential articles to the enemy, the governor and his ADC hurled billiard balls through the pictures.

Outside, the so-called 'last ditchers', mainly British and Anglo-Burmese businessmen and junior officials, were setting about destroying their life's work in a dismal replay of the events in Malaya. The telegraph and telephone offices, the central city barracks, the so-called Moghul Guard, and especially the docks and the great oil storage units across the river mouth went up in flames.[35] Huge explosions ripped the air with pillars of fire shooting heavenward. Shattered cranes and derricks hung at unlikely angles on the skyline. One correspondent remembered seeing the wrecked house of a rich Chinese Christian. Chairs, tables and wireless sets lay on the floor shattered. Only a picture of the Sacred Heart lay untouched on the wall. Even the religious buildings around the Shwedagon pagoda had been reduced to ashes by bombing and arson. The Shwedagon, cherished symbol of Burma, had itself barely escaped the conflagration.

Particularly painful for the last ditchers was the feeling that they were abandoning their old Burmese servants. They had been ordered to take no Burmese personnel on the final transports and motor boats which left the stricken city. There was an unspoken assumption among them that British prestige in Burma had been dealt a blow from which it would never recover.[36] Other 'old friends' were also left to their fate. While a large part of the Anglo-Burmese population were able to join the British retreat, many Anglo-Burmese and Anglo-Indians stayed on. They continued to man the essential services in Rangoon and elsewhere until the very last moment. A correspondent wrote that 'The Anglo-Indians have been the backbone of the defence of Rangoon' when others, especially the British, had run away. Those who were trapped by the advancing Japanese or elected to stay on in hospitals or schools were to be treated harshly by the Japanese over the next three years. The honour of the British Empire was upheld by some of those most widely disdained within its hierarchies of race and class.

# FROM SCORCHED EARTH TO
# GREEN HELL

From the moment that the first bomb fell on Rangoon on 13 December 1941 there began an exodus from Burma of the Indian, Anglo-Indian and Anglo-Burmese population which was at the time the largest mass migration in history. By the autumn of 1942 in the region of 600,000 people had fled from Burma into India by land and sea. Of these as many as 80,000 may have perished of disease, exhaustion or malnutrition.[37] These events have only paled into insignificance by comparison with the even greater horrors that were to be visited on South Asia over the next six years. They have been eclipsed by memories of the Bengal famine of 1943, by the riots, migrations and massacres that accompanied the partition of India in 1947 and by the Burmese civil war. Two conditions contributed to the scale of the disaster. First, the immigrant population of Burma was very large on the eve of the Japanese invasion because coolies, plantation workers and merchants were all anticipating the Burmese legislation which would restrict the number of new immigrants. People from all over India were desperate to get themselves and their families into Burma before the restrictive legislation was passed so that they would count as old rather than new immigrants. For so many families across India from the Khyber Pass to Cape Comorin, the few extra rupees earned by relatives working in the often appalling conditions of Burmese mines, factories and plantations made the difference between life and death.

The other condition was the vulnerability felt by the whole Indian population. When they fled from the cities, the Burmese could take shelter with relatives among the villages of the interior, or, if they were too far distant, in the hospices of the Buddhist monasteries. The civilian Chinese were on the whole a tightly organized and relatively egalitarian community of traders and skilled artisans. When the death knell of the British began to sound, many of them were systematically evacuated to Yunnan and China by their homeland associations, the regional and sectarian self-help organizations. Many undoubtedly perished in air raids and the nationalist soldiers had to endure appalling conditions, especially if they were wounded. Yet the Chinese devised an effective escape plan. Indians did not have this option. Shelter in India was far distant; with the collapse of industry and agriculture it was doubtful whether they could even find food, let alone a livelihood. They remembered the riots of 1930 and 1938 when large parts of the Burmese population turned on them with savage hostility. The British would not help them. More than one of the vaunted *ma-baps*, the 'mothers and fathers' of the people among the civil servants, had already precipitously fled in their motor cars ahead of the advancing Japanese. The only thing ordinary Indians could do, therefore, was to tie up their pathetic possessions in a bundle and get on the road or make for the ports where they might at least be able to squeeze on a boat as a deck-class passenger. For many, this decision was to prove fatal.

Having some sense of how hazardous the overland journey was likely to be, many Indian residents of southern Burma made for the ports through which they had entered the country. The situation at Rangoon, which had a large percentage of the total Indian population, quickly became impossible. Panicked by continuing air attacks and rumours of the rapid advance of the Japanese, people mobbed the shipping offices in early January. At this point the government of Burma still thought that it was a going concern and wanted to stop the exodus of labour. It prohibited the sale of deck-class tickets to males.[38] This measure fell hard on the poorer Indian labourers, but also on their wives and daughters, because Indian women could never be expected to travel without male escort. Charges of inequity and racism soon began to be heard. Ticket prices soared. Many officials of the Scindia Steamship Company fled on the first boat. Those who remained were accused of favouring their former customers. The pervasive racial basis of so much colonial life was even more evident in the crisis. On one typical ship, 800 deck berths were reserved for Anglo-Indians and 2,000 for Indians. This was apparently generous, but wildly out of line with the relative percentages of the population. Elsewhere, however, Anglo-Indians themselves were consigned to their usual status of 'non-persons' in between 'proper whites' and Indians. They were debarred from the decks because this was demeaning, but unable to get places in the ships' saloons, which were reserved for 'pure' Europeans.[39]

Another problem was the indifference of many of the wealthier

Indians to the sufferings of their impoverished countrymen. Those who could well afford it refused to take cabin berths, even if it meant denying deck places to poor coolies who could not. Rekindling his inherited prejudices, one British official reportedly saw 'fat bunniahs [merchants] travelling in carts while poor women and children dragged their weary limbs along the tracks' to the ports. This was borne out by H. K. Mukherji, a clerk who had tried to get his mentally ill son to India. He wrote to a Calcutta newspaper, 'big merchants, Chettis, Gujarati Bhatias, paid huge bribes to get themselves on the steamships but poor men even with families were refused tickets by the steamship companies'.[40] Mukherji acidly contrasted this with fine talk from the same people about 'independence' and 'brotherhood'. Yet there was perhaps a hint of admiration in another account which noted that one cloth merchant continued to do his business and sell cloth in the midst of the anarchy. Wealth and strength generally won out. Unattached males forced women at the refugee camps to pass off as their wives in order to secure passages.

The press of people was soon so great that the agent of one shipping company had to be rescued from his office by the police. The situation got out of control at all the other ports, too. Tens of thousands of people crammed into camps on the outskirts of the towns. They lived without even the most basic sanitation or adequate water supply. Cholera was rampant within a few days, but there was no help at hand because the medical staff were among the first to run away. At the port town of Taungyup, half-way between Rangoon and Akyab, people pressed as close as possible to the boats. Women and children were crushed against fences or lacerated on barbed wire. Others drowned as they tried to jump from the wharves on to the ships. When one district magistrate attempted to move the milling crowds to the outskirts, they sat down and shouted in defiance 'Gandhi ki Jai!' 'Victory to Mahatma Gandhi!'[41]

The refugees' attempt to flee through Taungyup proved to be one of the early disasters of the war. Between 9 February and 25 March 1942, 64,000 people with possibly another 10,000 small children left the place by ship. Another 10,000 despaired and wandered north to try to find boats at Akyab. But at least 5,000 people died of cholera or exhaustion on the high mountain pass into the town while innumerable others perished unnoticed and unattended on its outskirts.[42] Similar scenes were played out in other towns along the eastern seaboard. In Akyab, itself a place much nearer to the Indian border, the dead lay unburied in the streets. At the hospital the doctors were left without nurses or servants and the health officials had run away. Chaos reigned in the town and men from the neighbouring villages came in to steal what they could. The British commissioner said there was nothing he could do and left on the first available ship, despite the pleas of his subordinates to remain. One of them, a Burmese deputy commissioner, stayed on to try to control the communal trouble between Buddhists and Muslims which soon broke out, only to be murdered a few weeks later.

Meanwhile, the Japanese and their allies went from strength to strength. The Thakins, now commanding the Burma Independence Army, moved into Burma in the vanguard of the Japanese advance. They had built up their strength south of the Thai border where the earliest recruits were often second-generation residents of Thailand who did not even know how to speak Burmese.[43] Fighters of the Shan ethnic group were also prominent in the early days. As Ne Win, a senior commander and later Burmese dictator, crossed the frontier with the advance guard, his men changed their Thai uniforms for Burmese ones. Their Japanese mentor Suzuki told them 'The enemy is weak ... Until now we have lived like beggars, but now we must assume the role of ministers.' In Tavoy and the towns of the south, they were greeted as heroes by crowds buoyed up with patriotic fervour.[44] Thousands rushed to their colours as the army passed through the districts of the southern delta which had offered fierce resistance to the British in 1886 and again in 1931. Rumours abounded. The Japanese were coming to help Burma. A Burmese prince was marching in the vanguard of the Japanese army.[45] By the time they reached Rangoon, the BIA was about 12,000 strong and its numbers swelled to about 18,000 by the end of the year. The numbers were, of course, quite small by comparison with the roughly 300,000 Japanese troops in the country by the same time.

Some Thakins who had been jailed by the British as war broke out and had not escaped like the Thirty Comrades to join the Japanese were released from jail and joined their brothers. So too did a number of more substantial politicians of the pre-war days. Ba Maw had spent the last months in the jail at Mogok, plotting his escape with the deputy jailer, a covert nationalist, and the prison medical officer. During midnight meetings in the jail, the prisoners told the staff that the British were now collapsing and would not pay their salaries. Ba Maw pledged that he would secure their pay.[46] As the Japanese reached Toungoo in the central valley of the Sittang river, Ba Maw was quietly allowed to wander in the prison garden. He later recounted how he had 'walked swiftly into the nearby woods, walked up a nearby hill and on the road Mrs Ba Maw and a car were waiting for me'. Very soon he was talking to wary but bullish Japanese officers. Given their suspicions of the young and undisciplined Thakins and in the absence of their oldest contact, U Saw, the plausible and eloquent Ba Maw seemed the man for them.

As the BIA marched on into their homeland, Burmese patriotic fervour sometimes took on a tinge of inter-communal hatred. The big Indian moneylenders and bankers of the Irrawaddy delta were the target of great resentment and some were attacked by their Burmese creditors and enemies. The scale of the killing is still unknown, because so many were believed to have died as evacuees. Still, there are some stray bits of evidence. An Indian doctor wrote from Rangoon to his relatives in India in May 1945, after the British reoccupied the city, reporting: 'In Rangoon the Burmese people ruthlessly murdered the Indians, but that was stopped by the Nippons on their arrival here.'[47] The Japanese were not averse to killing the Chinese if they thought them a threat, or wounded Allied soldiers if they thought they would cause logistical problems. But with the formation of Indian Independence Leagues across East and Southeast Asia, the Japanese had begun to see Indians as potential allies during a future invasion of India and stopped the assaults on them.

A few Burma Independence Army officers also took the opportunity to pay off old scores with the Christian Karen population of the lowlands whom they believed had been specially privileged under British rule. They were joined by local bandits. The Karen law minister of the government of Burma neither fled to India with the British, like two of his colleagues, nor co-operated with the Japanese as many more did. Instead, he went off to the delta and attempted to organize an anti-Japanese Karen strong-point. He and his English wife, along with hundreds of other local Karens, were eventually murdered by hangers-on of the BIA.[48] When the BIA entered Arakan to the north a few months later, gangs also took it out on the local Muslim population and instigated Buddhist–Muslim riots as years of resentment were vented in violence. Some of the worst massacres of civilians in the war in Burma were carried out not by the Japanese, but by local Burmese gangs loosely associated with the BIA. This ignited a smouldering hatred which was to blight Burma for a generation and more.

Though outwardly cordial, relations between the BIA and the Japanese remained edgy. The Japanese supplied the BIA with no more than 1,000 rifles and 100 army pistols at the start. The new force built up its firepower only by capturing British weapons and stores. The majority of recruits to the force, as British Burma began to disintegrate, were not really pro-Japanese as British propaganda made out; they were simply enthusiastic and frustrated nationalists. In Moulmein, the capital of Tenasserim, there were a few clashes between Japanese and BIA troops. As the victorious armies swept north a kind of rivalry developed between Burmese and Japanese as to who would liberate Arakan first. A Japanese mechanized column raced a BIA infantry regiment. One memoir recorded that 'the BIA regiment marched without sleeping for one night and ignoring two meals. Eating green leaves instead, so that they could gain time over the Japs.' Entering Akyab first, the Burmese commandeered the booty, including two and a half million rupees, a bone of contention between the two armies.[49]

In general, the Japanese won these races in their trucks and motorboats, but the BIA made a point of staging rapid marches to all the major towns of central and northern Burma. This helped to weld them into one force and also acted as political propaganda in the districts through which they moved. Most of the recruits were young students, Thakin political activists with a sprinkling of working-class men and peasants. The army had no catering corps. Instead, it lived on the country and this also provided a political education for the troops and local inhabitants. Buddhist monks, well trained in begging, helped to collect donations for the BIA and also to provide information and co-ordination. This was happening even before the British evacuation was complete. BIA commanders also broke their force into eating units to be billeted on the towns and villages through which they passed. In principle at least, poor families were given money to buy provisions for the 'guest troops', while richer ones were supposed to provide the food free. Local associations also opened messes for regiments as they passed through.

In many ways these early months of 1942 recreated Burmese society. Since 1886 British rule had had a fragmenting effect on political and social life. Villages and townships had become the basic units of administration while the towns and cities were almost unconnected satellites. Now, a link had been forged again between the army and Burmese national politics and between the villages and the Buddhist priesthood. Country people looked up in pride to the young men in their blue uniforms speaking of free Burma. Maung Maung, who later joined them, remembered 'how thrilling it was to see Burmese soldiers and officers wearing assorted uniforms, bearing assorted arms, tri-colour armband on the shirtsleeve, seriousness on the face'.[50] For seventy years real Burmese soldiers, they thought, could only be num-bered in the hundreds. The students and urban Thakins of the army began to find supporters, girlfriends and wives in the villages and small towns. The BIA became the effective government away from the Japanese gaze. Dacoits or bandits always took the onset of *kitpyet*, or the breakdown of social and political order, as an appropriate signal to step up their looting. But the BIA ruthlessly suppressed dacoity, resorting to savage public executions in village and town squares, as had been common under the Burmese monarchy. Later some com-manders had a better idea and, rather than public bayoneting, began to form convicted or suspected dacoits into labour gangs. The BIA also tried to protect ordinary people from looting by Japanese troops. Thein Pe, a young communist who later wrote about these early days, noted that the incidence of Japanese plunder and atrocity was much lower in districts where the BIA had a firm presence, though he was, of course, referring only to the safety of the ethnic Burman population. All this helps to explain the later strength of Aung San and his political movement, the Anti-Fascist People's Freedom League, after 1944. Despite their growing suspicions, the Japanese could not move against him because he effectively controlled the villages. On their return the British found themselves to be ultimately powerless for the same reason. The link between the village and the army keeps the Burmese regime in power into the twenty-first century.

The Japanese onslaught drove on up the coast and the Irrawaddy valley pushing a vast wave of refugees before it. By late March the refugees' only escape route was overland, through Manipur, or even further to the north, through the Hukawng valley, over the hills and into northern Assam. That so many, including British and Anglo-Indians, were forced through the mountain passes and mud, facing death, testimony to the speed of the collapse of British power. Dorman-Smith and Wavell had both hoped that some sort of resistance could be mounted in north Burma. It was essential to allow time for the evacuation of the defeated army and the destruction of the oilfields and mining installations in the Mandalay area. At the back of their minds also was the worry that if the hectic pace of the Japanese advance continued, the enemy might reach east Bengal before the monsoon. British government in the subcontinent was fragile in the spring of 1942. Churchill had unwillingly sent the socialist intellectual Stafford Cripps to negotiate a settlement with the Indian National Congress. The mission quickly reached an impasse and the annihilation of British power in the East looked a distinct possibility. In the event, the monsoon set in before the Japanese reached the Indian border. But the defence of north Burma proved a forlorn hope. The human line which held back the tide of defeat was the one scratched together by the resolute hill people of the north, the Chins and Kachins who gave the British a vital few days of grace.

The reasons for the speed of the collapse were stark. Once the British lost Rangoon it was all over. The city had provided essential supplies for the whole country: cloth, kerosene, cooking oil and food. The destruction of the oilfields meant that the retreating army was desperately short of fuel. Most important, once the south of Burma was occupied, the Japanese controlled the best airfields. The one bright spot in the Allied campaign, the air war, was now over. No new crews and planes could be embarked through the port of Rangoon. The precious radar early warning system and the code-breaking machinery had been withdrawn to India.[51] Magwe airfield south of Mandalay and Myitkyina to the north now had virtually no early warning as the large numbers of Japanese fighters and bombers streamed north. The air commanders realized that if they were to have any chance of fighting an air war from Assam and continuing to supply the Chinese over the northern mountains, they would have to withdraw their machines. A race began between the Japanese air attacks on the northern cities and the flights of Allied transport planes and Chinese commercial airlines which were attempting to get the refugees out.

Mandalay, the northern capital city, had felt itself above the crisis. It had been doing well as Chinese and British soldiers and richer refugees threw money around. Maung Maung recorded: 'Mandalay, business-like as usual, decided the war had its blessings.'[52] The city had a brutal awakening, coming under fierce air attack in April and May. To the delight of Tokyo radio, one of the first buildings to be flattened was the Upper Burma Club, where a luncheon party was taking place. A guest said: 'We didn't know what hit us. One minute we were seated at table, the next, the roof caved in, tables, chairs, food and ourselves were scattered all over the room.' The Burmese were very anxious about the nearby royal palace complex.[53] The air-raid protection organization of which Dorman-Smith had been so proud collapsed almost immediately. The Japanese fighters soared in and 'leisurely fixed the town under their sights as a scientist fixes a bug beneath a microscope'.[54] The administration and fire services broke down as British and Indian officials fled and the Burmese melted away into the countryside.

The retreating British destroyed some important installations in the city, but in the blistering Mandalay heat, accidental fire did most damage. As he watched the painted roofs of the old royal palace disappearing in smoke, Thein Pe anxiously wondered whether the English had 'actually gone so far as to set fire to the palace for no good reason at all'.[55] In fact, as Maung Maung saw, Japanese fighters and bombers had set fire to the city. They had swooped low and sprayed the people with machine gun bullets. Thousands of men, women and children were killed. Lady Dorman-Smith wrote to her daughter: 'Acres and acres of the city are burnt flat – a few walls standing here and there – all the trees burnt and broken – words just cannot describe the desolation. Rangoon was nothing to it.'[56] Many of the wounded struggled to the American Baptist hospital but the blood transfusion machine was broken and the power plant had been destroyed. Kerosene soon ran out so that operations could not be performed. There were persistent rumours that those British officers who remained in the city were drunk and incompetent. Madame Chiang Kai Shek, who was visiting the town and trying to raise the morale of the struggling Chinese troops on the front, was scandalized to see dead bodies lying in the roads days after the air raids.[57] Contempt for the military and political failure of the British began to spread ominously around Chungking, fuelled by American war correspondents who bridled at the disdain which the dying British administration was still able to direct at them.

Ruth Donnison, wife of the civil servant Frank Donnison, remembered vivid flashes of the nightmare: the terrible smell of death and decay; the flowers in the public gardens dying for lack of water. The poor Indian coolies refused to use the camps because they expected them to be bombed, 'so all along the roads out of the city and for many miles around the fields were littered with the filth of thousands'.[58] The trains were filled with scrambling passengers trying to move north to the nearest Indian road connections. These roads were jammed full of civilian cars and military lorries inching their way forward over straining bridges as Burmese villagers looked on in bewilderment. The British faced an acute dilemma. If they evacuated, they faced the charge of running away as some had done earlier in the south. If they stayed on, they risked capture, imprisonment and probable death. One senior employee of the Burma Corporation related how 'bitterly humiliating' it was to tell the loyal Indian, Burmese and Anglo-Indian staff 'that they would have to do their best to save themselves because the Corporation could do nothing for them'.[59] Donnison remembered breaking into tears when he was urged by a colleague to leave when he felt he should stay with his charges. He set off for India all the same.[60]

Residents of the Mandalay hill station of Maymyo, complete with manicured gardens and golf courses, were astonished to see Japanese planes flying in low to bomb their happy sanctuary. Stephen Brookes, son of a retired British Indian army officer and a Burmese mother, remembered the traumatic weeks when paradise vanished. The road to hell began as the small boy heard his mother crying aloud in anguish.

She had received news of the death in battle of his elder brother. Within a few days the first Japanese Zero fighters came sweeping in, devastating the peaceful hill station where they believed the Allied leadership might be hiding. He remembered people 'emerging from their ruined homes, and I can still hear their cries of despair. I picked up a piece of shrapnel from the assortment at our feet, feeling the weight and running my finger over the jagged, killing edge, my sense of bewilderment and fear about the future growing.'[61] The European residents' difficult situation was made impossible by the Shan traders who normally brought food into the town refusing to venture anywhere near it.[62]

Soon the retreating British, their American and Chinese allies, their Indian clients and the remnants of the civil administration were boxed up in the far north of the country around the airport at Myitkyina. This soon came under heavy attack. Hundreds of refugees were killed on the airfield itself as the Japanese cratered it with bombs. Stephen Brookes and his family were once again caught in this bombing. They had come down into the plains from the Chinese border, where they were relatively safe, because Mrs Brookes refused to leave her husband. He writes of the frenzied attempts of a gaggle of British, Indians and Anglo-Indians to get into the last Dakota as its propellers whirred. The crowd became frantic with anxiety as people fought to reach the door of the plane. Brookes himself screamed obscenities in Hindustani, pushing and shoving to get on. At the last moment his mother begged him pitifully to stay and he turned back from the plane. Almost immediately the Japanese fighters were on the scene. The two taxiing Dakotas were hit and all the women, children and wounded soldiers on board were killed.[63]

To the northwest the British forces made a hasty and apparently disorganized exit over the high passes which linked north Burma with Assam in India. With the Japanese army hot on their heels and its air force pounding them from the skies, General Alexander and his staff, led by General William Slim, were able to save a surprisingly high proportion of the retreating troops. They had vehicles, supplies, some air support and fast passage before the routes became virtually impassable. Yet little was done for the tens of thousands of civilian Indian refugees who were also attempting to struggle across into Assam without food or transport. Alexander had already survived one utter defeat at Dunkirk in 1940. As he and Slim pulled out, he vowed he would never again be called upon to command an army 'armed with umbrellas and hurricane lamps'.[64]

Dorman-Smith himself barely escaped in one of the last RAF planes out of Myitkyina airfield. Obese and unfit by his own account, he could not have made the overland route. He was ordered out at the last moment by Churchill himself. The PM did not want another of his governors forced to parade sheepishly in front of the victorious Japanese. As the plane circled precipitously above the pitted aerodrome, he clutched in his hands a few files of official codes. Precisely one year earlier to the day, in full finery and pomp, he had arrived at Rangoon with forty-three containers of clothes and personal possessions.[65] 'I was kicked out of Burma on the anniversary of the day I was sworn in as Governor – which was rather extraordinary,' he later mused.[66] British rule in Burma was over as suddenly as the Burmese monarchy had ended nearly sixty years before when the old quarter of the royal palace in Mandalay had been torched by drunken British soldiers.

## BURMA'S FALSE DAWN

The triumphant Japanese and their Burmese allies drove north. Victory parades were held in Rangoon and Mandalay. Leading the Japanese troops into Rangoon were soldiers carrying a white bag which contained body parts of fallen comrades, usually fingers. This allowed the spirits of the dead to take part in the day of glory. The remains would later be taken back to Japan to be interred in its sacred soil. Rangoon was filthy and depopulated but most of its buildings were standing and the population began to drift back as the food situation improved a little. With Colonel Suzuki in the vanguard, fraternity between Asian peoples seemed guaranteed. The colonel was a great admirer of all things Burmese. He managed to locate Po Sein, one of the greatest exponents of the Burmese classical theatre, the *zat* tradition. This Burmese Laurence Olivier was already close to Ba Maw. He speedily taught his children some Japanese. Within a few weeks a great performance had been organized in the Palladium Hall at Rangoon. In the presence of 2,000 guests and many representatives of the Japanese military, religious themes were celebrated, binding the two Buddhist peoples together. Then the classical singing and dancing routine commenced. Children sang:

> Let us dance happily.
> And if we dance happily,
> It will be in the heart of Tokyo,
> Joy! Joy!
> In the midst of Tokyo flowers.[67]

Japanese soldiers spoke of Burmese civilians mobbing them with pleasure, waving Burmese flags, certain that the day of Burma's freedom was at hand. But this was not to be. There were already disagreements between the army and the navy over control of the Burmese forces and their Thakin leadership. As the fighting developed, the Japanese at the front became intolerant of the Burma Independence Army. They regarded it as a distraction and were enraged when several less committed units – 'schoolboys out on an adventure' as one British officer called them – surrendered without firing a shot. Suzuki and the Minami Kikan found themselves subordinated to the military command. For the professional soldiers, Burmese independence was far down the list of priorities. In Moulmein port, the Japanese army had already roughly pushed aside the provisional government of free Burma which the BIA commanders had established. They also refused the Burmese permission to distribute a leaflet declaring the independence of the country.[68] When the invaders reached Rangoon, the BIA demanded the right to occupy government house as its headquarters, but was refused.[69] The Japanese general staff let it be known that there should be no talk of Burma's 'promised' independence. The war must come first. Some co-operation with the Burmese was, however, necessary, if only to secure supplies for the army from a population much of which had melted away into the countryside. But which Burmese? The Japanese began to make much of the fact that, like the Japanese, they were Buddhists. A Buddhist conference was hurriedly convened. This policy had mixed results. For one thing, there were deep differences between Japanese and Burmese Buddhism and Burmese monks were very wary of taking a direct role in government. The Buddhist tilt was also something of a liability because so many of the population were Christian or Muslim or held to their own popular 'animist' religions. In the early phases of the occupation there is some evidence that zealous Burmese Buddhists aggressively sought to 'convert' members of the minority groups to their faith. This exacerbated existing animosities. The Japanese also hesitated about the form of local government they would introduce. In 1942, and again in 1944, there was talk of establishing a member of the last Burmese king Thibaw's family as a client monarch. But the British had done such a thorough job of dispossessing the Burmese royal family that using compliant members of a ruling dynasty as the Japanese had done in Manchuria, French Indo-China and Malaya was simply impractical.

Ultimately, the Japanese commander General Shojiro Iida decided to form a Burmese advisory council with the flamboyant Dr Ba Maw as its head. Ba Maw, as a former prime minister, was a well-known figure on the political platform as well as being a consummate socialite and charmer. Besides, Iida was already suspicious of the Thakins. They were very young and inexperienced and, after all, were communists or crypto-communists. Elements associated with the BIA had already got the Japanese into trouble by massacring Karens in the delta and central Burma, so earning undying hate for the invaders. Sugii Mitsuru, a Minami Kikan operative, added another reason for the military's disregard of the Thakins. Aung San was simply too unimpressive: 'Maybe if Thakin Aung San was big statured like Dr Ba Maw, he might have attracted the attention of GHQ, but as he was small statured, he was practically unnoticed.'[70] In the short run, Iida was successful in persuading Aung San to act as Ba Maw's subordinate. In the longer run, the Japanese would have reason to regret a decision which firmly planted the seeds of resentment among the Thirty Comrades and their troops.

Terrible as was the human tragedy which accompanied the loss of Burma, the economic devastation was longer lasting and was to impoverish more than one generation. The British scorched-earth policy in 1942 destroyed most of the country's oil and mining installations, along with tens of thousands of boats and motor vehicles. Something was saved from the disaster. Employees of Steel Brothers, the huge logging company working in the Bhamo and Myitkyina areas of the northern hills, managed to round up and move north a large proportion of the 400 elephants which they owned there. The animals were the only reliable form of transport along the mountain roads in the monsoon season. These later proved invaluable in building the new road through the Hukawng Valley and distributing relief to refugees.[71]

## DEATH OF THE INNOCENTS

As the summer approached, the fate of the refugees worsened. A British 'last ditcher' wrote furiously of the total failure of the authorities, civil and military, to give any help or authoritative advice to the hundreds of thousands now on the move. There was no co-ordination, no organization, mainly a terrible fatalism, the sort of fatalism which the British had long imputed to Asian people, in fact. 'Those dumb masses who plodded day and night along the roads leading out of Rangoon were leaderless. They trailed like herds of animals before a forest fire.'[72] There was no attempt to provide proper sanitation in the refugee camps and cholera spread rapidly. With ghastly irony, this fact was then used by the authorities as an excuse for more than once halting Indian evacuation, while British and Anglo-Indian evacuation went ahead unimpeded. The attitude of the local Burmese population varied. There were some instances of Burmese peasants paying off scores against rich Indian moneylenders in the delta and around Mandalay. In a few cases poorer Indians were robbed on their way out by dacoits or by youths from local villages. This was built up into one of the charges of 'treachery' against the Burmese civilians by which the military justified its failure. Yet there is much evidence that individual Burmese displayed Buddhist compassion towards the Indian and British refugees. 'At many stations the Burmese gave cups of iced sherbet and aerated water' to the evacuees crammed into the trains going north.

The escape from the Burmese cities was etched in the minds of many who later wrote memoirs and personal accounts. One group hid on a launch as it struggled upriver from Mandalay. Japanese planes refrained from strafing it only because their pilots took the people lying on deck to be Indians. Captain Coutts, an employee of the Irrawaddy Flotilla Company, took passage on a Chinese army hospital ship. Conditions were terrible. 'The decks were littered with sick and wounded and the stench of filth and gangrenous wounds was indescribable.'[73] He escaped from Chinese officers who wanted to impress him as a pilot only to encounter Myitkyina airport at its worst, shortly before the final planes took off leaving thousands of women and children stranded without food, water or medical supplies. Conditions on the route across the hills were worse than any that he had encountered in the Mesopotamian campaign during the First World War. There were no medical supplies or medical aid. Coutts arrived in Calcutta a few weeks later with nothing but the shreds of clothing he stood in. The government of Burma had hurriedly appointed an officer to oversee the civil evacuation of the country, but the staff was tiny and the official aim seems to have been to prevent the spread of disease and to avoid hampering the progress of the retreating troops, rather than to provide aid or advice to the refugees themselves. Some civil officers stayed on in a private capacity to help direct people to refugee camps and organize the distribution of food. The officers of the Burma Forest Department were particularly important. They knew the pathways through the forests and where food was to be found in the villages along the wayside.

By the middle of May, with the monsoon beginning, the situation was desperate. Thousands had already died and the survivors were almost all diseased, starving and totally demoralized by the constant rain. The route through the Hukawng valley to Assam was the worse of the two remaining escape routes. It was a green hell of mud, human excrement and chaos snaking through the hills.[74] The lower parts of the valley consisted of huge tracts of thirteen-foot-tall elephant grass or stretches of near impenetrable jungle, broken up by small paddies which quickly became lakes of mud. Higher up, the track became more precipitous and the jungle thicker. Near-starving people ate poisonous fruits from roadside shrubs or rotting food from tins. If they collapsed with diarrhoea, they were left behind to perish. Even healthy males could travel no more than eight miles a day in a sea of mud which stretched for mile after mile across the mountains. The only way to make progress was to slither along the roots of trees by the side of the track. Women and children collapsed and drowned in the mud. Cholera became epidemic as exhausted people sheltered in bivouacks to escape the rain and relieved themselves on the floors. Porters refused to touch the dead so they lay decomposing until medical staff arrived with kerosene to burn them. The butterflies in Assam that year were the most beautiful on record. They added to the sense of the macabre as they flitted amongst the corpses.

Some people managed to make a terrible situation worse. An incautious RAF officer spread panic by remarking to a group of refugees that the Japanese were immediately behind them. Others said that the enemy was moving up the Manipur road so fast that they were machine gunning their own troops from the air. A false rumour went round that Gibraltar had fallen to the Germans, further demoralizing the British.[75] Indians believed that the Congress Party was sending workers to help them, but none came. Bodies were looted. 'Respectable women' were numerous among the dead and these were systematically stripped of their jewellery and ornaments. One sepoy had Rs 2,000 on his person and was accused of selling stores at an extortionate rate. A doctor on the route sold medical supplies stolen from the air drops.

Certain British officials showed themselves at their worst. One man requisitioned large numbers of Naga coolies and pack animals to bring over inessential personal belongings while Indian women and children died by the roadside. Others cornered far too large a proportion of the supplies which had been dropped, pulling rank on Indian and Anglo-Indian subordinates. Among the expatriates the general feeling was 'save yourself'. Many contemporary memoirs express horror at the plight of the Indian labourers. But what could be done? A. C. Potter, Dorman-Smith's secretary, who had escaped from Rangoon via Maymyo and Myitkyina, made it through the Hukawng valley: 'The track and campsites were sickening, with the bodies of the dead and dying. Mostly starvation and exhaustion and mostly lower class Indians. One could do nothing to help the dying and had to pass on callously.'[76] When he finally arrived back in Assam, Potter had dropped from twelve and a half stone to nine, had virtually no clothes and possessed only a razor, a signet ring and a fountain pen.

Some brave people helped others. Frank Sinclair Gomes, an Anglo-

Indian telegraphist from Maymyo, three times rescued people from the river at Mogaung, on the southern edge of the valley, saving a Gurkha and a Madrasi woman and her child as their boats overturned. Two Gurkhas died as they tried to rescue starving people on the far side of another river by putting a rope across.[77] All along the route hundreds of Kachin and Naga villagers helped, providing food and transport. They were the mostly unacknowledged heroes of the civilian evacuation, as they were to be heroes of the later military resistance to the Japanese. Hundreds of thousands of refugees tramped through their lands, polluting their homes and bringing disease and death with them, but their traditions of hospitality were too strong to wither even in this crisis.

At the Assam end of these two lines of suffering through Manipur and the Hukawng valley, the situation was on a knife edge. Pathetically weak in social services of all sorts, the Indian authorities had to fall back on one of the few efficient organizations in the subcontinent: the Assam Tea Planters Association. Alongside forest officers it was the planters who gave a semblance of order to the chaos. As Justice Braund remarked, the rescue was a story of 'tea and teak'. The civil service played a lesser role. Before the war Assam had been home to one of the elite expatriate societies of the British Empire. A rigid hierarchy had once prevailed, symbolized by placements at cricket lunches, where the young bachelors, who often kept Indian women in their homes, paid court to the senior planters and their memsahibs. All this changed abruptly as war approached. Thousands of tea labourers were drafted in to civil and military works on the front, expanding the airfields or beginning the construction of the long road which was eventually to take Allied troops back into Burma. Wives and daughters of tea planters became Morse code signallers and clerks or were drawn into the massive relief effort.

These people, many of whom were Scots, seemed to come into their own in the crisis. 'Planters', one wrote, 'are practical, early rising, hard-working people', good at dealing with scholarly government officials as well as 'mobs of ignorant workers'.[78] Many had fought in the First World War and were from factories and business, not from universities. They were particularly adept at handling 'men, materials, money and motor transport'. Despite their reputation, they had long since given up polo and fishing trips. The planters supplied their greatest resource, labour. As early as February 1942 the government asked the Tea Association for assistance on military projects in the northeast, 25,000 men for the Manipur road and 75,000 for the northerly road from Ledo into Burma.[79] By March every small railway station had its contingent of tea-garden labourers ready to entrain. Each one was equipped with a hoe, two blankets, sufficient food for a fortnight and a hurricane lamp.[80] They were sent off to build roads and carry supplies but many never returned, dying of cholera and exhaustion.

The Assam planters were joined by Anglo-Indian and Anglo-Burmese nurses. These women could easily have fled to their home villages in Burma, but they walked or flew in to help with the war effort. A system of reception for the refugees was quickly organized. The Assam Women's Voluntary Service and the Marwari Association were particularly active. 'There is a hut for those who prefer to eat puris, run by the Marwari Relief Committee while the WVS at Pandu provides a variety of other foods.'[81] The tea gardens were used as casualty clearing stations. Many of the military wounded were too ill to be moved and died in makeshift stations in the gardens. In addition to British and Indian troops, as many as 20,000 Chinese soldiers thronged the area and they were riddled with lice and typhus. The smell of rotting flesh was pervasive for months afterwards. Civilian refugees fared even worse. Veronica Westmacott, who lived on a tea estate, noticed that refugees who had survived the terrible flight through the jungles and valleys of death would suddenly lose momentum, sit down and die. For some reason the ever-present gorgeous butterflies would settle on people near to death.[82]

The airfield at Dinjan was so busy that it first became a massive sandpit and then a sea of mud. The makeshift graves scattered around the area became waterlogged and bloated corpses floated free. Chinese National Airlines flew in all weathers, getting people out from Myitkyina until the airport was overrun by the Japanese. Tea planters' wives dashed up the pass in their motor cars to rescue some of the European refugees. Some motored day and night up into the hills, covering fifty or sixty miles a time on dreadful roads, to collect the refugees. Private activity eventually began to fill the gap left by official neglect. On the Indian side, 'Captain Bose's' Congress volunteers appeared at the Pandu camp to work alongside the Marwari Association. The president of the Assam WVS, Amy H. Reid, asked the swamis of the Ramakrishna mission to help.[83] They put in continuous service amongst the refugees and went on to save many lives during the famine of the following year.

The RAF dropped supplies at some of the intermediate camps which had been set up on the route over the Hukawng pass, but these were soon overwhelmed with floods of diseased and desperate refugees. Stores ran out almost immediately but supplying the relief camps by land was desperately difficult as the monsoon lashed down in full fury. Garo and Khasi hill people who had been recruited for road building were pressed into service as porters.[84] They resented this. Sickness set in. At one camp alone there were 400 porters sick with cholera and malaria. The death rate among the mules struggling along the quagmire which was once a track reached 50 per cent.

It was scarcely possible for the British reputation in Asia to fall lower, but it did. Stories filtered out about racial discrimination on the escape routes. Europeans and some Anglo-Indians had been let out along well-supplied tracks with plenty of porters. Indians and Anglo-Indians who looked particularly dark were held back and allowed to starve or die of disease in the squalid transit camps. One of the worst was Shingbwiyang. Here the authorities had attempted to stem the flow of refugees, ostensibly because there was not enough food and because the crush of people would impede the last stages of the military evacuation. Stephen Brookes, with his ageing British father and Burmese mother, ended up in a tribal longhouse in this squalid place, having escaped ambush by marauding Chinese troops and the mud and disease along the way. Brookes remained convinced that a racial bar prevented his family continuing on the route, while Tommy Cook, Dorman-Smith's ADC, and his party had been allowed to continue a few days earlier. He remarked bitterly: 'Meanwhile, those responsible for the debacle in Burma sipped their sherries in the comfort of Simla, Delhi and London. After all, Burma was a "side-show". There was no glory or promotion there.' The Indians, Anglo-Indians and small numbers of British trapped at Shingbwiyang sat out the drenching monsoon of 1942 in the camp without medicines, hope or, for long periods, food. Many died of malaria, malnutrition, blackwater fever or maggot-infested sores before the survivors were rescued by jeep or elephant in October as the rains cleared. These tales of despair and betrayal were never erased even by the striking British victories of 1944.

Jawaharlal Nehru travelled up to Assam and gave these accounts further currency. The nationalists were furious with the British for refusing to make political concessions to the Congress. Nehru pointed to what he saw as the solidarity of Indians during the crisis as evidence of the ever-rising unity of his country. By contrast, he and other Congress politicians claimed Indians had suffered racial discrimination during the evacuation, especially from petty officials in Burma.[85] The rumour went round that there had been a 'white road' and a 'black road', the former taking precedence in the eyes of officials. MPs in London began to ask questions of the secretary of state. Official India and what remained of the Burmese government put out denials.[86] It only *appeared* to be racial discrimination, they said. The real issue was food. Only one route into Assam was properly supplied with 'Indian food'. So in the middle of April, Indians were refused permission to proceed beyond the Burmese border. By contrast, there was plenty of 'European food', that is tinned bully beef and so on, available in the camps along the route. So Europeans and some Anglo-Indians and Anglo-Burmans were allowed to proceed.[87] Besides, the officials argued, there was a great danger of cholera and dysentery spreading along the route and infecting the military personnel and road-building labourers if the mass Indian evacuation was allowed to continue. Whichever way one looks at it, these policies effectively condemned thousands of Indians to death.

Some private accounts speak of acts of kindness between races. Ruth Donnison said that there had been no racial discrimination. Pregnant women regardless of race had been flown out of Myitkyina. She herself had lent a shawl to an Indian woman and had slept beside her.[88] An executive in Burma Oil came away with a good impression of Anglo-Indians and Anglo Burmans, many of whom were actually of American and Burmese descent. 'Readers of Kipling', he wrote, 'who do not know the East at first hand may well have formed an impression that the half-caste in India was a poor type, with the weaknesses of both races. My own experience was very different. In Burma in particular, the sons of Oklahoma drillers and their Burmese mistresses were upstanding, honest and vigorous types, and none of them let us down in that trying time.'[89]

Be that as it may, the truth was perhaps more gloomy. For every example of help being offered across the racial divide there was an example of the opposite. The pervasive racial categorizing of colonial society persisted even *in extremis*. One Anglo-Indian man was refused permission to board an aircraft because his wife was wearing Indian clothes. There is a good deal of evidence that an important discriminator between those who were allowed along the 'white' as opposed to the 'black' route was whether or not they wore trousers, 'those insignia of European civilisation', as the *Amrita Bazaar Patrika* of Calcutta acidly put it.[90] Yet trousers did not always do the trick. Supercargo Paxton, an Anglo-Indian manager of the Irrawaddy Steamship Company, struggled across the mountains on foot, assailed by leeches, bamboo bugs and sand flies. Reaching Assam he went to the European canteen in the first rescue station he came to. He was 'refused entrance as he was not a European' and was told to go to the Indian canteen by a British military officer.[91] He was presumably too dark in appearance.

Beyond this there was pure tragedy. Large numbers of Anglo-Indian and Indian families were divided. The men moved more quickly and escaped. Women and children were trapped in Myitkyina. A mother set out across the Hukawng valley with her two eldest daughters aged eighteen and sixteen, a boy of seven and an infant. She did not know that her husband had set out two days before with another son. The infant died very quickly and the rest of the mother's party were robbed of their money and rations. Only eighty miles from Ledo and safety, the mother and her other son died. The two eldest daughters completed the route without food, clothing or a male protector. An Anglo-Indian and Anglo-Burman refugees and evacuees office opened up at 8 Chowringhee, Calcutta, to try to bring together such scattered remnants of families.

Some had no relatives at all. One of the worst stories of the war in the East was the fate of the Eurasian orphans of Bishop Strachan's Girls Home. Several of the nearly seventy girls had been killed when their train was bombed as it stood in Pyinmina station on the way north. Almost all of the older girls died in the transit camp at Shinbwiyang of disease and hunger or on the final trek over the Naga hills. Another twenty-five of the younger ones fled into the jungle behind the northernmost town of Suprabum. They were discovered and fed by Japanese troops, but the food soon ran out, and seven more died. The others suffered terrible hardships before they were rescued by British officers on elephants in October and finally flown out to India. Scarcely a handful of the seventy survived the war.[92]

Chaos reigned as soldiers and civilian wounded were shipped across the country from Assam or flooded into Chittagong and Calcutta. In some cases, trains went right across the country for days and nights without any food supplies. It was only the kindness of the civilian population in the stations they passed through which ensured that the refugees did not starve on the final stretch. For those British and Indian soldiers who survived the evacuation and initial reception camps, the situation was by no means rosy. The military, like the civil authorities, were simply overwhelmed. There were seven poorly staffed base hospitals scattered across the Indian subcontinent. Those in Bihar and the United Provinces bore the brunt of the influx. There was a serious lack of trained staff of all sorts and particularly of senior medical officers. In Ranchi, Bihar, for instance, there were only seven senior staff for 1,300 patients. By June 1942 the situation had become critical because a large proportion of the men who had escaped from Burma had developed malaria after their return or were still suffering from dysentery.

Mrs G. Portal wrote to her friend Mrs R. A. Butler about the 'heartbreaking' conditions in the Ranchi hospital. The letter caused ructions in the administration because Mrs Portal was sister-in-law to the air chief marshal of that name and Mrs Butler was wife to the Conservative politician. There were, she said, no modern conveniences of any kind and only one water tap. As for medicine, 'we haven't even got an aspirin'. There were seven nursing sepoys by day and three by night. The staff were 'bolshy' and overworked. There were three water-carriers and five sweepers or waste-removers during the day. 'The medical wards are like "Gone with the Wind" – pallets touching each other, people moaning for water and sicking up and so on everywhere.' She was referring to the great scene in the most famous motion picture of the day, when the camera tracks upward to reveal acre after acre of wounded Confederate soldiers lying in the squalor of the ruins of Richmond, Virginia. She concluded: 'It's all a shocking crime and may God forever damn the Eastern Command Staff', who must have known that the Burma army was finished a month before.[93] Responding to angry questions in India and Britain, the viceroy found a way to blame the Indians for what had happened. Medical standards in India were low and 'the sense of patriotism is not great'. People would not come forward for service unless they were paid at a certain rate, he said.[94]

## WOULD INDIA HOLD?

In an admirable piece of wishful thinking, India Command began almost immediately to plan for the reconquest of Burma, while the last malarious troops hobbled into the safety of Assam. The mighty machine could not yet deliver. The reminiscences of David Atkins give a sharp insight into why this was so.[95] Atkins was a major, reluctantly put in charge of a road transport company which was attempting to establish a line of communications up into Assam. The plan was to build up a huge dump for stores at Dimapur in Manipur state, the jumping-off point for Burma. For Atkins, everything that could go wrong went wrong. The massive Canadian-built lorries with which he was issued sprang electrical and mechanical faults in increasing numbers. As lights failed, many lorries fell into the deep ravines on the crumbling roads, killing their Indian drivers. Higher authority insisted that the men spend the night in an infected train on the way up to Assam and later camp in grounds swarming with malaria-carrying anopheles mosquitoes.[96] Within a month all but eleven of his 433 men had contracted malaria. The disease weakened them and they became even more likely to collapse at the wheel or drive over an embankment to their deaths. One of the consequences of the fall of Malaya was the complete cessation of supplies of quinine, which had been produced there. The only prophylactics were the mosquito net and a Kenyan pyrethrum-based spray.

Atkins's unit was mainly from south India. They spoke little of the army's common language, Urdu, but a polyglot mixture of the south Indian languages Tamil, Telugu and Malayalam, and some English. The VCOs (Viceroy's Commissioned Officers) were not themselves necessarily competent in either English or Urdu. Racial misunderstanding compounded the linguistic problems. Some of the British officers fell out with the men. One subaltern, reduced to fury by disease and frustration, kicked over his men's food, for which they never forgave him. The British other ranks often adopted a disdainful attitude to Indians. As a Women's Army Corps (India) officer later wrote of the military chaos of 1942, 'If the Japanese had known, one division landed in the south of India in late 1942 would have been unstoppable.'

Yet this was not the whole story. Atkins and others writing about this disastrous juncture still point up some of the strengths of Britain's eastern empire. These would make it possible for Britain's Indian army, at almost the last point of its existence, to become one of the most formidable fighting machines in the world, one capable of taking on and defeating not only the Japanese, but the Italians and Germans as well. Officers noted the determination of the Indian soldiers to honour their salt and fight for the king-emperor, whatever they might have thought of the activities of the British Empire in India. British reserve and racial intolerance often softened in the face of the obvious competence and the vivid personalities of the Viceroy's Commissioned Officers with whom they served. The VCOs and King's Commissioned Officers, loyal and increasingly well trained, were not only the last soldiers of the British Raj, they were the advance guard of the new Indian nation. Even though British and Indian officers had separate messes in base areas, they mingled freely in action, sharing luxuries such as tobacco, white rum and Carnation tinned milk. On the north-eastern front Atkins and his Indian subalterns attended troop entertainments in which Manipuri dancing girls paraded on the stage singing:

> We love the British Empire,
> We love it very much,
> It gives us peace and happiness,
> It gives us clothes and such.[97]

It was, however, months, if not years, before these strengths were seriously drawn upon and the British Indian army delivered its bee's sting to the enemy. In the meantime, the moral and physical collapse of Britain's eastern empire was an event so extraordinary and unprecedented that panic spread through the civilian population across thousands of miles. Even before the first bombs fell on Singapore and Rangoon, the population of the cities of eastern India had become very jumpy. Panic set in as soon as the British battleship the *Prince of Wales* was sunk on 10 December 1941. John de Chazal, a police officer stationed in Madras, recorded that traders immediately began to stockpile grain and prices shot up. On 30 January Vizagapatnam, a naval base 200 miles up the east coast, was bombed from a Japanese aircraft carrier.

In Vizag hundreds of yards of trenches had been built over the preceding months to shelter people from air raids. For the convenience of the Japanese, the trenches had been built in neat straight lines. The bombers just flew straight up them, dropping their load and creating havoc among the terrified population. Several ships were sunk in the harbour. De Chazal noted that the lack of British retaliation made a deep impression on the population. 'They lost their confidence in the British and some two-thirds left the city that night including the labour coolies.' Soon a rumour went around that a Japanese battle fleet was actually sailing from the Andamans in the direction of Madras and the city seized up again. Madras, as R. K. Narayan the renowned Indian writer noted, had not itself seen military action since the campaigns of Robert Clive in the 1750s, barring a few shells from the German battleship *Emden* which had fallen on the city during the First World War.[98] A large part of the population decamped as it had done in Singapore and Rangoon. Richer people moved their families permanently to the inland hill stations, fearing an immediate Japanese invasion. Thousands of Indian refugees from Ceylon, which was also feared to be vulnerable, crossed into the southern part of the presidency, further stirring alarm.

In fact, the danger of a naval invasion quite quickly passed. Since the sinking of the *Prince of Wales* and its sister ship the *Repulse*, Japanese warships could roam freely in the Bay of Bengal. The new constraint on the Japanese navy, however, was the quick and, for them, deeply ominous regrouping of the US fleet after Pearl Harbor. In early May the Americans had repelled a concerted Japanese naval thrust against Port Moresby in the Battle of the Coral Sea. The Japanese could not afford to deploy too many capital ships in the secondary Indian Ocean theatre. Yet the significance of this was not understood. India remained tense.

Calcutta had its own initial panic early in December as the news of war in Asia filtered through. Marwari businessmen, who were originally from central India, felt no great affinity with the city where they made their money. They sold up their stocks and moved en masse to central and north India. There was massive congestion on the roads. When news of the bombing of Rangoon was received further panic ensued: there was a run on the banks and grain prices shot up.[99] The government was alarmed because there was absenteeism from the Ishapore Rifle Factory and the Cossipore Gun and Shell Factory. Letters from Bengalis in Burma brought a trickle of bad news about loss of life in bombings and Japanese naval movements back to Calcutta, though people began to go back to their jobs again. In January and February Calcutta returned to relative calm, though a defence exercise misfired when Allied planes got the wrong target and 'attacked' a suburban village, leading to a mass exodus from the area.

In April the first real bombs fell on Calcutta. Up to that point the atmosphere among the whites in the city had been like that in Singapore, Rangoon or Honolulu before the bombs started falling: 'dressing for dinner, races, bridge, cocktail parties – all the hooh-ha without which life becomes unbearable for the conscientious bearer of the white man's burden'.[100] Up-country, Arthur Dash, a Bengal civil servant greatly unimpressed by his superiors, recalled how long British complacency lasted: 'Soothing rural conditions were very persistent and only slowly did it become necessary to ration supplies of scotch whisky and bottled beer.'[101]

The Japanese bombed trains, trams and buses and dropped large numbers of propaganda leaflets urging Indians to rise up and liberate themselves from the British yoke. Congress propaganda further fed people's fears. Subhas Bose's former allies in the Forward Bloc predicted the imminent destruction of British colonialism. The slip trenches in the Maidan and along Chowringee, Calcutta's great central boulevard, were a constant reminder of the immediacy of war and scarcity as refugees poured back into the city from Burma by sea and overland. The Sisters of Loreto Convent became a clearing house for ill and starving refugees and dozens of other associations from Muslim charities, through the Marwari Relief Agency, a business community organization, to militant Hindu organizations. Suddenly Calcutta felt that it was in the front line for the first time since the last Burma war of 1886. The political situation was tense. Despite the imprisonment of many supporters of Bose, many radical anti-British nationalists were still at large. They had been given hope by their leader's escape from house arrest and reappearance in Germany. There were bomb attacks in Dacca where a communist-inspired anti-fascist conference was held. Two students were stabbed during a violent affray, allegedly by 'the fascists'. One Tarpada Bose wrote to the *Statesman*, perhaps embarrassed by his name, drawing attention to the large numbers of 'fascists and fifth columnists' in Bengal and demanding that they be suppressed by the Special Branch.[102]

The main reaction to the stepping-up of activity, with the governor's National War Front and the expansion of air-raid precautions, was fear. Would the British flee Assam and Bengal as they had Burma and Malaya? Would they institute a scorched earth policy as they had done there, destroying the hard-won fruits of the province's limited modernization? It was already known that the evacuation of British women and children and 'non-essential personnel' from Ceylon had begun. George Donovan wrote a pamphlet 'If Japan Attacks Calcutta'.[103] He concluded that, unlike the 'cardboard city' of Singapore, Calcutta was better built and could sustain heavy air attacks and mortality. This conclusion was hardly designed to instil much confidence. Wavell, as commander-in-chief, India, tried to improve morale in a speech in late May. He insisted that more than four-fifths of the troops sent from India and Burma to oppose the invasion had returned to India. They had been outfought by the Japanese, who had much more appropriate equipment, but the 'picturesque story told by a member of the House of Commons of our troops wading waist-deep through snake-infested water and living on unripe limes is fantastic'.[104] Self-confidence was not so easily repaired. E. C. Benthal, one of the leading British commercial men in India, thought the issue was too close to call. Elaborate plans for the evacuation of his jute mill personnel were in place by the end of May. Benthal continued to hope that the Japanese had 'just about reached the end of their tether' and everyone was desperately hanging on for the rains.[105]

Arthur Dash, the acerbic and critical Bengal civil servant, later poured scorn on his superiors' plans for withdrawal and a scorched earth policy in the spring of 1942. 'Unaccustomed to scorching, the Government of Bengal limited its scorching to boats, bicycles and elephants so as to deprive the Japanese of these valuable modes of transport.' He himself had 'scorched' a few elephants from the plains up to the Assam hills. The result of this was simply to deny people some basic tools of agricultural operations and increase the severity of the gathering scarcity. The Bengal government then went on to make a fool of itself a second time. Drawing on Burmese experience, it sent round a circular ordering officials to avoid capture to deprive enemy forces of translators and other forms of expertise. At the same time it insisted that officers should stay in place to the last possible moment. The circular, he wrote, 'combined the absurdities of Gilbert and Sullivan with the incomprehensibilities of the Athanasian Creed'.[106] Dash decided that an appropriate response might be to scorch himself off to Tibet.

Initially, war measures were simply sucked into the usual steamy pit of Bengal politics. The minister of labour and commerce, H. Suhrawardy, whom Dash described as 'a well connected womaniser ... blackguard and political gangster',[107] began to profit from war supplies. High-handed British officials and officers were locked in barely concealed racial confrontations with their Indian colleagues. One of Dash's district officers used wartime powers to try to requisition his own daughter's school for the use of British troops. This was because he was having a dispute with its headmistress. Dash refused this order and instead requisitioned a house belonging to the Raja of Rajshahi, a local magnate.[108] The Raja protested that the house was to be used by the ladies of his family, who were about to be evacuated from Calcutta because of the bombing. When Dash persisted, lo and behold!, the image of a Hindu deity was found in the house. The Raja now said that his property could not possibly be inhabited by beef chewing, alcohol drinking British soldiers. Meanwhile, Dash became increasingly apprehensive as food began to disappear from the bazaars.

The phoney war in India had some of the tragicomic features of the equivalent period in Britain. As British rule in Burma fell through the trapdoor of history, General and Air Head Quarters India found it necessary to circulate an antiquarian disquisition to all British commanding officers. It concerned the design of the swastika. This symbol of Nazi pride and Aryan racial dominion had, of course, an older use as a Sanskrit symbol of good health and religious faith. Many Indian shopkeepers, a notably pious section of the population, had swastikas displayed in their shops. On more than one occasion British troops newly arrived in India had noticed this and jumped to the conclusion that the shopkeepers were Nazi sympathizers. They had invaded the shops and torn down the offending symbol to the outrage of the proprietors. GHQ circulated descriptions and pictures of the Sanskrit swastika showing how its angle and design differed decisively from the Nazi equivalent.[109]

Under the surface of crumbling morale and Indian resentment the British had managed to salvage something from the disasters and humiliations of early 1942. As the rains finally blanketed the protective hills in a dense, foggy mist, they could congratulate themselves that most of their troops in Burma had made it back through the passes to India without the mass captivity and death which had accompanied the Malayan campaign. In Assam it was the civilian refugees, not the soldiers, who had died. Recruitment into the Indian army was holding up reasonably well, partly as a result of the prevailing economic hardship. Eastern Command, caught napping in the spring, was belatedly beginning to regroup on the Arakan front and around Imphal. There was even talk of an offensive southward from Chittagong before the Japanese completed their military occupation. More than 23,000 Chinese troops, broadly under the command of Stilwell, were camped at Ramgarh in Bihar. This and the Assam airfields were to be the jumping-off points for American aid to be flown to Chiang Kai Shek, now that all land routes were closed. Of course, the British were suspicious of the Chinese. They had established a little extraterritorial concession in the middle of Bihar. They demanded special training and supplies. They were already 'showing a most embarrassing disposition to meddle in internal Indian politics' on the Congress side. They had even begun to influence the marketing practices of local villagers. Small boys soon found that they could catch the huge, plump frogs that wallowed in the monsoon rivulets and sell them to the Chinese troops as a delicacy.[110] The Chinese, as one British official put it, 'are poker players. Their sole interest in this business is the future of China.'[111] They were, in fact behaving exactly as the British had been behaving in China for the previous hundred years.

Only slightly less suspect, but considerably more useful in the minds of the Indian army were the Americans. As the British had withdrawn from Burma, Stilwell's American troops, the AVG and other personnel had withdrawn in two directions. Some had moved into China from where they continued to raid and patrol into north Burma in the Fort Herz region and around Kengtung to the south. Here Stilwell began a long campaign to try to get Chiang to commit a significant number of troops to the reconquest of Myitkyina and its airfield. Wisely, Chiang refused to do so until the British were equally prepared to commit their troops to an amphibious landing in central or south Burma. Another body of Americans retreated into Assam and to Ramgarh in Bihar. Joined by air-force and transport personnel, they were about 8,000 strong by the end of the year. The Americans in India flew supplies over the Hump, the high mountain ranges, into China and began to drive a road into Burma from the old Italian mining settlement of Ledo. The defences of eastern India were gradually building up. But what had really delayed the Japanese were the monsoon and the quick rebound of the American fleet in the Pacific.

## TOTAL DEFENCE IN THE HILLS: THE LUSHAI LEVIES

One other circumstance contributed to the survival of British India. A substantial section of the hill people of the Burma–India border were themselves providing tough resistance to Japanese patrols and 'providing material assistance to the Allied war effort'. All the British efforts at gerrymandering and political balancing in India's hill regions were blown apart in 1942 when the hills and the forest became the main arena of warfare throughout the whole region. Previously soldiers had sometimes penetrated into the hill people's fastnesses. Now whole armies tramped across and fought on their lands, requisitioning or forcing labour to carry food and munitions, seizing their animals and burning their forests. To the hill men these new conditions required epochal decisions. How far should they support their old masters against the new invaders? The chiefs and many of their followers were relatively satisfied with the old order. However much they had resented or even resisted the initial imposition of the Raj, they came to find that the British presence was not too intrusive and even gave them some advantages. In many cases they had come to dislike the assumption of the plains politicians that they would easily merge into the new Burmese or Indian nations, forfeiting their political privileges and long-cultivated special identities.

The rapid expansion of the Christian confession had also given them a point of contact with their white masters which few other Asians had. In the hills, some long-serving officials and missionaries had created networks of friendship and patronage which their indigenous friends and clients felt shame in violating. Most of all, however, the hill people on both the Burmese and Indian sides were deeply hostile to the intrusion into their territory of new and often violent predators, be they Japanese or local Chinese nationalist warlords. To this extent the British were able in the hills to draw on a reserve of qualified good will relatively rarely encountered in other parts of their Asian empire. Still, unpalatable dilemmas faced the local leaders and their British mentors when making the decision to resist the Japanese and summon up this spirit of ethnic patriotism in support of the empire. Was it ethical to encourage resistance and expose whole populations to Japanese reprisals, when the British were themselves evacuating as quickly as possible, sometimes in near panic? How, in fact, could an authoritarian and paternalistic system of rule foster the sort of popular guerrilla war which had broken out in Greece, Yugoslavia or even parts of China during the Axis invasions?

This sharp dilemma faced A. G. McCall, the local administrator, and the people of the Lushai hills, set high above Arakan, during 1942.[112] The British had paid little attention to the Lushai until the mid 1930s, when officials established a village welfare scheme with the aim of 'bringing together chiefs and non-chiefs, Christians and non-Christians'.[113] Village crafts and hill products found a market in the outside world and a trickle of Lushais began to serve in the Assam

Rifles and other imperial units. McCall believed he had a mission to create a kind of Lushai nationalism in the hills by bringing the chiefs and people together in *darbars* or consultative councils. Local nationalism would inculcate a code of morality and hygiene and prevent wasteful forms of customary slash-and-burn agriculture in the hills. This 'guided democracy' of the Mongolian people of the hills would create a new British Empire and hold at bay the Indian and Burmese agitators from the plains. McCall probably overestimated the British role. The real moving force in the hills was the Christian Lushai of the Young Lushai Association at Aijal, the headquarters town. In their congregational meetings the young men had replaced the raunchy old tribal ballads with uplifting moral ditties in order to face the modern world:

> Oh! YLA go on, ever on.
> Give of your best in doing good.
> Strive now for all generations to come.[114]

Now this little world faced great danger. As the Japanese pushed up towards the fringes of Burma, taking Akyab and threatening Chittagong, their patrols came within a hundred miles of Aijal. Officials and Anglo-Indian newspapers talked of mobilizing the people and denounced the old stick-in-the-muds or so-called *koi hais* who opposed such schemes. The Calcutta *Statesman* pointed to the terrible example of Malaya. The new governor of Assam, it argued, should 'kindle the patriotism of the province and silence the jeremiads of the boys of the old brigade. The jungle, instead of being a death trap for our own soldiers can be made to come alive with hostility to the creeping ants', the Japanese.[115]

McCall decided to try to draw on Lushai local patriotism and loyalty to the crown and create a territorial fighting force. His model seems to have been the citizen armies of Finland which had offered stiff resistance to the Nazis. The British home guard, 'Dad's Army', may not have been too far from his mind either. He called the scheme the Total Defence Force and it was composed of two sorts of *pasaltha* or rifleman amounting to more than 3,000 men. Large numbers who already held licensed weapons from muskets through to locally made hunting rifles were paid Rs5 per month to mount a watch-and-ward operation from their own lands.[116] The British army supplied another smaller group of men with more advanced weapons and paid them Rs10 per month to act as a mobile force which was ready to move to any area where trouble was expected. The officials and Lushai headmen drew up plans for the hiding of food and slaughter of animals as a prelude to a sustained guerrilla war in case of an invasion.

The territorial troops were given basic military training. In the event of an air attack they were 'not to look at any plane. Not to stand up. But immediately to run to a nullah [ditch] and to fall down at full length, open mouth, and rest head in hand, resting on elbows.'[117] Everyone remembered the terrible execution in Burma when guileless people stood up and waved at the Japanese planes. Many of the Lushai chiefs signed up eagerly to this display of loyalty. They proclaimed that they would fight against the evil enemy who 'had murdered the people of China for five years'. They would create a defence on the 'same basis of total defence as the peoples of the [sic] England, Scotland and Wales'. Enthusiasm for the war effort was helped along, too, by counting the oracles in a more traditional fashion: 'Two snails are procured from the river sides, and one is called Britain, the other the enemy.'[118] The snails were placed in a battlefield, a hollowed-out bamboo trough. Even in villages where the larger snail was called 'German', the British snail always won in the end.

The Lushai Hills Total Defence Force was never put to the test to the same extent as the Shan, Chin, Kachin and Naga resistance in the Indian and Burmese hills to the north and east. But it certainly raised morale and gave people the impression that the Raj remained resilient and virile. The diaries of Bruce Lorrain-Foxall, a missionary further to the south in the Lushai hills, give a sense of the foreboding and fear which reigned throughout 1942.[119] Lushai people reported planes flying over and bombing down towards upper Burma. Lungleh, centre of the South Lushai mission, was itself bombed. Fleeing sepoys and others passed on rumours of mass death and evacuation. In August 1942 one of the men went south, where he 'saw 50 Japs and said that as soon as September sets in 1000 Japs are coming up to nearby Paletwa'. It was important to have some sense that the authorities in Aijal knew what they were doing. In Lushai, McCall's wife Jean stayed on beside him at her post during the crisis of May, 'sharing the risk of mutilation and death accepted voluntarily by the families in the hills', while other *ma-baps* across British Asia had decamped in their motor cars. McCall believed that his reward was that the people stood resolutely beside him.

Yet the failings and problems of the Total Defence Force also provided a sharp example of the difficulties in which an autocratic and paternalist power found itself when trying to organize a democratic resistance movement. British military support from Eastern Command was minimal in the hills because there was no road and transport by animal or manpower was deadly slow. As McCall found to his irritation, there was a constant tension between the desire of the military authorities to press-gang people into portering and labouring jobs and their wish to have an effective civil defence force. Squabbles arose between McCall and the military. He really wanted local supreme power, perhaps a little like the great servants of the East India Company who had become virtual kings in their districts a century earlier. He had the problem of weaving a path between the Assam authorities, the exiled Burmese government and the split military commands in the plains. These continued to bedevil British military efforts until late 1943.

Local politics also played its part. Relations between the Lushai and the inhabitants of the Chin hills, where the Japanese presence was a reality, were strained.[120] Some chiefs here had decided that discretion was the better part of valour. Within Lushai itself there were a few people such as schoolmasters and those who were regular visitors to the plains who saw eye to eye with the Congress. They did not see why local people should stick their necks out and risk Japanese reprisals in the event of an invasion when British power itself was still in the process of ebbing away. By September 1942 McCall had lost control of defence in the Lushai hills. The military would not properly co-operate with him and had decided to move towards a system of bigger and more costly levies of local men like the ones they were operating in the Chin hills and Manipur. But the effort was not entirely stillborn. Nearly 5 per cent of all men in the hills served in the armed forces during the war and many of the others participated in the various territorial defence schemes. The Lushai met the demands for labour, porterage and support put on them during the guerrilla wars in the nearby Chin hills. McCall himself believed that the Japanese did not strike through Lushai in the 1944 campaign precisely because they knew of the great readiness of the local population. In a subtle way, indeed, the Lushai began to act as citizens. One of their leaders, Buchawna, wrote that voluntary enrolment and payment for service contrasted sharply with the old 'slave-servant' mentality which the nationalists so much disliked.[121] Ironically, the mobilization of hill peoples across the region and the spread of the idea of people's rights were by no means an unmitigated blessing for the bureaucratic and military regimes which were to emerge in independent South and Southeast Asia.

## THE NAGAS, THE KACHINS AND THE ANTHROPOLOGISTS

Two hundred miles to the north of the Lushai, in the Naga hills, a British anthropologist, Ursula Graham Bower, was experiencing a different type of encounter with a more famous and colourful people of the hills. The Lushai levies provided a valuable buffer for British India but the Nagas were on the front line of the retreat of the British army and the refugees in 1942. Two years later they were once again at the heart of the war. The scene of these terrible events was one of the most beautiful and picturesque places in the world. Bower recalled her first visit to Nagaland a few years earlier. She had passed up and beyond Imphal with its thirteen European residents, ruined palace and tennis club, later to be the scene of one of the bloodiest battles in south Asian history. In the highlands, way beyond the reach of the Raj, she had stood on a mountain top. From this point 'the hills stretched away as far as the eye could see, in an ocean of peaks, a wilderness of sheep fields and untouched forests, of clefts and gulfs and razor backs which merged at last into a grey infinity'.[122] She had marvelled, too, at the people of the hills with their extraordinarily vivid coloured shawls, black kilts and cowrie necklaces. In 1942, however, the horrors of war eclipsed these picturesque scenes. Now, rather than taking anthropological photographs, she was down at the Assam railhead helping to prepare quantities of tea and sandwiches for the famished and ill refugees struggling over from Burma. She worked alongside Indian nationalist volunteers feeding their own even more desperate country-men.[123] With a few Naga orderlies she penetrated filthy troop trains of wounded soldiers who were too weak or too ashamed to come out to the canteens of their own accord. While the Lushai were scarified by rumours of war and the occasional bombing raid, war thrust like a horrible gouge right through the centre of Nagaland. The new and virulent form of dysentery brought by the refugees had wiped out thousands of Nagas, especially in cases where the village elders had refused to accept doctors, instead sacrificing pigs to appease the spirits of disease.

By the late summer, as the monsoon reached its height, the British began to go back on the offensive and to raise armed levies of local people as they had done in the Chin hills to the southeast. This was easier said than done. Some of the Zemi Nagas among whom Bower was now working were pro-British, especially some of the older men who had fought in the First World War or had served in the Assam Rifles. A few were actively hostile, remembering earlier British punitive raids when white men had burned their villages and slaughtered their cattle. The majority wavered. As her Naga interpreter put it: 'They say this isn't our war, and we ought to leave it alone. We aren't Japs, we aren't British, we are Zemi.'[124] Anyway, what would happen to his wife and children if he helped the British and then the Japs came? Bower was much less sentimental about loyalty and the benevolence of the Raj than McCall down in Lushai. She well understood that recruitment into the levies was a matter of complicated local politics. She attended a meeting at which fierce debates had broken out amongst the Nagas. People stood up and threw insults at each other. Some asked why they should fight for the British when they had never fought for the local Hindu ruling dynasties or the Naga local bosses. Others said that they owed the British something for stopping raiding and giving the hills a few roads and salt markets: 'Don't we owe them something for that?'[125] Bower perceptively noted that when a trickle of recruits came in it was from the helot classes, bound as field workers to the Naga aristocracy, or very poor people attracted by the low pay the British levies offered. Inter-tribal and inter-village rivalry deter-mined how people would jump in this crisis, not vague ideas like loyalty and patriotism.

Bower, as one of the few British people who understood anything about the hills, laboured hard to expand the size of the levies. She helped distribute weapons and replace the dangerous, ageing muskets which some families had hidden when the British disarmed the population after earlier revolts. Yet she was constantly on the defensive, patronized or ignored by male officers who simply would not believe that a woman could organize men for war. As one of the more sympathetic observed, she was always wrong twice: 'Once for being wrong, and once for being a woman.'[126] By the following autumn, however, Bower had helped to put into place the rudiments of a defence force which would be of great service in the battles of 1944 and '45. The legend of the 'Queen of the Nagas' was born, though as she always herself admitted, the prime actors were the Nagas and not Britons acting out the romances of Rider Haggard. She was, as she later wrote, built up as a propaganda tool.

A third zone of tribal resistance and Allied guerrilla activity lay a further 200 miles even further to the east in the hills of northern Burma beyond the upper Chindwin. This tract was important because it remained the only tenuous land connection between India and China, once the Japanese occupied Myitkyina. Here lived the Kachin peoples. On the east, their high, remote forested lands bordered on the Chinese province of Yunnan. This was a kind of no-man's land of shifting populations interspersed for part of the year with waving fields of red opium poppy, the fabled Golden Triangle. Following the collapse of the defence, the Chinese armies had retreated northeast into Yunnan, living off the land – or 'plundering as they went', as the British put it. Chinese soldiers established themselves semi-permanently near the southern Shan state of Kengtung and also further north in the Shan country north of the Shweli river. Until the early 1950s Chinese 'deserters' or settlers, depending on the point of view, were to carry on a kind of tug-of-war for territory along this northeast border, first with the Japanese, then with the British and finally with the government of independent Burma.

Throughout the war an Allied strong-point called Fort Herz held out in the far north of the triangle. Japanese patrols were present in force. They had a direct interest in holding on to the strategic airfield at Myitkyina in the south from which Dorman-Smith had made his exit in May. If the Allies regained Myitkyina, they could pour supplies into Chungking and strengthen the Chinese nationalists much more easily than they could from Assam. Yet as early as the summer of 1942 the Japanese were already themselves feeling the pain of 'imperial over-stretch'. They could never field enough troops to control fully this doggedly independent land. Some Chinese too crossed the hills from time to time. These were deserters from the nationalist army who regularly looted the Kachin villages and sometimes created more permanent settlements on the wrong side of the border. The British had never established more than a loose sovereignty over the Kachin hills, reasserted from time to time by armed patrols and the occasional punitive expedition. The area was part of the Burmese Frontier Areas Administration. This authority had spawned its own legendary body of scholar administrators who knew the local languages and sometimes married local women or took them as mistresses.

Both the Indian and Burmese authorities realized that it might be possible to co-ordinate a popular movement against the Japanese along the difficult terrain bounded by the Chin and Kachin hills. After the British rout it became critical. If the Japanese once got the feeling that the forested rim of the Indian empire was easy to penetrate, they might be tempted to set aside forces for invasion as soon as the monsoon was over in September. Once Rangoon had gone and the fall of Mandalay seemed not far behind, Dorman-Smith had sent one of his most trusted Frontier Service officers, Henry Noel Cochrane Stevenson, to co-ordinate guerrilla units in the hills known as the Chin and Kachin levies. Stevenson had been in the hills since 1926. He was extraordinarily well-connected with the local chieftains and Christian pastors, and was widely regarded as an almost fanatical supporter of the hill peoples, their way of life and their claims to independence from the 'effeminate' plains Burmese. His enthusiasm was given a scholarly edge in London University where he trained with the world-famous Polish-born anthropologist Bronislaw Malinowski. The young London-educated anthropologist Edmund Leach, who had learned Kachin and Shan before the war, later joined him.

Leach's service in the hills, as he himself freely admitted, was of much more significance to anthropology than to the course of the war. He first found himself recruiting Kachins for the Burma army and then after the Japanese invasion he was seconded to what he called the 'crazy cloak-and-dagger outfit' run by Stevenson. Leach carried out intelligence work on the site of his earlier anthropological investigations, but this became pointless when his party lost its stores and radio. After seven weeks of walking he struggled into Kunming and was flown off to Calcutta, weak with dysentery. To the quiet relief of the military, Stevenson himself was also out of commission for months as the result of a parachuting accident and his place was taken by a retired Australian officer of the Burma police. Soon, Leach was again lurking in the hills around Fort Herz with a radio set. But relations with his chief became so bad that he was reduced in rank and shunted off into the Civil Affairs Department for the duration of the war. Leach's adventures were, he wrote, 'a strange mixture of the absurd and the horrible', but he had learned to appreciate the great variety of the types of Kachin society and language and this became the basis of his later academic writings.[127]

## THE MONSOON OF 1942:
## AN UNNOTICED TURNING POINT

In the short term, the early monsoon of April 1942 and the stubborn resistance of the tribal levies on the hills of the northeast gave British India a breathing space. No one realized it at the time, but this was one of the turning points of the war. Far distant in the Pacific Ocean on 4 June, Admiral Yamamoto stood horrified and groaning with apprehension on his quarter-deck as he learned that the Japanese navy had lost three aircraft carriers in a great battle near Midway island. But even if the long-term outcome of the war had already announced itself, the medium term was still fraught with danger. In Delhi the authorities were deeply pessimistic about India's chances of survival should a full-scale Japanese attack develop again in the autumn. India did not have enough troops to prevent invasion and penetration at all points along the east coast and Ceylon, if, as seemed likely, the British had permanently lost naval supremacy. Strategists argued that India Command should attempt to put in place an impregnable defence at two points. Calcutta was to guard the critical coal and iron resources and the munitions industries of Bengal and Bihar. Colombo, which, after the loss of Hong Kong, Singapore and Rangoon, remained the only first-class naval base in the East, should also be defended. In addition, most experts wanted to put together a mobile defence force. This would strike back at a Japanese invasion on the coast around Madras. It was also essential, they thought, to build up the Indian air force as rapidly as possible. Claude Auchinleck, now commander in the Western Desert, pondered on the fate of the Indian empire which had been the scene of his whole career. He was convinced that, should the choice between holding India and holding the Middle East present itself in earnest, India must be saved first: 'India is vital to our existence – we could still hold India without the Middle East, but we cannot hold the Middle East without India.'[128] Most of his military colleagues would have said that withdrawal from the Middle East would have been a virtual declaration by Britain that the war was being lengthened by three years. Churchill himself bridled in fury whenever Auchinleck counselled caution in the Middle East and the reinforcement of India. These huge strategic dilemmas pointed up the excruciating military problems which had now all but buried the British Empire as a world power.

# 4

# 1942: The Abyss and the Way Back

## THE RAPE OF MALAYA

In the silence of the fall, the people of Singapore waited anxiously to see how their new masters would reveal themselves. Many were to remember the sound of Japanese troops singing in the distance. By the agreement between Yamashita and Percival at the Ford factory on the evening of 15 February, Yamashita's men were ordered to keep out of the city. However, in the front-line suburbs the victors began to seize the spoils. Weary and hungry, ill-shod, suddenly in a city legendary for its sartorial elegance, the Japanese visited homes and demanded food and clothes. Some tried to pay for what they took; most did not. People remarked on the Japanese fondness for bicycles, watches and pens. Private cars were requisitioned. The zealot Masanobu Tsuji went on a personal crusade, taking the names and slapping the faces of soldiers negotiating larcenous 'bargains' in luxury shops.[1] The Japanese responded brutally to any looting by the general population. In Singapore and Kuala Lumpur and elsewhere, heads were placed on display at strategic intersections, to perhaps most shocking effect in front of the ultra-modern Cathay Cinema in Singapore. The Raffles College student and future prime minister Lee Kuan Yew speculated 'what a marvellous photograph this would make for *Life* magazine'.[2] At Fort Cornwallis in Penang, two men were beheaded in public while ghoulish crowds gathered to watch. In Kuala Lumpur, where heads were displayed on spikes on Batu Road, someone placed 'Craven A' cigarettes between their lips; others had set up a gambling stall across the street to capitalize on the spectacle.[3]

Singapore city was placed under the Kempeitai, the military police, who moved into a Japanese hotel, the Toyo on Queen Street, and set up road blocks. These checkpoints were volatile places. The soldiers manning them reacted violently to the confusion and resistance that ensued when people began to move around again in search of family and food. But people had learned from tales of the China campaign that a sentry was a 'mighty lord', and that to bow to him was to show the respect due to the Emperor himself. This offended the Muslims: to them, it was 'as if we pray'.[4]

Malaya had been bombarded with the crude racial stereotypes of Japanese in British propaganda and in the cartoon art of the National Salvation movement. People were unprepared for the tough, bearded men they encountered in the first wave of the occupation; they were noxious too from two months in the field. They were not prepared either, despite the grim predictions, for the full savagery of their arrival. The hospitals were the first target. At Alexandra Hospital in Singapore, after the bitter fighting nearby on the western outskirts of the city, a terrible retribution was taken. The doctors who met the Japanese at the hospital entrance were slaughtered and many patients were bayoneted in their beds. Around 400 others were crowded into an outhouse overnight, later to be killed. The Asian doctors on duty were aghast as they watched the soldiers smashing the X-ray machinery. 'Why were they like lunatics, their eyes, just like lunatics?'[5]

In the first euphoria of conquest the Japanese took the women they found. There is evidence that, in China and elsewhere, Japanese commanders at least tolerated rape as part of a 'scorched earth' policy and to encourage aggression in their men. In 1941 only two soldiers in the entire Imperial Army were convicted of rape.[6] As Low and Cheng wrote in 1946 in a vivid memoir entitled *This Singapore: Our City of Dreadful Night:*

The raping varied in intensity. Some localities suffered more and some less. As was natural, it varied also according to the characters of individual soldiers. Some did it sadistically and brutally, booted and belted as they were, the Knights of Japan, without fear and without reproach; some did it indifferently as men answering mere calls of nature; some shame-facedly, mindful perhaps of the mothers who had borne them and the wives who were suckling their young in Japan. Their victims steeled themselves to accept the inevitable in as seemly a manner as their philosophy and good sense dictated. It would have been foolish to shout their disgrace from the house-tops.[7]

There were men who sought to ingratiate themselves with the new masters by pointing out where pretty girls were to be found. In the Singapore Improvement Trust flats in Tiong Bahru, soldiers seemed to know where to locate the cabaret girls who lived there. Residents thought that the watchmen had tipped them off.[8] Taiwanese pimps saw easy money to be made supplying the officers with women. Families took refuge in the rural outskirts of the city, such as the rubber plantations of upper Serangoon. Here a bush intelligence system operated. 'Yee lai lo', was the cry: 'They are coming'. The women would then hide in air-raid shelters. In the midst of more general reprisals on their community, Chinese girls were most at risk: some dressed as Malays and hid in their kampongs.[9] In Penang there were rumours that some women from respectable families had been attacked. The military command punished offenders here, at least. Up-country their soldiers perhaps behaved with less restraint; in Johore they were said to have raped systematically, but there were also better prospects to evade them: parents shaved off their daughters' hair to pass them off as boys, or dyed it grey. If caught, the girls' clothes were shredded and their breasts and genitalia exposed. The scale of the rape of Malaya is unclear. Many local accounts speak of it, but do so in veiled and general terms, just as the eye-witness accounts were themselves spread at the time. So it was left to pass out of the memory of the living. 'For', as a Chinese chronicle of the occupation put it, 'this is one of those things in life concerning which the stark truth is neither desirable nor relished.'[10]

In Singapore, Yamashita installed himself in Raffles College and surveyed the situation. The diarist 'Mr Nakane' was with him. British soldiers were still in the grounds, playing ball: 'they seemed so glad for no war, any more'.[11] But no delegations of local notables came to receive Yamashita. He faced a sullen, hostile population. For Yamashita, the last-ditch defence of the island, particularly the tenacious resistance of the Chinese irregulars at the end, had convinced him that the entire Chinese population of Singapore was a security threat to the Japanese Empire. His 25th Army intended to move on, to Sumatra; only a much smaller defence force was to be left behind. He therefore ordered a mopping-up operation, a *genju shobun* or 'severe disposal', of the hostile Chinese. There has been intense debate as to what this term meant: as to how far Yamashita's men exceeded his own intentions, and as to who was ultimately responsible for what followed. This issue dominated the war crimes trials after the war, and demands for accountability since. Yamashita claimed that he had no knowledge of how his orders were implemented. He was hanged for other crimes, but not tried for those in Malaya. Other evidence suggests that Lieutenant Colonel Masanobu Tsuji played a key role in prosecuting the policy from the outset. He too was never indicted for his part in it.[12] The senior military hierarchy tried to distance itself from the event. As the order was passed down to the chief of the defence force, Major-General Kawamura Saburo, he questioned it, but was told that it had Yamashita's firm sanction. He authorized the Kempeitai commander in the city, Lieutenant-Colonel Oishi Masayuki, to carry out the task according to 'the letter and spirit of the military law': justice should be the guide for punishment. But it was unclear what legal process, if any, was to be followed. In the urgency and fury of the conquest, the implication of the orders was clear: it was a licence for summary killing. Those outside the city claimed to know little of the ferocity that was unleashed.[13] 'Mr Nakane' reported the event in a matter-of-fact way on 21 February. 'F and I went out to cruise around the streets to see how the personal examination is being carried on. Those who were to be killed . . .' he noted, 'were [ . . . ] in the separate group'.[14]

The *sook ching* – or 'purification by elimination', as it became known – was well underway by this date. It began on 18 February, when Chinese were ordered to report to screening centres. Some felt it was a call for registration for work. In some places the women, children and aged were summoned; where this occurred they were the first to be dismissed. In one case, a few hundred 'very young girls and young women' were concentrated in a machinery workshop store. They were released following the intercession by priests with a high-ranking officer. But the main targets were men of military age, aged fifteen to fifty. Some of the screenings lasted hours, or even days. The scene at Victoria Road was typical. The men squatted in the street. At its end, there was a long table, behind which sat an officer and very young Japanese lady, a resident from before the war, dressed in a local *sarong kebaya*, who asked questions about language, schooling and residence.[15] An individual's answers to these questions were critical. A key category of men who were separated out were those who had been active in the China Relief Fund. The Japanese had collected their names from the newspapers and even, it was said, from records seized from the Bank of China which listed the office-holders. A man who had worked for its head, Tan Kah Kee, as a motor-repair mechanic was tied to a motor-cycle and dragged away. But the 'King's Chinese', who pleaded that they were less involved in the struggle for China, were also marked men. Many Straits Chinese had served in the Volunteers, and the Japanese made no distinction between the enlisted men of the Volunteers and the irregulars of Dalforce. Government servants were all at risk. Also vulnerable were Chinese schoolmasters. To wear spectacles was dangerous. So too was to bear tattoos, the indelible mark of a Triad connection. Men who spoke the Hainanese dialect were another target, as the Japanese believed them all to be communists.

There was an arbitrariness and haphazardness to the process. Contradictory orders arrived for the officers involved. In some cases men were sorted *en masse* on the basis of their response to general questions with a simple show of hands, or they were sorted by category: *towkays*, government servants, hawkers, students.[16] Some were given slips of paper stamped in Chinese, 'Examined'; others were not. Those whose skin was stamped dared not wash for long afterwards. People who avoided the screening tried to take an impression of the mark from others. A gesture of the hand, the nonchalant swish of an officer's rattan cane, and an individual would be led away. At some screening centres the men were paraded before hooded informers. These were said to be renegade Taiwanese, betrayed communists and police detectives. Men searched their memories for people they could have offended. There were lucky escapes. The Indonesian communist Tan Malaka, incognito as a Chinese schoolteacher, walked through with his school students. The Raffles College student, and future prime minister Lee Kuan Yew was singled out once, but dodged back in the crowd on the pretext of fetching his belongings and passed through at a second screening unchecked. The veteran Straits Chinese leader Lim Boon Keng was hauled out of a line. Only the intervention of a Japanese officer who knew him from before the war saved him. The soldiers involved were under intense pressure to complete the process quickly. Some Japanese officers tried to intercede. The former press attaché Mamoru Shinozaki, newly released from Changi jail, was now working for the Foreign Ministry protecting neutrals; he began to issue safe-conduct passes to Chinese.[17]

The lucky ones filed through the gates of the makeshift screening centres and made it home. It was only very slowly that the fate of those who were taken away was known or, rather, began to be imagined. Few of those taken survived and no bodies were recovered to be buried by their families. The story is known only in fragments. The Malacca Volunteers, for example, were kept at Race Course Road on rice and water and what they could buy from hawkers until the morning of 28 February, when they were marched to Tanjong Katang, and then taken by truck to Bedok on the east coast. Their belongings were stripped from them. There, B Company and some stragglers from other groups, around ninety of them including five Malay officers, had their hands tied behind their backs. They were marched to stand alongside three trenches. The Japanese troops then opened fire: ten rounds, and then they moved on to the next group.[18] Memoirs of Chinese who survived these screenings and the massacres that became known as the *sook ching* speak of the difficulty of recording the emotions they felt. There was a silence to the proceedings. One account of another massacre on the beach at Changi recalls that there was no calling out or wailing. The handful of people who escaped did so by playing dead under the bodies of their comrades. British troops were put to work burying the victims. It took nearly three weeks.[19] Indiscriminate massacres occurred in outlying areas of the island until early March. A spectral presence would be felt at these places for several generations; the killing field at Telok Kurau was known as 'haunted hill' thereafter. Its residents would turn up in their vegetable plots the bleached bones of those gunned down.[20] 'Digging in the outer fringe of the town', wrote one prison diarist, 'we turn up a skeleton: was this a friend?'[21]

The killings moved up the peninsula. Again, violence was perhaps at its bloodiest and most indiscriminate in Johore. The Chinese of Johore Bahru were marched through a gate. One in five were removed and taken to dig their own graves at the Civil Service Club. Others were machine-gunned along the sea front. The Eurasian community was massacred in a house in a small village just outside the town. In the main settlements of the state, mass graves and memorials mark the terrain; in smaller Chinese villages entire communities perished, including many refugees from Singapore.[22] The white terror also followed the Malacca Volunteers home. Those who escaped the fall of Singapore were handed over to the Japanese on their return. Japanese sentries would feel their shoulders to see if they had been carrying a rifle. Many Volunteers were spared on the intervention of a Japanese woman resident, now working for the chief of police. As searches went on in Malacca photographs of Chinese personages, even of the royal family on walls or stashed in doors, became incriminating evidence. Men used acid to remove their tattoos, leaving tell-tale scars.[23] There were further extensive killings all along the line of the Japanese advance: in Seremban, Taiping and other towns. In Ipoh it came later, in April, when suspects were concentrated in the local amusement park. In Penang, where the Japanese did not have to fight their way into the city, there were still intermittent round-ups throughout the early period of the occupation. The full toll is not known. The war crimes trials put the figure at 5,000 – Chinese sources at ten times this, for Singapore alone, and perhaps 20,000 more for the southern states of Malaya. Given the lack of information about the rural areas, the larger estimates seem to be closer to the truth.[24]

It was under the threat of a second series of screenings, and perhaps a wholesale massacre, that the Chinese leaders sought to come to terms with the Japanese Empire. In the wake of false reports that Tan Kah Kee and others had been arrested or killed, the Japanese cast around for a community leader. Lim Boon Keng, after his rescue from the massacres, was sent to a meeting with a Japanese commander. He declined the role on the grounds of age (he was seventy-two) and ill health. When his wife, or in some reports his son, was detained by the Kempeitai, Lim capitulated. He was asked how the Chinese thought they could atone for their opposition to the Japanese. To frame an answer, Lim went to a 'millionaires' club' of the Chinese community, the Goh Loo Club, where some of the China Relief Fund leaders were congregating after the screenings, some of them bloodied. An approach to the Japanese was brokered by two men who became self-styled protectors of the Chinese community. One was a Taiwanese translator, Wee Twee Kim, who had been in Japanese employment before the war as a store-keeper in Singapore for the Japanese retailer Nanyo Shoko. He posed as an ally of the China-born residents who had been closest to the China Relief Fund. The other was the omnipresent Mamoru Shinozaki. He was to have a rather broad role in the municipality in Singapore as head of the Education and later the welfare departments, but he acted principally for the Straits Chinese. Shinozaki would later claim that this role stemmed from his name: *Sino*, China and *zaki*, cape. He had a fondness for Western women and waltzes. Shinozaki had been kicked out of an earlier posting in Berlin after a romantic liaison with a local woman had upset the Japanese ambassador's wife. In Singapore, Shinozaki's Eurasian mistress was also a line of intercession which helped preserve her community. These kinds of relationship would be vital to surviving the occupation.[25]

A series of tense meetings followed in the Kempeitai headquarters. At the first, the Chinese leaders asked for their countrymen to be released. The Kempeitai colonel Oishi Masayuki dismissed them: 'This is not for you to request. Get out of here, all of you!' A second interview, with Takase Toru, an intelligence officer, at which the Chinese community offered to put its wealth at the disposal of the Japanese administration, broke down in a similar vein. '*Bakayaro* [Bastard]. All your money and even your lives are at our disposal.' The tension deepened with news of the massacres in Johore and more arrests of leading *towkays*. After a few more tense meetings, a way forward was found. It was clear that the Japanese did not merely want cash, but atonement.[26]

At a final meeting the Chinese leaders signalled this, putting both their wealth and their lives at the Japanese government's disposal. Takase told the leaders, through a translator: 'I am an authority of Southseas Chinese and the part they play in development of Malaya. Now that you are willing to offer your lives and property, it shows that you now appreciate our kindness and respect our regime.' The Chinese of Malaya had given billions of dollars to the war effort in

China; they would atone by a gift of 50 or 60 million Straits dollars to the Japanese. Lim had the courage to protest that never before in the history of warfare had such a thing been demanded. This was not strictly true. The idea of *misogu*, or ablution, was a key element in the thought of the principal strategist of the military government, Watanabe Wataru, a veteran of the administration of conquered peoples in China. As he told the Total War Institute in Tokyo in 1941: 'The fundamental principle of my nationality policy is to require them to account for their past mistakes and to make them ready to give up their lives and property.'[27] But how were the Chinese to pay? The British had left only $120 million circulating in Malaya; on the eve of the capitulation, the currency reserves had been incinerated. Malacca, for example, had to raise $5.5 million, but the British had left only $1.5 million in its banks. Many wealthy Chinese had remitted funds abroad before the fall, to India, Australia and London. They were given a month to raise the money.

An Overseas Chinese Association was hurriedly formed to collect the 'donation'. This threw the disparate Malayan and Chinese-born leadership together as never before. Subscriptions were allocated on a state-by-state basis, but the actual assessment was organized by committees drawn from the different dialect groups. Each community was to be scrutinized by another; for instance, the properties of the Teochew Chinese were assessed by the Hylam; the Hylam by the Hokkien, and so on. Individual liabilities were assessed as a percentage of property value; in Singapore this was 8 per cent. Others were levied a tithe of the stock in their shops. Although the climate of fear led many to declare their assets, there was much evasion and the returns were slow, not least from the leadership. Lim Boon Keng himself failed to pay by the agreed deadline. Some former pupils raised his share. Singapore raised only 30 per cent of its quota and other states fared even less well: the Malacca representatives were detained. After an extended deadline of 25 April passed, just over half the amount had been found. The mood was desperate. Newspaper advertisements begged for cash, and for information on those who were evading payment. Chinese leaders from across the peninsula were summoned to Singapore, there to confront each other: 'Penang! What have you been doing?' At the eleventh hour, the 'life-redeeming' money was raised by sleight of hand. The Yamahama Specie Bank advanced the balance of $21.25 million on loan. It was the largest single bank loan in Malaya's history. At a solemn ceremony at the Fullerton Building, now the seat of the new administration, Lim Boon Keng, flanked by the other Chinese leaders, presented a cheque in a casket to the 'Tiger of Malaya', General Yamashita. The language of the 'gold offering' address to accompany it was abject:

During the past, the Chinese had been 'running dogs' of the British imperialists. They have maltreated the Japanese and they have helped Chiang Kai Shek to put up resistance against Japan. Now that the Imperial Forces have arrived, we are willing to repent and to respect the orders of the Japanese Military Administration. We now voluntarily offer herewith a sum of $50,000,000 to the JMA as token of our sincerity.

At the eleventh hour Chinese leaders had tried to substitute the word 'puppets' for 'running dogs', to save a modicum of dignity. They were in no position to negotiate. At the ceremony Lim fainted, but revived to read the address. Yamashita responded with a speech which concluded that the Japanese were descended from the gods, the Europeans, as fully explained by Darwin, from the monkeys. In the war between the gods and monkeys, there could be only one victor. Lim Boon Keng told friends that he was spending as much time as possible drunk. However, this first pan-Malayan Chinese movement, born out of terror, would have lasting consequences. So too would the memory of the *sook ching*. Thereafter, the watchword of the Japanese in regard to the Chinese was 'severity tempered with some benevolence'.[28]

## THE 'NEW MALAI'

The killing could not last indefinitely. The Japanese needed to govern. They now commanded all of maritime Asia and, indirectly, most of the mainland. Without air protection the Borneo colonies of the British Empire had fallen to Japan in early December 1941. The vital oil wells in Brunei and Sarawak had been destroyed. There had been a brief defence of Kuching, but the civilian population were terrorized from the air. Charles Vyner Brooke, the last White Rajah of Sarawak, took sanctuary in Australia, and the defending forces withdrew over the border to the territory of the Dutch East Indies. The Netherlands Indies had always been seen as a weak link in the chain of imperial defence in the Indian Ocean. There had even been talk, in the inter-war years, of offering some of its territory to appease Japan. But Japan's interests lay in the core areas of Dutch control, especially its oil reserves, which were desperately needed to fuel its war machine in China and Burma. Japan launched a determined three-pronged attack. First, towards Sumatra, where a fresh naval assault tore to pieces the British exodus from Singapore in small ships. Secondly, Japan moved to seize the vital oil wells of Borneo. Here Dutch scorched earth brought bloody reprisals down on the heads of civilians. The third strike was on Sulawesi and the spice islands, to sever communications with Australia and to isolate the island of Java. Although this had been Wavell's command headquarters in the last stages of the conflict, there was never a sufficient concentration of forces on Java to offer any hope of serious resistance. Like Singapore before it, the Allies could not reinforce the island fast enough by sea or air. The disastrous Battle of the Java Sea on 27 February made it futile to attempt to do so. When the Japanese landed on Java the Dutch position was untenable. On 8 March the final buttress of the much-vaunted 'Malay barrier' capitulated, and the flotsam of British Asia who had gathered there found themselves interned. The final link was Thailand. Thai forces had resisted the Japanese landings at Singora in the south, but the tide of war, and the British decision to bomb Bangkok in late January, gave Prime Minister Pibunsongkhram motive and opportunity to align Thailand with the Axis: 'Plainly speaking amongst Thais', he told his Cabinet, 'it is about time to declare war with the winner.'[29] A new imperial crescent in Asia had arisen.

Much more than with the old British crescent, war impelled the Japanese to draw these diverse lands into a unified system. A blueprint for this had emerged after 1940: the 'Greater East Asia Co-Prosperity Sphere', a regional system with Japan as its nucleus governed by the spirit of *hakko ichiu* [eight corners of the world under one roof]. The meaning of these terms was unstable and contested by imperial servants. What is more, the different corners of this world seemed to have a very different political status. Their prospects of 'independence' within the sphere were governed, according to the Total War Research Institute in February 1942, 'in consideration of military and economic requirements and of the historical and political elements particular to each area'. The future of the Buddhist lands of the mainland diverged from the mostly Islamic lands of the Malay archipelago. The latter were politically 'underdeveloped' and home to large concentrations of hostile Overseas Chinese: they were to remain 'permanent colonies'.[30] India lay beyond this system. There is little sense that the subcontinent ever loomed large in Japan's imperial vision. Its ambitions there were strategic: to strike at the root of British power in Asia, the Indian army, to break the mule trains of supply to China and, ultimately, to deal a death blow to Western influence in Asia by linking up with a German thrust to the Middle East. But in this global struggle the Russians checked Japanese ambitions in Asia at Stalingrad. After this point the impetus westward faded, to the disillusionment of Subhas Chandra Bose. And by the time the Japanese advance to the east had reached its limits in Timor, the tide of war had begun to turn with the American victory at Midway in early June 1942.

In his first declaration to the people of Malaya after the fall of Singapore Yamashita invoked 'the Great Spirit of Cosmocracy', by which he alluded to some vague ideal of unity. But this was in perpetual tension with the desire to strip Malaya of its assets of vital raw materials for an increasingly desperate war effort. There were deep divisions within the Japanese administration between the civilians, some of whom had happy memories of Malaya before the war, and the professional soldiers.[31] Yet, for a short period of time, Japanese rule entered a stage of constructive imperialism. Malaya and Singapore had been showpiece colonies of the West. In this sense, for all their perceived political backwardness, they occupied a symbolic place in the Japanese new order. Singapore had a special status. The Japanese well understood its opulent modernity. It became a laboratory for some of their most elaborate experiments in social and political engineering: an exemplary centre for the whole region. This was marked by the great Shinto shrines – monuments to Japan's 'national religion' – that were commissioned in the aftermath of the conquest. A war memorial was constructed on a forested side of the central reservoir, dedicated to the Amaterasu Omikani, the Sun Goddess, and the

Chureito, a wooden obelisk, reared up on top of Bukit Batok hill. They were built by British and Australian prisoners of war and became centres of pilgrimage for the Japanese soldiers and civilians that began to pass through Singapore once again in large numbers. On civic holidays, they became sites for orchestrated processions of loyal Malayans. They were ready for the first anniversary of the invasion, and Christmas 1942 was marked by the anniversary of the death of the father of Hirohito and of the fall of Hong Kong.[32] The Japanese refounded Singapore as Syonan-to–or 'light of the South'. It was unfortunate for them that the mandarin rendering of Syonan-to, 昭南島, could be punned with 受難島, *shou nan dao* – 'island of suffering'. Penang was renamed after the premier, Tojo-to – but this never had quite the same resonance.

By the end of 1942, the peninsula had become 'Malai'. A military command structure was grafted onto the pre-war Malay States, and whilst civilian governors were appointed to them, they were subordinate to the army. Watanabe's policy was formally to acknowledge the sovereignty of the Malay rulers. But they were to surrender their effective powers to the emperor; the analogy was the abdication of the Tokugawa Shogun in the Meiji Restoration of 1868 that had created the modern state in Japan. Ironically, one of the most ardent advocates of this approach was the last of the Tokugawa line, the Marquis Tokugawa Yoshichika. The 'Tiger Hunter' had been a regular visitor to Malaya in the inter-war years, and had been given royal honours by the Sultan of Johore, and this friendship brought him to the fore as a political adviser to the military government. He wanted to rationalize the great wheel of kingship by creating an expanded Johore monarchy which would encompass most of the central peninsula, including Kuala Lumpur, alongside four smaller kingdoms in the north. The Malay rulers would retain only religious powers and would be obliged to 'give the way of Shinto a concrete expression in their realms'. However, as the political and military situation deteriorated by the middle of July, Premier Tojo instructed military administrators to draw back from such schemes. They were not to impose Buddhism or Japanese morality on conquered areas, and to practise non-intervention and circumspection with regard to local religion and customs. Nevertheless, US intelligence reported in 1944 that the Japanese viewed the rulers as 'minor officials'.[33]

The Malay sultans resented Japanese encroachments on their status, but there was little they could do to prevent it. The Sultan of Johore's relations with the Japanese were cordial – in an early gesture he presented three zebras and one Australian cassowary to Tokyo Zoo – but little more; he retired to his estates and spent his time riding. It was said that his son had fled Malaya to avoid being manipulated onto the throne in his father's stead.[34] Indeed, in Selangor, where a succession dispute before the war over an unsuitable candidate had ruffled Anglo-Malay relations to an unusual extent, the existing sultan was removed and replaced by Raja Musa Uda, a man whose accession the British had blocked in 1936 on the grounds that he was unfit to take the throne. The Japanese festooned these arrangements, as had the British, with ornamental pageantry. But when, after a conference in Singapore, the sultans were impelled to visit the Syonan Jinja and Chureito, the Shinto shrines, the underlying tension was plain. The Japanese were less respectful of the etiquette of the Malay courts, which some British residents had made their life-long study. At one point the old Sultan of Johore was rebuked for leaning on his stick before Japanese officers. 'Mr Nakane' described taking tea and cakes with the ruler of Negri Sembilan in July, where he was entertained by traditional dancers clothed in the yellow of royalty: 'one of them had such a big tits swelling and hanging which made me so hot. I touched it and burnt my passion awfully.'[35]

Unlike in Burma, there was no national army in the baggage train of the Japanese conquest of the Malay peninsula, and the group of indigenous fifth columnists who had gravitated to the Japanese were already steeped in disillusion. In Singapore they joined forces with more young radicals who had been freed from jail. Among them was the Kesatuan Melayu Muda (KMM) leader Ibrahim Yaacob. He and his associates donned armbands and elegant military-style attire, and volunteered their services to the new regime. They gathered at a house set aside for them, many of them at sea in the big city. The Indonesian radical Sutan Jenain confronted Ibrahim Yaacob: 'Now that you are captain of the ship, Ibrahim, where are you taking these KMM members?'[36] There was no clear answer. Many leading Malays were arrested, including the editor of the leading Malay daily *Utusan Melayu*, Yusof bin Ishak. Soldiers of the Malay Regiment faced internment or worse. The KMM vice-president, Mustapha Hussain, interceded for them, but he did not manage to save them all from execution; this was a failure that would haunt him for the rest of his life. The Japanese made it clear that they saw Ibrahim's party, as 'a cultural association' and little more. By June the KMM was banned. Ibrahim continued to play a propaganda role for the Japanese, but most of the activists left Singapore for the smaller towns of the peninsula, where they took the organization underground.[37] Much of the old Malay elite had drawn back in a similar way. The scourge of Sultan Ibrahim, Onn bin Jaafar, like many of his kind, took modest employment as a food-control officer. In the north, Tunku Abdul Rahman, who had prevented his father the Sultan of Kedah from becoming hostage to the British, settled to the role of district officer. He was an able man. He had, after a protracted period of study, acquired a law degree at St Catharine's College Cambridge, but had a reputation as a playboy in the state. He used his new role to build up a reputation for a genial style of administration, and honed what was a well-disguised political shrewdness. In a sense, such men moved back to the land and closer to the people. If they could not always protect their areas from some of the worst excesses of Japanese administration, such as the labour mobilization for the Burma–Thailand railway, they were able to challenge, from their position of local knowledge, the wholly unrealistic Japanese demands for peasants to grow crops such as cotton instead of rice. This cost Tunku Abdul Rahman his job. As the occupation progressed, these strategies of obstruction became more aggressive.[38]

Most of the other communities of Malaya were viewed by the Japanese with suspicion. The Eurasian population was particularly exposed. Within the ethnic division of labour of British Malaya they were seen as a central collaborating group. Their leaders were particularly aware that any signs of defiance would spark reprisals. The community did not have the wealth of the Chinese as a buffer to protect them. In April the Eurasians of Singapore were told to report as a community for screening. Many first-generation Eurasians of European parentage were interned and a red badge was given to those of Eurasian parentage. They were the target of vitriolic attacks. 'The majority still cling to their old idea of "European respectability" and superiority', sneered 'Charles Nell' in the *Syonan Times*; the community had to prove that they were 'men and not spineless gutter-snipes'.[39] Throughout the occupation this community experienced unrelenting anxiety. The Singapore Eurasian leader, a medical doctor, C. J. Paglar, earned himself much enmity, and later a treason trial, for coming forward to head an All-Malaya Eurasian Welfare Association.

The notables of Malaya who had not fled the country were in an impossible position. In Penang, for example, it was those most closely associated with colonial rule who had been forced to surrender the island; they had boxed up the statue of Queen Victoria and come forward to restore order. Thereafter they sought to step back and continue to serve their communities in a modest way. The Cambridge-educated Lim Cheng Ean, who had named his house Hardwicke after an English lord chancellor, took up a magistracy in the outlying settlements of the island. Much of the fabric of law and administration would be unchanged. The Japanese were content to allow the civil courts to continue to implement the legal codes of the Raj, if according to 'Nipponese spirit and the Nipponese laws'.[40] The workings of the courts were capricious and dangerous for those representing the accused. Some lawyers stayed away, but professionals like Lim learned that in the implementation of the old law there was a measure of protection for themselves and their communities. Chinese *towkays* who signed up to the Overseas Chinese Association argued that they had bought time and protection for the community. But the dilemmas they faced would become more acute as the occupation wore on, and the Japanese made renewed demands upon them.

Meanwhile, over the fear a veneer of normal living had to be restored. The people of Malaya had to adjust to their new masters. The new arrogance of the Nippon-zin was alarmingly at odds with their complaisance as barbers and traders. In Johore, for example, many Japanese officials, including the chief civil administrator Naka-jima, were ex-businessmen with interests in the state. But whilst some friendships were resumed, there was more often discomfort at the new role of Japanese who had been well known before the war. The architect of the $50 million 'gift', Takase, crowed at Chinese leaders: 'I had been to Malaya three times before, and I had seen many of you at dinner table. I know many of you but you had not paid any notice to me then.'[41] Getting to know the Japanese was fraught with cultural incomprehension. Their unbending obedience to orders was completely alien to the natural anarchism of local urban life. From an early stage the Japanese military sought to pass on their ethic of discipline. All-too sensible of their dignity, they were quick to inflict indignities on others. The culture of face-slapping appalled Malayans, as it did Burmese, Vietnamese and Thais. Lee Kuan Yew would later argue that it was this that turned him into an anti-imperialist. Yet in other ways, the Japanese could be disturbingly informal. Lee's fellow student Lim Kean Siew was astonished at the sight of soldiers un-buttoning their trousers everywhere, mostly along the roadsides, 'peeing willy-nilly and farting openly'.[42] The fabled cleanliness of the Japanese seemed to be a myth. Much later, there was private mirth at the affectations of the new rulers, such as the officers' penchant for wearing tweed in a tropical climate, the inevitable effects of which they disguised with liberal usage of eau de cologne. Yes, a Japanese writer in the *Syonan Times* responded: the Nippon-zin were a vain people. But 'vanity has little by little carried us beyond [our] proper realm'.[43]

The heavy-handedness and sudden violence of the regime often stemmed from ignorance and linguistic frustration. After the fall of Singapore, the translator and diarist 'Mr Nakane' was put to work getting the fire brigade back to its feet. In private, he inveighed against administrative incompetence. At one meeting with fire officials he noted that 'Tsuji stood the official on his head. I did not approve of his excitement.' He was snooty about fellow officials who could speak neither a local language nor English. This kind of man was also 'extravagant in his style of living'. The war had been an excuse for 'robbing and misconduct'.[44] One source of expertise was an ex-residents' body in Japan known as the Malayan Association: about 500 of its members were persuaded to return with bank loans of $5,000 each. The regime received a further injection of talent and experience in October 1942, when 720 Japanese civil internees and 64 consular officials at Purana Qila in northern India were repatriated to Singapore in an exchange of prisoners via Portuguese Mozambique. Michael Sasaki was one of them. He had been born in Malaya, in Kedah in the north, and educated at an Anglo-Chinese school and

Raffles College in Singapore. On repatriation he was given his old job back as a purchasing agent for the Nippon Mining Company. Others went back to work in their hotels. Michael Sasaki was disdainful of the newer arrivals and of 'high officials' generally: 'They are fond of girls, wine and money. They were poor in Japan. And mostly those who were poor and not such important figures in Japan came to Malaya. They give certain privileges and rights to people and thus get bribes.' But Sasaki, like many of the repatriates, was recruited as a civilian interpreter for the Burma campaign; many more became intelligence officers. They had a hard time fitting into the new order. The Japanese-American former editor of the *Singapore Herald*, Johnny Fujji, was put into custody and sent back to Japan 'for further indoctrination with the Japanese spirit'. So too was a former Japanese interpreter with the Singapore Special Branch. Sasaki himself would later desert to the British.[45] There were also some repatriated Japanese Americans in the Imperial Army who could not speak Japanese and had no sympathy with its struggle.[46]

The deadly reprisals had died down by the middle of 1942, after which the Japanese military administration began to soften its approach. Yet in tandem with this, it wove elaborate webs of regulation. The Japanese undertook the registration of the entire population, something the British had never contemplated. Certificates were needed for residence, movement and purchase of food supplies. In the very early stages of the occupation, the first ever registration of bicycles was carried out. There were 125,000 registered in Selangor alone.[47] There was a proliferation of permits, permissions and licences for trades and services, including for dance hostesses; these were a source of income, as were licensed lotteries and the older monopolies enjoyed by the British on *toddy* and opium. To maintain the precarious good will of the regime, people had to play an active role in the creation of neighbourhood groups to acquire the insurance of 'good citizen' certificates. Known as the Jekeidan, they organized communities at all levels: divisions, sections, and heads of families. All males between eighteen and forty-five were members and eligible for military service. This added a phenomenal new reach to an administration which had hitherto ruled at a distance. In Kuala Lumpur, for example, the Chinese Jekeidan was divided into thirty-three sections with an aggregate of

20,300 members. In troubled areas they were used to restore order through vigilante action. In Perak, the pressure generated by the *sook ching* led to some bloody incidents and settling of some old scores between the wealthy property holders and criminal gangs seeking to take advantage of their vulnerability.[48] But in many cases these initiatives were cosmetic. As one member of the neighbourhood watch in Singapore put it, most of the comings and goings were not reported, it was too much trouble to do so. The watches were passed in drinking *goh kah pi*: brandy made from pineapple skins. The wealthy paid for stand-ins.[49]

For all its ambition, an understaffed, inexperienced and monoglot Japanese administration was more dependent on local knowledge than the British had been. Initially, the Japanese attempted to slash the bureaucracy down to one-tenth of its pre-war size, and dramatically lower salaries. But this could not be achieved given the new demands on government. Beginning with the police, the civil servants came back to work, often in higher positions than they had occupied before the war. The Japanese saw them as new cadres for the Greater East Asian Co-Prosperity Sphere. At the highest level, candidates were selected for an elite government college, the Syonan Koa Kunrenjo, which opened in mid May 1942. The Japanese modelled this in part on Chiang Kai Shek's *alma mater*, the Whampoa Military Academy. It looked to the small elite that was already being formed by the British at Raffles College and elsewhere. A small number of a particular pedigree were given 'Tokugawa scholarships' for study in Japan itself; some kin of the Sultan of Johore were among the first recruits. The regime was strict: long hours, callisthenics, codes of allegiance, and edifying tales of the Nippon *sheisin*, or élan. They were compelled under threat of punishment to speak Japanese. Their sports were kendo (stick-fighting) and sumo wrestling. The Malay students found it hard to adapt to bathing in public. In just over a year some 280 cadets had passed from the school in Singapore, and by the end of the war over 800 from a similar body in Malacca.[50]

Work was seen as liberation from old colonial ways and thought: 'Collars and ties go by the board', proclaimed the *Syonan Times*. Clocks were moved two hours forward to Tokyo time; the year to 2602, the seventeenth of Showa rule. Streets and public buildings were renamed and rededicated overnight. 'Stupid', thought 'Mr Nakane'. But the main weapon of cultural warfare was the promotion of the Japanese language. The clerical classes were told: 'Your future depends on a knowledge of *Nippon-go*'.[51] Classes became a thriving business, and schoolteachers rushed to learn it. The argument that Japanese would make a natural lingua franca for the people of Malaya was based on its similarity to Chinese. But in fact the Chinese-based *kanji* script was little used in schools; the *katakana* script was more successful. The results of this were mixed but, given that this was a society of great linguistic adaptability, particularly amongst the young, and well-attuned to the pragmatic acquisition of language skills for advancement, there were indications that, had the occupation continued, the Japanese language would have played a major role. More generally, war taught young nationalists the transformative power of language. A generation later, students would still remember the songs and slogans through which Japanese was taught, as well as their ironic counter-points: 'Nippon-GO!'

People eagerly embraced such opportunities to escape suspicion. 'The main thing is to have a badge: whether it's a school badge or whether it's a working badge.'[52] Gradually demand for local staff rose in some of the new branches of government. In addition to this there were the various companies and monopolies, the *butais* and *kumiais*, that were being established in Malaya. Many new recruits had no previous experience of administration. Older civil servants complained that young men and more particularly, young women, were pushing them out. As one civil servant complained: 'pudgy inexperienced girls were preferred to men who had all their lives been in clerical service'.[53] This trend was later reversed in the government service, but there remained a great demand for secretaries in the offices of Japanese commercial firms. Known as 'flower vases', they could not be taller than the Japanese. 'Syonan girls like their new jobs as waitresses', the *Syonan Times* claimed. Although the hours were long, from 10 a.m. to 11 p.m., there were many perks for women. One café, it was reported, offered free cosmetics, 'so that they can maintain a fresh complexion throughout the day'.[54] Through the 'Eyes of a Woman of Nippon', the women of Malaya were urged to emulate the Japanese women who were beginning to reappear: dress simply, they were told, seek 'enjoyment in housekeeping'.[55] Yet despite these admonitions, the war was to expand women's experience of waged employment.

The main target for Japanese policies of social engineering was youth. After the fall of Singapore the Japanese were obsessed by the vision of young people roaming uncontrolled on the streets. They were quickly blamed for the petty theft and vandalism that came with the collapse of civil order, and for the delinquent Western culture of the towns. Education was an instrument of order, but also of 'Nipponiz-ation': the shibboleths of the old colonialist thinking were to be swept away. When the schools began to be opened after May, the Japanese language was pushed hard, and teachers struggled to keep up with their pupils. Children in turn adapted to the new Japanese rituals and, by some accounts, gleefully subverted them by insisting on shouting, standing and bowing every time a teacher came and went from a classroom. War, for younger children, could be a time for curious and fascinating departures from routine and discipline as much as grinding hardship.[56] Teachers quietly worked to keep the established practices of colonial education going. Schools functioned around the older language streams and, in general, the English and Malay schools fared better than their Chinese counterparts. Initially, Chinese schools were abolished and the Chinese language was to be taught only as a subsidiary in new 'national' schools. When they were permitted to reopen, pupil numbers were low. Most of them had been subscription based, and resources were scant. Few Chinese schoolteachers were willing to put themselves forward; they had been among the principal victims of the *sook ching*. Many parents kept their children away from the schools, or taught them at home. Some never returned. Over the course of the occupation, book-learning became less important than learning to trade or grow food. Children grew up too fast.

The one exception to this was technology. For the first time the technocratic powers of the colonial state, diminished as they were by the war, were put into the hands of Malayans. The Japanese challenged the liberal-arts tradition of colonial education that sought to create clerks and peons. With the relative collapse of post-primary education in the form of the middle schools, which trained students between the ages of fifteen and nineteen, the main opportunities lay in technical schools. A college of engineering, Koto Kogyo Gakko, was set up in Kuala Lumpur in 1942. Government servants from the old technical departments constituted a third of the intake; most of the rest were Indians, a disproportionate representation, especially in a railway training school. Yet Malays too emerged from this in much larger numbers than pre-war. Malays were brought from the *kampongs* of Trengganu to the technical schools of Singapore. Their average age was twelve. They were then sent to the factories.[57] This substantially helped to create the blue-collar class on which the British were wholly dependent for the reconstruction of their colonies after the war.

This technocratic dream was punctured by the austerity of the war years. Only by early October was street lighting restored in Kuala Lumpur. The British scorched earth retreat had been dramatic, but it was not an all-consuming fire. Asian businesses had, for the most part, been left intact. There were also ample food stocks. The British had built up rice supplies, one of the more impressive achievements of Anglo-Malayan bureaucracy before it rolled up in late 1941. Although rubber and mining were slow to revive, other industries emerged. Kuala Lumpur and Port Swettenham, it was claimed, were becoming the 'veritable Osaka and Kobe of Malai'.[58] The area was a centre of import substitution industries. By 1943, forty different types of industry were established there, the biggest being soap manufacture (sixty different factories produced 23,000 cases a month) but also cooking oil, aerated water and biscuits. Penang was said to be producing 500,000 cigarettes and cigars a day from around seventy manufacturers. New Chinese and Indian entrepreneurs began to emerge. Local exhibitions advertised new products, and cash prizes for innovation: one winner was A. R. Menon of Selangor, for an electrical appliance of use in the rearing of pigs and an onion-based insecticide. In the case of rubber, the key was in finding new uses for it, rather than increasing its production.[59] This was satirized as mere 'soda effervescence'.[60] But it was also prophetic: it proved that, given the opportunity, the people of Malaya could demonstrate to the world that this land of tin, rubber, copra, timber and rich forest produce need not always remain a supplier of raw materials but could also be a large-scale producer of manufactured goods.

The great cosmopolitan worlds were slowly reviving. Raffles Hotel reopened as the Syonan Ryokan, an officers' club; the Chinese million-aires' club, the Ee Hoe Hean, the seat of Tan Kah Kee's resistance, opened an exclusive restaurant and bordello. By the end of March 'Mr Nakane' was to be moved out with Yamashita to the deadly campaign in the Philippines. On the weekend before he left he explored the city, one month after its fall. He went to dinner on the Saturday night with some of the recently arrived German and Italian officers. He spent the Sunday translating his diary and went out on the town. The consumerism of the city was in full flow. John Little had became 'Daimaru', and the choicest goods were marked 'For Nippon-zin only'. 'The stores were full of soldiers,' he observed, 'especially the watch shops.' So too were the brothels. The entry for the day carries the title: 'Fucking a Chinese girl for $3.00'. Already large numbers of women were being dragooned for the 'comfort' of Japanese soldiers. Nakane's departure was more sombre. He went back to the golf course where he had hidden in his foxhole during the last furious battle for the city. 'The garden was large and the water glittering. Could not think but the time when we passed here about a month ago. Very quiet. No bombardment, no shooting, we proceeded on it some way along its links . . .' He travelled on to the Straits of Johore, to the spot where he had landed. 'Still there were helmets floating on the seaside.'[61]

## DESPERATE JOURNEYS: BURMA IN LATE 1942

For ordinary Burmese, the events of the spring and summer of 1942 were as stunning as they were for the Malayans. Only one thing was certain: the days of British rule were over. The Burmese had always been world champion clairvoyants. Ancient prophecies had correctly predicted the overthrow of the Burmese royal house. Some of these went on to drop hints about the fall of the alien successor regime following a lightning strike. People now interpreted this to mean the Japanese invasion. Tin Tut was very sensitive to the Burmese popular mood. This senior ICS man had ended up in India with the exiled Burmese government after the British decided that he had had no part in U Saw's overtures to the Japanese. Pondering on the course of events after he arrived in Simla, Tin Tut drew attention to the profusion of apparently ancient sayings which predicted that the period of British rule would be short. One saying which was in circulation shortly after the fall of King Thibaw in 1886 ran like this: 'When Pan-Ni-I comes into power, the peacock banner will flutter.' Teahouse gossip insisted that Pan-Ni-I meant Germany, Nippon and Italy.[62] Peasants in remote areas took to tattooing themselves with symbols designed to make them invulnerable to weapons. This had also long been a sign that momentous events were in train. Tattooing had spread like wildfire before the 1886 revolt against the British conquerors and again during the 1930–31 peasant revolt led by the monk Saya San. This time, though, the gnomic prophecies which accompanied these outbreaks, such as 'The paddy bird eats the rice', began to give way to 'Asia for the Asians'.[63] To Ba Maw this meant 'Burma for the Burmans'.

By May 1942 it had become clear to the Japanese that they needed to work through civilian politicians. They needed a counterweight to the Burma Independence Army of which they were already deeply suspicious. Ba Maw saw an opportunity here to consolidate his position on the political stage. He helped organize a relief committee for the thousands of Burmese refugees who had gathered on the Sagaing ridge north of Mandalay. Many of these people were quite wealthy and were afraid of being robbed by their poorer compatriots. Ba Maw also got essential services going in Mandalay and Rangoon. On 4 June he delivered a clever speech over Japanese radio. He said: 'When I addressed you two years ago, I said we had a friend in the East. At that time I was not in a position to disclose that that friend was Japan. Burma is a nation in the making . . . The rapid progress of Japan fills in the breast of every Burman hopes of living a fuller political life.'[64] Ba Maw certainly contemplated a 'fuller political life' as he manoeuvred himself into a key position between Iida, the commander of the Japanese force which had occupied Burma, and the BIA.

Amongst hill people such as the Karen, Kachin and Shan political counsels were divided. In January 1940 the Shan chiefs had passed a loyalty resolution and declared their 'spontaneous and unanimous desire . . . that a territorial battalion should be raised in the Federated Shan States to give Shans the opportunity to undergo military training'.[65] But the complete collapse of British power in Rangoon and the south put a very different complexion on this. The chiefs of the southern Shan states knew only too well that if the Japanese controlled Rangoon, there really was no choice but to offer them allegiance. All the food and essential supplies for the more southern hill areas came through the port. On the borders of Chinese Yunnan Karen, Shan and Chin fought a long guerrilla campaign against the Japanese invaders, not so much out of love for the British but because the Japanese were invading their sacred territory alongside ethnic Burmese to whom they were deeply antagonistic.

Most communities were torn by doubt and seething with rumour. Amongst the Karen population in the eastern hills something called the Thompson Po Min movement had been spreading for some time in the atmosphere of crisis brought on by the Japanese advance north. Thompson Po Min seems to have been a millenarian shaman leader who with his brother Johnson Po Min were apparently associates of U Saw. Thompson predicted that the second coming and the end of the world would follow the Japanese invasion in short order.[66] He also preached a more mundane salvation. The leaders persuaded people that by buying a picture of Thompson and putting it in their houses with a Japanese flag, they would assure their protection from the invaders. This seems to have been both a money-making racket and a religious movement, a variant of what anthropologists call an invulnerability cult. Other Karen leaders remained loyal to the British and opposed the Po Min brothers. The authorities were slow to react and many families uprooted themselves in the course of a kind of schism and moved off to the mountainous parts of the Karenni states,[67] where the Japanese soon arrived. The fractious politics of faction and lineage, held in check for two generations by British frontier officers, broke out with a vengeance. Old political disputes and social divisions among the people often determined reactions to the war in all the hill and jungle territories.

In areas of south and central Burma which were directly affected by the fighting between the retreating British and the Japanese forces anarchy reigned. As the Indians left on their long and fatal trek to Manipur and Assam, the Burmese population had fled into the countryside, taking shelter in their home villages or in monasteries. A few attacks on Indians were recorded. Poor villagers looted the rich Indian merchants, the Chettiars, who had bought up their land during the Great Depression. Burmese women who had married Indians were sometimes the targets of abuse and derision as they trudged hopelessly along the roads. Yet many Burmese sympathized with both Indians and British. As Buddhists, they had compassion for the suffering refugees and put out small parcels of food for them or fed and gave them water as they waited exhausted at railway junctions waiting for the northward bound trains to start.

In general, the Japanese troops treated the Burmese population reasonably well in these early days. They tried to prevent local hoodlums in the train of the BIA murdering the Karens of the Delta and the Muslims in northern Arakan. By contrast, they behaved with exemplary savagery where they felt vulnerable and surrounded by enemies. Anglo-Indians and Anglo-Burmans were badly treated. The Japanese murdered all the wounded British soldiers they found as they entered Myitkyina and then proceeded to behead a large proportion of the male population of the town on the suspicion that they were British collaborators.[68] Most ordinary Burmese were still safe so long as they co-operated. Labourers quite liked the high prices paid for their services and there were even examples of marriage between Japanese and Burmese. Quite soon, however, local people became more wary. The Japanese military police or Kempeitai were to be avoided. Even ordinary troops had developed the habit of slapping the faces of Burmese for minor infringements of discipline or for irritating them in one way or another. To the Japanese this probably meant little. They slapped their own servants or menials in this way, but to Burmese Buddhists, for whom the head was the seat of divine wisdom, this was deeply offensive.

Thakin Nu, nationalist and later Burmese leader, gave a telling example of Japanese stupidity in this regard. Early in 1942 a group of villagers he knew decided to welcome the advancing Japanese with gifts. They were poor people and had little else to offer the liberators except bowls of rice, a traditional sign of welcome. When the villagers tried to present their little gifts, the Japanese brusquely slapped them, taking this as a silly distraction, or even an insult.[69] Nu turned this event to the credit of the Burmese peasants. He saw them on their return, bringing back their smashed rice pots and laughing helplessly at their own gullibility. Despite their proclamations of pan-Asiatic solidarity, the Japanese seemed hardly more culturally sensitive than the British and were certainly more brutal. Face slapping became a major issue. In the following year, the Japanese command, rather than prohibiting it altogether, forbade anyone below the rank of lieutenant-colonel to behave in this way.

Japanese troops indulged in other offensive activities: they bathed naked by water hydrants on the streets, to the horror of Burmese women. In some cases they were surprisingly cavalier with Buddhist shrines, stripping them of wood for cooking fires and otherwise violating them. As he escaped overland to India, Thein Pe viewed the eating and living habits of the Japanese soldiers with disgust: 'we cannot say whether or not they knew what a bed pan was. They were seen eating rice from one', he reported.[70] A later British compilation of anecdotes noted ponderously, 'The Japanese gastronomic habits had served them ill: that they ate dogs was observed to their discredit.'[71] But Japanese soldiers were extremely popular with the Burmese young. The troops were genuinely fond of children. They 'had made much of Burman boys and girls, given them sweet meats, taught them baseball, played football with them and taught them Japanese songs'. It was to be a 'golden age for children'.[72] Parents worried that their offspring were being alienated from them and that the Japanese were using their children to spy on them.

The middle-class Burmese of the cities, often distant from their rural roots, suffered particularly badly. Khin Myo Chit was married to a man who had been an employee in the Bombay Burma Trading Corporation but later joined the Criminal Investigation Department as a translator. Brought up as a strict Buddhist by her grandmother, she went through an atheist and communist phase as a Rangoon student in her early twenties. She frequented Thakin Nu's Book Club on the corner of Scott Market and knew most of the young radicals. Khin Myo Chit escaped the bombing of Rangoon as the couple were up-country desperately looking for a plot of land to buy. Later, as the Japanese invasion powered through central Burma, her family retreated to a monastery. They crouched under the pilgrims' shelters as explosions sounded all round them. Japanese troops burst into the compound in pursuit of the fleeing British, but they only seized her mosquito net and passed on. As the weeks passed, the community of refugees clinging to the security of the monastery grew larger and more diverse. Powerful men began to buy themselves special services and rights by making 'donations' to the monks. 'A sense of proprietorship' set in, violating the basic teachings of the Buddha, in Khin's view.[73] Infuriated by petty ritual and the hypocrisy of the monkhood, she fell out with her relatives and sulked on her own in a corner of the pilgrims' shelter.

Even the news from outside was troubling. An old friend who had enlisted in the BIA arrived at the monastery during the heat of June 1942. He whispered to Khin that no one really trusted the Japanese, despite their noises about Burmese independence. She resolved to leave the despised monastery and make the hazardous journey along the shattered railway system to Rangoon, where she still had friends. On the way she saw Japanese soldiers slapping the faces of Burmese civilians for no good reason. 'Everywhere we looked there was fear and anxiety.'[74] Reaching the shattered capital with Rs10 to her name, she saw pony-cart drivers going about with revolvers strapped to their belts because they had become administrative officers of one sort or another. The city was beginning to return to life, but huge revolutions had taken place in people's circumstances. Some had become rich overnight, trading in vital commodities such as cooking oil and cloth. Many professional people like Khin were reduced to poverty since they had no capital with which to buy commodities. British and Japanese paper money was now virtually worthless. Khin Myo Chit set herself up selling slippers in the bazaar. But she was a hopeless businesswoman, cheated by most of her customers.[75] Others fared even worse. Christians, Anglo-Indians and Anglo-Burmese, Karens – anyone, in fact, that the Japanese police believed might favour the British – were pushed to the bottom of the social scale. One Anglo-Burmese judge spent much of the war cutting wood. Some were imprisoned and killed by the Kempeitai. Indian Christian servants of the British population of Maymyo escaped into the nearby forests and remained there for much of the war.[76]

Burmese social life did not collapse completely over these months. During the summer and autumn of 1942 a semblance of normality returned to some of the southern towns and people who had fled the bombing slowly drifted back to any employment that remained. By early June General Iida had decided to work through Ba Maw and any other Thakins who were not too openly recognized as communists. He set up a 'preparatory committee' to consider the form of a future civilian client government. This was eventually to come into being a year later. As a former prime minister under the British, Ba Maw was skilled at finding cronies, friends and party members to fill offices in the districts evacuated by the colonial regime. In most localities the new political order emerged as a kind of compromise between the local Japanese commander, the local Burmese (or sometimes Chinese or Indian) 'big man' and an apparatchik sent out from Rangoon or Mandalay.

One of the latter was U Shwe Mra, Indian Civil Service, who was deputed to become district commissioner of Sandoway in southern Arakan, on the west coast of the country. To get to his new posting, he had to take a boat to Akyab and go south. His memoirs of this journey give a vivid picture of life in the early, confused months of Japanese rule in Burma.[77] Shwe Mra's new status and a signed letter from the Japanese commander quickly came into their own while he was still in Rangoon. A Japanese air-force officer arrived at his house to purloin his wife's piano. Having taken a look at the letter, the Japanese decided not to loot the piano after all. Despite the fact that it was Iida's and not Ba Maw's signature which carried the day, Shwe Mra and the other new appointees decided that bowing to the Japanese was not a solemn enough assumption of office. They went to the Shwedagon pagoda and 'solemnly pledged ourselves to serve our country to the best of our abilities'.[78] Since the only way to get to Sandoway fast was by Japanese troopship Shwe Mra was faced with the humiliating prospect of going to the Jubilee Hall, stripping off his clothes and lining up with hundreds of naked Japanese soldiers in order to get the required medical certificate. Only his Japanese interpreter saved him from this fate.

In early August, U Shwe, his interpreter, Mr Saito, along with a Japanese colonel and a mixed body of soldiers and civilians set off in an aged British freighter from the Sule Pagoda wharf in Rangoon for the port of Akyab. One telling feature of the voyage was the fact that two Japanese *bosans* (Shinto priests) and a Burmese Buddhist monk accompanied the colonel. Their job was to walk up and down the ship all day singing chants to keep evil spirits, and the RAF in particular, at bay. When they reached Akyab, they found that the local Japanese commander was already working through a body called the Peace Preservation Committee, which was later to become the kernel of Ba Maw's administration in the area. It consisted of teachers from the National High School, Akyab, and one fairly junior civil servant. Shwe Mra was concerned about how he, a former ICS officer, might be received. But Akyab had other, more pressing problems. This once bustling seaport now had a population of fewer than 500 people excluding the Japanese soldiers. Even the administrators slept on the floor and ate at a communal table where they were served with little more than rice. Sesamum oil, an essential for Burmese cooking, was virtually unobtainable, as it was to be for most of the war. In order to get their belongings off the boat the newly appointed district officer had to 'round up' a few stray Indian coolies, 'but it was no use relying on them. They were so weak and famished that we actually had to move the boxes from the ship to the wharf with our own muscle power.'[79]

Since almost all the staff of the local launches before the invasion had been Indians from Chittagong, U Shwe Mra had difficulty in getting an onward passage to Sandoway. His problems were compounded by the extreme caution of the Japanese colonel who was accompanying him. The colonel refused to leave until a particularly auspicious day had dawned. He again insisted on being accompanied by his chanting monks and Shinto priests as he journeyed even further into what he obviously regarded as a malevolent and spirit-infested countryside. The colonel's superstition was not without reason. Arakan must have been one of the grimmest places on earth in mid 1942. It had been the scene of mass deaths among refugees earlier in the year and then vicious communal rioting between Muslims and Buddhists. It was the first area to be subject to aerial attacks once the British had regained their balance. An epidemic of rinderpest had wiped out much of the cattle population, including the herd belonging to U Shwe Mra's mother. Only the arrival of a few administrators like him and the efforts of local people in the peace committees prevented the outlying parts of Burma collapsing into bandit-infested anarchy.

During almost the same period another Burmese, almost the opposite of the ICS man, was also making a journey and one that took him politically in precisely the opposite direction. This was Thakin Thein Pe Myint, the communist leader and close follower of Thakin Soe. Thein Pe hated the British. He was among those who watched the great palace of Mandalay going up in smoke in April, believing that the British were responsible for a final act of scorched earth barbarism. His hatred of the Japanese fascists was even greater. His decision to flee Burma was at least in part brought about by the fact that he had published diatribes against their policy in China and felt he was bound to be on the Kempeitai hit list. The political motive was also clear. Britain was now an ally of the Soviet Union against the Axis. The people's liberation struggle demanded that communists work with the Allies, at least until the anti-fascist war was over. For some weeks Thein Pe moved around Burma in disguise. At one point he floated down the Irrawaddy on a raft pursued by bandits. On another occasion an aggressive Japanese soldier forced him to clean his rifle. All the while he observed the living and eating habits of the Japanese with contempt. Finally, when the coast was clear, he decided to escape into India via Arakan. He took the route which the Burmese crown prince had taken in the war of annexation against Arakan in 1785. On his triumphal return, the prince had brought with him to the royal capital a great statue of Buddha Mahamuni, one of the most revered icons in the whole country.[80] Every Burmese schoolchild was brought up with this geography etched on his memory. So Thein Pe counted off the stopping points of the statue one by one on his mental map.

Braving leeches and avoiding Bengalis, who might, he thought, be Bose sympathizers and betray him, Thein Pe moved slowly north. Finally, he crossed Lushai military police lines into British territory and down into the Chittagong plains. He and his companions gave themselves up to Indian soldiers who 'looked at us as though we were untouchables'.[81] Thein Pe's reception by the British was mixed, to put it mildly. A young colonel who interviewed him seemed to be favourable to Indian independence and wanted an anti-fascist alliance. Later, 'Mr Fann', a former deputy commissioner in Tavoy and recently escaped from Burma, snarled at him, 'You Thakins are traitors.'[82] Finally, a short, fat British soldier who was guarding his detention cell turned out to be a communist and saluted him as a comrade.

Thein Pe's political difficulties were hardly resolved when he reached Calcutta. He needed to make contact with the Chinese nationalists in the city, if only to make sure that he was no longer dependent on the British alone amongst the Allies. He could not really confide in Indian nationalists, however, because he felt that they were so blinded by their anti-imperialism that they failed to appreciate the true horror of the Japanese regime. He noted ruefully how, 'having left Burma in order to be free of the fascists, we were captured by the Allied imperialists. Now we were endeavouring to regain our freedom with the help of the Allied imperialists' soldiers, Indian Communists and those who were on Chiang Kai Shek's side' and hostile to the Chinese communists.[83]

Thein Pe must have been one of the most frequently debriefed and interrogated Burmese of the whole wartime period. The British did not know what to make of him, instinctively distrusting communists, and by now wary of all Burmese. But he clearly had value at such a critical point in their fortunes. He was shunted from Calcutta to Delhi and then on up to Simla where the Burmese government in exile had come to rest in July. On the way up into the Himalayan foothills, Thein Pe visited Sir Paw Tun, the conservative former Burmese prime minister, at Solan. Here this slightly dotty representative of the old order lived close to the town's famous beer factory. In Simla itself Thein Pe spent much of his time sleeping and watching films in warm cinemas. He also cast a jaundiced eye on the dispirited assemblage of his former colonial masters. Dorman-Smith was, he believed, simply plotting to bring back capitalism to Burma. The senior Burmese ICS man present, Tin Tut, was, he wrote caustically, 'as patriotic a person as the ICS regulations allowed. He carried a bamboo hat and wore *hanza* [native] clothing.'[84]

As his health recovered, the young communist began to compose his polemic against the Japanese, *What Happened in Burma*. He gave extracts of it in lecture form to groups of disbelieving Indians, whose countrymen were already convulsed by the biggest revolt against British rule since 1857, the Quit India movement. His aim, as he put it, was to stop the British saying that all Burmese were traitors and to get the Indians to see the truth and not to romanticize the Japanese. He had not achieved much success in this before he moved off again to Chungking the following year. Here he worked as an anti-Japanese propaganda expert amongst the large Burmese and Sino-Burmese population that had been evacuated to south China in early 1942.

The hill station of Simla was a bizarre place at the best of times. Since the nineteenth century it had been summer camp for the whole government of India. The gothic pomp of the viceroy's house, the secretariats and numerous colleges and Christian churches had been unceremoniously plonked down on a typical precipitous Himalayan settlement, where hill men and traders in mountain produce met the entrepreneurs from the plains. Maharajas and other hangers-on of British rule had congregated there, spawning clubs, billiard rooms, cinemas, drinking haunts and southern counties-style general stores full of English jams, cheeses, cakes and preserves. During the Second World War the 'Magic Mountain' was a place alternating between staid pomposity and frenzy. One visitor noted aghast that 'society' still dressed for dinner, a practice which even the British king and queen had abandoned for the duration. The pressure on housing and service was acute. A whole host of newcomers came up from the plains: American journalists, Chinese generals, Special Operations Executives bristling with weapons. They mingled with a constant flow of Allied officers moving from the Middle East and the Staff College at Quetta to Calcutta and Assam, or vice versa.

Into this precipitous ant hill ventured, like unloved poor relations, what remained of the government of Burma. Journalists had played up the 'treachery' of the Burmese and the failures of the civil government. Dorman-Smith tried to salvage his unjustly maligned reputation while his wife contemplated her empty wardrobe. On 5 August she wrote 'Everything depressing up here – foul weather torrential rains and thick mists.' She set about making up new clothes from 'gorgeous Indian brocades'.[85] Meanwhile, rage and frustration drove these British and Burmese civil servants to a most extraordinary reappraisal of the whole history of British rule in the country. They instituted a kind of academic seminar which started in the autumn of 1942 and continued in minutes and meetings for the rest of the war. Their discussions gathered some urgency as it became clear in 1944 that a British reoccupation of the country was not only possible but now imminent. How could a revitalized and rebuilt Burma be retained within the British Commonwealth? The basic premise of all these outpourings was that the British Empire in Asia would be rebuilt as surely as day followed night. To a later generation, this confidence of mastery in the midst of defeat is quite extraordinary. One telling detail is that on 5 August 1942, while Indian refugees were still dying by their hundreds in camps on the Burmese border and Indian nationalists were about to rise in revolt, the British were not only talking about reoccupying their Southeast Asian empire, but actually extending it. Dorman-Smith, Leo Amery and Anthony Eden discussed by air letter the availability of civil administrators for the eventual occupation of Thailand. This was still a Victorian generation and the 'hell of a licking' administered to it by the Japanese had done no more than scratch the outer paintwork of its indomitable self-confidence.[86]

All this started as pie in the Simla sky. As Dorman-Smith said, the soldiers looked on the Burma civilians 'as more of a nuisance than a potential help'. What remained of the Burma army was scattered in camps all over India, leaderless, demoralized and often despised. The civil administration was dispersed between Calcutta, Delhi and Simla. Many of those Anglo-Indians who had survived the 'green hell' of the escape were concentrated in refugee hostels in the city of Lahore. One straw in the wind, though, was the fact that one of the shrewdest members of the former Indian commercial community in Burma, Vellayan Chettiar, came to seek out the exiled governor as early as August. He informed Dorman-Smith that the Indians all wanted to get back into Burma as quickly as possible as it was so much more 'attractive' than India.[87] He urged the British to deal with the Burmese 'traitors' who had handled the Indians so harshly during the evacuation. Chettiar had already heard that the Japanese had established an Indian Independence League in Rangoon and said that the British should be harsh with that, too. Dorman-Smith felt 'he was not very convincing on this point'. Chettiar's clarion call to subdue the Burmese traitors did not extend to Britain's enemies within India. He said that the whole Indian commercial community was in thrall to Gandhi and urged the British to make an immediate declaration of dominion status for the subcontinent. Cripps, Churchill's emissary to the

Congress, was getting on famously, he said, until London undermined him.

In 1942 the Simla seminar on Burmese history rapidly became an embittered debate about such 'traitors', racialism and the failure of British government. One of the early minutes was writen by Reginald Bertie Pearn, an old hand of the purest water, who had been professor of history in Rangoon University. He had written a history of Rangoon which had been, some said conveniently, destroyed in the Japanese invasion, though, in fact, this descriptive piece turned up again after the war. Dorman-Smith must have come to wish that his had not been the first contribution. Pearn took a lofty view of the question of Burmese loyalty to the Raj. The problem was that the old Burmese society had been destroyed, he wrote, and that everything had been fragmented down to village level under the British.[88] The Burmese could not conceive loyalty to anything beyond the parochial. Western education had offended the monks who had previously run the local schools. The European was regarded as 'a rascal and at best a money-grubber' because it was the worst British firms and 'impoverished mining prospectors' who had flooded into the country during the Depression years.[89] Immediately before the war anti-British propaganda had been allowed to flourish so that everyone began to think that 'socialism' and even the Japanese would be the saviours of Burma.

There was a lot of truth in what Pearn wrote. But when he described popular unrest as the product of economic disenchantment and alienation he was underestimating the widespread Burmese desire for independence. This was an independence which many Burmese could themselves remember, or which had been described to them by their fathers and mothers. Tin Tut replied to Pearn powerfully. The Burmese, he said, were astonished and horrified to be under foreign rule. This was the key to events in 1942. 'A Burmese child is brought up on history and traditions which have as their background the ancient glories of the past and it is with a shock that he realises in his adolescence that he is a member of a subject race.'[90] People remembered the independent Burma before 1886. This memory of old Myanmar (Burma) was a living tradition in a country where there was a high percentage of literate people who could read newspapers and books, while dramatic performances and monks' speeches renewed the sense of loss even amongst simple and illiterate people in the villages.

Tin Tut also drew attention to the cultural clash between Europeans and their subjects: 'The European in Burma dresses for his dinner, the Burman undresses for his', and so on. Anyway, how could the British denounce the Burmese for failing to defend their country against the Japanese when they had deliberately been excluded from the Burmese armed forces since 1886? What had really sparked Tin Tut's outrage, though, was the insouciance with which Pearn, this historian of Burma, had described the Burmese as a 'primitive people.' In response to this slight, Tin Tut marshalled his best Dulwich College and Cambridge venom. A particular problem, he said, homing in on Pearn, had been the racialism and incompetence of the Rangoon University academic staff. This had driven so many students into the Thakin camp: 'The European professors of the universities were frankly regarded by the students as cranks and as the leavings of British universities.'[91] Tin Tut had personal experience of the colour bar. A fine rugby player, he had once been excluded from the shower room of the Gymkhana Club because of his race.

Pearn was duly stung by this slight and retorted that it was nonsense to regard Burma as a great antique empire and, besides, 'I don't know that the opinions of students about their tutors are of much validity.' Dorman-Smith decided that this was a good time to be an Irishman: 'On Mr Pearn's analysis, we Irish were and still are a "primitive people"' because hunger was a common bedfellow. It always came as a shock to the British that 'we' can be unpopular anywhere. But 'to the Irish freedom was more desirable than a full belly'.[92] They, too, were brought up on stories of Ireland's ancient glories when Irish kings ruled in the land, when the Irish language was a live and vigorous tongue. There was a good deal of blarney in this, but none the less Dorman-Smith remains an interesting, though by no means unusual, example of a conservative Irish nationalist working for and within the British Empire. And so the debate rambled on as winter settled in over the peaks around Simla and the snow leopards crept closer to the human settlement, searching for food as they did every year. Perhaps the wisest words were spoken by those officials who denounced the immobility and inefficiency of the former British government of Burma, overwhelmed, especially after 1937, by a sea of paper. This was a system where 'strong men worked fourteen hours a day and achieved nothing . . . Progress was swamped in a sea of paper . . . centralisation ran wild.'[93] It was not surprising that in 1942 about 10 per cent of the population favoured the Japanese, 10 per cent the British, while the rest simply watched and waited, concerned only with the security of their own families. What else could be expected?

## INDIA ABLAZE

Most of the officials who contributed to Dorman-Smith's academic seminar in Simla made the assumption that British prestige in the East would ultimately be restored. In the monsoon season of 1942 that seemed a forlorn hope. Even though the forested rim of the great subcontinental empire was still holding, for a considerable time the Raj seemed on the point of collapsing from within. The proximate cause of this was the failure of Sir Stafford Cripps's mission of the previous spring to win over moderate Congressmen into a wartime government of Indian national unity under the British crown. As a high-minded and independent socialist, Cripps was quite close in many of his views to the thought of Jawaharlal Nehru and the more self-consciously modern of the leaders of the Indian National Congress.[94] Like Nehru, Cripps believed that the world's real divisions were not those of race and religion, but of class. Eventually, the working classes of the world would claim their inheritance, but in the meantime the war against fascism must be won. Churchill, of course, had little time for Indians and saw political debate with them as a waste of time. In the early months of 1942, more and more dependent on American aid and pressed by the British Labour Party and even the Chinese, Churchill, too, had to make some serious concessions. Cripps was sent to India to try to broker a deal. He arrived there on 22 March 1942, at the very moment that British Asia seemed finally to be foundering.

The story of the Cripps mission, of its early promise and dismal failure, has been told many times. Cripps judged that Indian participation in the central executive bodies of the government of India should be greatly increased during the war so that the subcontinent's massive resources could be harnessed better. To all intents and purposes he was prepared to give India de facto dominion status, like Canada or Australia. With this the Americans agreed, informed by President Roosevelt's man in Delhi, Colonel Louis Johnson, who arrived in India two weeks after Cripps and threw himself into the discussion. At first there seemed real hope of a settlement, but by 10 April negotiations were dead in the water.

Indian nationalists and some British radicals then and ever since have indicted Churchill's behind-the-curtain wrecking for its failure. Officials at the time blamed Congress for demanding too much. There was no question, they said, that the defence of British India could be handed over to a responsible Indian minister during the crisis of a world war. All other ministries could go to Indian representatives in a cabinet chaired by the viceroy, but the war ministry was not up for grabs. Muslims, for their part, blamed Congress for rejecting the deal because Leo Amery, the secretary of state for India, had apparently offered the Muslim League some kind of right to secede from the Indian Union, if not to form an actual 'Pakistan', within this scheme. The most authoritative recent study has decisively disproved the 'Churchill factor'.[95] Churchill, like the viceroy Linlithgow, hated the emerging deal, but he did not sabotage it at this point. The fundamental problem was simply lack of trust on both sides. The British had led the Congress up the garden path too often. Congress did not trust Cripps's private engagement to get rid of Linlithgow if a deal was struck. Nor did they trust the British to let Indian ministers get on with the job. They were understandably deeply uneasy with the veto over the whole process that Amery seemed to have given to the Muslim League. The British, for their part, simply did not believe that Indian ministers would have the will to win a war which many Indians believed was not in India's interests. On 6 April, while a dejected Cripps, his friendship with Nehru in tatters, was still in India, the first Japanese bombs were falling near Calcutta.

By this time the Congress rank and file was dangerously angry. The leadership still vacillated about whether or not to announce a full-scale campaign of civil disobedience. The British got hold of Congress Working Committee papers.[96] These revealed agonized debates among different groups. Gandhi, who was not at the meeting, wanted to call on the British to leave immediately. Indians should trust to 'soul force' alone if the Japanese invaded, which seemed more likely day by day. Vallabhbhai Patel, a hard man from peasant Gujarat, also wanted a showdown with the colonialists. On the other side, Nehru was deeply concerned. What would the world think of Indian democrats if they even tacitly supported the Axis powers against the Western democracies? He was supported by liberal Congressmen, such as C. Rajago-palachari, former chief minister of Madras, who trusted the apparent British commitment to concede self-rule at the end of the war.

Some sections of wider Indian public opinion also accepted the need for at least temporary co-operation with the British. Many middle-class Indians continued to deplore the Japanese policy towards China. Chiang had recently visited India to drum up support for his war effort against the Japanese. Congress activists had received him warmly, especially when he irritated the British by himself demanding political concessions in India. Though the Indian communists were still committed to an anti-capitalist rebellion, they were badly thrown by the German invasion of the Soviet Union. Trades unionists with Burmese and Southeast Asian connections were already tacitly working with the British. There were other ideological positions of a less modern sort which predisposed people to co-operate. Several tribal mullahs in the Muslim northwest helpfully declared the war to be a kind of jihad once the Japanese threat materialized. Badshah Gul, spiritual leader of the Mohmand tribal area, described the Japanese as 'enemies of Islam' and said it was the duty of all Muslims to fight alongside the British against them.[97] The right-wing Hindu organization the Hindu Mahasabha had something similar in mind when it began cautiously co-operating. One leader said, 'If the Hindus are armed, trained and equipped in their millions, then and then alone they shall be in a position to defend their hearths and homes from the ravages of the war and suppress any internal anarchy.'[98] V. D. Savarkar, a yet more intransigent proponent of 'Hindu empire', demanded the 'militaris-ation of the Hindus'.[99] Even Jawaharlal Nehru at first refused to make statements directly against the British. As late as mid April he mused: 'it distresses me that Indians should talk of the Japanese coming to liberate India. Japan comes here either for imperialist reasons straight-forward or to fight with the British government . . . it does not come to liberate.'[100] He continued to doubt Gandhi's position and even accepted the need for a scorched earth policy should the Japanese invade India.

By late July and August 1942 the deadlock following the failure of the Cripps mission left the moderate Congress politicians and those who opposed the Axis out of principle with nowhere to go. Gandhi's call to civil disobedience gained support. Ultimately, what happened was not decided by the politicians at all but by ordinary people in the streets and villages of eastern India. In early August there broke out a massive challenge to British rule. Huge crowds began to attack police stations, government offices and other public buildings. Students and schoolchildren were at the heart of the protests. Many of these had been influenced by the example of Subhas Bose who was known to be in Berlin. Some old disputes about the right to land erupted in rural Bihar. Whole villages further to the east protested against the arbitrary expropriation of their land to make way for airfields. The most important point about the Quit India movement was not the way in which it drew on the disgruntled and resentful across India but that, at root, it was an unorganized, popular movement. Quite suddenly the feeling of awe for the state, the *izzat* or 'face' of the British Raj, which more than troops and police had sustained foreign rule, simply vanished, melting away in the warm monsoon rains.[101] People along the railway lines and in the small bazaars had seen the defeated and demoralized white troops struggling back through Assam to Calcutta. The Indian troops had told them of the superhuman bravery and discipline of the once-despised and oriental Japanese. A rumour flashed round that not only did the Japanese rain down from the skies in their parachutes, but they could use their parachutes like rockets and power back upwards on them. The malarial and diseased sepoys passed on the news that the Japanese advanced columns were only a few hours' march behind them on the road. They had come to free India, as they had already freed French Indo-China, the Dutch East Indies and British Burma and Malaya.

Quit India began as another of Gandhi's great non-violent displays of 'soul force'. There were huge demonstrations and sit-ins (*hartals*) in major towns in the first two weeks of August. These were put down with police firings and baton charges. Labour unrest was quelled with particular vigour because the government was fearful of its consequence for war production. Within a few weeks this popular movement had taken on a rather different character. An organization began to appear at the grass roots rather than among the homespun-clad leadership, who were by now almost all in jail. By 15 August a new pattern had emerged of a systematic attempt to sabotage Britain's war effort based on smaller population centres along major lines of communication or near important factory complexes. Telegraph lines were cut, railway lines were ripped up and bridges dynamited.[102] In all 66,000 people were convicted or detained, of whom about a quarter, including most of the Congress leadership, were still in jail in 1944. About 2,500 people were shot dead.[103]

This was undoubtedly a serious revolt, and one that directly threatened the war effort. Armed groups attacked several of the weakest points of the Indian railway network, derailing trains and bombing signal boxes at essential junctions. In one incident two Canadian military officers were pulled off a train and murdered. The government worried particularly about central Bihar, where the most important railway link from Delhi up to the Assam front and Bengal passed through miles of desolate and formerly bandit-infested countryside. At a time when the Japanese were expected to be on the point of invading Ceylon, the essential supply route through Coimbatore in the far south was hit by sabotage. In Madras, 'Burma refugees' were said to have been prominent in an outbreak of sabotage to trains and cutting of telegraph wires. Even sixty years on it is still difficult to say whether this month-long campaign was organized to a plan or whether the enraged local political leadership was reacting to British repression on the hoof. The savagery of the British response – police shootings, mass whipping, the burning of villages and sporadic torture of protesters – was testimony to the fact that the Raj was seriously rattled.

Linlithgow and the India Office quickly got into the spirit of things. Reacting to the news that the viceroy was on the point of sanctioning the aerial machine-gunning of saboteurs, an official noted that this was 'an exhilarating departure from precedent'.[104] Bomber patrols began over the affected areas. One serious concern was that the Indian element of the army, particularly the VCOs, was wobbling. There were a few examples of officers refusing to obey their orders to confront Indian demonstrators. T. B. Dadachanji was a young Parsi who had joined up to fight the Nazis when he was in England at the beginning of the war. He disobeyed an order to take a mobile column into a riotous city on the grounds that he might be forced to shoot his own people. He was arrested on a charge of treason but subsequently released and allowed to resign. 'Jick' Rudra and the senior Indian officers thought that a court martial might spark a major revolt. This was a time when much of the army had reacted with 'dismay and consternation' to the news that was trickling through about the formation of the INA in Singapore. The Dadachanji incident and others like it were hushed up.[105] It was important, though, that many of the Indian troops were critical of the movement. One soldier commented: 'I do not know what harm this wicked destruction is doing to the sirkar [government]. I do know that it is causing much misery to my family.'[106]

As a precautionary move, the Second Suffolk Regiment was brought down from Lahore to Lucknow.[107] If a new Indian Mutiny were to break out, would it not be in Lucknow where the Union flag still waved over the ruins of the old British residency? With the unusually large number of fifty-two battalions of soldiers for deployment in India at this time, a substantial proportion of which were British nationals or Gurkhas rather than Indians, the authorities were never in danger of losing control. Yet the diversion of manpower from the war fronts could have been serious. Perhaps the worst moment of the Quit India movement for the British was in late August and early September. The main cities of Bihar and Bengal had been quietened by police shootings and collective fines, but like a bush fire, smaller conflagrations kept breaking out further from where the fire started. Substantial numbers of Gurkhas and British troops were now deployed in Bihar and Bengal. Villages suspected of harbouring 'terrorists' were punished with fines or in some instances torched. One of the officials most prominent in this counter-insurgency was one of the few British personnel whom Nehru later declared should have been hanged. In fact, he became vicar of a Cambridgeshire village.

By mid September the big demonstrations were suppressed and Gandhi, Nehru and the other leaders had resumed their well-rehearsed jail regimes of reading, writing and exercise. The army and police had, despite all the fears, remained solid. The large Muslim element among the Viceroy's Commissioned Officers was intensely suspicious of the

Congress, often seeing it as a Hindu organization. Many of the Hindu, Sikh and Indian Christian officers genuinely feared the consequence of a Japanese invasion and felt that they had, after all, sworn an oath of allegiance to the king-emperor. Equally important, the railways held firm. By 20 September rail travel was more or less back to normal. But serious labour trouble broke out in Tata Iron and Steel in Bihar and production was falling in the Raniganj coalfields. These events were 'really serious for the war effort' and stringent measures were taken to keep them out of the press.[108] L. W. Russell, a police officer of Gaya in Bihar, believed that he had helped to avert the crisis by stopping dead the spread of demonstrations in his area. Russell came from an old Indian family and believed in decisive action. He arrested large numbers of demonstrators and had them whipped on the spot by executive order. This was preferable to jailing them or shooting them, so creating martyrs, he believed.[109] The growing incidence of floggings and the rising tally of people shot dead by the police or seriously injured by *lathis*, metal-tipped bamboo staves, raised serious worries in Britain where tales of Nazi 'dreadfulness' were legion. Amery explained in the House of Commons that the floggings were being carried out not with an eighteenth-century-type cat o'nine tails, but a light rattan cane in order to 'deter hooligans'.[110] This only faintly reassured Labour and Liberal MPs, for anyone who had seen the 'light rattan canes' employed by the Indian police would have remained sceptical of this clemency. Out in the districts where villages were being burned and people beaten, several Indian and a few British members of the ICS, particularly magistrates, attempted to put some restraint on the doings of their more savage colleagues.

The British government and Churchill in particular remained adamant that the movement must be suppressed vigorously and immediately. They were in no mood to compromise. The Japanese might just resume their attack as the monsoon clouds lightened. In North Africa, British and Indian troops were still stalemated and General Auchinleck's advance after he held El Alamein failed to materialize. Churchill assailed the Congress in Parliament. The Quit India movement, he said, had as its main aim not political advance but 'to hamper the defence of India against the Japanese invader who stands on the frontiers of Assam' and may well have been aided by Japanese fifth columnists. The Congress was not even a Hindu body, he announced: 'It is a political organisation built around a party machine and sustained by certain manufacturing interests.'[111] This was the sort of sentiment which had so annoyed Mr Chettiar when he had spoken to Dorman-Smith. Churchill insisted that all Muslims, untouchables and the populations of the princely states opposed the Congress. There were also 'many loyal Sikhs, Christians and Hindus'. Altogether, there must be at least 300 million Indians who supported the Raj. There was a little truth in these charges. The pattern of rebellion definitely suggests a desire to damage Britain's military communication to the eastern front. By contrast, recruitment into the British Indian army held up well and even increased somewhat, especially in the northwestern Muslim areas, during the political troubles. Be that as it may, Congress still managed to attract a huge amount of support across the country, from all classes of the population. The main activists were not 'fifth columnists' but students, shopkeepers and other ordinary people who could not wait to see the back of the British in India.

Churchill's view of India turned from scepticism and dislike to a near hatred. It became what Amery was to term his 'Nazi-like attitude' to the country. The antagonism generated by the Quit India movement affected people right the way down the hierarchy of British government. Faced with growing evidence of a food shortage, officials averted their gaze and insisted on the primacy of the war effort. Russell, the man responsible for the flogging at Bhagalpur, consistently blamed the Congress for starving its own people by urging farmers and merchants to withdraw support from government. Certainly the domestic panic which accompanied the political disturbances did little to encourage the markets. Some district Congress committees put out posters advising people that the government was on the point of collapse and that they should store their grain.

Premonitions of the coming great starvation were already in the air in the spring of 1942. A Bengal food conference was held to assess the situation. Sir John Herbert, the governor, took the chair. He was 'more than usually ineffective' in getting the chief minister, Fazlul Haq, to act, according to the increasingly acerbic Arthur Dash.[112] By December Linlithgow was writing of a 'disastrous deterioration of supplies'.[113] Early in January, even Amery became aware that a serious problem was developing. The loss of Burma deprived India at a stroke of nearly 15 per cent of its rice supplies. War panic and political unrest made smallholders, landlords and merchants all hedge their bets. This was not a developed market economy. The morale of the seller remained of critical importance. If the peasant felt that food for his own family might not be available a few months on, he would not sell. If the grain merchant or moneylender expected the government to clamp down on grain prices because of the war, he would neither buy nor sell. Victor Bayley's prediction that the defenders of India would 'never again face famine' was already sounding hollow.

After three years of gloom, Christmas 1942 saw some real cause for cheer for the British at home and scattered round the world. The American recovery, following their decisive defeat of the Japanese fleet at Midway in June, had taken the pressure off Australia and New Guinea. The string of British defeats and fiascos had finally come to an end at the Battle of El Alamein in October and Indian troops had distinguished themselves in North Africa. The Japanese advance had temporarily ground to a halt even on the Assam front. Trapped up in the snow of Simla among the disdainful Indian bureaucrats, Dorman-Smith and his wife found comfort in their dogs. The exiles sustained their morale by planning for the coming reoccupation of Burma and playing host to the men of British and American special operations units who came from the upper Chindwin and the Assam hills. The visitors passed on news of tenacious Chin, Karen and Kachin resistance to Japanese advances. Sir Paw Tun delivered an impassioned address to the Burmese people over All-India Radio, recounting Japanese atrocities in China and the violation of Buddhist shrines in the Burmese homeland.

Meanwhile, a British forward patrol had recently penetrated as far as Mogaung on the route from Burma to India, where so many had perished earlier that year. They reported on the eerie silence among the dense, overhanging forest vegetation. Thousands of skeletons, the majority Indian, lay along the road or in nearby bushes. A few months later British troops ventured as far as Tamu, grimly nicknamed 'city of the dead'. Here, skeletons still reclined in derelict cars, sat at decaying tables, lay in collapsed beds.[114] Yet for Indians, the horrors of war and civil conflict had scarcely begun. In eastern Bengal cyclones and flooding devastated the autumn harvest. The best rice crop was destroyed up to forty miles inland 'while huge trees and telegraph poles were uprooted blocking the Grand Trunk Road'.[115] The scorched earth policy had destroyed all the vehicles, carts and animals on which the people relied. In early December the Indian government estimated that the total food supply in India was more than one million tons short. Already children and the elderly were beginning to die.

## THE FORGOTTEN ARMIES MOBILIZE

The Indians of the Japanese Empire followed these events anxiously. There were monster meetings in Malaya, Medan, Shanghai and elsewhere to attack British treatment of Congress and the hypocrisy of the Atlantic Charter. On 12 August 1942 an estimated 125,000 people gathered at Farrer Park in Singapore to hear Rash Behari Bose announce: 'Mahatmaji, Nehru, Azad and other leaders are arrested. The real fight for Indian freedom has begun.'[116] With the Raj in crisis, and with its collapse in Southeast Asia, there was a tremendous sense amongst the Indians in the region that this was a moment when they could play a crucial role in India's struggle for freedom: in the words of one young activist 'a force from outside can give a great impetus to the movement inside India'.[117] By mid 1942, they had the means to do so. The Indian Independence League had at its conference in Bangkok in May 1942 taken the political initiative to unify the scattered leadership of the overseas Indians in East and Southeast Asia. The embryonic Indian National Army that had emerged from the mass capitulation of Indians at Farrer Park six months earlier had also begun to take on a firmer form.

These bodies came together in the person of Rash Behari Bose, chairman of the League and commander-in-chief of the INA. 'Fat Babu' possessed a legendary status amongst Indian exiles. He had been involved in some of the most dramatic direct actions of the pre-First World War period, such as the attempted assassination of Viceroy Hardinge in 1912 and the 'Delhi conspiracy case' of 1915. Like many Asian revolutionaries of the era, he took sanctuary in Tokyo, where he married a Japanese woman. Other young students there fell under his spell. One such was an engineering student at Kyoto University, A. M. Nair, who, like his great mentor, married a Japanese. Nair portrayed his life as that of a *ronin*, a wandering samurai of Japanese legend, and indeed, travelled as a 'living Buddha' and a camel dealer on various assignments. He worked for the Japanese-sponsored Five Races Unity Movement in Manchukuo and on the attempt at Dairen in 1934 to organize a Pan-Asian Conference, and acted as Rash Behari Bose's secretary. Both men were close to Japanese intelligence officials in Tokyo.[118]

The Japanese role in the movement divided Indian civilians and soldiers in Southeast Asia. Rash Behari Bose argued that co-operation with the Nippon armies did not mean control by them. Tojo, in a speech to the Diet, had mentioned India in the context of a 'spirit of non-attachment'. This phrase came from an attempt by a Japanese professor of Indian philology to render into Japanese the League's motto: *Anasaktha karma* – 'Action without attachment'. Yet the Japanese association was very damaging, and had bitterly divided delegates at the Bangkok conference. Their dependence on the Japanese was vividly demonstrated by the Japanese having brought them together; an original conference on 28 March had been postponed because of a shortage of transport.[119] The leaders of the League in Malaya were men who had been active in the Central Indian Association of Malaya before the war. The Penang leader, N. Raghavan, was a Cochin-born, London-educated lawyer who had set up practice in Penang in 1920. He anguished over 'honourable self-preservation of the community'. In Kuala Lumpur S. C. Goho was another lawyer, whom the British had contemplated putting under arrest before the surrender, who had formed an Indian passive defence force. They worried over the technicalities of the League's relations with the Japanese, and mistrusted the Japanese citizens who were at the heart of its organization. Yet without the League they had no natural mass appeal of their own. At the Farrer Park rally in August, one of the platform speakers, the Singapore journalist K. P. K. Menon had been met with what he termed a 'rising tide of uncontrolled anger sweeping over the large crowd'. This was because there was no speech in Tamil, the language of most of the Indian workers in Singapore and Malaya. He was forced to issue an embarrassing apology (in English) in the newspapers, and pledge his commitment to the Tamil language. Was the Indian Independence League, the *Syonan Times* asked, a mere 'hot-air merchant association'?[120]

The Indian Independence League posed an acute dilemma for the Ceylonese community, who were concentrated in government employment or worked as clerks and managers of European businesses. Although the Buddhist Ceylonese had been initially treated gently by the Japanese, the Ceylonese Tamils, who were predominantly Hindu, remained very exposed through their English-language education and status. The Bangkok conference had not mentioned the cause of Ceylonese independence. Prudence had dictated that, for the purposes of the occupation, they identify themselves as 'Indians', and leading members of the community were organized to tour and promote the League, including M. Saravanamuttu, the newspaper editor who had lowered the Union flag in Penang. These men were under some compulsion. Some took the view that, as civil servants, they were loyal to the government of the day. Other harboured a secret loyalty to the British, but joined the League to protect their communities and families. A membership subscription included a protective certificate to be pasted on the member's front door. Ceylonese lawyer S. Chelvasingham-MacIntyre described his initiation into the Indian Independence League after a visit to a Chettiar temple in Batu Pahat. General Mohan Singh was there, 'reserved and modest'. So too was Fujiwara: 'he cut a splendid figure. Tall, handsome and resplendent in uniform, he created a stir by solemnly kneeling before the Hindu shrine in silent prayer.' Before he realized it, he found himself enrolled as a local committee member of the League.[121]

The co-operation between Fujiwara's intelligence operation and Mohan Singh had secured better treatment for Indian troops from Japanese commanders in the field than the other fighting forces had received. But the future relationships between an Indian National Army and the Japanese divided Indian officers. Mohan Singh determined to raise the INA into an effective fighting force. In April 1942, with a group of officers at Bidadari prisoner-of-war camp in Singapore, he issued a statement of intent – a united India, above caste, community or religion – and announced recruitment for the INA. It was also a stipulation that the army would fight for India only when Congress and the people commanded it to. However, many still mistrusted Mohan Singh and disparaged his personal leadership qualities. Mohan Singh had joined the Indian army as an infantryman and had worked his way up through the ranks at Dehra Dun. He was a captain at thirty-two and remained so in 1942. Indian officers resented the fact that a more senior man had not been anointed. When Fujiwara conferred on him the rank of general, this and other promotions were seen as debased, coming through, in A. M. Nair's words, 'the crazy action of a Japanese major'. Opponents were suspicious that intelligence officers such as Fujiwara, acting on their own initiative, could not guarantee that their actions would be endorsed by the high command. As the INA expanded its recruiting drive there was at least some intimidation and persecution to make sure that troops joined. Many officers and *jawans*, or rank and file, hesitated. Many were Muslim, and determined to keep Muslim troops out of an INA led by a Sikh. But how far could this opposition be sustained? Some officers took their men in to avoid their being divided and becoming easy prey to Japanese labour recruitment schemes. Others felt that it was useless for senior officers to be sitting humiliated in a concentration camp whilst the juniors lorded it over the INA. They joined the INA to restrict Japanese involvement and, if unable to do so, 'to sabotage the movement from within'.[122] Not only was a soldier's loyalty to his salt at issue, but to India. The decisive question was what would India do if the INA crossed its borders? For many, Quit India settled the matter: if India fought, how could they stand idle?

Mohan Singh wanted twelve infantry battalions in four regiments: a force of around 8,000 men with support units of around 2,000 more. The recruits that came forward were stripped of their old regimental distinctions and placed in new units called Azad, Nehru and Gandhi. More promotions followed to create a new officer corps. The INA delivered its commands in Hindustani, but the force remained governed by the martial traditions of the Raj. It also had no new arms, or even uniforms. Nevertheless, by the time it paraded on the Padang in Singapore on 2 October, Gandhi's birthday, Mohan Singh argued that the first division was ready for deployment to Burma and that more were ready to be raised. Other initiatives too were bearing fruit. N. Raghavan had established a Swaraj Institute in the Free School building in Penang. From the beginning of August it took in a first batch of over thirty students for training in intelligence, espionage, photography and surveying. Many of its graduates were Malayan-born; for some the lure was adventure, for others it was a way of getting back to India. They undertook penetration work, landing by submarine in India and Ceylon. But a number were arrested and hanged as 'enemy agents'.[123] They were the first casualties of the INA's war of independence. Mohan Singh was ambitious for his army and could be a high-handed generalissimo, especially to civilians. The Japanese began to be more high-handed in turn. His relationship with Fujiwara had been superseded by the establishment of the more powerful Iwakuro Kikan, a new intelligence organization that had replaced the Fujiwara Kikan, and which had little sympathy for Indian independence. The Malayan leaders of the League were horrified by reports of the treatment of Indian people and property in the wake of the fall of Burma. Raghavan closed his school in fury when Japanese sent his agents into the field, to their deaths, without his permission. He was promptly placed under house arrest. Mohan Singh suddenly became more cautious about the Japanese connection. There were worrying reports that the Japanese were taking over once again the camps of Indian prisoners of war who had not joined the INA. Rash Behari Bose and his entourage arrived in Singapore and took up residence in the Park View Hotel. He became bent on keeping what he saw as Mohan Singh's dictatorial tendencies in check. He charged that troops numbers had been inflated, and that many of them had opted to return to the camps. To Rash Behari Bose, the INA had become a divisive force, and this was undermining the policy of using co-operation with the Japanese to secure better conditions for all Indians. Indeed, the indications are that Rash Behari Bose did not see the INA as a fighting force at all; he saw it more as an auxiliary to the League, raising morale and giving practical support to the Indians in Southeast Asia.[124]

Mohan Singh began to assert his independence from both the League and the Japanese. He was perhaps not politician enough to achieve this: he ended in head-to-head confrontation with them both. The lawyer and INA propagandist, J. A. Thivy, recorded a furious exchange with Major Ogawa on 2 December after an advance party of INA personnel had been embarked for Burma without Singh's approval:

OGAWA: Why have you suddenly become suspicious?

SINGH: Your sudden and straight refusal to a genuine demand re Bangkok resolutions and moreover, by seeing your ideas in Malaya and Burma.

OGAWA: You cannot compare India with Malaya and Burma. India will be more independent.

SINGH: What do you mean by 'more'? India will be absolutely independent. No one can stop it . . .[125]

After another Sikh officer was arrested by the Japanese for treason, Mohan Singh's men refused to embark for Burma. At a crisis meeting on 29 December Rash Behari Bose dismissed Mohan Singh and the Japanese arrested him as he left the room. An armed confrontation between Japanese and Indian forces was narrowly averted only by Fujiwara interceding with Mohan Singh with the promise that he would do his utmost to have Subhas Chandra Bose brought to Asia. The Swaraj Institute was disbanded. The Malayan leadership of the League was brushed aside. Mohan Singh spent the rest of the war exiled to Pulau Ubin, an island off Changi Point, and then in Sumatra. The first Indian National Army and its members reverted to prisoner-of-war status. Rash Behari Bose appointed new commanders to keep it alive: a colonel, J. K. Bhonsle, with Lieutenant Colonel Shahnawaz Khan as his chief of staff. But the old revolutionary was sinking; he was gravely ill with diabetes and pulmonary tuberculosis. He had never captured the imagination of the Indian masses in Malaya and Singapore. As one activist put it: 'Everyone knew that he was more of a Japanese than of an Indian'.[126]

With the creation of the Indian National Army, the connections that colonial rule had forged along the crescent were beginning to resurface. Nor was it just the politics of the Japanese Empire that were doing this, but also a small flow of refugees that was beginning to make it across the crescent to territory still held by the British. Among the hundreds of thousands of displaced persons wandering through Burma in the later months of 1942 were a few members of the Indian army who had evaded capture in Singapore. These men brought valuable but disquieting news of the Indian National Army to the British. They included Captain Pritam Singh of 2/16 Punjab Regiment. Having seen Indian officers slapped and beaten by the Japanese in a 'demonstration of love towards the Asiatic races', as he put it, he decided to escape north by taxi and train in civilian clothes. He bought a false Japanese passport in Penang and got into Thailand. Further north, he stayed for some time with a Kiplingesque character called Khan Zada. The Khan was a Pathan who had spent twelve years in jail in Calcutta for murder, but ended up as a butcher on the Thai-Burmese border. Now aged seventy, he had recently shot his son in the thigh for some mild misdemeanour. Evading Japanese spies and staying in gurdwaras (Sikh temples), Pritam Singh eventually ended up in Kalewa, where the refugees had recently died in thousands. He shaved his head and beard to be less conspicuous and finally escaped into British India via Imphal.[127]

Others followed. Two Indian lieutenants who had refused to attend the Bidadari meeting in April with Mohan Singh made a long overland journey to Penang armed with false Indian Independence League cards. They were disguised as Chettiar merchants and slipped through southern Thailand to Victoria Point in Burma, reaching Delhi at the end of August. They brought some of the first news of the conditions of Indian prisoners of war in Malaya and perhaps the first reports of the mass prostitution that was appearing in the towns. They also reported others on the move: sepoys disguised as waiters or drivers.[128] There were Chinese too, filtering back through China. They were interrogated at length by a British military suddenly starved of information. Peoples in exile too had an inordinate amount of influence in policy-making. By building on such resources the Raj slowly began to turn back on the offensive.

It did so initially by subterfuge and by encouraging others to wage war on its behalf. The British looked to new sources for specialists to replace those lost in the fall of Singapore and Burma and to answer for new needs. In May 1942 a number of pupils in their late teens were recruited from British grammar schools for an intensive course in Japanese at the London School of Oriental and African Studies. They were selected on the basis of their proficiency in classical languages. They were known as the 'Dulwich Boys', lodged as they were at Tin Tut's *alma mater*, Dulwich College. They were trained as 'service interrogators' or 'service translators'. They came from a range of backgrounds – the son of Bertrand Russell being one. In all 648 students passed through the scheme, with a 90 per cent success rate. They became many of the post-war British scholars, diplomats and industrialists with interests in the region, and one distinguished novelist, Richard Mason, the author of *The World of Suzie Wong*. A number of them spent a lifetime writing the history of the conflict they had experienced as young men. The British instructors were men with a deep love of Japan: one of them, Frank Daniels, had spent time on Hokkaido island teaching C. K. Ogden's new global inter-language, 'Basic English'. The father of another, Francis Piggot, had advised on the drawing up of the Meiji constitution. The son, himself a diplomat, had attended Hirohito on his 1921 visit to Europe and was a military attaché in Tokyo between 1935 and 1939, where he had lobbied for a less confrontational approach to Japan. There were even several Japanese, including two who had been released from internment on the Isle of Man: Daniels's wife Otome, who had to be accompanied by SOAS students on outings in London for protection, and the exotic beauty Aiko Clarke, immortalized by Mason in his novel *The Wind Cannot Read*. These instructors taught respect for Japanese culture and life. Otome Daniels's parting words to pupils leaving for India were 'please look kindly on my people'.[129]

On the eastern front itself, Britain's secret war got off to a slow start, as spies and agents recruited by Special Operations Executive HQ in Baker Street made their slow way around the Cape of Good Hope to Bombay. Recruitment on the spot was in the spirit of Evelyn Waugh's *Officers and Gentlemen*: a trawling of the old school networks and chummeries of the eastern empire, from the clubs and officers' messes of Calcutta. SOE's India Mission was led by a Scot, Colin Mackenzie, a classics scholar from Cambridge, who had worked in Asia for J. & P. Coats, of which Linlithgow, the viceroy, was a director. It also recruited from the survivors of SOE's ill-starred Oriental Mission, the second in command of which, Basil Goodfellow, an ex-ICI man, became head of the Malaya Command.[130] Two key operatives were Richard Broome of the Malayan Civil Service and the policeman John Davis, who had organized the last 'stay-behind parties' in Malaya. They were nicknamed Tweedledum and Tweedledee, and this supplied their codenames: Dum and Dee. They quickly concluded that, in Davis's words, 'it wasn't much good trying sabotage in a country like Malaya 2,000 miles . . . from the recent war front or nearest fighting'. It was decided in October 1942 that the priorities were reconnaissance and infiltration: in the trade jargon, there were to be no 'pin pricks', other than the 'removal' of selected pro-Japanese figures. Operations were deferred to a time when they would yield the greatest results and would be in conjunction with military operations, at some later date.[131] There was an exception to this: a former Japanese fishing vessel, MV *Krait*, which had been used in an improvised search-and-rescue operation for the disastrous evacuations from Singapore, was boxed up and sent to Australia for a planned hit-and-run raid on Singapore harbour. This would have disastrous consequences.

Meanwhile, Davis and Broome searched the bazaars for local allies. These were in short supply. The British consul in Bombay even resorted to providing blood money to buy out of jail a stranded Malay pilgrim who had been working as a chef in a restaurant and had killed a customer.[132] Chinese recruits were even harder to find: some Canadian and American Chinese were recruited, but the breakthrough came with Dum and Dee's connection with the Kuomintang leader Lim Bo Seng. Lim was one of the few Chinese evacuated from Singapore; he was a successful businessman, running the family concerns of a biscuit factory and a brickworks from the age of twenty. He was active in Chinese commercial circles, but had also headed the labour section of the Kuomintang. He was well known to the British, and had met Goodfellow during the escape from Singapore. Lim went to Chungking to mobilize Malayan Chinese students there. But until these first KMT exiles began to appear in the early spring of 1943, the British were in almost complete ignorance of conditions on the ground.

In Malaya the planters and miners who had been hastily recruited as guerrillas for SOE were scattered and equally isolated from any news of the broader course of the war. They were part of a considerable number of groups at large in the forests of the peninsula at the fall of Singapore. There were many stragglers who had gone to ground when separated from their units. Until 1943, there were persistent rumours of large bands of Australians. But of the hundreds of men moving through the jungle in early 1942, only two British, three Australians and four Gurkhas made it out. The Japanese swiftly picked up the rest, or they died squalidly from disease or starvation in an environment that holds little natural provender for humans.[133] Even the organized groups had supplies for only three months, in expectation of a rapid British and American counter-attack. Many of the men had been killed in the last stages of the fighting. There was only one radio transmitter in British hands, with a Secret Intelligence Service group in Johore in the south. The nominal leader of the SOE forces was Freddy Spencer Chapman. In the last stages of the Malayan campaign, he and some associates waged a short campaign of sabotage on roads and railways in northern Selangor. But as Japanese patrols closed on him, he was forced to retreat and seek shelter in the central range. There were a number of graduates of 101 Special Training School at large, but there was no way of knowing which parties were still in existence, or whether any rendezvous would be possible. Chapman's small party met up with two rubber-estate managers, both veterans of the First World War and over forty-five years of age, W. S. Robinson and Robert Chrystal, who had volunteered when their plantations were overrun. They took to the forest with the intention of blowing up the east coast railway. In the event, the bridges on the northern stretches were already destroyed and the Japanese had bypassed it entirely by heading down the west coast. The rationale for the original mission gone, they were stranded with one radio receiver but no transmitter, waiting for a British counter-attack that never came. The Europeans were dispersed and depleted by arrests and illness. They were also divided on how to proceed. Chapman wanted to steal a junk, sail to India and re-establish contact with the British command. By April, contact came, in the form of Chin Peng of the Malayan Communist Party, and they fell effectively into the hands of the Chinese guerrillas of the Malayan Peoples' Anti-Japanese Army.

Chin Peng was assigned as the liaison officer between the MPAJA and Spencer Chapman and his men, who arrived in their camp in April 1942. Their relationship was to be a vitally important one in the years that followed. It was eased by the fact that Chin Peng had known of Chrystal before the war. He had attended a Chinese middle school in Sungei Siput, that had bordered Chrystal's vast Kamunting estate. The rising star of the party was to be a principal guarantor of the Europeans' safety and kept a reputation for fair dealing. In the months that followed, Chapman would move around searching for supplies and other units. In July Chapman travelled from Selangor to spend the next year with the 6th Independent Regiment in West Pahang. Chrystal and Robinson moved with a unit of the 5th Independent Regiment up above the Kinta valley to a limestone ridge at Bukit Rimau, HQ of the Perak MPAJA, where they undertook, though comparative novices themselves, to train the guerrillas. There, jetsam from the towns began to join them, including a Chinese orchestra from Ipoh. The guerrilla bands brought together labourers and the sons and daughters of merchants. The Europeans were fascinated by the great seriousness of purpose and high intensity of life in the camps. The days were strictly regulated by a timetable of lessons and communal events: exercises, singing lessons, debates and concerts. Outside of military matters, Chapman made himself useful by drawing pictures of Stalin and Gorky from books, and joined the concert parties with a repertoire of Eskimo songs. There were many young women in the camps, who lived and worked on equal terms with the men. The proprieties of relations between them were strictly preserved. The discipline was most rigid with regard to security. Commanders took brutal reprisals against those who were thought to have collaborated with the Japanese. In the early stages of the war there had been heavy losses, particularly in Singapore and the south. Virtually the whole of the Central Committee had been arrested, including the party's leading intellectual and number two, Huang Chen. Under these conditions, release after arrest by the Japanese carried with it an assumption of guilt. Loyal cadres could expect no quarter from the Kempeitai. One of the feared instruments of revolutionary discipline in Perak, Lai Lai Fuk, the son of a Sitiawan merchant and one of the original fifteen graduates of 101 Special Training School, was himself to meet a violent end, executed by the Japanese in mid 1943 in Taiping jail.[134]

Perak was to be the greatest security problem for the Japanese, although for periods Johore too was turbulent. The MPAJA pursued a policy of hit-and-run attacks on police stations and railways, harassing Japanese patrols. At the same time it developed its underground, building webs of supporters and informers in the towns. Chin Peng took responsibility for this, making long and dangerous journeys:

'I lived in rented rooms. I slept in tin mine offices. I stayed with schoolteachers.'[135] This policy could cut both ways: in the second half of 1942 the Kempeitai began to fight back, through a combination of reviving the local police forces under Japanese commanders, turning communist agents, and by drafting in specialists. In Perak the police force was under the command of a former employee in Malaya of the beer company Suntory, whose sole qualification was an ability to speak Malay. However, the pre-war police, who did know their business, were called back to work. The police were supported by the Kempeitai, who developed jungle missions. Neither side inflicted great damage on the other, although there was a general mood of terror in large parts of Perak.[136]

In late July messages went out from the Malayan Communist Party secretary-general Lai Teck for a council of war. Each state was to send its most senior representatives to a meeting that was to be held on 1 September at a jungle fringe location in a village called Sungei Dua, near Batu Caves, a pinnacle of limestone just north of Kuala Lumpur and the site of a major Hindu temple complex. As leaders gathered the night before the meeting at the temporary camp, it came under heavy attack from a large Japanese force. The fighting was furious, only a few communists managed to get away, mainly under covering fire from a young female cadre who perished in the attack. At a stroke, most of the senior leadership of the party was wiped out: twenty-nine were killed and fifteen more arrested. These included the senior military commanders of the MPAJA, and men who had been through the Yenan training school and returned to Malaya from there. Lai Teck was to have been at the meeting, but had been delayed; his car had broken down. A second, follow-up meeting involving Lai Teck, near Kampar in Perak was also compromised. These were major breakthroughs for the Japanese, and had resulted from an extraordinary coup.

In March, on a tip-off from two former Chinese detectives, the Kempeitai in Singapore had arrested a man called Wong Show Tong in a house near the Sultan mosque. He was interrogated by Major Satoru Onishi, a man instrumental in the *sook ching* on the island. The detainee revealed another alias, Wong Kim Gyock: the name by which, Onishi knew, the secretary-general of the Malayan Communist

Party was known. When confronted with this Wong Kim Gyock/Lai Teck agreed to provide information in return for his life. It does not appear that Lai Teck revealed that he had been a British agent, and knowledge of the new deception was confined to very few Japanese. After no more than ten days in detention Lai Teck was released. He then exposed, piece by piece, the organization of the party in Singapore and south Malaya, including the information that the senior cadres and military commanders of the party were planning a meeting at Batu Caves on 1 September.[137]

In the short term, the resultant massacre rendered unassailable Lai Teck's position within the party. It also wiped out an entire generation of party leaders most of whom were China-born. In the longer term the massacre allowed younger, Malayan-born cadres to come to the fore. Many of these had adopted a more Malayan outlook to their struggle. With the demise of the Singapore and Selangor organizations, the more independent Perak organization came to the fore, and with it the young state secretary of the party, Chin Peng. But in late 1942 and early 1943 the MPAJA was fighting for survival. It was not until May 1943 that the Central Executive Committee reconstituted itself.

Even before the Batu Caves massacre the MCP was facing difficulties. Documents prepared by the Perak party for the Batu Caves conference spoke of the poor political work and lack of specificity in propaganda and of dissension in the ranks. The position of the Europeans with the MCP became increasingly difficult. They abhorred the MPAJA's brutal revolutionary justice. They restricted their activities to military training and resisted any political role, although Chrystal penned anti-Japanese propaganda addressed to Indian labourers. The pretence that they were there as advisers and allies was dropped; they were vagrants, dependent on the guerrillas' charity. For the propagandists in the camp, they were kept as living exhibits of the decadent and degraded colonial planter class. They were no longer to be addressed as 'Tuan', were relegated from the top table and were ordered to eat with chopsticks. They resented that their health suffered as a result of a conflict over food practices: the Europeans were not adept enough with chopsticks to take their share from the common pot; the Chinese objected to a spoon being placed in the pot having been in a person's mouth.[138] For many of the Chinese, this was their first direct encounter with Europeans; in colonial Malaya there had been few circumstances in which Europeans would live so intimately with Asians, and for so long.

Spencer Chapman was later to write a minor classic of war literature about the campaign in which he emphasized the torturous self-reliance of jungle survival: 'The truth is that the jungle is neutral. It provides any amount of fresh water, and unlimited cover for friend as well as foe – an armed neutrality, if you like, but neutrality nevertheless. It is the attitude of mind that determines whether you go under or survive.'[139] This was indeed one of the last great adventures of the British Empire. Wavell, in his introduction, compared Chapman to T. E. Lawrence, and he had known both men. 'What boy has not longed to blow up trains?', Chapman himself would later write. 'What man too; especially if he has read *Seven Pillars of Wisdom*!'[140] But his tale is misleading in many ways. Britain's secret fighters were for most of the time rather marginal to the guerrilla war. They were for long periods seriously ill and incapacitated, and in truth did very little fighting. His friend Chin Peng admired the book, but he warned: 'you will find his text peppered with slurs against Asians. Interestingly enough, though, Chapman seemed to pride himself on the relationships he established with us.' Chin Peng resented that Asians were portrayed as betrayers and as innocents in warfare: the treachery and military incompetence lay on the British side.[141]

Of course, the jungle was never neutral. It was the hereditary domain of communities of forest peoples. Marginal in most British accounts, they were to emerge as crucial players in the struggles for control of the peninsula's interior. They were dragged into a political turmoil not of their own making, and this would mark the beginning of the end of their relatively autonomous existence. There were around 26,630 of them according to a 1941 census, of whom over 24,000 were in Perak, Pahang and Kelantan.[142] The Orang Asli, literally the 'original people' of Malaya, can be divided into three broad groups. All of them kept the modern world at a distance and fought to protect their way of life. There were what the ethnographers termed the 'proto-Malays'; groups that had assimilated to some extent with neighbouring Malays, and followed a similar economy. That these groups would and should evolve in this direction was the central assumption (both then and now) of official thinking towards them. Then there were the main forest communities of north and central Malaya – the Semai and the Temiar – who followed shifting cultivation around a cycle of sites, but who also traded with other communities. Finally, there was the forest nomadism of the Negritos, who were mostly to be found in the deep jungle of Ulu Kelantan. Before the war, like other communities on Malaya, the Orang Asli had their protectors: mostly paternalistic district officers and Malay chiefs; anthropologists were drawn to study the 'primitive socialism' or the 'non-violence' of the Semai. In Perak, which had some of the largest concentrations of Orang Asli, there had been established in 1938 a 'Protector of Aborigines'. The field ethnographer who held the post was Pat Noone. He had taken a First in Archaeology and Anthropology from Cambridge University, and in Malaya, a Temiar wife. He launched a series of investigations through which he went some way to gazetting Orang Asli lands: firstly in the Telom valley where he incidentally had had his first contacts with the Temiar and stocked the river with English trout.[143]

The war propelled the Orang Asli into the modern world with sudden violence. In Perak, in particular, they were under pressure from the Chinese agriculturalists who were moving into the forests to escape the Japanese.[144] They traded with them, and this included the supply of food – particularly meat from hunting – to guerrilla camps. But towards the end of November an event occurred that was to have long-lasting repercussions for the Orang Asli. Pat Noone, his hair cropped short, naked save for brief shorts and a black cummerbund tied loose in the Temiar style, and accompanied by a six-man Temiar bodyguard, marched into the camp of the 5th Independent Regiment. On the British retreat, Noone, trusting to his local knowledge and connections, had taken to the forest with the Temiar communities. He had been in isolation from the other Europeans, and from the war, but had been in contact with some British officers in Kelantan. Noone's military experience was limited to Officer Training Corps at Cambridge, but he knew the Orang Asli as few outsiders did. He applied the principles of the British school of structural-functionalist anthropology to the understanding of Orang Asli social organization and leadership. He imparted this to the Malayan Communist Party and they applied it to their revolution. From the outset the communist leaders were deeply impressed by Noone's intellect. He was asked to write a paper on the Malays and to give a lecture to camp leaders on the Orang Asli; flattered by the fuss, he agreed. More significantly still, Noone possessed the only detailed map of the interior of Malaya. This, with his personal knowledge, made him a major asset to the MPAJA. He made introductions to Orang Asli leaders, and on New Year's Eve 1942, they held a party for MPAJA forces.[145]

At the end of 1942 the broader shape of the war in Southeast Asia was only dimly revealing itself. The Japanese had achieved astounding successes, destroying the myth of the British Empire which had prevailed for nearly two centuries. Even in India, the underpinnings of the Raj seemed to be crumbling away and it was now threatened by a militant Indian nationalism based in Singapore, Penang and Rangoon. In Burma and Malaya themselves, the status of Europeans and the local people who depended on them had undergone an astonishing transformation. The malnourished British were locked up in prisoner-of-war camps, despised by their Japanese captors. Anglo-Burmese and Malayan Eurasian former judges and civil servants were selling trinkets in the streets or working as coolies. The tribal and hill Christian communities, clients of the British, were deeply suspect to the Japanese, and often the targets of their violence. There were distant signs that the worst was over. Allied arms were making headway in North Africa; the Soviets were regrouping at Stalingrad. Admiral Yamamoto's great Pacific fleet had suffered a massive American counter-strike. Forgotten armies of Allied supporters and their communist allies were coming together in the Malay forests, and even in Burma the young men of the Independence Army were beginning to plot against the Japanese. Yet in the crescent 1943 was to be a year of horror. No true dawn was to appear on the Allied horizon for many months.

# 5

# 1943: Valleys of the Shadow
# of Death

As the New Year of 1943 dawned, the British and the Americans looked to the future with restored confidence. In Britain the sound of the November church bells celebrating the victory over the Germans at El Alamein in North Africa was still ringing in people's ears. Stalingrad had held against the Nazi onslaught. The German army was beginning to taste the bitterness of the greatest defeat in its history. In the Pacific, the US fleet seemed once again to have the upper hand. Alan Brooke, Chief of the Imperial General Staff, began to feel that the Allies might be 'beginning to stop losing this war'. He confided to his diary: 'We start 1943 under conditions I never would have dared to hope.'[1]

There were patches of failure amidst the emerging pattern of Allied success. The eastern land front against the Japanese was one area of continuing gloom and worry. Somewhere at the back of Brooke's mind lurked the fear that a British collapse in India might come at the same time as a renewed German eastward push, this time against the Allied oil resources in Persia at Abadan. If this were to happen, the whole grand strategy might unravel again before the end of the year. Of course, even in mainland Asia things could have been worse. At least India had held the Japanese advance as the monsoon and civil disobedience movement of 1942 petered out. The first Chindit expedition, which penetrated far behind enemy lines in north Burma, was about to give morale a significant upward blip. Kachin, Shan and Nagas were already fighting heroic guerrilla wars to protect their homelands. Yet India Command and Whitehall knew very well that the real reason the Japanese advance had stopped was that they simply did not have the resources to fight the Chinese, the US and British India at the same time. The British still did not really understand what they were up against. It required a further comprehensive 'licking' in 1943 for them to realize how much effort they would have to put into defeating this brave, desperate and ruthless enemy.

The faint stirrings of optimism in Southeast Asia were soon stilled by series of crises as corrosive and deadly as the collapsing house of cards of 1942. In an ascending order of danger, the threats were, first, local British and American disagreements about strategy and aims on the north Burma front; secondly, the dismal failure of the first British push forward in Arakan in the spring of 1943; thirdly, and most insidiously, India began to starve. The crisis was so severe that it became touch-and-go as to whether the subcontinent could ever again be the base for a military campaign. By the end of 1943 a few visionary individuals were even urging that the whole British effort should be moved to Australia. India, Britain's 'barrack in an oriental sea', had become her oriental charnel house.


## UNEASY ALLIES

The British and American disagreements over the future of the Burma front which were to smoulder through to the middle of 1944 were minor spats when compared with the titanic problems of the Allied grand strategy. Yet they did indicate how difficult it would be for the Allies to co-ordinate a joint plan when American resources were so hugely in excess of Britain's. Joseph 'Vinegar Joe' Stilwell was determined to avenge the defeat that his American and Chinese forces had suffered during the withdrawal of 1942. His ostensible aim was to capture the aerodromes in far northern Burma, especially the one at Myitkyina through which Dorman-Smith had recently made his unceremonious exit. From here the US could supply China's front against the Japanese with materiel from the Anglo-US base at Ramgarh in Bihar. A huge engineering effort was already underway at Ledo to extend a road eastward from Assam into Burma and at the same time to push south from Chinese territory against the Japanese. Stilwell wanted to concert a Chinese–American move south with a British and Indian army push eastward into Burma. There were two problems

about this. The first was Stilwell's aggressive and misanthropic character and, in particular, his contempt for his allies; the second was that
neither move was particularly strategically desirable.

Stilwell was a professional soldier who had spent much time in
China, but long service had not instilled in him any great respect for
the Chinese. As commander-in-chief of Chiang Kai Shek's nationalist
armies he carried on a running war with Chiang's other commanders.
His disagreements with Chiang over strategy soured relations between
the two to the point where the continuation of Stilwell's command
was constantly in question. In Stilwell's letters home, Chiang became
'Peanut', corrupt, obstinate and dominated by his wife, 'Madame',
and later by his mistress, a nurse several decades his junior.[2] Stilwell
portrayed Chiang as hesitant and defensive, unwilling to commit his
troops to an attack against the Japanese on the Burma front, afraid
both of the Chinese communists and of his own generals. In fact,
Chiang was a more astute general than might have appeared. He knew
that the real danger to his government lay in a Japanese attack from
the north against embattled Chungking. He did not want to send his
best troops off to Myitkyina and was perfectly correct in his assessment
of the communists, who were hoping to infiltrate into Nationalist
China's territories from the north in the rear of any Japanese advance.
Chiang refused to do anything much in Burma until the Allies agreed
to put in an amphibious expedition on its southern coast. This again
was sensible. Under intense pressure from Stilwell and Washington,
Chiang did finally agree to give over the Chinese forces at Ramgarh in
India to Stilwell's control and to a move into Burma from the north.[3]

Stilwell's view of the British was scarcely better than his view of the
Chinese. He regarded them as effete, defensive and disorganized. In a
later visit to India he marked down Wavell as a beaten man.[4] The India
of which the British were so proud was a pit of famished inefficiency,
even more backward than China. The British were, as he charmingly
put it, 'mother fuckers' who 'always try to cut our throats'. Mountbatten, who assumed the position of Supreme Commander Southeast
Asia in the summer of 1943, was simply a 'glamour boy', a matinee idol
with 'nice eye-lashes'. This was ironic since Stilwell's own reputation in
America and outside was partly a media creation. He was the gritty
American fighter struggling against Chink and Limey obstruction to

take the war to the Japs, a poor man's General MacArthur. The disdain was mutual. Alan Brooke recorded: 'Except for the fact that he was a stout hearted fighter suitable to lead a brigade of Chinese scallywags, I could see no qualities in him.' He was an inept tactician and 'did a vast amount of harm by vitiating the relations between the Americans and British both in India and Burma'.[5] The British high command were very dismissive of the Chinese, too. They suspected them, as Wavell had done in 1942, of having 'imperial' designs on north Burma. A secret intelligence memo of late 1943 caught the tone of this Allied mutual respect: 'Chiang, known to most Americans as "Chancre-Jack", is a stern iron-willed man who takes little heed of advice except from his wife.'[6]

As in the case of China, the real question was the feasibility of a British assault on Burma in 1943. Shipping for military supplies or even for feeding the civilian population of India was in perilously short supply before full-scale American war production developed in the autumn of the year. The lines of communication up into Assam or southeast into Arakan were extended and rickety. The perennial problem of finding high-quality British officers bore on both the Indian and the British armies, as Brooke realized. He thought it would not be until late 1944 that experience on battle fronts and rapid training courses would bring on enough junior officers to make up for the '1914–18 gap', the vast hole caused by casualties amongst the best junior officers in the First World War. And it was not until the final eighteen months of the Second World War that sufficient numbers of King's Commissioned and Viceroy's Commissioned Indian officers came on stream. A huge effort had to be put in by the Allies to refurbish India for a modern war. Up to that point, as Churchill colourfully told Brooke, an attack on Burma by land was a very doubtful proposition: 'you might as well eat a porcupine one quill at a time.'[7]

## ANOTHER FIASCO IN ARAKAN

Churchill kept his mind occupied with the thought of a variety of seaborne assaults against Japanese Southeast Asia via Sumatra and other unlikely ventures. Meanwhile, one attempt was made to eat a few quills of the porcupine. In the winter and early spring of 1942–43 the British tried to take the offensive in Arakan. India Command moved forces forward along the waterlogged coastal strip and also down the inland mountain ranges in an attempt to recapture Akyab, one of the most important ports of northwest Burma. The attempt was a total flop and the British had eventually to concede most of the gains they had made.[8] The Indian troops were too raw, inadequately trained and led and often suffering from malaria. The British troops did not really want to be there, failing to see why they should be defending an impoverished Indian population which did not want them when Britain itself was still under deadly assault. The Japanese, by contrast, still hoped for a significant victory. They were well protected in foxholes and even concrete bunkers. They also had fast motorboats, easily manoeuvrable in the coastal waterways of Arakan.

The British and Indian troops found themselves once again out-flanked and forced to retreat in a dismal replay of the events of 1942. India Command still seemed to be unable to understand the nature of total war. Stories of disorganization drifted back to Calcutta, Delhi and London. One typical story concerned the brigadier who had moved forward to a dangerous position in order to direct fire onto Japanese lines. He was brusquely called back behind the front lines to answer a call from HQ staff. They then engaged him in a long discussion about a certain committee of enquiry which was being planned. Witnesses heard the brigadier threaten to resign his commission with the words: 'I am here to fight a war, not to waste time fiddling about unnecessarily with sheaves of papers. You can tell the General from me to shove them up his rectum!'[9] The Allies had already achieved air superiority over this front, which was an augury for the future. In the meantime, air bombing of enemy forces was the usual hit-and-miss affair based on inadequate ground intelligence. A civilian assessment spoke of pilots boasting about bombing people with 'suspicious bundles'. In fact they had killed innocent refugees and a number of British agents.[10]

On the eastern front in 1943 about 450,000 Allied troops faced perhaps 300,000 Japanese troops across Burma. British and Indian battle casualties had been relatively light, about 5,000 killed and wounded, though thousands more contracted malaria.[11] The troops who had actually borne the brunt of the fighting were said to be in reasonable heart. They realized that the problem was less the super-human qualities of the Japanese than their own poor training, equipment and command. But the effect on morale in the rest of the army, and particularly among Burmese and Indian civilians, was disastrous. In Burma, many important local leaders who had supported the Allied war effort gave up and began to look to the Japanese. Expatriate opinion became uneasy again. At the end of the previous year 'Jick' Rudra had been sent to Arakan to see what was wrong. Over the next month or two he found out that morale amongst the Sikhs was terrible and there had been a string of desertions. Japanese propaganda and news of the Indian National Army were factors here. More important were local failures. The British officers had more or less given up, lacking direction from above. In one case, a Viceroy's Commissioned Officer had indulged in 'intrigue', favouritism for people from his own village or district and 'high-handedness'. This, conventional wisdom had it, usually happened when VCOs were left without adequate supervision.[12] Many British troops were equally demoralized and panicky, but no one in authority was really listening yet.

On 6 April the Calcutta *Statesman* mildly denounced 'muddled planning' in Arakan. General Noel M. S. Irwin, commander of the Eastern army, summoned a press conference. Irwin was certainly faced with poor morale and inadequate resources, but what offended observers was his blaming everyone except himself and his staff. Many officers believed he was unable to delegate and constantly intervened in their decisions. The debacle was a consequence, Irwin said, of lack of ships and lack of outboard motors for local communication. The troops should have stood and fought. 'Our men are not fit like the Jap is, and not constituted like the Jap is', and it would take generations to get them to that standard.[13] Worse, the Japanese had had the bad taste to 'run away' at an inconvenient time: in other words withdrawing and regrouping while British communications were stretched to breaking point. Irwin was deeply pessimistic: 'In Japan the infantryman is the corps d'élite; in England we put our worst men into the infantry.' As for Indians, it would take years to train them.[14]

The government of India leaned on the *Statesman*, according to its deputy editor Ian Stephens, and refused to allow the despatch of this news from India 'by any means of communication, telegraphic, postal mule, and whatnot'.[15] This infuriated the foreign correspondents whose disparagement of the military reached new heights. The left-wing Australian journalist Wilfrid Burchett spoke for many in his particularly virulent denunciation of India Command and the government of India. He wrote that 'thousands of British and Indian troops had to be sacrificed before the idea was drummed into the Delhi Brigade that a tank is stronger than a mule, a motor launch faster than a sampan, a concrete pill box is resistant to bayonets, even if the tanks, launches and pillboxes are manned by undersized people with yellow skins and buck teeth, who have not even heard of the playing fields of Eton or seen a cricket match'.[16] India Command in Delhi was, he raged, 'an antiquarium of Colonel Blimps ... All the inefficiency, orthodoxy, stodginess, inertia, complacency and snobbishness in the British army seems to have gravitated to India and found a congenial resting place' among the ponderous and self-satisfied civil bureaucracy.[17] The constant refrain was 'you can't get anything done with these people in this blasted climate'. The Indian army had no idea what privations people in Britain were facing. A typical comment by an expatriate returning to Delhi from Britain was, 'Tell you the truth, old man, I was glad to get back here and have a decent meal. Food's terrible over there.' It was not surprising, Burchett thought, that India Command was soon relieved of its fighting role and relegated to supply functions by an exasperated British government.

The debacle did have two important longer-term consequences, one positive and one negative. Whatever his personal style of command, Irwin's diagnosis was certainly right. In England on sick leave and relieved of his command, he met and briefed Lord Louis Mountbatten, soon to be supreme commander of the whole theatre. Mountbatten later acknowledged that his action plan for the 'forgotten army', an assault on the three weak points, 'malaria, monsoon and morale', owed much to Irwin's advice. British and Indian troops needed better medical attention, they needed to fight through the monsoon and morale had to be greatly improved.[18] The negative consequence of the first Arakan campaign was further to envenom relations between the Arakanese Buddhists and the local Muslim population. Zainuddin, a Muslim civil officer posted to the areas which the British temporarily reconquered in Arakan, wrote a confidential account of the hostility between the communities. The British Baluch troops in the area treated the local Buddhist population very badly, he recorded, telling them that the Muslims who had suffered at their hands during the Japanese invasion of the previous year 'would take full revenge on the Arakanese "Mugs"'.[19] The coolies and other camp followers who flooded into the region in the wake of the British stole large numbers of local boats and brutalized the people. Zainuddin compared the British treatment of the civilian population very unfavourably with that of the Japanese. Indeed, Wavell himself was worried by rumours that British troops had shot out of hand village headmen in Japanese-occupied areas.[20] All in all, these events seem to reverse the usual stereotypes of Japanese brutality and British solicitude for the civilian population. They were also part of a pattern common to the whole crescent: inter-community conflict became endemic in the wake of the fighting and would persist for at least a generation. Finally, Zainuddin delivered his most savage observation. On the appearance of the Japanese the indifferent and lethargic British troops 'began to run as no deer had ever run when chased by a tiger'.

## INDIA IN THE DOLDRUMS

Graft, pomposity and inefficiency really did seem to hold large parts of the Indian establishment, civil and military, in its grip. This was the perception not only of the newcomers, but also of many of the military and civil servants of India's governments, particularly the government of Bengal. The strain of war had brought this nineteenth-century system to the point of sclerosis. Petty failures abounded amongst the big disasters. For example, when the soldiers and refugees fleeing from Burma had arrived back in India, they naturally wanted to telegraph their relatives to announce that they were still alive. Not only were they charged full rates, their messages took between three days and a month to reach Calcutta alone. Many were still to be delivered as 1943 began. Some soldiers later reported of the Army Section of the Calcutta Sorting Office: 'the place is an absolutely chaotic state, letters anything up to five months old are just lying in heaps all over the floor in no sort of order. I feel certain that there are some letters for us in this country somewhere, probably stuck in a dump like this and receiving the same scant attention.'[21] At an airfield near Calcutta a random inspection revealed that the contractors had hoodwinked the air force by supplying non-reinforced cement two inches thick rather than reinforced cement six inches thick. Worse, many first-hand accounts indicate that no one was prepared to take responsibility. Large numbers of officers remained at ease in up-country stations far from the fronts with no idea how bad things were.

This pervasive rot in morale had a political dimension. The Quit India movement of August and September 1942 had been ruthlessly suppressed. More than 30,000 Congressmen and other political activists were in jail. They included Gandhi, Nehru and most of the high command. In some ways, though, a leaderless movement was more dangerous. Political activity had gone underground. Throughout 1943 and 1944 political gangs were active in the poverty-stricken 'badlands' of south Bihar, where they had been driven by police attacks on villages in 1942. Sporadic sabotage of the railways and telegraphs continued throughout 1943. In March, for example, Special Branch reported that one K. N. Bhattacharya was laying plans for widespread sabotage in Assam because 'the Indian Army would be greatly influenced by carrying on propaganda there'.[22] He was planning guerrilla attacks on a hydro-electric plant which generated electricity for the front and had apparently met both tribal leaders and a Muslim deserter from the Sappers and Miners. Pamphlets urging the population to rise against the government surfaced regularly. Bengal remained particularly restive. The British worried, as they had worried every year since the great Mutiny and rebellion of 1857–9, that political malcontents would begin to affect the army. A letter was in circulation from the new Indian National Army:

Dear Indian Brothers, The Japanese forces do not wish to fight against their Asiatic brothers, therefore you should not fight against us. It will be foolish to lose your lives by fighting for Britain who has been keeping you in slavery for years and has been ill treating you.[23]

Intelligence reports in early 1943 suggested that Indian officials of the government were secretly aiding demonstrators and others sentenced to death for political crimes. Even the government's friends were of concern to it. Congress propaganda against air-raid precautions as an 'imperialist ploy' had damaged recruitment to the services. The Communist Party, uneasy ally of the government since the Nazi invasion of Russia, stepped into the breach. Not only was it largely ineffective in getting the lower-caste and Muslim recruits that the government wanted, but officials also feared that some type of seditious 'people's committees' might be forming.[24] The terrors of the early summer of 1942 seemed to be returning.

In one respect the British had much to fear. Subhas Chandra Bose, their most resolute and resourceful Indian enemy, was on the move. On 27 or 29 May of the previous year he had finally met Hitler for the one and only time.[25] It was hardly a meeting of minds. The Führer had often expressed admiration for the British Empire and its dominion over 'lesser races'. Bose wanted the Axis powers to issue a declaration of Indian independence. Stifling his beliefs as a democrat, he greeted Hitler as 'an old revolutionary'. Bose had already written to Joachim von Ribbentrop, the German foreign minister, arguing that 'it is absolutely essential that I should be in the East'.[26] Hitler agreed. He would send Bose to his Japanese ally and solve a minor diplomatic problem that seemed likely to become a nuisance. Then it was the turn of the Japanese to vacillate. Did they really want Bose in their sector?

It was not until 8 February 1943, after months of meetings, journeys and speeches across Nazi-occupied Europe, that Subhas Bose and an aide clambered aboard a German U-boat on their way to Tokyo. As he left, he scribbled a note from Germany to his brother Sarat, then under house arrest in Calcutta, with little hope that the letter would ever reach him. He mentioned that he had married and had a small daughter in Europe. He was once again 'embarking on the path of danger'.[27] Before leaving he recorded an address in the Hotel Kaiserhof, Berlin. It commemorated the Amritsar massacre of 1919 when British troops had shot down unarmed Indians attending a political rally. Bose compared this to the Quit India movement. 'Machine gunning, aerial bombardment, tear gas, bayonet charges, capital punishment – none of these ruthless measures has succeeded in cowing down the unarmed masses of Indians.'[28] Bose had decided that he must move closer to the war front which was most critical to India. Hitler's Indian

Legion, recruited from Indian expatriates and POWs from North Africa, could achieve only indirect successes from its base in Germany. Bose would need to take hold of the Indian Independence League and the Indian National Army in Malaya and Burma and transform them. He himself had long since averted his eyes from features of fascism and Japanese imperialism in China that he had once found offensive. All that mattered was the liberation of India.

For both the Allies and the Axis in Asia, early 1943 was a time of hiatus. One bright spot, according to Burchett, was the first Chindit campaign in February. In fact, this campaign was not all it seemed at the time. It had originally been planned as a deep-penetration expedition to accompany a serious British push into north Burma from the Manipur area. Wavell, however, had to countermand that push because lines of communication were still poor and the Arakan offensive was going so badly. He was in two minds about abandoning the Chindit attack, too, but decided that this might be the last straw for Allied morale. The expedition went ahead as a kind of exceptionally costly training exercise. Frank Donnison, the former Burma civil servant who was to become an inveterate critic of the Chindit commander Orde Wingate and his posthumous reputation, believed that vital stores were diverted from India Command proper. Later, Alan Brooke himself was to complain about Wingate's 'continuous and excessive demands'. The campaign, however, did achieve a number of things. It reminded the Japanese that the British were still there, and it significantly improved British morale at a low point. It also gave the Chindit columns valuable experience which they were to draw on in future campaigns.[29] The columns of British, Indian and Gurkha troops made contact with Kachin and Shan guerrillas, learned how to cross the Chindwin river, live off the land and use small bazaars still run by Chinese and Indian businessmen in the distant hills.[30] The campaign could not be maintained for more than a few weeks, however, and the forces, emaciated and exhausted, crossed back across the Chindwin and struggled back into India. Still, the Chindit legend was born. It provided a glow of warmth for the British eastern army during the dog days of 1943. William Slim, later commander of the victorious 14th Army, credited Wingate with significantly improving morale.

Even further to the north and east another extraordinary saga of hardship and resolve was working itself out. After the Japanese invasion of 1942, the Allies had lost control of the original Burma–Yunnan road which had brought supplies up to the Chinese national-ists. For a year everything had needed to be flown to Chungking from India over the Hump or northern mountains, a dangerous and costly exercise. The Americans decided early on that it was imperative to build a new road from India across the northern tip of Burma into China as part of their support for the fragile nationalist regime. Wavell and Stilwell initiated the project in late 1942 and it was agreed that this would be an American show. Starting at the Italian mining settle-ment of Ledo in Assam, the road would thrust for 500 miles through Allied-controlled territory to Bhamo in north Burma and then on eastward to Kunming in China.[31] The plan was to get this road finished before the monsoon of 1944. The task seemed impossible. On the Chinese end of the route the road had to cross deep ravines and the Chinese engineers were forced to build miles of wooden causeways. At the Burmese–Indian end of the route, average rainfall was 150 inches per season. Any human being who inhabited this terrain was prey to leech bites which became infected and festered, as the 1942 refugees had discovered. Problems of labour control were acute for the road builders, especially at the Indian end. Coolies from the Assam tea plantations and others from Travancore in what is now Kerala, mingled with Kachins and porters from the Darjeeling hill tracts. Since there was no common tongue most orders had to be given by sign language. An attempt was made to use the small Indian horses which pulled *tonga* carriages along the roads of the subcontinent. This failed when many of the undersized animals suffered broken legs. Some progress had been made by February 1943, but then the rains washed the embankments away. Worse, early in the 1943 monsoon, Japanese patrols approached to within eighty miles of Ledo on the Assamese side, though at this point their own native drivers and elephants deserted them. By September 1943 the whole project had ground to a halt. It had progressed only forty-two miles during the whole year.

Then on 13 October General Lewis A. Pick arrived on the scene. Chosen personally by Stilwell following an interview in a rain-sodden tent, he had been in charge of flood control works on the Missouri river during the 1930s. Pick drove the project forward at the Chinese end with extraordinary energy. He relied heavily on black troops of the US Engineer Corps and was later acknowledged as having improved race relations within the US forces as a whole. He disciplined and organized the fragmented Indian, Chinese and Burmese labour force. He instituted twenty-four-hour shift working. During the night flares were lit in buckets of oil placed every few yards along the road. Pick achieved the extraordinary progress of one new mile of road per day. By New Year's Day 1944 he had got as far as Shingbwiyang, the ill-fated refugee camp where so many Burma refugees had died the previous year. It was through this route that Stilwell and his Chinese troops were to enter north Burma that year.

Wingate and Pick were two beacons shining through the gloom of 1943. Assam was protected by little more than the monsoon and gallant hill levies. In Arakan, to the south and west, things were still going no better. The British were hampered by poor artillery support and were still being caught out by the Japanese tactics of infiltration and turning the flank of the enemy. The result of the campaign was deeply dispiriting and did much to cancel out the morale-boosting effects produced by the Chindits' and Americans' long-range penetration forces further north in Assam. Churchill was particularly displeased. He had already summed up Wavell as a man better suited to running a provincial golf club than a major command. His biased view of the Indian army was that it was a massive and inefficient force that ought to be cut back severely. When Wavell returned to London and was consistently baited by Churchill, it was all that Alan Brooke could do to stop him resigning. Brooke confided to Wavell that if he had felt obliged to resign every time Winston had slighted him, he would have resigned every day and, anyway, 'resignation would not result in reforming Winston's wicked ways'.[32] The failure at Arakan, like the Indian army's great failures in the 1915–16 Mesopotamian campaign, did ultimately lead to dramatic changes in personnel and attitudes but before this deathbed reformation of the Indian empire came about its administrators were to face one great final humiliation. It was seen by many as the ultimate demonstration of the hollowness of the British claim to be running a competent government amidst the inefficiency of the Orient. This was the great Bengal famine of 1943–4 which killed an estimated 3 million people.

## THE GREAT STARVATION

For many poor Bengalis the nightmare began in October 1942 when a cyclone devastated the coastal parts of east Bengal, especially the district of Midnapur. Abani, a fisherman, later recounted his story. On the night of the cyclone, 16 October, his married sister had come to visit:

The storm blew up because God (Bhagaban) wanted to kill all humans. Everything – trees, people, houses – was blown away; people were thrown about on top of walls and into trees. My father and sister died in the flood. My father was crushed under a collapsed wall. My sister could not swim and was swept away, but we found her corpse the following day.

After the cyclone and flood, Abani had to give up fishing for two years. 'We could not afford to buy a net, which cost Rs400 and had to be replaced every year. The moneylender would not give me a loan. The moneylender himself had no money. Our family possessions had been destroyed in the flood: of eight cows we only saved one.' Abani turned to day labour and salt making. The remains of the family survived the gathering famine by supplementing a little grain with gruel from relief kitchens and root vegetables.[33]

A year after the cyclone struck, famine and disease peaked across the Bengal countryside. Arangamohan Das, a relief worker, reported of one of the worst affected areas:

In the morning of October 24, I with a small party of my colleagues reached the Terapekhia bazaar, situated on the river Haldi. There I saw nearly 500 destitutes of both sexes, almost naked and reduced to bare skeleton. Some of them were begging for food or asking for pice [small coins] from the passers by, some longing for food with piteous look, some lying by the wayside approaching death hardly with any more energy to breathe and actually I had the misfortune of seeing 8 peoples breathe their last before my eyes. It shocked me to the bottom of my heart.[34]

In September 1943 this was the situation in the town of Manikganj as reported to the Bengal Relief Committee by D. C. Majumdar, a local attorney:

Dear Sir,

Without much introduction regarding the gravity of the situation, the harrowing details of which beggars description, I, on behalf of Manikganj relief committee beg to draw your attention to the following state of things arising from want to subsistence.

Some famished people are taking gruel from free-kitchens. But there are hundreds of little children, both orphans and those deserted by parents. They cannot take gruel and are only fit for using mother's breast. They are rolling on the street. Some of them are dying and the dead bodies lying by the roadside – none to look after these. They require milk, barley, water, etc. if the innocent creatures are to be saved.

Cholera in the form of an epidemic has broken out both in this town and in the mofussil [country] areas of this subdivision. People attacked by cholera are lying here and there, spreading germs of diseases all over the locality, groaning in agony for days together with no one to look after them.[35]

War, which was the broad context of the famine, was intertwined with it in malignant ways. The Bengali novelist Bhowani Sen wrote:

In Chittagong, women from the families of fishermen, scavengers and others were forced by the distress in the wake of the famine to join the Military Labour Corps in large numbers. From there, many have come back infected with venereal diseases. This is true not only of Chittagong; in many famine-devastated areas of Bengal, womanhood has been dishonoured. A section of the contractors has made a profession of selling girls to the military. There are places ... where women sell themselves literally in hordes, and young boys act as pimps for the military. After having tolerated meekly theft, bribery and deception we have come to a stage where we fail to stand up even to this barbarism.[36]

Sen told the story of Majada, the wife of a poor peasant. During the famine, her husband had deserted her. Later he came home, an invalid who could no longer work. She joined the Labour Corps and soon realized that she would have to sell herself to survive. She revolted at the filth and corruption and deserted with thirteen other women, but hunger drove her back to the Corps again. Sen saw Majada one last time as she lay dying in her village. He wrote, 'Standing on the Arakan Road, I felt I was standing amid the devastated ruins of a great and ancient civilisation. Under this heap of ruins lay buried all its precious legacy – kindness and compassion, mutual respect and comradeship – all bruised and broken to bits.'

How had this situation arisen? The roots of the famine were deep in the past. Bengal was a rice-growing province which could support two crops a year. Less exposed to drought than the drier areas to the north, its population had crept up slowly but steadily since the last great famine of 1769–70. Peasant farmers were under pressure to pay rents to a class of landowners deeply dug into village society and itself growing rapidly in numbers.[37] The British government had done little or nothing to promote sources of income other than from agriculture in the province. Indian nationalists, indeed, accused it of 'deindustrializing' the country, destroying the indigenous artisan textile industries and failing to provide the conditions for industrial development. To feed their families and pay the landlords and the government which stood behind them, peasants had switched to growing jute and other cash crops, abandoning the cultivation of low-value rice. They had already suffered terribly during the Great Depression when the value of jute and other cash crops had plummeted. With further growth of population in the 1930s, the food situation was balanced on a knife-edge. Scarcity was always a possibility. But in Burma, with its relatively smaller population, the rice acreage was rapidly expanding. By 1940 something like 15 per cent of India's rice was coming from Burma, and much of this was finding its way to Bengal. Then, during 1942, an unparalleled set of problems hit Bengal.

The government was already worrying in an indecisive way about the food problem when British Burma fell to the Japanese. Too much of India's rice had been shipped off to help the war effort in the Middle East and Ceylon. The appearance of large numbers of Allied troops had not helped matters. But the fall of Burma was a double blow. Not only did it cut off an important supply of rice at a stroke, but the authorities also panicked themselves into a scorched earth policy. The nearer the Arakan frontier, the more officials urged the destruction of the boats that plied along the great network of canals which linked producer, bazaar and consumer. Not only all motor vehicles and carts but even elephants from Chittagong and its surrounding countryside up to the Assam border had been 'scorched'.[38] Farmers and merchants who were already terrified of invasion and price controls could not get their produce to market even if they had wanted to. But things got worse. The usually plentiful wheat harvest in the Punjab and north India was rather poor in the autumn of 1942. The Punjab government itself moved to impose price and movement controls on wheat. Of course, Bengalis did not eat wheat; the poor could not even digest it very easily, but wealthier people, north Indian immigrants and soldiers could have eaten it if it had been available, so taking the pressure off the poor.

Then on 16 October 1942 the whole east coast of Bengal and Orissa was visited by the cyclone described by Abani. A huge area of rice cultivation was flooded up to forty miles in from the sea. This almost complete failure of the autumn rice crop meant that people had to eat their surplus and the seed that should have been planted in the winter of 1942 had been consumed by the time the hot weather began again in earnest in May 1943.

At this point, a competent and independent government might have intervened to bring in food supplies and provide people with seed for the next harvest. But this was wartime and the government of Bengal, far from being independent, was weak and corrupt. Indian provinces which had suffered devastating famines in the nineteenth century were better prepared. Bengal however had no 'famine code' and little organization to deal with the impending food shortage. Its ministry was a sleazy machine for patronage, split by hostility between Hindus and Muslims. According to Arthur Dash, its British members and advisers were lazy and incompetent. The esprit de corps found in the Punjab civil service was lacking. The higher levels of the British government had been warned constantly from the early months of 1942 that a serious crisis was building up. It was a matter not only of public welfare but of military security that the second most important base of Britain's world power should be adequately fed. But government was deaf at the highest level. Nor were local agencies in better shape. There were many complaints about the province's British and Indian doctors who, as one official put it, 'make astonishingly heavy weather of everything and persist in sticking strictly to the letter of every instruction to the exclusion of any initiative'.[39]

The British War Cabinet refused to countermand orders to send

Indian food overseas. It had not the slightest intention of diverting shipping from the war front to send food to Bengal. Britain was grossly overstretched and the ships were needed to feed the United Kingdom and supply the critical war front in the Middle East. Leo Amery, the secretary of state, who had the responsibility of justifying the doings of Indian government in Parliament, began by adopting a lofty political economist's perspective. He argued that growing hunger was the 'natural' result of the long-term growth of the Indian population and Bengal's climatic problems, as if this somehow justified the government's lethargy. By the early summer of 1943 he was, however, becoming seriously concerned. Penning ever more alarming reports on the food situation for his Cabinet colleagues, he tried to rouse them to action. He predicted that India's future as a base of military operations would be threatened if the population of Bengal continued to starve and die in the ensuing epidemics. Morale in the Indian army was in jeopardy. A soldier wrote in an intercepted letter: 'We come home to our own villages to find the food is scarce and high priced. Our wives have been led astray and our land has been misappropriated. Why does the Sarkar [Government] not do something about it *now* rather than talking about post-war reconstruction?'[40] An even more urgent tone was heard after British and Indian press reports began to use the forbidden word 'famine' in July and August 1943. Yet the Cabinet remained unwilling to release more than a quarter of the food tonnage and shipping which the viceroy and secretary of state were now demanding.

Quite apart from the demands of war, it is difficult to escape the impression that the War Cabinet was simply hostile towards India. The prime minister believed that Indians were the next worst people in the world after the Germans. Their treachery had been plain in the Quit India movement. The Germans he was prepared to bomb into the ground. The Indians would starve to death as a result of their own folly and viciousness. Churchill got the implicit support of the government's scientific adviser Frederick Lindemann, who seems to have thought the Bengalis were a weak race and that overbreeding and eugenic unfitness were the basic reasons for the scarcity.

In Bengal the situation deteriorated rapidly during May and June. It became a 'familiar sight to see crowds of ordinary honest country people gathering in their hundreds for a poor handout of food and soon to see many dying in the streets'.[41] Disease was as much of a scourge as hunger itself. Cholera hospitals were overcrowded and people died in the streets and parks where they lay. Seeking the city as their last hope, they flooded into the terminals by bus and train, collapsing on the platforms and near the bus shelters. As they did so, they spread more cholera to the suburban quarters. Air-raid posts were transformed into temporary shelters and food distribution points, as a limited charitable operation got underway. This was constantly disrupted as Japanese air raids continued. Then the shops closed and already weakened people fled in their thousands back towards the villages. Some Europeans and wealthy Indians gave up eating rice or provided free food to the poor. A wide range of Indian voluntary associations from the Ramakrishna mission through to the Marwari Association and the Arya Samaj attempted to collect food and bring it into the province.[42] Government remained weak and directionless. The governor, Sir John Herbert, was dying of cancer in Government House while his people died around him. After his retirement, there was a hiatus of several months before he was replaced by the Australian administrator, R. G. Casey.[43]

The famine hit the most vulnerable hardest. It was people who were dependent on food or wages from others in the villages who starved first. Those who died were 'the village washerman, cobbler, blacksmith, tailor, mason, labourer and his wife and his dependants and children'.[44] These people were predominantly of low caste, of course. Inequalities within the family as well as between social groups were brutally exaggerated. Many starving families tried to preserve young males, sacrificing their daughters and grandmothers. Hundreds of thousands died in their own homes, too proud to embarrass others with their fate. People lay down in the street and died, rather than resisting or looting the grain stores in the way the radicals wanted. This was not because they were 'fatalistic', as the British and high castes asserted. It was because they were good subjects, good parents, good children. Their rulers, elders and betters, husbands and fathers had cut them adrift.

Mrs Pandit, Nehru's sister, toured the relief centres in Bengal in September. She wrote of 'rickety babies with arms and legs like sticks;

nursing mothers with wrinkled faces; children with swollen faces and hollow-eyed through lack of food and sleep; men exhausted and weary, walking skeletons all of them'. Worse still was 'the look of utter resignation in their eyes. It wounded my spirit in a manner that the sight of their suffering bodies had not done.'[45] By mid October the death rate in Calcutta alone had reached over 2,000 per month, this compared with under 600 a month in a so-called normal year, though for the poor of Calcutta all years were abnormal. The journalist Wilfrid Burchett wrote that 'each morning the trucks rolled around the suburbs of Calcutta like the plague carts of seventeenth-century England . . . by September and October they were picking them up – mainly women and children – at the rate of a hundred a day.' The air was tainted with the smell of the dying, the 'distinctive sourish odour which the victims give off a few hours before the end'.[46]

Muslim burial parties too weak to carry the bodies to a cemetery simply tipped their friends and family members into the river and let them float down to the sea. But still famished people continued to arrive in the city. Some arrived at Howrah station on the point of death, too weak even to pull themselves off the trains. Those who could make it often collapsed in the freight yards where they huddled picking tiny grains of rice out of the mud where they had fallen from the bottoms of the few boxes of grain which had arrived. Others trooped into the city hoping that the government would do something for them: 'lines of dusty scarecrows, predominantly women accompanied by children with bloated bellies and shrivelled limbs moving towards the magic capital where surely food must be abundant'.[47]

Much of the country outside Bengal was now aware of the events in the province. Indian relief agencies in the Punjab, social service societies and religious associations were beginning to mobilize to send in food. Some of this aid reached Calcutta, but out in the districts of the southeast the situation was even worse. In towns such as Faridpur and Barisal 'armies of the destitute and starving' roamed up and down the roads. Relief kitchens had been closed down for lack of supplies. The poor of the villages were forced to sell their lands and houses for just a few pounds of rice which they consumed in days. People died in the streets and cholera was rampant. Bloated and rotting bodies were torn apart by jackals and vultures, so spreading the disease further. No aid reached these areas because no transport was available.

Only government action could have had the slightest impact on the situation. The *Statesman*, Calcutta's leading British-run newspaper, which had already denounced the incompetence of the army, now began a courageous campaign against the civil authorities. It denounced the appalling ineptitude and corruption of the previous provincial government of Fazlul Haq, adding pointedly that it was British as well as Indian officials that had advised it. In an editorial on 23 September it fulminated: 'This sickening catastrophe is man made', a consequence of the 'shameful lack of planning capacity and foresight by India's own civil Governments, Central and Provincial'.[48] More dramatically, its editor Ian Stephens began to publish pitiable photographs of dead and dying women and children.[49] T. G. Narayan of the rival *Hindu* wrote to him that 'by that single act you have done more to impress both on Government and the people the seriousness of the situation than all other newspapers with their verbose editorials'. There was a spontaneous outpouring of private charity though this did little to alleviate the situation. Grieving children at the New School in Darjeeling launched an appeal and collected Rs800 for the victims by saving up their pocket money. Sudhir Ghosh, a former political activist, found some peace of mind working with the Friends' Ambulance Unit in the dreadful conditions of Midnapur district.[50]

For months the word from Calcutta had been that there was no real problem. Arthur Dash was sure that the basic difficulty was the lack of any consistent policy on the part of the provincial government. The administration, often operating on autopilot, passed contradictory orders. It was too timid to interfere with the vast profits made by local politicians trading in rice. Dash realized that he himself was contributing to the problem in a small way. He had bought up two months' supply of rice for his own servants at the inflated price of Rs50 per maund and sold it to them at Rs20.[51] This was happening across the country where district magistrates, industrial companies and landholders were hoarding grain for the use of their own dependants. The people who suffered most, of course, were those who had no protector and no avenue of patronage. Now H. S. Suhrawardy, the new minister for civil supplies, a man more competent, but perceived by some as even less financially fastidious, than Fazlul Haq, had himself used the phrase 'unprecedented famine'.[52]

The ire of Stephens and his Indian staff was directed more forcefully yet against the central government. For a full year after the Japanese declaration of war, there had been no government of India food department. Ineffectual attempts to control prices had given way suddenly to a freeing of the market. Provincial governments with surplus food were no longer allowed to prevent its export. The centre, said the *Statesman*, already had the power to intervene against the provincial governments, but did not have the guts. The argument about local self-government was simply 'an excuse for its lack of foresight and its failure to take an all-India view of food as a munition of war'. Amery, 'habitually smug', had to take ultimate responsibility for this desperate failure, moral and administrative, of British government, the newspaper asserted.

The sight of this tragedy all around them was beginning to sap the morale of British as well as Indian troops. Some young British newcomers 'feel personally disgraced that such conditions should have been allowed to develop among the helpless and ignorant of a great province for whose welfare Britain still carries a great share of responsibility'.[53] As the stilted words of one intelligence report had it, the troops were 'adversely affected by the visible evidence of the result of famine conditions. Among British troops there has been some open criticism of government.'[54] One British military unit fed a hundred children, while an Indian battalion collected Rs100 as food aid. Against orders, some troops began to share their own food with the starving. W. A. Barnes later recorded,

I have heard many homeless little children of between 5 and 10 crying bitterly and coughing terribly outside my room in the rest camp at Chittagong at 3 and 4 in the morning in the pouring monsoon rain. They were all stark naked, motherless, fatherless and friendless. Their sole possession was an empty tin in which to collect scraps of food. We were strictly prohibited from helping any of these refugees in any way under heavy penalties. Many could not endure to see this suffering and helped surreptitiously.

Barnes, in contrast to the editors of the *Statesman*, blamed 'well-fed and well-paid Bengalis' for the tragedy and largely exonerated the British government.[55] Congress and the INA laid responsibility squarely at the feet of the government. At a rally in Singapore on 15 August Subhas Bose offered to supply Burmese rice to India. The news was spread across India by Japanese radio. Even a body such as the Bengal Provincial Hindu Mahasabha, which looked relatively favourably upon the war effort, urged the government to consider this offer.[56]

In the end it was the implications of the famine for the war effort that tipped the balance from neglect to action. Linlithgow's belated but growing alarm seems to have woken up people in London. The chiefs of staff began to hear that India would not be able to serve as a base of operations against Japan in 1944 if its civilian economy collapsed. The troops themselves might even face shortages. But Linlithgow was too old and tired to achieve very much. He had already served a full year more than the normal viceroy's term. Six feet six inches tall, 'long hours spent at his task had given him a stoop and his eyes were the eyes of a tired man'. In early autumn Amery had finally managed to extract a commitment from the War Cabinet to send a million tons of food to India and divert some shipping for that purpose. This was still no more than a quarter of what the government of India was demanding.

## THE SLOW FIGHT BACK BEGINS

Now, finally, British government within India was changing. In extremis, the Raj returned partly to its origins as a government of military occupation. This was first signalled by the arrival of Admiral Lord Louis Mountbatten at Delhi airport in September to take up his post as Supreme Allied Commander South East Asia. The war effort against Japan was now taken out of what Churchill saw as the sclerotic grip of Delhi.[57] In retrospect it might seem that Mountbatten was appointed SAC for positive reasons. His royal status would impress the Indians; he was knowledgeable about amphibious operations; he understood logistics, and so on. But many of the reasons were actually negative. Mountbatten was chosen because the Americans were prepared to allow a Briton to hold this position as a quid pro quo for

British acceptance of an American Supreme Allied Commander in Europe. Churchill realized that he could not insist that Alan Brooke or any other British general fill this command, given that the US was to provide most of the troops and war materiel for the coming invasion of Europe.

Brooke remained doubtful about the appointment. He was initially more favourable than Churchill, but privately recorded that Mountbatten had none of the qualities of a supreme commander and that he was unimpressed by his enthusiasms. Just before the appointment was made, the 'Supremo' designate had been touting around Whitehall a bizarre plan to build aircraft carriers out of ice floes ('Operation Habakkuk'). At an Allied chiefs of staff meeting in Canada he had even attempted to win over his audience for this plan by shooting at large chunks of ice with a pistol to demonstrate their resilience. An officer waiting outside was heard to remark, 'Good heavens, they've started shooting now!'[58] This incident appears to have confirmed Brooke in his judgement of Mountbatten's lack of soundness for command. But there were bigger issues at stake. Brooke was convinced that the occupation of Italy had to be completed before an invasion of northern Europe, let alone Southeast Asia. He was afraid that an alliance of forces was building up to frustrate this. There was continuous American pressure to aid Chiang Kai Shek by opening up a land route to Chungking through north Burma. Worse, Churchill had become a sudden convert to the idea of a seaborne invasion of Southeast Asia via the northern tip of Sumatra. Brooke worried that all this might coincide in some obscure way with one of 'Dickie Mountbatten's bright ideas' and lead to the diversion of vital resources into some madcap scheme in Asia. In the event, Brooke had won the point before Mountbatten even touched down at Delhi. By 1 October Brooke had forced Churchill and the Americans to ignore pleas from India to send landing craft and other supplies from the Mediterranean to the East. He was able to hold this position for another six months.

This meant that Mountbatten's arrival in Asia did not signal the opening up of a new amphibious Asian front. It meant only that, slowly and painfully, Southeast Asian land forces would have to prepare themselves to confront the increasingly desperate Japanese Imperial

Army over some of the worst terrain in the world. To return to Churchill's picturesque metaphor, they finally began preparations to eat the porcupine quill by quill. Yet Brooke had misjudged the impact of Mountbatten in one vital respect.[59] He had charisma. This was vital for a demoralized sector of the war where the British felt themselves failures, the Americans felt marginalized and the Indians were smarting under a historic sense of grievance. As a member of the royal family Mountbatten did at least impress the Indian princes, the aristocracy and the ridiculously class-conscious British society in India. As a skilled public performer and speaker he gave morale a much needed shot in the arm.[60] The denizens of New Delhi were prepared to be uncharmed. One contemporary recorded that the 'brass hats' went to meet Mountbatten at the aerodrome 'including several American generals who did not seem too impressed', in part because they wanted the job themselves. Then there emerged from the plane a tall, bronzed man with sleeves rolled up, but sporting his medals. 'He shook hands all around with a dazzling smile. He was so handsome – no Hollywood star in admiral's uniform could have looked more striking – and the American generals' resistance melted in the glow of his personality.'[61] Mountbatten quickly established a large staff in Delhi and began to address the critical problem of how to improve the lines of communication between plains India and Assam. The troops had to be fed properly before they could fight. Monsoon, malaria and morale: these were the most deadly enemies.

In those first few weeks the old and new establishments of the British Raj did not mix well. Mountbatten's charm and energy only went so far to assuage the wounded feelings of India Command, which had been relieved of operational responsibility for the Assam and Arakan fronts. Even the Indian soldiers felt that it was unreasonable for the Indian army to take all the blame for the dismal showing of the spring when they had been so poorly supplied and inadequately trained. The differences of style grated badly at first. One small incident brought out the contrasting attitudes between the new supreme commander and the leathery, paternalistic establishment of India Command. Shortly after his arrival in Delhi, Mountbatten's ADC phoned Auchinleck on a private matter. Where did the General Officer Commanding India get his hair cut? The Auk's ADC replied that his boss's hair was cut by his military barber, Naik Ram Gul. Mountbatten's ADC replied, 'Oh! Supremo wouldn't like his hair cut by a native.' Instead, a man from Trumpers, the gentlemen's shop near Piccadilly Circus in the fashionable part of London, was drafted into the RAF as a sergeant and flown out.[62]

One reason Admiral Mountbatten seemed to be a good choice as head of South East Asia Command was that the Allies originally envisaged a seaborne invasion of Burma and Malaya. The demand for ships and landing craft in the Mediterranean scotched this. The brunt of the fighting was, therefore, to fall on Southeast Asian land forces. SEAC had at its disposal roughly a million men in late 1943 and early 1944, exclusive of the large force garrisoning or being trained in India, which remained under Auchinleck's India Command. SEAC's total compared favourably with the million-odd men the Japanese had in Southeast Asia as a whole. In addition, the Japanese could call upon about 80,000 friendly troops in the Indian National Army and the Burma Independence Army, though the latter proved distinctly unreliable in the long run. In late 1943 and early 1944 the British forces under SEAC constituted the fleet, the air force and the 11th Army Group under General Giffard. The heart of this force, which included troops in Ceylon and the Indian Ocean islands, was General William Slim's 14th Army. This was a force which numbered between 80,000 and 100,000 men and which was to fight a brilliant defensive campaign against the Japanese invasion of India in 1944. It went on to reoccupy Burma, French Indo-China, Malaya and the Dutch East Indies in 1945–6.

The 14th Army was composed of three army corps of about 30,000 men each and the special forces under Wingate. The troops came from British, Indian army, Burma army and African units. Some of these were the same men who had retreated from Burma in 1942, now retrained and re-equipped. Others were new units brought in from Europe and Africa or raised in India and Nepal. Indian Army units were composed of one-third British soldiers and two-thirds Gurkha or Indian troops. Though figures fluctuated and are difficult to pinpoint, about 70 per cent of soldiers in the 14th Army were Indians, Gurkhas, Burmese peoples (mostly Kachins, Karens and Shan) or east and west Africans. While Mountbatten, Stilwell (now his deputy) and George

Giffard played a part in energizing this polyglot force, it was William Slim who was responsible for turning it into a well-trained fighting force. Slim, a Gurkha officer by training, was one of the most admired British soldiers of the twentieth century. Slim had helped organize the retreat from Burma in 1942, receiving scant thanks from the irascible Irwin. Thereafter he began patiently to plan for victory. Liked by his fellow officers and the Indian and Gurkha troops, he became a skilful strategist and propagandist for a series of campaigns in which neither the British soldiers nor the Asian and African troops had any strong national interest.

In the following spring, finding the atmosphere of Delhi torpid, Mountbatten moved his whole staff off to Kandy in Ceylon, which became the headquarters of SEAC. India was reduced to a supporting role and the commander in chief, the patient but chastened Auchinleck, spent the remainder of the war organizing India as an effective centre of supply and control. With unrivalled knowledge of the Indian army and of Indian and Nepali society, Auchinleck finally came into his own.[63] He flew around the subcontinent from base to base encouraging the troops and trying to hold up recruitment which in the later months of 1943 sagged as the harvest came in. He visited and cajoled the Indian princes who remained vital for the supply of troops and civilian labour. He established contact with the Imam of the Delhi Jama Masjid, and even, on one occasion after the war, received Gandhi at his house in central Delhi.[64]

On the heels of Mountbatten came Archibald Wavell, the Harley Street medical practitioner with his travelling bag, sent to tend another dying patient, this time as penultimate viceroy and governor general of India. On 20 October 'Archie' was installed as viceroy at a stately ceremony in the gigantic sandstone and marble palace in Delhi, surrounded by bejewelled princes, turbaned warriors of the bodyguard and British officials in full civil regalia. Less than a week later he arrived in Calcutta. This was something his predecessor had not done since the beginning of the famine. Visiting a relief centre where a few minutes earlier air-raid precaution workers had still been carrying the dying to hospital, he and the vicereine stood sympathetically 'amidst the famished in their filthy rags on Calcutta's less attractive streets'.[65] Visibly moved, he toured the emaciated groups of people asking about the food and where they had come from. Wavell already had a good deal of information about the famine. Through Auchinleck, he had sent 'Jick' Rudra down to Dacca a few weeks earlier. Rudra had confirmed the impression that the civil authorities were either complacent or incompetent. One district officer had at first refused to see Rudra about relief efforts because he was going to the tennis club for a game.[66]

Wavell announced the first concerted action which had yet been taken in the months of famine. He ordered the speeding up of food deliveries from within India, especially of wheat from the Punjab. The destitute were to be sent to properly managed relief camps outside the city. Military vehicles and personnel were to be used in a co-ordinated plan to send food to the outlying villages. The army said that it had not been asked to help with famine relief by the civil power at any point before Wavell's speech. Very soon, though, military convoys were in action moving food around the countryside in lorries emblazoned with the words 'Food for the People' in Bengali and English.[67] In more remote areas army mules took bags of rice to villages which had been virtually cut off from the outside world since the panicked 'scorched earth' policy of spring 1942. Military intelligence reports claimed that Indian morale immediately began to improve. Most Indians were said to consider civil administration corrupt and inefficient, while the military was still held in high regard.

Wavell fired no magic bullet. Of the viceroy's commandeering of stocks a British commentator recorded, 'So the famine ended and honour was restored.'[68] It was not as simple as that. The death rate in Calcutta was still over 1,500 per month, three times normal, at the end of 1943. Across Bengal as a whole up to 10,000 people a week were still dying of starvation and many of those who apparently recovered from malnutrition succumbed easily to the waterborne diseases rampant in the months after the monsoon. One major problem was the fact that the first food supplies to come on line consisted of wheat from the Punjab rather than rice imported from overseas. Desperately weak and famished people who were used to eating rice could not digest wheat and died even when food finally became available. Perhaps the most terrible irony was that the rice harvest of the autumn of 1943 was one of the best on record. The 'luscious profusion' of ripening crops swayed gently in the southeast winds. But instead of the babble and jollity of the women and children harvesting the crop, there was an eerie silence. In village after village there was no one left alive to harvest it. A reporter who visited the Twenty-four Parganas district encountered many childless girls of about fifteen 'wearing the white borderless sari of the widow'. One woman's husband was found lying dead in a hut where he had gone to look after the crops.[69]

Calcutta during these awful, critical months was a strange place: a dying world, but also the centre of a major war effort. Tens of thousands of Allied officers came through the city for briefings and meetings. The press was muzzled, but cinemas showing Hollywood love stories remained open for the troops while starving Bengalis died outside their foyers. The limited number of hotels were crammed with beds, sometimes four men to the same room and bunks in the corridors. Other ranks came into the city for rest and recreation. As in other sectors of the war front, racial tensions sometimes exploded when Indian, British, American, Free French and Chinese troops were in close proximity. Black American troops, often driving around in large jeeps and sporting larger wallets than even British and Indian officers, were resented by whites and high-caste Indians. The black soldiers for their part complained of an Indian and white colour bar. There were occasional scuffles and fights around restaurants and hotels.[70] Meanwhile, even in the crisis of the war, many British continued to discriminate against mixed-race Eurasians, the most loyal of the empire's subjects, who had suffered most from the Japanese and kept all the major services running even in the face of the Quit India movement. The ever-outraged Burchett railed against the pomposity and bad faith of sections of Calcutta society. One woman told him that while it was all right to sleep with Eurasian women, 'flaunting a half-breed' set a man beyond the pale.[71]

Yet the tenacity of racism appeared a mild social evil compared with destitution. British and Indian officers who went to Calcutta during 1943 and '44 hated seeing the poverty and the beggar-ridden streets. The newspapers complained that the famine had led to a great explosion of disease, but the authorities allowed the streets to remain filled with 'huge, stinking heaps of garbage, whereon crows and kites and mangy dogs, cattle and human scavengers scramble for sustenance'.[72]

Arthur Dash, who had begun to work for the Public Service Commission in Calcutta a year before, was like many others disgusted by the luxury that he still saw at the Bengal Club. He recalled seeing an American admiral demanding and then consuming a second helping of langoustine in the well-stocked dining room. Going out into the town by the Russell Street entrance, he encountered an emaciated Bengali villager. The man was 'picking over the contents of the club garbage cans and trying to get some nourishment by sucking the empty skins of the cray fish which had fallen from the tables of the rich men lunching at the Club'.[73] A few months later A. C. Potter, Dorman-Smith's former secretary, now a brigadier, recorded his own shame. The meals at the club were still at their luxurious pre-war standard. He wrote, 'how people can accept such luxury nowadays beats me. I wonder if there was any lowering of the standard of meals when the streets of Calcutta were littered with destitute and starving people last autumn.'[74] W. A. Barnes, too, later noted down the seven-course meals on offer at the Grand Hotel on Chowringee. The dishes included 'tronçons de bekhti Allenby', and 'quartier de mouton rôtie à la Metternich'. The cooks were apparently Egyptian and Austrian, with a penchant for allusions to the martial and diplomatic. Guests complained when there were only two instead of four eggs each at breakfast.[75] In England the ration was two eggs a month. Calcutta's poor could afford none.

Despite this, many Calcutta expatriates and upper-class Indians did rally to help with the war and relief efforts. Volunteers flooded to the Red Cross, Salvation Army, YMCA and church groups. Hindu and Muslim charitable organizations worked overtime and some big businessmen donated money for famine victims and troop welfare. The Hospital Welfare Service helped to give patients companionship and keep them occupied. European women ran tea stalls at Howrah terminus. They took medicines to airports and bus stations and looked after the huge numbers of orphans who had survived the escape from Burma in the previous year. Though it hardly made a dent on death rates in the city, let alone in the villages, the volunteers donated and distributed food to the famine victims through ARP units and relocation camps.

However sickening the conditions around them, men about to be sent to one of the most vicious and uncomfortable war fronts in history expected a little luxury, drink and, of course, sex, before departing to what might very well be their deaths. Eastern Command, unprepared in almost every way in 1942 and early 1943, did not have troop entertainment high on its list of priorities. The volunteers stepped in here too. The Calcutta amateur dramatic societies in the city formed the Bengal Entertainment for the Services Association. BESA put on plays, dances and concerts, drawing on the large pool of talented eastern European Jewish and other refugees from Nazism who had found their way there during the 1930s.[76] Small groups were created to visit troops on the Arakan and Assam fronts. Indian entertainers, jugglers, acrobats and dancing girls were brought in from the villages to give the proceedings an oriental tinge. One night a pre-war comedy artist sang 'A Nightingale Sang in Berkeley Square' to completely drunken troops in from the Arakan front. Some of the earlier and most courageous visitors from Britain were the singers Elsie and Doris Waters and Vera Lynn. Later, in 1944, Noël Coward charmed his way through the empire's second city.

Sex was a trickier issue. Some lucky young men of the European and American officer class struck up liaisons with the wives and daughters of businessmen and civil servants. Others had surreptitious flings with Eurasian nurses and volunteers, while being abjured not to 'flaunt' them in public. Dash remembered seeing a GI and an Anglo-Indian woman having sex in the back seat of a taxi while the Sikh driver sat impassively in the front.[77] Indians and British other ranks were less fortunate. Calcutta and the other eastern garrison towns during the war years provided uniquely favourable conditions for mass prostitution. A huge number of men of many nationalities, almost all far from their homes, lived for brief periods in close proximity to a civilian population in which a large part of the middle class was destitute and the poor were starving. Young Indian women were particularly hard hit by the famine and tens of thousands had fled into the city in search of food. Senior officers were alarmed by the huge explosion of uncontrolled pimping. Young boys would pursue soldiers in parks, near temples and churches and in secluded streets to make assignations with their impoverished elder sisters or other family members. Medical officers were overwhelmed as venereal disease spread among the soldiers returning to the Arakan or Assam fronts. Up in Gauhati, Assam, one enterprising officer actually set up his own brothel serviced by women from the nearby hills. The local authorities turned a blind eye and he amassed a healthy nest egg for his retirement. The British army did not need 'comfort women' like the Japanese. Free enterprise did it all for them.

At first, commanding officers seem to have tacitly accepted the development of controlled brothels near military bases where medical officers could give the women a basic health check. This ran against the strict morality of the age. The Association for Moral and Social Hygiene, India, was a powerful and active body which brought together Indian and Briton, imperialist and nationalist. Its patroness-in-chief was the vicereine, Lady Wavell, and other patrons included Mrs Brij Lal Nehru, Dr H. Patel and sundry bishops and worthies of various Indian religious groups. Affiliated to the International Abolition Federation of Geneva, the association had local connections which included the Calcutta Vigilance Association and the Mahila Seva Gram (Woman's Service Society), Pune. In 1943 the Calcutta press began to hint that the army was running licensed brothels. The guardians of morality saw to it that questions about the upsurge of vice were asked of ministers in the Central Assembly, Delhi, and in the British Parliament. Even the Archbishop of Canterbury intervened in this dispute about morality, while millions around the world were being gassed, bombed, tortured or starved to death.

Stung by charges that brothels were nests of spies and sedition, the British army and the US War Department were forced to agree to a statement that 'no recognition is permitted to any system of prostitution, to the installation and control of brothels, or to any inspection of women'.[78] Brothels were declared out of bounds to the troops. The rates of venereal disease amongst the poor women of Calcutta and the Allied forces suggest that these measures did little to promote celibacy. On 1 March 1944, Major W. A. Barnes was staying at the Grand Hotel in Calcutta. This time he was under arrest, having denounced his superiors in the Intelligence Department for incompetence once too often. He noted in his diary: 'The American and British military police raided a section of the hotel which was largely being tenanted by American officers at half-past one in the morning and removed from their rooms a goodly number of Eurasian and coloured girls aged between fourteen and sixteen.'[79]

Yet already somewhere beneath the surface of the shattered society, India's great reserves of energy and entrepreneurship were beginning to stir. Indian business, like Indian labour, was used to making the most of dire situations at home and abroad. Indian labour, poorly fed as it was, began to work harder and harder. The usual sources of labour, Travancore in the south, Chota Nagpur in the east and the Santal tracts in Bengal, gushed forth more men. Every tea estate in Assam undertook to provide free one labourer for each ten acres and to recruit several others at government expense under the Shadow Force Labour Scheme. From the end of 1943 onward the estates maintained a steady force of about 80,000 men.[80] At one critical point in 1943 the scourge of flood was added to those of famine and pestilence. On 13 July 1943 the Damodar river burst its banks and threatened to cut the only rail link between north India and the Assam front. A massive engineering effort began which Margaret Stavridi, who was married to an official in the railways, compared to D-Day. Tens of thousands of labourers, men, women and children of the Santal 'tribal' group, were drafted in to help the East India Railway operatives repair the line.[81] General Sir George Giffard, commander in chief of the Eastern Army from May 1943, before Mountbatten arrived, had already begun to improve military amenities and logistics.[82]

The spending of Allied soldiers gave a considerable boost to consumption and to the income of the middle class, even when the poor were still dying in Bengal. People were prepared to invest money and there was a surge of import substitution – in other words, people suddenly found it profitable to make advanced components and machines which had previously been imported from abroad. Even as late as 1942 the Indian engineering business had operated on a jobbing basis. It existed almost entirely to maintain other industries, and not for mass production. That began to change in mid 1943 as demand from the Burma front gradually began to pick up.[83] Indian railways were now run on military lines and began to produce armaments and parts.[84] Tata Iron and Steel rapidly expanded to create new factories producing motor engines, parts for aircraft, landing craft and large quantities of munitions. Tata had one big advantage: so important was it for the war effort that the authorities had kept it well stocked with food even during the worst of the famine. That meant it had the pick of skilled and semi-skilled labour now cowed into quiescence by wartime ordinances and fear of starvation. Workers in the factories of Bengal, Bihar and Bombay worked weeks of sixty or seventy hours, but earned large bonuses.[85] Some of these benefits spilled out into the surrounding rural communities. By 1943, India was producing upward of a million blankets for troops in all parts of the world, but particularly the Middle East and Burma fronts. That was the produce of more than 60 million sheep. It put back into the pockets of shepherd communities across the subcontinent something of what they had lost by the rise in prices of food and kerosene. India had been hard hit by the loss of rubber imports from Malaya and the Dutch East Indies, but by 1943 there had been a rapid expansion of rubber production on the south-western coast of the country in the princely states of Cochin and Travancore. By the autumn the first of the huge number of young trees were ready for tapping. Even rural Bengal benefited a little as demand for jute sacking to protect fragile war materiel soared.

This forced industrialization was very unbalanced, as businessmen with nationalist credentials, such as the jute and textile magnate, G. D. Birla, constantly complained.[86] A little like the Soviet space programme of the 1960s and '70s, it exaggerated a bias towards heavy industry and away from the consumer sector which was later to plague the independent government of India. But just as the new Indian army was to produce hundreds of thousands of trained men, so the military-industrial boom generated a new class of managers. For this was very much an Indian operation. The European business leadership of the pre-war days in the agency houses and the factories of the port cities was overwhelmed by a new tide of Indian talent. Often it came from the sons of the old business classes, but sometimes from local men of lower status and caste. Lorry entrepreneurs, those who cannibalized and built things in sprawling outhouses near railway yards and those who had the cunning to buy up large stocks of valuable commodities at the beginning of the war all prospered. This huge Indian enterprise was topped out by the imposing figure of the Bombay Parsi and former chairman of the Association of Cement Companies Ltd, Sir Homasji P. Mody, KBE, Member for Supply of the Government of India.

Even if the supplies were now beginning to flow, in terms of morale and fighting spirit the new command and the reinvigorated viceroyalty had a mountain to climb. The disasters in early 1943 in Arakan were accompanied by a miserable drooping of morale. Military intelligence was alarmed. It read the soldiers' mail, snooped near the front and in major recruiting districts such as Rawalpindi on the North West Frontier. One soldier's letter to his CO said that 'in the eyes of Mahatma Gandhi all are equal but you pay a British soldier Rs75/- and to an Indian soldier you pay Rs18/- only'.[87] Another wrote 'An Indian subedar salutes a British soldier, but the British soldier does not salute an Indian subedar. Why is this so?' He went on vividly we 'get from the Sarkar [government] Rs18/- out of which Rs5/- are forcibly deducted for milk, Rs3/- for soap and Rs2/- for polish. In addition we do not get sufficient food to fill our stomach . . . work night and day like a sweeper.'[88] One retired subedar stated that he did not care whether the Japanese or the British ruled the country, provided his pension was paid.

The problems were not only economic. The war had already been a long one, with Indian soldiers fighting a hard campaign in North Africa for nearly two years before the war in the East even started. Soldiers could not get home on leave very often. The result was the inevitable affairs between soldiers' wives and local men, particularly when farmers in the Punjab began to benefit from higher grain prices. There were many serious domestic disputes and army welfare officers were hard put to prevent murder or the escalation of sexual rivalries into conflicts between soldiers' clan groups. When illegitimate children were born the problems became serious. Babies were given to military hospitals or left on verandas overnight. Women were sometimes thrown out of their husbands' homes, but their own families refused to take them back because of the dishonour they brought. If their lovers refused to support them, they would become destitute.

Despite the authorities' sedulous attempts to keep politics out of the army, politics crept in. The war was also a propaganda war and raised more political questions than it answered. The men were aware that a good part of the political leadership was either opposed to the war or neutral. In the key recruitment area of the Punjab, Abdul Ghaffar Khan's Red Shirt movement tried to enlist the military virtues of the

Pathan soldiers on the side of Mahatma Gandhi's non-violence. The British fought a long battle with the Red Shirts, jailing many and treating them with great brutality in a few cases.[89] But they could not altogether still anti-recruitment propaganda. Besides, Indians did not need openly to side with the nationalists in order to believe that India's freedom was now inevitable. After all, Cripps and Amery had said as much. An Indian officer from a 'martial race' who was also secretary to the soldiers' entertainments committee confirmed that 60 per cent of all Indian commissioned officers regarded themselves as nationalists and expected immediate independence after the war. Forty per cent were non-political, but had many grouses about pay, living conditions and racial discrimination in clubs, restaurants and trains.[90] The danger of all this discontent for the army was that it coincided with the Bengal famine. Soldiers were seriously worried about the welfare of their families, even in relatively well-off areas like the Punjab. Over the summer the Indian National Army began to step up its propaganda war both at the front and by radio from Singapore and Rangoon. Subhas Bose's arrival in Burma in mid June had transformed the situation, giving the INA a much more powerful and defined political aim. One of his most telling blows against the British was his offer to send Burmese rice over the lines to help feed starving Bengalis. It was not just the INA but Indian army troops themselves who circulated stories of the British 'drain of wealth' from India. Its consequences were, people thought, plain to see not only in Bengal and Assam, but in far distant labour-recruiting areas such as Madras where people were also dying in the streets.

The British propaganda fight back was difficult. It was clear that the food situation in the country as a whole would not begin to improve for many months. 'If India's civil economy collapses, so does India's war effort and the war effort of the United Nations in India', said a gloomy intelligence report.[91] Soldiers would continue to see their countrymen dying before their eyes. The particular problems of supply on the eastern front began to improve a little over the summer as some Punjab wheat reached Assam and supplies began to trickle in by sea. In the absence of any decisive advance by the Allies on the Southeast Asia land front there was little positive propaganda to build on. The Chindits' shadowy successes were played up and much was made of the fact that Gurkha, Indian and Burmese troops took part in the raids. The relative successes of the American advances in the Pacific and the Allied gains in Italy were too far from home to interest the average Indian soldier. The best that the army could do was to build up morale from below. The Indian army had always been quite good at looking after recruits. It now insisted on best practice throughout the force. Officers were aware that most Indian recruits were farm boys who needed an old soldier to shepherd them to their training units and raise morale. *Bhaibands*, friendship groups, from their village or area kept the new men interested and sympathetic. NCOs helped them to draw food, clothing and pay. Officers believed that plenty of ceremonial helped to build up the young soldier's sense of his own importance.

More overtly political measures were also adopted. There were daily explanations of war news. 'Jap Orientation courses' were established for British and Indian officers. The ever-busy 'Jick' Rudra helped set these up along with Lieutenant Himmatsinhji, a soldier who had been returned from Tokyo after a prisoner exchange, and Ali Noon, brother of Sir Feroze Khan Noon, a member of the Viceroy's Council. These explained emperor-worship and the Japanese samurai ethos.[92] Vernacular language pamphlets titled 'Against Japan' were distributed. These dwelt on Japanese atrocities in Burma and Malaya. They hit a chord with some soldiers, for stories of Japanese-sponsored massacres of Karens, Kachins and Gurkhas were trickling through as Indian prisoners of war straggled back to India. So-called 'josh groups' – informal regimental discussion forums – were established to promote hostility to the Japanese and to 'JIFs', Japanese influenced forces. The idea was to make the Japanese the personal enemies of the Indian soldiers in the way that the Germans and Italians had become in the Western Desert. Indian captains or majors gave anti-Japanese and anti-Bose lectures in Urdu or Gurkhali to the troops. They set up local morale circles which were supposed to discuss problems and emphasize India's stake in British war aims. These moves seem to have had some success in the longer run, particularly when victories began to be registered against the Japanese in 1944.

Gradually, too, the British began to step up the propaganda war behind the lines. Touring war buses and tea canteens were a start, but more serious efforts were needed to deal with soldiers' problems. The number of army welfare officers, often sensible middle-aged women, was increased. They visited women in their homes, many of whom, both Hindu and Muslim, were in *purdah* or seclusion. They began to talk over the issues. It was found, for instance, that a much larger percentage of the wives and families of ordinary soldiers were used to taking tea than the British had imagined. Tea and sugar rations for the private soldiers' families were therefore considerably increased. In a district such as Rawalpindi, near the present capital of Pakistan, Islamabad, the problems were peculiarly complex. This was because an astonishing 100,000 soldiers or nearly 4 per cent of the army's total strength was drawn from this single district. Soldiers' dependants accounted for nearly a third of the district's population. So huge was the human and administrative problem here that the Punjab government established a special network of post offices for dealing with soldiers' mail and another office to deal with the complaints and petitions of soldiers' families.

In 1943 Simla, where they still dressed for dinner, continued its bizarre existence. Linlithgow shuffled off the stage and Wavell made his entrance as viceroy. More cinemas opened and the number of American Special Operations personnel, Chindits and Force 136 officers slowly increased as the Arakan debacle gave way to long-range penetration operations into the upper Chindwin valley. The Burmese government in exile stirred uneasily. Officers who had been scattered in 1942 straggled back to join Dorman-Smith's post-war planning exercise, Burma's equivalent to the Malayan exercise happening less exotically in Wimbledon. Others, meanwhile, moved off, taking up temporary commissions in the Indian Army after training at Quetta or Saugor. The recriminations about Burmese 'treachery' and the collapse of civil administration the previous year rumbled on, but Dorman-Smith and his officials gradually regained their sense of humour and sense of purpose. Whatever happened in the Far East, it was clear from the invasion of Sicily that the Allies were beginning to win in the West. The excitements of special forces activity also began to stir the draughty corridors of Simla's rented hotels and commandeered gothic cottages. It was still not clear, though, how the bloody stalemate in the East could possibly be resolved. One of the most awful years in Indian history, 1943 drew to a close with a whimper.

# 6

# 1943: Personal Wars

## BA MAW'S APOTHEOSIS

The 1943 Arakan campaign was a cue for local political change in Burma. The Burmese knew first hand that the advance had been a shambles. What remained of the Raj's prestige in the region crumbled. Even moderate leaders in Arakan decided that it was politic to play along with the Japanese and their Burmese supporters.[1] The alternative seemed to be increasing banditry and a resurgence of communal violence between Muslims and Buddhists. Sir San C. Po, a long-time proponent of Karen autonomy and confidant of the British, was seen more and more in the company of Ba Maw. In Rangoon, the pro-Japanese newspaper *Greater Asia* dwelt on themes of patriotic unity between the Japanese and Burmese Buddhist people as they strode towards independence. It painted a picture of all communities, 'Indians, Chinese and Nipponese', participating in prayers, processions and the presentation of addresses to leaders of various communities. People took part in 'the feeding of pongyis [monks] and public dance performances, pwes [dramas], wrestling matches . . . motion picture exhibitions, musical contests and lectures'.[2]

Slowly, however, the significance of more distant events began to register with the Japanese and their Burmese supporters. Despite the dismal showing of the British army in Arakan and the gathering crisis in Bengal, the Japanese Cabinet itself was by now aware of their nation's military limitations. The Japanese commanders had become increasingly pessimistic since Pearl Harbor and knew very well that the defeat of one particularly hidebound and ineffective arm of the Allied alliance was ultimately of little importance. Their small island empire was challenging the United States with twelve times Japan's gross national product. Even the British Empire, when fully mobilized, exceeded their own GNP five to one. It was pointless to dispute the obvious, though this could never be said in the hearing of the emperor. Worse, the Axis powers seemed on the point of losing Italy to the Allies. New Guinea had been wrested back from Japan's grasp by the Americans and Australians. The Japanese navy had been decisively defeated at the Battle of the Bismarck Sea in March 1943. Even on the Indian front, Wingate's first Chindit campaign had proved much more than a pinprick to the Japanese forces, sending them scurrying around upper Burma and diverting important resources from the war front. In the Japanese-occupied countries of Southeast Asia, the conditions for civilians were gradually deteriorating. Shortages of cooking oil and cloth began to develop and inflation surged ever upwards. However skilful the propaganda broadcasts of Tokyo Radio and its allies and offshoots in Manila, Saigon, Singapore and Rangoon, it was difficult to continue to hide from listeners the fact that the Allies were inching forward on all the main war fronts. How vulnerable the Great Co-Prosperity Sphere really was became all too evident by April 1943 when British and American bombers began to fly more and more sorties from Assam over central Burma. Air raids became common and the already damaged Rangoon to Mandalay railway line received a regular pounding.

In Burma people began to read the propaganda sheets dropped in their hundreds of thousands over the populated areas. Apart from this meagre fare, though, reading matter was scarce. Khin Myo Chit read Shakespeare and P. G. Wodehouse over and over again. She and her husband had been trying to scratch together a living in Rangoon since the previous summer. Working in the market had not been a success. Her mental arithmetic had failed her as she tried to reconcile British annas and rupees with the 'dollar' currency introduced by the Japanese and the couple had been turned out of Scott market in disgrace. Thakin Than Tun, whom she had known as a frequenter of the Left Book Club in pre-war days, introduced her husband to people in Dr Ba Maw's government. In time she herself was offered a position as head of the women's section of Dobama Sinyetha Asi-ayone, the organization of nationalist leagues patronized by Ba Maw's Burmese government.[3]

Burma's independence was a tactic employed by the Tojo government in Tokyo to shore up its crumbling prestige in Burma. As the Japanese became further and further stretched, it became imperative to draw more heavily on local manpower for day-to-day administrative tasks. The Japanese hoped that Burmese officials would find it easier to procure local labour for their railway- and airport-building projects. Precisely what sort of quasi-independence was to be conceded remained uncertain until late in the day. Some Japanese officers hankered after a 'royal solution' and wanted to install a son of the last-but-one Burmese king, Mindon, who still lived in Mandalay.[4] Many officers found that Ba Maw was not as pliable a puppet as they hoped. Thakin Nu thought that elsewhere, as in Manchukuo or Taiwan, they would have got rid of him with a single blow.[5] But Ba Maw, who had been currying favour with the Japanese in Singapore and Tokyo, had the upper hand. He had good contacts with the military liaison committee led by General Isumara, described by a Burmese as 'not a brilliant officer'. This man had previously been counsellor at the Japanese embassies in Italy, Germany and Russia. More formidable was one Mr Saito, born and educated in the US, who became a key figure in the negotiations because of his excellent American English. Both sides prevaricated for a long time, using their language difficulties as a smoke screen. The Japanese made some concessions. They agreed to give the Burmese rather more control over internal policy. They agreed to the establishment of a special railways department to deal with the problems of hard-pressed travellers. They declared they would restore 'enemy', that is Indian, property seized in 1942, though this was never fully implemented. Finally, after several months of wrangling, the Japanese lost their tempers and ordered the committee to draw up plans for a Burmese dictatorship under Japanese control.

Under the terms of 'independence' agreed in June 1943, the Japanese military continued to have the power of veto over all policies.[6] The Japanese broadcast reporting the change of governance gave the game away. It said that the new military governor appointed in February 1943, Lieutenant General Masakazu Kawabe, had himself 'convened the assembly and recommended Dr Ba Maw to it'. The new constitution specified that the interests of the Japanese war effort were always to take priority. The Japanese kept in their own hands the administration of the frontier areas and relations with the non-Burmese minorities, as the British had. The agreement included special provisions for the treatment of fraternal Burmese business. There is plenty of evidence, too, that the Japanese military and the Kempeitai were deeply suspicious of Ba Maw. They distrusted his associates, above all Aung San and his increasingly restive Burma Defence Army, the former BIA. They had good reason to. Aung San burst in on Ba Maw at one point during the negotiations and denounced the whole thing as a sham. This was simply the good old British policy of 'home rule' with a Japanese gloss to it. It was duping the people. Ba Maw reminded Aung San, who was often now called Bogyoke or 'General', that politics was the art of the possible. No foreign power, whether British or Japanese, would give them full independence in the middle of the war. This was the best they would get.[7]

In the event, the elaborate declarations and ceremonies that attended the installation of the Burmese government in August 1943 did act as a considerable stimulus to the national pride of the Burmese people, even though the majority of them knew that these were largely a sham. British and American intelligence reports admitted as much. The declaration of independence was 'founded on the union of blood and aspiration of Burmans'. It proposed a stronger relationship between the state and a new, popular Buddhist movement. Indians and other minorities were to be protected, but everything said made it clear that the Burmese majority was to have the dominant voice. Even a flawed declaration that they were now masters in their own house appealed to many Burmese. Though some of the old guard, notably Ba Maw himself, remained in power, Thakin Nu, the foreign minister, was only thirty-six and Aung San eight years younger. The rickshaw pullers, oil workers and farmers could at least identify with some members of the new government. Above all, the British were gone. People did see some merit in the official propaganda which predicted that Burmans would finally come into their own as the grip of the British, the Indians and the Chinese was prised off the levers of the economy.[8]

Ba Maw was in his element. As Khin Myo Chit wrote: 'handsome, brilliant, debonair, he seemed to have a way with people',[9] even though many speculated that Mrs Ba Maw was the real power behind the newly erected throne. Intensely impressed by his own appearance, Ba Maw set about designing costumes for himself and his officials which reflected the grandeur of the first independent Burmese government since 1886. There was something more to this than showmanship. Ba Maw was competing with the memory of the royal house, which many older Burmese still remembered. He was also aware that royalist legitimist movements continued to spring up in different parts of the country from time to time and that many conservative Japanese thought that monarchy was the natural order for Asian peoples. Rather than style himself prime minister or president, Ba Maw took the ancient Sanskrit title Adipadi, or 'he who stands first'. He choreographed the elaborate installation ceremony. This was followed by a declaration of war on the Allies and a pledge of eternal friendship with the Japanese people.

Coloured cloth and silks had always been a passion for the Burmese and now that so many of them were dressed in rags, even more so. The Adipadi's costume rose to the occasion. An Anglo-Burman student described Ba Maw dressed in 'a glossy, black long-sleeved silk shirt under a blood red silk waistcoat, blood red silk pyjamas tightened at the waist and ankles with elastic and black velvet Burmese slippers. The strange *tout ensemble* was completed with a black beret and both his cheeks were rouged.'[10] This reminded the British intelligence officer who received the report that Ba Maw had always been noted for his effeminate dress. 'It is not surprising that the British crowd at the Coronation' in 1937, which he had attended as prime minister of Burma, 'took Ba Maw to be the wife of the virile and hirsute representative of another Empire country who shared the state coach with him'. This had apparently been one of the Indian princes. Ba Maw thought it important to stress the Asian nature of his new regime, so other officials were dressed in workaday versions of the Adipadi's garments. Burmese patriotism had always been tempered with a sense of humour, though. Khin Myo Chit had difficulty in keeping a straight face when she saw people dressed in these costumes. Many of the local officials who had to swear allegiance to Ba Maw with a pompous oath were reported to have collapsed in laughter afterwards. The new government lived up to its Gilbert and Sullivan inauguration. The Home Department spent much time minuting itself and discussing matters which were then brusquely rejected by the Japanese commanders. The most important work of the Foreign Office 'was sending telegrams to dignitaries like the Emperor of Japan or Hitler on auspicious days or writing speeches for ministers'. The new Burmese government and Subhas Chandra Bose's government of Free India made constant courtesy calls on each other, discussing such 'important matters' as whether Bose should be seated on the right or left of Ba Maw at formal dinners.[11]

However bizarre some of the activities of Ba Maw and his cronies, there were important movements taking place under the surface of Burmese society. Things had changed out of all recognition since 1939. The Burmese *Who's Who* had been torn up. Before 1936 cronyism with the British, their Indian clients and Burmese Indian Civil Service men was what had counted. After 1936, Burmese ministers became a new source of patronage, making massive fortunes from speculation and 'buying up' minor British officials and the agents of major local companies. From 1942, however, Christians, Anglo-Indians, Anglo-Burmans and senior former officials who had stayed in Burma were at a discount. All were under surveillance. Some were brutalized by the Kempeitai. People who controlled goods and services, rather than those who had Japanese paper money or even rupees, were the ones who survived and prospered. If you could build up a sufficient credit with the Japanese military and commercial firms by supplying railway cars, women and liquor, you could make a fortune. For example, hiring a railway carriage cost Rs1,000. The loot was then divvied up among all the railway officials and the Indian agents. An Arakanese observer wrote of the 'undesirable people who had become millionaires in Japanese paper currency'.[12] Even the later leader of the Burmese Communist Party, Than Tun, was alleged to have done well out of the supplies which were controlled by his father-in-law, a leading timber merchant. People who had preserved stores of cloth, cooking oil and medicines became rich overnight. Anyone who could strong-arm labour for the Japanese or the Ba Maw government made a killing. A massive prostitution racket developed which by the end of the war had given Burma one of the highest rates of VD in the world. Thein Pe noted perceptively that officers of the Burma Defence Army and connections of ministers now 'bid high in the marriage market like the ICS men of the old days'.[13]

Ironically, in view of their slogan 'Asia for the Asians', the Japanese began to sell opium in the best British imperialist style. They brought in quantities of it from sources in Taiwan and north China and their Burmese rural middlemen profited. For these changes were not seen only amongst the middle classes. During 1943 the links between the villages and the Burmese military which had been forged during the 1942 campaign were strengthened. Large numbers of unemployed young men were recruited into the BDA. Even the harsh training they were subjected to by Japanese instructors, casual beatings with rifle butts, constant face slapping and abuse, created a bond between them and the Thakin leadership. Men from the far south served in the Chin hills and on the Arakan front where previously few ethnic Burmese had ventured. Villagers fed and housed Burma Defence Army men from distant parts of the country, learned to follow their version of the language and listened to what they said about 'Myanmar' or Burma.

The propaganda which poured out from Japanese and Ba Maw-run radio stations and newspapers had an insidious effect which both the communists and the British were later to notice. The president of the International Buddhist Society of Tokyo harped on the affinity of all Buddhists, urging 'patriotic priests and monks and heroic people' to work together against the Anglo-Saxon enemy. The radio and newspapers were replete with stories about Allied desecration of pagodas and bombing of monasteries.[14] Articles derided the British claim that the Japanese were attempting to spread their own Shinto religion among the Burmese and pointed to the signs in Japanese outside pagodas reminding soldiers to take off their shoes before entering. Monks urged building teams on to greater labours and helped people enlist for the so-called 'sweat army' of 30,000 which supplied labour for Japanese war works.[15] In order to combat the insidious effects of British 'divide-and-rule', different groups of monks merged to form a united Buddhist *sangha*, or church, of more than 100,000 members. The link between Buddhism and the nation which was to become a powerful long-term resource for Burma's independent rulers was greatly strengthened at this time.

So too was the theme of race. The Rangoon propaganda organ *Greater Asia* prosed on and on about the fate of the 'Mongolian' races and their partnership with the Aryan Germans and the Latins. It wrote 'when the present war broke out our deepest racial instincts told us that Burma's day had at last come and Nippon would be our liberator'.[16] These effusions took on a practical aspect in the burgeoning of youth and health associations throughout the country. 'Burmans: now is the time to build your body . . . the key to the building of a great nation is to have its people build a healthy body and a sound mind.' The radio intoned: 'Hands on hips, heels together, body erect!'[17] The variety of old Burma's dress also became a matter of contention. While the Adipadi indulged his sartorial antiquarianism, younger men proclaimed their Nippon-loving modernity. The Toungoo Youth Association began a 'dress reformation' movement and pledged to wear only 'short trousers and short-sleeved shirts as a universal dress'.[18] Women vaunted their freedom through the Women's National Service Movement. Burmese women were 'more free and independent than any other women in Asia'.[19] But Burmese women also had a place in the home. Stressing hygiene and health, Aung San's wife Daw Khin Kyi urged them on to 'produce more sons for the war'. Even the ever faction-ridden Buddhist priesthood was persuaded to put on a show of unity, denouncing its earlier schisms as a product of British 'divide and rule'.[20] Nationalism was now more than an aspiration. It became a routine which long outlasted the departure of Nippon's armies.

The Burmese viewed these events with a curious mixture of patriotic pride and amusement. There was little else to laugh at in Burma in 1943. Their former rulers jeered in the wings. Sweltering in the heat of his place of exile in India, Sir Paw Tun spilled out his bile. Ba Maw was 'a twicer', he wrote. His supporters included 'a vernacular man of no social standing', 'a human parasite and hanger-on', 'a Sino-Burman who drank like a fish', an 'ex-excise officer who threw lavish parties', a 'Jap-leaning woman' and 'an eccentric fellow from Myingun – a man of doubtful education and rude behaviour'. The Thakins as a body were 'almost entirely composed of the lowest type of Burmese element, some of whom are riff-raff and scum of society; some are menials, motor-car drivers, omnibus drivers and labourers, some are rogues and hooligans who have no employment of any sort, some are young students of shady character.'[21] Paw Tun's particular animus against students and the drivers of wheeled vehicles concealed an aversion to nearly all the social changes that had overtaken Burma in the previous quarter century. More seriously, many of these prejudices were shared by British officials, fighting their own frustration and the scarcely concealed disdain of their ICS colleagues on the Olympian heights of Simla. Even the lame-duck governor Dorman-Smith, Irish nationalist as he often claimed to be, was apparently becoming more rigid in his views. At the end of the previous year, he had let slip to a startled Leo Amery that he expected the returning forces to shoot most of the Thakins they captured. Amery replied, more rapidly than was his wont, that he thought this rather a bad idea: much better to turn them and use them against the enemy.[22] The battle lines of post-war Burmese politics had already been drawn.

## THE 'SPIRIT OF ASIA' AND THE MALAY NATION

The Japanese had promised less to the Malays than they had to the Burmese, but by early 1943 they seemed to be offering a little more. The Marquis Tokugawa's scheme to reform and diminish the Malay sultanates was abandoned, and the Japanese became more solicitous towards the rulers themselves. They also began to dabble in Islamic affairs. On 5–7 April 1943, the *ulama*, Islamic religious leaders from across the peninsula and from Sumatra, were summoned to a conference in Singapore. The ninety-one delegates were housed at the Sea View Hotel. On their first night the Marquis Tokugawa entertained them at the Syonan Club; the next evening the mayor of Syonan gave them dinner at the Nanto Hotel, the old Adelphi, where Jean Cocteau had stayed a few years earlier. The mayor even went to the trouble of having a room set aside for the delegates' evening prayers. The *ulama* were regaled with a show, a film presentation and speeches on the progress of the war. The Japanese impressed on the Malays that Nippon was the true defender of faith. The Marquis incanted:

'I resign unto God, the Most Powerful and Great who will direct the one hundred million and three thousand [sic] followers of Islam to the right path and favour them with the true spiritual guidance so they will unite into one

315

solid body and soul and co-operate fully with Nippon. It is only in this way that a New Asia that will cast brightness on Islam can be built.'

The delegates were each sent home with a white commemorative medal, enamelled in scarlet, embossed with a crescent and a star, surrounded by twelve cherry blossoms. The Malay phrase *Sehiduplah dengan Nippon* – 'Live with Nippon' – was inscribed on the back in Arabic script. The *ulama* left giving formal expressions of satisfaction at Japan's commitment to protect Islam and of support for the war.[23]

The gestures were token on both sides. Before the Mufti of Pahang had left for the meeting he had met with his sultan and the Japanese governor of the state. The governor had posed the question: 'Can the Malay States declare a holy war (*jihad*) against the British and her allies?' The question was referred to the mufti. He quickly answered: 'Yes, provided that the Japanese emperor is a Muslim.'[24] And there the matter rested. There was confusion and anger when the Japanese followed through their initiative by thrusting prepared texts on *kathis* to be included in their Friday sermons and by encouraging prayers for the emperor and the success of the war. On occasion, Japanese officers themselves invaded mosques and interrupted prayers with speeches, even ordering the worshippers to turn their prayer mats 180 degrees away from Mecca and towards Tokyo. This propaganda became more subtle over time, but it generated anxieties. In some areas attendance at the mosque for Friday prayers fell. More generally, religious values were felt to be under threat; divorce rates, gambling and opium use were dramatically on the rise. These were profane times. Like all Japan's efforts at political engineering, the most important effects of the Islamic conference were unforeseen by its initiators. It realized a long-held ambition of many clerics: the creation of a more unified voice for Islam, outside the control of the rulers and their courts. This was to have far reaching implications for politics of religious reform in Malaya after the war. The real significance of pan-Asianism lay not in what it achieved for the Japanese Empire but in what it allowed others to achieve for themselves.

The political future of the Malays looked ever more uncertain. In October 1943 the Japanese ceded the four northern Malay states of the peninsula to Thailand. This was a blow to the cherished vision of a greater Malay nation held by the radicals. The states involved – Kedah, Perlis, Kelantan and Trengganu – were the rice-bowl of Malaya. As Ibrahim Yaacob's increasingly disaffected second-in-command Mustapha Hussain put it: 'Malaya was to me a fish the Japanese had cut into two; the better part of mouth, eyes and breathing organs being presented to the Siamese on a silver platter. The other half, though it had plenty of flesh, most of it did not belong to us Malays.'[25] The creation of a new tier of Thai administrators, and the promotion of the Thai language in public life, was resented in states which possessed proudly independent political traditions. But Thai supervision was lighter than that of the Japanese and, over time, the main effect of the transfer was to weaken central control of these areas. Throughout the peninsula the Japanese remained reliant on the existing machinery of rule and, after 1943, the Malay elites upon whom it depended began to claw back some of the initiative. Some administrators in the localities came to tacit agreements with the communist resistance to keep the peace in their areas. In Johore, where Onn bin Jaafar worked as a food controller, lorries and their supplies began to go missing in guerrilla territory. Some officials went further in hedging their bets on the outcome of the war. The transfer of northern states provoked the young Raffles College and Koa Kunrensho graduate Abdul Razak bin Hussein into making contact with a movement called Wataniah, a name drawn from the Arabic for 'homeland'. It was led by a civil servant, Yeop Mahidin, who had received the secret blessing of the Sultan of Pahang to set up a cell of Malay fighters. Abdul Razak and others in the administration began to feed it information. There were similar bodies in Kedah and Kelantan. Their existence was entirely separate and largely secret from the guerrilla forces of the Malayan Communist Party.[26] Malays were taking the defence of their communities into their own hands.

Even the Malay radicals were becoming disillusioned with the Japanese. Mustapha Hussain had retired up-country to Perak. The bohemian journalist Ishak Haji Muhammad confined himself to work on the Malay newspaper *Berita Malai*, 'Malai News'. He too was later to return to the land. But although the larger political ambitions of these men had been contemptuously brushed aside by the Japanese, they were given unprecedented access to the press. Malay newspapers and periodicals brought the new generation of writers and critics together in a common purpose as never before. In the pages of magazines such as *Fajar Asia*, 'East Asia', and *Semangat Asia*, 'Spirit of Asia', alongside the crude propaganda and reports on political developments in Burma, Indonesia and elsewhere, was a new idiom of writing by Malays. Many of the writers and poets who after the war would reinvent Malay literature and reshape the language itself first found space in their columns: in vivid portraits of social conditions; reflections on the spirit of the age, and exhortations to love and serve the homeland.[27] They experimented with the relatively new genre of the short story and free-form verse. The rule of Nippon had taught Malay radicals that 'through language the race is known'. Poems were primers for a new age. *Fajar Asia* adopted a new form of romanized Malay spelling and, after the war, the British were driven to issue primers to re-educate European civil servants in what was a new language of politics. Two of the principal keywords were *pemuda*, youth, and *semangat*, spirit. These terms had special associations in Malay thought: where existing leadership had failed the nation, or the nation was in crisis, the spirited youth had a particular role in its defence and resurrection. This idea stood in stark contrast to the understated bureaucratic finesse of the pre-war Anglo-Malay partnership. This was a new idea of politics itself; in the new language, it had moved from *siasat*, being merely the problem-solving of administration, to become *politik*: something ideological and alive.[28] The richly allusive style of Malay editorials was impenetrable to Japanese censors. It offered messages in formulas that satisfied the Japanese but which, to the attuned ears of a new generation of Malay readers, said a lot more.

This was the fate of all Japanese policies towards Malay nationalism. In December 1943 the Japanese announced a fresh initiative to recruit support for the regime: a volunteer corps, a *giyu-tai*, and a *giyu-gun*, or standing force. Although multi-ethnic in conception, the initiative fell to the Malay radicals. They seized it as an opportunity to enlist Malays to defend their patrimony. The writer Ishak Haji Muhammad invoked the legendary hero of the golden age of Melaka in the fifteenth century: 'Malay *pemuda* must seize this opportunity to show the world that within their breasts flows the blood of Hang Tuah who once reminded us: "The Malays shall not vanish in this world".' Ibrahim

Yaacob was installed as its chief of staff and Mustapha Hussain brought back to Singapore from Perak by the Japanese police to take a somewhat reluctant lead in its formation. The first batch of recruits was around 2,000 strong.[29] The *giyu-gun* was never to achieve the scale and the independent momentum of the Burma Defence Army. Yet the militarization of the Malays was one of the most profound effects of the occupation period. All society was infected by the new military ethos. Students, employees, fighters in the forest – all had hats and badges of every colour and design. 'Never in the history of Malaya were bald-heads more respected and feared than at this period', reported Chin Kee Onn. 'For a man with a clean shorn head might be anything: he might be an MP, a high-ranking military officer; or he might be a goose or an idiot.'[30] This aspect of Japanese military style disappeared among the young at the war's end. But the regime of drill, marching and uniform left a distinct mark: it would be adopted by most post-war political movements, and even by Islamic militants. The necktie, too, never really made a comeback in Malaya. Lee Kuan Yew's socialists would adopt the open-necked, short-sleeved shirt as their political uniform. To echo the historian Rudolph Mrazek's description of Indonesia in this period: 'dressing gaily and behaving bohemian, the Japanese occupation, and the apocalypse of standard and uniform, made even the billiard generation appear, for awhile at least and to some extent, serious and meaningful'.[31]

This was a time of music and pageants. The jazz age was declared to be at an end. In January 1943 a list of 1,000 proscribed British and American popular songs was published, from 'Colonel Bogey' to 'Aloha De' and 'Kisses in the Dark'. They had, it was claimed, acted as an 'anaesthetic agent' on the minds of Malayans.[32] Only such standards as 'Auld Lang Syne' and 'Home, Sweet Home' which were already embedded in the Japanese consciousness escaped censure. Yet the Japanese worked energetically to fill the silence. The musicality of the occupation left its residue: songs sung in schools, the lilting languor of the romantic music heard in restaurants and nightspots, all became popular. The Japanese tried to police every aspect of popular culture. After August 1942 all British and American films were banned. But the cinema remained popular and Japanese films did well. 'The attractive feature of Japanese films', one critic mused later, 'was not the planes or big games or their splendid troops but their richness in natural scenery of an Eastern atmosphere, and the beautiful and serene mountains.'[33] They offered a different kind of 'instant Asia' to the 'Road' movies of Bob Hope and Bing Crosby. Malaya's own styles fared well. The theatre of the *bangsawan* grew in importance as well as the scripted *sandiwara* that emerged from it. Bachtiar Effendi, a Sumatran-born student lawyer, had been arrested in the sweep of Japanese sympathizers in December 1941. He emerged under Japanese rule as a new type of cultural warrior: his theatre troupe Sahara's Bolero, named after his wife, took on a propaganda role touring the peninsula. Its plays celebrated Japan's 'New Asia', but also advanced other themes: cruel and insane rulers, the predicament of ordinary men and women; the conditions of the age; and the spectacle of a multi-ethnic society on stage. The actresses, writers and musicians involved would graduate to the cinema screen after the war. They connected the popular culture of the 'Worlds' to the new politics. A young Malay in Perak, Ahmad Boestamam, working for the Japanese as a propagandist, would develop a connection with the Sri Nooran Opera that made it an effective arm of the radical nationalist movement after the war.[34] On a larger scale, the Japanese seized the public spaces of the old colonial regime in order to Nipponize the civic life of Malaya. They played baseball on the Padang in Singapore; they turned the Cathay Building into a propaganda centre. To mark a series of anniversaries in 1943 of the fall of Singapore and the emperor's birthday they staged elaborate public parades and processions in every town of the peninsula.

The great spectacular of life in war time reached its climax in the middle of 1943 with a new arrival on the Syonan stage. On 6 July there was tight security across the city. A fixed number of people from each community was told to assemble on the Padang: 50,000 Chinese, 10,000 Indians, 5,000 Malays and 5,000 from other communities. They were not told why, and some feared another massacre. When all were given a Rising Sun flag, the mood eased somewhat. The sultans were there, without their retinues. They had just been told the news of the transfer of the northern states to Thailand. They were left standing with the crowd for several hours. At 4 p.m. an announcement came: premier Hideki Tojo himself was in Singapore on a tour of inspection, and was about to appear. When he materialized on the dais in front of the Municipal Building the crowd shouted *banzai!* three times. Then Tojo was gone. All the shophouses along Orchard Road, near Government House where he was staying, were ordered to close their doors and window shutters. Soldiers lined the route facing the crowd. It was, remarked one witness, 'a Godiva's ride . . . Like a dream he came, like a dream he passed.'[35] But Tojo had already been upstaged by a supreme piece of political theatre: the previous day, along his ceremonial route, hordes of people, including many Indian soldiers and labourers, were making their way down Orchard Road to the Padang. They were carrying placards and chanting 'Chalo Delhi!' [To Delhi!] It had been the cry of the Indian rebels of the great Mutiny of 1857.[36] They were going to welcome Subhas Chandra Bose.

## THE SECOND COMING OF THE INDIAN NATIONAL ARMY

It began quietly. In mid May 1943, after a long journey by Japanese submarine via Madagascar and Sabang on the northern tip of Sumatra, Subhas Chandra Bose slipped unnoticed into Singapore. He crossed the causeway to stay at Sultan Ibrahim's palace at Bukit Serene, and then, with Rash Behari Bose, flew on to Tokyo. The revelation of Subhas Bose's presence in Japan was an epochal moment for the overseas Indians of Southeast Asia and the day of his second landing in Singapore on 2 July 1943 was a political awakening for all communities. He arrived at Kallang aerodrome in a silk suit and a grey felt hat but within three days he had abandoned this attire for the military uniform and top boots he would almost exclusively be seen in thereafter. On 4 July a press conference was called in the auditorium of the Cathay Cinema. The old revolutionary Rash Behari Bose was the first to speak: 'You might now ask of me what I did in Tokyo for our cause, what present I have brought for you? Well, I have brought for you this present.' With this he transferred leadership of the Indian Independence League to the younger man. From the outset Subhas Bose's demeanour was presidential. There was an almost Churchillian cadence to his first speech: he warned his audience they would have to 'face hunger, thirst, privation, forced marches and death. Only when you pass this test will freedom be yours'.[37] At this meeting Bose's supporters ruffled the sensitivities of Japanese journalists by calling him 'Netaji', an Indian word, meaning leader. To the Japanese present it smacked of impiety; it echoed the word 'Führer', and seemed to herald some sort of challenge to Japan's leadership of Asia.[38]

The people of Malaya had never before experienced a political presence in the mould of a giant of the Indian National Congress. Subhas Bose drew crowds to public rallies on an unprecedented scale: Chinese and Malays as well as Indians. The first, on the Padang on 5 July, was followed by an appearance at Tojo's side the next day, and another rally on 9 July. This was the true dawn of mass politics in Malaya. As one young Indian recalled: 'It was really the first speech, you see, I had heard in my life. Like magnetic power . . .' For decades afterwards witnesses would relive the symbolism of the scenes. On 9 July it was raining heavily. Bose, it was said, was offered an umbrella. He refused it, and asked: 'Who will offer an umbrella to all these people?'[39] But others would remember a more disturbing piece of imagery. In the parade, as a Japanese tank passed, draped in an Indian tricolour, the flag became tangled in some wires and fell under the tracks of the vehicle. Bose was visibly angered.[40]

In the wake of the opprobrium that had confronted 'General' Mohan Singh, Subhas Bose took no military rank. But he resurrected the Indian National Army. Since the dismissal and arrest of Mohan Singh in December 1942, the Indian soldiers had returned to their internment camps. In February 1943 the intelligence chief Iwakuro told the Indian officers that the INA could not be dissolved, and anyone attempting to do so would be treated as a mutineer in the Japanese army. A second Indian National Army began recruiting. Many soldiers joined willingly, but others did so under the threat of forced labour overseas for Indian troops. The Gurkhas who refused to join were put to menial work in Singapore. One Chinese observer recalled seeing them bent under heavy loads, barefooted in the freezers of Cold Storage.[41] This deepened their solidarity with the British and Australian prisoners of war they occasionally met as they were transported around town. By December 1942 some Indian units began to depart for the island of New Britain in the southwest Pacific. The first transport ship was torpedoed and sunk; for others who survived, it was a gruelling journey into desperate conditions.[42]

Shahnawaz Khan was one of the Indian officers canvassed by the Japanese. A Muslim Rajput, he had been suspicious of Mohan Singh, had stayed out of the first INA and continued to resist the second. He was taken aside by Iwakuro and asked what a real INA should be. He replied that it should be a 'holy thing'; 'a formidable fighting force and not merely a propaganda army'. Like Mohan Singh before him, he claimed that only Subhas Bose could lead it. In trying to protect men who stayed out, he realized that his own continued abstention from the INA was not an option. 'I had committed myself too far and could not retrace my steps.' But when Bose arrived Shahnawaz's position changed: 'I was hypnotised by his personality and his speeches . . . I knew in his hands, India's honour was safe, he would never barter it for anything in the world.'[43]

The second INA involved Indian society in Southeast Asia in a way its earlier incarnation had failed to do. Most crucially, in the words of one volunteer, 'it had a sense of independence from Japanese manipulation'.[44] Men were recruited locally, and in an attempt to break with martial race theory special emphasis was placed on the Tamils of Malaya. Bose's presence energized the civilian organization. He would sit up much of the night in *darbar*, in the traditional style of a Bengali gentleman-politician, with visitors to his house in Katong on the east coast of Singapore. He launched a furious drive for funds on the peninsula and further afield, visiting in a short space the principal cities of the Japanese Empire: Rangoon, Manila, Bangkok, Shanghai and Nanking. His speech in Kuala Lumpur was a repeat of the triumph in Singapore two months earlier. Wealthy Indians donated beds and carpets, sandalwood soap and expensive china to the bungalow that was to house Bose for his short stay. The officer responsible recalled how Subhas Bose admonished him for the display: 'Who do you think I am? A Prince or a soldier in the INA?' Out of such stories the legend grew. On the day of the speech, the roads to and from the *padang* in front of the Royal Selangor Club in Kuala Lumpur were jammed. The crowd numbered around 60,000, and again included many Chinese and Malays. Subhas Bose arrived in an open Dodge car flying the Indian flag. He spoke for an hour in English, and then in Urdu, which few present understood, for another hour. Yet the crowd stayed to listen. Then, when he asked for funds: 'there was a great rush towards the rostrum. Men were throwing their rings, women their jewellery and those who did not have gold ornaments, whatever money they had'.[45] Bose moved swiftly to make connections with Indian businessmen. There was an element of opportunism in the response. As one Singapore storekeeper candidly admitted: 'I do everything and see everything and do nothing. I was that type. Just to be in the line like that, that's all, they took me in.' He gave $20,000 to Subhas Chandra Bose and Netaji's good offices helped his business, not least by granting him the contract to supply paper and stationery to the INA.[46]

The rhetoric of the INA was inclusive. It reached out to the Muslims: Bose replaced the wheel of the Indian National Congress with a symbol of a springing tiger which evoked Tipu Sultan, the Muslim ruler of Mysore who had resisted the British conquest of southern India. He retained Mohan Singh's use of Hindustani as a language of command. Bose also argued that 'Ceylon was the pendant in the Indian chain', a view Nehru was to echo in 1945, and established a Lanka Unit within the Indian Independence League. The community had been prominent in the colonial administration, and was vulnerable under the Japanese, especially after SEAC moved its headquarters to Ceylon. Some members felt coerced. One propagandist on the Burma front would later describe how broadcasts would round off with a message in Sinhala: 'all this is rubbish'. A leading figure in the Lanka movement was Gladwin Kotelawela, kinsman of Sir John Kotelawela, a future prime minister of Ceylon. He was stranded in Malaya at the outbreak of war and ran the Kangaroo Store in Tampin, Malacca. He had known Bose before the war, and co-operated with the IIL. His motives were, ostensibly, to protect the community; but he controversially embraced the active pursuit of Ceylonese independence through the INA. An opportunist to some, he possessed a bust of Winston Churchill in his home, a cause for some embarrassment when entertaining Japanese officers. On the reoccupation he was arrested, released and awarded an MBE on his return to Ceylon after the war. Many enthusiastic Ceylonese youths were genuinely inspired by Bose, and joined the Lanka Unit either through a spirit of adventure or as a way of gaining a clandestine passage back to Ceylon and their families. A mutiny of Ceylonese troops in the remote Cocos Island garrison and its surrender to the Japanese was seen in patriotic terms. The jeweller B. P. de Silva – whose employees provided several recruits to the INA – made officers' badges in silver, with a map of India on them. Ceylon did not appear on this map.[47]

On 21 October, within three months of his arrival in Malaya, speaking in the auditorium of the Cathay Cinema, Subhas Chandra Bose announced the formation of the provisional government of Azad Hind: 'But with all the Indian leaders in prison and the people at home totally disarmed – it is not possible to set up a Provisional Government of Azad Hind within India, or to launch an armed struggle under the aegis of that Government. It is therefore the duty of the Indian Independence League in East Asia, supported by all patriotic Indians at home and abroad to undertake this task . . .'[48] Three days later Subhas Bose addressed another exultant crowd on the Padang: 'The British know very well that I say what I mean and that what I mean I say. So, when I say "War" I mean WAR – War to the finish – a war that can only end in the freedom of India.'[49] Bose stated that he would be on the soil of India by the end of the year. Azad Hind had already acquired territory. On 6 November the Japanese ceded the Andaman and Nicobar Islands to the provisional government, and on 30 December, the tricolour was hoisted above them. They were renamed Shaheedi (Martyr) and Swaraj. This came with no formal transfer of administration, but in the eyes of the Indians overseas it added legitimacy to their war in India's name.

The INA had to be welded into a fighting force. The officer training school at Nee Soon passed out former NCOs as second lieutenants and second lieutenants as first lieutenants, and forty-six recruits were sent to the Imperial Military Academy. New recruits streamed in. Other youth training camps were established in Kuala Lumpur, Seremban and Ipoh. Young men from well-to-do Indian families lied about their ages and signed up for these camps.[50] But there were intrinsic difficulties in finding them equipment and in training young and middle-aged civilian volunteers who knew nothing about soldiering. The movement for India in Malaya was a massive opening of horizons for the Indian masses on the rubber estates. They were all the more isolated by the war and the collapse of the rubber industry. They lacked a leadership to voice their collective concerns. The INA offered a new opportunity for this. Yet there were other motives. As the rubber estates ran down, it was dangerous to be seen to be unemployed. Those who were became prey to Japanese forced-labour schemes. The INA was often the only alternative to the Siam–Burma railway. Many proletarian recruits were 'rice soldiers', not patriotic idealists. The estates were riven with tensions. The tier of clerks and *kanganys* that controlled the labour force for the British planters gained status in their absence, but they often sent the husbands of recently married women away and took the women under their own 'protection'. Retribution for this would come during the labour upheavals of the post-war period.[51]

The tensions and sexual predation on estates were at odds with the visionary rhetoric. In October 1943, partly to counter the charge that Indians were being coerced into rebellion against the Raj, Subhas Bose announced the formation of a women's brigade. It was to be called the Rani of Jhansi Regiment, after the heroine of the Mutiny-rebellion of 1857. It was headed by a young doctor, Lakshmi Swaminathan, who had settled in Singapore shortly before the war and had been alienated by its affluent indifference to the cause of colonial freedom. Bose approached her with a proposal for a fighting force. The Japanese refused to issue it with weapons, but Bose insisted that the INA would provide. As one recruit put it in a radio broadcast in January 1944: 'I am not a doll-soldier, or a soldier in mere words, but a real soldier in the true sense of the word. I am a soldier in boots and uniform, armed with modern weapons.'[52] There was a progress around provincial towns to enlist volunteers: speeches were made in English, Hindi and Tamil, and the platform dignitaries were drawn from all communities. Young girls, too young to serve, donated their pocket money. Of the volunteers at the Women's Training Camp in Singapore, most were local born, and one was as young as twelve. Recruits were urged to give up all ties of love and family. A proud father from Seremban said on visiting the camp: they look 'like seasoned soldiers'.[53] The first contingent of 500 women and girl soldiers left Singapore, reaching Burma in late 1943. There they were given training in jungle warfare and nursing and soon took responsibility for the care of the vast numbers of wounded from the front.[54]

Rash Behari Bose had left the field to the younger Bengali. He returned to Japan in October, but before he left had one last meeting, in private, with Subhas Bose. This time it was the old man's turn to urge caution in the alliance with the Japanese: they had claimed right of conquest in Manchuria, they would do so in India. Quit India had shown that this would not be accepted by the Indian nation. He tried to persuade Netaji to abandon the belief that the British could be defeated militarily, and use the INA to give moral support to the struggle already going on within India. Rash Behari Bose reported the conversation to his long-standing aide, A. M. Nair. Netaji, said Nair, made no comment. But 'he did not put up a cheerful face'.[55] When the INA went to war in November 1943, the first troops – Shahnawaz's 'Subhas Brigade' – were filled with a strange mix of fervour and fatalism. As one Singaporean recruit, P. K. Basu, who had served in the Singapore Volunteer Corps before the war, put it: 'I did not believe that the INA would actually succeed, but I believed in the INA.'[56] For the Indian officers, the Imphal campaign of the following year was to be Malaya 1941 all over again.

## LIFE IN THE TIME OF TAPIOCA

Across the great crescent new connections continued to be forged. The holocaust in Bengal was part of a connected series of famines that were continental in compass, stretching to Honan, China and Tonkin. The hollowness of the Greater East Asian Co-Prosperity Sphere was exposed by the breakdown of regional mechanisms for the supply of food. The memoirist Chin Kee Onn described the situation in his vivid 1946 memoir, *Malaya Upside Down*: 'The economic structure of Malaya rests on a grain of rice ... every activity contributing towards the wealth of Malaya, depends on labour and labour depends on rice. Therefore, whoever controls the rice-pot of Malaya, controls the destiny of the country.'[57] The rice-pots of Malaya were the Irrawaddy and Chao Praya deltas. British Malaya had been dangerously dependent on imported rice: imported foodstuffs accounted for 1,400 of the 2,562 calories in the average Malayan daily diet in 1940.[58] The situation was aggravated by the loss to Thailand of the few states that could produce a surplus of rice locally.

Rice became a hard currency in a time of escalating inflation. Prices were astronomical. By the end of 1942 general prices in Penang and Singapore were twelve to fifteen times their pre-war level. Few people had faith in the 'banana currency' issued by the Japanese. It was so termed for the fruits that appeared on it; it was shoddily printed, with ink that faded; by the end of 1942 the serial numbers had disappeared from it. It was easily forged, as the British in India soon realized. Yet the 'tiger' notes of the Straits Settlements were hard to obtain. The barter trade revived: doctors were paid in rice and eggs. Smuggling was rife. The islands of the eastern littoral of the crescent from Victoria Point in Burma to the limestone outcrops of Phuket and Phang Nga bay, to Langkawi and down to Penang – now popular beach resorts – offered many havens for illicit trade. Pangkor island just offshore of the industrial heartland of Perak was another centre, especially for trade in scarce hardware such as nails, copper wire and tin. These were the quiet sea lanes through which the British agents of Force 136 would enter Malaya.

The scarcity was felt at all levels of Malayan society. By early 1944 even the wealthiest families were down to one rice meal a day. Most families were forced to seek substitutes. The most ubiquitous was the tuber known locally as *ubi kayu*: tapioca. It became inextricably associated with the times. The writer A. Samad Ismail wrote in 1944 a tale of Syonan life entitled 'Ubi Kayu': 'In this period, everyone feels affection for tapioca; embraces, exalts and extols tapioca; there is nothing else that they discuss other than tapioca, in the kitchen, on the tram, in a wedding gathering – always tapioca, tapioca and tapioca; until they even dream sometimes of things tapioca.'[59] People swapped recipes to make it palatable. These would be satirized after the war: skinned and chopped 'Syonan style'; 'a taste not inferior to Irish soda biscuits and good for Christmas presents'. There were other crops too, such as sweet potato; it could be made into chips: 'after eating, drink water copiously so as to have good bowel movements'.[60] Tapioca gave vital calories, but not essential vitamins, particularly those that were needed by young children for growth. The seeds of chronic malnutrition were sown over the years of occupation. People on the whole did not starve as they did in Bengal, but appearances could deceive: by the end of the war a child of ten looked like a normal, healthy child of six.[61]

The Japanese launched a 'grow more food' campaign. Office hours were changed to allow townspeople time to tend their allotments. The Japanese attempted to reverse the drift of the Malays to the towns: they were told to abandon the mentality of the clerk and 'get back to the land'. Some Malays responded to the call, many of them to get out of the tense atmosphere of the towns. But there was also resentment that, like the British before them, the Japanese interest in the Malays was merely directed at making them better cultivators and fishermen. There were official colonization schemes on some rubber estates and aborted British settlement schemes were resumed. A new high-yielding strain of Taiwan rice was planted in Kedah. Yet it failed and brought with it 'paddy blast', a disease which affected other crops. Generally the new lands opened up to cultivation were poor, half-cleared and at risk from pests. As people began to scrape food from marginal urban land, fertilizer was in short supply, and eventually human waste was used, entrepreneurs collecting night-soil for this purpose. The risks of epidemics of cholera or typhoid increased dramatically. In the rice-producing areas, the Japanese *mata-mata padi*, or rice police, forced peasants to sell rice to government and monopolies at a fixed price. Peasants found ways of holding on to rice. Smallholders were short of cash; many sold what food they could on the black market; they pounded rice in secret. The harvest of late 1941 had already been hit by the war; by 1945/46 rice yields had shrunk to 227,000 tons from 335,000 tons in 1939/40.[62]

In later times local writers and historians would struggle to encapsulate adequately these years of hardship, to make sense of the divergent fortunes of different communities and of the infinite textures of personal experience. The problem of 'collaboration' stood in the way of a full reckoning, and the needs of nationhood often demanded amnesia.[63] Yet two broad currents of narrative would emerge. There was the theme of powerlessness in the face of trauma; of peoples trapped between two warring empires. There was also that of self-sufficiency and of opportunity. But if war brought out the innate genius and resourcefulness of the people of Malaya, opportunity fell unevenly and was constrained by the ever-present threat of sudden, arbitrary violence. The balance of experience was to shift at several periods in the war. The first frenetic period of conquest from December 1941 until the second half of 1943 saw, on occasion, everyday social relations collapse in an elemental way. Trust between and within communities was at its lowest ebb. Ironically, this was the period of Japan's constructive imperialism, when some elements within the military administration tried to reshape Malaya. In these conditions they could not but fail. After late 1943, as the tide of war turned against them, the Japanese had to accommodate more effectively with local communities. By this time too, social relations were being repaired, a new way of doing things was being worked out and a degree of trust was returning. But it was at this point, by later 1943, and in many different ways, that the people of Malaya began to turn the trauma of war into an experience of their own fashioning. The fragile local compacts that emerged could be overturned. In the fraught last months of the war, a renewed and terrible uncertainty arose to threaten the internal peace of Malaya.

Initially, townspeople were perhaps the hardest hit by the war. The burgeoning bourgeois civilization of Singapore seemed to have its veneer stripped away. Many old ties of hierarchy were broken; many old truths seemed to fail. Making money was no longer so honourable and respectable as it had been before the war. Nor did possessing it confer security. It was a world upside down:

The former social order was reversed. The 'nobodies' of yesterday become 'the big shots' of today. The former scums and dregs of society, such as ex-convicts, notorious gentleman-crooks, swindlers, and well-known failures, became the new elite, riding high in official favour and power. Legcarriers, puppets, pimps, informers, flatterers and nothing-to-lose adventurers were persona grata with the Japanese, and they rose in the new social order.[64]

The salaries of public employees in particular were torn down to a humbling level by the Japanese. The $50 million extortion stung the Chinese, and many had to dispose of property to pay their share, such as rubber land or urban shophouses. The middle class could be quite helpless in its poverty. Respected men of civic affairs were unable to put their skills to use in the volatile new conditions; men of business found, to their chagrin, that they lacked the right entrepreneurial touch for the black market. As one Cambridge law graduate reflected from his prison cell, 'in every respect we were dealing with a new currency'.[65] Many families employed brokers to do distasteful tasks for them. The young Lim Kean Siew, a scion of the elite, from the very outset of the occupation found himself among the mansions of the super-rich of Penang, on the heights of the Hill. He realized that they had no conception of how supplies could be brought up to them. Here was work to be done. It was, for Lim, a first lesson in socialist principles: 'I could see myself not only in isolation but as part of a society on whose health ours depended.'[66]

There were various routes to new affluence. 'Upstarts' who did not have to contribute to the Overseas Chinese Association stole a march on their rivals. Access to small plots of urban land helped; whilst some profiteers hoarded 'banana' currency, savvier individuals bought up real estate at bargain prices. Rentals soared. Not all civil servants were inept under the new conditions; some found sudden scope for private business. In Selangor, where bureaucrats were given better rations and got their supplies direct from the warehouse, a small surplus could be sold on. Bosses and employees were often brought closer together: old clerks 'would bring their wives' ornaments and costly sarees and give them to their juniors to sell on a commission basis'.[67] Everyone bought and sold. Prim Straits Chinese housewives took to hawking their cakes and dainties on the streets. To a degree never before seen the households of the middle classes brought together both the formal and the informal economy. For many townspeople survival meant a change of work, the taking on of low-status tasks. A variety of new sub-professions emerged, such as queuing. People with cars ran them as 'charcoal taxis', carrying up to a dozen people at a time. The Johore lawyer, S. Chelvasingham-MacIntyre, in addition to the market garden and small dairy business he ran with his wife, worked as a taxi driver and used this valuable resource to trade drugs and cigarette papers. He even set up a manufactory on the first floor of his legal office which produced 'Diamond'-brand cigarettes and employed as many as sixty workers.[68] By a variety of such arts the Malayan middle classes waited on better times. Some would later even glamorize this experience, as recalled from the relative calm of prosperity.

During this period the invisible city came into its own. The 'now-becoming towns' on the fringes of the main settlements were particularly well placed to benefit from the expanded informal economy. They were away from the centres of Japanese power and closer to opportunities for small-scale cultivation and trade. Without the Europeans, and without some of the old community bosses, urban life reconstituted itself. Neighbourliness and trust were fostered amongst the kaleidoscopic societies of Malaya. After the war British intelligence officers struggled to understand the new ties that were formed between the people who now 'took the same *makan* [food] and went to the same places'.[69] Over time this took on a political meaning. Up-country doctors such as A. C. Kathigasu and his wife Sybil in Papan, Perak, who found guerrillas knocking at their back doors, received payment in protection and were drawn into the resistance organization. The revival of the sampan trade to Indonesia and Thailand kept the black market alive; it also sharpened the political connections between worlds that had been sundered in the colonial period. The Malayan and Thai communist parties set up a joint venture. Smuggling networks were expanded to support the Indonesian republic after the Dutch reoccupation in 1945. In pre-war Malaya there had been perpetual tension between colonial attempts to create order and the anarchical improvisations of urban life. The Japanese occupation was a constant battle of subterfuge against restriction and regulation, food control and monopoly. It formed part of the wider culture of resistance. The Malayan Communist Party, after the war, made this kind of buccaneering 'free trade' a central platform of its programme. The experience of war was undermining the old rigidities of the plural society. It was, amongst migrant communities, creating a rooted, shared local experience. The emergence of the 'invisible city' lies behind the phenomenal rise and scope of the united front radical politics after 1945.

Later, 1943 would be remembered as the year when the black market began to overshadow the formal economy entirely. At this point, 'everyone became a broker'. The Singaporean Heng Chiang Ki elaborated on the system:

You have got a group of friends, some would be looking for Aspro, some would be looking for lipsticks, some would be looking for whisky, some would be looking for brandy, so you just go around and start hunting. Get the supplier to supply to the buyer through these brokers. So it goes around all the time: buy-sell, buy-sell, buy-sell . . . it goes round and round because that tin of cigarettes may cost say, $1,000; finally you can let out at $25,000. So I buy I pay a higher price. Then I sell it to you, you pay me at a higher price that it goes on until finally it reaches the consumer. And the consumers are mainly those collaborators or high-ranking Japanese officers.[70]

There were opportunities, but there were also terrible dangers. Lipstick was one thing; controlled materials were another. In August 1943 the Japanese brought in legislation to halt the traffic in a wide range of vital goods. It was riskier still to deal in money itself: buying up Straits dollars with 'banana' money. Police investigation was brutal, rules of evidence cursory in the extreme and the courts corrupt. As people had learned to avoid all kinds of authority, they looked to other types of patronage to protect their transactions, enforce contracts and collect debts. Petty gangsterism was rife, and although for a Chinese man a tattoo meant sudden death at the time of the *sook ching*, the secret society underworld began to make a comeback. Private opium dens proliferated. Both major and minor players on the black market lived in constant fear of denunciation to the Kempeitai. Many old rivalries were prosecuted in this way. 'The "reign of protectorship" had begun', and it reached right to the top.[71]

Japanese stood to make a great deal of money in Malaya. The preference given in the purchase of goods to Japanese individuals and *kumiais*, groupings of companies in certain fields, gave rise to new business partnerships with Malayan entrepreneurs. So too did the competition to supply the *butais*, the garrison forces. The lynchpins of this business were the brokers and agents who advised the Japanese; they received 10–15 per cent sweeteners as 'introducers' from sellers, shopkeepers and other dealers. The Japanese buyers began to connive with agents to split these 'commissions'. Japanese companies and individuals competed fiercely with each other. This forced up prices further. There were the big men behind the scenes, the 'armchair brokers', operating with special passes from the military and emerging only at night to entertain their clients. Then there were the 'field-brokers', with their runners who ferreted out supplies to order from sources up and down the length of the peninsula. With each find of goods, the price would rise as it was reported up the chain.[72]

At the base of this elaborate web of scams, there was the occasional, opportunistic broker. Employees at Japanese ports and warehouses were constantly vigilant. One servant in a canteen on the Singapore naval base described how he would give sailors extra issues of drink in return for watches and cigarettes to sell, or even a bag of rice. 'The Japanese are very fond of beer. They drink a bit of beer, they feel drowsy, they feel tipsy, they're quite happy. Now if I give him say 10 cups of beers, it's only 20cts a cup, it's only $2. But that bag of rice is a few thousands of dollars in those days. And they know it.'[73] There was risk involved; Japanese contacts varied in access and influence. Brokers could threaten sellers with exposure to the *butai* officers. But this was the basis of a system that Japanese scholars would later identify right across Asia as 'ersatz' or 'crony' capitalism. The rapid resurgence of Japanese business networks in the region after the war would take full advantage of this earlier experience. The unpalatable aspects of the trade were sweetened by treating and pleasing on a lavish scale. As one Eurasian civil engineer reported: 'I went to more Chinese dinners during '43 than I did before the war.'[74]

The social gyre of the towns began to get back into gear. By July 1942 race meetings were resumed in Kuala Lumpur and elsewhere. In Syonan, the Cathay Cinema became a preserve of the Japanese, but the Shaw Brothers did well as the leisure industry revived. The 'Worlds', the great amusement parks, were reopened by the end of 1942, to the disgust of the haute bourgeoisie but to the relief of the troubles of virtually everyone else. A new park appeared near the battlefield of Bukit Timah: Beauty World. In some ways, they were a shadow of their former selves; many of the old attractions were closed, but new ones sprang up. People would walk round them in the evening, peering at the stalls that sold almost anything. Visitors to the New World in Singapore remembered around 300 to 400 stalls of all kinds. The most popular new attraction was gambling. Lottery mania swept Singapore and the peninsula: 'Poor Today, Rich Tomorrow'. The first winner, a Chettiar banker from Kuala Lumpur, had bought 223 tickets.[75] By 1943 the Japanese had begun to license gambling farms. The biggest and noisiest was in Ipoh. Chin Kee Onn estimated that an average of 30,000 people a day visited it, and that it employed 2,000 people or more as clerks, guards and detectives. About three in ten of the workforce were girls to sweeten the clients. The Chinese syndicate that controlled it was said to pay $8,000 a day in tax; the stallholders, collectively, $30,000 more. Fortunes were made by the operators; more were lost by their clients. Of all the games, *chap je kee* – Chinese literary riddle-puzzles based on the twelve pieces used in Chinese chess – was the most popular. All sorts of ancillary trades were attracted. Goh Huan Bee worked as a 'substitute gambler' at the New World. He was given $10 to gamble and $10 a month to get people to play at the stalls. Others worked as pawnbrokers for the stalls. 'They were places of ceaseless motion, ceaseless noise, ceaseless smoke.' The vendors of red candles and joss sticks and the *yim-po*, the paper currency of the underworld, also made money; so did roadside soothsayers and interpreters of dreams. 'Opium was given to the people to dull their minds', Chin Kee Onn wrote scornfully, 'and gambling farms were given them to dull their souls'.[76]

But in the Worlds there was a rare freedom, and for this reason they loom large in the memoirs and oral testimonies of Malayans. They were out of bounds to Japanese, though parties of soldiers would come in from time to time looking for people. In New World, the *ronggeng*, the Chinese opera and the restaurants had reopened. Prices were high: at the Tai Thong restaurant a dumpling cost $10. There were fewer women customers than before the war: it was not so safe for them to go out at night. But there were plenty of dancers, and at the stalls of the New World there were 'coffee girls', respectable women who would engage the customers in conversation.[77] For those with money, or with the occasional windfall, there was, despite the austerity, hedonism in the air. 'Charles Nell' of the *Syonan Times* might complain that 'westernized Orientals still debauch in cabarets',[78] but as the INA businessman Abdealli K. Motiwalla put it, drinking and dancing were a staple of life in Syonan and the new Malai: 'that was the only way to keep ourselves . . . at least we were alive.'[79] During the war, much of Malaya's life was lived out on the streets and in the Worlds. After the war, the denizens of the Worlds would seize the political limelight.

# 'LIFE WITHOUT SALT'

The Europeans had disappeared entirely from view. In Singapore, prisoners of war had been seen in early 1942 on various works projects in the town. Thereafter there were very few sightings at all. Few of their relatives at home knew where their loved ones were, particularly those troops who had arrived in Singapore in its final days. When the 18th Division left Britain in late October 1941 it was headed for the Middle East via Cape Town but was diverted off the East Coast of Africa to Singapore. The 45th Indian Brigade had been en route to Burma. For the last telegrams that got out from Cable and Wireless, servicemen had been able to choose three stock phrases from a list of 142. Not all troops were given this privilege; few of the Indians were. In the whole theatre of war, over 250,000 people were missing and still to be traced by the Japanese. Slowly names were sent out by radio, or on lists through the protecting powers: first through Argentina, then Switzerland. The International Red Cross Committee received the first list of prisoners from Singapore only in November 1942. By May 1943 Australia had been notified of only 3,000, or one-seventh, of its POWs.[80]

Some Europeans remained outside the wire. In the hours before the fall, the governor of Singapore, Shenton Thomas, had issued dispensations for some key technocrats to remain at their posts; they included a fisheries officer and some medical doctors. The Bishop of Singapore, John Leonard Wilson, was not detained until 29 March 1943. One man, E. J. Horner, later professor of tropical botany at Cambridge, remained at large for virtually the entire duration. By his own admission, Horner was an eccentric. He saw Singapore's colonial society as a 'Sodom and Gomorrah'. He presented his decision to remain at his post at the Botanical Gardens as the triumph of scientific rationality over the barbarism of conflict between nations. Sixty years later there were still debates in the newspapers about his conduct.[81] For all Europeans in authority during the years of internment, the line between necessary co-operation and collaboration was a fine one. Neutrals also resurfaced: the Europeans had to wear white armbands with a photographic identification. Danish planters went about their business. The press paraded neutrals who had defected from the cause of colonial society and expressed sympathy towards Nippon, such as 'Free Irish seamen' and even a Hungarian member of the Malayan Magic Circle. There were reports of a European passing as a Eurasian working on the English-language *Syonan Times* and of an Irishman called Dan Hopkins conducting the band in Raffles Hotel in 1944.[82]

In Singapore civilian internees were moved to Changi prison and the military prisoners of war into Changi military encampment: an area of six square miles, with sea on three sides. There were, at the outset, 52,000 soldiers there and initially they were not wired in. This was work the POWs would have to undertake for themselves. Their status was an uncertain one. Japan had not signed the Geneva Convention of 1929, but had stated that it would follow it *mutatis mutandis*. A Privy Council meeting attended by Emperor Hirohito on 21 December 1941 established a Prisoners of War Bureau. The gulf in perceptions between captives and jailers was vast. If the POWs believed they were victims with rights, to the Japanese they were a sullen, disgraced mob, who had lost their rights as individuals and were to be treated as such.[83]

The fate of the Japanese in India threw a shadow over the whole business, and the British believed, with some justification, that the ill-treatment of Allied prisoners of war was a reprisal for this. By December 1942, there were 2,115 Japanese internees, the vast majority from Singapore, in Purana Quila camp outside Delhi. They were housed in tents that gave little protection from the cold in winter, or from temperatures that rose to 120 degrees in summer. The Japanese government protested that the food and the cooking, washing and sanitation facilities were inadequate. The British dismissed this: the Japanese were 'notoriously unable to cope with extremes of heat or cold'.[84] 'According to Asiatic standards', officials observed, the rations were 'adequate for proper nourishment'.[85] But the predominantly middle-class Japanese internees found them insufficient and unpalatable. By the end of 1942 the Indian government was 'shocked' to discover that 106 of them had died (55 men, 42 women and 9 children), some of beriberi. This was higher than the 29 deaths amongst all European civilian internees in Changi in the same period. The number of cases of dysentery, the major killer, was a grim reflection on health care,[86] and the old were particularly at risk.[87] The situation was not helped by the deaths of some of those chosen for repatriation in August 1942. The survivors brought with them reports that the cadavers of Japanese were left in a makeshift hospital, and that when they were returned for burial they had been mutilated, dissected by doctors who refused to explain the causes of death.[88] British officials later acknowledged that the treatment of Japanese internees had been scandalous. It would soon be overshadowed by the appalling deterioration of conditions in the prison camps of Japanese Asia.

Yet the initial regime in Singapore was relatively mild. The POWs were at first concentrated by the Japanese in horrendous conditions in the Selayang Barracks where a parole was extorted from them, but thereafter, experiences of life behind the wire were to differ dramatically. Initially, there was freedom of movement around the concentration area in Changi camp. However, the area was then sub-divided under an HQ of Malaya Command, and military life and discipline reasserted itself in reaction to its collapse at the fall of Singapore. It was through the Allied officers that the orders of the Japanese were delivered. The complex dynamics within the military that had undermined the defence of Malaya continued within the camps. The rival groups nursed their enmities and rehearsed their apologias. The rigid sense of order followed in Changi was tested by visitors from other traditions. The British officers did not impress American soldiers, to whom it seemed as if 'they lived in splendour and have their "dog robbers", or soldier servants do their bidding.' The British were jealous of their supplies. They charged the Americans double the price for black-market food (although it was an American trader in the camp who was to be the model of James Clavell's novel of incarceration, *King Rat*). Relations broke down when an enterprising Japanese-American, Frank 'Foo' Fujita, caught and ate an RAF canine mascot that had survived the evacuation of both Dunkirk and Crete.[89]

Changi was to be remembered as something of an idyll for the men who stayed there in its early days and experienced debased conditions in other camps. There were games, theatricals and hobby classes, even a 'Changi University'. Some Dutchmen ran a restaurant and musical café, Smokey Joe's, with a palm-leaf partition in it to separate officers from other ranks.[90] But by the end of 1942 a crisis had arisen. White prisoners had been scattered around the empire as symbols of Japanese triumph and the humiliation of the white man. The fittest remaining began to be shipped out of Changi for the Burma–Thailand railway, although they did not know their destination at the time. They were moved in railway cars marked 'livestock'.[91] Such scenes would have a profound impact on Asians: 'We always thought they were somebody up there where we couldn't reach. We always felt that they were superior to us. The Japanese opened our eyes; because they were there sweeping the floor with me . . . walking without shoes and without this and without that.'[92] After this, conditions deteriorated in Changi. Officers lost their batmen, who for the first time were put on general duties. Soon officers themselves were under pressure to take their turn in the vegetable plots. As men began to drift back from the Burma railway, the full horror of the experience began to deepen and mortality rates quickened. As 'Foo' Fujita wrote in his diary: 'Life without salt was a whole new experience'.[93] Interaction with the world beyond the wire was the key to survival. Chinese traders cashed POW personal cheques for 10 per cent commission. On the railways, when the officers arrived it was their pay that kept things afloat.

By late March 1942 there were 2,585 civilians, including 354 women and 49 children, in Changi prison. By early September 1943 the number was 3,458, including 527 women and 116 children. At the end of the war the total had risen to over 4,500. The population of civilian internees would remain a shifting one, as the Japanese were confused and inconsistent as to the status of some neutrals and Eurasians. There were nationals of twenty 'enemy countries' and ten neutral countries.[94] Married couples were separated; there were only irregular contacts between the women and the men; the Europeans lived under the shadow of intense anxiety as to the fate of the last evacuees from Singapore. If the soldiers fell back on the routines of camp life, the civilian men's camp was run something like an English public school: the cell blocks resembled school houses, with rival sports teams and concert parties. This at least alleviated the enervating tedium of captivity. There was bridge, crosswords, theatricals and a great deal of community singing. There was scholarship too: the camp saw something of a final flourishing of the tradition of 'Malayistics' within the Malayan Civil Service. Scout troops and even golf clubs continued their meetings. So too did the various freemasonry lodges that had been so strong in colonial Malaya. They met in secret, and minutes of meetings were disguised as toilet paper.[95] All this eased tensions. An official medical report on the internees in Hong Kong – where Europeans had originally been held in Chinese brothels – placed particular emphasis on 'the nervous strain resulting from the sharing of rooms by social and racial incompatibles'.[96]

Resentments would be carefully nursed over the coming years, especially over the last-moment departures from Singapore. The verb 'to bissecker', deriving from the name of the second in command of civil defence, was used by internees to mean 'to depart from a place where one should have remained'. The police felt stigmatized on this in the eyes of the army, although there had been departures from both. Yet the camps remained a microcosm of the larger colonial society. On 7 April 1943 there was another arrival of internees. The chief surveyor of Singapore, Thomas Kitching, recorded the moment in his secret diary:

'What a collection,' someone remarks. 'It's like the East End'. They are Jews – 110 of them – and the manner of their being taken into custody is disgusting. They were roused at 5 a.m. today with no previous warning and torn from their wives and families. They have come in with wardrobes and Heaven knows what junk. And their conditions in here are disgraceful – 110 in the rice store. There is one toilet in the room . . .

But, as early hopes of repatriation and exchange faded, social tensions eased. Poverty was a great leveller. 'It is remarkable,' Kitching mused, 'that so many hard drinkers have settled down with no ill effects.' Internees pooled resources for purchases of food and other supplies. Old servants and underlings helped keep internees alive through the wire in Changi.[97] In May 1944 the civilians were moved to a former RAF camp at Sime Road, near Bukit Timah.

The women lived apart from the men and built their own world. In the organization of the women's camp, British birth or marriage to a British man dictated subtle racial hierarchies. The women themselves ranged from housewives to nurses to cabaret dancers. For the young it was an extraordinary rite of passage. Sheila Allan, the daughter of an Australian mining engineer and his Malayan wife, entered Changi aged seventeen and kept a remarkable chronicle of the experience: of powerful solidarities formed, of the underlying tension. 'This is war and war seems to change people and being in here in close proximity to other human beings can destroy our good intentions.' Reflecting on it years later she suggested that 'it was a perhaps very British air of formality that helped keep our community together'. Within the camp, there was an elaborate social round of issuing cards and invitations, concerts and other entertainments, even on one occasion a circus. The American wife of a colonial servant published a typewritten 'newspaper' called 'Pow Wow'. Through it all ran the enervating lack of privacy under the leering gaze of the Japanese sentries.[98] The most vulnerable of the women were those who had fallen into the camps in Sumatra. In the Dutch East Indies there were cases of European women being forced into prostitution as 'comfort women'.[99] This was a fear shared by all women internees.

One of the provisions of the Geneva Convention that the Japanese followed relatively scrupulously related to prisoners' mail. This was perhaps a reflection of the prestige attached to modern communications; it was a mark of civilization. The British mail went from London to Tehran, and then to Moscow on the Trans-Siberian railway, through China to Tokyo. From Australia, the route was Colombo–Basra–Tehran. The first large batch of mails to arrive was on 6 March 1943: forty mailbags containing upwards of 250,000 letters. It had taken nine months to arrive.[100] For those who did not receive any mail, it was a crushing blow. Prisoners were wholly reliant on news from outside, from snatched conversations on fatigues in the city, and a number of clandestine radios in the camps. One measure of the changing fortunes of war was the attitude of the Japanese themselves. They became increasingly paranoid about internal security. When Force 136 staged a raid on Singapore harbour from Australia, with the MV *Krait*, a survivor of the small-ship exodus from the fall of Singapore, the Japanese rounded on what they saw as a network of internees – male and female – who had passed information to the Allies. The arrests began on 10 October 1943, mostly of internees who had held high rank in the pre-war administration or who had worked outside the camp. Most were subjected to extreme forms of torture, including the acting colonial secretary Hugh Fraser, who died of his injuries, and the Bishop of Singapore: fifty-seven internees in all, including three women, suffered at the hands of the Kempeitai: fourteen died of their injuries.[101]

The beatings and torture of Europeans was only the tip of the iceberg. The Kempeitai believed there was a web of conspiracy across Singapore island, but there was a capriciousness to the arrests, often made on the basis of a scribbled name and false information. The rumour, the fear of informers this engendered, became a collective hysteria. It caused many to flee Singapore. T. L. Thean published the first vivid memoir of the experience immediately after the war, which he called *Kempeitai Kindness*. 'Evidently', he observed, 'the Japanese authorities regard imprisonment as some form of retribution: our cells were places of expiation.' It was a particular humiliation for the service elite who saw themselves as exemplars of probity and public service and might, in different circumstances, have rendered loyal support to the new regime. The public privy; the niceties of food hygiene; the constant sounds of others; the bestial conditions; the beatings and the starvation diet – all were remembered. The Straits Chinese were denied the use of a spoon. Between the long waits for interrogation, prisoners were made to sit for long hours, facing the bars with their legs drawn up against their bodies; excruciating cramps resulted. On the YMCA wall there was a notice that read in English:

NOTICE TO DETAINEES
1. Always keep quiet.
2. Don't move about at random.
3. Don't converse with each other.
4. Don't do the following.
    a. Preaching
    b. Membling [sic]
    c. Groaning[102]

The Japanese licensed non-Japanese to give beatings. The police system would take a long time to recover from this. After the war the China Relief Fund would provide a list of forty-five practices of torture: sand forced down the throat, electric shocks, lips sewn together, burning with cigarettes or incense sticks, piercing of nipples, and worse.[103] Entire families could be caught up in the terror. In one case around forty arrests were made over the possession of a wireless and suspected possession of guns. The innocent could not be released because they had witnessed the atrocities perpetrated on the others.[104]

Heroic acts of defiance were to be important to the later memory of the experience of occupation. In Singapore the dignity and resolve of Elizabeth Choy, a prominent Chinese who was detained along with the Europeans and other suspected fifth columnists in Changi and elsewhere on what became known as the 'Double Tenth' (10.10.1943), would make her a heroine to both communities. She was tortured whilst her husband had been made to kneel at her side.[105] There was a swoop in Malacca on a network of professionals who listened in to the radio. Fourteen prominent citizens were arrested, including two teachers of the principal English school of the settlement. One of them, P. G. Mahindasa, wrote movingly from his cell before his execution: 'I have always cherished British sportsmanship, justice and the civil service as the finest things in an imperfect world. I die gladly for freedom. My enemies fail to conquer my soul. I forgive them for what they did to my poor frail body. To my dear boys, tell them that their teacher died with a smile on his lips.'[106] One of the most potent symbols of the shared suffering of Japanese rule in Malaya was Sybil Kathigasu, the Catholic wife of a Perak doctor, who was arrested as a sympathizer of the Malayan Communist Party and was tortured in Taiping jail. As her Japanese jailers sought to extract information from her, her daughter was hung from a tree over a fire. She shamed them into releasing her child but emerged herself crippled and ill.[107]

## WAR BY PROXY

These tales were only one component of a growing resistance tradition. By this stage the communists in Malaya had established both a guerrilla army and an underground organization outside the forest. The young teacher Ho Thean Fook, who had introduced Sybil Kathigasu to the guerrillas, described the terrain around her home town of Papan in Perak in which the local communists' secret camp at Gunung Hijau was found. It was the ideal landscape for irregular warfare.

Gunung Hijau [Green Mountain], which loomed over the town, was covered by thick jungle made even more inaccessible to trespassers by the secondary growth which stretched out from its foot to the edge of the town itself. On the approach to the left of the main hill, the first of the great peaks, was a squatter settlement called Tampoi. To the right of this settlement was an elongated rubber estate which, like a ribbon of cultivated trees, ranged along the foot of the hill and ended near the Wah Chiao Chinese school in Siputeh. The whole area was connected by bridle paths. They were used by rubber tappers, lumberjacks, charcoal burners, illegal 'wild rat miners', booze distillers and wild-game hunters.

In the remoter stretches of this jungle lived Orang Asli communities who had never been contacted by the British administration. Through such a landscape guerrilla forces and their supplies could move with stealth. Ho was driven into the forest underground by the arrest of Sybil Kathigasu and the Papan network. He was a non-communist, branded as a bourgeois, and ill at ease with the Party's iron discipline and political paranoia.[108]

By early 1943 this paranoia was at its height. The betrayal and massacre of most of the Malayan Communist Party's leadership at Batu Caves in September 1942 had weakened the links between the jungle and outside world. The Selangor organization went to ground in the leper colony at Sungei Buloh. It turned out to be an inspired choice for a base: the Japanese gave it a wide berth. The crisis left the Perak guerrillas almost completely isolated for the rest of the war. Here, party leaders began systematically to weed out suspected informers and target Japanese collaborators with assassination. Yet there was tension between the military and political wings of the guerrilla organization over this. The de facto supremo of the MCP in Perak, Chin Peng, still only eighteen years old, argued that the killings needed to be sudden and dramatic: his watchword was 'daring precision'. However, the jungle fighters were unwilling to be dictated to, and Chin Peng was forced to form secret 'mobile squads' of a handful of men for such work. He commanded one himself. This was, he would later argue, legitimate war, not 'terror'. 'We were involved in a free-flowing war . . . When we worked with the British during the Japanese occupation and killed people – essentially in Britain's interests – we were neither bandits nor terrorists. Indeed we were applauded, praised and given awards. You only became a terrorist when you killed against their interests.' Chin Peng was here referring to the OBE he was awarded after the war. He did, however, concede that 'perhaps from time to time errors were made'. Ho Thean Fook recalled the suspicions and the petty jealousies, sometimes over women, that often played a role in internal purges. Chin Peng estimated that perhaps 150 people were eliminated during the war in Perak in this way, most of them Chinese.[109]

The MCP's strategy of eliminating party members who had fallen into the hands of the Japanese military police also had the effect of choking off the rumours that were spreading around the party's secretary-general, Lai Teck. These grew as two other central committee leaders were arrested by the Kempeitai on the way to rendezvous with him. Ng Yeh Lu, another captured leader, was kept isolated from Lai Teck, but over time he too became suspicious. The Kempeitai would release other communists in the full knowledge that they would be disbelieved and executed. Lai Teck was ordered to lie low. It was only later in 1943 that he began to travel up-country again, in dark glasses and a white suit, using women couriers to contact the various regional organizations of the MPAJA. He would stay in Kuala Lumpur at the old planters' hotel, the Coliseum, or at a hotel in Chinatown, meeting cadres at safe houses or business premises on the Ipoh Road. Chin Peng was summoned to meet him for the first time in June at a hilltop bungalow north of Kuala Lumpur. They conversed for two days:

I noted the Secretary General's strong Vietnamese accent. Lai Te[ck] was obviously not Chinese. He didn't look Chinese; he didn't sound Chinese. To me he looked almost Eurasian. He was dark and quite small in stature – no more than 1.65 metres. He looked ill.

Thereafter Chin Peng would acquire the reputation of being Lai Teck's protégé. They corresponded in romanized Chinese, from which Lai Teck occasionally slipped into incomprehensible Vietnamese. This intrigued but did not disturb Chin Peng. It was by this means that Chin Peng sent news in July 1943 of the arrival of British officers from India, under the operation codenamed Gustavus.[110]

Until this point, the British in India had no inkling of developments on the ground. Malaya was completely isolated from the rest of the war. Spencer Chapman, the most senior Special Operations Executive officer in the field, was cut off in the central range with no radio to contact India. His superiors in India assumed he was dead or captured. The difficulty was compounded by the fact that there were various secret worlds within South East Asia Command, and they tried to have as little to do with each other as possible, notwithstanding the fact that they all operated out of the same airbase, Jessore in Bengal. There was the ISLD – the Inter-Services Liaison Department – essentially the Indian title for the Secret Intelligence Service. There was D Division, specializing in radio deception, under the travel writer Peter Fleming. Jessore was also a forward base for the American Office of Strategic Services, which ran its own operations in the region. In fact the first parachute drop of personnel into Malaya was an OSS operation – Cairngorm – in December 1944, involving a Liberator flight that lasted over twenty hours. For a long period there were only two ISLD parties in Malaya with radios. These were landed separately by submarine in early 1943, and they were within hailing distance of the spot when SOE finally made contact with Spencer Chapman. SOE heard nothing of this from the ISLD. In the interim, nine men were lost in a Liberator mission trying to get a radio to Chapman.[111]

The fight back to Malaya could begin only after local agents had been found. The richest sources of recruitment for the secret war in Southeast Asia were the patriotic Overseas Chinese in Chungking-held territory in China. The dapper, charismatic Singapore businessman Lim Bo Seng had left Calcutta in late 1942 on a recruitment mission for the Malaya section of SOE. He found veteran fighters who had been part of the pre-war anti-Japanese movement in Malaya ready to join the patriotic struggle in China. Others were young students. One of them, Tan Chong Tee, had been a champion badminton player and was studying art when he was recruited by Lim. He was also recruited by the Kuomintang regime to report back to them on Lim's mission.[112] Recruits began to arrive in India for training by Force 136 in the early part of 1943. In May the initial party, Gustavus, under the leadership of the Cantonese-speaking policeman John Davis, went into Malaya by submarine. The first attempt failed as local fishermen were unwilling to take them in. The only achievement was to acquire Japanese money as a specimen for counterfeiting. Davis and his small party eventually got in by dinghy on 24 May and went to ground on the coast just north of Pangkor island. He returned to India with intelligence of the guerrilla operation and landed again on the same stretch of coast on 4 August; his colleague Richard Broome followed a month later. They found themselves stranded at a hill location, Bukit Segari, on the coast and unable to move further inland, wholly reliant on their Chinese agents to make contacts in the towns to secure food and a junk to rendezvous with future parties. One agent found work as a waiter in a coffee shop, another as a fisherman. One of the Chinese, Tham Sien Yen, returned to his home in Ipoh and began to set up a network with old friends in the towns; he also made contact with the communists. By the time of Broome's arrival the local leaders of the MCP were resident in the Segari camp. The KMT man, Tan Chong Tee, was furious with what he saw as Davis's high-handed decision to ally with the communists: he and the other Kuomintang men vowed to keep their identities and contacts secret from the MCP.[113]

South East Asia Command's first contact with a senior figure of the resistance came when a young cadre, Chen Chin Sheng, made contact with Davis and Broome. Chen Chin Sheng was an alias of Chin Peng. For the next two years he was to act as the principal liaison officer between the guerrillas and the British, and he was to gain their trust. He was also to establish a better relationship with the Chinese Kuomintang agents. As Tham Sien Yen was later to recall: 'his vast knowledge and far-sightedness won us over. Chin Peng had no overbearing mannerisms and he spoke in a voice so full of passion and power that it had all of us spellbound.'[114] But it was unclear what Force 136 had to offer the MCP. Until the end of January 1945 Operation Gustavus had no functioning radio. The transmitter it brought in was too heavy to be easily moved and too weak to reach Ceylon. Chin Peng moved the British and their five Chinese officers inland. He prepared a special camp, with handpicked cadres to guard them, near the 2,200-metre peak of the mountain known as Blantan, above Bidor, a town where John Davis had served as a police officer before the war. It commanded a magnificent view of the coastal plain, but was a tough two-hour trek from the nearest road. The main force of the Fifth Independent Regiment of the MPAJA was nearby in the Cameron Highlands but the British were kept in quarantine from it and from other forces in the state.

There were long periods of inactivity. Broome was stricken by illness. He made a set of Monopoly cards, and scrounged for reading materials. The Europeans had no contact with Chapman, who was still with the guerrillas in Pahang. There he was frustrated and bored. He was, Chin Peng wryly observed, less a 'stay-behind' than a 'left-behind'. The British attempted to build their own network with their Chinese agents. One of the first batch of guerrillas, Wu Chye Sin, had set up as a front the Jian Yik Jan rice-trading company in Ipoh, with a branch in Lumut on the coast. The campaign was boosted by a fresh rendezvous with a submarine. Broome and Davis wanted to meet it, but Broome was ill, and the roads were unsafe. It was Chin Peng who boarded the submarine, where he met another Force 136 operative, Claude Fenner, a man who later, as chief of police in Malaya, was to be Chin Peng's principal antagonist. Chin Peng refused to take the white men ashore. He did agree to take a radio and a man introduced to him as an influential Chinese under the alias 'Tan Choon Lim': this was Lim Bo Seng. The radio had to be abandoned, but Lim Bo Seng joined Davis and Broome at Blantan.[115] He found that the KMT's network was falling apart. The life of peninsular towns was stultified by rumour and the presence of informers. The Japanese had strung road blocks across the coastal plains which made movement difficult. There had been sightings of submarines. The KMT's liaison man in Ipoh was not on speaking terms with his fellow agent in Pangkor. More than this, their key man in Ipoh, Wu Chye Sin, had for his cover immersed himself in the debauched culture of corporate hospitality there. Through this he hoped to extract information from befuddled Japanese businessmen and officials. He affected the air of a playboy and, in a breach of security, moved in with a taxi-dancer with whom he had fallen in love. To his colleague Tan Chong Tee, it seemed as if the lifestyle was taking its toll. The intelligence blurted out by his contacts was useful to the Allied cause, but there was no way of getting it to India.[116]

Chin Peng mistrusted all this and in any case his thoughts had already turned in a different direction, to boosting the fighting forces in the forest. In early 1943 the appearance of the anthropologist-gone-native Pat Noone had opened up new possibilities for the communist Malayan Peoples' Anti-Japanese Army in northern Malaya. Previously the Temiar communities of the region had been a closed world to them, but Noone sent out messages to Temiar leaders, urging them to support the guerrillas. The larger numbers of fighters needed the Orang Asli for supplies of food and for their local knowledge. Some co-operated willingly; there were old trading relationships between the Orang Asli and the Chinese that could be built on by exploiting the Temiar tradition of mutual co-operation: this was a crucial element of understanding that Noone passed on to the MPAJA. It helped sustain the MPAJA during what was its darkest period. The real problem began when the Orang Asli began to face Japanese reprisals for giving succour to 'bandits'. The Japanese forces were further unable to distinguish between Orang Asli and guerrilla camps: both adopted similar sites and bamboo structures.

Noone's personal intervention in the war was to have tragic consequences for himself and for the Orang Asli. Robert Chrystal, the stay-behind planter who spent a lot of time with him during this period, saw Noone as a naïve fantasist: T. E. Lawrence in a loincloth. Noone was flattered to be accorded the unique privilege of being invited to become a full member of the Malayan Communist Party. Chrystal warned Noone that the main enthusiast for the Temiar work – a student leader called Low Mah – was not himself a full party member, and not perhaps fully trusted, or to be trusted. But Noone was not to be restrained. He only broke with the MPAJA in July 1943; by then the damage was done, and cadres such as Low Mah had learned to work without him. This connection did much to keep the Malayan resistance alive in a period of betrayals and Japanese harassment.[117] It was fatal for Noone: he was murdered. The precise circumstances of his death remain a mystery. In one sense it was a crime of passion by a jealous suitor of his Temiar wife, but it was also a result of the unease the Temiar felt at the extent to which Noone was implicating them in battles that lay beyond the forest. The death of Noone was a terrible trauma for the Temiar. A great taboo was placed over the business. When Noone's brother Richard, himself a Force 136 veteran and later Protector of Aborigines for the whole peninsula, attempted after the war to discover what had happened to him, he found no clues. The memory of this violence on a peaceable community proved difficult to live with. It also created a pattern that was hard to break. Noone had organized the Orang Asli in *asal* networks and had imparted this technique to the MPAJA. They would employ it to some effect when they returned to the jungle.[118] 'They are,' acknowledged a leading party cadre in 1945, 'the real patriots of Malaya.'[119] But by the last stages of the war they were in a desperate state; close to starvation by some accounts, and desperately short of the supplies they took from outside the forest.[120]

At the end of 1943, on Christmas Day, 'Dum' and 'Dee', Davis and Broome, finally were united with Freddy Spencer Chapman, who was brought into the camp by Chin Peng. The meeting had a Livingstone and Stanley quality about it. At the same time, after a long, frustrating delay, Chin Peng received word that the secretary-general would nego-tiate with the British in person, but incognito. Lai Teck arrived north of Bidor in his black Austin motor car, where he was met by Chin Peng. Chin Peng noticed that Lai Teck was very weak. He struggled to make the walk up to Blantan camp, and used a crutch. He made it clear to Chin Peng that he would take sole responsibility for the negotiations. Lai Teck was introduced to the British as 'Chang Hong'. It is clear that, although both Davis and Broome had heard rumours of Lai Teck's relationship with the British before the war – 'it was', Davis said, 'a good story' – they did not connect the Lai Teck legend to the man they met at Blantan. Chapman, however, had met Lai Teck shortly before the fall of Singapore, and may had known of his background. If he did, he kept this to himself. The British referred to 'Chang Hong' as 'The Plen'. It is unclear whether Lai Teck recognized 'Tan Choon Lim' as Lim Bo Seng. The two sides faced each other across a wooden table, hastily constructed from forest materials. Davis, a malaria-stricken Broome, Chapman and 'Tan Choon Lim' for SEAC; 'Chang Hong' and Chin Peng for the Malayan Communist Party, the MPAJA and its affiliates.[121]

An agreement was drawn up on two sides of a page torn from a school exercise book: 'C[hang] H[ong] agrees that his party will fully cooperate with the Allied Forces while retaking Malaya and for this purpose will follow the instructions of the Allied C-in-C in so far as military operations in Malaya were concerned.' 'Chang Hong' haggled over the last phrase. An original draft had used 're-occupying'; he would only accept the less permanent 'retaking', which carried with it no associations of legitimacy. 'Co-operation' was to continue whilst the army were responsible for civil order in Malaya. Beyond that, the political issues regarding the future status of Malaya and the MCP were scrupulously avoided. The MCP gained arms, supplies and a subsidy of $50,000–70,000 a month. The agreement was signed by Davis, Broome and 'Tan Choon Lim' for SEAC, and by 'Chang Hong' for the MCP.[122] There has been much speculation about Lai Teck's motives. Had Lai Teck decided to switch his allegiance from the Japanese to the British? Yet there were more betrayals to come. After the communists left, Orang Asli arrived with musical instruments and the treaty was celebrated with dancing.

Similar sets of calculations were occurring right across the crescent. In Burma 1943 was a hiatus year before the massive battles of 1944. Whilst 1943 did not bring the scale of misery seen in India, an impoverished Burma teetered apprehensively towards a kind of independence under the Japanese, its northern hills alive with the sound of gunfire. Indeed, the special forces operations by the Allies among the hill peoples of the Assam–Burma frontier proved to be one of the most memorable aspects of the Second World War. Numerous volumes of memoirs recount the activities of the American special forces, Stilwell's troops and British Force 136 operatives among the Shans, Nagas, Chins and Kachins, as also in Malaya to the far south. The American image of the 'tough guy' and the British muscular Christianity of the 'Sanders of the River' sort provided a mythical background against which real acts of great bravery and endurance were played out.

Yet as the intelligence historian Richard Aldrich has suggested, the special operations on the Burma front did as much to envenom relations between the British, Chinese and Americans, and even within the British and American camps themselves, as they did to advance the cause of the war.[123] Right from the beginning the more conventional officers of the British and Indian armies viewed Wingate's Chindit campaigns with alarm. As Alan Brooke complained, Wingate demanded huge quantities of arms and supplies in a very difficult situation. Because he got first the attention of Wavell and then of Churchill himself, he seemed to them to have an unfair advantage in the distribution of military resources. The situation in north Burma quickly became a quagmire of contention between the British, Americans and Chinese. Stilwell's slow advance into Burma in the second half of the year reignited Burmese worries about Chinese claims on their northern borders, besides putting the local populations at risk from pilfering and looting of their crops by Chinese troops who had no option but to live off the land. Chinese soldier settlers penetrated far into north Burma in June 1943 until they encountered a force of Gurkhas which turned them back. The Kachins of Force 136 fought several pitched battles with Chinese infiltrators in between their engagements with the Japanese.

The background to the Allied trials, tribulations and local successes was, indeed, the extraordinary resilience of the hill people themselves. By the end of 1943 Kachin resistance to the Japanese had become a popular movement. At the outset of the war, many Kachins had been stunned by the British defeat. According to J. L. Leyden of the former Frontier Areas Administration, '[t]hey concluded that the Japanese must be a race of super-Europeans'. The tide began to turn in October 1942 when a Kachin jemadar (sergeant) just returned from the Indian army began to organize more effective resistance amongst the poorly equipped levies.[124] Rifles, shotguns and flintlocks were brought out of their hiding places all over the country. As Japanese patrols came into the hills, stealing cattle and forcing people to work, admiration began to turn to hatred. The Japanese did little to endear themselves to the local population. Particularly suspicious of churches, in more than one place they turned Kachin Baptist meeting halls into military brothels. By now the Kachins had killed more than a thousand Japanese and they considered them less brave. This was because they squealed like pigs when shot, fired aimlessly into the air in terror and herded cows before them in order to avoid ambushes. News of Allied victories was beginning to seep back into the Kachin and Karen territories occupied by the Japanese, too. The old idea of British invincibility was on the rise again. The British began to supply the now thousand-strong levies from India and activity behind the lines was stepped up. An effective espionage network was started deep into Japanese territory in Bhamo and Suprabum. Two Kachin schoolmistresses acted as collecting posts for information. Leyden reported 'We held our own in the hills because the Jap could never get any of his agents through to obtain co-operation from the Kachins.' This was because the Kachins 'made the war their own war and thought of themselves as allies of the Allied nations, they were a people under arms and at war.' One Kachin chief being tortured by the Japanese shouted defiantly. 'Kill me if you want to, but the guns remain for the people and the government. I am a Kachin!'[125]

In the far northern hills, where British authority had survived the Japanese invasion, a furious row broke out between American military commanders at Fort Herz and the local British administrators. The Americans were recruiting and training their own special forces from among the Kachins and seemed to have imposed their own martial law on the hills. On one occasion some Kachin levy recruits shot a cow and were arrested by the British magistrate. The American commander, Carl Eifler, a former customs official and 'G-Man', accused the British of obstructing the war effort. The British accused the Americans of virtually creating extra-territorial rights in what was still a part of the British Empire. Dorman-Smith and his staff had to damp things down while keeping up some slight element of prestige. Eifler, wrote one of them, 'flies off the handle at the slightest provocation, but really wants to get on with the war'.[126] Ultimately the British on the ground in the far north had to be diplomatic.

American and Chinese meddling at the highest level, though, was another matter. Amery engaged the governor in a little Colonel Blimp-like badinage: 'By Gad! Sir. I am not at all prepared that anyone Yank or Chink, should poke either projecting or flat noses into the problem of the reconstruction of Burma.'[127] Still, a modus vivendi was eventually reached between the American Force 101 and British Force 136 special operations operatives. Dorman-Smith recorded one apocryphal example of a truce with honour among the contending parties. Carl Eifler, armed to the teeth, was visiting Simla. He encountered 'Wally' Richmond, a small, short-sighted, British former employee of Steel Brothers who spoke Burmese and Kachin and was working with Force 136. Doing his John Wayne act to put the Limeys in their place, Carl stood Wally up against a wall, took aim and blew a tobacco tin off his head with a revolver. Wally returned the compliment and Carl had a bad moment when the tin was duly blown off his own head. Wally then put a cork from a gin bottle on Carl's head and made ready to fire. At this point Carl, fearful of Wally's myopia, finally chickened out and cried 'No!' to the triumphant joy of the British onlookers.[128]

Amidst the tedium and occasional high jinks of Simla, the unhappiest men of all were probably the Burmese. Tin Tut, still smarting after his encounter with the 'old hands', lived in virtual seclusion at the incongruously named Braeside. In the Himalayan foothills near the Solan beer factory Sir Paw Tun, the last pre-war prime minister, wrote the obituary of the old order in a long, rambling series of letters to Dorman-Smith, part combative, part self-pitying. He wrote as an Arakanese who had imbibed some at least of Britain's imperial ideas and had tried to reconcile them with Buddhism and his deep sense of Arakanese and Buddhist Burmese identity. He recalled that during his school days in a Christian convent he had read Samuel Smiles's essay on 'character'. He had prayed daily for his governor, his king and his country. 'My mother taught me to be absolutely loyal to the British crown', he wrote. But this was difficult when many British officials acted with arrogance and racial pride. It was natural for well-brought up Burmans to bow before superiors. But more than once he had 'straightened up from my bending posture to show that he [the British official] no longer deserved respect because he was bullying me'.[129] Mortal man, he said, was liable to be blinded by greed, passion and ignorance. That was particularly true of the old British administration in Burma which knew little of the people or their religion. The British, of course, were not as corrupt as the Burmese ministers such as Ba Maw and U Saw. They were less tempted by money as such, but they still fell victim to 'other attractions – in some cases women, and in other cases, flattery, platitudes and kow-towing'.

Paw Tun loathed British racism and arrogance, but he believed the Thakins were beneath contempt, merely low-class upstarts. What worried him was the way in which the Thakins and Japanese had rallied the monkhood and the faithful in his 'priest-ridden country'.[130] He noted how the Japanese were giving liberal donations to the Shwedagon pagoda and how their commanders had liberally fed the monks and taken part in Burmese religious ceremonies. Despairing of the British, because Dorman-Smith seemed intent on bringing back the old unfettered bureaucracy, and profoundly out of sympathy with the new plebeian Buddhism of the Thakins, Paw Tun slowly came to see that he had no future. It was this that lay behind his increasingly erratic behaviour and protracted bouts of illness.

Worried about the fate of their relatives in Burma and uncertain about the country's future, the Burmese ministers and officials in India began to turn their minds to the reconstruction plans that the British were drawing up to keep themselves cheerful. Writing to Ernest Bevin, the governor acknowledged that after the war there was likely to be little left of Burma except its soil. What was needed, he thought, was a serious attempt to root out corruption and create an honest administration at the local level. Only then could national life restart and taxation for development be justified. J. S. Furnivall, the socialist former administrator who knew the Thakins well, was more radical. He had made his reputation before the war with a book describing the 'plural' and segregated societies of Southeast Asia. What the British had to do was repair the damage that their economic and 'divide-and-rule' policies had created by binding the different cultural groups together in a new style of national entity. This was the sort of policy that the Malayan officials gathered in Wimbledon were now urging. A new, humane, Fabian, socialist empire of benign nation-building was now looming in their consciousness.

Events on the ground were to make all these schemes academic. For a start, there were serious disagreements between the British about what the future shape of a British government in Burma was to be. While Dorman-Smith was keen to get civil administration back into the saddle, Wavell wanted a long period of military administration. When the two met, as they did from time to time over the next two years, Dorman-Smith kept saying things that annoyed the viceroy. Frank Donnison, who was present, remembered that each time the governor prattled on, 'I could see a deep purple flush rise above the collar of Wavell's bush shirt and spread up the back of his neck into his hair', until the conversation moved to safer topics.[131] When he visited London, the governor pressed for a declaration of the date for Burmese independence after Allied reoccupation. It would be a good number of years in the future, but still this was not enough to assuage Churchill. The prime minister thrust his face towards Dorman-Smith at their meeting, barking, 'So this is the man who wants to give away Burma!'

# HIGH COUNCILS: TOKYO, CAIRO AND TEHRAN

The year 1943 had been one of the most terrible in history for the whole of east Asia, but especially for the people of the great and embattled crescent of land which stretched from Calcutta to Singapore. The cities of Japan had tasted the first fruits of American mass bombing. In China, millions had died in the famines in Kwantung province and tens of thousands in the bloody slugging-match between the Nationalist and Japanese armies. Scarcities and forced labour flayed the people of Burma, Malaya and Indo-China. A whole generation died in Bengal. Yet the region was still gripped by a kind of stasis. The two sides, the Japanese, the Burma Defence Army and the Indian National Army on the one side, the British, Americans and Chinese, on the other, were still fencing cautiously as the monsoon came to an end. For the Allies, Southeast Asia was still on the back-burner. The slow build-up to the invasion of Europe absorbed most of Alan Brooke and Marshall's time. The Japanese and their allies were still unsure of their next move: with the war in China unresolved and the American fleet steaming forward across the Pacific, some strategists decided they could still afford one final thrust against the British in India, whom they still regarded with disdain. But it could not come yet.

Thus it was in the absence of decisive military activity that three conferences, three tense encounters between the most powerful men in the reeling world, staked out the political future of south and east Asia in the autumn and winter of 1943. The first, held in Tokyo from 5 to 8 November, was a conference of Japan's Greater East Asian Co-Prosperity Sphere. Here gathered all the leaders of Japan's sponsored Asian governments from Manchukuo in the north to the Philippines, Indo-China, Burma in the south and, of course, Subhas Chandra Bose, leader of Free India, but as yet ruler only of the Andaman and Nicobar Islands. General Tojo had organized a range of impressive ceremonies which included audiences with the emperor, visits to the shrine of the Meiji emperor and the Yasukuni shrine for the Japanese war dead, and a mass rally in Hibiya Park. Hundreds of journalists gathered from the nations of the new Asia for 'the greatest assembly in world history'.[132] The aim was to persuade the representatives of the dependent nations of Japan's continued determination to lead Asians to their freedom from Anglo-American domination. Independence was real. The Co-Prosperity Sphere would bring benefits to ordinary people, once the war began to be won. The Anglo-Americans, it was hoped and believed, would soon see the futility of the stalemate and agree to a peace settlement which would guarantee the future of the 'Mongoloid and Indic races'. Ba Maw, attending as Adipadi of Burma, was impressed. In retrospect he claimed to see at this conference table the origin of the independent spirit which took Asians into the non-aligned movement in the 1950s. At the time he spoke not of economics but of the 'call of Asiatic blood. This is not the time to think with our minds; this is the time to think with our blood.'[133] Subhas Bose remained in high spirits at this 'family party'. His army was ready. The cry 'Chalo Delhi!' was already on his lips. This, he said, echoed the recent German war cry 'To Paris, To Paris!' and the Japanese 'To Singapore, To Singapore!' There was a deeper historical resonance. The war cry had been used by the Indian sepoys of 1857 who converged on the old imperial capital of Delhi during the great Mutiny and Rebellion. In Japan, Bose was met with a welcome bordering on adulation by the large community of exiled Indian nationalists, students caught in Tokyo by the war and the Indian Independence League.

In public, the Japanese emperor seemed more powerful than any of his revered ancestors. He was the leader and central focus of a Japanese commonwealth of armed, anti-Western nationalities. His quiet support for the imperialist elements in the Japanese navy since the 1930s seemed to have brought unequalled honour. Pearl Harbor was only two years behind. Privately, though, Hirohito was a troubled man. In July, the Allied invasion of Italy, a country which he had visited as a young man, shocked him into the realization that Germany might not win after all. Closer to home, he was perplexed by his navy's apparent failure to stem the American advance across the Pacific. It was the army which was now taking over the vital defensive role. Learning that the Solomons were about to fall to the Americans, he angrily demanded from his commanders: 'Isn't there some place where we can strike the United States? When and where are you people ever going

357

to put up a good fight? And when are you ever going to fight a decisive battle?'[134] His staff mumbled their apologies.

Less than a month later, on 22 November, the British, Americans and Chinese met in Cairo. This was to be a preliminary conference to set the agenda for a future summit with Stalin.[135] A communiqué was later issued in which the Allies vowed to 'punish the aggression of Japan' and demanded its unconditional surrender, but in private there was little meeting of minds. The Americans were already determined to push for a full-scale invasion of France and fend off British demands for more resources to be poured into the Mediterranean. Neither Churchill nor Roosevelt was prepared to put the reoccupation of Burma any higher up their list of priorities. Relations within the various national leaderships were not too happy either. The permanently irascible Stilwell found he left one interview with the president 'puking', by his own account, while Roosevelt disliked Stilwell's habit of referring to Chiang as 'Peanut'.[136] Brooke was fascinated by the ferret-like qualities of Madame Chiang, but found the Chinese appropriately inscrutable and wondered why they were at the conference in the first place. The Americans were stone-walling so nothing much was decided.

Stalin began his journey to Tehran by train. He passed through but did not stop at the shattered though victorious city of Stalingrad. Russian soldiers and secret-service agents flooded into Tehran for his arrival. Roosevelt flew in on 26 November, now sure that the American view would prevail. Churchill arrived later by air and stayed at the British embassy, which was guarded by a regiment of Sikh troops. A brittle sense of celebration pervaded the first face-to-face meeting between the wartime Allied leaders. Churchill presented Stalin with the Sword of Stalingrad to commemorate the city's heroic defence. The delegations toasted Churchill's sixty-ninth birthday. Stalin traded sly insults with his generals and Brooke over tumblers of vodka. But what really happened was that Roosevelt and Stalin formed an axis which put Churchill in the shade.[137] They focused Allied strategy on an early invasion of France, the famous 'second front' in the west. This meant that Churchill's Italian campaign and the campaign in Greece he had hoped to begin were downgraded in importance. Burma virtually disappeared from view. Any troopships and landing craft diverted from the Mediterranean would now go to France and Operation Overlord. Mountbatten's amphibious attack on Burma or Malaya and Churchill's plans for 'the tip of Sumatra' became pipe dreams. South East Asia Command's forgotten armies were forgotten again. What its frustrated commanders did not yet know, however, was that Tokyo's very desperation would quite suddenly set the Burma front alight in the New Year of 1944.

# 7

# 1944: The Pivot of the Fighting

## JAPAN'S FINAL THROW

In Tokyo, on the last day of September 1943, a conference of Japanese Imperial Headquarters had been convened in the presence of Emperor Hirohito. The tone of the meeting was sombre and quite at odds with the celebrations of Asian unity the following November. American naval forces were massing to the west and driving like a trident into Japanese positions. To the north, they had destroyed the garrison on the Aleutian Islands. In the centre, they were gathering to assault the Marshall Islands. In the south, a third prong of American and Australian forces was thrusting by land and sea along the coast of New Guinea. Japan needed 40,000 aircraft a year to compensate for the numbers being steadily shot down by the Allies. Tojo told the despondent emperor that in 1943 only 17,000 or 18,000 had been built. After a tense debate, the conference issued a communiqué. The new policy for carrying out 'the Emperor's war' was to establish an impregnable perimeter which ran from the Kurile Islands in the north through the inner south Pacific, to 'the western parts of New Guinea, the Sunda Strait and Burma'.[1] Though apparently defensive in posture, the troops on this perimeter would bide their time and launch massive local assaults against the Allies. The overall plan was still to knock the Chinese nationalists and British India out of the war and to inflict crushing defeats on the American naval forces. Japan would fight on to the end regardless of the fate of Germany. With American resolution wilting, she would then be in a strong position to extract concessions at the peace conference which was expected to follow.

Far to the southwest in the pretty Burmese hill station of Maymyo,

Lieutenant-General Renya Mutaguchi, General Officer Commanding, Japanese 15th Army, pondered among the dilapidated villas and gardens of what had once been Dorman-Smith's favourite spot in Burma. Mutaguchi was an extreme nationalist and a fighting general. In his diary he wrote:

I started off the Marco Polo Incident which broadened out into the China Incident and then expanded until it turned into the great East Asian War. If I push into India now, by my own efforts and can exercise a decisive influence on the Great East Asian War, I, who was the remote cause of the outbreak of this great war, will have justified myself in the eyes of our nation.[2]

Mutaguchi had several reasons to expect success. The Wingate expedition, which had struggled back into India a few months before, showed that a strong landward invasion through Assam was a distinct possibility. As the Arakan campaign of 1943 had demonstrated, the British army in India was still underperforming and the Burma frontier seemed to be the weakest sector of the whole long Allied perimeter. India was seething with discontent. Newly inspired by Subhas Bose, the Indian National Army was now a fighting force of 40,000 men, spurred to greater efforts by news of the suffering of the famine. If it appeared on Indian soil shouting 'Chalo Delhi!' it might spark a rebellion greater than the Quit India movement of 1942. The Japanese had more than a million troops scattered across Southeast Asia as a whole. It was possible to imagine a major thrust against India using as many as 200,000 of them without significantly weakening the defensive posture.

Other generals had been cautious, even hostile, to this philosophy of the final throw. One had dryly told Mutaguchi, 'It would no doubt satisfy you to go to Imphal and die there. But Japan might be overthrown in the process.'[3] Yet Mutaguchi was quite sure that the highest authority, the emperor himself, was in favour of a thrust into India. The fact that Prime Minister Tojo acquiesced in the attack on Imphal, the most easterly British base in India, suggests that this was probably so. Herbert Bix, Hirohito's biographer, writes: 'Although no documents indicate that Hirohito himself actively promoted this particular offensive, it was just the sort of operation he had pushed for all through the war – aggressive and short-sighted.'[4] So began, in mid March 1944, the battle which was to initiate the last major campaigns of the British Indian army and see the greatest land defeat of the Japanese armed forces in their history. It was a struggle that was to determine the form of Indian, Burmese and Malay society far into the future. It was a struggle which mobilized vast armies of nurses, porters, labourers, prostitutes and animals down the length of the great Southeast Asian crescent to service the half a million fighting men who struggled in the mud and the high jungle passes between India and Burma.

## INDIA ON THE OFFENSIVE

As the New Year of 1944 dawned in Calcutta, the auguries for the British remained very mixed. People were still dying in the streets and the word 'famine' was now used officially. Even though Wavell and the army were securing more rapid deliveries of food, and Churchill had finally relented about sending relief shipping to India, in Bengal people were weakened by malnutrition and were easily carried off by the Indian winter ailments. Even when they could get food, their stomachs were too withered to digest it. Well into 1944 the authorities still worried about a recurrence of famine when the monsoon once again proved erratic. Wavell, fortified by the office of viceroy, nagged, berated and threatened the British government: 'Please tell your colleagues that they have been warned!'[5] The old complacent routines of Anglo-India were beginning to change. Junior officers were now sleeping four to a room in the great hotels along Chowringee. From their windows they could see camouflaged anti-aircraft guns along the whole length of the street. The great paddock, or Maidan, once the scene of equestrian events, had now become an airstrip. The denizens of the Calcutta Club had become more reticent about their luxurious meals.

Now, finally, India's war effort began to kick into gear. War production increased. Munitions factories were properly supplied with food and raw materials. The minor acts of sabotage and strikes of the previous summer and autumn died away. However, engineering surveys showed that the Assam lines of communication were still very weak and that the rail network in eastern India was groaning under the strain.[6] Numerous voices in Whitehall and in Washington continued to predict that India would never make a strong base for an offensive against the Japanese, or at least not in the foreseeable future.[7] Amery and Brooke were still muttering to each other about transferring the whole war effort to Australia. But things were moving on the ground. The Ledo road from Assam into Burma was pushing ahead. There was a big effort to improve the roads and bridges in Assam. The Americans began to pour resources into India, rebuilding a large part of Calcutta Port and further developing airfields for the Burma–China Hump. As the summer approached they put in five battalions of military railway engineers and effectively took control of the Assam railway's northern section.

Predictably, this led to a severe outbreak of tension between the British and Americans. There were also occasional conflicts between US soldiers and Indian shopkeepers. On one occasion GIs occupied and searched a Bengali village without police permission. Black Americans were regarded with particular suspicion. As on most war fronts, the British resented the intrusion of the Americans into their patch, especially when they had better railway carriages, better beer, better films, more and prettier women. According to the British, they never seemed to realize how difficult it was to pull further resources out of India: 'you can't tighten the belt of a skeleton', as one senior official had put it.[8] American commanders were determined that US resources should not be used to 're-build the British Empire'. This infuriated the British because it was so difficult to disentangle the civilian from the military use of newly installed generators, roads or port facilities.[9] Serious conflicts over resources were compounded by silly disputes over protocol. At one station where American airmen were quartered, the local British club's band had taken to playing 'The Star Spangled Banner' along with 'God Save the King'. Some British army officers objected 'because our anthem lasted about three seconds less than the American'. They asked the club chairman to abandon the American anthem. Wisely, he refused.[10]

Americans for their part were often brash and generally utterly dismissive of the Indian civil and military authorities. They had different war aims and were not concerned to Save England's Asian Colonies, as their acronym SEAC (South East Asia Command) had it. They had been taught to mistrust and dislike the British by Stilwell, who was still smarting over his defeat in 1942. Many Americans were also offended by what they saw as the overt racism of the British Asian empire. An American surgeon working in Burma thought that the carrying of 'thunder boxes', or portable latrines, for British officers by low-caste Indian servants was deliberately instituted by the colonials to humiliate the natives. Americans voiced their disapproval apparently oblivious of the way that the United States, and particularly its army, was still rigidly segregated on racial lines. Naturally the British pointed this out. By no means all Indians liked the Americans' confrontational manner either. K. K. Tewari remembered being flown into Akyab by a gum-chewing American sergeant: 'He was surprisingly courteous for an American,' wrote Tewari.[11]

One friendly American officer had written a memo which caused a stir as far up as the British Cabinet. Americans, he said, thought that the government of India 'is not concerned about winning the war and is hopelessly inefficient, tangled in red tape, short-sighted, reactionary, uncooperative and strongly anti-American'. He went on to say that the average US civil or military officer saw GHQ India and the government of India 'as a sort of composite of the Dual Monarchy [Austria–Hungary] and the Third [French] Republic in their last days'.[12] Both of these polities had been bywords for incompetence and corruption. More generally, 'most Americans in this theatre, as elsewhere, disapprove vaguely of "Imperialism" in about the same way as they disapprove of sin. At the present time, however, there is virtually no sympathy with the Indian Nationalists even amongst the most advanced liberals here. Everyone is disgusted and fed up with the Indians.' In Whitehall there were splenetic notes on files inveighing against the 'usual shallowness of Americans'. Wavell penned one of his weary minutes reflecting on how difficult it was to get anything done in India. Relations did not really improve much until later in the year when finally a major British effort was being made on the Burma front. Even the congenitally hostile American war correspondents came round to some degree at this point.

It was not only the Americans who complained about British India. The military censors reported a worrying 'leftward trend' in the attitudes of ordinary British soldiers in India in late 1943 and 1944.[13]

Intercepted letters and reports by commanding officers revealed persistent grumbling about the inefficiency and incompetence of everything in India and about the incredible amount of basic paperwork which bedevilled every move. Soldiers contrasted the failure of the British front in Burma to move forward even a few miles with accounts of the great successes that the Soviets were achieving on the eastern European front. The lesson seemed obvious. Socialism was more efficient than Britain's class-ridden and imperialist society. Though the censors seem to have been less aware of it, youthful members of the officer corps were openly espousing socialist and communist causes, teaching the troops about the need for an end to imperialism in Asia and radical political change at home. Some, like the future Urdu scholar of London University, Ralph Russell, had known Indian communists at Cambridge. Russell later resumed his contacts with the Indian party while on active service near Kohima.[14] Sydney Bolt, another Cambridge communist, working behind the lines in Assam to rally Indian opinion to the Allies, was denouncing the racism and exploitation of the Raj to his colleagues and Indian contacts.[15] The Indian communists' wartime anti-fascist alliance with the British made it difficult for the authorities to clamp down hard. The government of India was worried enough to institute in Delhi a lecture series for officers on 'The Constitutional Issue in India'. The word went out that Stafford Cripps's offer to the Congress in 1942 had just been 'too good to be true'.[16] The British were doing their best, but the Congress simply would not trust them.

India's key resource, and one slowly being exploited to the full, was labour. Poverty and the need to buy food pushed people into civil and military labour schemes, but control was difficult, sub-contractors often corrupt and sometimes brutal. There were conflicts of interest. Was it more important to build the new roads or finish the aerodromes? When the military used excessive amounts of civilian labour, other parts of the Indian economy began to creak. For instance, Assam and Bihar coal-mine owners complained that the military was drawing off labour and this was impeding steel and munitions production. They also bleated about the excess profits tax. The underlying problem was the labour market. Poor villagers and agricultural labourers would only come and work in the coal mines for cash with which they could buy kerosene and other necessities. But by 1944 civilian shortages meant there was little left to spend their money on and the supply of labour began to dry up.

More important still was the work of keeping up the flow of recruits to the army. During the critical period of January and February 1944, more than 720,000 new recruits were signed up. The authorities regarded this as adequate rather than good. At under 5 per cent, desertion rates were remarkably low for an ill-educated mercenary army, but it took a relatively long time to train and very large forces were required for the build-up on the northeast frontier. Ironically, an improvement in economic conditions actually made it harder to recruit good troops. As the Punjab began to reap the benefits of food production during the winter harvest of 1943–4, farmers who stayed home began to prosper at the expense of those in the forces and pay rates in the army slipped behind: soldiers felt their families were getting a raw deal from the rationing authorities; soldiers' lands were partitioned in their absence; their women ran off with village layabouts.

Politics also continued to affect recruitment. Congress and its Red Shirt supporters in the North West Frontier Province recruiting areas were almost entirely in jail at this time, though some of their local cells were still operational. The communists spent more of their effort warning the working class to be ready for revolution than helping the recruitment drive.

Another political menace to recruitment was the electoral and factional conflict in the Punjab between the Unionist Party and Mahomed Ali Jinnah's resurgent Muslim League which made much of the running while so many of the Congress membership was in jail.[17] The Unionists represented the conservative and pro-war Muslim and Jat 'yeoman' caste landowners of the province who could always be relied on to put a little pressure on local headmen to raise the recruitment level. The All-India Muslim League, by contrast, had hedged its bets at the beginning of the war. Jinnah wanted plenty of Muslims in the subcontinent to be trained for warfare, but did not want to help the British too much. By 1944 the League was trying to outbid the Unionists and take over the Punjab as its power base. The policy of its local organizers towards recruitment vacillated from week to week.

As 1944 wore on, therefore, the army and civil authorities made strenuous efforts to improve village-level propaganda and troops' amenities. In April Indian troops were given a rise in their so-called 'proficiency pay' which applied to combatants and non-combatants alike. Travelling propaganda vans visited villages and attempted to get veiled women to visit them. One ploy was to send tanks into the villages of the Punjab and North West Frontier Province where they would cause an immediate stir and demonstrate the continuing power of the Raj. They also reminded the young peasant farmers of the villages that motorized vehicles were key to the future and that the army could teach them vital mechanical skills. One visitor described such a visit: the village landlord followed by a non-commissioned Indian officer of the Armoured Corps addressed a large, expectant crowd as a fleet of tanks and armoured personnel carriers roared into the dusty village square. Nearby, a group of eighty or ninety women were swarming over a 35-ton tank in their brilliantly coloured saris. 'Yesterday, an old lady of eighty insisted on climbing into the Lee and looking through the periscope and the gun sights and sitting in the driver's seat. She said her favourite grand nephew was a tank gunner.'[18] The influence of the village women in encouraging the men to join up was crucial according to recruiting officers. District soldiers' boards and liaison officers tried to make sure that soldiers' families were in good order.

The Indian army had become a curious hybrid. The most modern psychological theories jostled with old concepts of race and *izzat*, or honour. By the third year of the Japanese war, the army had in place an effective system for rapid training. This taught basic skills to illiterate recruits who as yet had had no contact with machinery beyond the pump of the village well. Recruit reception centres in North West India and Nepal provided the men with radio and gramophone records. They could hear popular music or play games and get a sense of military life and modern inventions. After basic training in drill and the use of weapons, 'group testing officers' gave them psychological and practical tasks and graded their fitness for different types of service. The old idea that some 'races' were more martial than others was officially abandoned. Once they were recruited and trained, efforts were made to improve the variety of the soldiers' food. The army provided books, Urdu and Punjabi films and American film projectors. The village uplift enthusiast Frank Brayne, subject of Clive Dewey's book *Anglo-Indian Attitudes*, became inspector-general of amenities for the troops. Brayne tried to get the men active in base camps and hospitals by popularizing Indian games. He had an Indian prince draw up a rulebook for a kind of North West Frontier 'tag' called *pir kaudi*.[19] He toured India, Egypt and Iraq lecturing Indian soldiers and officers on changing society after the war. These 'splendid young men at the peak of physical fitness' were the shock troops who would finally transform the Indian village and sweep away generations of ignorance and backwardness.

Despite these new psychological methods of making the modern soldier, the old prejudices of the Raj died hard. Canadian doctors investigated the diet of the Indian army. They reported that commanding officers were the least likely to want to add nutritious new foods to the 'class' or 'caste' diets their men had traditionally been fed.[20] Young British officer cadets still learned about the plucky characteristics of 'their' Pathans, Dogras, Sikhs, Jats, Punjabi Muslims and, above all, Gurkhas. Some displayed the zeal of the newly converted. Eric Stokes, the Cambridge historian, later wrote of his delight during the war in the easy, paternalistic relationship between officers and men 'so different from twisted western ideas of equality'.[21] This was still the English public school or grammar school at war in the East. But Indian commissioned and non-commissioned officers were also happy to put themselves forward as representatives of caste traditions and the honour of the dead fallen in past battles. These visions of stability and persisting values were easier to contemplate than the reality of contemporary India, with its starvation, inter-communal massacres and seething urban anti-colonialism.

Much of this old-style Raj agonizing about food and customs was probably misplaced. The Indian soldiers themselves simply wanted to be fed properly. In 1942 and early 1943, there had been little to eat besides the reviled Shakapura 'dog biscuits', various types of goat meat and, for those who could stomach it, tins of bully beef. The famous American self-heating tins of soya-bean chunks had gone down like a lead balloon. Things improved in 1943. Bully beef became 'bully mutton'. More nutritious foods and even vegetables began to appear as far east as Dimapur. Some troops complained that the stores were still poor, though watches, Christmas supplies and so on, were being parachuted in for their officers. As the army advanced into Burma, dog biscuits, Australian Kraft cheese and tea remained the staples. The British did seem to be trying though. The tins were all given *halal* labels for Muslims or *jhatka* labels for Hindus and Sikhs. Basically they were the same and the Indians did not seem to care much.[22] Later, American 'K rations' arrived – breakfast, lunch and dinner, with chocolate thrown in, but not everyone appreciated these either.

As the British Indian army learned to stand and fight, rather than withdraw before the Japanese advance, it became necessary to treat serious wounds on the front. The authorities developed a flexible system of well-supplied forward field hospitals. Supplies and personnel could be parachuted into the fiercest battle areas. Things had improved in the base areas as well. The four military hospitals at Secunderabad in the Deccan were now among the best in the world.[23] There were spacious X-ray rooms and new tropical drugs were available. The most important change was the rapid development of the Indian nursing service during the war. Before 1940, the tour diaries of the British nurse Diana Hartly paint a depressing picture.[24] The hospitals were being rapidly Indianized, yet Indian nurses were mainly recruited from local social-service bodies. They usually received no salary and yet were made to pay up to Rs20 per month for their own training. They lodged in low-grade housing. Worse, the nursing profession still had a stigma about it. In these impoverished hospitals nurses had to carry bedpans around and personally wash the patients. In a society where ideas of caste purity were still strong, nursing was a lowly occupation, suitable only for widows, orphans, Anglo-Indians, Indian Christians and partly educated members of the so-called scheduled castes. High-caste Hindus regarded all these groups as virtual untouchables.

During the war this changed quite fast. Some girls from 'sheltered homes' joined the Red Cross and Hindu and Muslim social-service organizations as a patriotic act and in defiance of Congress propaganda about the 'imperialist war'. Nurses were recruited from this pool of volunteers. The authorities in Madras set up a state nursing service with standard uniforms and rules for pay and leave. Medical schools established courses in nursing. Finally, in 1943 the first post-graduate course in nursing management was established in the Delhi School of Administration.[25] But even though the mass recruitment of nurses was going ahead, most of these facilities only had about half the staff they needed. There were simply too many other demands for women's labour. The aftercare for British and particularly Indian troops also left a lot to be desired. Even at the end of the year, the artificial limb centre at the Kirkee hospital under Lieutenant Colonel Chaudhary was overwhelmed. He only had one trained man and a small number of Barhais, men of the local carpenter caste, to deal with 400 patients. The light Japanese trench mortars did terrible execution on the Indian army throughout the war. The carpenters had to make prosthetic limbs out of unseasoned wood and give them heavy metal fittings because the hospital could not get hold of quality woods or aluminium. When Edwina Mountbatten, wife of the Supreme Commander, visited the unit towards the end of the campaign she reported that Chaudhary was doing 'a wonderful job' but was on the verge of a nervous breakdown.[26] Over these same months, a blood donation scheme got into gear despite attempts of the Congress to restrict its use to air-raid victims rather than the 'imperialistic' army.[27]

## BATTLE COMMENCES: IMPHAL
## AND KOHIMA

So the Indian military and civil order, Kipling and Lord Curzon's mighty machines for doing nothing, were finally creaking into action. The authorities in Delhi, Kandy and London had their eyes fixed on the winter of 1944 for the start of a major campaign in Assam. As so often in the past, the Japanese caught them on the back foot. What they thought was mere probing of the defences in Arakan and on the Manipur border developed into Japan's last great offensive in Southeast Asia during March and April 1944. Why did Mutaguchi and the Japanese high command initiate this incredibly costly attack just at the time when they were also undertaking the Ichigo offensive against Chiang Kai Shek in South China? Why did they contemplate a major land push when they were under intolerable pressure from the US Pacific fleet?

The Japanese themselves saw this as the final throw in Southeast Asia. They hoped to knock out British India and had been told by Subhas Bose that once they penetrated the Bengal plains there would be a mass revolt on a larger scale than in 1942. They seem to have believed that Germany was about to counter-attack the Allies in Italy and frustrate a potential invasion over the Channel. If they knocked out Britain and China, they could hope for a negotiated peace with the Americans. If, instead, they waited until the autumn, their air power would have dwindled further, their food and raw material situation would have collapsed and the Allied build-up in India would have reached its peak. The Japanese plan, as in 1942, was for rapid deep penetration and they expected the British armies to fall back as they had always done previously.

There were now also strong political reasons for giving the commanders in Singapore and Rangoon the go-ahead. In Tokyo the position of Prime Minister Tojo, the super hawk, was in the balance. The Greater East Asian Co-Prosperity Sphere was running into trouble with shortages of essential commodities, soaring prices and labour problems. On the ground there were signs of restiveness on the part of the Burma Defence Army and the Indian National Army. In fact, the BDA was already plotting against the Japanese. Some of its leaders had approached the British as early as the end of 1943. The Japanese were already suspicious and a faction within the local military and intelligence services even took the view that Ba Maw was contemplating treachery, making a ham-fisted attempt to assassinate him and replace him with a more compliant character, a prince of the former Burmese royal house.[28] Wiser counsels prevailed, however, for the last thing the Japanese high command needed during the assault on India was a political coup in the rear.

The INA remained steadfastly anti-British but officers and men bridled at being used as a kind of coolie corps by Japanese troops who had never really taken to them, finding Indian food customs and the long hair of the Sikh troops, for instance, completely incomprehensible. Subhas Bose himself knew that this was the critical moment and was putting great pressure on the Japanese high command. His men were ready. The INA had trained specialists in sabotage and infiltration in its academy in Penang. Some agents were already in place across the

Indian border. It was now or never. From the moment Bose had arrived in Rangoon, a large proportion of the city's remaining Indian residents had been glowing with pride. The previous November the anniversary of the death of the last Mughal emperor of India had been celebrated. He had died in exile in Rangoon where the British sent him in 1859. The chairman of the Burma branch of the Indian Independence League had vowed to present Netaji, the affectionate name for Bose, with earth from the emperor's grave in a silver casket to accompany him on the march to India.[29] Now Indians mobbed the trains packed with INA troops as they steamed out of the city's stations to cries of 'Chalo Delhi!' and 'Azad Hind Zindabad!' 'Long Live Free India!' Preparations were made for a 'Netaji week' from 4 to 10 July to celebrate Subhas Bose's assumption of leadership of the freedom movement in East Asia a year earlier.[30]

The commanders of the three armies now facing each other in the Assam hills intensified the propaganda effort amongst their own troops. How to keep the civilian population on their side was the key issue. The Japanese commanders were particularly worried about priests, women and cows. A pamphlet was produced for Japanese soldiers entitled 'Everyday Knowledge about India'. It cautioned them against acts of violence, especially against temples and priests. The British had been vilified for going into religious buildings with their boots on. The pamphlet also confidently reported that 'there is probably no place in the world where women are more bother'.[31] In other words, the procurement of 'comfort women' in the subcontinent was going to prove a problem. Above all, soldiers should leave cattle alone, even when hungry. British counter-propaganda had constantly harped on the way in which Japanese troops had casually slaughtered and eaten any cow they came across in their passage through Burma. The Japanese took the hint. A document captured later revealed that Japanese officers had been sent on a special course to learn about goat breeding preparatory to the advance. Huge numbers of the animals were rounded up. They were to be the staple food of the army as it advanced into Assam, 'to avoid offending the scruples of Indian people' by eating cattle.[32] As it turned out, the Japanese infantrymen faced less complex issues of cuisine as they began their great assault. A captured diary reported of one feint, 'We were ordered to withdraw – many dropped out of the ranks due to weakness from lack of food. We have to chew uncooked rice to satisfy our hunger. The enemy certainly eat well. I wish I could have a stomach full of such good food.'

Japanese morale was still high, but it was the morale of desperation. Captain Shosaku Kameyama of the Japanese 31st Division said that most of his comrades were aged between twenty and twenty-two. They came from the devoutly Buddhist Niigata prefecture. He bewailed the fact that most of these young men were unmarried. They could not become ancestors after death and were later forgotten by the younger generation. In 1944 they 'fought for their country, to save their country. They believed that their country was in a serious situation. When they left their home town, many schoolchildren and local people cheered their departure, singing songs and waving flags. This had greatly impressed the soldiers, who had a strong obligation to their family and local folk.'[33] It was this unquestioning belief that, even in the distant jungles of Burma, they were literally defending their native soil that explains the almost fanatical bravery and self-sacrifice commented on by so many of their British and Indian adversaries. It was harder for the British or Indians to believe that they were doing the same thing. To the British, the enemy of their homeland was Hitler and even poorly educated Indian soldiers were now deeply ambivalent about the Raj. For the Allies, the offensive spirit was kept up by regimental loyalty and, by 1944, by a fierce and cold hatred of the merciless Japanese.

Alongside the Japanese now stood about 40,000 men of Subhas Bose's INA. Its commanders launched a major propaganda offensive too. They told their men in numerous political talks about British atrocities in India. They spoke of the bloody suppression of the 1857 rebellion, the massacre at Amritsar in 1919 and the recent and still unrolling famine in which millions of their countrymen had starved to death as a result of British neglect. The British Indian battalions would, they were told, desert the moment they met a truly Indian army. The British, it was said, were so worried by the unreliability of their own troops that they had brought in nearly wild West Africans to keep an eye on them. The commanders knew they had their own vulnerabilities. Subhas Bose constantly invoked the Mahatma in his messages to the troops and radio broadcasts. The Congress leaders were national icons even for those who wanted to liberate India by force of arms. Yet Gandhi and Nehru had persistently rejected the tactics of the INA, even when they were immured in British jails. This was because the one opposed violence and the other opposed fascism. Even before the defeat at Imphal and Kohima, there were signs of fractiousness and worry amongst the INA commanders. A captured letter from the Officer Commanding, North India Guerrilla Regiment, to Subhas Bose in April 1944 said that the troops had set off in high hopes for the liberation of India. When they got to the front line, the Japanese assigned them to tasks such as road making, repairing bridges, driving bullocks or, worse, carrying rations for Japanese soldiers. Often they had to eat Japanese food. Malaria was tightening its grip in the absence of medicines. The Japanese commander said they would eventually fight, but he was often being asked 'Sahib, when the Japs are advancing into the sacred soil of our motherland, what are we doing sitting in remote corners of Burma?' In an ironic recapitulation of the relations between British and Indian troops, the Japanese refused to salute INA officers.[34]

The British behind the lines began to be jumpy as February turned to March. There were sporadic acts of sabotage across India. In districts such as Midnapur in Bengal and the 'badlands' of southern Bihar revolutionary nationalists had gone underground in 1942 to escape arrest. From here they carried on a stubborn campaign of anti-British propaganda, attacks on communications and the occasional murder of Indian government officials. On both the east and west coasts parties of INA special forces had been landed from Japanese submarines. The Criminal Investigation Department lost sight of them for days at a time and they found many sympathizers among ordinary people in bazaars and villages.

Up in Simla, Dorman-Smith idled away his exile, taking his dachshunds for walks. He continued to argue with officers of South East Asia Command about the role of civilians in the reconstruction of Burma. He listened to INA propaganda broadcasts. In his letters to his wife, he ridiculed the 'March on Delhi': 'Poor old Netaji [Bose], he still slaughters the 7th Indian Division nightly over the radio and is most pained that their imminent surrender never takes place.'[35] As S. A. Ayer, Bose's minister of information, recorded afterwards, Netaji, who also had a stout sense of humour, listened to the British broadcasts out of Delhi with equal amusement.[36] British morale was boosted by 'Wingate's stout show'. Dorman-Smith was referring to the Chindits' second great campaign to strike behind the Japanese lines with gliders, a campaign which saw the death of Wingate himself in a plane crash on 24 March. Here and there, though, there was a note of concern; as Dorman-Smith wrote to his wife, 'it may be that your old pal Bose's propaganda is having a bit of an effect'.[37] On 23 March as the Japanese push on Imphal developed, Dorman-Smith and the deskbound military became increasingly concerned. An 'anxious time' was coming.[38]

The British stepped up the propaganda effort. 'Old Burma hands' recruited from Steel Brothers and other major firms toured the British regiments giving them pep talks. There was little need to stress the hatefulness of the Japanese enemy to these troops. But the attitude to be adopted to the Burmese when the breakthrough finally came was a more touchy question in view of the constant barrage of denunciation directed against them since 1942. In their briefings to the troops, the old hands gave little quarter. According to one, the Burmese were close to 'primitive savagery' and this had been demonstrated by their treatment of Indian coolies in 1942.[39] Other morale-building talks urged that though there were very large numbers of 'bad hats' in the country, these were concentrated in a few particular places. Shwebo north of Mandalay was one black spot, for here the Burmese kings had sent their most troublesome subjects into exile.[40] The Delta had always harboured 'bad hats' too. Here the British had encountered the fiercest opposition in 1886 and 1930–31, and they were likely to do so again. All the same, a pep talk opined, 'the average Burman will be found to be a gentleman if treated as such'. Another improving talk warned British troops against constipation and consequent hypochondria. It added: 'half our trouble with the natives is due to their remaining constipated for several days without asking for medicines'.[41] Perhaps this was just a conceit, but the writer's tendency to equate native political problems with bowel complaints was a bad augury for the future. Within a year these same old Burma hands were to be in action against the Japanese alongside the Burmese fighters they now denounced as 'quislings' and 'fascists'. For some of them, the mental leap would be too great.

Among Indian troops, morale was rising. Indian officers were taking over the 'josh groups' or regimental chat sessions. This was a new breed, better educated and more independent than the old corps of native officers. They felt on a par with the British and began to convey a new confidence to the troops. The soldiers began to put memories of Arakan behind them. Increasingly, they were being taught to fight as thinking men rather than automata. Commanders of the Indian divisions, notably Frank Messervy, built on Auchinleck's new training programmes for Indian soldiers at base camp. Units held regular post mortems on the fighting, discussing ways to counter Japanese jungle warfare tactics and teaching individual soldiers to think independently.[42] General Slim, shrewd as ever, sensed the change and spent much more time talking to the Indian and Gurkha soldiers. He began his campaign 'not so much like a general and more like a parliamentary candidate' trying to get the ear of his electors, 'except that I never made a promise'.[43] Speaking to groups of soldiers and officers along the front and in base camps, Slim came to think that Indian troops responded even better than British troops to appeals on abstract grounds to religion and patriotism.

On 15 April 1944 Mountbatten moved his headquarters from the 'marble palaces' and intrigue of Delhi to the *bashas* (hutments) of Kandy in Ceylon, which he insisted were nearer the front.[44] His aim was to counter the 'forgotten army' feeling that particularly affected British troops immobilized for months in the dust or rains of India or stuck in the mud and malaria of Assam. The army's propaganda and entertainment wing had a good time targeting this. 'Laugh with SEAC' printed a little poem, 'Sticking it out in Delhi', which summed up the sense of boredom. It began:

> Fighting the Nazis from Delhi,
> Fighting the Japs from Kashmir,
> Exiled from England, we feel you should know,
> The way we are taking it here.
> Sticking it out at the Cecil,
> Doing our bit for the War,
> Going through hell at Maiden's Hotel,
> Where they stop serving lunch at four.[45]

The previous autumn, Mountbatten had recruited Frank Owen of the London *Evening Standard* to run South East Asia Command's propaganda newspaper, the *Phoenix*. Its editor, 'Supremo' said, would hold 'by far the most important job that a lieutenant has ever held in the army'.[46] Mountbatten tried to instil into the troops, by way of Owen's editorials, a sense that Kandy represented a new beginning. Later in 1944, the two arch-propagandists began to work on the Americans. Owen tried to cajole Frank Capra, the Hollywood film director, to put a better gloss on British and Indian troops in one of his films of jungle warfare. By the end of the year plans were afoot to produce a joint Anglo-American forces magazine for SEAC.

In a sense, the more difficult propaganda war for the British was inside India itself. Starvation continued in some parts of Bengal. Perversely, a return to relative agricultural prosperity in the Punjab discouraged enlistment there. A huge and apparently accidental explosion ripped apart the Bombay dockyards at the beginning of April. Indian labour fled into the hinterland, anticipating Japanese bombing. The enemy advance into Arakan raised memories of 1942 and their propaganda was believed even when Kohima's capture was announced more than once in their broadcasts. To cap it all, there was a serious shortage of coal in eastern India, labour was scarce and the Indian merchant classes were rattled. Yet somehow the Allied victories in Europe meant that morale never plummeted as low as it had done two years before. Officials noted that bank deposits outweighed withdrawals by two to one. The opposite had been the case in 1942. The political situation remained deadlocked with the Congress leadership still languishing in jail. But the Muslim League was now becoming more and more positive on the issue of recruitment, hoping to cut the ground out from under the ruling Unionist Party ministry in the Punjab. The communists were also very active in promoting recruitment and countering Congress propaganda against the war. In the long run, they told would-be recruits, the real battle would soon be against imperialism and capitalism.

Where the two armies encountered each other, the propaganda war between the Indian army and the INA was as sharp as the fighting. INA commissars lectured Indian army POWs with stories of British atrocities and won some of them over. A young Gurkha of the INA

Bahadur Group infiltrated British lines. On capture he wept copiously in front of the commanding officer and said he was a refugee and had lost both of his parents at the hands of the Burmese. The officer believed him, gave him a certificate of good conduct and set him free. He continued spying for the INA. Other INA men made contact with former supporters of Bose's Forward Bloc as they moved into Assam and began to hatch plans for a general rising in the event of a Japanese breakthrough.

But these local political successes were offset by the grave situation of Axis forces even before the advance on Imphal ground to a halt. The Japanese had finally tested their logistical capabilities to destruction. Less and less food was coming up from the Burmese plains. Soldiers in both the armies were living on tiny parcels of rice supplemented with roots. INA troops were fed with Japanese food to which many were allergic. Disease was now rampant among Indian and Japanese soldiers as the supply of medicines dwindled to nothing. This was at the very time when the Allied armies were beginning to get the benefit of wartime advances in tropical medicines made in Canada and the United States. In 1942 disease rates in the British and Indian armies had been over 20 per cent during the flight from Burma. By June 1944, they had fallen to 6 per cent. Still, morale among the INA seems to have held up well. Bose remained invincible in his optimism, announcing that the march on Delhi was making slow but steady progress even as the Japanese began to withdraw from the Assam front. British intelligence itself reported that the INA was still overwhelmingly anti-British. It was also reported, though, that relations between the INA and the Japanese had begun to sour further. The Japanese commanders were dubious of the INA's tenacity as a fighting force. This was probably unreasonable as the INA were never properly supplied and remained dependent on captured British arms and ammunition which were now harder to come by.

The first test came once again in Arakan. Japanese forces began to probe and push against the positions to which the British had been forced back during the dismal fighting of the previous spring. Their aim was to direct attention away from Mutaguchi's forces which were now building up for their push on Imphal. The assault began on 6 February 1944, about three weeks before the great U-Go offensive to the north. Japanese forces moved north and began to encircle the British HQ of Lieutenant-General Messervy at Launggyuang. As the battle developed, something unusual happened. Rather than retreat, the British held their ground. Their Spitfires knocked the Japanese fighters out of the sky. Ammunition, medical supplies, food and even Frank Owen's newspaper *SEAC* were parachuted to the British strongpoint at Sinzweya. Tanks and heavy artillery, in which the British were now overwhelmingly superior, turned the course of the battle in their favour. By 26 February the Japanese offensive had been broken. For the first time a British and Indian force had met and decisively defeated a major Japanese offensive, leaving 5,000 of the enemy dead on the field. The army, gloomy and apprehensive as it had been a mere nine months earlier during Irwin's watch, had now massively improved morale.

There was something else. On 7 February a Japanese assault had entered one of the field hospitals. They massacred the Indian and British medical team and bayoneted the wounded in their beds. News of this and other similar atrocities spread along the whole eastern front. British, Indian and African troops began to loathe the Japanese with a hatred almost unparalleled in modern warfare. Thereafter, Allied soldiers often casually killed any Japanese they encountered without the slightest compunction. Hatred of the enemy appears to have become one of the great causes of the Allied army, a more potent force by far than loyalty to the king-emperor. Indian troops extended this hatred even to their former comrades of the INA. When they encountered them in battle, Indian troops shot INA men in large numbers, to the relief of British intelligence officers.[47]

The next major event to unroll on the Burma front was Orde Wingate's second Chindit expedition, Operation Thursday. Its purpose was not so much to help the British push into central Burma but to cut off the Japanese forces in the north of the country and relieve pressure on the Chinese under Stilwell to the north. Popular with Churchill and Mountbatten, Wingate had dramatically built up his forces since the previous year, even though some senior officers worried about the diversion of men from the main battle front. Thursday drew on more than 10,000 combat troops, supported by US commandos and equipment. This large force was deployed by means of glider drops far into north Burma, around Indaw. The campaign proceeded at a slower pace after Wingate himself died in an air accident early in the operation. Mountbatten paid tribute to 'one of the most forceful and dynamic personalities this war has produced'. The results of the operation remain a matter of controversy in the military-history literature. Yet there seems no question that the sudden appearance of such a large Allied force at his rear disrupted Mutaguchi's plans and unnerved his commanders, even though he initially dismissed the attack as a sideshow. The disruption of Japanese communications and battle plans in the north also significantly aided Stilwell's advance on Myitkyina later in the year, though he, too, was highly sceptical of Thursday. Most important, perhaps, was the psychological effect of the expedition on British and Japanese morale. Once again, Wingate had created a morale-boosting legend precisely at the time when the British were under maximum pressure. The Japanese never entirely regained the advantage of surprise and flexibility which had served them so well early in the war. Over the next two years, they were constantly looking over their shoulders, fearing attacks by the Chindits and other Allied special forces.

The Arakan attack was the curtain raiser to the far more massive battle that unfolded a few weeks later to the north. Imphal and Kohima were, for the British, the defining land battles of the war in the East. Mutaguchi planned a typical two-pronged attack. One thrust was to the south on Imphal. The northern advance was intended to drive through Kohima and ultimately encircle the massive base being built up at Dimapur, where David Atkins and his transport corps had met its Waterloo the previous year. The Japanese attack on Kohima almost succeeded. On 17 April the garrison of 2,000 men nearly fell. This would have been another terrible blow to British morale and prestige, but the garrison was initially relieved on 19 April.[48] According to Ba Maw, Bose had an Indian governor and even a new Free India currency ready for the captured strong-points. Ba Maw added that a joint INA–Japanese advance was delayed by wrangling between the two sides over who should take the credit. Bose wanted to raise the Indian flag while the Japanese wanted the first towns to fall in British India as a gift for the Emperor Hirohito on his forty-third birthday.[49]

In the end, though, it was military factors which saved the day for the British. The British had tanks in the sector and the Japanese did not. This can be attributed to the huge improvement in both land and sea communications that had occurred on the Allied side since the previous spring. An animal-based Japanese army was quite suddenly facing a mechanized British Indian one. Another key factor was the formidable fighting power of the revitalized Indian element of the army.[50] It was Punjabis and Gurkhas, in particular, the men of the 5th, 17th and 23rd Indian divisions, who came to the rescue of the embattled garrisons. These troops were better fed, better led by the hardened elite of Viceroy's Commissioned Officers and better directed as a result of effective unit-based propaganda work. Once the Kohima garrison had been rescued the British battled to retake the Kohima area throughout April and May. Eventually, in June, the Japanese offensive began to crumble and their troops, out of food and ammunition, began to fall back southward towards Imphal. There were, of course, many episodes of British heroism and grit, notably the battle on the Kohima tennis court in May where, for instance, Sergeant J. Waterhouse of B Squadron, 149 Tank Regiment, kept dozens of attackers at bay. After the battles of April 1944, however, the British army began to use Indian troops to stiffen the morale of the British in particular circumstances, reversing a generations-old practice of the Indian army at war. Here, on India's jungle-clad eastern frontier as much as in Whitehall or the Congress Working Committee, the Raj really came to an end.

Imphal showed the Allies using another of their decisive advantages: air power. In the first two weeks of April the Japanese attack on the southerly strong-point was as fierce as it was anywhere during the whole war. The Japanese wanted to neutralize the local airfields and push on towards the Indian plains where they hoped to spark off a popular revolt. With Mutaguchi in personal command, massive and well-trained forces were available. Again, the garrison held its ground. This time the air drop was on an equally massive scale. Against resistance from some American officers, Mountbatten diverted US transport planes from supplying Chiang Kai Shek over the Hump to China. With the garrison consolidated by parachute drops in brigade strength, tanks again switched the battle in the Allies' favour. Lacking food and ammunition and decimated by cholera and malaria, the Japanese attacks began to slacken by the third week of April. In late June the siege of Imphal was raised.

The Japanese had no transport aircraft and few mechanical vehicles by this time. Instead, they mobilized the animal power of north Burma and the hills on a scale unprecedented since the time of the old Burmese kings. They also brought their own horses. In Operation Imphal 12,000 horses and mules, 30,000 oxen and more than 1,000 elephants crossed the Chindwin. The scale of animal fatality was colossal. During the campaign Japanese horses survived only fifty-five days on average and mules seventy-three days. All the horses and mules had died by August and the cattle had also perished or been eaten. Only the elephants survived.[51]

While Imphal and Kohima suddenly awakened the world to the titanic scale of the military conflict in mainland Asia, the other front in Arakan burst further into life. Here the British had even more ground to make up in terms of morale and self-esteem. SEAC, keeping up pressure on the Japanese command in Akyab, sent in a mixed division of men from Hyderabad in the south and from the North West Frontier during early 1944. It was supported by the motor launches of the Royal Indian Navy, moving up and down the Naf river with supplies. The air force, too, was much more in evidence than it had been the previous year. This allowed British troops to hold out and fight back when surrounded by the Japanese because they could be supplied from the air. The aim in this third Arakan campaign was straightforwardly to kill as many Japanese as possible.

Gaining territory in Arakan was very difficult because of the intricate nature of the waterlogged plain and its paddy fields and the low hills of the interior. The planners had already decided that the push into Burma by land had to go over the northern mountains. By contrast, the Arakan fighting was a war of attrition during the monsoon season. The British river craft and artillery were not much better than they had been in the previous year. Conditions remained appalling. One officer recorded his memories: 'leeches in the jungle, chaungs [paddy field streams] in spate that he had to cross with ropes; socks that shrank because they were never dry; the whiskers that grew overnight on his boots and the fungus that grew on his binoculars'.[52] Eastward in the drier, higher land a fierce battle raged along tunnelled railway lines that were the only route down into Burma. The Japanese were dug into individual foxholes and kept up a random mortar fire on the *bashas* or temporary hutments built by the Allied troops. These were constructed out of dripping tarpaulins and rusting sheets of corrugated iron. In this climate and terrain, wounds turned septic within hours and as many as eight men were needed to carry a single casualty over many miles.

## THE POLITICS OF WAR

This third Arakan campaign was broadly a success in the end. By September the Japanese were retreating south as their command concluded that it was no longer possible to hold north Burma. Still, it was a costly campaign, bedevilled by military and political problems. The air war was a hit-and-miss affair. It consisted mainly of bombing already ruined towns into the ground. An intelligence officer recorded that Paletwa, the largest town in northern Arakan, was now no more than jungle. It had been completely bombed out by the RAF. 'In all these bombings there was not a single soul in the place and the only casualty was a Japanese officer who lost an eye.'[53] The town and environs had already been squeezed for labour and produce by the Japanese who worked through the corrupt local police. It was then occupied by a British West African force and things got even worse for the local people. Everyone commented favourably on the Africans' fighting qualities, but they appear to have been used to living off the land. The people were terrified of them and they happily looted village after village, committing more than fifty rapes for good measure, or so it was reported. Their officers apparently turned a blind eye. 'The African generally seems to have a touch of kleptomania', someone noted, after troops had made off with a cow and brought it into their camp without a single British officer stopping them.[54]

This was an area where there had been fierce clashes even before the war between incoming Bengali Muslims and the local Arakanese Buddhists. The Thakins had found much support among the embattled Buddhists and had instigated or turned a blind eye to communal massacres in 1942. In 1943, during General Irwin's abortive offensive,

Muslim militias 'bent on loot and revenge' had moved into the region on the heels of British troops. The Muslims massacred Buddhists and when the British moved out again the vicious cycle was reversed with Buddhist massacres of Muslims.[55] The scene was set for nearly ten years of conflict during which armed Muslim militants carried out a guerrilla war first against the incoming British and then against the government of independent Burma.

The coming of the Civil Administration (Burma) was not an unmixed success either. Initially, the administration's main aim was to collect labour and supplies for the advance to the south. This proved difficult. The population was mobile. Timber workers were used to migrating between Chittagong in India and Arakan, depending on the price of rice in the two regions. During the famine they had dispersed into Arakan. Labour had to be coerced into service. The 'old hands' now working for the Civil Administration found it difficult not to revert to tried, pre-war ways. The former Burma civil servant, Frederick Pearce, onetime secretary to the governor of Burma who was now chief civil affairs officer, wanted to collect the land revenue in classic ICS form despite the fact that the population was malnourished and in rags. Conflicts soon broke out between civil and military officers. Such was the demand for coolies to work on the new military roads that the army began to pay piecework rates well above those of local day labourers. The only way the Civil Administration could get off the ground was to impress labour under the Defence of Burma Rules and starve agricultural operations of manpower. This caused deep dissatisfaction and was psychologically damaging. The returning British administrators expected to find themselves greeted as heroes. To many local people they seemed little better than the Japanese, if at all. There was a strong Thakin element in Arakan and the news spread fast to central and southern Burma. It was one reason why relations between the British and the nationalists deteriorated so quickly after the Japanese were beaten.

The Nagas and other hill peoples played a key role in the fighting. As the Japanese pushed towards Manipur, the hill people found them-selves right in the front line. The Naga levies and the exiguous British forces sent to aid them – V Force – had set into something of a routine since 1942. They drilled, exercised and listened. But the fighting on this front was over two hundred miles distant in 1943 and the first months of 1944 as the Chindits of the second Wingate expedition and Shan and Kachin levies carried on hazardous operations behind enemy lines. The main enemies at this time were cholera and smallpox, which stubbornly revived during the 1943 monsoon. But at least V Force now had food, clothing and ammunition. A particular hit amongst the Nagas, who had a keen sense of colour, were red blankets. These were specially coloured for use in the region and were used as gifts and payment throughout the hills. Amongst the Nagas, a leader was only first among equals and his honour and respect depended on his courage and his generosity in distributing prized items such as these.

Suddenly, the calm was broken. Ursula Graham Bower recalled two sergeants coming up to her on 28 March 1944 with chilling news. 'Fifty Japs crossed the Imphal Road about a week ago and they ought to be here by now. We wondered if you had heard anything of them.'[56] The defensive belt had suddenly been rolled up and she and the local Naga chiefs were facing the advancing Japanese army with 150 native scouts, one service rifle, one single-barrelled shotgun and seventy muzzle loaders. There was a nagging fear that they would all be boxed in as the Japanese tide flowed round them on both sides. The code 'one elephant' was devised to signal that ten Japanese were approaching. A near panic set in when someone arrived in the locality with forty real elephants. On this occasion, the only 'Jap' sighted was an unfortunate squirrel which was shot out of a tree by an over-eager scout. But the danger was real enough. Several Naga scouts in the Imphal area went over to the Japanese and led the Japanese to British arms dumps. Bower noted that they were from communities that had taken part in a rebellion during the First World War. There was always the fear that the whole scout force would break and flee as the attack proceeded. After all, these men were scouts and not a fighting force. Meanwhile, refugees once more tramped through the hills. Among them were Bengali and Madrasi pioneers evacuated from Imphal. Then came newly recruited and ill-disciplined Indian support staff, artisans, drivers and mechanics, who all stumbled by with Naga porters and children, sometimes accompanied by escaped Japanese prisoners. Morale hung on a knife-edge until a platoon of Gurkhas came up to support Bower's detachment. They maintained calm until Kohima was relieved.[57]

The sense of chaos and panic among the defence units of the hill people hid a more important fact. This was the extent to which Naga, Chin and other personnel contributed to the defence of Imphal and Kohima and to the shattering victory that British and Indian forces subsequently won against the Japanese. Army intelligence wrote in the summer: 'The quantity and quality of operational information received from the local inhabitants has been a major factor in our success to date. A high percentage of our successful air strikes have been the direct result of local information.'[58] The loyal Nagas gave the Japanese false information about British troop numbers. They guided British and Indian troops through the jungle and pointed out Japanese entrenchments and foxholes to them.

Finally, the great Japanese strength as jungle fighters was being turned against them. Ironically, the Japanese high command was in part betrayed by its own racial ideology, as the British had been two years earlier. The Japanese found it difficult to see the Nagas and allied tribes as anything more than illiterate primitives, more backward even than the aboriginal groups that they encountered in Hokkaido island or Taiwan. Nor could they believe that any Asiatic could reject the idea of 'Asia for the Asians' unless they had been bribed or bullied into doing so. No native people could possibly support the British of their own volition. Nagas and Chins were therefore allowed to wander around the Japanese camps even at the critical time when the Imperial Army was moving against Manipur.

Slim told Ursula Graham Bower a revealing story about Naga support. The Japanese commanders on the Manipur front employed a number of Naga orderlies as batmen in the early months of 1944. Naturally, they treated them as illiterate numbskulls. Two of these Nagas decided to steal an operational map which they saw lying around in a commander's tent. Only too well aware of the estimate the Japanese put on their brainpower, they covered their tracks by pretending that this had been an ordinary theft, and made off with clothing and small pieces of equipment as well as the map. Within a few hours the map was on Slim's table at British headquarters. As the attack developed, Slim was astonished to find that the Japanese commanders had not modified their plan one iota, so sure were they that no mere Naga orderly could have understood the significance of a battle plan. Slim told Bower that this intelligence was of very great importance in the defence of Imphal and Kohima. Indeed, the debt of the British to the tribal people of the hills was incalculable. Smith Dun, the four-foot tall Karen officer, remembered how dependent he had been on intelligence supplied by the local people during the fighting in the Chin Hills in 1943 and '44. By chance one of the unit's batmen was the son of a member of the local Chin levies. Dun's force was able to move around behind Japanese lines using the information supplied by family members. But vendettas were also in the air. Smith Dun believed that the batman was eventually betrayed by a rival Chin family.[59]

In Simla during June and July, Dorman-Smith among many other officials was aware of the critical situation in Manipur. Their optimism waxed and waned day by day as they read intelligence appraisals and spoke to soldiers returning briefly from the front. They listened to the English-language propaganda broadcasts from Japanese and INA sources with a mixture of amusement and anxiety, unable to evaluate what they heard. The governor still had a lot of minor political skirmishes to fight and this kept his mind off the war. There were the constant battles with Simla officials over accommodation for his government. Would this irritate Archie Wavell? 'Who would be an exile!' he wailed. Then again news came that 'Uncle Joe Stilwell is by no means the popular figure that he was with his own Yank forces' because of his cavalier attitude to the Chinese troops' brutal way with the civilians of north Burma. Best of all, 'Chancre Jack' and his corrupt cronies were in trouble. 'I expect you have heard that Chiang is engaged in an affair with some chit of a nurse who is about to produce an infant. Hence Madame's disappearance. Just what repercussions all this may have, I do not know. But I do not like to think of a Madame scorned set loose upon the world.'[60]

The mood across India remained apprehensive. Yet there was still no panic as there had been in response to every rumour during 1942. Censorship was tight and the Information Bureau of the government was by now so skilled in packaging news of the campaign that, as an intelligence official recorded, 'even the civilians in Delhi failed to realise its importance'. He remembered looking out over a quiet and peaceful Janpath, Delhi's triumphal thoroughfare, during these weeks and later recorded that it was impossible to conceive of the vast Arakan battle, still less the looming fact of the independence of India and Pakistan. British India seemed to have survived once again as it had survived every challenge since the Maratha invasions of the eighteenth century.

## JAPAN'S FORGOTTEN ARMY

Once the monsoon had begun in earnest the Japanese reverse in Assam became a rout and the scenes of horror were even worse than the green hell of the Hukawng valley in 1942. The 14th Army had become a cold, efficient killing machine. Very few prisoners were taken on the Allied side. The British, Indian and African troops methodically and ruthlessly killed all Japanese, enraged by cases of atrocities against their own wounded. The enemy were rooted out of their foxholes and shelters, shot down or burnt to death with the new American-made flame-throwers. British, Indians, Gurkhas and Africans took tallies of the numbers of the dead. Those Japanese who stumbled into Kachin and Shan levies sometimes had their heads taken as grim tokens of the new barbarism. Of these operations, Slim wrote laconically: 'quarter was neither asked, nor given'.[61] Worse even than the condign Allied vengeance were the ravages of disease, monsoon and malnutrition. The Japanese army thrown against Imphal and Kohima was a kind of mass suicide squad. When it was defeated by the vastly increased firepower of the British and Indian armies and American air power, it was cast aside and abandoned by its commanders. There were no reserves, little transport for the withdrawal, no food and medicines. The Japanese air force was almost entirely a fighter force and could not supply its troops by air. The Japanese had aimed to live off the land and 'Mr Churchill's rations' – captured British supplies – as they had done in 1942. But there was little left on the land by this time and Mr Churchill proved very much less obliging. Even during the advance, the Japanese were on completely inadequate rations, except where they encountered the few remaining herds of cattle belonging to the hill peoples. Now, in July and August, they simply starved or drowned, sucked into seas of mud and filth. One Japanese soldier remembered:

In the rain, with no place to sit, we took short spells of sleep standing on our feet. The bodies of our comrades who had struggled along the track before us, lay all around, rain-sodden and giving off the stench of decomposition. Even with the support of our sticks we fell amongst the corpses again as we stumbled on rocks and tree roots made bare by the rain and attempted one more step, then one more step in our exhaustion.

Thousands and thousands of maggots crept out of the bodies lying in streams and were carried away by the fast flowing water. Many of the cadavers were no more than bleached bones. 'I cannot forget the sight of one corpse lying in a pool of knee-high water. All its flesh and blood had been dissolved by the maggots and the water so that now it was no more than a bleached uniform.'[62]

For many their only recourse was suicide. Groups of soldiers huddled together over a grenade by the side of the road, while one pulled out the pin to end their misery. A British officer of the King's African Rifles remembered encountering thousands of the dead or dying enemy. There were 'strewn over gaseous, bloated bodies family photographs, postcards of cherry blossom and snow capped Mount Fujiyama and delicate drawings of flowers had fallen from dying hands as life ebbed away in the roar of the unceasing rains'.[63] Near Tamu, scene of mass refugee deaths two years before to the month, the King's African Rifles warily entered a village recently occupied by the Japanese. 'At the far end of the village a small shrine beneath a rusted corrugated-iron roof housed a statue of Buddha gazing across the paddy fields. Lying at the foot of the Buddha was a naked Japanese soldier, a barely living skeleton, with an empty water bottle by his side. Glaring at us, he croaked some words before his head fell back on the mud floor.' Later, in the British camp, a Japanese-speaking intelligence officer wrote down the dying man's delirious ravings: 'Lieutenant Hazaki! Lieutenant Hazaki, where are you, you bastard? Shoot me with your pistol! Come and shoot me! You useless fool! For the sake of the Emperor we came to these filthy hills to be disgraced. Dragged on my behind by blackamoors! We came from Indo-China to be disgraced and clowned by blackamoors. Lieutenant Hazaki, you bastard, bring a machine gun and mow them down. Ah, the disgrace. A Japanese officer dragged in the mud.'[64]

It is estimated that more than 80,000 Japanese died in this campaign as a whole, making it the worst defeat in Japan's military history and in terms of personnel killed a greater one than any suffered during the main battles of the Pacific naval war. After their failure at Imphal, the Japanese were beaten back at Manipur and the Manipur road was reopened. The 17th Indian Division moved forward on Tiddim, taking Tamu on 4 August. This finally obliterated the memory of the division's mauling at the Sittang bridge in 1942. The rolling-up of the Japanese position in the northeast was accompanied by a new push by Stilwell and the Chinese from the north. This assault was led by the US Army's 5307th Composite Unit, the famous Merrill's Marauders, built up to strength with Kachin and Chinese soldiers. This long-range penetration unit, urged on by Stilwell, took nearly 80 per cent casualties from enemy action and disease as it pushed down from the north through rain-soaked jungle.[65] By 3 August, however, Myitkyina and its airfield were once again in Allied hands, recaptured as the Japanese garrison withdrew.

Finally, the Allies on the Burma front had something to celebrate. Leo Amery, the secretary of state, visited the war front. He spoke to Gurkha troops in Urdu, revealing that it was 'a language I learned with my Ayah's [nurse's] milk nearly seventy years ago',[66] a perfect example of how the whole British ruling class of those days was shot through with memories of India. Wavell later flew to Manipur and knighted Slim and Auchinleck on the field. He then held a durbar, or official audience, with the Naga chiefs, as the Japanese were finally cleared south into Burma, chased by deep penetration forces.

In the distant Punjab, the province from which such a large proportion of the troops came, there was quiet rejoicing. The National War Front published advertisements in newspapers and distributed posters proclaiming 'Salute the Soldier!' The Maharaja of Patiala met returning troops and moved amongst them, chatting. Recruiting posters harped on the modernity of the armed forces: 'Pilot today. Airline executive tomorrow!' But that quiet rejoicing was tempered by anxiety. The Railway Board published a notice depicting emaciated villagers staring at a railway carriage: 'Travel less'. It urged people to refrain from leisure journeys when food distribution remained a priority. Rationing remained severe. The black market burgeoned.

The poisonous fires of Hindu–Muslim hatred were stoked across the Punjab as Jinnah denounced Gandhi's most recent political plans as 'a death warrant to all Muslims'.[67] It was as if the callousness of wartime killing was seeping into Indian political debate and polluting it.

As the Japanese perished in their thousands, the Punjab and Delhi were suffering a particularly punishing 'hot weather'. Despite its appearance of blithe normality and the distance from the crisis in Assam, things were gradually deteriorating in the capital. The last few years of the Raj were far from the 'cushy billet' that expatriates had come to expect. Wartime restrictions on imports meant that people were forced to make do with poor-quality Indian goods: electric light bulbs that exploded with monotonous regularity, Indian beer which had to be upended in pails of water to let the toxins drift off. The cost of living had risen 200–300 per cent in a few months. Private servants were in very short supply because of the demand for labour from swollen government offices and the military.[68] Several officials suffered nervous breakdowns because of the pressures of extra work. Race relations deteriorated further. Indians were resentful of the new influx of British and Americans and their own declining standards of living. The imprisonment of Gandhi and the other Congress leaders was regarded as a national insult and the prospect of Gandhi's death from a hunger strike had threatened public order. The British, for their part, were tense. They knew that the eastern war was still in the balance, but were poorly informed about what was actually happening. They tended to take it out on Indians, who were regarded as secretly seditious. Water shortages became worse. Pumping stations could not cope with the greatly increased wartime population. Cholera made its appearance as people drank bad water and started to spread as the rains began.[69] Police cordoned off the coolie camp near the city and 3,000 people were inoculated in the course of a few weeks.

Then, quite suddenly, with the coming of the rains, the mood lightened. People sensed that the crisis had passed. Noël Coward arrived in Delhi and began to entertain the troops.[70] He appeared at a cocktail party at the viceroy's house, while lower ranks were entertained all over town with sausages, fruit juice and cigarettes. Around the middle of July All-India Radio began to broadcast news of the Japanese retreat from Imphal. British India was saved for its final three years of existence. Not everyone rejoiced. The victory at Imphal and the Normandy landings in Europe triggered a slump on Indian stock markets. This was because 'India was one vast black market' and the fun would end with the war.[71] One Indian merchant wired his agent: 'Situation Changing. Don't buy anything . . . the future is not at all promising. It seems the war is drifting towards its end.'

# 8

# 1944: The Nemesis of Greater East Asia

As he learned of the destruction of the Imperial Army before Imphal and Kohima, a young Japanese soldier remembered the discussion he had had with a captured British officer before the offensive. Even though he was smoking one of his cigarettes, the Briton stated categorically the 'Japanese army will be defeated. The British Army will finally win without fail.' The reason was simple: 'mechanization'.[1] The Allies' superiority in mechanized warfare and industrial production had already turned the tide decisively in the West. Now in the autumn of 1944 it was doing the same in the East. Yet the war remained a curious hybrid. The most advanced scientific techniques of killing were deployed alongside almost medieval patterns of bravery and brutality. The Japanese emperor still believed that the Allies could be denied victory if his samurai were brave enough. Soon the high command would unleash kamikaze attacks on the US fleet. Subhas Bose also believed, against all odds, in the triumph of the will. As the Japanese and the INA began to fall back on Mandalay, well versed in British history, he seemed to echo Robert the Bruce. He told Indians in Burma 'neither the INA nor he was the least disheartened: he would immediately set about preparing for another attack on Imphal. If need be, he must attack Imphal ten times . . .'[2] Indian civilians in Southeast Asia poured even more money and resources into the hands of the INA after the disaster in the north.

## HEROISM AND MURDER IN THE HILLS

Amongst the British, too, memories of the war would dwell on individual bravery, the heroism of special operations personnel and the men of the hill levies. Colonel Balfour Oatts spent much of his war fighting with the Chin levies east of the Lushai hills where McCall had organized his total defence scheme in 1942. The hill villages, which had already suffered two years of scarcity, had been ravaged again by Japanese patrols while their young men had been off fighting the guerrilla war. Following Oatts's intervention, the British made a gesture of support as the Imphal–Kohima campaign began to go their way: 'In spite of a rice famine in Bengal and a general shortage everywhere, the authorities agreed to flying in a hundred tons of rice "as a gift to the Chins in acknowledgement of their gallant services".'[3] From then on no one in the northern hills doubted that their side was winning.

Personal bravery was attended by a very personal style of atrocity. As the Japanese occupation of northern Burma frayed and dissolved, the pressures on its people intensified. From the first days of the occupation, the Japanese had randomly visited violence on the Burmese population, especially Karens, Christians and other minority groups. With the exception of purges of the Chinese, like the ones that took place in Singapore in 1942, these did not have the chilling, mechanical character of Nazi mass murder. Instead they were face-to-face outbreaks of brutality, often instigated by local Japanese commanders and the Kempeitai military police, rather than by murderers from on high. Late 1944 saw a climax of attacks against civilians. The area around Namtu in the northern Shan states seems to have suffered particularly badly. This was a place about a hundred miles from the Chinese border and two hundred from the Chindwin river, a happy hunting ground for the Chindits and Allied special forces. It had a mixed population, basically Christian and non-Christian Kachin, but with a scattering of Anglo-Burman, Indian and Chinese commercial or professional people. In June 1942 thirty Chinese residents were summarily machine-gunned by the incoming Japanese. Others were abducted for forced labour. A Japanese mining company was established nearby and the locals were forced to work for it and for the Japanese occupying force. Minor infringements of discipline were met with torture and beatings. In 1943 the first Wingate expedition infiltrated the area and was offered a good deal of help by the brutalized inhabitants. Ba Gya Spurgeon, a Karen pastor of the American Baptist mission and an important community leader, helped a sick Indian non-commissioned officer left behind by the Chindits.[4] The Kempeitai got to know of this.

In the following year, Allied special forces distributed arms to the local population north of the Shweli river and Kachin levy patrols became more and more active. As the scale of their defeat in Assam became apparent, the Japanese became more vicious. In the autumn of 1944 things came to a head when a member of the Namtu Kempeitai was killed in an ambush. A score of local people were tortured and murdered. Spurgeon was brutally interrogated. An Indian doctor, B. C. Dey, died of torture and Mr Zacharias, an Anglo-Indian resident, was imprisoned in Mandalay jail and later burned to death, when the Japanese guards set the building alight in the face of the advance of the Allies. The Indian population, though, was split. The English interpreter present at Japanese interrogations was a member of the Indian National Army. Later, in November, as the Allies surged into north Burma, the Japanese began a scorched earth policy in Namtu. They locked up 700 members of its Indian population in what was called the Black Hole of Hsipaw. Perhaps this name was an ironic reference to Subhas Bose's pre-war celebration of Siraj-ud Daulah, initiator of the Black Hole of Calcutta. A third of these people died of dysentery and starvation. In a nearby village, long a Gurkha colony, the Japanese bayoneted women and children as they withdrew, saying that 'the Gurkhas were fighting against us'.[5] Japanese officers confessed to these war crimes when they were in detention in Rangoon and Singapore later in the war. By then, many of the main perpetrators had already died in Allied bombing or in fighting with the Burma Defence Army when it revolted in the following year.

Across this vast landscape of hill and jungle millions of men were fighting and labouring in dreadful conditions. Terrible atrocities were perpetrated daily on innocent civilians and every major city in the region was suffering random punitive bombing by the Allies and

Japanese. Yet even here, at the apex of the great crescent, there were huge areas of quiet, so remote that they were barely affected by the war. Far up beyond Gauhati in Assam, north even of the Hukawng valley where the refugees had perished in their thousands two years earlier, lay the hills of Sadiya. Here, on this remotest frontier of the old Indian empire, lived the Mishmi people, mingling with Tibetans who trekked across the frontier with their wares. Patches of slash-and-burn cultivation suddenly gave way to brilliant red fields of waving opium poppy. British and Indian political officers patrolled this distant landscape, settling disputes and trying unsuccessfully to stop the buying and selling of slaves.[6] Life continued as usual, interrupted only by rumours of war. Far in the sky above, huge American transport planes snaked over the Hump to land supplies for Chiang Kai Shek as he faced his final bloody struggle with the Japanese. During a tour of several months, one civil officer recorded that only one Mishmi asked him how the war was going.[7] Were the US personnel at the ground signals bases monitoring the transport planes 'sarkari men' (British officers) or not, he asked. Sporadically, Chinese deserters would rob and loot a village; the occasional US airman sought shelter after baling out thousands of feet above; the US forces had recently begun to recruit coolies as a permanent labour corps. But no one really knew what the war was about, or who was fighting it.

## THE CRUMBLING OF 'FREE BURMA'

As the death struggle proceeded on Burma's northern and western rim, conditions deteriorated rapidly in the interior. There was no mass starvation as there was in India, south China or even parts of Malaya, but people were desperately short of basic commodities.[8] The Japanese military diverted most medicines to their own troops. Hospitals and clinics were deserted as doctors and nurses turned to private practice in order to buy food for their own families. Burmese women, traditionally proud of their deportment and attire, refused to go out of doors because they had nothing but rags to wear. A longyi worth a quarter rupee was now selling for Rs1,000.

Meanwhile Japanese firms, which had obtained privileged access to the country under the terms of the independence declaration, progress-ively pillaged the forests of timber. Their agents sealed up paddy stores, purchased rice mills and profiteered from the consequent shortages. Japanese cotton manufacturing enterprises forced each household in cotton-growing areas to produce a certain quantity of raw cotton.[9] Particularly irritating to the Burmese was the fact that Japanese entre-preneurs began to muscle in on the trade in dried fish and *ngapi*, a pungent fish sauce. These were trades in which women had tradi-tionally had a large role. As military supplies began to dry up, the requisitioning of goods and labour became more and more common. Young men were forcibly enlisted in the 'sweat army' building roads and bridges for the Japanese, or worse they were taken south to the infamous 'death railway'.

Japanese intelligence officers and censors had an increasingly diffi-cult job. At first they were able to cover up the Imphal and Kohima defeats, but from the early months of 1944 the Allied propaganda offensive became more determined. The Indian army remained very jumpy about the INA. A propaganda newspaper, *Hamara Hindustan* ('Our India'), was prepared in Calcutta and dropped in large quantities. In September 1944 alone 31,000 copies along with 23,000 copies of pamphlets in various Indian languages were dropped over Burma.[10] Altogether half a million copies of propaganda leaflets in various Asian languages were flown in. There was some debate about the effect of this blitz. Some officers said that since the INA was demoralized and beginning to surrender anyway, it was rather pointless. They suggested concentrating on the civilian Indian population. Reports from the Burmese side also suggested mixed results. Probably what was most important was not the content of the literature but the way it worked as a kind of visiting card for the British and Americans.

Ba Maw and the Japanese tried to respond in kind. They were said to have planted Japanese corpses dressed in Allied uniforms in downed planes in order to improve morale. They also made good use of Burmese *pwes*, or theatrical performances, to spread pro-Axis stories and play up their successes. Rangoon radio controllers shrewdly recog-nized the importance of women in Burmese society and their increasing disenchantment in the face of air raids, shortages and the forced conscription of their men into labour schemes.[11] The number of 'women's interest' broadcasts and women presenters significantly increased. The Japanese and their aides also played the Buddhist card for all they were worth. The danger to the great Buddhist religious site at Pagan was played up. The *New Light of Asia* and other publications harped on the RAF's bombing of pagodas and British troops' looting of monasteries to the north. But the truth was more and more difficult to conceal. When the Japanese reported their own successful bombing of a northern town it became clear that in fact the Allies had already taken it. The fall of the Pacific island of Saipan to the Americans in June 1944 demonstrated to even the most pro-Japanese Burmese that the Co-Prosperity Sphere was foundering to ruin.

Not, of course, that everyone was malnourished or filled with gloom. People who were able to get their hands on stores of valuable commodities and hangers-on of the Japanese forces continued to do extremely well. People were still being promoted to government offices with plenty of servants and access to government stores. Politicians, in denial as they might have been, continued to politick. Up and coming fixers used 'dinner parties, *pwes* and entertainments, courting favour through women and wine'. Prostitution took off on a massive scale for the delectation of Japanese troops, Burmese officials, army and police personnel.

The regime decided to capitalize on what remained of the feelgood factor, planning a huge celebration of the first anniversary of Burma's independence. Pagodas throughout the country were packed with people praying for the continuation of Burma's freedom, or more accurately praying that it would begin. A mass rally was staged in Rangoon with march pasts by the BDA, Subhas Bose and the INA and Japanese troops. The cinemas were declared free for the day. Japanese manufacturers presented cloth to the wives and daughters of war workers.[12] Ba Maw continued to develop the fascist-style Burma Youth Leagues. He also got the central Buddhist authorities to appoint 1,500 preachers who were to go around the country and lecture against the return of the British, warning of even harsher economic exploitation at their hands. Word was put about that the British were intent on securing massive reparations from Burma as they had from Germany after the First World War. In his Independence Day speech, Ba Maw said that this would be achieved by seizing jewels from

18, 19. Indian refugees
fleeing Rangoon, 1942

## — BENGAL'S FOODLESS —

We publish on this page photographs showing typical daily scenes in and around Calcutta, to illustrate the present plight of thousands of human beings throughout India's distressed Province, Bengal. Such scenes are commonest on the "Second City's" outskirts, where a moving population wanders pitiably in search of food.

Government's plans to feed and shelter these people on the outskirts, and thus in some measure to check the distress within the city, appear urgently to need enlargement and acceleration. Commendable efforts, which have been described periodically in our Calcutta editions, are being made inside Calcutta by non-official public bodies, women's organizations, and beneficent private persons, to establish free kitchens and cheap feeding houses for the destitute and starving. But neither these efforts, nor the authorities' undertakings on the city's outskirts are sufficient. The task is so great that in any case personal philanthropy could touch only its fringe, the main responsibility necessarily resting on Government, by which is meant not only the Bengal Government but the Government of India in New Delhi.

A young woman, overcome by the strain of waiting for food, faints by the roadside. This and the pictures below were taken in Calcutta a few days ago where such sights are not rare.—Statesman.

20. Two pictures from the *Statesman*'s coverage of the Bengal famine, 1943

These emaciated children were the central figures in a poignant scene at a free kitchen where they had been taken by their mothers.—Statesman.

21. Lord Wavell at a Rotary Club soup kitchen, Calcutta, 1943

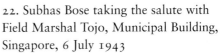
22. Subhas Bose taking the salute with Field Marshal Tojo, Municipal Building, Singapore, 6 July 1943

23. Malayan Peoples' Anti-Japanese Army propaganda leaflet

24. 'Comfort women' from Malaya liberated in the Andaman Islands, c. 1945

25. Subhas Chandra Bose with Ba Maw in Rangoon, 1943

26. Louis Mountbatten with General Giffard, Air Chief Marshal Peirse
and General Auchinleck

27. West African troops arriving in India for the Burma front, 1944

28. General Slim addressing the troops

29, 30. Indian troops (Punjab Regiment) and British and African troops in Arakan, 1944

31. A Sikh patrol charging a foxhole, 1945

32. Surrendered Indian National Army troops at Mount Popa, Burma

33. Aung San delivering a speech in Rangoon, c. 1945

34. Chinese fighters of Force 136, 1945

pagodas and temples. Victory, he claimed, was still possible: 'once the war is over, you can have all the longyis and all the pork and chicken that you desire'.[13]

Under the surface gaiety, the political world was changing fast. The Japanese had never really trusted Ba Maw, whom they regarded as a corrupt office-seeker. Their intelligence continued to register concern about the reliability of Aung San and his former BIA, renamed the Burma Defence Army following 'independence'. But they needed Ba Maw's officers to continue to provide labour and they needed Aung San's troops to plug holes in their battered northern battle front. The Japanese commanders believed that if Ba Maw's henchmen were put into positions in the BDA, it would become even less effective as a military force. They therefore protected Aung San's monopoly over the appointment of senior officers. This increased tensions among the Burmese leaders.

The Ba Maw administration began to show cracks. Aung San detested Ba Maw and made no secret of it. He would openly quarrel with the Adipadi in front of the Japanese military, but in public, at least, he deferred to him. His own position was a difficult one. Since 1942 he had suspected Japanese intentions towards Burma's future. If later accounts are to be believed, the Thakins had already begun to plot against the Japanese when they were fighting on the Arakan front in 1942. But Aung San was determined that his plot would not go off half-cocked. The British had made a mess of the Arakan campaign and there might be something in the 'ten anna' (half-baked) independence. By late August 1944, with the tide turning decisively after Imphal and Kohima and Japanese-sponsored independence proving more and more of a sham, Aung San was ready to act. His soldiers were becoming restive. They were young and ignorant. A Burmese observer recorded that many seemed to think that Japan would withdraw all its troops from Burma after Imphal and that they could rise against them. One plan they had was to 'get an air force from Russia by walking a few days through China'.[14] This time, however, it appears to have been the British who urged caution. Slim and Mountbatten passed on the message to wait through contacts of the communist Thakins who had gone directly to India in 1942 and Thein Pe, who was now in Chungking. The 14th Army commanders were afraid that a premature uprising of the BDA would play into Japanese hands and allow them to tighten their grip on Burma's resources.

During the summer and autumn of 1944 Aung San had little option but to bide his time. In fact, he put it to very good use. It was in these months that Aung San completed the transformation of the BDA from the old Thakin-led, southern Burmese force of 1942 to an all-Burma organization with a strong recruitment drive among the youth of the villages. The Burmese loved to see young men in uniform and, given the deterioration of economic conditions as Allied bombing intensified, the young men were delighted to get a suit of clothing and a couple of decent meals a day. Aung San also enlisted the civilian population to his cause. This is because the BDA had control of commodities secured through its connections in the cities and the countryside. People were paid in commodities, not cash. Aung San even had small quantities of the now incredibly rare sesamum oil to distribute, an essential ingredient for any decent Burmese dish.[15] The BDA could also provide that equally precious commodity, news. Their radio operators listened in to forbidden Allied broadcasts and got hold of Reuters telegrams.

People spontaneously gave Aung San their allegiance. Songs were composed in his honour without any official encouragement. Before long many tea houses, play houses and milk bars had posters up saying 'BDA men at concession rates'. By this time, most people were aware that the real target of the strengthened BDA was the Japanese and not the British. The Japanese began to arrest people they suspected and to extract confessions by torture. But they had little success. One day Khin Myo Chit was going home in Rangoon from her job in the Education Department when she saw a young soldier she knew in the street. 'Why are you in civvies?' she asked. He put his finger to his lips and told her under his breath that he knew that the Japanese were about to disarm and arrest the BDA and some of them had gone underground with their arms.[16]

Ba Maw desperately tried to curb Aung San's ambitions and reassert his control over the army which was now infinitely more popular than the government. He married his daughter to Bo Yan Naing, a hero of the BIA of 1942.[17] He tried to have Aung San removed as commander-in-chief and made war minister instead. Despite his suspicion of Aung San, the Japanese commander would not countenance any change. He was also aware that the Adipadi's authority was draining away day by day as the British forces followed up their successes and swept down from Arakan and into the lower Chindwin valley. As the reckoning drew closer, Ba Maw's rhetoric became grandiose, bordering on the hysterical. Dr Goebbels became his long-distance tutor. The war, he declared in October, was 'a racial war' between the Anglo-Saxons and the pure Teutonic race, fortified in the support of its allies, the Mongolian and Latin races.[18] Nippon was leader of the Mongolian race and the Burmese were proud to be a member of it. The Adipadi's fascist slogan 'One blood! One voice! One command!' echoed across the airwaves and in public meeting places. Meanwhile, many of his officers laughed up their rose-coloured satin sleeves. In view of the shortage of paper, one little game they played was to use the backs of the tons of Allied propaganda posters dropped over the country for writing inter-departmental minutes. This practice was eventually forbidden.

After Imphal and Kohima, relations between the Japanese and the Indian National Army also began to deteriorate further. This was accompanied by disagreements between the INA leaders and the IIL and between the INA leaders themselves. For one thing, many INA leaders from the days of Mohan Singh, its first leader in 1942 and 1943, had always been more anti-British than they were pro-Japanese. They began to feel that they were misused and humiliated by the Japanese, being treated as coolies and camp-followers. Others secretly disliked the paraphernalia of 'Asia for the Asians' under Japanese leadership. Defeat turned these flea-bites into sores. Bose himself had been surprised and astonished by the Japanese order to withdraw from Manipur and the removal of INA wounded back to Mandalay.[19] He had been far too optimistic about the campaign and persistently overestimated Japanese resources. There were also differences between the Hikari Kikan, the more official successor to the Minami Kikan, and the INA. Bose really saw himself as an ally of the Japanese emperor and General Tojo. He wanted a direct line to Tokyo and distrusted the 'Manchurian' local Japanese commanders.[20] The Hikari Kikan, at least after Suzuki's loss of influence, saw the INA as its own baby, a subordinate part of the imperial war machine.

Matters came to a head in October 1944 when the Japanese were concerned about an amphibious landing in Malaya. They had obviously got wind of Mountbatten's endless procession of unlikely sounding and aborted invasion schemes – Zipper, Dracula and so on. The Japanese command ordered an INA division in Malaya to assist in the defensive operations under their command. Subhas Bose was furious, insisting that the INA were allies and not subordinates of the Japanese. He argued that only on the Burma front were they under Japanese control, and then only for operational purposes. He threatened to fly straight off to Tokyo to complain to Tojo. But Tojo's own position had crumbled. When he visited Tokyo for the final time in October, Bose tried to insist that the INA should be regarded as the army of an independent government, not as an appendage of the Hikari Kikan, which he wanted replaced by a Japanese ambassador to Free India.[21] He also demanded supplies, aircraft and medicines, none of which his Japanese hosts could supply. They were further annoyed by Subhas Bose's efforts to get in touch with Soviet diplomats in Tokyo, believing rightly that he saw that the writing was on the wall for Japan. Relations were restored, but in reality the INA's brief moment on the stage was over. Some units fought resolute and brave battles as they retreated south into Burma. Some melted away or gave themselves up. At any rate, the INA was to become a much more powerful enemy of the British Empire in defeat than it had been during its ill-fated triumphal march on Delhi.

As the monsoon of 1944 drew to its close, Slim's 14th Army pushed rapidly into northern Burma, supported by now overwhelming Allied air power. The situation was changing rapidly. Stilwell was recalled in an American effort to appease Chiang. Sir Oliver Leese took over from Mountbatten as Commander, Land Forces, South East Asia, though the former remained Supreme Commander. Mutaguchi and other Japanese generals on the Burma front were recalled to Tokyo. The Japanese were falling back on the river Chindwin and retreating south from Myitkyina into the central plain of the Irrawaddy. Prices soared throughout the region. The Allies discovered a wounded country in which social life had been massively distorted. At Myitkyina, where the Americans were now firmly based, the local Kachin school had been turned into a brothel of 'twenty-five Japanese, Korean and Chinese prostitutes' for the use of the Japanese army. In Arakan the returning

British found that Karens and Chinese had been subject to much surveillance and harassment by the Japanese. Ba Maw's henchmen had seized the property of the Chinese refugees to India and China, while the property of Indian refugees had been handed over to the Indian Independence League.

Christians of all sorts, whether from combatant or neutral countries, were particularly badly treated. A letter from a nun at Kalaw to her headquarters in Philadelphia brought out the picaresque horror of the situation.[22] A Japanese commander burst into the convent one day and demanded to use an organ. He sat down at it and played first 'Auld Lang Syne' and then, to their terrified amusement, 'God Save the King'. Though the nuns were not slapped and beaten like ordinary people, the Japanese officers invaded the convent time after time and interrogated them. The problem was how to keep quiet an elderly and gaga nun who insisted on launching into loud, rambling eulogies of the British and talking about writing to Winston Churchill. At one point, everyone in the settlement was ordered to bow to the Japanese and raise the Rising Sun flag from their houses. The sister instead raised the papal flag from the roof of the convent. When questioned she stated that it was the flag of Eire, a neutral country.

For much of the war, relations between the Japanese and the Burmese civilians, as opposed to civilians of the minorities, had been reasonably good. Stories of atrocities circulated by the British referred to the Gurkhas, Karens and Shan, in the main, and were often exaggerated. Women were generally not molested. Face slapping had been reduced. But things began to change as the Axis crisis deepened. Once the Japanese peace preservation committees began to demand labour in the villages, examples of resistance and brutality multiplied. So bad had the Burmese railways become that 3–4,000 Japanese military engineers and civilians were brought in to run them. Labour was brought from north to south and when the supply of Indian Oriya coolies dried up more and more Burmese labour was recruited.[23] Headmen were often threatened with punishment if they did not supply young men. One of the problems for the ordinary Burmese citizen was the inordinate amount of money the Japanese spent on espionage as their position weakened. The Japanese civilians, Burmese collaborators and Indian Independence League personnel who acted as their spies were hard pressed to find enough treachery to justify their handsome bonuses and went out of their way to dig it up or implicate people in any way they could. The former judge Maung Maung had survived the war by selling his shopping-mad wife's cache of longyis, built up over many years.[24] He now found himself under constant investigation by one Mr Iwata of the Fuju Gasu Cotton Spinning Company. This gentleman kept visiting his house on one pretext or another. Later, the Kempeitai turned up and would walk into his bedroom at all hours asking for a drink. 'Respectable people' were shot, he said, during the Allied advance simply because they were found to possess gold sovereigns or British currency. The physical hardships during these months, he concluded, were nothing to the continuous mental strain.

The Japanese themselves began to regard the Burmese as lazy and stupid. They failed to get them to learn Japanese. The Japanese found themselves paying extortionate amounts for supplies in the bazaars, especially for the opium on which many of them had become dependent. The Burmese in turn began to loathe the Japanese. One told the incoming British military administration, no doubt to curry favour, that the Japanese 'look like dogs, they eat like dogs and now they are dying like dogs'. Even the BDA, 'gallant allies of the Nipponese race', were treated badly in brutal Japanese military training camps. Khin Myo Chit's brother told her that he and other erring cadets were repeatedly beaten not just with sticks but with light machine guns. One young man was beaten to death by the Japanese instructors because he kept fainting on parade. He died muttering deliriously 'Hancho [instructor] please stop beating, oh, Hancho, please excuse me.'[25] Hatred of the Japanese slowly built up inside the BDA. Most ominously for the Ba Maw government, new 'ancient prophecies' began to appear among the astrologers and soothsayers. Shortly after a star had gone through the horns of the moon, the Japanese had arrived and in February 1944 this phenomenon had been glimpsed again, signalling their departure. Quite soon everyone had heard of this omen.

## ROADS TO THE DEATH RAILWAY

It was during 1944 that conditions on the Thailand–Burma railway deteriorated badly. The building of this line had become central to Japanese strategy, as they tried to link up the disparate units of the great crescent. Stories of the Second World War and the 'Bridge over the River Kwai' have concentrated on the suffering of Australians, Britons and Americans. Perhaps 14,000 European troops were starved to death, killed by their guards or died of untreated disease. Asian doctors and medics serviced the camps. They were appalled by the scene. Tan Choon Keng was from a prominent Singapore family; he had spent some time in medical school and volunteered to work as a medic to escape from his overbearing father. He was sent to the railhead. 'Most of the POWs had lost their personal belongings. They sold off their trousers, singlets, shirts, watches anything to the Thais. Some had to use banana leaves as sarongs. It was a real pitiful sight. Imagine that they were once our colonial masters.'[26] He found that about 90 per cent of the POWs had malaria, which was aggravated by malnutrition and chronic exhaustion to a fatal degree.

Horrible as these conditions and atrocities were, ten or perhaps twenty times as many Burmese, Indians, Chinese and Malays perished, largely unrecorded in films and memoirs. There were also Korean and Taiwanese 'comfort women' for the Japanese officers and men on these stations. From early 1943, death rates from disease and malnutrition began to soar, both among Allied POWs who were unused to Asian food and among the Asian labourers, who were chronically under-nourished from birth. The Burmese authorities were certainly aware that many of their citizens who had joined the 'sweat army' or been coerced to labour on the railway were suffering appalling privations. Thousands of escaped labourers from the camps spread news of the conditions and this badly dented the government's prestige. So quickly did labourers flee or die that the authorities began to round up whole villages for work. Soon, on the approach of the police, villages became suddenly depopulated as their inhabitants fled to the hills where the policemen were too frightened to follow. Many years later in an interview, U Kyaw Nyein, a close associate of Aung San, admitted the guilt of the government. The Ba Maw administration just closed their eyes to the matter; 'none of them really cared'. All of them, including himself, 'were responsible and shamelessly unconcerned, mainly trying to survive or avoid Japanese Military Police arrest for themselves'.[27] As local labour became short or ran off, men were brought from further afield. In 1943 and '44 large numbers of workers were recruited by means of advertisements and circulars from Singapore, the southern Malayan cities and Burma for work on the railways. They were promised good wages – as much as $3 a day – and free meals and accommodation. But as news began to filter back about the poor conditions, the Japanese resorted to strong-arm methods of recruiting: using village headmen or labour overseers to identify victims. Tamils, redundant on the rubber estates now trade had all but ceased, were easy prey. Malays were also recruited, mostly from the northern states under Thai rule. There were levies amongst the townsmen of Singapore. Some came from further afield, from Sumatra and Java. They included numerous refugees, beggars and homeless people who could hardly survive in the conditions of scarcity then prevailing. Many of the workers took their wives and children with them to live in primitive circumstances in makeshift camps.

Medical workers sent up from Singapore spoke of how labourers 'died like rats' carrying water for anti-cholera work. 'We cannot do anything. There's no medicine. We just left them alone. They first passed motion, then vomited and they died off. Then they got the labourers to bury the labourers – a mass grave. No single grave there, impossible. They kept one portion opened, just fill up, fill up and fill it up.'[28] Some of the most abused labourers were the dark-skinned Tamils. They were treated by the Japanese as entirely dispensable. The Japanese would not allow them funeral services or, in some cases, even a burial. In one epidemic in June 1943 at Nieke on the Burma–Thailand border, around 6,000 people were struck by cholera. Tan Choon Keng and his colleagues were ordered to fire a barracks of the stricken with oil. There were nearly 250 Tamils and Javanese men, women and children inside, tempted by a six-month contract and the promise of good conditions. Horrified, he asked the Japanese medical officer: 'Are you sure? Can something else be done?' 'These people are dying,' he was told, 'nothing can be done.'

We did the job very quickly. I dared not look into their eyes. I only heard some whispering '*tolong, tolong*' [help, help]. It was the most pitiful sight. God forgive me. I was not happy to see them being burnt alive. All Asian labourers with their wives and children. They could not walk, all their nails blackened. As the fire engulfed the hut I could not hear them crying out because of the loud crackling from the burning wood. The heat was intense and we ran and ran. After this incident, I used to say to myself, is there a God on earth? If there were a God he would not allow all this to happen.[29]

Allied prisoners and Burmese, Indian, Malay and Vietnamese survivors tell of Japanese atrocities against Asian women and children, the burial of living cholera victims and death on a massive scale, with perhaps as many as 150,000 victims over two years.[30]

In the case of Malaya alone, the best available statistics show that of the 78,204 recorded as being sent to Thailand, 29,638 died and 24,626 were recorded as having deserted. Not all of the latter made it back to their homes alive.[31] The full scale of what had happened only became clear after the war, in many cases long after the war. At the time, the evidence was anecdotal; the horror came first as rumour, and later in the trickle of survivors home. It took many of the Asian forced labourers months, even years, to get home. Some had to walk. Attending to their welfare became a major preoccupation for Malay elites in the northern states. In Kedah, Tunku Abdul Rahman organized *bangsawan* theatre shows in the state capital Alor Setar to raise funds for their relief.[32]

By the spring of 1944 rumours of mass deaths were spreading amongst the Indian community throughout Southeast Asia. So dangerous did Bose consider this to the reputation of his Japanese allies that he sent a fact-finding mission up into Thailand in July of that year. Amar Singh, a merchant in Bangkok, was secretary in charge of social welfare in the Indian Independence League. He travelled north to Kanchanaburi on the railhead with another Indian, a Japanese captain and two Japanese journalists. The investigators confirmed all the worst rumours. Amar Singh later made a deposition in which he said that even Japanese sympathizers were unable to conceal the appalling conditions.[33] Officially there had been 60–70,000 Indian coolies on the railway at this time, but 20 per cent of the Indians recruited from

Malaya and Thailand had already died, 30 per cent had deserted and 10 per cent were in what passed for hospitals. The observers concluded that nearly 40 per cent of all labourers who had worked on the railway in a twelve-month period had died of disease or exhaustion. To the harshness of the labour and the poor quality of the food were added other factors. By this time almost no prophylactics against malaria and encephalitis were available. There were hardly any trained doctors. Cholera could be treated only with herbal remedies. Poor food gave rise to an epidemic of tropical ulcers and primitive sanitation spread all the diseases. People were forced to work even when they were gravely ill. The standard day was ten hours of continuous hard labour, but workers were supposedly paid overtime if they volunteered to work for another two or three hours.

The Japanese, themselves desperate, poorly fed and aware of the mass mortality of their comrades on the Assam frontier, treated the labourers with indifference and often brutality. One Japanese officer, later confronted with statements that the Japanese had called the workers 'dogs', deposed disingenuously that the Japanese for 'worker' sounded very much like the Burmese word *koin*, 'dog'. The Indian and Chinese labour contractors also stole the money which the Japanese paid the workers for food and accommodation. Subhas Chandra Bose put in a strong complaint to the Japanese army. The Japanese apologized. Malay and Chinese labour was unreliable, they said. The Indians were best.[34] The Japanese promised that things would improve. The Burmese government also established camp welfare officers to look after their own people. A system of rewards came into operation. Ordinary workers were dressed in gunny sacks and matting. 'Excellent workers' got special longyis. Still the deaths continued, and by June 1944 a further horror along the railroad was bombing by American B-29s.

By contrast with the experience of the Burmese people, December 1944 saw the best Christmas the Allies had had for five years. Between August and December the volume of war materiel going to China and down into north Burma doubled. There were still bottlenecks and infuriating examples of incompetence. Yet the Ledo Road had come into its own, the American reorganization of the Assam railway and the rebuilding of Calcutta docks were beginning to bear fruit. With the crossing of the Irrawaddy towards the end of December, the Allies knew they had effectively won the war in Burma, but for how long and how far down the great crescent would they have to fight? The Japanese were stubbornly defending their conquests. There were British, Indian and American casualties by the thousand. The auguries were still mixed.

## SILENT ARMIES

As the test of arms in the crescent reached its last desperate stages, and the full horror of the forgotten armies began to emerge, there were other, silent armies whose stories have yet to be fully told for the shame of telling them. The provision of 'comfort women' for Japanese soldiers had been an accepted facet of the Japanese way of war from the beginning of the Sino-Japanese conflict. After the 'rape of Nanking', the Imperial Army subscribed to a brutal logic: if men could not be kept from women, to prevent such excesses it was necessary to regulate the provision of women for soldiers. Military commanders got involved in the traffic of women to brothels for their men. Some were brought from Japan; Chinese women were found, but in the fear that they might act as spies the net was cast wider. Tokyo brothel owners were employed to recruit Korean women for China, although in what were termed 'front line' stations local women were still used. There is compelling evidence that the women in these stations were coerced.

The scale of this sexual enslavement was enormous. It was an integral part of military planning for the Southeast Asian war. A document by the head of medical affairs of the medical branch of the Japanese Ministry of War, dated 3 September 1942, gave the following statistics for 'comfort stations': 100 in North China, 140 in Central China, 40 in South China, 100 in Southeast Asia, 10 in the Southwest Pacific and 10 in South Sakhalin. Japanese planners estimated a provision of one woman for every forty soldiers. This would suggest that 80,000 to 100,000 women were involved; on the best statistical evidence perhaps 80 per cent of them were Korean. But there were many local women ensnared, forced by trickery, taken as hostages to be released on a ransom, or just snatched from their families. In 1942 32.1 million condoms were supplied to units stationed outside Japan. The preferred military brand was called 'Assault No. 1'.[35] The Japanese military were not alone in managing the traffic in women in Asia. The British army had regulated barracks prostitution in India in the past, and was to do so again during the great Asian war. It had its own problems: 35,000 Allied servicemen contracted venereal disease in 1943; that is sixteen times the number who fell in battle.[36]

The 'comfort houses' became a notorious feature of Southeast Asian towns. A report by a former Japanese resident of Singapore who surrendered to the Allies highlighted this: 'The inmates of the brothels are Chinese, Malayan, Korean, Japanese, Indian and Eurasian. In my opinion the brothels were the biggest change made by the Japanese in Singapore.'[37] The Singapore Chinese Girls' School became a geisha house and in Cairnhill Road a row of houses was barricaded off for the Japanese. Similar houses in Tanjong Katong seemed to observers to have a grimly functional aspect: the girls were 'all dressed in white, no makeup, nothing . . . no kimono . . . something like a nurse's uniform . . . simple, plain. A plain Miss.' The Japanese would buy their tickets and quietly sit outside waiting their turn.[38] In Penang, Lim Kean Siew argues that the prostitutes of the port were used by pimps to fill the 'comfort houses' to spare other women.[39] But it is clear from other evidence that coercion was used, and that by no means all the women were prostitutes. In mid 1942, the Japanese interpreter 'Mr Nakane' recorded his regular visits to the kimono-clad women at the 'Girl's House' and the 'New Girl's House' in Seremban, where he was posted, and reported a 'Miss Kiku who was amateur and very good'.[40]

Fifty years after the fall of Singapore, as former 'comfort women' from Korea and China began to speak out, an official in a Malaysian political party attempted to collect testimonies from local people who had been victims of Japanese atrocities. Some 3,500 letters were received. None has been published, but the Japanese historian Nakahara Michiko managed to interview a number of the women who came forward to say they had been in 'comfort houses'. They spoke of rapes and abductions; where parents tried to resist, they were killed in front of their daughters. Girls were kept in seclusion from other girls in the comfort stations and given a Japanese name. There they were repeatedly raped. When women did not submit to sexual acts, they were kicked and beaten. One woman who came forward in Penang spoke of being raped by thirty soldiers a day. The physical and psychological injury would stay with these women for the rest of their lives.[41] As with the 'rape of Singapore', in the memoirs of the times the comfort women linger as an unwelcome ghost, writers hesitating to probe too deeply, women fearing the stigma of coming forward and of rejection by their communities or even their families. A Dutch victim who published her story in 1994 related how she had told it once before in 1945 to the highest authority at the British army police headquarters in Java, 'but I never heard any more about it'.[42] The chroniclers of Syonan life, Low and Cheng, reported the return of fifteen young women from a 'comfort station' in Java shortly after the war. On disembarking from the docks, one girl was heard to remark to the official receiving them: 'Will my father accept me back?'[43]

During the last stages of the war people began to move of their own volition to avoid forced relocation by the Japanese, or worse. Many Singapore residents migrated with their families to smaller peninsular towns to see out the war in quiet and safety. A former victim of child prostitution, Janet Lim, was evacuated as a nurse from Singapore in the small-ship exodus shortly before the fall; she was one of the few to escape the sinking of the *Kuala*. She spent an uneasy sojourn in Sumatra, in constant fear of being taken as a 'comfort woman'. But when she returned to Singapore she fled back again to Sumatra, because 'the underlying fear and mistrust in Singapore were terrible'.[44] Middle-class Chinese and Eurasians felt this most acutely. Mamoru Shinozaki, the Syonan administrator who seemed to have taken the welfare of these people to heart, announced a series of settlement schemes whereby townspeople would be given the resources to fend for themselves. The unproductive and crypto-British clerical classes were to be turned into peasants and to redeem themselves through manual labour. Many seized upon this opportunity to escape the daily scramble for scarce resources and the threat of arrest. The settlements were built along ethnic lines. For the Malays there was a scheme in Bintan island, just south of Singapore. The journalist Ishak Haji Muhammad was an early, enthusiastic pioneer. The Chinese were given Endau, on the jungle fringe of the eastern coast of Johore. The third settlement was a mixed one, but principally for the Eurasians. It was at Bahau in

Pahang, dead in the centre of the peninsula. This was inhospitable country, much of it controlled by the guerrilla armies of the Malayan Communist Party.

The Bahau project was conceived as part of a grander Japanese settlement plan for central Malaya that encompassed four sites, each of 150,000 acres, and a million settlers. The pioneer colony was a Roman Catholic initiative in which Bishop Devas of Singapore played a major role. Pope Pius XII himself, it was reported, had sent a blessing for the enterprise.[45] The head of the settlement was the lawyer and former legislative councillor Pat de Souza. It was conceived in late 1943, and most of the settlers arrived in early 1944. The site had originally been chosen for an airfield but had been abandoned because it was highly malarial. The young men went ahead to prepare the ground, digging primitive drains and erecting bridges. The amenities were basic: there was a cookhouse and two longhouses; later two more appeared with a small chapel and a church. The Eurasian community of Singapore divided on whether or not to go. Many who went did so in the belief that with the priests there would be safety. There were also around fifteen de la Salle Brothers and nuns with some Chinese girls in their care. They ran their part of the settlement as a convent.[46] Despite the hard conditions there was a holiday atmosphere amongst the settlers who travelled there, and the arrival of each new batch was an occasion for communal celebration and campfire singing. There were monthly dances, fuelled by *toddy* in five-gallon bottles and rice wine. One settler even brought a piano. By the end of the war 8,500 acres of land had been opened up for 5,167 settlers. Although mixed, the colony was segregated: there were distinct areas separated by virgin rainforest for Catholics, Protestants, Chinese and Neutrals, who were also keen to get out of Singapore. There were Danes, Swedes, Spanish, even a White Russian couple there. The Eurasians despised them for their snobbishness.[47]

Bahau was one of the driest parts of the peninsula, an enclave of scarcity in the midst of abundance, and the settlers had to resort to divining for water. An ambitious plan to irrigate the land by damming the powerful Muar river with a timber construction had to be abandoned. Two graduates from the government agricultural college south of Kuala Lumpur were on hand to advise on planting; one settler had

had a spell at Kew Gardens. The Japanese demanded that they grow cotton, but the overwhelming need was for food: mostly tapioca and sweet potato. There was no top soil. The Brothers grew ragi successfully over ten acres, but the output was small and the settlement was kept alive by barter trade with local Malays, as settlers were forced to dispose of the goods they had brought with them from the city. They initially spoilt the market in doing so. The alternative was fishing and trapping in the forest. Nobody made a real success of it. Some had enough money to pay others to build houses, and to get by, but prices skyrocketed so far that by the end of the war settlers could pay \$1,000 in banana notes for a pair of white trousers. Mamoru Shinozaki distributed blue tunics of the kind worn by Chinese labourers, but as one settler concluded: 'Eurasians are not tillers'.[48]

Bahau was to become 'a living hell'. By April 1944 the first settlers began to die of malaria and beriberi. Survivors likened what followed to the Ten Plagues of Egypt. 'It was a case of malaria in every house, wave after wave of malaria there. Then came a period when there was a funeral every day, at least one, sometimes two a day.'[49] Endemic disease preyed on frames worn down by malnutrition. The most virulent strains of malaria attacked people's spines: 'some of them went temporarily insane. They used to run around, throw their clothes off, run naked on the road. Until they had a quinine injection in the spine, and then they came to their senses.'[50] The bishop himself would die of diabetes resulting from a cut that became gangrenous. On one estimate, a quarter of the Eurasian population of 2,000 died. The community life diminished. But yet, to those who survived, Bahau was a haven. 'You felt you were free . . .' recalled Herman da Souza, an inspector of English schools who had gone to Bahau to flee the Kempeitai. '[We] all talked quite freely there. But you couldn't do that in Singapore. That was the most important thing that I was concerned – the freedom. Sunsets were beautiful. The morning was fresh and beautiful. It was only the malaria.'[51]

A similar optimism had marked the arrival of the first Chinese settlers at 'New Syonan' in Endau in September 1943. For most of them too it was a means of escape. Chu Shuen Choo was a young woman fleeing from becoming a kind of Tokyo Rose for Japanese radio. She remembered the journey to Johore as being like that of an

American pioneer. On arrival settlers were confronted with a military-style communal barracks, thatched with leaves. To begin with, normal family life was impossible. Saws, *changkols* (scythes) and baskets were doled out to settlers. Each family was given two acres of wet rice paddy and two of dry land. The settlers learned rice farming from the local Malays. The settlement swelled to around 12,000 by the end of 1943. Chu Shuen Choo concluded that 'it was quite a good life'. She prospered in a small way by paddy planting, fishing and trading in a night market. The only drag was her husband: 'every day he wait there under the tree, reading Shakespeare, reading stories'.[52]

This scheme that gave land legally to Chinese to cultivate was the first of its kind in Malaya. 'You leave the Chinese alone for finding food for themselves,' argued one settler. 'They will never starve. That's the wonder of it all.' Some of the settlers were already enterprising agriculturalists from the rural areas of Singapore, but many were intellectuals. The principal of the school ran a coffee shop. It was famous for its iguana soup and as a meeting place for the lawyers, doctors and university men who moved to Endau. A chemistry PhD brewed whisky. There was a remarkable structure of mutual support in Endau, which transcended the divide between the middle class, English-speaking Chinese and the various different dialect-speaking groups. Endau was unusually tranquil in another sense. Shinozaki had cut a deal with the local guerrilla commanders: peace for the settlement in return for rice.[53]

## THE PENINSULAR WAR

The bourgeois settlers at Bahau and Endau left behind many testimonies of their experience. We know far less of the more general movement to the hills of the western peninsula by Chinese from the towns, mines and estates. They opened up new land independently, although to some extent the Japanese tolerated and even encouraged them to take over neglected rubber estates. By the end of the occupation, Chinese occupied perhaps 70,000 acres of plantation.[54] They had also cut into around 150,000 acres of forest reserve.[55] They grew hill rice, but also vegetables and cash crops such as tobacco; some had fish ponds and ducks and pigs. They had no legal claim to their lands. The British government had tried to keep the Chinese away from this kind of agriculture, but in the Depression it had offered a life-line in times of low wages. It allowed a worker to sit out a strike. During the war, it was a route to relative freedom, and the 'squatter' settlements had taken on a more permanent character. New hamlets were formed on a strongly egalitarian basis; there was rarely a headman in evidence. For a while at least, the power of the *towkays*, the bosses, and their labour contractors was broken. The spirit of these settlements was a return to older traditions of mutual support in times of adversity. A myriad of 'little republics' had emerged. This movement was vast in compass: perhaps as many as 4–500,000 Chinese were involved, particularly in the hinterlands of the industrial areas of Perak, Selangor and Johore. It would take the state and the bosses many years to bring these people under control. To reverse this movement after the war by forced resettlement, the British undertook what was at the time the largest planned population movement in recorded history. In the interim, it brought the squatters into the orbit of the guerrillas of the Malayan Communist Party who used them as sources of supply and information, and their noisy livestock as a system of alarms.

The communists spread their influence in these areas through a mixture of skilful propaganda and old-fashioned protection. Ho Thean Fook witnessed a 'people's convention' in his area of Perak: a night meeting in a cleared area of rubber trees. An opera stage was assembled with planks on benches, lit by pressure lamps and with a set improvised from sticks and pieces of cloth. There were speeches, music and a play showing Japanese atrocities and the heroic resistance of the guerrillas. 'A carnival spirit prevailed.' The highlight was the singing; the audience was encouraged onto the stage, the village belles especially. This was a big draw for youths in a remote place, and the guerrillas skilfully presented themselves so as to offer an enticing new vision of life. But in the business of protection the communists had their competitors. The world of the squatter was a volatile one. In many areas, other kinds of Robin Hood figures emerged to protect their settlements, and to take money from them. In Pusing, there was a man known as 'The Rat', Low Choo Chai, who moved from running urban extortion rackets to set up in the forest during the occupation with a sizeable band of men. Squatter communities fell under his sway. His guerrilla band was a much less disciplined affair than the communists'. The men lived with their wives and mistresses, which was unheard of in a communist camp. The communists repeatedly attempted to bring men like Low into their orbit, but with little success.[56]

Many of these other gangs were, like Low Choo Chai's men, nominally affiliated to the Kuomintang's Overseas Chinese Anti-Japanese Army. They were recognizable by the single star they wore in their forage caps, as opposed to the three stars of the communists. They were mainly concentrated along the Thai border with Perak and Kelantan. There were rich pickings to be had here, particularly from the smuggling trade and from the Chinese communities in the area around Pulai. This was a settlement of hardy Hakka Chinese that dated back two centuries. They were said to have intermarried with the Orang Asli and called themselves the Hakka-hai. The communists tried to expand their influence in what was perhaps the most naturally well-designed base area on the peninsula, potentially a little Yenan. The Kuomintang too were in the region, around Kundor, an area of more recent settlement by Kwongsai and Cantonese tappers and woodcutters. But when the Kuomintang raided the neighbouring town of Gua Musang early in the occupation, the Japanese took reprisals against Pulai. The communists tried to gain influence by protecting the local people. The area became perhaps the most contested ground of the peninsular war. A Malayan Civil Service officer, J. K. Creer, spent most of the occupation with the Kuomintang-affiliated guerrillas in the highlands of this area. He witnessed whole communities caught up in brutal internecine violence. He was present on one occasion when a gang fried and ate the heart and liver of a suspected communist spy, and drank some of his blood with *samsu* liquor. In September 1944 the arrival of another Kuomintang leader from the south with a more 'soldierly' bearing, Lee Fung Sam, ignited a fresh round of fighting between the two Chinese factions. Not least amongst the tensions in this area was the fact that the violence spilled out into the Malay *kampongs*.[57]

Despite the indiscipline of the hill gangs, Creer rated the fighting potential of the Kuomintang quite highly. Another stay-behind man, Robert Chrystal, joined him from the communist camps in Perak, because, as Creer explained it, 'he was tired of the monotonous round of traitor-killing, hymn singing and heart-searching à la Oxford Group Movement'.[58] The Kuomintang appealed to Chrystal as 'a band of rough, swashbuckling bandolieros, who drank, whored and gambled hard'. Their leader Yong Kong, a sixty-year-old opium addict, resisted all communist propaganda. The communists in the area were led by a *towkay*'s son, an educated man from outside the region. He operated a more puritanical regime of propaganda and mock battles in the paddy fields with old pirate rifles, and exercises in two-infantry-ranks firing: a staple of British drill before the First World War passed on to them by Chapman in his elysian wanderings. Here, as elsewhere, the British were for long periods hostage to the MPAJA, who demanded their help in training troops and ground them down with political polemics.[59]

The year 1944 was another period of hiatus for the secret war in Malaya. Early in the year, Davis and Broome moved further into the central range, away from their camp at Blantan. There were growing tensions within the town network their Chinese agents had built up the previous year. A plan to get in touch with the POWs in Singapore was abandoned. There was still no radio contact with the world outside the forest. The Kuomintang operative Tan Chong Tee, for one, was becoming increasingly suspicious of the British: he felt that they had turned their back on the Kuomintang intelligence operation and pinned their hopes on their relationship with the MCP. What is more, they were brushing aside the growing concerns about the security of the operation. Davis, he concluded, 'was a typical arrogant British col-onialist bureaucrat'.[60] In March 1944, under pressure to bring the situation to order, the senior Kuomintang man Lim Bo Seng made a fateful decision. He decided that he needed to make contact with the wealthiest Chinese to work on old friends to revitalize the underground struggle. To exercise the necessary personal sway he had to go out of the jungle. 'It would have been a marvellous thing,' Davis mused years later, 'It was a real dream.'[61] His Kuomintang comrades were later to recall Lim's last night in camp. They talked of opening a factory together after the war, and of philanthropic schemes to dispose of the wealth it would generate. 'There was a feeling of doom in our hearts as if we knew that this was an ominous farewell.'[62]

Lim went to ground in a private house in Ipoh. But the Kempeitai, acting it seems on a local tip-off rather than information directly from their agent Lai Teck, had begun to roll up the network. They made a series of arrests along the coast and raided the rice-trading business front in Ipoh on 26 March. One of the Chinese Force 136 men whom the Japanese had planned to turn into a double agent escaped custody and made it back to the jungle by taxi. The others were arrested one by one. Lim Bo Seng and an accomplice attempted to get out of Ipoh by car, but it was stopped at a road block by the Kempeitai and Lim was given away by the Force-136 steel wristwatch he wore. He tried to bribe his way through but was arrested by the same Kempeitai sergeant who had captured Lai Teck in Singapore two years earlier.[63] With the rest of the Kuomintang agents Lim was detained, interrogated and ruthlessly tortured. He died in Batu Gajah prison of dysentery on 29 June 1944. He was to be Force 136's only casualty of war. His wife would be given a bounty of £2,700. Lim's remains were exhumed immediately after the Japanese surrender and carried to Singapore for a hero's funeral; in time he would become Singapore's national martyr.

The British operation was exploded by the loss of Lim and the other Chinese agents. The recriminations as to who betrayed Lim Bo Seng persist to this day. Davis refused to engage in lengthy post-mortems with the communists over this. 'I didn't want to start probing individuals who had served me so well.'[64] On top of this, their camp was attacked by a large Japanese force and, although Davis and Broome were absent, the code book and other secret documents were lost. The collapse of the Kuomintang operation made the British entirely dependent on the Malayan Communist Party. Their claims to represent SEAC were redundant in the absence of radio communication. The party reappraised its position: in October 1944 Chin Peng and another senior Perak commander, Colonel Itu, were summoned to meet Lai Teck just north of Kuala Lumpur. It took them two weeks to get there on foot, by the jungle route. At the meeting Lai Teck announced a strategy of dividing the party into an open and a 'clandestine' army. The party would, on the opening of a Southeast Asian second front in Malaya, move to seize country towns and establish its own administration, in the name of a National Liberation Army. He heartened cadres hungry for a step-up of action against the Japanese. Years later Chin Peng would see in this a cynical plan to play off all sides, but the strategy was accepted by the party, and withheld, too, from Lai Teck's Japanese handlers.[65]

By now news was filtering through that the Axis was on the wane. Perhaps the first public intimations of this came from the radio speeches of Subhas Chandra Bose from mid June to mid August reporting the collapse of the offensive at Imphal and Kohima. They stirred the imagination of all who heard them. In Singapore there was an illicit sheet news service run by Chinese, culled from BBC broadcasts intercepted on illegal short-wave radio sets. The English version was known as 'The Voice of Freedom'. Those people who listened to radios did so at a terrible risk, but there were those who monitored the channels for the Japanese radio stations, and so news was not in short supply. Elsewhere, the news came by other means. Escaped POWs reported that news of the Allied landings in Normandy spread with incredible speed. As POWs passed through Taiping station, a Eurasian stationmaster pasted up a board: 'Second Front: France Invaded'.[66] From November 1944 Allied B-29s took Bahau as a mark, dead centre of the peninsula, and flew south to bomb Singapore naval base. By this time the settlers 'were just waiting for the end'.[67] By the early part of 1945 bombs were falling again on the residential areas of Singapore and the sickening prospect of more civilian casualties raised itself once again.


## NEW BALLS AT WIMBLEDON

The British dared to plan for the re-establishment of their Raj in Malaya. Like the seminars in the gardens of Simla, the post-mortem on pre-war rule had a detached and unreal quality about it. It was prepared at the Military Administration School at Wimbledon, and by a Malayan Planning Unit at Hyde Park Gate. The planners were ordered in 1943 to draw up policy directives for everything from law to electricity to assist the restoration of British government in the event of the Allies invading Malaya. An initial military administration by SEAC would be rapidly superseded by a new civil government; the question as to its form was very open. The Malayan Planning Unit's blueprint for the future of British Southeast Asia would provoke the inevitable retort from the die-hard 'Old Malaya' lobby, 'what do you expect coming from Wimbledon: all balls'.[68] What emerged in fact was one of the most comprehensive attempts to refashion colonial government in the history of the British Empire. But it was drawn up in almost complete ignorance of the situation on the ground.

The debate on Malaya's future had begun immediately on the fall of Singapore, with a series of articles in *The Times*, including most strikingly Ian Morrison's charge that the British had 'no roots in the life of the people of the country'. This provoked a debate on Britain's imperial intentions that ranged much wider than Malaya itself.[69] It was, in particular, a catalyst to attempts to recast the image of British imperialism in the United States. When Singapore fell, Victor Purcell, a Malayan civil servant seconded to the Ministry for Information, was on a speaking tour of the United States where he had been sent on leave to promote Malaya's cause. He was summoned to meet Dorothy Lamour – the saronged star of *The Road to Singapore* – at Twentieth Century Fox Studios to promote her picture, but was also lionized as a 'New Deal' kind of politician.[70] Purcell would play an influential role in the Malayan Planning Unit, and in the remaking of Malaya after the war. The 'new imperialism' that emerged from the war would have a keen eye on United States opinion.

A debate was also underway in India. There, a community of Malayan notables had gathered in exile. Perhaps most eminent of these was the Straits Chinese leader, Tan Cheng Lock. Prior to the war his political star had been on the wane, and he lived in Bangalore relatively humbly. As his daughter reported: 'the household's domestic helpers had to be reduced from twenty down to three'. Tan Cheng Lock was reduced to washing his own underwear and carrying pails of hot water for his own bath.[71] As he did so he planned a paper on Malaya's future: it urged the granting of full political rights to the Chinese, but also expected from the Chinese a greater identification with Malaya. Along-side this there was the Kuomintang group. Its leading light was the Selangor tycoon H. S. Lee, who served in China, and acquired the honorary rank of colonel from Chiang Kai Shek's regime. Another group of exiles, Europeans, Singapore Jews and Straits Chinese, came together as the Malayan Association of India. It was headed by the son of the Sultan of Johore, Tengku Abdul Bakar. It was a somewhat rancorous body and the Chinese broke away from it with Tan Cheng Lock emerging to lead them.[72] They vied to get the attention of the British. It is not clear that they did.

Important voices were absent from these discussions. The undisputed leader of the Overseas Chinese, Tan Kah Kee, had escaped the fall of Singapore but had gone to ground in occupied Java. The Rulers had all remained in Malaya. The most senior Malay outside of Malaya was Tengku Mahiyideen, a relative of the Kelantan royal family, who had been bundled out with a bottle of whisky for luggage and was active in Force 136 recruitment. The legendary figures who had helped build Old Malaya, such as Sir George Maxwell and the redoubtable T. S. Adams, hastened to speak for the Malays. They feared that the Malays would be swamped under any changed arrangements. Senior Malayan Civil Service men who had escaped internment flooded the planners with detailed memoranda on the intricate balances of the old order.[73] The new men were not listening. By the time the Malayan Planning Unit had moved from Wimbledon to India in 1944 the key decisions had been made and the expertise on the spot was largely superfluous.

The exclusion of the Old Malaya hands was entirely deliberate. It was said by them that the Colonial Office was disappointed that so many of the Malayan Civil Service had survived the war. Some twenty-five of a service of 169 were at large in 1943. Of over 2,000 government officers generally, there were about 230 left, half of whom were in the forces. It was, the head of the unit admitted, very much 'the second eleven'.[74] It would be a point of bitter resentment that policy would be drawn up by men largely outside the Anglo-Malay condominium that had governed Malaya for seventy years. Perhaps the most influential of the planners was Edward Gent. He was an experienced but entirely deskbound Colonial Office man. He was one of a series of men in Whitehall who had advocated a reformed colonialism in the 1930s, and were determined to use the war to push it forward. Another influential and senior voice was Victor Purcell, who advised on Chinese affairs; he was dismissed by critics as a maverick of the Chinese-language stream of the Malayan Civil Service. In this sense, the Malayan Civil Service establishment was paying for the blunders of 1941 and 1942.

The new policy hammered out in 1943 and 1944 had two main thrusts. The first was a transfer of sovereignty in Malaya from the rulers to the British crown. The fall of Malaya, it was argued, had showed that 'the people had no organised connection with government'. The old systems of indirect rule – through sultans, protectors of Chinese and estate managers – was obsolete: they could not deliver what a modern government should deliver. The remedy for the ills of imperialism was more and better colonial government. The people had not defended Malaya because they lacked any central object of loyalty. Most Chinese and Indians lacked citizenship rights: so what was Malaya to them? The British reconquest had as its key aim the creation of a centralized state structure – a 'Malayan Union' – with a common citizenship that would override the jumbled system and confused loyalties of the pre-war period. Chinese, Indians and others would share citizenship with the Malays, and the creation of a multi-racial 'Malayan' nation was a long-term goal. Within the Malayan Union, the sultans would retain a ceremonial role, but they would no longer rule.

There was a second, more visionary, aspect to the plan. The second colonial occupation was also conceived as a kind of controlled experiment in freedom. It was driven by a Fabian socialist agenda: paternalist, gradualist, but seeing the future of empire in a partnership with colonial peoples. It was an early experiment in 'nation-building'. To this end, and largely through the influence of Purcell, the stifling legislation by which the British had controlled Malaya's emerging politics – the control of societies, speech, assembly, publications – was to be relaxed. This seemed to herald a Malayan spring for colonial peoples. The victory of the Labour Party in the British general election of 1945 would raise expectations further. However, these ideas would generate an unprecedentedly hostile reaction from Malay nationalism that would put Britain's entire position in the region in jeopardy. The expectations for colonial freedom it raised were dashed as the post-war crisis deepened.

# 9

# 1945: Freedoms Won and Lost

The Greater East Asian Co-Prosperity Sphere was dissolving and the transnational movements that it had helped to foster were faltering. On 21 January 1945, the legendary freedom fighter Rash Behari Bose died in Tokyo. He was given full honours by the Japanese at his funeral, which Premier Tojo attended. But the Indian Independence League which he had briefly energized was failing. There were many who had never, at heart, accepted the way in which Subhas Chandra Bose gave precedence to his dream of an armed liberation of India over the civil affairs of the Indians in Southeast Asia. There was criticism of the high-handedness of the military; K. P. K. Menon, who had led the movement in its early days and vocally fell out of sympathy with it, was arrested. Even Subhas Bose himself was not immune from censure. Rash Behari Bose's secretary A. M. Nair attacked both the pretence of Netaji's entourage and his aloofness, which Nair saw as the product of an engrained 'master–servant complex'. Above all, '[h]e functioned as though the community could be looked after by speeches'.[1] The war-weariness was general. The mood of the Indian community shifted to one of mourning. At an emotional ceremony in Singapore on 8 July Subhas Bose laid the foundation stone of an INA memorial on Connaught Drive beside the Padang. One of the first acts of the returning British forces two months later would be to pull it down.

A second, sure register of the changing fortunes of war was the black market. After the end of 1944 people began to turn their assets into commodities and properties. The price of urban land rose astronomically. The cost of shophouses in Singapore rose thirty-fold in some accounts. People spent more freely in the coffee shops, tea houses and nightclubs. The Japanese government tried to stem the trend with patriotic saving schemes, and even a new lottery. In December 1944 the Japanese acknowledged the futility of this by issuing a $100 note. This just helped people dispose of them quicker. The British dropped $750,000 in false banana money overprinted with 'Japanese money will die with the Japanese'.[2] The heavy raids on Singapore stopped. The city began to clear for the second battle of Singapore that was soon to begin. But this time more people opted to remain, the terrible conditions of Bahau and Endau becoming a deterrent. Those who had nowhere to go and no assets to trade waited anxiously for the end.

## INDIA MOBILIZED

In India too the rich did quite well out of the later years of the war. Contractors and industrialists prospered, subjected to relatively low rates of taxation. Military families and many farmers in the Punjab were comfortably off. But the government of India was an impoverished administration presiding over a largely impoverished people. In the main it was Britain and America that were now footing the huge bill for the expansion of the Indian port, road and railway systems. One thing India was not short of was manpower, but the labourers were badly malnourished. A Canadian medical team conducted a survey of Indian pioneer labour on the Assam front in late 1943 and early 1944. They examined various well-represented groups: Bengali Muslims, low-caste Hindu Chamars from Bihar and the United Provinces and Madrasis from the far south. All classes were undernourished. The average Indian's weight fell short of a twenty-year-old Englishman's weight by between fourteen and twenty-three pounds and the average English labourer working in England was in any case shorter and lighter than, for instance, a North American.[3] The Indians had been brought up in poverty, suffering from endemic malaria and consequent anaemia. Local customs and practices made things worse. Most Hindus were vegetarians and even those who did eat meat were on short rations because of the long lines of communication. Severe vitamin deficiency caused by the absence of germinated wheat had produced conjunctivitis in nearly 50 per cent of the Madrasis. Cooking at the labour camps was done by untrained cooks who had a tendency to boil the food until it had lost all its nutritional value. Many British officers were excessively worried about respecting the food taboos of their pioneer labourers and refused to intervene to improve the diet. Perhaps they were thinking of the Great Mutiny of 1857, when violations of dietary taboos were supposed to have led to rebellion. Finally, these men were working in debilitating conditions 3,000 feet above sea level. It is not surprising that the Canadians concluded that output of the average labourer in India was only about one third that of his English counterpart.

In addition to the nearly 2 million men directly under arms, the Indian empire furnished hundreds of thousands of men to work in pioneer and military labour corps. Then there were the many thousands of extra labourers taken on in civil engineering projects away from the war fronts in Arakan and north Burma. The huge mobilization of manpower is one of the untold stories of the Indian war effort. Contractors raised large amounts of labour from eastern India. But the impact of this demand fell very unequally on the poor, the 'tribal' groups such as the Santals of Bengal and the Garos of Orissa or the Nuniyas of Bihar. Nearly 200,000 Nagas were working as porters and carriers on the Assam front at any one time in 1944 or 1945. Areas which had hardly been touched by the outside world before the war, such as McCall's little fief in the Lushai hills, were called on to supply men to carry, scout or fight with matchlocks and bayonets. Across the Burmese border Karen, Kachin and Chin had been fighting and sacrificing their lives since 1942. Major H. Seagrim died heroically at Japanese hands in 1944. He had given himself up voluntarily to avert Japanese atrocities against Karens. Yet there were thousands of other villagers from the minority peoples shot down in jungle fire-fights or massacred by the Japanese in retaliation for aiding the Allies. As in Malaya, the life of the forest and hill peoples would never be the same again after this brutal conflict with the outside world.[4]

Older established bodies or organized labour were also drawn on over and over again as the war progressed. The Assam Tea Association continued to provide so much labour that the owners began to worry that not enough of this commodity, so essential to the war effort of the British Empire and Commonwealth, would be produced. The Assam Civil Porters' Corps also swelled in size, working close to the front line. The cost of the campaign in lives of the tea workers was huge. Iris Macfarlane, who grew up in the apparently idyllic world of the tea planters, was horrified to find out in later life how many coolies had perished of disease and overwork. Then again, the ever-loyal Indian princes, some based far from the front, made available state labour corps. Puddukottai, a small state in the dry southern tip of the peninsula, did particularly well. It had been in alliance with the British for exactly 200 years, though it was soon to be abandoned to the exigencies of the politics of decolonization without a thought.[5] One of the most intriguing organized units involved in road building was the Italian Auxiliary Pioneer Corps. This was raised from so-called Italian 'co-operators'.[6] During the 8th Army's campaigns against the Italians in 1941 and 1942, thousands of Italians had been brought to POW camps in India as they could not be taken to Britain. At first, the Italians were something of a nuisance in a jocular sort of way. They were adept at spreading anti-Allied propaganda to the Indian population – for example on the backs of cigarette packs with one or two cigarettes left in them. British military intelligence was particularly struck by one jape. The POWs had fabricated an Italian fascist flag from old clothes. They captured a vulture which flew into their compound and tied the flag to it. The unfortunate bird was seen flapping around the surrounding villages for hours displaying the insignia of Mussolini's new Roman Empire. After the fall of the dictator and the German invasion of Italy, however, many Italian soldiers who were not committed fascists agreed to work on the Allied side. The valleys of Assam were alive with the sound of the songs of Sorrento.

As the 14th Army trenched into north Burma, the labour situation became more precarious. This part of Burma was relatively lightly populated and most able-bodied men were needed for agricultural work. Families were often only prepared to send off young boys to work in public works gangs. More and more Indian labour was sent in and, as the end of the war approached, this began to pose a political problem for the emerging civil affairs administration. Burmese hackles began to rise once again about Indian immigration. The few exhausted British administrators who returned to this war-torn land quickly realized that they were back at square one.

## BA MAW'S LAST STAND

As 1945 began Ba Maw contemplated his fate. The British and Indian armies were pouring into Arakan. Early in January they had reached the periphery of the great Irrawaddy plain and in late February they took the important strong-point of Meiktila. Mandalay and Rangoon were subject to constant bombing, and Mandalay itself was to fall to the 14th Army on 20 March.[7] The populations of these cities, which had crawled back to the pre-1941 level, began to run away again. Rangoon radio continued to assure its listeners that Nippon was shortly to win the war. It claimed that the retreats by Japanese forces, which even the dimmest listener could now easily trace on the map, were no more than strategic withdrawals. In his extremity, Ba Maw summoned up some of the deepest and most ancient themes of Burmese fear and pride. In his speeches he claimed that the Allied armies were already looting the Buddhist pagodas of their images and treasure and that no monk or temple would be safe on their return. He urged people across the country to pray and make offerings and called on the Buddhist priesthood to give sermons which would stiffen the morale of the heroic people. Even Buddhism was not enough. Ba Maw had a bucketful of 'victory soil' brought from Shwebo and deposited near Mandalay. The soil was supposedly from the place where Aulangpaya, the great founder of united Burma, had begun his victorious march in the mid eighteenth century.[8]

By the end of January Ba Maw, a Buddhist of Christian lineage, was even invoking the *nats*, those dangerous and powerful spirits of the Burmese cosmos feared even by the medieval Buddhist monarchs. He named a number of crack regiments after the most bloodthirsty of them. But neither the Buddhist nor the animist card came up trumps. The only thing that really kept the Burmese at their posts now was fear of the Japanese. For in its extremity, the Kempeitai turned on the Burmese population with even greater ferocity. As all failed around them, the Japanese, who were quite prepared to die themselves rather than surrender, brutalized many in the civilian population who were not strengthened with a matching commitment. Many Burmese officials were rounded up, tortured or executed. Nu himself had to step in to save a number of his friends and Thakin colleagues who had come to the attention of the Kempeitai because they were listening to Allied broadcasts or had let slip stray anti-Japanese remarks. In her shabby compound in Rangoon, Khin Myo Chit lived a life of near terror. By day all around her was pounded by the RAF. By night, even though she was still technically a member of Ba Maw's government, she feared the tread of Japanese boots coming to arrest her.[9]

Indians in Burma were equally apprehensive, but for different reasons. Civilians who had distanced themselves from the Japanese feared their desperate vengeance. Those who had sided with them feared the Allies. Following Imphal and Kohima, some Indian National Army soldiers had quickly surrendered, shocked that Indian troops treated them as enemies not liberators. Lieutenant-Colonel Riaz surrendered a regiment of 300 to 400 men to the British when the latter crossed the Irrawaddy river in late 1944. 'Bose was greatly shocked at this action and Japanese criticism of the INA increased.'[10] The remaining core, however, held fast. Morale was sustained by the invincible self-confidence of Subhas Bose himself. Whatever his personal fate, he was convinced that the independence of India was not far off and that he had played a major part in it. The Indian National Army fought gallantly against the British Indian army, especially at the great *nat* shrine of Mount Popa, as the invaders moved south from Mandalay. There were, by this time, deep divisions in the INA between the pro- and anti-Japanese elements and about whether to withdraw into Malaya. American bombing of the INA hospital on 10 February outraged the rank and file.[11] A horrified Ayer, Bose's minister of information, said, 'In less than an hour the whole hospital had been razed to the ground . . . a large number of patients had been killed on the spot and most of the rest had sustained severe burns.'[12] If anything, this strengthened the resolve of the INA leadership to fight to the end, though by now they had even begun to suspect the intentions of their Burmese allies.

Aung San and the Burmese Defence Army had, in fact, been cultivating covert connections with the Allies for eighteen months and planning an attack on the Japanese. By the autumn of 1943 it had become clear to him that Burmese independence was a sham under cover of which the Japanese army and Japanese companies were continuing to exploit Burma. By the summer of 1944 the ultimate defeat of the Axis was plainly signalled even to the most pro-Japanese Burmese. In August, following the Japanese rout at Imphal and Kohima, members of the Army Young Resistance Group began to plan a rising against the Japanese. They tried to link up with Thakin Soe, the communist leader who was hiding in the Arakan countryside and trying to create a civil resistance movement. The civil and military arms of Burmese resistance together formed what was called the Anti-Fascist People's Freedom League (AFPFL). This body planned a concerted military and civilian rising which seems to have been modelled on the contemporary French resistance to the Germans.

At a meeting between Soe and the BDA conspirators a long proclamation entitled 'Drive Away the Fascist Japanese Marauders' was read out.[13] This rambling document was to form the basis of the AFPFL's policy for the next four years. Significantly, it denounced the plans of Dorman-Smith and his staff in Simla, who were reported to be preparing to bring back British capitalism to Burma. The AFPFL's constitution denounced Japanese exploitation of Burma's resources. It also harped on the Japanese army's insults to Burmese religion: 'The Japanese are pillaging the pagodas, monasteries and shrines. Some of our religious buildings are being used by the Japanese as barracks, stables and wash houses. Our phongyis [monks] are knocked on the heads, are told to climb the trees, to kill rats, etc.'[14] The young revolutionaries made elaborate plans which divided Burma into eight resistance areas, each to be commanded by a military officer and a political commissar. Together they planned a rebellion for October 1944. But Soe himself never really had his heart in the idea of an early rising, even though many of his younger followers were eager to take up arms. Why was this? One point is that the communist leadership was at this time closer to the Allies. Thein Pe, who had slipped away to India in 1942, was the first to throw in his lot with the Allies, at least for the medium term.[15] Mountbatten and his commanders, Oliver Leese[16] and William Slim, were trying to persuade the young Burmese not to move until the Allied invasion of the north was in full swing. South East Asia Command did not want a rising within Burma to go off half-cocked. They judged it to be in their interest for a revolt to disrupt the Japanese rear, but only after Allied forces had made significant inroads into Arakan and the upper Chindwin valley. Judging by later comments, Mountbatten was also apprehensive that if the Burmese revolt went ahead early and succeeded in liberating a large area of the country, the incoming Allies would be faced with a fully fledged, and probably communist, Burmese provisional government which they would then have to unseat. In fact, this was exactly the scenario which the British were to face later in French Indo-China and in Indonesia. So Force 136, which had already been distributing arms to the Burmese rebels in Arakan, was forbidden for several months to arm the Burmese further. It was not only the British who counselled caution. Delay was also in the communists' interests. Soe was too canny an operator to believe that the Japanese were completely finished. Even if the Burmese patriotic forces were able to stage a successful guerrilla war against them, he reckoned that the Japanese could still act with great ruthlessness against pro-communist communities and smash the base areas which Soe and his comrades had painstakingly built up since the 1930s.[17] As in Malaya to the south, this hiatus may eventually have proved fatal to the future of doctrinaire communism in the country.

As the Japanese collapse in north Burma gathered speed in January and February 1945, Aung San himself became restive. He made frequent speeches implicitly criticizing the Japanese. On 3 February, at the funeral of a battalion commander who had fallen in battle, he recalled the soldier's sympathy for the Chinese cause and his hatred of fascism. The crowd wept. No one seemed to worry that the Kempeitai was watching and listening. Aung San also made closer and closer contact with the incoming British through Force 136 and the communist networks. He had now decided that the national revolt would come in March 1945, and that nothing could stop it. In this he had an ally in Mountbatten, who now disregarded the objections of some of his own officers and the background teeth-gnashing of Dorman-Smith and the civil officers. Their hatred of Aung San seemed to harden even as he made his move over to the Allied side.

Mountbatten was at his best in dealing with the politics surrounding Aung San's rising. Many officers were deeply suspicious of the good faith of what they still regarded as the 'quisling army'. This was particularly true of the old Burma hands among the Civil Affairs Secretariat (Burma) officers drawn from Steel Brothers, the Burmah

Oil Company and the former Burma administration. Mountbatten decided to intervene decisively. He addressed his commanders on 27 March, saying that before the end of the month there would be a 'nationalist revolt'. It would be 'a spontaneous movement which has not been evoked by us'.[18] On the contrary, as some of his senior staff knew, the BDA had been straining at the leash for nearly a year. It was the British who had urged them to wait. Anticipating the anger of the old hands, he conceded that there could be political trouble in the future and that British support for Aung San would annoy 'respectable elements' of the population. But these had been inactive, whereas a Burmese rising would materially help the progress of the Allied reconquest. The Burmese knew that Force 136 had armed Karens, Kachins, Lushais and Nagas in the hills. If they now refused to accept the only ethnic Burmese resistance force in the field, how much co-operation could the Allies expect when they returned to Rangoon? Colin Mackenzie, the Force 136 commander, personally urged an alliance with Aung San.[19]

Mountbatten was always good on historical analogies.[20] Later he was to compare Aung San with Jan Smuts, the former Afrikaner enemy of Britain who was now the grand old man of imperial defence. On this occasion he cleverly noted that by sending in Special Operations people to make contact with and help Aung San, 'we shall be doing no more than has been done in Italy, Roumania, Hungary and Finland'.[21] He might have added Yugoslavia, for the Allied compact with the supposedly communist leader Marshal Tito almost exactly paralleled the end of the war in Burma. Again, if no aid was given, Mountbatten warned, the news would soon get to the United States and the usual denunciations of 'British imperialism' would be heard. Life would be easier if the civil affairs administration were dealing with people who had been given help to free their own country.

Mountbatten's position was not simply opportunistic. He really believed that Burma had been exploited by the British. A great burden of debt had been lifted from the shoulders of the peasants by the Japanese invasion and the retreat of the Indian moneylender. He would 'be sorry to think that its re-imposition would synchronise with our return'. As a member of the royal family, he could afford to strike the vaguely leftist note which was so common amongst the British rank and file. The relationship between Bogyoke and Supremo went from strength to strength. At some point Aung San presented Mountbatten with a Japanese sword. General Sir Montagu Stopford, who had commanded the 33rd Indian Brigade at Kohima, later reassured his commander that, although this was a small stabbing weapon on the pattern used for hara-kiri, it should not be interpreted as a hint.[22] The chiefs of staff in London, who had little real leverage on the man on the spot, entered a note of caution. It was all right to aid Aung San's men as a military force, they said, but the AFPFL should not be allowed to become an incipient government, like the communists in Greece. In Burma itself, former government of Burma civil servants turned military officers such as Frederick Pearce bit their tongues for the time being. Dorman-Smith agreed with Pearce that it was 'sheer madness' to build Aung San up.[23]

Having convinced himself and his immediate supporters, Mountbatten countermanded Leese's earlier orders and directed Force 136 to begin issuing weapons to the Burma Defence Army or Bama-Tatmadaw as it was in Burmese. The war cabinet in London reluctantly went along with the Supreme Commander, but so cautious were his officers that only 3,000 weapons were dropped or issued to the BDA under very restrictive conditions. Burmese politicians took note of the fact that at least four times as much weaponry had been issued to the Karen levies in the Karen hills alone. Force 136 officers were told to remind the BDA and Anti-Fascist People's Freedom League leadership that they had to 'work their passage' and that their past offences would not simply be washed away. On their side, the Burmese forcibly reminded the British that they had left Burma undefended against the Japanese and had forfeited all rights to regard themselves as the legitimate government. It was the BDA who now represented the people of Burma. On the ground, the high politics was generally forgotten. Force 136 officers, concerned above all with defeating the hated Japanese, worked well with the BDA, determined that it should kill as many of them as possible.

## AUNG SAN'S REVOLT

The reaction of the Burmese to the striking and quite sudden change in their allegiances is difficult to gauge. Young Burmese had always been ambivalent about the Japanese. They admired their soldierly virtues and patriotism, but detested their brutality and bad manners, especially face-slapping. None were more ambivalent than those, like Maung Maung, who had gone through training, comradeship and physical abuse with the Japanese at the newly established military academy at Mingaladon near Rangoon. Before his passing-out parade in front of Aung San and the Japanese commanders in January 1945, Maung Maung had gratefully thanked his Japanese instructors, including those who had slapped and abused him. They had helped recreate Burmese manhood by passing on their military skills. Yet within weeks he and his comrades were ambushing and killing the Japanese. It was their total loyalty to Aung San, embodiment of the nation, which allowed these young men to perform an act of such spectacular treachery without any real qualms of conscience. Maung Maung remembered their commander's demeanour at the passing-out ceremony. He wrote that Aung San 'was brief, almost abrupt. He mounted the rostrum with sudden steps. He did not look a smart general; his cap seemed too large for his high domed head. Yet there was an intensity in his eyes, in his whole being.'[24]

When it did come, the Japanese were curiously unprepared for the uprising of the BDA against them. This was possibly because only the hard-line anti-communist elements in the army and the Kempeitai really believed that the Burmese would willingly welcome back 'British imperialism'. Most of the Japanese ignored suspicious activities by Aung San and his colleagues and even information about conspiracies extracted from victims of the Kempeitai under torture. As the Thakins and their troops marched out of Rangoon into the jungle on the pretence of moving against the invading Allies on 26 March 1945, many of the Japanese commanders cheered on their supposed allies. What remained of the Japanese air force flew overhead and tipped its wings. Ba Maw drove past in a big car and Burmese wept to see their beloved army stride out to its destiny.

The following day, 27 March 1945, the Burmese suddenly attacked Japanese positions in the Rangoon area. The date was to become the most important day in the calendar of the new Burmese nation. Over the next five months before the atom bomb terminated the Japanese war, the BDA claimed that they killed 8,826 Japanese, including a lieutenant-general and two major-generals, with several thousand wounded. It was only after mid May that they co-ordinated closely with the advancing British forces or secured significant Allied air support. The BDA forces fanned out into the countryside, escaping the vengeance of the pursuing Japanese, for the British were still a hundred miles away. Here the links with the villages which they had cultivated since the spring of 1942 came into their own. Maung Maung remembered: 'Partisans, young men from villages, left their homes to march with us. We ate the food that the villagers offered us, wooed their daughters, brought danger to their doors and took their sons with us.'[25] One Thakin Than, 'a devout Buddhist who counted beads by night and courted women by day', managed to get hitched three times before the force left Henzada district.

The British noted the help they had received with different degrees of reluctance. Slim, who was in the best position to know, thought most highly of the BDA, arguing that they had helped tie down large numbers of Japanese troops and had speeded the British reconquest of Burma by many weeks. In May 1945 he met Aung San for the first time and was impressed by him, as many soldiers were. Aung San apologized for his poor English and rustic manners. Slim graciously turned the apology, saying that it was the British who should apologize for not knowing Burmese. He congratulated the BDA on its successes and began to discuss an arrangement by which the BDA could become a full part of the Burma defence forces after the war. Aung San, he believed, was 'an honest nationalist'. It was possible to do a deal with him and he would keep his side of the bargain.

## RANGOON FALLS AGAIN

Events were running fast on the ground. The Allied advance into central Burma had run into heavy Japanese resistance when it forced its way down to Mandalay. As the spring wore on, Slim became concerned that the Japanese might try to hold Rangoon. If the British were held up until the rains came, he faced the possibility of being literally stuck in the mud in front of the devastated capital with an increasingly precarious supply situation in his rear. Might the spectres of 1942 return again? As it turned out, the Japanese commander decided to evacuate Rangoon in late April in order to fall back on and reinforce the troops in Malaya. An odd spectacle ensued. For nearly three weeks Rangoon became a no-man's land. A group of emaciated British officers who had been cooped up for three years in the central jail were released. They unsteadily took command of Rangoon.[26] To their surprise, Indian National Army officers in the city surrendered to them and offered to help maintain law and order. The Indians apparently feared that an outbreak of lawlessness and banditry would put the remaining Indian population of the city in peril. These British officers' relations with the incoming BDA were much more tense. A provisional government of independent Burma came into being in the city, owing allegiance to Aung San. Neither group of Rangoon's would-be rulers recognized the other's legitimacy. As the situation deteriorated, the British painted the roof of one of the prison buildings with the huge legend: 'Extract Digit'. It was spotted by one of the British reconnaissance aircraft and relayed back to Allied command, which duly got its finger out and moved on the ravaged city.

Before Slim arrived there took place a number of significant final journeys down the crescent. Since Aung San's revolt, Ba Maw and what remained of his government were even more suspect to the Japanese. He did, however, perform one final service to his country by strongly supporting those members of the local Japanese command who wanted to abandon Rangoon rather than fighting street by street. He managed to get countermanded a Japanese order to build a gun emplacement around the Shwedagon pagoda.[27] Then Ba Maw decided to retreat with the Japanese, leaving some of his ministers to negotiate with the incoming British. He was not sure whether he might not be shot out of hand and he was certainly correct in surmising that Dorman-Smith, for one, would have been only too happy to take this course. Ba Maw took flight south in his car accompanied by his wife and pregnant daughter as the RAF bombed and strafed the retreating Japanese troops. Ba Maw's daughter went into labour and had to be left with her mother in a wayside village. Ba Maw himself escaped to Tokyo where the Japanese Foreign Office hid him in a monastery. Later in the year he surrendered to the British occupation forces in Tokyo and was sent to prison. In his later memoirs, the former Adipadi recorded that even in this extremity he knew that freedom for Burma was imminent and that he had played a major part in it. He comes over as a dejected and frightened man, blaming the Japanese for all that went wrong, according to the transcript of his British interrogators.[28]

Subhas Bose, by contrast, was deeply reluctant to pull out of Rangoon. For him the city was a symbolic staging post for the march on Delhi, the burial place of the last Mughal emperor. As the Japanese retreat began, he realized he had no choice. On 24 April he appointed a deputy leader of the provisional government of Azad Hind, and began to evacuate his personnel in the direction of Bangkok.[29] The forced march south was hazardous. Bose refused to take transport when so many of his men and women were walking on what rapidly became monsoon-soaked tracks. He pressed on with blistered feet through the villages of Pegu which had been set alight by the Japanese. More than once Bose's party was nearly caught in the open by RAF fighter aircraft harassing the Japanese columns. His main concern was to secure from the Japanese transport and protection for the several hundred women of the Rani of Jhansi Regiment of the INA who were retreating with him. Several weeks later Bose and some of his supporters reached the Thai capital. He still believed that the international situation was so fluid that he could play a part in India's imminent move to independence, perhaps in alliance with the Soviets. These final illusions were dispelled, first by the Soviet Union's declaration of war on Japan and then, a few days later in August, by the unconditional surrender of Japan itself.

Back on 15 May 1942 General Harold Alexander, fighting a grim rearguard action against the advancing Japanese, had crossed the Burmese border near Tamu, accompanied by his corps commander General William Slim. Almost three years later to the day, on 2 May 1945, Sir William Slim re-entered Rangoon 'the hard way', that is overland. The evacuation of the Japanese from Rangoon and its environs was marked by the depressingly familiar atrocities. Japanese troops burned down the jail in which their Burmese prisoners had been housed, murdering many of them, including some of those who had helped the Chindits at Namtu and elsewhere. Several British soldiers still in their hands were summarily executed hours before the liberation. The Japanese were no more merciful to their own side. Just before the evacuation they blew up St Philomena's Convent, which they had used as a hospital for wounded Japanese soldiers. Four hundred men died. The officers responsible told the mother superior that they could not take the patients with them and could not bear to see them fall into enemy hands.[30] The Burmese turned on the Japanese with equal savagery. A party of Japanese nurses were bayoneted and shot as they tried to flee the city. Allied planes meanwhile bombed civilian properties they thought were connected with the 'quisling' government. Ba Maw and Thakin Nu barely escaped with their lives and many innocent civilians perished.

The Japanese were driven out of the Irrawaddy delta and back down through Tenasserim from where they had come in January 1942, this time pounded by the RAF all the way. The Burmese, who had once treated the retreating British with pity and garlanded the invading Japanese, gave the Allied troops a rousing welcome. T. L. Hughes vividly described the situation.[31] Most people were wearing rags and even though there was no fighting in Rangoon itself, as there was in Manila in the same month, the city was the scene of extraordinary levels of destitution. No public transport existed. There was not a single train, tram or bus in existence, except on the outskirts of the city where 'a few dilapidated pony carts, pulled by mangy scarecrows of ponies were plying for hire at exorbitant rates'.[32] The streets were two feet deep in filth and open drains had long since ceased to be anything other than a depository for garbage. The city suffered complete blackouts at night because there was no electricity or even kerosene. All heavy moorings in Rangoon harbour had been destroyed during the scorched earth campaign of 1942 and the signalling system on what remained of the railway had collapsed. Whole blocks at a time had been demolished by Allied bombing and the once pretty residential areas around the lakes were unbelievably dirty and unkempt. The little of value that remained in February 1945, down to doorknobs and panes of glass, had been looted in the anarchy before the British entered the city. Central and Lower Burma were two of the areas most ravaged by the Second World War. Dorman-Smith's great cosmopolitan city was a shambles.

The condition of the people was more shocking even than the physical depredation. Whole cities such as Bassein and Prome had simply disappeared and were now no more than creeper-infested ruins. The population of Rangoon was reduced to two fifths of its previous level. Unlike the case in 1942, many people had fled permanently, to escape the Kempeitai and the bombing. Hughes found 'old friends so changed as to be unrecognisable; many were emaciated and shrunken; many were white-haired prematurely and many continued to cast an anxious eye over their shoulder on the look out for the Japanese Gestapo'.[33] This was particularly true of Ba Maw's officials and supporters who had lived in terror over the previous few months because they were secretly in touch with the resistance. People with no connection with politics were simply emaciated and diseased. While rice remained available, as it was not in contemporary Indo-China, cooking oil was unobtainable and people used to meat were half starved because the Japanese had butchered herds of cattle and other animals for themselves. Tuberculosis and scabies took off at an alarming rate because people were denied vitamins. Venereal disease was rampant because so many women had been forced into prostitution during the later days of the occupation. Leprosy had become a public scourge again because leper clinics, like all other hospitals, had effectively ceased to work and their inmates had fled away to their homes, sometimes to infect other people.[34] The collapse of the export market meant that many of the labourers in town and country had turned to crime, a situation exacerbated by the Japanese who, as their armies disintegrated, handed out many weapons randomly to foment problems for the invading Allies. The result was an extraordinary upsurge of banditry or 'dacoity' as the British perennially termed it. Dacoit gangs were particularly prominent in the delta and on the route between Rangoon and Mandalay. They attacked towns, looted cars on the main roads, murdered headmen in peaceable villages and broke open weapons stores at police posts. At the end of the year 20,000 dacoits were awaiting trial.

Many groups of people in the country had been brutalized and harassed because of their assumed support for the return of the British. The Chinese, of course, were persecuted from the first day the Japanese arrived. One Chinese national reported to friends and relatives in North America that 'the belongings of 80 to 90% of the Chinese people in Burma had been stolen, burnt or destroyed'. Whole populations of villages or quarters of towns had been dispersed. Many had been systematically massacred in strategic areas such as Myitkyina. The Anglo-Indians and Anglo-Burmans were treated almost as badly. The largest concentration of them was around Maymyo, the old hill station. Here there were so many that the Japanese authorities simply interned them and many succumbed to disease or malnutrition. Railway workers were kept under constant surveillance and occasionally brought in for routine beating and interrogation, though some of them managed to smuggle information to the Allies. One interned Anglo-Indian wrote, 'I forgot to tell you that poor old Dad had no more clothes to wear towards the end and had to lie on gunny bags – he used to say "This is killing me" – and you won't believe, we could not get rags to wipe him.'[35] Indians, too, were under suspicion if they were Christian, spoke English or had close relatives in India. One wrote from Sagaing to India: 'Our enemies told the Japanese that I was a British agent. They arrested me and imprisonment consisted of tortures like beating me up, pouring hot water on my head and burning me with fire. These were the lighter forms of their tortures.' Burmese too were sometimes trapped by the paranoia of the Kempeitai. One wrote to another: 'During the time of the Japanese occupation my elder brother went down to lower Burma. He was searched by the Japanese at Ku-Me and was killed by them because they found British notes in his possession.'[36] This brutalized population now faced new hardships. A Rangoon resident wrote, 'the prices of things have gone up, greater than during the time of the Japanese. At first the prices came down with the arrival of the British. Then a kind of control was attempted, and as a kind of pure cussedness, the prices went up until they reached a point never before seen.'[37]

Relations between the different communities in Burma had never been entirely cordial as the Burmans proper accused the Karens in particular of being stooges of the British. The war had burned hatreds into people's minds which were not to heal in a generation of Burmese independence. In the Karen Christian town of Kappali where the Bishop of Rangoon had once lived, the church had been Japanese brigade HQ and the school building was turned into a Japanese brothel.[38] During the occupation some Burmese Buddhists had taken the opportunity to pay off old scores. Karens had been afraid to go out after dark, living in terror of being denounced to the Kempeitai. What laid the ground for the future Karen–Burmese civil war, though, was the attitude of young Karen soldiers who had escaped to India. Returning with Wingate and later the 14th Army, they were stirred to fury by the atrocities which had been perpetrated on their villages, and especially by the 'moral degradation of their women and girls' by the Japanese and Burmese. The Revd Captain W. J. Baldwin wrote to Aung San himself, taking him to task for claiming the British had stirred up these hatreds. The Karens, he said, now doubted Burmese good will. The young fighters had come to weep at his house in Calcutta about what they had seen during their long-range penetration campaigns. Now political separation was the only option.

Into this minefield drove the Civil Affairs Secretariat (Burma). CASB was like other military administrations which the British established in territories conquered from the Axis. These included North Africa, Sicily and southern Italy where Alexander, commander in Burma during 1942, and many Indian troops were now operating. The idea was that civil administration could not be fully restored in territories where enemy forces were still active and martial law was in operation. CASB had begun operations in 1943 and 1944 in Arakan. It had been responsible for combating disease and dealing with thousands of refugees. Its scope increased massively as the British moved down into Burma in the autumn and winter of 1944. But it was in the more populous southern parts of the country in the spring of 1945 that the immensity of the problems of reconstruction became clear to it. Some portfolios of government were handed back to the civil administration as early as 16 October when Dorman-Smith formally took over again. These included justice, police and education. Others, where technical expertise was more important, such as signals, posts, medical affairs and the railways, stayed with the military administration until the beginning of 1946, as did administration as a whole in Tenasserim, the southern archipelago. CASB operated in one part of Burma or another for the best part of three years. It profoundly marked the country, inheriting many features of Ba Maw's administration and many of its personnel. It intervened like no other British administration before it had ever done simply to get the rice mills and saw mills working, the revenue collected and the harvested crops moving. It earned the contempt of many for its congenital graft and corruption. But the fact that anything was happening in Burma at all was largely the result of its Burmese, Indian and British officers.

One problem emerged early. CASB officers were mainly taken from the old administration and British firms, then put into uniforms with military rank. Over the months before the reoccupation, in Calcutta and on the front, they had painstakingly combined old files of intelligence information with their own personal knowledge. The long memories of former employees of Steel Brothers in the frontier and inland teak forests were particularly useful. Lists of prominent citizens were drawn up, with their pro-Japanese and anti-British sympathies in the pre-war days noted.[39] Sketchy information gleaned during the Japanese occupation was stirred in to give a riveting picture of local networks of power at a level way below the district office. In the Pakkang subdivision of Prome, for instance, the occupying forces were told to expect to deal with U Lu Wa. He was a 'political bully' who had been briefly arrested in 1942 by the Pegu commissioner for making anti-European and pro-Japanese speeches in the precincts of the Shwe Zandaw pagoda.[40] They were most likely to get help from 'friendly and influential villagers' who had been contractors for Steel Brothers and had opened shops in their villages under the firm's aegis. A high level of support was expected to come from the 'senior elephant headman' in Paungde, who was 'very pro-British and very deaf'. Again, the contours of the 1931 rebellion were still marked on the political map.[41] The old rebel areas were still prey to a particularly high level of dacoity even fifteen years on and after Japanese occupation. In Myitkyina to the north, one key local worthy whose influence had survived the deluge was U Ba Maung who had married the daughter of the largest local Chinese food business house. Dismissed for dishonesty as a pawnbroker, he had joined U Saw's party in 1939 and done well in the occupation. More likely to be favourable was S. B. Singh, a rich, English-speaking Indian who had a large shop in Myitkyina and had lent large sums to local European businessmen. Some of Steel Brothers' own local Karen employees were known still to be active in the area.

These officers often came back into Burma with a lot of baggage in the form of old scores to settle and old prejudices to vent. Most of them hated the Thakins and popular militias which were in de facto control at the village level over much of the country. Aung San later complained to Montagu Stopford that the first CASB officer who landed at Rangoon had insulted him. They spread a rumour that Aung San had boycotted the governor's first reception, which was not entirely true. Stopford wrote to Mountbatten of the sequence of events over the six months between May and October 1945 that it 'very much confirms your own suspicions regarding the sabotaging of your policy at the lower levels'.[42] Several members of CASB set out deliberately to antagonize the Thakins. They ran up against not only the Burmese nationalists but also in the British army the leftist soldiers, air force officers and 'progressive' followers of Mountbatten who had no time for the 'old hands'.

The political situation was balanced on a knife edge. The irreconcilables of the civil administration were faced on the Burmese side by Burma Defence Army men and new volunteers who wanted to take the war to the British immediately the Japanese had been driven out. Some rank-and-file Burmese communists were pushing for an immediate uprising, as their colleagues in Malaya were doing. Aung San and the leadership were convinced that this would be a disastrous mistake. Even though the immediate food situation in the country was somewhat better than it was in Malaya, Burma was even more devastated and could not afford a civil war. The police got hold of a pamphlet that the leadership secretly distributed. 'Why We Should not Continue to Revolt' argued that it was imperative that a rising be undertaken by the whole nation. For 'the temper of the masses was not ready'.[43] Headmen and lower government servants were 'ogling' the British and most people were just too dispirited and hungry to persevere with a revolt.

Besides, it said, the Anti-Fascist People's Freedom League was in a good position to face the returning British. Burmese patriots had liberated Rangoon and attacked the Japanese enemy's divisional head-quarters. 'English vested interests' were still too weak to grab back what they had lost in Burma. They would need to invest in the UK. Europe was turning socialist. On a practical level, the pamphlet urged people to join the new Burmese Defence Force that the British were forming. That was much better than hiding their weapons in the ground where they would rust. Aung San himself even made it clear that he saw no particular problem in taking an oath of allegiance to the king when joining the BDF. In the event, he resigned from the army to take up the political leadership of the AFPFL before the issue really came to the fore.

Other problems were more mundane. Many Burmese resented the fact that their civil rights remained in abeyance for many months after the Japanese had left the scene. Others simply had unrealistically high expectations, believing that a huge flow of basic supplies would pour into the country when much of Asia was hungry and in tatters. The civil administration faced many tricky problems in trying to get even a semblance of normality back to Burma. Take the issue of cloth. Cloth was essential: most Burmese were living in rags and were too humiliated by this to go out. This made it impossible to get the bazaars moving again. Cloth was also an 'inducement good', that is to say people would work for it even when they had totally lost faith in all paper currency.

But it was terribly difficult to get hold of supplies of cotton goods even with the muscle of the 14th Army. Madras, a major centre of textile production which had long supplied Rangoon, was loath to release supplies because consumer goods were scarce in India itself and serious political trouble felt imminent across the subconti-nent. The Americans were another option, but the British mission in Washington had difficulty in getting supplies through the Combined Production Board. The American contention 'was briefly: why should we give cotton to the Burmese who have done nothing for the war at the expense of the Philippines who have fought magnificently?'[44] So serious was this impasse that the War Office in London had to send to Washington a memo entitled 'Assistance given to the Allies by Burmans during the war'.[45] This pamphlet sneakily omitted much about the BDA and the ethnic Burmese, dwelling instead on the exemplary courage of the hill peoples fighting the Japanese in the jungles and 'called upon to perform prodigies of road making and transportation', while saving the lives of refugees and Chindits. Washington released some cloth. This was later supplemented with supplies from Australia and South Africa.

Even when cloth was available, it was by no means clear that the Burmese would accept it. There were examples of Burmese consumers rejecting white Madras cloth because its colour was associated with Indians. Only blue or red cloth was acceptable. This could be made into the jackets for the longyis on which Burmese women prided themselves. Monks were a particularly difficult proposition. Gifting the temples was deemed essential to restore the battered legitimacy of the British regime. Only saffron coloured cloth was acceptable in the temples and saffron dye was in short supply. CASB procurement agencies in London struggled with this problem and the equally intractable problem of razors. Razors, too, were in short supply, but it was found that Burma had an unusually voracious appetite for them at a time of acutely low production. Not only did the lay population shave their faces, but the more than 300,000 monks in the country also needed to shave their heads. Such anthropological niceties did not apply to toothbrushes. These were required by the 'majority of the European-clothes-wearing population and Chinese and urban natives'. The requirement for can- and bottle-openers was calculated at one for every 150 of the population.

While the war went very well in the course of April and May, it is important to remember that victory in Europe and the reconquest of northern Burma did not spell its end in the minds of either the Allies or the people of Asia. Many felt that the Japanese would fight on, perhaps for years, and that thousands of Allied troops would die. This was the justification for the dropping of the atomic bomb. Huge numbers of Japanese troops were still armed and fighting in Southeast

Asia and China. A massive battle to take the Japanese islands seemed to be looming. In Burma, the Japanese commanders had evacuated Rangoon, but they were still holding the difficult country around Tenasserim and were arming local people to fight against the incoming British. To the Allied commanders it seemed politic to continue to work with the Burmese nationalists while at the same time concerting plans to disarm them in the longer term. In Kandy in May, at a meeting presided over by Mountbatten, the BDA was given recognition as the Patriotic Burmese Forces.

On 15 June, more controversially, the BDA took part in a victory parade in Rangoon. To the distaste of many of the British officers present, and in particular the old Burma hands in uniform, Aung San and his troops goose-stepped in their Japanese-style uniforms between the Sule and Shwedagon pagodas.[46] The new AFPFL flag, a white star in the upper left side on a red background, flew alongside the Union flag. Mountbatten's toast to the victorious powers also underlined the political delicacy of the liberation of Southeast Asia. He raised his glass to 'The King, the President, the Generalissimo, Queen Wilhelmina [of the Netherlands] and France!'[47] All but one of these powers would be driven by armed insurrection from one or another part of Southeast Asia within ten years. The exception, America, would follow within a generation.

Mountbatten and his commanders in Burma had more immediate political problems in the wake of the victory celebrations. In the spring, the British government had released a White Paper, or statement of intent, on Burma's constitutional future. It conceded that Burma would move towards dominion status – self-government within the Commonwealth – in due course, but was irritatingly unspecific, as far as Burmese politicians were concerned, about the time frame. What was envisaged by the British was a fairly rapid transition within a few months from military administration to civilian rule headed by the governor, but under the pre-war system. This was an equally sore point with much of the Burmese population. Rightly or wrongly, they believed that the Burma Defence Army had played a major part in the liberation. They had freed themselves and nothing was more repugnant to them than the thought of the return of Dorman-Smith and the pre-war civil servants. They also feared that British and Indian firms had been given a guarantee that they would be able to resume their money-making activities in Burma.

The governor was itching to get back to his job. During the years of exile in India and abuse from British and American journalists, iron seemed to have entered his soul. He was profoundly antagonistic to the Thakins and disapproved of the tilt by Mountbatten and his staff towards them. On 20 June Dorman-Smith arrived on the Rangoon river and held a kind of durbar on board HMS *Cumberland*, as constitutional proprieties debarred him from going ashore.[48] Aung San was there, but so were many conservatives, Burmese, Karen, Anglo-Indian and British. Ominously for Burmese socialists and communists, Sir Paw Tun and Tin Tut had joined the sea cruise. The Thakins were now well aware that the old order was by no means dead and buried. Mountbatten had written two days earlier: 'We must act in the light of HM Government's policy, and not as though we are going to keep Burma under Crown Colony Government for another hundred years.' To many, it did not seem that the governor-in-waiting had yet adjusted to that policy.[49]

In the meantime the reoccupation of Burma was cause for celebration. In the hills the chiefs, levies and scouts celebrated victory with loyal durbars, Christian services and tribal festivals. Pledges of loyalty to the king-emperor were made by people who two or three years later were to find to their consternation that the government of that same king-emperor was about to abandon them to the Indian and Burmese majorities with scarcely a second thought. Lieutenant-Colonel Oatts of the Shan levies certainly saw the writing on the wall as he contemplated with disgust Aung San and his followers parading through Rangoon's streets. Many others, British, Naga, Kachin and Karen, had their gaze concentrated on the massive task of rebuilding the hill economies which had been isolated and degraded to an extent unparalleled even in the plains. As all over the world when the war ended, people also began to rebuild their personal lives. One such was a British officer 'on the wrong side of 40', Tim Nicholson. Throughout the last months of the war he had become entranced by the story of 'The Naga Queen' – Ursula Graham Bower – which had already taken on a truly Rider Haggard glow. Nicholson decided that he would marry his 'She'. Struggling up high into the Naga Hills he found her and requested an interview. Then, to the astonishment of the Naga onlookers, he clinched her in a passionate embrace at their first meeting. They were married on 7 July 1945, during the short interval between the liberation of Rangoon and the war's sudden climax.[50]

The joy of the victory celebrations among the British and Indian troops in India base and Rangoon could not conceal apprehension about the future. The Japanese seemed determined to fight on in a desperate attempt to protect their home islands. Would the reoccupation of Malaya be as bloody as the dreadful battle recently fought by American marines on the Pacific island of Iwojima? Even in Tennaserim, from which they had invaded Burma in 1942, the Japanese seemed to be preparing to hold out. The rapid fall of Rangoon might have been a fluke. Quite apart from this, there was the question of the future political status of India and Burma. British soldiers felt that the Indians in Burma were still hostile and were only pretending to welcome their return. The British were by now impressed with Indian soldiers, however. One soldier wrote, 'I am all in favour of giving India her freedom if these chaps I have mixed with and spoken to are an example of her qualities.'[51] Indian soldiers were obsessed with the issue of the INA. Some men thought that the INA was being treated too leniently for fighting against their own army. Some felt that Bose's troops had been misled. Others believed that they were real patriots. The INA men certainly protested under interrogation that they had fought as patriots and not because of any love for the Japanese. One officer pointed to the INA's fierce defence of the great precipitous *nat* shrine of Mount Popa even after the fate of Burma was sealed. Not everyone bothered with politics, though. When he was questioned, one late recruit among the Pathans said that after the war he would become a bandit, 'or rather, a better bandit than he had been before'.[52] The general peace, when it finally came, was going to be difficult to manage.

India, like Burma, was divided and uncertain as the baking heat of that summer gave way again to the monsoon rains. Most people in the Punjab already expected the European war, though not the Japanese war, to end quickly. They greeted Victory in Europe Day with relief, if not joy. Not everyone was pleased. Irreconcilable nationalists put round an odd rumour to the effect that the Germans were still fighting on, but could not contradict stories of their defeat because their radio equipment was all destroyed.[53] By contrast, die-hard 'loyalists' and the 'martial classes' complained that Punjab's heroes still fighting in Burma were not getting their fair due because of the obsession with local Hindu–Muslim politics. The Muslim League tried to use the heroism of Punjabi Muslim soldiers in Burma as a bargaining counter against the Congress. The Indian National Army, which contained a significant number of Punjabis, also came to the top of the agenda. On 30 June a train carrying captured INA personnel happened to be passing through a Punjab railway station just as people were awaiting a visit by Jawaharlal Nehru. To the fury of the British, people in the crowd waved pictures of Subhas Bose.[54]

If the Punjab had applauded VE Day and the fall of Rangoon in a muted way, Bengal was restive as ever. The last Japanese bomb had fallen on the port of Chittagong as late as March. In the base areas, conflicts between soldiers and civilians flared up from time to time. In January a letter from an Indian published in the *Statesman* denounced US soldiers as 'venereal disease ridden and seducers of young women'.[55] Black marketeers made huge profits from war supplies while the malnourished population still bore the heavy imprint of the famine. Periodic conflicts broke out between Hindus and Muslims in and around Calcutta. The province's politicians seemed as venal and divided as ever. There remained deep suspicion of British intentions. Why had Churchill spoken only of liberation in Europe in his VE Day speech? Why had the king's broadcast mentioned only Europe? Would the new Labour government make any difference? 'Perhaps messages of Freedom, Democracy and Lasting Peace, liberal as they are will have application to no wider area than Europe', mused a newspaper.[56] Another wrote ominously and presciently: 'the war in the East will not come to an end with the defeat of Japan'.

## THE FADING LIGHT OF THE NEW ASIA

In the south of the crescent, as peace became a prospect, a great uncertainty gripped peninsular Malaya. Mustapha Hussain, now a veteran of many campaigns, had retired to his farm in Perak. It lay in an area that was more or less controlled by the communists. He was worried that the guerrillas would identify him as an officer in the Japanese volunteer army, and as a collaborator. He was anxious for the safety of his family. He tried to shy away from politics and made himself useful to the village community; in his neighbours lay security. His first intimation of the impending Japanese defeat came with a meeting with a Malay in Allied uniform, a former student from Mecca who had parachuted in with Force 136. To prove he had come from overseas the soldier had brought with him small bottles of *minyak atar*, a rich perfume.[57] In Mustapha's home state of Perak the Malays had been caught up in the cycle of killings and counter-killings between the communist Malayan Peoples' Anti-Japanese Army and its 'Kuomintang bandit' rivals. Goods were seized, houses burned, and in the general mood of lawlessness, denunciation and reprisal there were wholesale killings. Chin Peng wrote that as many as 400 Malay villagers had been killed in upper Perak in a series of attacks, after Japanese military operations in the area.[58] There were rumours, too, that the Chinese troops of Chiang Kai Shek would be assigned the task of liberating Malaya. This further alarmed the Malays. All around there was a palpable sense of forces mobilizing for a confrontation; a general dread of a new war for control of the peninsula.

The actions of the Japanese fuelled this unease. For the last year or more there had been no political initiatives on the part of the Japanese, beyond a general softening of approach. But faced with continuing military defeats in Asia and the Pacific, they began to look to rally last-ditch support. On 13–15 December 1944 the military administration convened a second conference of religious leaders. This time the gathering was held in the royal town of Kuala Kangsar in Perak. The senior Japanese administrator, Fujimura Masuko, adopted a direct tone: 'Is it not the case that the holy land of Mekka has been neglected all this while under the power of the Anglo-Saxons? The way of the resurgence of East Asia is to reach all the way to the holy land of Mekka until it is under the hand of Muslims.' The message was reinforced more crudely when the delegates paid a courtesy call on the Japanese military commander at Taiping. They were told that the Greater East Asian war was a holy war: a *jihad*. The general sermonized on: he stressed the similarities between the Quran and the *Tenno*, the

Japanese emperor. He compared the emperor's war to that of the Prophet and his companions. This was blasphemy, or close to it: the general trespassed on issues that both sides wanted to evade. The *ulama* had no wish to adopt the language of *jihad*; more temperate Japanese had wished to play down the divinity of the emperor so as not to offend the sensibilities of Muslims. However, Japanese propagandists began to impose this kind of rhetoric on the mosques.[59] They also played on the threat posed by the Malayan Peoples' Anti-Japanese Army.

There were undercurrents of religious unease in the villages. However, these found expression not in calls for *jihad*, but in a surge of support for spiritual teachers at a local level, who seemed to offer protection to a community by the possession of special powers. This often took the form of invulnerability to bullets and charms to be worn, usually inscribed with quotations from the Quran which made it clear that the charm was effective only by God's will. A popular charismatic figure was Kiyai Salleh of Batu Pahat, Johore. He headed a movement of *sabilillah* – 'The Path of God' – which, although not a *jihad* in an orthodox sense, mounted a fighting response from March and April 1945 to what was seen as a threat to Islam and to the Malays. It was a movement of self-protection against MPAJA attacks on Malays who had been identified as collaborators. These were most often policemen and village headmen, and in June the Malay district officer was killed by the MPAJA. The Sultan of Johore appointed the leading Malay, Onn bin Jaafar, as his successor. This proved to be a shrewd move. Onn's intervention and mediation stabilized matters somewhat. In turn, it strengthened Onn's own prestige. Kiyai Salleh's aura became legendary and at the war's end *sabilillah* movements spread to other parts of the peninsula.[60]

The guerrilla armies of the Malayan Communist Party had from the end of 1944 stepped up their attacks on Japanese police stations and convoys, and quite often Malay policemen were the victims of this. The communists were emboldened by the arrival of supplies from India. On 1 February 1945 the Force 136 leaders, or rather their Chinese radio operator, had finally got the transmitter working, fourteen months after it had arrived in Malaya with Lim Bo Seng. The terms of the alliance with the MCP could now finally be reported to

SEAC. Buoyed up by the contact with the outside world, Davis and Broome called another conference with Chang Hong, alias Lai Teck. It took two months to organize. The meeting, on 15 April, was a much grander affair than the first plenary meeting. 'They had built "kong-si" houses in the jungle', recalled Broome. 'And they had got a number of their young Chinese communist girls to be waitresses and maids inside the house, looking after us, and the food was terrific.'[61] Given the more practical focus on the implementation of the earlier agreement, the influential military commander of the 5th Regiment, Colonel Itu, also attended. It was decided that the MCP would receive arms and supplies in return for accepting liaison officers from Force 136. Each officer would be accompanied by a platoon of Gurkhas. The idea of Chinese liaison officers was dropped entirely. Afterwards, Broome would deny that the political future of the Malayan Communist Party was discussed, but the Force 136 officers had been allowed to go further in promising that the MCP would not be required to register as a political party after the war, as part of the new liberal imperialism of the Malayan Planning Unit. In India it was further argued that they should not be disarmed immediately upon victory, but should play a policing role. These were substantial signals of future intent. Later the British would try to obscure this issue, claiming that they had no record of whether guarantees were in fact made or not.[62] The seeds of future confrontation were sown. But neither side had any illusions about the other. 'You must realise', Chin Peng told Broome, 'that our ultimate aims are very different from yours.'[63]

Drops of arms and supplies began to be arranged. In April, Broome and Chapman returned to Colombo, where they were fêted. Chapman went back to England, where he seems to have backed into the limelight much as his hero T. E. Lawrence had. '[A] few of my friends found it necessary to form a special protection society to keep me safe from designing females.' He also experienced, after three years in jungle isolation, the 'Rip van Winkle effect' that thousands of Allied prisoners of war and detainees were to experience.[64] Chapman and Broome were to return to Malaya after the end of the war. New men came in as liaison officers, many of them old Malaya hands: policemen, planters and game wardens. By the end of the war over 300 men, with at least 2,000 rifles, had arrived from Ceylon. This included some Malay parties that linked up with the emerging Malay resistance organizations such as Wataniah. One of the first in was Broome's 'boy' Ah Choon, who had escaped with him from Singapore and Sumatra at the beginning of the war. He parachuted in shortly before Broome's departure, announced himself – 'Reporting, sir' – and offered Broome a cigarette.[65]

The new liaison officers swiftly gathered intelligence on their allies. They discovered a young army of extraordinary fortitude, ground down by malaria, nutritional anaemia, tropical ulcers and skin conditions such as gaping tropical sores. In Perak infection rates were practically 100 per cent in the case of malaria. They also, in some cases, found young people traumatized by all the moves, violence and betrayals. In one week a doctor noted 'hysteria' in the case of three of the women and one of the men from the same company of guerrillas.[66] This was one of the first encounters on any scale between British soldiers and Asian Marxism. Officers who already knew Malaya were confronted with a new world: their impressions of the MPAJA varied dramatically. A report from Johore emphasized the 'formidable spirit' of the fighters. Another from the same area saw them as 'unwarlike': 'the average age of these men seemed to be around fifteen years'.[67] Some Europeans admired the egalitarianism of jungle life: 'wherever we went we ate and slept with them. There was no discrimination and we asked for none.'[68] Others – the old Malaya hands in particular – found this very aspect of it an ordeal. In Kedah two former planters virtually withdrew unilaterally from Force 136 because of their aversion to the task in hand. Their commanding officer reported that they did not like Chinese, and had even begun to investigate MPAJA killings of Japanese to the extent of exhuming bodies.[69] British officers sent in patronizing assessments of communist leaders. They read like school report forms. Of the Johore leader Chen Tien it was written: 'he should prove a useful man in civil service once outlook broadened'.[70] The senior Force 136 commander in the field, Lieutenant Colonel J. P. Hannah, wrote of his opposite number 'Colonel Itu': 'Itu is a compete moron and nothing more than a political agitator of low cunning but without the brains of a louse.' His colleague, I. S. Wylie, dismissed Itu as 'a rather stupid, intolerant hypochondriac obsessed with a sense of his own importance'. Yet by their own admission, Itu had, in his 5th Independent Regiment, raised and maintained a force of 700 fighting men and women who were armed, trained and uniformed.[71] Hannah had been a businessman in pre-war Malaya; in the post-war regime Wylie would rise to become acting commissioner of police. Later conflicts would become extremely personal.

The Malayan Communist Party did not, of course, reveal its full organization to the British. Its army was about 5,000 strong at the end of the war. There were substantial units that did not have European liaison officers, such as the 7th Independent Regiment in east Pahang. Like everyone else, the MCP was waiting on events. But the political theatre of the Greater East Asian Co-Prosperity Sphere had one last act to play out. The Japanese Empire made a final great push to mobilize Southeast Asian society behind it by making rapid concessions to Asian nationalists. Indonesia set the pace for change: plans there were far advanced for the creation of a quasi-independent regime. The pre-eminent national figure, Sukarno, was, in a sense, everything Ibrahim Yaacob in Malaya aspired to be. Under Japanese rule he had pushed the cause of Indonesian independence and of his own charismatic claim to national leadership. Although Ibrahim Yaacob and the Kesatuan Melayu Muda youth union had been increasingly marginalized, they hoped, at the last, to gain freedom for Malaya in the slipstream of the advance of Indonesia. Ibrahim's opportunity came when a new political adviser to the Japanese government, Professor Yoichi Itagaki, began to recant on the previous treatment of the Malay nationalists. At a meeting of Ibrahim Yaacob's men in Singapore a new movement was formed. The movement was known as KRIS. The acronym is significant: a *kris* is a Malay dagger; a weapon that demonstrates some of the highest levels of Malay art and craftsmanship. The *kris* carries great symbolic meaning, and individual weapons can possess magical properties. These kinds of dynamic acronyms became very common. They took precedence over the precise name of the organization itself. It is a measure of the confused intentions on all sides that the name of the movement was to be unclear and contested. KRIS was variously rendered Kekuatan Rakyat Istimewa ('The Special Strength of the People') or Kesatuan Rakyat Indonesia Semenanjung ('The Union of Peninsular Indonesians'). These meanings suggested rather different 'notions of intent'.[72]

Ibrahim Yaacob's former deputy Mustapha Hussain was enlisted to the cause. He was put to work writing a constitution for an independent Malaya. Mustapha afterwards maintained that at no point was the independence of a Malaya integrated within Indonesia on his agenda.[73] But it seems that Ibrahim Yaacob actively sought this. After Sukarno and his deputy, Hatta, had travelled in August to Dalat in Indo-China to meet the Japanese supremo in Southeast Asia, Count Terauchi, on their return they stopped in Malaya at Taiping airport. Ibrahim hurried to meet them. There he committed the Malays to the struggle in the archipelago, to Sukarno's leadership and to a Greater Indonesia: 'Indonesia Raya'. He laid plans to be in Jakarta to witness the declaration of independence. The provisional date for this was 7 September, and the first meeting of the planning committee was scheduled for 18 August. There is little indication as to how seriously Sukarno took this. Malaya was peripheral to his world vision, which remained focused on events in Jakarta. He would tell Ibrahim later that he had no wish to commit himself to fighting both the Dutch and the British. However, for radical Malay nationalism this was an epochal moment.

But time was running out. KRIS delegates began to assemble at the Moorish fantasy of the Station Hotel in Kuala Lumpur for a conference to decide the independence of Malaya. It was scheduled for 17 August. However, travelling to Kuala Lumpur on 15 August, Ibrahim was told of the surrender of Japan. A meeting of the main figures was hastily convened. Plans were made to press ahead, and to announce the formation of a Malayan Democratic Republic. Its figurehead was to be Sultan Abdul Aziz of Pahang, but it would also include the sultans of Perak, Johore and Selangor as well as the leading nationalist leaders. Many of these men were committed *in absentia*. The Sultan of Pahang had been detained by Force 136, 'for his own protection', and was quarantined in a jungle camp for over three weeks.[74] Events in Indonesia threw these plans into disarray. On 17 August, kidnapped by his own radical *pemuda*, determined that the new nation should not be seen as a Japanese puppet regime, Sukarno took a bold initiative. In the courtyard of his house in Jakarta he announced: 'We, the people of Indonesia, hereby declare Indonesia's independence'. There was no mention of Malaya, or Indonesia Raya.[75] For the Malay radicals this was a bitter blow; in the minds of many members of KRIS the two causes had been indissoluble. There was talk of seizing strategic institutions. Ibrahim Yaacob even harboured a chimerical notion of uniting his *giyu-gun* standing force in common cause with the MPAJA. But they had run out of time. Mustapha Hussain recorded his reaction many years later:

I cried when I heard that the Japanese had surrendered on 15 August 1945 simply because there were only 48 hours separating us from the declaration of Independence for Malaya. This was indeed a tragic case of 'So near yet so far.' I regretted the matter deeply as Malaya would once again be colonised and gripped by Western power. Even tears of blood could not rectify the situation. That was one of the most bitter moments of my life.[76]

In the meantime, the communists had their own plans: across the peninsula they were coming out of the jungle and starting to move in on the towns. On the evening of 17 February Professor Itagaki gathered the Malay *pemuda* and told them that 'Indonesia Raya' would not be realized. He also acknowledged that Japan's dream of a Greater Asia was over. 'Malayan independence is now your problem. You are on your own.'[77]

# 10

# August 1945: An End and
# a Beginning

On the morning of 6 August 1945 Matsushige Yoshito, a young photographer, was trying to cool himself down in the summer heat at his house in Hiroshima. This was a military city, full of army and navy facilities. Many Japanese troops had passed through here on their way to Southeast Asia over the past four years. Suddenly Yoshito 'heard a tremendous cracking noise, like trees being torn apart, and at the same instant there was a brilliant flash of immaculate white'.[1] Struggling dazed into the city, he saw '[p]eople's bodies were all swollen up. Their skin, burst open, was hanging down in rags. Their faces were burnt black. I put my hand on my camera, but it was such a hellish apparition that I could not press the shutter.' Later, he took the only five photographs in existence of the immediate effects of the atomic bomb on Hiroshima at ground level.

Some of the first Allied troops on the scene were from Japanese work camps. An Australian soldier, Kenneth Harrison, liberated himself after the surrender from a coal mine at Nakama. He had fled behind enemy lines after the battle of Malaya, and was one of the few to make it out alive. He had been a prisoner in Johore, in Pudu jail in Kuala Lumpur and a slave labourer in Thailand. Now, in the company of a Malayan Chinese, an Australian Chinese and a Malay soldier, Puteh Marican, Harrison went joyriding around Japan. They wore fake Military Police armbands and collected, as many soldiers did, officers' swords: they took twenty-three in all. They boarded a train to Hiroshima. There was a strange normality to the civilian rail travel, and they sat among the commuters in silence. When they disembarked they walked ankle deep in ashes. A Japanese policeman asked Marican if he was 'The Utmost Commander of the American Army'. They surveyed 'the listless people; the scarred people; the burnt people; the apathetic people'. 'Poor, poor bastards,' commented one of the Chinese. 'Now, as we left Hiroshima', wrote Harrison, 'our hatred of the Japanese was swept away by the enormity of what we had seen.'[2] The cruel great Asian war was coming to its horrific end.

## FINAL JOURNEYS DOWN THE CRESCENT

The dropping of atomic bombs on Hiroshima and Nagasaki took the whole of the great crescent by surprise. Mountbatten had only been told in strictest secrecy of the plan to use the bomb, on 24 July at the Potsdam conference, when Churchill took him aside and announced that Japan would surrender on 15 August. In the interim, the plans for reconquest could not be emended and had been pressed forward. The surrender was a colossal relief. In Burma the 5th Indian Division reacted to the news with wild celebratory firing. Few Allied commanders wanted to fight their way to Malaya and beyond. The last-ditch resistance that both commanders and men feared would not now occur.

Japanese field commanders, far from the reality of the American pounding of the Japanese mainland, were by turn confused, devastated and recalcitrant at the news of the emperor's surrender. Some wanted to fight on: the Japanese had a million men in the South East Asia Command. The Imperial Army and Navy remained in control of large territories which possessed sufficient resources to fight on, and to the end. Individual commanders feared Allied retribution: propaganda had made it clear that war crimes would be prosecuted. It was unclear how far SEAC's preparations for an assault in Malaya were advanced. The Australians were still bogged down in eastern Indonesia. In Malaya the commander, Lieutenant General Itagaki, refused to submit. It was only the arrival of a prince of the imperial house, with a personal order from Hirohito himself, that persuaded him to summon his senior officers to his headquarters at Raffles College and order them to stand down. In the jungles of the Philippines, Yamashita, the 'Tiger of Malaya', continued to fight on until 2 September; General Percival was despatched to attend his surrender. Some of Yamashita's former lieutenants disappeared. The psychotic 'king of strategy', Masanobu Tsuji, went to ground in a Buddhist temple in Bangkok, and from there to nationalist China. It has been estimated that around 200 Japanese troops took to the jungle with the Malayan Communist Party. In 1989 there were two of them still to be repatriated. The fellow-travellers, too, dispersed: on 19 August 1945 Ibrahim Yaacob fled to Indonesia on a Japanese aircraft. Many of his former followers left independently and some would join the Indonesian war of independence against the Dutch. In time, some of these men were to bring its radical doctrines back to the Malay peninsula, but Ibrahim Yaacob himself did not return to Malaya, save for two short visits shortly before his death in 1979.

In the occupied lands there were rumours of a last stand by the Japanese, perhaps a final, murderous *sook ching*. In Singapore in particular there was great unease. Just as on 15 February 1942, there was no formal announcement of the end, there was only the back-alley news of the emperor's broadcast. The Europeans at Changi heard from a Eurasian singing to himself cycling past an outside working party, without taking his eyes off the road: 'The Japanese have surrendered. The Japanese have surrendered'.[3] When the welfare officer Mamoru Shinozaki broke ranks to tell a public meeting that the war had ended, he had to hide to escape some hothead officers who wanted to kill him.[4] 'We did not know what they intend to do', recalled one witness. 'There were a lot of rumours – they might slaughter us before the surrender – then they kill themselves, or they might just surrender, nobody really knows.' In the event, 'we tried not to be in contact with them. They in turn avoided us.'[5] In Malacca some Chinese revellers were brutally punished, but on the whole, as N. I. Low and Homer Cheng reported, most Japanese met their fate with quiet resignation: 'once again we remembered the courteous Nip shopkeepers of Middle Road of pre-war days, who used to bow a customer in and bow him out again with equal affability, even if he bought nothing'.[6]

But for others the strain was too much. In Singapore there were suicides in the Cathay Building; by hand-grenade in Killiney Road. At a bungalow on Newton Road some officers had a final *sake* party. At an appointed hour explosives were detonated under the house by a timer. Most Japanese stayed at their posts, maintained order, and waited for the humiliation of surrender. Inoue Tsuneshichi, a private in the garrison, told how his company commander had prepared them for the end in July after the fall of Okinawa: 'I order you to do this: do not allow yourself to die in the War. Alive you can be of use to your country someday . . . don't obey any orders to commit suicide. It's no longer the era of Kusunoki Masahige.' (Kusunoki was a warrior hero of the thirteenth century held up as a model for Japanese soldiers.)[7] A Eurasian employee of a Japanese firm was summoned to a meeting where the Japanese boss read the news to his workers, the female Japanese telephonists fainted. He then addressed the local workers in Malay: 'Being the first atom bomb dropped in Japan, our people . . . they just died and [were] killed by the American bomb . . . they just died like dogs. But we Japanese will never forget what is happening by the Americans.'[8] These scenes were played out across Singapore. At the military brothels on nearby Cairnhill, 'there were the Japanese ladies sitting on the five-foot way, looking very bored, nothing more to do'.[9]

The Japanese burnt archives and silenced witnesses to their atrocities. One of the most tragic cases was that of the poet Yu Dafu. After his escape from Singapore he ran a rice wine business with the communist writer and critic Hu Yuzhi, working under assumed names. Their First Love and Gunong Fuji brands were popular with Japanese soldiers. The Japanese used Yu Dafu as an interpreter and he had interceded for many local Chinese by improvising translations to clear suspects under interrogation. He had settled in Bukitinggi with a young Indonesian Chinese wife. It seems the Japanese were made aware of Yu Dafu's true identity. A week or so after the surrender, and on the eve of his wife's giving birth to a child, he was called from his house in his pyjamas. He was never seen again. It seems he had witnessed too much to be left to live. The mystery of his disappearance was a staple theme of local writers for many years afterwards.[10] This was just one disappearance amongst many. Many local police fled, fearing reprisals. The hated Taiwanese auxiliaries went to ground: many were killed, including the man who had brokered the $50 million 'gift' in Singapore. The brutal logic of vendetta took over: 'You done me harm. I don't like you. Now is the chance.'[11]

In the towns people took their 'banana money' for a sudden spending spree. The canniest businesspeople used the cash to pay off their overdrafts, others withdrew it, to buy such goods as they could find. The price of 'Tiger' notes rose from 12:1 to 30:1 against the Japanese currency. In Singapore Japanese profiteers opened the warehouses and sold off their stock. Military and civilians withdrew to the Jurong area in the west, the opposite corner to the European internees at Changi, in trucks loaded with refrigerators and bedding and carpets. The rumour was that they were preparing a scorched earth of consumer goods in advance of the British. All eyes turned to the Cathay Building, where the Japanese flag still flew until 5 September when the first British warships appeared in the Singapore Roads. But on the streets Chinese flags appeared; a few days earlier, possession of them would have brought the Kempeitei down on their owners' heads. Now the Kempeitei were nowhere to be seen. There was one even more profoundly symbolic event. The night the war ended, the three great amusement parks – New World, Great World and Beauty World – were ablaze with neon: the jazz bands struck up 'The Beer Barrel Polka' and hits of the Andrews Sisters. 'Announcements were made in English again. With such attractions, thousands flocked to these parks to celebrate and spend.'[12]

In remote Bahau the Eurasian settlers had their own celebration. The news of the surrender had filtered through the jungle telegraph, but not of the bomb that had caused it. The small garrison of Japanese and Indian police disappeared. The settlers ran up a Union Jack, and threw a party. They sang 'God Save the King' and 'There'll Always Be an England'. As one of them. F. A. C. Oehlers, remembered: 'many of us got drunk that night. You know, how music would travel through an area like that – jungle. And you would hear it for miles. You could hear the singing for miles.' But there were others who heard, and who were displeased to hear the British songs: the 'three-star' guerrillas of the Malayan Peoples' Anti-Japanese Army. They marched into the camp the next day, demanding 'Who told you to put up the Union Jack? We'll tell you what flag to fly.' They raised their own flag with its three stars of the communist resistance. Then came another order: 'No more *mahjong* playing'; an end to gambling. The people came forward with their grievances of war. The guerrilla forces moved through the villages and neighbouring towns, looking for collaborators. Oehlers's father-in-law, who had been a leader of the Eurasian association in Singapore, was arrested. He survived revolutionary justice to face that of the British military.[13] Many others were summarily executed.

In country towns across the peninsula the communist fighters were taking over. British and Indian troops would not land in Penang until 3 September. Not until five weeks after the surrender did they enter the remoter areas. In the interregnum, Malaya belonged to the forgotten armies. In the key battlegrounds of the peninsular war, in Perak and elsewhere, townspeople put up triumphal arches and banners: 'Welcome to the MPAJA'. The first encounter between the British and the Japanese was immediately after the surrender at Forest Lodge in Ipoh, the house of the Chinese magnate Eu Tong Sen. In Perak the senior officer of Force 136, J. P. Hannah, had twenty-one British officers, nine sergeants and around eighty Gurkhas. He was backed by the 5th Independent Regiment of the MPAJA, 800 men strong, under its now-legendary commander Liao Wei Chung, alias Colonel Itu. Hannah went alone to the meeting, escorted by Onishi Satoru, perhaps the most feared Kempeitai operative in Malaya: the man who had captured both Lai Teck and Lim Bo Seng. Hannah refused to shake his hand. 'Even a Rotarian', he commented, 'could not have described the meeting as cordial.' However, he secured from the Japanese governor of Perak an undertaking that the Japanese would not hand out arms to 'unauthorized' persons. The governor relinquished authority with the words, 'These people are pig-headed and deceitful and strong measures are the only things they understand. You are very welcome to them.'[14]

In late August and early September Malaya was on the brink of revolution. The communists began their own negotiations with the Japanese for arms. In several states, including Perak, Negri Sembilan and Kedah, Japanese commanders sent messages that they would be prepared to make them available and fight alongside the communists. Many of the local communist commanders, in the knowledge that the struggle against Japan was already won, were prepared to listen, and held back from attacking them. 'Nothing was further from the Chinese mind', commented one Force 136 officer, many of whose colleagues reported guerrillas making bids for Japanese arms.[15] In the event, most of the party's secret caches of weapons were acquired in this way rather than from the British. Chin Peng was appointed to the Central Military Committee of the party. On the surrender he was summoned to Kuala Lumpur to meet Lai Teck. He intended to report that the party was ready to confront the British. He did not see the secretary-general, but there learned that Lai Teck had other plans.[16] Lai Teck's treachery was yet to be unmasked and many have argued that his foot-dragging at this critical time aborted the chances of a Malayan communist revolution once and for all. Meanwhile, in the most troubled areas, Malay villagers began to mobilize to defend their *kampongs* and their people; at meetings in the mosques there was talk of *jihad* against the Chinese. These conflicts were neither general nor inevitable: in many ways the war had brought the multi-ethnic communities of the region together to an unprecedented degree, in the everyday struggle for survival and in broad anti-imperialist fronts. As the British landing forces headed for their old colonies, they expected to be embraced as liberators. However, with the surrender of Japan, a new phase of the great Asian war had begun.

## FORGOTTEN ARMIES, FORGOTTEN WARS

Victor Purcell, a Chinese-speaking official working in Malaya, remembered what a closed little world Southeast Asia had been before the Second World War. An intricate hierarchy of race and status gave a false sense of permanence. Singapore had experienced an early consumer boom and Japanese economic colonization by stealth. Rangoon was a cosmopolitan city linked to the world beyond by exports of oil, teak and rice. But whole swathes of the region were tied only intermittently to the outside world, while politics was something that lawyers did in the towns. Only deep economic hardship stirred the countryside to action, as had happened during the great peasant revolts of the early 1930s.

This congeries of little worlds was ripped apart and totally reconstructed by the experience of war. The Japanese had violently united the enclaves of British Southeast Asia, imposing on it new uniformities of government and economic management. The social life of the crescent was drawn together by the desperate journeys of armies of fighters, labourers, comfort women and nurses. Indians from Singapore had been propelled far north into Burma to fight alongside Japanese and Burmese from the southern deltas. Coolies from southern India and Chinese slave labourers from Malaya found themselves building a railway on the border between Burma and Thailand.

The British and the Americans then punched two new corridors into the crescent from the north. By the time the atom bomb fell, Pathan soldiers from near Kandahar were serving alongside Africans, British and Australians in the hills and river valleys of southern Burma. Soon they would erupt into the peninsula pursuing the last Japanese and Indian National Army units fleeing south into Thailand and Malaya. The idea of Southeast Asia as a region was itself a product of this violent series of unifications. For many months from 1944 to 1946 Allied South East Asia Command ruled a large part of the whole area from the borders of Bengal and Assam to Singapore and on to the seas north of Australia. Its writ even temporarily penetrated into south China, Indo-China and Indonesia. This was the first time in history that the region was forged into a political unit.

The wrenching of geography into new patterns was nothing compared with the dramatic change in people's ideologies, attitudes and assumptions which had occurred in the short space of four years. The prestige, the face, the *izzat* of British rule had barely survived the Japanese typhoon. In Burma it was never restored and in Malaya it would be restored only because Malays and Chinese businessmen saw it as in their interests to give the British Empire a temporary new lease of life. In India, as almost everybody knew, war, the Bengal famine and the Indian National Army had made independence inevitable. The question was simply what type of independence it would be and when. How far would a residual British influence survive? It was an Indian army, Indian business and Indian labour which had played the major part in the British victory on the Burma front and Indian initiative would now flow strongly into politics. There had also been deeper changes in the way government and politics were regarded. Before the war large parts of the state across the whole region had been content to operate as the classic 'night watchman'. People thought private enterprise was the way to get things done. Now, from left to right, from Malayan communist to Indian businessman, everyone believed that planning and state intervention was the way of the future. Production and organization for war, whether by the Americans, the British Empire or the Japanese, had given people a belief in the state's competence which would become almost a religion.

A new militant nationalism invigorated this renovation of the state. The uniforms, the marching, the drilling and the flag-waving of wartime had indelibly imprinted themselves on the minds of the region's youth. Where in the past Indians, Burmese, Malayans and Nanyang Chinese had at best been led by lawyers tiptoeing around British constitutional provisions designed to render them powerless, now all these nations had martial leaders who embodied a historic form of militant patriotism: Subhas Chandra Bose, Aung San, or, secretly in the jungle, Chin Peng. Even the British had emerged from the war with a new clutch of military heroes, some of whom such as Mountbatten or Slim were surprisingly robust in their views of what an energized and constructive state could achieve at home and abroad. The problem was whose nation and whose state was it to be. Everywhere up and down the crescent the war had mobilized ethnic minorities, indeed it had even created them where they had existed earlier only as categories for anthropologists. Nagas, Kachins, Karens, Lushai, Shans and the Orang Asli of the Malay peninsula had acquired arms and leadership along with a sense of brotherhood, sisterhood and identity. Myriad units of the forgotten armies reforged themselves into the armies of militant small nationalisms. The contest between the big state ruled by the dominant Hindu Indian, Buddhist Burman, Muslim Malay nations and the militant minorities was to play out over the next generation, as the British temporarily regained and finally relinquished their long-lived dream of an eastern empire.

# Notes

## PROLOGUE, PART I: ESCAPING COLONIALISM

1. Herbert P. Bix, *Hirohito and the making of modern Japan* (London, 2000), pp. 384–5.
2. See images in the Japanese Association in Singapore, *Prewar Japanese community in Singapore: picture & record* (Singapore, 1998).
3. Nogi Harumichi, verbal testimony, in Haruko Taya Cook and Theodore F. Cook (eds), *Japan at war: an oral history* (New York, 1992), p. 51.
4. Rana Mitter, *The Manchurian myth: nationalism, resistance and collaboration in modern China* (Berkeley, 2000).
5. Bix, *Hirohito*, pp. 361–6.
6. Ibid., p. 353.
7. 'Burma–Yunnan Road', notes and cuttings, Papers of Sir John Clague, Mss Eur E252/42, OIOC.
8. Robert Slater, *Guns through Arcady: Burma and the Burma Road* (Madras, 1943).
9. The most accessible recent account, based on new Japanese documents, is in Bix, *Hirohito*, pp. 375–83.
10. S. Mitsuru, 'History of the Minami Organ' ('Minami Kikan Geishi'), April 1944, Mss Eur C614, OIOC, f. 1.
11. Statement by Japanese Army Press Chief, reported by Reuters, *Leader* (Allahabad), 3 September 1941.
12. The best description of this activity is found in post-war Allied interrogations of Japanese personnel; see, for example, the depositions of Toshio Otsuka and others in WO203/6312, PRO.
13. 'An analysis of the Malay people', *Al-Imam*, 27 September 1908, in Abu Bakar Hamzah, *Al-Imam: its role in Malay society, 1906–1908* (Kuala Lumpur, 1991), p. 181.
14. Ismail Zain, OHD, SNA.

15. Tomoko Yamazaki, 'Sandakan No. 8 Brothel', *Bulletin of Concerned Asian Scholars*, 7, 4 (1975), pp. 52–62; James Francis Warren, *Ah Ku and Karayuki-san: prostitution in Singapore, 1870–1940* (Singapore, 1993).

16. Clement Liang, 'The Japanese in Penang 1880–1940', The Penang File, 28, http://thepenangfileb.bravepages.com/may-2003/histr282.htm.

17. 'Read This Alone – And the War Can Be Won', Appendix to Masanobu Tsuji, *Singapore: the Japanese version* (London, 1962), p. 302.

18. Virginia Thompson, 'Malayan iron ore for Japan', *Far Eastern Survey*, 10, 11 (1941), pp. 130–1.

19. Sjovald Cunyngham-Brown, *Crowded hour* (London, 1975), pp. 81–2.

20. Izumiya Tatsuro, *The Minami Organ* (Rangoon, 1981), p. 12.

21. The best short English account of the origins of the Minami Kikan, based on Japanese sources remains the classic military history by Louis Allen, *Burma: The longest war* (London, 1984), pp. 17–24.

22. Khin Myo Chit, 'Many a house of life hath held me', Mss Eur D1066/I, OIOC, p. 23.

23. Ibid., pp. 28 ff.

24. Ibid., p. 22; see also U Nu's biography *Saturday's son* (Bombay, 1976).

25. The most up to date and accessible biography of Aung San, which uses many Burmese language reminiscences is Angelene Naw, *Aung San and the struggle for Burmese independence* (Copenhagen, 2001).

26. Ba Maw, *Breakthrough in Burma: memoirs of a revolution 1939–46* (New Haven, 1968), p. 65. Cited Naw, *Aung San*, p. 62.

27. U Ba Than, *The roots of the revolution* (Rangoon, 1962), p. 10.

28. 'History of the Minami Organ', Mss Eur C614, OIOC, f. 6.

29. Aung San, 'Burma's challenge', in Joseph Silverstein (ed.), *The political legacy of Aung San* (Ithaca, 1976), p. 46.

30. Than, *Roots of the revolution*, p. 17.

31. Naw, *Aung San*, p. 78.

32. Robert H. Taylor (ed.), *Marxism and resistance in Burma 1942–1945: Thein Pe Myint's 'Wartime Traveler'* (Athens, Ohio, 1984), pp. 107–10.

33. Memoir of P. E. S. Finney, Special Branch, Calcutta Police, 1939–40, Mss Eur, D1041/4, OIOC, ch. 16, esp. ff. 7–10.

34. 'A general survey of the Indian Independence League and the INA, 30 March 1943', L/WS/1/1576, OIOC.

35. Cited in Leonard A. Gordon, *Brothers against the Raj: a biography of Indian nationalists Sarat and Subhas Chandra Bose* (New York, 1990), p. 329. This is the most accessible recent biography of Subhas Bose.

36. The words were those of the political leader Humayun Kabir, in an

amendment to the war resolution of the Bengal Legislative Council, Office of the Governor of Bengal, R/3/2/10, OIOC.

37. Hugh Toye, *The springing tiger: a study of a revolutionary* (London, 1959), p. 53.

38. Gordon, *Brothers*, p. 412.

39. *Amrita Bazaar Patrika*, 3 July 1940.

40. Assembly debate reported in *Amrita Bazaar Patrika*, 16 July 1940.

41. The house is now a memorial to Subhas Bose, 'Netaji', 'Our Leader'. Impressions have been re-created of Bose's footsteps on the escape route as he stole out on this fateful mission.

42. A. H. C. Ward, Raymond W. Chu and Janet Salaff (eds), *The memoirs of Tan Kah Kee* (Singapore, 1994), pp. 208–27.

43. C. F. Yong, *Tan Kah Kee: the making of an Overseas Chinese legend* (Singapore, 1989), pp. 229–79.

44. Tan Malaka, *From jail to jail*, trans. and intro. Helen Jarvis, vol. II ([1946] Athens, Ohio, 1991), pp. 95–6.

45. Marco C. F. Hsü (trans. Lai Chee Kien), *A brief history of Malayan art* (Singapore, 1999), pp. 64–5; Tan Meng Kiat, 'The evolution of the Nanyang art style: a study in the search for an artistic identity in Singapore, 1930–60', M.Phil. thesis, Hong Kong University of Science and Technology, 1997.

46. Yeo Song Nian and Ng Siew Ai, 'The Japanese Occupation as reflected in Singapore–Malayan Chinese literary works after the Japanese Occupation (1945–49)', in Patricia Lim Pui Huen and Diana Wong (eds), *War and memory in Malaysia and Singapore* (Singapore, 2000), pp. 106–22.

47. C. F. Yong, *The origins of Malayan communism* (Singapore, 1997), pp. 266–7.

48. Ibid., pp. 241–68; Aw Yue Pak, 'The Singapore Overseas Chinese salvation movement', in Foong Choon Hon (ed.), *The price of peace: true accounts of the Japanese occupation* (Singapore, 1991), p. 226.

49. *Singapore Herald*, 21 January, 1941.

50. Virginia Thompson, 'Japan frozen out of Malaya', *Far Eastern Survey*, 10, 20 (1941), pp. 237–40.

51. Chin Peng, *My side of history* (Singapore, 2003), pp. 41–56.

52. Yong, *Origins*, pp. 250–4.

53. Stephen Leong, 'The Kuomintang-Communist United Front in Malaya during the National Salvation period, 1937–1941', *Journal of Southeast Asian Studies*, 8, 1 (1977), pp. 31–47.

54. Yong, *Tan Kah Kee*, p. 57.

55. Tai Yuen, *Labour unrest in Malaya, 1934–41: the rise of the workers' movement* (Kuala Lumpur, 2000), pp. 161–73.

56. Ban Kah Choon, *Absent history: the untold story of Special Branch operations in Singapore, 1915–1942* (Singapore, 2001), pp. 221–8. Dr Ban has been given access to Singapore Special Branch files that are unavailable to other scholars.

57. Mamoru Shinozaki, *Syonan – my story: the Japanese occupation of Singapore* (Singapore, 1979), pp. 1–10.

58. Fujiwari Iwaichi, *F. Kikan: Japanese intelligence operations in Southeast Asia during World War II* (Singapore, 1983), pp. 9, 41; Iwa Iwao Hino and S. Durai Rajasingam, *Stray notes on Nippon–Malaysian historical connections* (Kuala Lumpur, 2004[1944]), pp. 79–81.

59. Cheah Boon Kheng, 'The Japanese occupation of Malaya, 1941–45: Ibrahim Yaacob and the struggle for Indonesia Raya', *Indonesia*, 28 (1979), pp. 85–120.

60. *Syonan Times*, 1 October 1942; Giles Playfair, *Singapore goes off the air* (London, 1944), p. 60.

## PROLOGUE, PART II: JOURNEYS THROUGH EMPIRE

1. Mustapha Hussain, 'Malay nationalism before Umno: the memoirs of Mustapha Hussain, 1910–1957', translated by Insun Mustapha and edited by Jomo K. S., ch. 21. This is a forthcoming translation of a longer Bahasa Melayu published version, Insun Mustapha (ed.), *Memoir Mustapha Hussain: kebangkitan nasionalisme Melayu sebelum UMNO* (Kuala Lumpur, 1999).

2. Sir Shenton Thomas, 'Malaya's war effort', July 1947, BAM papers, RCS; Li Dun Jen, *British Malaya: an economic analysis* ([1955] Kuala Lumpur, 1982), pp. 13–24, 104.

3. Timothy Lindsey, *The romance of K'tut Tantri and Indonesia: text and scripts, history and identity* (Kuala Lumpur, 1997). For Bali's allure more generally, Adrian Vickers, *Bali: a paradise created* (Singapore, 1996).

4. Desmond Pereira, *The sun rises, the sun sets* (Singapore, 1993), pp. 54–5.

5. Jack Edwards, *Banzai, you bastards!* (London, 1990).

6. All quotations are from Jean Cocteau, *Around the world again in 80 days (Mon premier voyage)* ([1936] London, 2000).

7. Philip Ziegler, *Diana Cooper* (London, 1981), p. 208.

8. Lim Cheng Ean memoirs, 'The Penang File', http://thepenangfileb.bravepages.com.

9. Lim Boon Keng, *The Great War from a Confucian point of view* (Singapore, 1917), p. 115.

10. Alice Scott-Ross, *Tun Dato Sir Cheng Lock Tan: a personal profile* (Singapore, 1990), pp. 57–60.

11. Li, *British Malaya*, pp. 62–108.

12. See entries in Victor Sim (ed.), *Biographies of prominent Chinese in Singapore* (Singapore, n.d. [1950]) and Lee Kam Hing and Chow Mun Seong, *Biographical dictionary of the Chinese in Malaysia* (Kuala Lumpur, 1997).

13. Tai Yuen, *Labour unrest in Malaya, 1934–1941: the rise of the workers' movement* (Kuala Lumpur, 2000), p. 10.

14. R. E. Vine, 'Memorandum on the medical aspects of the use of opium and allied drugs in Malaya', 5 December 1944, BMA/DEPT/1/14 Pt 1, Arkib Negara Malaysia [ANM].

15. Tai Yuen, *Labour unrest*, pp. 85–112; C. S. Grey, 'Johore 1910–1941: studies in the colonial process' (Ph.D. thesis, Yale University, 1978), p. 337.

16. Ravindra K. Jain, 'Leadership and authority in a plantation: a case study of Indians in Malaya (c. 1900–42)', in G. Wijeyewardene, *Leadership and authority: a symposium* (Singapore, 1968), pp. 163–73.

17. 'ITBA', *The Planter*, 23, 9 (September 1947), p. 235.

18. S. Arasaratnam, *Indians in Malaya and Singapore* (London, 1970), p. 101.

19. Note by W. L. Blythe to Colonial Office, 12 September 1948, Heussler papers, RHO.

20. Victor Purcell, memorandum, 22 January 1945, BMA/ADM/239, ANM.

21. A. E. Coope to Hugh Bryson, 6 May 1969, Heussler Papers, RHO.

22. John S. Furnivall, *Colonial policy and practice* (Cambridge, 1948).

23. 'A.J.S.T.' [A. J. Shelly-Thompson], *By-laws and history of the Lodge Johore Royal, No. 3946 E.C.* (Johore Bahru, 1922).

24. G. E. Gent, minute, 29 June 1940, CO717/141/7, Public Records Office [PRO]. See also, Grey, 'Johore 1910–1941'.

25. British Consul Jeddah to Foreign Office, 15 June 1942, CO273/671/4, PRO.

26. Syed Naguib al-Attas, *Some aspects of Sufism as understood and practised by the Malays* (Singapore, 1963), pp. 34–48.

27. Pamela Ong Siew Im, *One man's will: a portrait of Dato' Sir Onn bin Ja'afar* (Penang, 1998); Anwar Abdullah, *Dato Onn* (Petaling Jaya, 1971), pp. 50–60.

28. The classic account remains William R. Roff, *The origins of Malay nationalism* (Yale, 1967). See also, Anthony Milner, *The invention of politics in colonial Malaya: contesting nationalism and the expansion of the bourgeois public sphere* (Cambridge, 1995).

29. Mustapha Hussain, 'Malay nationalism', ch. 17.

30. R. H. Bruce Lockhart, *Return to Malaya* (London, 1936), p. 80.

31. Lim Kay Tong, *Cathay: 55 years of cinema* (Singapore, 1991).

32. Peter Fay, *The forgotten army: India's armed struggle for independence, 1942–45* (Ann Arbor, 1992), pp. 46–8.

33. Omar Mohd Noor, 'Three layers', in Edwin Thumboo (ed.), *The second tongue: an anthology of poetry from Malaysia and Singapore* (Singapore, 1976), p. 91.

34. Judith Djamour, *Malay kinship and marriage in Singapore* (London, 1965); Tania Li, *The Malays of Singapore: culture, economy and ideology* (Singapore, 1989), pp. 93–101, 135.

35. Tan Malaka, *From jail to jail*, trans. and intro. Helen Jarvis, vol. II ([1946] Athens, Ohio, 1991), esp. pp. 105–12.

36. In a letter to C. F. Yong, *The origins of Malayan communism* (Singapore, 1997), p. 188.

37. Yoji Akashi, 'Lai Teck, secretary general of the Malayan Communist Party, 1939–1947', *Journal of the South Seas Society*, 49 (1994), pp. 57–103.

38. Chin Peng, *My side of history* (Singapore, 2003), p. 157.

39. For this remarkable man see Henri Chambert-Loir, 'Les Nationalistes Indonesiens vus par un romancier Malais: Shamsuddin Saleh', *Archipel*, 12 (1976), pp. 147–74.

40. Jurgen Rudolph, 'Amusements in the three "worlds"', in S. Krishnan et al. (eds), *Looking at culture* (Singapore, 1996).

41. R. McKie, *This was Singapore* (London, 1952), p. 104.

42. Tan Sooi Beng, *Bangsawan: a social and stylistic history of popular Malay opera* (Singapore, 1993).

43. Mustapha Hussain, 'Malay nationalism', ch. 17.

44. Ong, *One man's will*, p. 50.

45. See Rudolf Mrazek, *Engineers of happy land: technology and nationalism in a colony* (Princeton, 2003).

46. A. H. C. Ward, Raymond W. Chu and Janet Salaff (eds), *The memoirs of Tan Kah Kee* (Singapore, 1994), pp. 193–4.

47. We owe this phrase to Dr J. E. Lewis.

48. C. E. C. Davis, 'Report on the VD situation in Singapore', 9 March 1946, BMA/DEPT/1/2, ANM.

49. H. B. M. Murphy, 'The mental health of Singapore: part one – suicide', *Medical Journal of Malaya*, 9, 1 (1954), pp. 1–45.

50. George Bilainkin, *Hail Penang!* (London, 1933), p. 55.

51. Lockhart, *Return to Malaya*, p. 117.

52. Jeffery Amherst, *Wandering aloud: the autobiography of Jeffery Amherst* (London, 1976), p. 178.

53. C. Blake to Robert Heussler, 5 September 1979, Heussler Papers, RHO.

54. Sir Richard Winstedt, 'Introduction' to Katherine Sim, *Malayan landscape* (London, 1946), p. 8.

55. Henri Falconnier, *The soul of Malaya* ([1931] Singapore, 1985), p. 3.

56. Letter of 17 October, 1941, in Jean Falconer, *Woodsmoke and temple flowers: memories of Malaya* (Edinburgh, 1992), p. 5.

57. McKie, *This was Singapore*, p. 102.

58. For responses, Ashley Gibson, 'Propaganda: report on statements of Malayan evacuees etc. Some observations on the "No roots in the country legend"', BMA/PR/1/6, ANM.

59. O. W. Gilmour, *From Singapore to freedom* (London, n.d. [1943]), pp. 12–13.

60. Bilainkin, *Hail Penang!*, p. 93.

61. Katherine Sim, *Malayan landscape* (London, 1946), pp. 141–7.

62. Lockhart, *Return to Malaya*, pp. 84–5.

63. Giles Playfair, *Singapore goes off air* (London, 1944), p. 49.

64. Maye Wood, *Malay for Mems* (Singapore, 1927).

65. *Straits Times*, 18 September 1933, cited in Christina B. N. Chin, *In service and servitude; foreign female domestic workers and the Malaysian modernity project* (New York, 1998), p. 72.

66. McKie, *This was Singapore*, p. 74.

67. Sir John Mattey to Lord Wigram, 10 March 1937, CO323/1478/3.

68. Gent, minute, 17 February 1937; W. G. Ormsby-Gore, minute, 8 March 1937; Gent, minute, 14 July 1937, CO717/126/9.

69. *Daily Mirror*, 6 November 1940.

70. *Singapore Herald*, 5 January 1941.

71. Barbara Hodgson (ed.), *Letters from Harry: Malaya, 1941–42* (Durham, 1995), p. 4.

72. Ibid., pp. 31–9.

73. Russell Braddon, *The naked island* (London, 1952), pp. 32–6.

74. S. Chelvasingham-MacIntyre, *Through memory lane* (Singapore, 1973), pp. 83–4.

75. David H. Jones, *The rise and fall of the Japanese empire* (London, 1952), p. 206.

76. Fay, *The forgotten army*, p. 65.

77. Gilbert Mant, *You'll be sorry* [1942], reprinted in *The Singapore surrender* (Kuala Lumpur, 1992), p. 152.

78. *INA heroes: the autobiographies of Major-General Shahnawaz, Colonel Prem K. Saghal and Colonel Gurbax Singh Dhillon of the Azad Hind Fauj* (Lahore, 1946), pp. 108–10; 150–51; Peter Ward Fay, *The forgotten army:*

*India's armed struggle for independence, 1942–45* (Ann Arbor, 1992), pp. 55–7.

79. The incident was first recounted in Peter Elphick, *Singapore: the pregnable fortress* (London, 1995), pp. 66–7.

80. Charlie Cheah Fook Ying interview, OHD, SNA.

81. Note of interview with Maj. J. C. K. Marshall, FMSVF, 15 May 1942, WO106/2550B.

82. Konrad Morenweiser, *British Empire civil censorship devices – World War II: British Asia* (London, 1997), p. 83.

83. Victor Purcell, *Memoirs of a Malayan official* (London, 1965), pp. 312–16.

84. *Singapore Herald*, 22 January 1941, 25 February 1941, 26 September 1941.

85. Sir Shenton Thomas, 'Malaya's war effort', July 1947, BAM Papers, RCS.

86. Chan Cheng Yean interview; Joginder Singh interview, OHD, SNA.

87. K. M. Rengavajoo, interview, OHD, SNA.

88. Gilmour, *From Singapore to freedom*, p. 12.

89. Jane Tierney, *Tōbō: one woman's escape* (London, 1985), p. 16.

90. Caroline Reid, *Malayan climax: experiences of an Australian girl in Malaya: 1940–1942* (Hobart, 1943), p. 15.

## CHAPTER I 1941: LAST OF THE INDIAN AND BURMESE DAYS

1. Herbert P. Bix, *Hirohito and the making of modern Japan* (London, 2000), p. 420.

2. Ibid., fn. 82, p. 738.

3. Ibid., p. 423.

4. Eric Stokes to his sister, 21 May 1945, Stokes Papers, Centre of South Asian Studies, Cambridge [CSAS].

5. Sydney Bolt, 'Pseudo Sahib', f. 3, CSAS.

6. Viceroy's Commissioned Officers (VCOs) were Indians who had generally risen through the ranks and had been trained at Indian military academies. King's Commissioned Officers were men who had trained as officers at military academies in Britain and the Dominions. Very few Indians were able to take this route.

7. Maj.-Gen. K. K. Tewari, *A soldier's voyage of self-discovery* (Auroville, 1995), pp. 1–5.

8. A. M. Bose to Ian Stephens, undated [October 1943], Stephens Box 20, CSAS.

9. D. K. Palit, *Major General A. A. Rudra: his services in three armies and two world wars* (Delhi, 1997), p. 252.

10. John Connell, *Auchinleck: a biography of Field-Marshal Sir Claude Auchinleck* (London, 1959), pp. 20–60.

11. Palit, *Rudra*, p. 72.

12. Smith Dun, *Memoirs of the four-foot colonel: General Dun Smith, first commander-in-chief of the independent Burmese armed forces* (Ithaca, 1980), pp. 8–10.

13. *Two years of war, being a summary of important matters connected with the Indian defence services with special reference to the year 1940–1* (Delhi, 1941), p. 15.

14. Margaret Stavridi, 'The civilian war effort in Bengal for the welfare of the forgotten army of the east, 1942–6', Stavridi Papers Box 1, CSAS.

15. *Two years of war*, p. 25.

16. Victor Bayley, *Is India impregnable?* (London, 1941), p. 208.

17. *Leader*, 4 September 1941.

18. *Leader*, 6 September 1941.

19. *Leader*, 3 September 1941.

20. *Leader*, 11 September 1941.

21. *Leader*, 13 September 1941.

22. Dr Percival Spear, 'The development of new ideas through danger and suffering', *Leader*, 23 September 1941.

23. *Leader*, 18 September 1941.

24. Goods provided 'on loan' by the Americans to help the Chinese war effort.

25. Note by J. A. Stewart, January 1942, Clague Papers, Mss Eur E252/44, f. 3, OIOC.

26. In 1947 when the future of the Frontier Areas was under discussion a large volume of documentation reaching back into the nineteenth century was put together, see Burma Frontier Areas Committee of Enquiry, Cmd. 7138 (1947) and related papers, Clague Papers, Mss Eur E252/23, OIOC.

27. 'Karen and Kachin Levies', Burma Governor's Papers, M/3/1221, OIOC.

28. 'The Kachins', note by J. L. Leyden, 8 January 1943, Clague Papers, Mss Eur E 252/44, ff. 29–36, OIOC.

29. Ibid., f. 34, OIOC.

30. Dorman-Smith, Memoirs, Mss Eur E215/32, a/b, f. 207, OIOC.

31. Ibid., f. 7.

32. Ibid, f. 10.

33. Maurice Collis, *Last and first in Burma* (London, 1956), p. 41. This is a politer version of Dorman-Smith's memoir in OIOC.

34. Lady Dorman-Smith to Miss Mary McAndrew, 18 May 1941, Dorman-Smith Papers, Mss Eur E215/46, OIOC.

35. Robert Slater, *Guns through Arcady: Burma and the Burma Road* (Madras, 1943), p. 12.

36. A. C. Potter to R. E. Potter, 7 September 1941, A. C. Potter Papers, Mss Eur C414/6, OIOC.

37. Donnison Memoirs, F. S. V. Donnison Papers, Mss Eur B357, f. 307, OIOC.

38. John Clague, Memoir, Mss Eur D252/72, pp. 3–4, OIOC.

39. Donnison Memoirs, f. 306.

40. Maurice Maybury, *The heaven-born in Burma* (Castle Cary, 1985), I, p. 82.

41. *Rangoon Times*, 15 August 1941.

42. Ma Than E, 'Burma's ties with China', *Statesman*, 8 March 1942.

43. *Rangoon Times*, 19 August 1941.

44. Notes on Indian Immigration by H.F. Searle, ICS, Commissioner of Settlements and Land Records Burma, Reforms Department, Government of Burma, Clague Papers, Mss Eur E252/38, OIOC.

45. Searle Report, Clague Papers Mss Eur E252/38, f. 6, OIOC.

46. Note by F. G. Beestra, Indian Police, 'Attitude of the Burmese People in the late campaign in Burma', Arnold Papers, Mss Eur F145/6b, ff. 61ff., OIOC.

47. E. J. L. Jackson, *Indian labour in Rangoon* (Oxford, 1933).

48. Searle Report, f. 14.

49. B. R. Pearn, *The Indian in Burma* (Ledbury, Herts., 1946), p. 18.

50. W. S. Desai, 'Burmese attitudes to Indian immigration', Clague Papers, Mss Eur E252/38, ff. 62–6, OIOC.

51. 'Report of the Committee on the Buddhist–Muslim Riots of 26 July 1938', Clague Papers, Mss Eur E252/48, OIOC.

52. 'Burma's ties with China', *Statesman*, 8 March 1942.

53. Slater, *Guns through Arcady*, p. 138.

54. 'Burma's ties with China', *Statesman*, 8 March 1942.

55. W. G. Burchett, *Bombs over Burma* (Melbourne, 1944) p. 86.

56. A. C. Potter to R. E. Potter, Bristol, 3 August 1941, Potter Papers, Mss Eur C414/6, OIOC.

57. Dorman-Smith, Memoirs, ff. 10–12.

58. Ibid., f. 14.

59. Jack Belden, *Retreat with Stilwell* (London, 1943) p. 47.

60. Governor Burma to Secretary of State Burma, and appended minutes, 28 Sept 1941, 'Visit of U Saw', M/3/1113, OIOC.

61. Governor of Burma to Secretary of State, 28 September 1941, M/3/1113, OIOC.

62. U Nu, *Saturday's son*, (Bombay, 1976), p. 91.

63. Ba Maw, *Breakthrough in Burma: memoirs of a revolution 1939–46* (New Haven, 1968).

64. 'Life of Ba Maw', in Peter Murray, British Ambassador to Burma, to B. R. Pearn, Foreign Office Research Department, 21 November 1950, f. 5. This letter appends the fragmentary ms account of his life and anti-British activities Ba Maw appears to have prepared for himself in 1943, Governor of Burma's Office, R/8/38, OIOC.

65. Ibid, f. 8.

66. General Alexander took part in the retreat to Dunkirk and in 1942 commanded the retreat from Burma into India. He went on to distinguished service in the Western Desert and in France.

67. Dorman-Smith, Memoirs, f. 281.

68. Tour notes, July 1941, Papers of E.T. Cook, Dorman-Smith Papers, Mss Eur E215/32b, f. 18, OIOC.

69. Ibid. f. 32.

70. A. C. Potter to R. E. Potter, 11 August 1941, Potter Papers, Mss Eur C 414/6, OIOC.

71. *Rangoon Times*, 4 September 1941.

72. A. C. Potter to R. E. Potter, 11 August 1941.

73. *Rangoon Times*, 4 September 1941.

74. *Rangoon Times*, 5 September 1941.

75. General and Air HQ India, intelligence summary, 30 September 1941, L/WS/1/317, f. 18, OIOC.

76. Note on the Karens, Clague Papers, Mss Eur E252/22, p. 4, OIOC.

77. Minute by C. G. Stewart, Director Burma Defence Bureau, 15 October 1941, 'Visit of U Saw', M/3/1113, OIOC.

78. Cook to Devonshire, 9 September 1941, Papers of Major E. T. Cook, Mss Eur E215/35b, OIOC.

79. A. C. Potter to R. E. Potter, 12 November 1941, Potter Papers, Mss Eur C414/6, OIOC.

80. Note by L. S. Amery, 24 January 1942, PREM 4/50/2, PRO.

81. Linlithgow to Amery, 19 January 1942, PREM 4/50/2, PRO.

## CHAPTER 2 1942: A VERY BRITISH DISASTER

1. 'An appreciation of the value of Singapore to Asia', n.d., DEF331 Pt 2, A981/11, NAA, SNA.

2. For the background we have drawn on two excellent new studies: M. H. Murfett et al., *Between two oceans: a military history of Singapore from first settlement to final British withdrawal* (Singapore, 1999) and Brian Farrell and Sandy Hunter (eds), *Sixty years on: the fall of Singapore revisited* (Singapore, 2002). See also, J. L. Neidpath, *The Singapore naval base and the defence of Britain's eastern empire, 1918–1941* (Oxford, 1981); Raymond Callahan, *The worst disaster: the fall of Singapore* (Singapore, 1991).

3. Mamoru Shinozaki, *Syonan – my story: the Japanese occupation of Singapore* (Singapore, 1979), pp. 1–10.

4. Some comments on the Malayan Campaign by G. Morgan, Senior Executive Engineer, Malayan Public Works Service, Bombay 23 July, 1942', WO106/2550B.

5. Sir Earle Page to A. W. Fadden, 16 November 1941, 475/1, A5954/1, NAA, SNA.

6. See Ong Chit Chung, *Operation Matador: World War II – Britain's attempt to foil the Japanese invasion of Malaya and Singapore* (Singapore, 2002).

7. Sir Josiah Crosby to J. F. Babbington, 15 July 1940, FAR 16, A981/1, NAA, SNA.

8. Callahan, *The worst disaster*, pp. 181–2.

9. Brian Montgomery, *Shenton of Singapore: governor and prisoner of war* (Singapore, 1984), p. 53.

10. For an extended analysis of Vlieland's views, see Louis Allen, *Singapore, 1941–42* (2nd edn, London, 1993), pp. 226–46.

11. For a well-balanced and sympathetic portrait see Clifford Kinvig, *Scapegoat: General Percival of Singapore* (London, 1996), p. 106.

12. Lt.-Col. Roland Frank Oakes, 'Singapore Story', November 1947, AWM, SNA.

13. 'Note on interview with Maj. J. C. Westall, RM, 15 May 1942'. Westall was formerly SOI Singapore, WO106/2550B.

14. Cecil Lee, *Sunset of the Raj: fall of Singapore, 1942* (Durham, 1994), p. 57.

15. Philip Ziegler, *Diana Cooper* (London, 1981), p. 208.

16. John Charmley, *Duff Cooper: the authorised biography* (London, 1986), pp. 156–7.

17. Lady Diana Cooper, *Trumpets from the steep* (London, 1984), p. 127.

18. Paul H. Kratoska, *The Japanese occupation of Malaya, 1941–45* (London, 1998), pp. 28–9; Lim Heng Kow, *The evolution of the urban system in Malaya* (Kuala Lumpur, 1978); J. Innes Miller, *Changi Guardian*, 55, 13 May 1942, BAM, RCS.

19. Dato Haji Mohamed Yusoff Bangs interview, OHD, SNA.

20. John Dean Potter, *A soldier must die: the biography of an oriental general* (London, 1963), p. 205.

21. Yoji Akashi, 'General Yamashita Tomoyuki: Commander of the Twenty-fifth Army', in Farrell and Hunter, *Sixty years on*, pp. 185–207.

22. Richard J. Aldrich, *Intelligence and the war against Japan: Britain, America and the politics of secret service* (Cambridge, 2000), p. 46.

23. 'Read This Alone – and the War Can Be Won', Appendix to Masanobu Tsuji, *Singapore: the Japanese version* (London, 1962), pp. 295–349.

24. Ong, *Operation Matador*, pp. 227–33.

25. J. Innes Miller, *Changi Guardian*, 55, 13 May 1942, BAM, RCS; Peter Elphick, *Singapore: the pregnable fortress* (London, 1995), p. 224.

26. There is a vast literature on the fall of Malaya and Singapore. The best single account remains Allen, *Singapore, 1941–42*; see also Alan Warren, *Singapore, 1942* (London, 2002).

27. Tsuji, *Singapore*, p. 263; 'Extracts from a letter to his father by a staff officer of the 18th Division – sent to the Prime Minister', 19 June 1942, WO106/2550B.

28. 'Some comments on the Malayan Campaign by G. Morgan'.

29. Entry for 29 January 1942, [Nakane] 'My Diary 1942', BAM Collection, RHO.

30. See the discussion in Warren, *Singapore*, pp. 65–77.

31. Lim Kean Siew. *Blood on golden sands: the memoirs of a Penang family* (Kuala Lumpur, 1999), pp. 25–32, 35.

32. A. H. C. Ward, Raymond W. Chu and Janet Salaff (eds), *The memoirs of Tan Kah Kee* (Singapore, 1994), p. 152.

33. A. L. Stallworthy, *Changi Guardian*, 27 April 1942.

34. E. A. Davis, 'The Blitz on Penang', 22 December 1941, WO106/2550A; Lim, *Blood on golden sands*, pp. 39–40.

35. Dr Oscar Elliot Fisher, Diary of Japanese Invasion of Malaya, 11 and 12 December 1941 http://freespace.virgin.net/sam.campbell/grandpa1a.html.

36. L. Forbes, resident commissioner, Penang, *Changi Guardian*, 20 May 1942.

37. 'Malaya Broadcast Corporation Monitoring Station, WIR 2', 24 December 1941, A981/1, NAA, SNA.

38. J. N. Cooley, 'Report on personal experiences in Penang', 13 January 1942; E. H. Bode, untitled memo, 29 December 1941, CO106/2550A.

39. Fisher, 'Diary', 16 December 1941; J. A. Quitzow, 'Penang experiences', 27 January 1942, CO106/2550A.

40. Described in Lim, *Blood on golden sands*, pp. 55–6, 59.

41. War Office to C-in-C Far East, 21 December 1941; War Cabinet, 'Evacuation of civilians from Singapore', 22 December 1941, WO106/2534, PRO.

42. A. E. Percival, *The war in Malaya* (London, 1949), p. 179.

43. Conclusions of War Cabinet, 22 December 1941, WO106/2534.

44. Diary entry, cited in Charmley, *Duff Cooper*, p. 160.

45. 'Statement of L. W. C. Byrne', CO273/673/7.

46. 'Speech of Pritam Singh on the occasion of the opening of the Indian Independence League in Bangkok requesting the Indians to refrain from helping the British War efforts', 9 December 1941, in T. R. Sareen (ed.), *Select documents on the Indian National Army* (Delhi, 1988), p. 3.

47. 'Capt. Mohan Singh to Major Fujiwara Iwaichi for the willingness of India prisoners of war to join hands with Japanese forces and to form the INA to fight the British', 31 December 1941, in Sareen, *Select documents*, pp. 4–7.

48. 'A note on the role of the Fujiwara Kikan volunteers in the surrender of the British forces in Singapore', in Sareen, *Select documents*, pp. 24–32.

49. C. C. Brown, 'The war in Pahang', *Changi Guardian*, 21, 3 April 1942.

50. N. Rees, *Changi Guardian*, 29 April 1942.

51. N. F. H. Matter, British resident Perak, *Changi Guardian*, 10 April 1942.

52. Felix Inggold to HH The Rajah of Sarawak, *Sarawak Gazette*, 10 October 1942, BMA Collection, RCS.

53. Ho Thean Fook, *Tainted glory* (Kuala Lumpur, 2000), pp. 23–34.

54. W. D. Brown, extract from the 'Madras ARP Journal for May: Exit Klang', W. D. Brown Papers, BAM collection, RCS.

55. Dudley Robinson, authors' interview.

56. Goh Eck Kheng (ed.), *Life and death in Changi: the war and internment diary of Thomas Kitching (1942–1944)* (Singapore, 2002), p. 32; N. R. Jarret, 'The war in Selangor', *Changi Guardian*, 8 April 1942.

57. Shenton Thomas, 'Malaya's war effort', July 1947, BAM Collection, RCS.

58. Tsuji, *Singapore*, p. 179.

59. Callahan, *The worst disaster*, p. 247.

60. This was a letter of 18 December, delivered by hand; it did not reach Churchill until 6 January. Discussed in Callahan, *The worst disaster*, p. 249.

61. Ziegler, *Diana Cooper*, p. 213.

62. Ibid.

63. Montgomery, *Shenton of Singapore*, p. 109.

64. Aldrich, *Intelligence and the war against Japan*, p. 45.

65. Cheah Boon Kheng, 'The Japanese occupation of Malaya, 1941–45: Ibrahim Yaacob and the struggle for Indonesia Raya', *Indonesia*, 28 (1979), pp. 99–100; Fujiwari Iwaichi, F. *Kikan: Japanese intelligence operations in Southeast Asia during World War II* (Singapore, 1983), pp. 99–100, 114–16, 201–11.

66. Mustapha Hussain, 'Malay Nationalism Before Umno: the Memoirs Of Mustapha Hussain, 1910–1957', translated by Insun Mustapha and edited by Jomo K.S., chs. 21–2.

67. H. W. Begbie to Mrs Begbie, 27 March 1942, WO106/2550B.

68. 'Note of interview with Maj. J. C. K. Marshall'.

69. 'Interview with Maj. W. H. Aucutt, FMSVF, 5 June, 1942', WO106/2550B.

70. Mahmud bin Mat, *Tinggal kenangan: the memoirs of Dato' Sir Mahmud bin Mat* (Kuala Lumpur, 1997), pp. 250–4.

71. 'Interview with Maj. W. H. Aucutt'; Col. J. Jones, memo, 1 February 1946, XL39794, NARA, SNA.

72. 'Some comments on the Malayan Campaign by G. Morgan'.

73. For this incident, Ian Ward, *Snaring the other tiger* (Singapore, 1996).

74. Callahan, *The worst disaster*, p. 257.

75. 'Some comments on the Malayan Campaign by G. Morgan'.

76. Maurice Baker, *A time of fireflies and wild guavas* (Singapore, 1999), p. 62.

77. Tsuji, *Singapore*, p. 213.

78. [Nakane] 'My Diary 1942', BAM Collection, RHO.

79. Ibid.

80. Inggold to Rajah of Sarawak.

81. Giles Playfair, *Singapore goes off the air* (London, 1944).

82. William Shaw, *Tun Razak: his life and times* (Kuala Lumpur, 1976), p. 41.

83. M. C. Hay, MCS, diary, 9 January 1942, BAM Collection, RCS.

84. Michael Moore, *Battalion at war: Singapore, 1942* (Norwich, 1988); Roland Frank Oakes, 'Singapore Story', November 1947.

85. 'Note of interview with Maj. J. C. K. Marshall'.

86. Oakes, 'Singapore Story'; Kratoska, *The Japanese occupation*, p. 43. For the military details of the final defence of Singapore, the best guide is Murfett et al., *Between two oceans*, pp. 215–38.

87. 'Note of interview with Maj. J. C. K. Marshall'.

88. Chin Peng, *My side of history* (Singapore, 2003), p. 65.

89. SOE (Meerut), 'OM Operations in Malaya', April 1942, HS1/115, PRO; Ban Kah Choon and Yap Hong Kuan, *Rehearsal for war: resistance and the underground war against the Japanese and the Kempeitai, 1942–1945* (Singapore, 2002), pp. 31–3.

90. A. H. C. Ward, Raymand W. Chu and Janet Salaff (eds), *The memoirs of Tan Kah Kee* (Singapore, 1994), p. 157.

91. Hu Tie Jun, 'A letter to the British advisor of Malayan affairs (The Parkerton open letter)' [1945], in Foong Choon Hon (ed.), *The price of peace: true accounts of the Japanese occupation* (Singapore, 1991), pp. 281–8.

92. Tan Malaka, *From jail to jail*, trans. and intro. Helen Jarvis, vol. II ([1946] Athens, Ohio, 1991), p. 115.

93. 'Note of interview with Maj. J. C. K. Marshall'; Frank Brewer, interview, OHD, SNA.

94. A. H. C. Ward, Raymond W. Chu and Janet Salaff (eds), *The memoirs of Tan Kah Kee* (Singapore, 1994), pp. 156–9.

95. Arthur Gerald Donahue, *Last flight from Singapore* (London, 1944), pp. 40–54.

96. 'Note of interview with Maj. J. C. K. Marshall'.

97. Jack Edwards, *Banzai, you bastards!* (London, 1990), p. 18.

98. Lee, *Sunset of the Raj*, p. xvi.

99. Charles Huxtable, *From the Somme to Singapore* (London, 1987), p. 54.

100. Mrs M. R. S. Segeram interview, OHD, SNA.

101. H. R. Oppenheim, diary, 8 February 1942, BMA Collection, RCS. Lee Kip Lin interview, OHD, SNA.

102. Edward William Burrey, 'A diary 1942–45: HQ Coy AASC, 8th Division AIF', AWM, SNA.

103. Oppenheim diary.

104. Playfair, *Singapore goes off the air*, pp. 105, 113–14; Montgomery, *Shenton of Singapore*, p. 132.

105. Lee Tian Soo interview, OHD, SNA.

106. Revd A. J. Bennitt, *Changi Guardian*, 10 June 1942.

107. P. C. Marcus interview, OHD, SNA.

108. Kheng, *Life and death in Changi*, p. 58.

109. 'The last days of Singapore, 8 May, 1942. By Val Kobouky', WO 106/2550B.

110. Described in Henry P. Frei, 'The island battle: Japanese soldiers remember the conquest of Singapore', in Farrell and Hunter, *Sixty years on*, pp. 218–39.

111. [Nakane] 'My Diary 1942'.

112. Oppenheim diary, 10 February, 1942.

113. 'Report by GSOI – Malaya Comd', WO106/2550B.

114. Here we have drawn chiefly on Callahan, *The worst disaster*, pp. 15–19, and Allen, *Singapore 1941–42*.

115. H. Fraser, 'The last days of Singapore', *Changi Guardian*, 19, 1 April 1942.

116. Kinvig, *Scapegoat*, pp. 217–20.

117. Tsuji, *Singapore*, p. 269.

118. Edwards, *Banzai, you bastards!*, p. 18.

119. Oppenheim diary, 15 February 1942.

120. Chan Chen Yean interview, OHD, SNA.

121. [Nakane] 'My Diary 1942'.

122. Gay Wan Guay interview, OHD, SNA.

123. Robert Chong interview, OHD, SNA.

124. Shinozaki, *Syonan – my story*, pp. 1–10.

125. Denis Russell-Roberts, *Spotlight on Singapore* (Douglas, 1965), pp. 143–4.

126. Ibid., p. 150.

127. Peter Ward Fay, *The forgotten army: India's armed struggle for independence, 1942–45* (Ann Arbor, 1992), pp. 69–70.

128. *INA heroes: the autobiographies of Major-General Shahnawaz, Colonel Prem K. Saghal and Colonel Gurbax Singh Dhillon of the Azad Hind Fauj* (Lahore, 1946), pp. 112–13.

129. Ibid., pp. 15, 43.

130. Ibid., pp. 3, 16–17.

131. Russell-Roberts, *Spotlight on Singapore*, p. 150.

132. For casualty figures see Allen, *Singapore 1941–42*, pp. 270–1.

133. 'The last days of Singapore, 8 May, 1942. By Val Kobouky'.

134. Joseph Kennedy, *British civilians and the Japanese war in Malaya and Singapore, 1941–45* (London, 1987), pp. 62–83.

135. Betty Jeffrey, *White coolies* (London, 1971 [1954]), p. 4.

136. This was Margot Turner, who later went to head the organization, see Sir John Smyth, *The will to live: the story of Dame Margot Turner* (London, 1978), pp. 28–48.

137. Capt. McPherson, Argylls, in 'Various people's views and assertions on some contradictory causes for the fall of Singapore', Oppenheim diary, 15 February 1942.

138. Stephen Gordon Tailor, 'Some notes on personal observations on the Malaya campaign written on the request of Room 055 War Office', 19 September 1942, WO106/2550B.

139. 'Note on interview with Maj. J. C. Westall RM', 15 May 1942; 'Note

on interview with Maj. T. Wardrop Army Audit Staff HQ Malaya Command on 7 May 1942'; 'Intercepted letter – H. K. Hardwick, Colombo, to A. F. Eaden, London', 5 May 1942; 'Report by GSOI – Malaya Comd', WO106/2550B.

140. David H. Jones, *The rise and fall of the Japanese empire* (London, 1952), p. 224.

141. W. G. Bowden to Dept External Affairs, 13 February 1942, 1/301/479, CRS A816/1, NAA.

142. W. S. Morgan, minute, 11 January 1946; Commissioner of Police to P. McKerron, 1 October 1945; J. C. Burn to A. Newboult, 20 September 1945, CO273/673/7, PRO.

143. A. H. Dickinson to Sir Edward Gent, 22 December 1945; statement by Boyle, 9 July 1942, CO273/673/7, PRO.

144. 'Excerpts from Lim Bo Seng's diary', in Foong, *The price of peace*, pp. 148–52.

145. Lee Hock Chye, *Comfort homes and earlier years* (Kuala Lumpur, n.d.), pp. 22–8.

146. Soon Kim Seng interview, OHD, SNA.

147. Foong Choon Hon, 'The intellectual's bayonet: an interview with Zhang Chu Kun, former deputy major of Xiamen', in Foong, *The price of peace*, pp. 202–4, 210–11.

148. Oppenheim diary, 28 February 1942.

149. Janet Lim, *Sold for silver* (London, 1958), and see the reconstruction in Richard Gough, *SOE Singapore, 1941–42* (London, 1985), pp. 169–94.

150. 'Note on the Malayan Chinese organisation up to the loss of Malaya', 16 November 1943; 'OM operations in Malaya', 15 October 1943, HS1/114, PRO.

151. Ho, *Tainted glory*, pp. 35–54.

152. Chin Peng, *My side of history*, pp. 68–72.

153. *Syonan Times*, 9 September 1942; *Syonan Shimbun*, 12 February 1943.

154. Harold Nicolson, *Diaries and letters, 1930–67* (London, 1980), entry for 17 February 1942.

## CHAPTER 3 1942: DEBACLE IN BURMA

1. Louis Allen, *Burma: the longest war*, (London, 1984) pp. 5–6.

2. Herbert P. Bix, *Hirohito and the making of modern Japan* (London, 2000), p. 446.

3. A major source for the following narrative is the semi-official 'Report on

the Burma campaign 1941–2' writen by Dorman-Smith and his staff in the autumn of 1943, see Dorman-Smith Papers, E215/28, OIOC. For the first air raids see ibid, p. 104.

4. Dorman-Smith to L. Amery, 19 January 1942, Dorman-Smith Papers, Mss Eur E215/1, OIOC.

5. Dorman-Smith to Amery, 25 January 1942, Mss Eur E215/1, OIOC.

6. Lt. Gen. Sir T. J. Hutton to Wavell, 7 March 1942, Laithwaite Papers, Mss Eur F138/75, f. 7, OIOC.

7. Dorman-Smith to Amery, 27 January 1942, Mss Eur E215/1, OIOC.

8. Jack Belden, *Retreat with Stilwell* (London, 1943), p. 7.

9. Diary of Lt. Col. W. E. V. Abraham, Liaison Officer from the Middle East, 5 March 1942, Abraham Papers, Centre of South Asian Studies, Cambridge [CSAS].

10. 'Report on the Burma campaign', pp. 105–7.

11. Dorman-Smith to Amery, 11 February 1942, Mss Eur E215/1, OIOC.

12. Dorman-Smith to Amery, 17 February 1942, Mss Eur E215/1, OIOC.

13. E.g. Hutton to Wavell, 7 March 1942, Laithwaite Papers, Mss Eur F138/75, f. 14, OIOC.

14. Hans J. van de Ven, *War and nationalism in China, 1925–45* (London, 2003), pp. 19–64.

15. For the background see, e.g., Felix Smith, *China pilot: flying for Chiang and Chennault* (London, 1995).

16. *Statesman*, 24 May 1942, 'The last days in Rangoon'.

17. Abraham diary, 5 March 1942, CSAS.

18. Dorman-Smith, Memoirs, MSS Eur 215/32, a/b, ff. 155–62, OIOC, presents by far the most dramatic picture of the fall of Rangoon, but is mostly unpublished.

19. F. B. Arnold, Note on the food supply in Burma, December 1941-April 1942, late 1942?, Arnold Papers, Mss Eur F145/2, OIOC.

20. Kenneth (Maung Khe) Sein and J. A. Withey, *A chronicle of the Burmese theater: the great Po Sein* (Indiana, 1965), p. 117.

21. Dorman-Smith, Memoirs, f. 293.

22. Dorman-Smith to Amery, 16 January 1942, Mss Eur E215/1, OIOC.

23. 'Report on the Burma Campaign', Dorman-Smith Papers, 28, pp. 111–12, OIOC.

24. Dorman-Smith, Memoirs, f. 156.

25. Appendix 5 to 'Report on the Burma Campaign', Simla 1943, Dorman-Smith Papers, Mss Eur E215/28, f. 10, OIOC.

26. Ibid., f. 158.

27. Ibid.

28. Dorman-Smith to Amery, 8 March 1942, Mss Eur E215/1, OIOC.

29. Donnison, Memoirs, Donnison Papers, Mss Eur B357, f. 374, OIOC.

30. Field Marshal Alanbrooke, *War diaries 1939–45*, ed. Alex Danchev and Daniel Todman (London, 2001), 19 February 1942, p. 232.

31. Ibid., 23 January 1942, p. 227.

32. Wavell to Hutton, 29 June 1942, cf. Dorman-Smith to Hutton, 24 January, 1943, Hutton Papers, 3, Liddell Hart Centre for War Studies, King's College London.

33. Governor to secretary of state, 28 February 1942, L/WS/1/706, OIOC.

34. Dorman-Smith, Memoirs, f. 161.

35. 'Report on the Burma Campaign', pp. 114–16.

36. The whole issue of the performance of the civil service during the invasion was discussed in an interesting correspondence between the former official and civil servant Philip Mason and W. I. J. Wallace, a Burma civil servant, after the war, see Mason to Wallace, 19 September 1949, etc., Wallace Papers, Mss Eur E338/7. See also Mason's conclusion in *The men who ruled India*, vol. II (London, 1963), the first edition of which was published under Mason's pseudonym Philip Woodruff.

37. The evidence was first reviewed by Hugh Tinker, see 'The Indian exodus from Burma 1942', *Journal of South East Asian Studies*, 6, 1, 1975, pp. 1–22. More official and other papers have become available since then and a mean between Tinker's rather low figure and the high figures given by Indian nationalists and British critics of the governments of India and Burma has been taken.

38. 'The Civil Evacuation', appendix to 'Report on Burma Campaign', p. 16. This is a major source for the narrative in the following pages, adjusted by private accounts.

39. 'Report on the Evacuation from Burma' by R. Hutchings, agent to the government of India (late 1942?), Hutton Papers 3/18, Liddell Hart Centre.

40. H. C. Mukherji, 'The rich at Rangoon', *Statesman*, 25 March 1942.

41. 'Civil evacuation', Dorman-Smith Papers, Mss Eur E215/28, p. 23, OIOC.

42. Ibid., p. 26.

43. Sugii Mitsuru, 'Minami Kikan', Mss Eur C614, f. 46, OIOC.

44. Izumiya Tatsuro, *The Minami Organ* (Rangoon, 1981), pp. 144–6.

45. Thakin Nu, *Burma under the Japanese: pictures and portraits*, ed. and trans. J. S. Furnivall, (London, 1954), p. 20.

46. Ba Maw's draft autobiography, 1943, in Peter Murray to B. R. Pearn, 21 November 1950, Burma Governor's Office, R/8/38, f. 27, OIOC.

47. 'Indian Censorship', 27 May 1945, Burma Governor's Office, R/8/40, OIOC.

48. Dorman-Smith, Memoirs, f. 37.

49. U Ba Than, *The roots of the revolution* (Rangoon, 1962), p. 32.

50. Maung Maung, *To a soldier son* (Rangoon, 1974), p. 17.

51. Abraham, Diary, 4 March 1942, CSAS.

52. Maung, *To a soldier son*, p. 18.

53. Maurice Maybury, *Heaven-born in Burma*, vol. II, *Flight of the heaven born* (Castle Cary, 1985), p. 120.

54. Belden, *Retreat with Stilwell*, pp. 49–50.

55. Thein Pe Myint, 'Wartime Traveller', in R. H. Taylor, *Marxism and resistance in Burma 1942–5* (Athens, Ohio, 1984), p. 107.

56. Lady Dorman-Smith to Cpl Patricia Dorman-Smith, 10 April 1942, Dorman-Smith Papers, Mss Eur E215/46, OIOC.

57. 'Report on the Burma Campaign', p. 133.

58. Ruth Donnison to her family, 6 December 1942, inserted in Frank Donnison, Memoir, Donnison Papers, Mss Eur B357, f. 367 (b), OIOC.

59. Frank to Percy Marmian (Burma Corp. Ltd), 16 June 1942, p. 12, Clague Papers, Mss Eur E252/44, f. 4, OIOC.

60. Donnison, Memoirs, f. 341.

61. Stephen Brookes, *Through the jungle of death: a boy's escape from wartime Burma* (London, 2002), p. 17.

62. Ann Purton, *The safest place* (Wells-next-the-Sea, 1982), p. 153.

63. Brookes, *Jungle of death*, pp. 73–6.

64. Dorman-Smith, Memoirs, f. 41.

65. Ibid., f. 168.

66. 'Survey of the situation in Burma during the Japanese invasion of Burma by Sir Reginald Dorman-Smith', July 1942, L/WS/1/568, OIOC.

67. Sein and Withey, *Chronicle of the Burmese theater*, p. 127.

68. Tatsuro, *The Minami Organ*, p. 149.

69. Mitsuru, 'Minami Kikan', f. 69.

70. Ibid., f. 6.

71. Records of Ms F. D. Edmeades concerning the Hukawng evacuation, 1942, Steel Bros. Records, Box B, Empire and Commonwealth Museum, Bristol.

72. 'A last ditcher' to the editor, *Statesman*, 1 April 1942.

73. Personal accounts of the 1942 retreat, Capt. Coutts, Mss Eur E375/11, OIOC. Material is also drawn from the accounts of A. G. McCrae, F. F. Musgrave and Supercargo Paxton.

74. There are numerous accounts of these horrors; see esp. that of Eric Battersby, Dorman-Smith Papers, Mss Eur E215/59, OIOC.

75. *Indian Tea Association report on the evacuation of troops and civilians*

*from Burma via the Pangsan route, Namyang River to Lekhpani, May to July, 1942,* (Calcutta, 1944?), p. 37.

76. A. C. Potter to R. E. Potter, 16 June 1942, Potter Papers, Mss Eur C414/7, OIOC.

77. *Tea Association Report*, p. 41.

78. Letter to *Statesman*, 17 April 1942.

79. Minute re. Tea Association Labour Officer, Indian Tea Association Papers, Mss Eur F174/1310, OIOC.

80. A. H. Pilcher, *Navvies to the Fourteenth Army* (Delhi, 1945), R. Palmer Papers, CSAS.

81. *Statesman*, 18 April 1942.

82. Memoir of Virginia Westmacott, Mss Eur C394, pp. 277–8, OIOC.

83. *Amrita Bazaar Patrika*, 17 April 1942.

84. *Indian Tea Association Report*, p. 7.

85. *Amrita Bazaar Patrika*, 26 April 1942.

86. Dorman-Smith to Amery, 6 May 1942, L/WS/1/706, OIOC.

87. Many official justifications are available in the records, see, e.g., Major-General E. Wood, Administrator General of Eastern Frontier Communications, 'Report on the evacuation of refugees from Burma to India (Assam), January to July, 1942', 1 October 1942, Pearce Papers, Mss D 947, pp. 25–6, OIOC.

88. Ruth Donnison to her family, 6 December 1942, inserted in Memoir f. 367 (b), Donnison Papers, Mss Eur B357, OIOC.

89. P. D. M. Lingeman, 'Memoir', f. 8, CSAS.

90. *Amrita Bazaar Patrika*, 26 April 1942.

91. Note of Supercargo Paxton, Personal accounts of the 1942 retreat, Mss Eur 375/11, OIOC.

92. W. G. Burchett, *Bombs over Burma* (Melbourne, 1944), p. 235.

93. Extract of a letter from Mrs G. E. Portal, Ranchi, to Mrs R. A. Butler, 7 June 1942, L/WS/1/886, OIOC.

94. Linlithgow to Amery, 11 July 1942, L/WS/1/886, OIOC.

95. The following paragraphs are based on David Atkins's lively memoir, *The reluctant major* (Pulborough, 1986).

96. Ibid., pp. 59–69.

97. Ibid., p. 86.

98. R. K. Narayan, *My days* (Delhi, 1974), pp. 46, 198. John de Chazal, 'Sunset of the Raj', f. 168, Mss Eur D1041/3, OIOC.

99. General and Air HQ India, intelligence summary, 10 January 1942, L/WS/1/317, f. 2, OIOC.

100. Burchett, *Bombs over Burma*, p. 178.

101. Arthur Dash, Bengal Diary 1938–42, Dash Papers, Mss Eur C/1885, f. 2, OIOC.

102. *Statesman*, 10 March 1942.

103. *Statesman*, 18 March 1942.

104. *Statesman*, 26 May 1942.

105. E. G. Benthal to Tom, 10 May 1942, Benthal Papers, personal correspondence, CSAS.

106. Dash Diary 1938–42, f. 8.

107. Ibid, f. 5.

108. Ibid., ff. 12–14.

109. Note from General and Air HQ India, 6 July 1942, India intelligence summaries, L/WS/1/317, OIOC.

110. L. W. Russell, Memoir, Mss Eur D1041/9, f. 23, OIOC.

111. Viceroy to secretary of state, 2 October 1942, L/P and O/4/24, OIOC.

112. A. G. McCall, Superintendent, Lushai hills to J. P. Mills, secretary to government, 7 July 1942, McCall Papers, Mss Eur E361/34, OIOC.

113. Manifesto, 6 May 1942, Mss Eur E361/35, OIOC.

114. A. G. McCall, *Lushai chrysalis* (London, 1949), p. 298.

115. *Statesman*, 10 March 1942.

116. General notice, May 1942, McCall Papers, Mss E361/36, OIOC.

117. Ibid.

118. McCall, *Chrysalis*, p. 293.

119. Diary of A. Bruce Lorrain-Foxall, 28 August 1942, Mss Eur F185/92, OIOC.

120. Later correspondence on the *pasalthas* and civil defence schemes in the hills can be found in McCall Papers, Mss Eur E361/37, 38 and 50, OIOC.

121. Note by Buchawna, Lushai magistrate, 2 July 1942, McCall Papers, Mss Eur E361/44, OIOC.

122. Ursula Graham Bower, *Naga path* (London, 1950), p. 4.

123. Ibid., p. 170.

124. Ibid., p. 167.

125. Ibid., p. 187.

126. Ibid., p. 195.

127. Edmund Leach, *Current Anthropology*, 27, 4 (1986), pp. 376–8.

128. John Connell, *Auchinleck: a biography of Field Marshal Sir Claude Auchinleck* (London, 1959), p. 491.

## CHAPTER 4 1942: THE ABYSS AND THE WAY BACK

1. Masanobu Tsuji, *Singapore, the Japanese version* (London, 1962), p. 279.

2. Lee Kuan Yew, *The Singapore story* (Singapore, 1998), p. 61.

3. Lim Kean Siew, *Blood on golden sands: the memoirs of a Penang family* (Kuala Lumpur, 1999), p. 98; Mustapha Hussain, 'Malay nationalism before Umno: the memoirs of Mustapha Hussain, 1910–1957', translated by Insun Mustapha and edited by Jomo K.S., ch. 21.

4. Robert Chong interview; Heng Chiang Ki interview; Madame Zamroude Za'ba interview, OHD, SNA.

5. T. J. Danaraj, *Japanese invasion of Malaya and Singapore, memoirs of a doctor* (Kuala Lumpur, 1990), pp. 78–80; Dr Benjamin Chew interview, OHD, SNA.

6. Yuki Tanaki, *Japan's comfort women: sexual slavery and prostitution during World War Two and the United States occupation* (London, 2002), p. 29.

7. N. I. Low and H. M. Cheng, *This Singapore: our city of dreadful night* (Singapore, 1946), p. 5.

8. Charlie Cheah Fook Ying interview, OHD, SNA.

9. Robert Chong interview; Ismail Zain interview, OHD, SNA.

10. Lim, *Blood on golden sands*, p. 98; Chin Kee Onn, *Malaya upside down* ([1946] Singapore, 1946), pp. 11–16.

11. [Nakane] 'My Diary 1942', BAM Collection, RHO.

12. For Tsuji's indictment, see Ian Ward, *The killer they called a god* (Singapore, 1992).

13. For an account based on Japanese sources, see Yoji Akashi, 'Japanese policy towards the Malayan Chinese, 1941–1945', *Journal of Southeast Asian Studies*, 1, 2 (1970), pp. 61–89.

14. [Nakane] 'My Diary 1942', Entry for 21 February.

15. Heng Chiang Ki interview, OHD, SNA.

16. Lee Kip Lim interview, OHD, SNA.

17. Lee, *Singapore story*, p. 56.

18. Chan Cheng Yean interview, OHD, SNA.

19. Michael Moore, *Battalion at war: Singapore, 1942* (Norwich, 1988), p. 25.

20. Charlie Cheah Fook Ying interview.

21. Tan Thoon Lip, *Kempeitai kindness* (Singapore, 1946), p. 86.

22. For a moving survey of the available evidence, P. Lim Pui Huen, 'War and ambivalence: monuments and memorials in Johore', in P. Lim Pui Huen and

Diana Wong (eds), *War and memory in Malaysia and Singapore* (Singapore, 2000), pp. 139–59.

23. Lee Hock Chye, *Comfort homes and earlier years* (Kuala Lumpur, n.d.), pp. 22–8.

24. Cheah Boon Kheng, 'Japanese army policy towards the Chinese and Malay-Chinese relations in wartime Malaya', in Paul H. Kratoska (ed.), *Southeast Asian minorities in the wartime Japanese empire* (London, 2002), pp. 102–3.

25. Mamoru Shinozaki, *Syonan – my story: the Japanese occupation of Singapore* (Singapore, 1979), p. 26; Gay Wan Guay interview; George Bogaars interview, OHD, SNA.

26. Y. S. Tan, 'History of the formation of the Overseas Chinese Association and the extortion by the J.M.A. of $50,000,000 military contribution from the Chinese in Malaya', *Journal of the South Seas Society*, 3, 1 (1946), pp. 2–4.

27. Yoji Akashi, 'Watanabe Wataru: the architect of the Malaya Military Administration, December, 1941–March 1943', in Mohd Hazim Shah, Jomo K.S. and Phua Kai Lit (eds), *New perspectives in Malaysian studies* (Kuala Lumpur, 2002), pp. 116–23.

28. Yap Pheng Geck, *Scholar, banker, gentleman scholar: the reminiscences of Dr Yap Pheng Geck* (Singapore, 1983), p. 67; Akashi, 'Japanese policy'; Tan, 'History', pp. 6–12.

29. For a summary account of these theatres see Nicholas Tarling, *A sudden rampage: the Japanese occupation of Southeast Asia, 1941–1945* (Singapore, 2001), pp. 80–124.

30. Willard H. Elsbree, *Japan's role in Southeast Asian nationalist movements, 1940–1945* (Cambridge, Mass., 1953), p. 26; Yoji Akashi, 'Japanese Military Administration in Malaya – its formation and evolution in reference to sultans, the Islamic religion, and the Moslem-Malays, 1941–1945', *Asian Studies*, 7, 1 (1969), pp. 81–110.

31. Classic academic studies are Paul H. Kratoska, *The Japanese occupation of Malaya, 1941–45* (London, 1998) and Cheah Boon Kheng, *Red star over Malaya: resistance and social conflict during and after the Japanese occupation of Malaya, 1941–1946* (Singapore, 1983), and the work of the Japanese scholar Yoji Akashi.

32. Kevin Blackburn and Edmund Lim, 'The Japanese war memorials of Singapore: monuments of commemoration and symbols of Japanese imperial ideology', *South East Asia Research*, 7, 3 (2001), pp. 321–40.

33. Akashi, 'Watanabe Wataru', pp. 123–6; Office of Strategic Services, Research and Analysis Branch, No. 2072, 'Japanese Administration in Malaya', 8 June, 1944.

34. *Syonan Times*, 1 October 1942; discussed in A. J. Stockwell, *British policy and Malay politics during the Malayan Union experiment, 1945–1948* (Kuala Lumpur, 1979), p. 11.

35. [Nakane] 'My Diary, 1942', entry for 17 July.

36. Mustapha Hussain, 'Malay nationalism before Umno', chs 22–4.

37. Cheah Boon Kheng, 'The Japanese occupation of Malaya, 1941–45: Ibrahim Yaacob and the struggle for Indonesia Raya', *Indonesia*, 28 (1979), pp. 85–120; Fujiwari Iwaichi, *F. Kikan: Japanese intelligence operations in Southeast Asia during World War II* (Singapore, 1983), pp. 189–90.

38. Mubin Sheppard, *Tunku: his life and times* (Kuala Lumpur, 1995), pp. 46–7. Discussed in Abu Talib Ahmad, 'The impact of the Japanese occupation on the Malay-Muslim population', in Paul H. Kratoska (ed.), *Malaya and Singapore during the Japanese occupation* (Singapore 1995), pp. 21–4.

39. *Syonan Times*, 24 March 1942.

40. Lim, *Blood on golden sands*, p. 100; Kratoska, *The Japanese occupation*, pp. 77–9.

41. Low and Cheng, *This Singapore*, p. 39.

42. Lim, *Blood on golden sands*, p. 100.

43. T. Ohnisi, 'Nippon-zin are a vain people but they are not petty', *Syonan Times*, 9 July 1942.

44. [Nakane] 'My Diary, 1942', vol. II.

45. OSS, 'Japanese administration in Malaya'; 'PW – interrogation report – Sasaki Masao (Michael)', XL3010, NARA.

46. Soon Kim Seng interview, OHD, SNA.

47. *Syonan Times*, 13 August 1942.

48. Ho Thean Fook, *Tainted glory* (Kuala Lumpur, 2000), pp. 70–7.

49. Heng Chiang Ki interview, OHD, SNA; Lee Kip Lee, *On amber sands: a childhood memoir* (Singapore, 1995), p. 147.

50. Yoji Akashi, 'The Koa Kunrenjo and Nampo Tokubetsu Ryugakusei: a study of cultural propagation and conflict in Japanese occupied Malaya (1942–45)', *Shakai Kagaku Tokyu*, 23, 3 (1978), pp. 39–66.

51. *Syonan Times*, 4 April 1942, 6 June 1942.

52. Heng Chiang Ki interview, OHD, SNA.

53. Tan, *Kempeitai kindness*, p. 88.

54. *Syonan Times*, 21 August 1942.

55. *Syonan Times*, 9 October 1942.

56. See the engaging memoir by Aisha Akbar, *Aishabee at war: a very frank memoir* (Singapore, 1990), pp. 141–2.

57. Harold E. Wilson, *Educational policy and performance in Singapore*

*1942–1945*, ISEAS Occasional Paper 16 (Singapore, 1973); Victor Kruse-mann interview, OHD, SNA.

58. *Syonan Shimbun*, 1 July 1943.

59. Karen Lee Li Yeng, 'Japanese occupation in Selangor, 1942–45' (BA graduation exercise, University of Malaya, 1973).

60. Chin, *Malaya upside down*, p. 179.

61. [Nakane] 'My Diary 1942'. After his stint of service in Negri Sembilan in 1942 the diary concludes. Nothing further, alas, is known of Mr Nakane or his fate.

62. Note by U Tin Tut, 2 October 1942, 'Attitude of the Burmese people in the recent campaign in Burma', Arnold Papers, Mss Eur F145/6b, OIOC.

63. Jack Belden, *Retreat with Stilwell* (London, 1943), p. 44.

64. Tokyo Radio, 4 June 1942, reported in 'Burma under the Japanese', Clague Papers, Mss Eur E252/44, f. 24, OIOC.

65. Resolution 5 January 1940, Clague Papers, Mss Eur E252/44, f. 1, OIOC.

66. Note of H. F. Smith, IFS, Chief Conservator of Forests, Burma, late 1942, 'Attitude of the Burmese People', Arnold Papers, Mss Eur F145/6b, OIOC.

67. A series of quasi independent states, ruled by indigenous rulers but 'protected' by the British. More than half the population were so-called Red Karens, hence the region's name.

68. Intercepted letter dated 25 October 1945 from L. K. W. Kweiyang to Miss S. T. Wu, Bombay University, Intelligence Report, 24 August 1945, R/8/40, OIOC.

69. Thakin Nu, *Burma under the Japanese: pictures and portraits*, ed. and trans. J. S. Furnivall (London, 1954), p. 21.

70. Thein Pe, 'Wartime traveller', in R. H. Taylor, *Marxism and resistance in Burma 1942–5* (Athens, Ohio, 1984), p. 135.

71. 'Memorandum upon conversations with Burmans newly arrived from Japanese occupied areas', 1943?, Clague Papers, Mss Eur E252/44, f. 155, OIOC.

72. Ibid., f. 186.

73. Khin Myo Chit, Memoir, Mss Eur D1066/1, f. 50, OIOC. A much abridged version of this was published as *Three years under the Japs* (Rangoon, 1945).

74. Ibid., f. 66.

75. Ibid., f. 68.

76. Ann Purton, *The safest place* (Wells-next-the-Sea, 1982), p. 169.

77. U Shwe Mra, 'Japanese interlude', *The Guardian. Burma's National Magazine*, 13, 11 (1966), pp. 9–19.

78. Ibid., p. 9.

79. Ibid., p. 10.

80. Thein Pe, 'Wartime traveller', pp. 115, 154 Thein Pe seems to be confusing this event with Mahabandula's invasion of Arakan in 1824.

81. Ibid., p. 165.

82. Ibid., p. 169.

83. Ibid., p. 171.

84. Ibid., p. 181.

85. Lady Dorman-Smith to Mary McAndrew, 5 August 1942, Mss Eur E215/46, OIOC.

86. Amery to Dorman-Smith, 5 August 1942, Dorman-Smith Papers, Mss Eur E215/2, OIOC.

87. Dorman-Smith to Amery, 31 October 1942, Mss Eur E215/2, OIOC.

88. Note by Prof. B. R. Pearn, 12 June 1942, in file 'Attitude of the Burmese people during the recent campaign in Burma,' Arnold Papers, Mss Eur F145/6 (b), f. 2, OIOC.

89. Ibid., f. 3.

90. Note by U Tin Tut, 2 October 1942, ibid., f. 6.

91. Ibid.

92. Minute by H. E., 7 November 42, ibid., f. 12.

93. Note by S. D. Jupp, Superintendent CID, ibid., f. 70.

94. Peter Clarke, *The Cripps version: the Life of Sir Stafford Cripps* (London, 2002).

95. Ibid.

96. Enclosure to Sir M. Hallet, Governor of the United Provinces to Linlithgow, 31 May 1942, no. 113 in Nicholas Mansergh (ed.), *Constitutional relations between Britain and India: the transfer of power 1942–7*, vol. *Quit India 30 April–21 September 1942* (London, 1971), pp. 158–60.

97. *Statesman*, 9 April 1942.

98. *Statesman*, 10 April 1942.

99. *Amrita Bazaar Patrika*, 11 April 1942.

100. *Statesman*, 13 April 1942.

101. Indivar Kamtekar, 'The shiver of 1942', *Studies in History* (Delhi), 18, 1, n.s. (2002), pp. 81–102.

102. The best narrative of the Quit India movement is to be found in 'India intelligence summaries', August–October 1942, L/WS/1/1433, OIOC. Some material in the following paragraphs is derived from this source.

103. J. M. Brown, *Gandhi: prisoner of hope* (New Haven, 1989), pp. 337–44.

104. Note on viceroy to secretary of state, 15 August 1942, 'Disturbances in India, 1942', WO106/3721, PRO.

105. D. K. Palit, *Major-General A.A. Rudra: his services in three armies and two world wars* (Delhi, 1997), pp. 252, 256–7.

106. India Intelligence Summaries, 16 October 1942, L/WS/1/1433, OIOC.

107. Note for CIGS, 23 August 1942, 'Disturbances in India, 1942', WO106/3721, PRO.

108. Ibid.

109. Memoir of Lawrence Walter Russell, Mss Eur D1041, p. 3, OIOC.

110. *Statesman*, 11 September 1942.

111. Ibid.

112. Dash Diary 1938–42, Dash Papers, Mss Eur C188/5, f. 22, OIOC.

113. Viceroy to secretary of state, 3 December 1942, 'Food Situation in India', WO106/3772, PRO.

114. *Statesman*, 14 July 1943.

115. Margaret Stavridi Memoir, Mss Eur C808, OIOC.

116. *Syonan Times*, 13 August 1942.

117. Damodaran s/o Kesavan interview, OHD, SNA.

118. A. M. Nair, *An Indian freedom fighter in Japan: memoirs of A. M. Nair* (New Delhi, 1985).

119. Ibid.

120. *Syonan Times*, 14 July 1942, 21 August 1942.

121. S. Chelvasingham-MacIntyre, *Through memory lane* (Singapore, 1973), pp. 116–17.

122. *INA heroes: the autobiographies of Major-General Shahnawaz, Colonel Prem K. Saghal and Colonel Gurbax Singh Dhillon of the Azad Hind Fauj* (Lahore, 1946), pp. 18–21.

123. Motilal Bhargava and Americk Singh Gill, *Indian National Army, secret service* (New Delhi, 1988).

124. Iwachi, *F. Kikan*, pp. 238–46; Nair, *An Indian freedom fighter*, pp. 193–211.

125. S. A. Das and K. B. Subbaiah, *Chalo Delhi! An historical account of the Indian independence movement in East Asia* (Kuala Lumpur, 1946), pp. 75–6.

126. Damodaran s/o Kesavan interview.

127. Testimony of Pritam Singh, 6 November 1942, note on Indian independence movements in the Far East, Appendix D, L/WS/1/1576, OIOC.

128. 'Escape report by Lt M. M. Pillai and Lt V. Radhakrishnan who left Singapore on 7 May 1942 and reached Delhi 25 August 1942', 25 August 1942, AWM.

129. Sadao Oba, *The 'Japanese' war: London University's World War Two secret teaching programme and the experts sent to beat Japan* (Sandgate, 1995), pp. 1–47.

130. Richard Aldrich, *Intelligence and the war against Japan: Britain, America and the politics of secret service* (Cambridge, 2000), pp. 156–8.

131. John Davis interview, OHD, SNA; 'Record of meeting on Malaya held at Meerut on 24 October, 1942', HS1/114.

132. Richard Gough, *Jungle was red: SOE's Force 136 Sumatra and Malaya* (Singapore, 2003), pp. 50–1.

133. Summarized in Janet Uhr, *Against the sun: the AIF in Malaya, 1941–42* (St Leonards NSW, 1998), pp. 209–11.

134. This section draws heavily on F. Spencer Chapman, *The jungle is neutral* (London, 1949); Dennis Holman, *The green torture: the ordeal of Robert Chrystal* (London, 1962).

135. Chin Peng, *My side of history* (Singapore, 2003), p. 78.

136. Yoji Akashi, 'The anti-Japanese movement in Perak during the Japanese occupation, 1941–45', in Paul H. Kratoska (ed.), *Malaya and Singapore during the Japanese occupation* (Singapore, 1995), pp. 83–118.

137. Yoji Akashi, 'Lai Teck, secretary general of the Malayan Communist Party, 1939–1947', *Journal of the South Seas Society*, 49 (1994), pp. 57–103; Chin Peng, *My side of history*, pp. 79–84.

138. Holman, *Green torture*, pp. 52, 62.

139. Chapman, *The jungle is neutral*, pp. 125–6.

140. F. Spencer Chapman, *Living dangerously* (London, 1953), p. 120.

141. Chin Peng, *My side of history*, pp. 74–5.

142. J. A. Harvey to DCS, 27 September 1946, MU/4119/46, ANM.

143. For a more or less contemporary account by Noone's successor see P. D. R. Williams-Hunt, *An introduction to the Malayan aborigines* (Kuala Lumpur, 1952).

144. DO Kuala Kangsar, 'Chinese squatters in Aboriginal Tribal Reserve in Mukim of Sungei Siput', n.d. [early 1948], Pk Sec/ 2777/47, ANM.

145. Holman, *Green torture*, pp. 58–60; Dennis Holman, *Noone of the Ulu* (London, 1958).

## CHAPTER 5 1943: VALLEYS OF THE SHADOW OF DEATH

1. Field Marshal Alanbrooke, *War Diaries 1939–45*, ed. Alex Danchev and Daniel Todman (London, 2001), 1 January 1943, p. 338.

2. Joseph W. Stilwell, *The Stilwell Papers*, ed. Theodore H. Wright (London, 1949).

3. The degree of Stilwell's grip on Chinese political realities is also thrown

into doubt now that the historian Hans van de Ven has shown how the Chinese nationalist army really worked: van de Ven, *War and nationalism in China, 1925–1945* (London, 2003).

4. Stilwell, *Stilwell Papers*, p. 68.

5. Alanbrooke, *Diaries*, 14 May 1943, p. 404.

6. 'The China Background', Clague Papers, Mss Eur E252/44, f. 214, OIOC.

7. Alanbrooke, *Diaries*, 19 April 1943, p. 394.

8. For an account of the battle see Louis Allen, *Burma: the longest war* (London, 1984), pp. 91–116.

9. Conversation recorded in W. A. Barnes, Diary, 7 January 1944, Barnes Papers, CSAS.

10. Civilian appreciation of the military situation on the Arakan front, mid 1943, Bell papers, CSAS.

11. Sir William Slim, *Defeat into victory* (London, 1955), p. 160; cf. N. Irwin, 'Note on our capacity to act offensively against Burma', Irwin Papers, Imperial War Museum, London; Allen, *Burma*, p. 638. Figures such as these must be considered highly approximate.

12. D. K. Palit, *Major General A. A. Rudra: his services in three armies and two world wars* (Delhi, 1997), p. 259.

13. General Irwin's Conference, 9 April 1943, Stephens Papers, Box 1, CSAS. Stephens was annoyed because the conference seems to have been held specifically to refute the *Statesman* rather than to explain the wider situation.

14. Rough shorthand note of Army Commander's Press Conference, 9 May 1943, Irwin Papers, Imperial War Museum (IWM), London.

15. Ian Stephens to Vyvyan Edwards, 18 April 1943, Stephens Papers, Box 20, CSAS.

16. Wilfred G. Burchett, *Democracy with a tommy gun* (Melbourne, 1946), p. 126.

17. Ibid., p. 123.

18. Mountbatten to Irwin, 28 June 1968; see also Irwin's 'Note on our capacity to operate offensively against Burma, May 1943', Irwin Papers, IWM.

19. Zainuddin, Assistant Liaison Officer, Kyautaw area, 'Confidential account of my experiences prior to and during the re-occupation of the Kyautaw area by the British', Irwin Papers, Imperial War Museum. The Baluch troops were Muslims from the far north west of the Indian empire; 'Mug' was a term for Arakanese Buddhists but it had a slightly derogatory connotation in India.

20. Wavell to Irwin, 15 January 1943, Irwin Papers, IWM.

21. Barnes Diary, 10 October 1942, Barnes Papers, CSAS.

22. Intelligence report, 13 March 1943, in Partha Sarathi Gupta (ed.),

*Towards freedom: documents on the movement for independence in India 1943–1944* (Delhi, 1997), Part I, pp. 53–4.

23. India intelligence summary, 31 December 1942, L/WS/1/1433, OIOC.

24. Government of Bengal (Home) file W58/43 Calcutta, in Gupta, *Towards freedom*, Part II, pp. 1542–6.

25. Leonard A. Gordon, *Brothers against the Raj: a biography of Indian nationalists Sarat and Subhas Chandra Bose*, (New York, 1990), pp. 484–5.

26. Bose to Ribbentrop, 22 May 1942, S. K. Bose and Sugata Bose (eds), *Subhas Chandra Bose, Azad Hind: writings and speeches 1941–1943*, Netaji Collected Works, vol. xi (Calcutta, 2000), p. 100.

27. Subhas Bose to Sarat Bose, 8 February 1943, ibid., p. 205.

28. Ibid., p. 200.

29. A huge amount has been published on the Chindits. A short account of the debates about Wingate and the Gurkhas is to be found in Tony Gould, *Imperial warriors: Britain and the Gurkhas* (London, 1999), pp. 251–61.

30. See Bernard Fergusson, *Beyond the Chindwin: behind the Japanese lines in Burma* (London, 1945).

31. There is a comprehensive account of the Ledo Road in the journal *Engineering*, 21 September 1945, pp. 223–5.

32. Alanbrooke, *Diaries*, 9 May 1943, p. 400.

33. Paul Greenough, *Prosperity and misery in modern Bengal: the famine of 1943–1944* (New Delhi, 1982) p. 150; interview, January 1979.

34. BRC records doc. no. 528–2/3, cited ibid., p. 151.

35. BRC records doc. no. 115–1/2, cited ibid., p. 164.

36. Bhowani Sen, *Rural Bengal in ruins*, trans. Chakravarty (Calcutta, 1945), pp. 29–30.

37. One of the best short sustained analyses of the roots of the famine is to be found in the Papers of L. G. Pinnell, Superintendent of Civil Supplies, especially 'Tabular History Statement' and 'Note to Famine Commission', MSS Eur D911/7, OIOC.

38. Dash Diary, 1938–42, Dash Papers, Mss Eur C188/5, f. 21, OIOC.

39. 'Memorandum submitted to the Bengal Famine Enquiry Committee by the Deputy Local Surgeon General', Pinnell Papers, Mss Eur D911/8, p. 52, OIOC.

40. Extract from GHQ intelligence report 86, 25 June 1943, in viceroy to secretary of state, 15 July 1943, WO106/3772, PRO.

41. Margaret Stavridi memoir, Mss Eur C808, f. 3, OIOC.

42. *Statesman*, 3 October 1943 and following issues.

43. Dash Memoir, part 2, Mss Eur C188/6, ff. 17–18, OIOC.

44. Barnes Diary, 22 March 1944.

45. *Statesman*, 2 October 1943.

46. Burchett, *Democracy with a Tommy Gun*, pp. 145–6.

47. Ibid., p. 147.

48. These were reproduced in a special issue of the *Statesman* in late October 1943 entitled 'Maladministration in Bengal', Stephens Papers, Box 1, CSAS.

49. The first pictures appear in *Statesman*, 22 August 1943.

50. *Statesman*, 20 September 1943.

51. Dash Diary 1942–7, Dash Papers, Mss Eur C188/6, f. 12, OIOC.

52. Khwaja Nizamuddin had replaced Fazlul Haq as chief minister this year and Suhrawardy had joined the ministry.

53. *Statesman*, 'The Bengal Famine' commemoration, November 1943, Stephens Papers, Box 1, CSAS.

54. Intelligence report, 1 September 1943, L/WS/1/1433, OIOC

55. Barnes Diary, 22 March 1944.

56. Intelligence report 102, October 43, L/WS/1/1433, OIOC.

57. Prime minister to viceroy, 19 June 1945, L/P and O/4/24, OIOC.

58. Alanbrooke, *Diaries*, retrospective comment, pp. 445–6.

59. Ibid., 6–20 August 1943, pp. 436–46.

60. Philip Ziegler, *Mountbatten: the official biography* (pb. edn, London, 2001), pp. 220–30.

61. John Robert de Chazal, 'Sunset of the Raj', Mss Eur D1041/3, p. 198, OIOC.

62. P. Warner, *Auchinlek: the lonely soldier* (London, 1981), p. 243.

63. Ibid. and John Connell, *Auchinleck: a biography of Field-Marshal Sir Claude Auchinleck* (London, 1959), esp. pp. 745–88.

64. Warner, *Auchinleck*, pp. 249–50.

65. *Statesman*, 31 October 1943.

66. Palit, *Rudra*, p. 269.

67. *Statesman*, 9 November 1943.

68. John de Chazal, 'Sunset of the Raj', Mss 1041/3, p. 192, OIOC.

69. *Statesman*, 21 November 1943.

70. Dash Diary, 1942–7, ff. 39–40.

71. W. G. Burchett, *Bombs over Burma* (Melbourne, 1942) pp. 217–18.

72. *Statesman*, 24 March 1944.

73. Dash Diary, 1942–7, f. 13.

74. A. C. Potter to K. A. Potter, 12 May 1944, Potter Papers, Mss Eur C414/8, OIOC.

75. Barnes Diary, 7 July 1944.

76. Margaret Stavridi, 'The civilian war effort in Bengal for the welfare of the forgotten army of the east, 1942–6', Stavridi Papers, Box 1, CSAS.

77. Dash Diary 1942–7, f. 40.

78. 'The Trained Nurses Association of India. Annual Report 1942–3', Diana Hartly Papers, Royal Commonwealth Society Collection, Cambridge University Library.

79. Barnes Diary 1 March 1944.

80. A. H. Pilcher, *Navvies to the Fourteenth Army* (Delhi, 1945), p. 34; R. Palmer Papers, CSAS.

81. Margaret Stavridi Memoir, Mss Eur C808, f. 6, OIOC.

82. Sir William Slim, *Defeat into victory* (London, 1954), pp. 161ff.

83. Geoffrey Tyson, *India arms for victory* (Allahabad, 1943), pp. 35 ff. This sort of propaganda work should be viewed sceptically, but not dismissed completely.

84. Rumer Godden, 'Bengal Journey', f. 3, Stavridi Papers, Box 1, CSAS.

85. See Tyson, *India arms for victory*, pp. 66ff.

86. Medha M. Kudaisya, *The life and times of G. D. Birla* (Delhi, 2003), pp. 206–13.

87. 17 Dogra Regimental Centre, Jullunder, to Staff Delhi, 28 March 1943, 'Indian National Army and Free Burma Army', L/WS/1/1576, OIOC.

88. Ibid.

89. See Mukulika Bannerjee, *The Pathan unarmed* (London, 2000).

90. Extract from Appendix 3 to GHQ India letter, 26 February 1943, L/WS/1/1576, OIOC.

91. India Intelligence Summaries, no. 90, 23 July 1943, L/WS/1/1433, OIOC.

92. Palit, *Rudra*, pp. 272–4.

## CHAPTER 6 1943: PERSONAL WARS

1. Note by I.G. Police Burma, 22 February 1944, Dorman-Smith Papers, E215/23, OIOC.

2. *Greater Asia*, 7 February 1943.

3. Khin Myo Chit, Memoir, Mss Eur D1066/I, f. 83, OIOC.

4. Typewritten note 'by someone who knows the BIA general staff well', Clague Papers, Mss Eur E252/44, ff. 154a–156, OIOC.

5. Thakin Nu, *Burma under the Japanese: pictures and portraits*, ed. and trans. J. S. Furnivall (London, 1954), p. 61.

6. The most important statement of the form of government was Ba Maw's 'A review of the first stage of the new order plan', 26 October 1943, in Frank N. Trager (ed.), *Burma: Japanese Military Administration, selected documents 1941–5* (Philadelphia, 1971), pp. 177–89.

7. Ba Maw, *Breakthrough in Burma: memoirs of a revolution 1939–46.* (New Haven, 1968).

8. See one of the few surviving official publications, *Financial and Economic Annual of Burma July 1943* (Rangoon, 1943), which airs all the themes of the old British leftist J. S. Furnivall against what he called the 'plural' society. The only available copy is in the Library of the School of Oriental and African Studies, University of London.

9. Khin Myo Chit, Memoir, f. 78.

10. Burma Fortnightly Report, 55, 28 October 1944, R/8/42, OIOC.

11. Khin Myo Chit, Memoir, f. 85.

12. Typescript by an 'unnamed Arakanese' on Burma under the Japanese, f. 152, Clague Papers, Mss Eur E252/44, OIOC.

13. Typewritten note 'by someone [a Burmese] who knows the BIA general staff well', Clague Papers, Mss Eur E252/44, f. 96, OIOC.

14. *Greater Asia*, 2 December 1943.

15. *Greater Asia*, 7 March 1943.

16. *Greater Asia*, 7 February 1943.

17. *Greater Asia*, 21 February 1943.

18. *Greater Asia*, 14 March 1943.

19. *Greater Asia*, 18 July 1943.

20. *Greater Asia*, 2 August 1943.

21. Paw Tun to Dorman-Smith, 25 August 1943, Dorman-Smith Papers, Mss Eur E215/13a, OIOC.

22. Amery to Dorman-Smith, 29 December 1942, Mss Eur E215/2, OIOC.

23. This paragraph and the next draw on Abu Talib Ahmad, 'Japanese policy towards Islam in Malaya during the Occupation: a reassessment', *Journal of Southeast Asian Studies*, 33, 1 (2002), pp. 107–22.

24. Mahmud bin Mat, *Tinggal kenangan: the memoirs of Dato' Sir Mahmud bin Mat* (Kuala Lumpur, 1997), p. 265.

25. Mustapha Hussain, 'Malay nationalism before Umno: the memoirs of Mustapha Hussain, 1910–1957', translated by Insun Mustapha and edited by Jomo K.S., chs. 21–2.

26. William Shaw, *Tun Razak: his life and times* (Kuala Lumpur, 1976), p. 41.

27. See the selections in Arena Wati, *Cerpen Zaman Jepun* (Kuala Lumpur, 1980).

28. J. N. McHugh, *Words and phrases related to political organizations and procedure at meetings* (Kuala Lumpur, 1948). For these Malay terms, see A. C. Milner, *The invention of politics in colonial Malaya: contesting nationalism and the expansion of the bourgeoise public sphere* (Cambridge, 1995), p. 265.

29. Cheah Boon Kheng, 'The Japanese occupation of Malaya, 1941–45: Ibrahim Yaacob and the struggle for Indonesia Raya', *Indonesia*, 28 (1979), pp. 106–7.

30. Chin Kee Onn, *Malaya upside down* ([1946] Singapore, 1946), p. 192.

31. Rudolf Mrazek, *Engineers of happy land: technology and nationalism in a colony* (Princeton, NJ, 2003), p. 156.

32. Paul H. Kratoska, *The Japanese occupation of Malaya, 1941–45* (London, 1998), pp. 142–3.

33. Hwang Lian, 'Film distribution services for the last three years in Malaya', *Allied Screen Review*, 1, 1 (1946).

34. Ahmad Boestamam, *Lambaian dari puncak: memoir 1941–45* (Kuala Lumpur, 1983), pp. 29–32.

35. K. R. Menon, *East Asia in turmoil: letters to my son* (Singapore, 1981), pp. 198–9.

36. Lee Kip Lee, *On amber sands: a childhood memoir* (Singapore, 1995), pp. 144–5.

37. S. A. Das and K. B. Subbaiah, *Chalo Delhi! An historical account of the Indian independence movement in East Asia* (Kuala Lumpur, 1946), pp. 129, 135.

38. A. M. Nair, *An Indian freedom fighter in Japan: memoirs of A. M. Nair* (New Delhi, 1985), pp. 225–6.

39. Damodaran s/o Kesavan interview, OHD, SNA.

40. Nair, *An Indian freedom fighter in Japan*, p. 228.

41. Heng Chiang Ki interview, OHD, SNA.

42. John Baptist Crasta, *Eaten by the Japanese: the memoir of an unknown Indian prisoner of war* (Singapore, 1999).

43. *INA heroes: the autobiographies of Major-General Shahnawaz, Colonel Prem K. Saghal and Colonel Gurbax Singh Dhillon of the Azad Hind Fauj* (Lahore, 1946), pp. 40–3.

44. Damodaran s/o Kesavan interview, OHD, SNA.

45. K. R. Das, 'The Bharat Youth Training Centre', in Netaji Centre, Kuala Lumpur, *Netaji Subhas Chandra Bose: a Malaysian perspective* (Kuala Lumpur, 1992), pp. 56–9.

46. Abdealli K. Motiwalla interview, OHD, SNA.

47. We have here drawn on the recollections in S.N. Arseculeratne, *Sinhalese immigrants in Malaysia and Singapore 1860–1990: history through recollections* (Columbo, 1991), pp. 275–319.

48. J. A. Thivy, *The struggle in East Asia* (n.p., n.d.), p. 62.

49. Das and Subbaiah, *Chalo Delhi!*, p. 175.

50. Dato K. R. Somasundram, 'My reminiscences of World War II and the

INA', in Netaji Centre, Kuala Lumpur, *Netaji Subhas Chandra Bose: a Malaysian perspective* (Kuala Lumpur, 1992) pp. 100–101.

51. P. Ramasamy, 'Indian war memory in Malaysia', in P. Lim Pui Huen and Diana Wong (eds), *War and memory in Malaysia and Singapore* (Singapore, 2000), pp. 90–105.

52. *Young India*, 23 January 1944.

53. *Young India*, 12 December 1943.

54. Janaki Athi Nahappan, 'The Rani of Jhansi Regiment', in Netaji Centre, *Netaji Subhas Chandra Bose*, pp. 42–6.

55. Nair, *An Indian freedom fighter in Japan*, p. 230.

56. P. K. Basu interview, OHD, SNA.

57. Chin, *Malaya upside down*, p. 55.

58. Kratoska, *The Japanese occupation of Malaya*, p. 248.

59. A. Samad Ismail, 'Ubi Kayu', in Arena Wati, *Cerpen Zaman Jepun* (Kuala Lumpur, 1980), p. 165. Our translation from the original Bahasa Melayu.

60. 'Recipes by Chou Pai', *New Democracy*, 20 December 1945.

61. T. Matthews to Victor Purcell, 22 September 1945, BMA/CH/7/45, SNA.

62. Van Thean Kee, 'Cultivation of Taiwanese padi in Perak during the Japanese occupation', *Malayan Agricultural Journal*, 21, 1 (1948), pp. 119–22. Halinah Bamadhaj, 'The impact of the Japanese occupation of Malaya on Malay society and politics, 1941–45', MA Thesis, University of Auckland, 1975), pp. 2–12; Kratoska, *The Japanese occupation of Malaya*, pp. 259–77.

63. See the excellent collection of essays in Lim and Wong, *War and memory in Malaysia and Singapore*.

64. Chin, *Malaya upside down*, p. 190.

65. Tan Thoon Lip, *Kempeitai kindness* (Singapore, 1946), p. 83.

66. Lim Kean Siew, *Blood on golden sands: the memoirs of a Penang family* (Kuala Lumpur, 1999), pp. 63–4.

67. Thomas R. P. Dawson, *Amusing sidelights on Japanese occupation (Malaya: January, 1942–August, 1945)* (n.p., 1946), pp. 33–4.

68. S. Chelvasingham-MacIntyre, *Through memory lane* (Singapore, 1973), pp. 104–18.

69. Malayan Security Service (KL), 'Memorandum on the present high cost of living', 9 January 1946, BMA CH/7/45, SNA.

70. Heng Chiang Ki interview, OHD, SNA.

71. Tan, *Kempeitai kindness*, p. 88.

72. Chin, *Malaya upside down*, pp. 40–3.

73. Heng Chiang Ki interview, OHD, SNA.

74. P. C. Marcus interview, OHD, SNA.

75. *Syonan* Times, 13 September 1942.

76. Chin, *Malaya upside down*, pp. 92–8.

77. Goh Huan Bee interview; Robert Chong interview, OHD, SNA.

78. *Syonan Times*, 20 September 1942.

79. Abdealli K. Motiwalla interview, OHD, SNA.

80. For a fascinating account of this see David Telt, *A postal history of the prisoners of war and civilian internees in East Asia during the Second World War*, vol. I: *Singapore and Malaya, 1942–45: the Changi connection* (Bristol, 2002), pp. 15, 63–8, 74.

81. E. J. H. Corner, *The Marquis: a tale of Syonan-to* (Singapore, 1982). See the discussion in E. G. Reisz, 'City as garden: shared space in the urban botanic gardens of Singapore and Malaysia, 1786–2000', in R. Bishop, J. Phillips and W.-W. Yeo (eds), *Postcolonial urbanism: Southeast Asian cities and global processes* (New York, 2003), pp. 123–48.

82. OSS, 'Japanese Administration in Malaya'; 'PW – Interrogation Report – Sasaki Masao (Michael)', XL3010, NARA.

83. Yoichi Kibata, 'Japanese treatment of British prisoners of war: the historical context', in Philip Towle, Margaret Kosuge and Yoichi Kibata (eds), *Japanese prisoners of war* (London, 2000).

84. 'Treatment of Japanese internees in India', 12 December 1942, FO916/477, PRO.

85. R. N. Gilchrist to under secretary of state, Foreign Office, 19 October, 1942, ibid.

86. Government of India, Home Department to secretary of state for India, 12 December, 1942, ibid.

87. 'List of Japanese internees who have died in the internment camp Purana Qila New Delhi (Up to 31.12.1942)', FO916/775, PRO.

88. *Syonan Times*, 7 October 1942.

89. Frank Fujita, *Foo: A Japanese American prisoner of the Rising Sun: the secret prison diary of Frank 'Foo' Fujita* (Penton, Tex., 1993), pp. 115–22.

90. See the new research by Robert Havers, 'The Changi POW camp and the Burma–Thailand railway', in Towle, Kosuge and Kibata, *Japanese prisoners of war*, pp. 17–36.

91. Dawson, *Amusing sidelights*, p. 36.

92. C. T. Retnam interview, OHD, SNA.

93. Fujita, *Foo*, p. 119.

94. Joseph Kennedy, *British civilians and the Japanese war in Malaya and Singapore, 1941–45* (London, 1987), pp. 93–4.

95. 'Transactions of the Quatuor Coronati Lodge – craftsmen in captivity: Masonic activities of prisoners-of-war by Bro. A. R. Hewitt', dated 1 May 1964, http://users.libero.it/fjit.bvg/prisoner.html.

96. Sir Selwyn Selwyn-Clarke, 'Hong Kong', in Sir Arthur Salisbury MacNulty (ed.), *The civil health and medical services*, vol. II: *The colonies, the medical services of the Ministry of Pensions, public health in Scotland, public health in Northern Ireland* (London, 1955), pp. 55–62.

97. There are a number of diaries surviving from Changi; we have drawn on what is perhaps the most vivid of them, Goh Eck Kheng (ed.), *Life and death in Changi: the war and internment diary of Thomas Kitching (1942–1944)* (Singapore, 2002). Kitching did not survive his internment.

98. Sheila Allan, *Diary of a girl in Changi, 1941–45* (2nd edn, Roseville, NSW, 1999), pp. 9, 74.

99. Jan Ruff-O'Herne, *50 years of silence* (Sydney, 1994).

100. Telt, *A postal history*, pp. 140–4.

101. Kennedy, *British civilians and the Japanese war*, pp. 94–7, 147–51.

102. Tan, *Kempeitai kindness*, p. 100.

103. 'Personal and eye witness reports of Japanese atrocities by victims, victims' families, and/or eye witnesses collected by the Singapore China Relief Fund', 19[?] November 1945, XL26928, NARA.

104. Lan Khong Kon interview, OHD, SNA.

105. Elizabeth Choy interview, OHD, SNA. Elizabeth Choy was presented to Queen Elizabeth after the war.

106. Ruth Ho, *Rainbow around my shoulder* (Singapore, 1975), p. 169.

107. For this extraordinary memoir, see Sybil Kathigasu, *No dram of mercy* (Singapore, 1983).

108. Ho Thean Fook, *Tainted glory* (Kuala Lumpur, 2000), pp. 61–2. Ho gives an extended account of his relations with Sybil Kathigasu.

109. Chin Peng, *My side of history* (Singapore, 2003), pp. 84, 103–5; Ho, *Tainted glory*, e.g. pp. 43–4.

110. Chin Peng, *My side of history*, pp. 91–2. See also Yoji Akashi, 'Lai Teck, secretary general of the Malayan Communist Party, 1939–1947', *Journal of the South Seas Society*, 49 (1994), pp. 57–103.

111. Terence O'Brien, *The moonlight war: the story of clandestine operators in Southeast Asia, 1944–45* (London, 1987), p. 110.

112. Tan Chong Tee, *Force 136: story of a resistance fighter* (2nd edn, Singapore, 2001), pp. 28–35.

113. Tham Sien Yen, 'Fighting behind enemy lines', in Foong Choon Hon (ed.), *The price of peace: true accounts of the Japanese occupation* (Singapore, 1991), pp. 71–3; Tan, *Force 136*, pp. 87–9.

114. Tham, 'Fighting behind enemy lines', pp. 78–80.

115. Chin Peng, *My side of history*, pp. 15, 96–8.

116. Tan, *Force 136*, pp. 136–46.

117. Dennis Holman, *The green torture: the ordeal of Robert Chrystal* (London, 1962), pp. 60–4.

118. See the account in Richard Noone, *Rape of the dream people* (London, 1972).

119. 'The following report is compiled from notes taken by William McDougall, American, United Press, during an interview with Wu Tain Want [Wu Tian Wang] spokesman of the Singapore City Committee of the Malayan Communist Party 23 Sept 1945 in Singapore', XL27129, NARA.

120. T. A. Kendall to Economic Adviser Malayan Union, 18 May 1946, MU/4185/46.

121. Chin Peng argues that Chapman *did* recognize Lai Teck, but kept this secret, *My side of history*, pp. 12–27. John Davis, when pressed on this point by a Singaporean interviewer, suggested no such connection was made, interview OHD, SNA. Chapman himself gives nothing away.

122. Ibid. The document is reproduced in facsimile on pp. 12–13.

123. Richard Aldrich, *Intelligence and the war against Japan: Britain, America and the politics of secret service* (Cambridge, 2000).

124. Leyden minute, 8 January 1943, Clague Papers, Mss Eur E252/44, OIOC.

125. 'Kachin Resistance', 1 December 1944, Clague Papers, Mss Eur E252/44, f. 92, OIOC.

126. 'Wally' Richmond to Dorman-Smith, 26 July 1943, Dorman-Smith Papers, Mss Eur E215/23, OIOC.

127. Amery to Dorman-Smith, 29 December 1942, Dorman-Smith Papers, Mss Eur E215/2, OIOC.

128. Dorman-Smith, Memoirs, pp. 284–5.

129. Paw Tun to Dorman-Smith, 2 April 1943, Dorman-Smith Papers, MSS Eur E215/13a, p. 5, OIOC.

130. Paw Tun to Dorman-Smith, 25 August 1943, ibid.

131. Donnison, Memoirs, Donnison Papers Mss Eur B357, f. 375, OIOC.

132. *Greater Asia*, 27 November 1943, cf. ibid., 20 December.

133. Ba Maw, *Breakthrough*, p. 343.

134. Herbert P. Bix, *Hirohito and the making of modern Japan* (London, 2000), p. 466.

135. Richard Overy, *Why the Allies won* (London, 1995), p. 142.

136. Joseph W. Stilwell, *The Stilwell papers*, ed. Theodore H. Wright (London, 1949), p. 230.

137. Overy, *Why the Allies won*, pp. 142–4, 245–7.

# CHAPTER 7 1944: THE PIVOT OF THE FIGHTING

1. Herbert P. Bix, *Hirohito and the making of modern Japan* (London, 2000), p. 470.

2. Louis Allen, *Burma, the longest war* (London, 1984), p. 154 quoting Katakura Tadashi, *Inparu Sakusen hishi* (Secret History of the Imphal Operation), p. 154.

3. Allen, *Burma*, p. 158.

4. Bix, *Hirohito*, pp. 474–5.

5. Wavell to secretary of state for India, 12 January 1944, Mss Eur D977/2, OIOC.

6. 'Lines of communication in Assam', WO203/322, PRO.

7. Chiefs of Staff Committee, 3 April 1944, 'Maintenance of India as a base', WO106/3836, PRO.

8. Statement of Financial Adviser Military Finance at Army Commanders' Conference, 9 July 1943, India intelligence summary, 23 July 1943, L/WS/1/1433, OIOC.

9. E.g. General Lindsell to Quarter-Master General India Command, 14 April 1944, WO106/3836, PRO.

10. Ellis Bee to Ian Stephens, 26 November 1943, Stephens Box 21, CSAS.

11. Major-General K. K. Tewari, *A soldier's voyage of self-discovery* (Auroville, 1995), p. 27.

12. The letter is undated but is from early summer 1944; Wavell responded to it in a private letter to Amery, 9 May 1944, L/P and O/4/24, OIOC.

13. SEAC and India Command weekly intelligence summary, 21 April 1944, L/WS/1/1433, OIOC.

14. Ralph Russell, *Findings keepings: life, communism and everything* (London, 2001).

15. Sydney Bolt, 'Pseudo Sahib', ff. 178–210, CSAS.

16. SEAC intelligence summary, 5 May 1944, L/WS/1/1433, OIOC.

17. Appendix C to SEAC intelligence summary, 21 July 1944, Political activities and the army, L/WS/1/1/1433, OIOC.

18. F. Yeats-Brown, *Martial India* (London, 1945), p. 26.

19. 'Pir Kaudi and Babbadi', Brayne Papers, Mss Eur F152/79, OIOC.

20. 'Nutitional survey of Indian troops', Appendix for March–April 1944, WO203/269, PRO.

21. E. T. Stokes to sister, February 1946, Stokes Papers, CSAS.

22. Tewari, *Voyage*, pp. 35, 38.

23. Auchinleck to Mountbatten, 28 September 1944, Mountbatten Papers 5 (microfilm), OIOC.

24. Diana Hartly diaries, e.g. Poona, June 1938, Diana Hartly Papers, RCS Collection, Cambridge University Library.

25. T. K. Adranvala, 'Developments in nursing 1947–57', in *Trained Nurses Association of India 50th Anniversary volume 1908–58* (Delhi, 1958), pp. 326–8 (copy in Diana Hartly Papers).

26. Mountbatten to Auchinleck, 13 February 1945, Mountbatten Papers 5, (microfilm), OIOC.

27. J. D. Tyson to his family, 31 January 1943, Tyson Papers, Mss Eur E341/36, OIOC.

28. Dr R. H. Taylor, 'Interview with U Kyaw Nyein, 29 October 1979', Mss Eur D1066/2, OIOC.

29. *Greater Asia*, 9 November 1943.

30. S. A. Ayer, *Unto him a witness: the story of Netaji Subhas Chandra Bose in East Asia* (Bombay, 1951), pp. 10–11.

31. Intelligence report 3 December 1943, Appendix C, excerpts from Japanese diaries, L/WS/1/1433, OIOC.

32. Burma intelligence reports, 18 November 1944, Clague Papers, Mss Eur E252/43, OIOC.

33. Memoir of Captain Shosaku Kameyama, in Kazuo Tamayama and John Nunneley (eds), *Tales by Japanese soldiers of the Burma campaign 1942–5* (London, 2000), p. 156.

34. Appendix A to WSIS N. 163, captured letter from Officer Commanding Number One Guerilla Regiment, INA, to Bose, April 1944, L/WS/1/1433, OIOC.

35. Dorman-Smith to Lady Dorman-Smith, 24 February 1944, Dorman-Smith Papers, Mss Eur E215/47A, OIOC.

36. Ayer, *Witness*, p. 183.

37. Dorman-Smith to Lady Dorman-Smith, 19 February 1944, Dorman-Smith Papers, Mss Eur E215/47A, OIOC.

38. Dorman-Smith to Lady Dorman-Smith, 23 March, 1944.

39. 'Guidance notes for talks between officers and men, Burma', Sir John Tait on Burma and the war, p. 27, Steel Bros Box B, British Empire and Commonwealth Museum, Bristol.

40. Lectures by F. D. Edmeades, J. C. Purdie and C. Lorimer, ibid.

41. Lecture by Mr Heath, p. 20, ibid.

42. 'Note by Messervy on the lessons of Arakan and Imphal', summer-autumn 1944?, Messervy Papers, 5/3, University of London, King's College, Liddell Hart Centre for Military Archives.

43. Sir William Slim, *Defeat into victory* (London, 1955), p. 184.

44. Mountbatten to Frank Owen, 29 March 1944, Mountbatten Papers, MB C/189, Southampton University Library; cf. Mountbatten to Roosevelt, 28 March 1944, Military correspondence 1944–5, Box 36, Franklin D. Roosevelt Presidential Library and Museum, www.fdrlibrary.marist.edu/online.14.html.

45. 'Laugh with SEAC' (summer 1944?), p. 58, Messervy Papers 6, Liddell Hart Centre.

46. Mountbatten to Frank Owen, 1 October 1943. Mountbatten Papers MB/C189, Southampton University Library.

47. E.g., India intelligence report 133, 19 May 1944, L/WS1/1433, OIOC.

48. B. Prasad, *Official history of the Indian armed forces in the Second World War*, 4 vols (Delhi, 1954–65), vol. I: *The reconquest of Burma*, pp. 260–82.

49. Ba Maw, *Breakthrough in Burma: memoirs of a revolution 1939–46* (New Haven, 1968), pp. 353–4. Ba Maw is a year out in his calculation of the emperor's age.

50. There are many good accounts of the battle. One of the earliest and best is Anthony Brett-James, *Balls of fire: the Fifth Indian Division in the Second World War* (Aldershot, 1951). See also Ian Lyall Grant, *Burma, the turning point: the seven battles on the Tiddim Road which turned the tide of the Burma war* (Chichester, 1993).

51. Tamayama and Nunneley, *Tales by Japanese soldiers*, p. 192.

52. Major-General G. N. Wood, 25th Indian Division history of the Arakan campaign, p. 12, WO203/315, PRO.

53. Notes, Arakan Hill Tracts, secret source to 'My dear Brigadier', 26 February 1944, 'Labour in Arakan' WO203/309, PRO.

54. Ibid.

55. DCCAO(B) Eastern Army to K. J. E. Lindop, 16 July 1943, WO203/309, PRO.

56. Ursula Graham Bower, *Naga path* (London, 1950), p. 206.

57. Ibid., p. 214.

58. Note on civil and military intelligence on the Arakan front, 27 June 1944, enc. in private secretary to viceroy's letter to secretary of state, 27 June 1944, L/PandO/4/24, OIOC.

59. Smith Dun, *Memoirs of the four-foot colonel: General Dun Smith, first commander-in-chief of the independent Burmese armed forces* (Ithaca, 1980), p. 41.

60. Dorman-Smith to John Walton, 24 July 1944, Walton Papers, Mss Eur D545/13, OIOC.

61. Slim, *Defeat into victory*, pp. 188ff.

62. Tamayama and Nunneley, *Tales by Japanese soldiers*, p. 178.

63. John Nunneley, *Tales from the King's African Rifles* (London, 2000), p. 127.

64. Ibid., pp. 139–40.

65. The best brief account is by Gary J. Bjorge, *Merrill's Marauders: combined operations in northern Burma in 1944* (US Army Center of Military History, Washington DC, 1996) available at http://www.cgsc.army/carl/resources/csi/Bjorge/BJORGE.asp. This account, however, takes Stilwell's position against his critics.

66. *Eastern Times* (Lahore), 12 September 1944.

67. *Eastern Times*, 13 October 1944.

68. J. D. Tyson to his family, 30 January 1944, Tyson Papers, Mss Eur E341/37, OIOC.

69. Tyson to family, 30 July 1944, Tyson Papers, OIOC.

70. Tyson to family, 16 July 1944, Tyson Papers, OIOC.

71. Intelligence report, 14 July 1944, L/WS/1/1433, OIOC.

## CHAPTER 8 1944: THE NEMESIS OF GREATER EAST ASIA

1. Kazuo Tamayama and John Nunneley (eds), *Tales by Japanese soldiers of the Burma campaign 1942–5* (London, 2000), p. 174.

2. S. A. Ayer, *Unto him a witness: the story of Netaji Subhas Chandra Bose in East Asia* (Bombay, 1951), p. 11.

3. Lieutenant Colonel Balfour Oatts, *The jungle in arms* (London, 1962), pp. 149–50.

4. 'Atrocities on the race course, Namtu', WO325/27, PRO.

5. Ibid.

6. Assam diary of I. Ali, political officer, Frontier Tract, 1945–6, Assam Tour Papers, Mss Eur D1191/7, OIOC.

7. Assam tour diary of F. P. Mainprice, ICS, assistant political officer, November 1943–May 1945, entry for March 1944, Mss Eur D1191/3, OIOC.

8. See the vivid 'Account of conditions in occupied Burma', by U Htin Wa, Clague Papers, Mss Eur E252/44, ff. 96–105, OIOC.

9. See the long typewritten note 'by someone who knows the BIA general staff well', Clague Papers, Mss Eur E252/44, ff. 165–8, OIOC.

10. Group Captain C. Bell, Director Psychological Warfare Division to SACSEA, 14 November 1944, Mountbatten Papers, 5 (microfilm), OIOC.

11. Burma fortnightly intelligence reports, 16–31 August 1944, Clague Papers, Mss Eur E252/43, OIOC.

12. Ibid.

13. Burma fortnightly intelligence report, 1–15 September 1944, Clague Papers, Mss Eur E252/43, OIOC.

14. Memoir of U Htin Wa, 'Conditions in occupied Burma', Clague Papers, Mss Eur E252/44, f. 98, OIOC.

15. Khin Myo Chit, Memoir, Mss Eur D1066/1, f. 88, OIOC.

16. Ibid., f. 96.

17. Typewritten note 'by someone who knows the BIA general staff well', ff. 175–7.

18. Burma fortnightly intelligence reports, 1–14 October 1944, Clague Papers, OIOC.

19. Hugh Toye, *The springing tiger: a study of a revolutionary* (London, 1959), pp. 122–47, has a useful section on this based on post-war interrogations of INA men.

20. The material here is based on British intelligence reports and interrogations of INA personnel after the end of the war. The inwardness of the conflict is expressed, albeit episodically, by Ayer, *Witness*, especially pp. 184–9; see also K. K. Ghosh, *The Indian National Army* (Meerut, 1969).

21. Leonard A. Gordon, *Brothers against the Raj: a biography of Indian nationalists Sarat and Subhas Chandra Bose* (New York, 1990), pp. 518–19.

22. 'India Censorship', 27 May 1945, Burma Governor's Office, R/8/40, OIOC.

23. Burma fortnightly intelligence reports, 1–16 September 1944, Clague Papers, OIOC.

24. Minute of U Tharrawaddy Maung Maung, 9 April 1945, M/3/781, OIOC.

25. Khin Myo Chit, *Three years under the Japs* (Rangoon, 1945), p. 37. This differs significantly from the much longer Ms version in OIOC; for one thing there is little about Buddhism.

26. Goh Chor Boon, *Living hell: story of a WWII survivor at the death railway* (Singapore, 1999), pp. 54–5.

27. 'Interview of U Kyaw Nyein by Dr Robert Taylor, 20 October 1979', Mss Eur D1066/2, OIOC.

28. Chelliah Thurairajah Retnam interview, OHD, SNA.

29. Goh, *Living hell*, pp. 79–83.

30. See 'Notes on the Thai–Burma Railway', part 2, David Boggett, 'Asian Romusha; the silenced voices of history', http//www.kyoto-seika.ac.jp/johokan/kiyo/pdf-data/no20/david.pdf.

31. Nakahara Michiko, 'Labour recruitment in Malaya under the Japanese

occupation: the case of the Burma – Siam railway', in Jomo K.S. (ed.), *Rethinking Malaysia* (Kuala Lumpur, 1997), pp. 215–45.

32. Mubin Sheppard, *Tunku: his life and times* (Kuala Lumpur, 1995), pp. 49–51.

33. Deposition of Amar Singh, 'Coolie camp conditions on the Burma–Siam Railway November 1943–August 1945', WO325/57, PRO.

34. Ayer, *Witness*, p. 200.

35. This account is based on Yuki Tanaka, *Japan's comfort women: sexual slavery and prostitution during World War II and the US occupation* (London, 2002), pp. 8–28.

36. 'Special meeting held at HQ SACSEAC to consider methods to combat VD in SEAC', 7 December 1945, BMA/DEPT/1/2, ANM.

37. OSS, 'Japanese Administration in Malaya'; 'PW – Interrogation Report – Sasaki Masao (Michael)', XL3010, SNA.

38. Robert Chong interview, OHD, SNA; Lee Kip Lee, *On amber sands: a childhood memoir* (Singapore, 1995), p. 150.

39. Lim Kean Siew, *Blood on golden sands: the memoirs of a Penang family* (Kuala Lumpur, 1999), pp. 111–24.

40. [Nakane], 'My Diary – 1942', entry for 21 August, 1942, BAM, RCS.

41. Nakahara Michiko, 'Comfort women in Malaysia', *Critical Asian Studies* 33, 4 (2001), pp. 581–9.

42. Jan Ruff-O'Herne, *50 years of silence* (Sydney, 1994).

43. N. I. Low and H. M. Cheng, *This Singapore: our city of dreadful night* (Singapore, 1946), p. 5.

44. Janet Lim, *Sold for silver* (London, 1958).

45. The figues are from Paul H. Kratoska, *The Japanese occupation of Malaya 1941–45* (London, 1998), pp. 280–1.

46. George Bogaars interview, OHD, SNA. Here we have drawn freely from the interviews cited below.

47. Dr F. A. C. Oehlers interview, OHD, SNA.

48. Herman Marie de Souza interview, OHD, SNA.

49. Ibid.

50. P. C. Marcus interview, OHD, SNA.

51. Herman Marie de Souza interview, OHD, SNA.

52. Chu Shuen Choo interview, OHD, SNA.

53. Gay Wan Guay interview, OHD, SNA; Mamoru Shinozaki, *Syonan – my story: the Japanese occupation of Singapore* (Singapore, 1979), p. 84.

54. H. K. Dimolene, United Planters' Association of Malaya to chief secretary, 25 March 1948, MU/4949/1947.

55. E. J. Shurbshall, minute, 13 September 1946, MU/5705/46.

56. Ho Thean Fook, *Tainted glory* (Kuala Lumpur, 2000), pp. 199–201.

57. J. K. Creer, 'Report on experiences during Japanese occupation', 3 November 1945, RHO.

58. Ibid.

59. Dennis Holman, *The green torture: the ordeal of Robert Chrystal* (London, 1962), pp. 77–81.

60. Tan Chong Tee, *Force 136: story of a resistance fighter* (2nd edn, Singapore, 2001), p. 152.

61. John Davis interview, OHD, SNA.

62. Tham Sien Yen, 'Fighting behind enemy lines', in Foong Choon Hon (ed.), *The price of peace: true accounts of the Japanese occupation* (Singapore, 1991), pp. 90–2.

63. Yoji Akashi, 'The Anti-Japanese movement in Perak during the Japanese occupation, 1941–45', in Paul H. Kratoska (ed.), *Malaya and Singapore during the Japanese occupation* (Singapore, 1995), p. 103.

64. John Davis interview, OHD, SNA. Chin Peng gives his own interpretation in *My side of history* (Singapore, 2003), pp. 106–8. See also Tan Chong Tee's response to Japanese accounts, 'Clinging on to the evil ambitious past: a critical analysis of Ishibe Toshiro's memoirs', in Foong, *The price of peace*, pp. 166–75. Interestingly, both Chin Peng and Tan exonerate Lai Teck from treachery in this case, at least.

65. Chin Peng, *My side of history*, pp. 111–12.

66. Statement made by 6137573 C/Sgt J.W. Beach, East Surrey Regiment, January 1945, CO273/673/2.

67. P. C. Marcus interview, OHD, SNA.

68. What follows draws on two definitive studies: A. J. Stockwell, *British policy and Malay politics during the Malayan Union experiment, 1945–1948* (Kuala Lumpur, 1979) and Albert Lau, *The Malayan Union controversy, 1942–48* (Singapore, 1991).

69. See, for example, Noel Sabine's minute on colonial public relations, 18 March 1942, CO875/14/9, PRO.

70. Victor Purcell, *Memoirs of a Malayan official* (London, 1965), p. 317.

71. Alice Scott-Ross, *Tun Dato Sir Cheng Lock Tan: a personal profile* (Singapore, 1990), pp. 57–60.

72. Tan Cheng Lock, *Malayan problems from a Chinese point of view* (Singapore, 1947).

73. For example, S. W. Jones, 'Notes on the government and administration of Malaya prior to the Japanese invasion', November 1943, CO825/21.

74. O. W. Gilmour, *To Singapore with freedom* (London, 1950), p. 28.

## CHAPTER 9 1945: FREEDOMS WON AND LOST

1. A. M. Nair, *An Indian freedom fighter in Japan: memoirs of A. M. Nair* (New Delhi, 1985), p. 255.

2. J. N. McHugh, 'Psychological warfare in Malaya, 1942–46', *Journal of the History Society of the University of Malaya*, 4 (1965/66), pp. 48–64.

3. 'Nutritional Survey of Indian troops', Appendix A, 12 November 1943, WO203/269, PRO.

4. A good summary of the events in these areas is to be found in Burma Frontier Areas Committee of Enquiry, Parliamentary Papers, Cmd. 7138 (1947).

5. Pioneer and Labour situation in SEAC, 16 January 1945, WO203/796, PRO.

6. Details of Service: Italian Auxiliary Pioneer Force, ibid.

7. There is a vivid account of these operations in John Masters, *The road past Mandalay* (London, 1962); cf. Louis Allen, *Burma: the longest war* (London, 1984), pp. 386–424.

8. Maung Maung, *To a soldier son* (Rangoon, 1974), p. 56.

9. Khin Myo Chit, Memoir, Mss Eur D1066/1, f. 99, OIOC.

10. This material from SEAC intelligence bulletins was collected together in 1946, see WO203/6312, PRO.

11. Burma intelligence reports, 24 February 1945, Clague Papers, Mss Eur E252/43, OIOC.

12. Ayer, *Unto him a witness: the story of Netaji Subhas Chandra Bose in East Asia* (Bombay, 1951), pp. 207–9.

13. Another version of this is published in Hugh Tinker (ed.), *Burma: the struggle for independence 1944–1948*, vol. 1: *1 January 1944 to 31 August 1946* (London, 1983), pp. 110–12.

14. Ibid., p. 111.

15. See note by Thakin Thein Pe Myint, 'Burma Patriotic Front [AFO] and the Communist Party of Burma', Tinker, *Burma*, 1, 54, pp. 107–8.

16. General Officer Commanding, Land Forces, South East Asia.

17. U Thein Pe Myint, 'Note to Indian Communists 1973, a critique of the Communist movement in Burma', Mss Eur C498, f. 8, OIOC.

18. Supreme Allied Commander, South East Asia to chiefs of staff, 27 March 1945, Tinker, *Burma*, 1, 108, pp. 197–8.

19. Colin Mackenzie to Mountbatten, 31 January 1945, ibid., 86, pp. 153–4.

20. HQ briefing, 2 April 1945, Tinker, *Burma*, 1, 114, pp. 207–8.

21. Mountbatten to chiefs of staff, 27 March 1945, WO106/4797, PRO.

22. Montagu Stopford to Mountbatten, 26 September 1945, Mountbatten Papers, Southeast Asia, 8 (microfilm), OIOC.

23. Dorman-Smith to Pearce, 25 May 1945, Pearce Papers, Mss Eur D947, OIOC.

24. Maung Maung, *To a soldier son*, p. 53.

25. Ibid., p. 61.

26. Lionel Hudson, *The rats of Rangoon* (London, 1987).

27. Allen, *Burma*, pp. 483–4.

28. Transcript of statement made by Dr Ba Maw before Lieutenant Col. J. G. Figges, 17 January 1946, M/4/2600, OIOC, partly published in Tinker, *Burma*, 1, pp. 596–7.

29. Ayer, *Witness*, pp. 15–65.

30. Typewritten note 'by someone who knows the BIA general staff well', Clague Papers, Mss Eur E252/44, f. 162, OIOC.

31. T. L. Hughes, 'Report on the Civil Administration of Burma, October 1945', Dorman-Smith Papers, Mss Eur E215/35B, OIOC.

32. Ibid., f. 2.

33. Ibid., f. 163.

34. *Times of Burma* (Rangoon), 26 June 1947.

35. Fortnightly intelligence report (civil censorship), Burma and Malaya, 24 August 1945, R/8/40, OIOC.

36. Ibid.

37. Intelligence report, 23 August 1945, R/8/41, OIOC.

38. 'Burmese, Christians and the war, pamphlets and notes about Christian churches, Burma', Dorman-Smith Papers, Mss Eur E215/54, OIOC.

39. E.g. 'List of prominent citizens, Pakkang Subdivision, Prome District', Steel Bros. Box E, British Empire and Commonwealth Museum, Bristol.

40. Ibid., p. 4.

41. Ibid., p. 6.

42. M. Stopford to Mountbatten, 26 September 1945, Mountbatten Papers, South East Asia 8 (microfilm), OIOC.

43. Enclosure to minute, Burma N. Army, Camp Pegu HQ, 29 May 1945, R/8/30.

44. BAS Washington to WO and SCSEA, 5 March 1945, 'Reoccupation of Burma', L/WS/1/568, OIOC.

45. WO to BAS Washington, 14 March 1945, 'Assistance given to the Allies by Burmans during the war', ibid.

46. Lieutenant Colonel Balfour Oatts was particularly vitriolic against the BDA, like many soldiers who served with the minority peoples, see *The jungle in arms* (London, 1962), p. 203.

47. W. R. Penney to Mrs Shirley Penney, 20 June 1945, Penney Papers 4, 18, Liddell Hart Centre.

48. 'Meeting between the governor of Burma and representatives of communities and organisations in Burma', PRO, WO203/5238, published in Tinker, *Burma*, 1, pp. 339–40.

49. Mountbatten to Major-General H. E. Rance (Director of Civil Affairs, Burma), 18 June 1945, Tinker, *Burma*, 1, p. 204.

50. Ursula Graham Bower, *Naga path* (London, 1950), p. 233.

51. SEAC intelligence summary, 29 June 1945, L/WS/1/1506, OIOC.

52. Ibid.

53. 'Report on the situation in the Punjab for the first half of May 1945', L/P and J/5/248, OIOC.

54. 'Report on the situation in the Punjab for the first half of July 1945', ibid.

55. 'Confidential note on the political situation in Bengal for the first half of January 1945', L/P and J/5/152, OIOC.

56. 'Provincial press adviser's report on the press for the first half of May 1945', ibid.

57. Mustapha Hussain, 'Malay nationalism before Umno: the memoirs of Mustapha Hussain, 1910–1957', translated by Insun Mustapha and edited by Jomo K.S., ch. 29.

58. Chin Peng, *My side of history* (Singapore, 2003), p. 110.

59. Abu Talib Ahmad, 'Japanese policy towards Islam in Malaya during the occupation: a reassessment', *Journal of Southeast Asian Studies*, 33, 1 (2002), pp. 107–22.

60. 'Sabilu'llah and invulnerability', supplement to Malayan Security Service, political intelligence journal, No. 9/ 1947, 15 June 1947, Dalley Papers, RHO. Discussed in Cheah Boon Kheng, 'Sino-Malay conflicts in Malaya, 1945–1946: Communist vendetta and Islamic resistance', *Journal of Southeast Asian Studies*, 12, 1 (1981), pp. 108–17.

61. Richard Broome interview, OHD, SNA.

62. Edward Gent to Colonel G. F. Taylor [SOE], 21 August 1944, HS1/115, PRO.

63. Richard Broome interview, OHD, SNA.

64. F. Spencer Chapman, *The jungle is neutral* (London, 1949), pp. 407–8.

65. Richard Broome interview, OHD, SNA.

66. 'Operational report by Major A. Rapport', 18 October 1945, HS1/107, PRO.

67. 'Operational report by Major H. H. Wright, Carpenter PLO, 28 December 1945'; 'Operational report by Major C. L. D. Newett, Carpenter Brown PLO, 19 December 1945', HS1/107, PRO.

68. 'Operational report by Major D. Sime AIF', n.d., HS1/107, PRO.

69. 'Operational report by D. R. W. Alexander, Sergeant GLO, 5 December 1945', HS1/107, PRO.

70. 'Operational report by Lieutenent Colonel I. S. Wylie, Carpenter GLO, 23 June 1945–18 October, 1945', HS1/107, PRO.

71. J. P. Hannah, 'MPAJA personalities 5th (Perak) Independent Regiment'; 'Operational report by J. P. Hannah Funnel GLO 27 February 1945–22 October, 1945', HS1/107, PRO.

72. For the account of the events that follow we are indebted, as are all historians of this period of Malaya's history, to Professor Cheah Boon Kheng. See 'The Japanese occupation of Malaya, 1941–45: Ibrahim Yaacob and the struggle for Indonesia Raya', *Indonesia*, 28 (1979), pp. 85–120.

73. Mustapha Hussain, 'Malay nationalism before Umno', ch. 28.

74. Mahmud bin Mat, *Tinggal kenangan: the memoirs of Dato' Sir Mahmud bin Mat* (Kuala Lumpur, 1997), pp. 271–98.

75. J. D. Legge, *Sukarno: a political biography* (Harmondsworth, 1972), pp. 181–202. In his dramatic account of the event, Legge does not mention the Taiping meeting, or Ibrahim Yaacob.

76. Mustapha Hussain, 'Malay nationalism before Umno', ch. 28.

77. From Itagaki's memoirs, quoted by Cheah Boon Kheng in 'The Japanese occupation of Malaya, 1941–45', p. 116.


CHAPTER 10 AUGUST 1945: AN END AND
A BEGINNING

1. Haruko Taya Cook and Theodore F. Cook (eds), *Japan at war: an oral history* (New York, 1992), p. 392.

2. Kenneth Harrison, *The brave Japanese* (London, 1967), pp. 258–68.

3. Preamble to A. M. Duncan-Wallace, 'Diary of a civilian internee in Changi, 1942–45', BMA, RCS.

4. Mamoru Shinozaki, *Syonan – my story: the Japanese occupation of Singapore* (Singapore, 1979), p. 95.

5. Heng Chiang Ki interview, OHD, SNA.

6. N. I. Low and H. M. Cheng, *This Singapore: our city of dreadful night* (Singapore, 1946), p. 165.

7. Frank Gibney (ed.), *Senso: the Japanese remember the Pacific war* (London, 1995), p. 164.

8. Patrick Hardie interview, OHD, SNA.

9. Lee Kip Lin interview, OHD, SNA.

10. Wong Yoon Wah, 'Yu Dafu in exile: his last days in Sumatra', in *Post-colonial Chinese literatures in Singapore and Malaysia* (Singapore, 2002), pp. 83–100. Thanks to Chua Ai Lin for this reference.

11. Lee Kip Lin interview, OHD, SNA.

12. Lee Kip Lee, *On amber sands: a childhood memoir* (Singapore, 1995), p. 164.

13. F. A. C. Oehlers interview; P. C. Marcus interview, OHD, SNA.

14. J. P. Hannah, 'The conference at Ipoh' n.d. [1946?], Appendix IV to Ban Kah Choon and Yap Hong Kuan, *Rehearsal for war: resistance and underground war against the Japanese and the Kempeitai, 1942–45* (Singapore, 2002), pp. 196–201.

15. Operational report by Major C. L. D. Newett, Carpenter Brown PLO, 19 December 1945, HS1/107, PRO.

16. Chin Peng, *My side of history* (Singapore, 2003), pp. 118–25.

# Bibliography

MANUSCRIPT SOURCES
Oriental and India Office Collection, British Library

Arnold Papers, Mss Eur F145
Assam Tour Diaries, 1945–6, Mss Eur D1191
Brayne Papers, Mss Eur F152
Burmese Politics Collection, Mss Eur D1066/2
Clague Papers, Mss Eur E252
Dash Papers, Mss Eur C188
Donnison Papers, Mss Eur B357
Dorman-Smith Papers, Mss Eur E215
Memoir of P. E. S. Finney, Mss Eur, D1041/4
'History of the Minami Organ' ('Minami Kikan Geishi' April 1944 by S. Mitsuru), Mss Eur C614
Khin Myo Chit, 'Many a house of life hath held me', Mss Eur D1066/1
Laithwaite Papers, Mss Eur F138
Lorrain-Foxall Papers, Mss Eur F185
McCall Papers, Mss Eur E361
Potter Papers, Mss Eur C414
Pearce Papers, Mss D947
Pinnell Papers MSS Eur D911/7
L. W. Russell Memoir, Mss Eur D1041/9
Margaret Stavridi Memoir, Mss Eur C808
Thein Pe Myint, 'Note to Indian Communists 1973, a critique of the Communist movement in Burma', Mss Eur C498
Tyson Papers, Mss Eur E341

Wallace Papers, Mss Eur E338
Walton Papers, Mss Eur D545
Wavell Papers, Mss Eur D977
Memoir of Virginia Westmacott, Mss Eur C394

## Centre of South Asian Studies, Cambridge

Abraham Papers
Barnes Papers
Benthal Papers
Sydney Bolt, 'Pseudo-Sahib'
P. D. M. Lingeman, Memoir
Ian Stephens Papers
E. T. Stokes Papers

## Royal Commonwealth Society Collection, Cambridge University Library

*British Association of Malaysia Papers:*
W. D. Brown papers
A. M. Duncan-Wallace, 'Diary of a civilian internee in Changi, 1942–5'
*The Changi Guardian*
Hartly Papers
M. C. Hay, diary
[Nakane] 'My Diary 1942'
H. R. Oppenheim diary
*Sarawak Gazette*
Sir Thomas Shenton Thomas, 'Malaya's war effort', July 1947

## Liddell Hart Centre, King's College, London

Hutton Papers
Messervy Papers
Penney Papers

# Imperial War Museum, London

Irwin Papers

# Rhodes House Library, Oxford

John Dalley Papers
Robert Heussler Papers

# Southampton University Library

Mountbatten and Edwina Mountbatten Papers

# British Empire and Commonwealth Museum, Bristol

Steel Brothers Records

# Franklin D. Roosevelt Presidential Library and Museum

Online resources: fdrlibrary.html

# Perpustakaan Universiti Sains Malaysia, Pulau Pinang, Malaysia

Microfilm collection: Office of Strategic Services, Research and Analysis Branch, No. 2072, 'Japanese Administration in Malaya', 8 June 1944.

# National Archives of Singapore

British Military Administration Headquarters, Singapore, 1945–6, BMA/ HQ
British Military Administration Chinese Affairs, Singapore, 1945–6, BMA/ CA

*Oral History Department, interviews, OHD:*
Dato Haji Mohamed Yusoff Bangs
P. K. Basu
George Bogaars
Frank Brewer
Richard Broome
Chan Chen Yean
Charlie Cheah Fook Ying
Dr Benjamin Chew
Elizabeth Choy
Robert Chong
Chu Shuen Choo
Damodaran s/o Kesavan
John Davis
Herman Marie de Souza
Gay Wan Guay
Goh Huan Bee
Patrick Hardie
Heng Chiang Ki
Ismail Zain
Victor Krusemann
Lan Khong Kon
Lee Kip Lin
Lee Tian Soo
P. C. Marcus
Abdealli K. Motiwalla
Dr F. A. C. Oehlers
K. M. Rengavajoo
C. T. Retnam
Mrs M. R. S. Segeram
Joginder Singh
Soon Kim Seng
Madame Zamroude Za'ba

*Microfilm collection:*
*Files from Australian War Memorial, Canberra (AWM):*
Edward William Burrey, 'A diary 1942–45: HQ Coy AASC, 8th Division AIF'
Lt.-Col. Roland Frank Oakes, 'Singapore Story', November 1947
'Escape report by Lt. M. M. Pillai and Lt. V. Radhakrishnan who left Singapore on 7 May 1942 and reached Delhi 25 August 1942', 25 August 1942

OFFICIAL PAPERS:
# Oriental and India Office Collection, British Library

Burma Office Papers: M/3
Governor of Burma's Office: R/8
Reforms Series: R/3
War Staff Files: L/WS/1 and 2
Judicial and Public Department: L/P and J/4 and 5
Burma Miscellaneous: L/P and O/4 and 9
Information Department: L/I/1

# Public Record Office, The National Archives, Kew, London

Colonial Office: CO273, CO323, CO717, CO825, CO875
Special Operations Executive: HS1
Foreign Office: FO371, FO916
Prime Minister: PREM4
War Office: WO106, 203, 208, 325

# Arkib Negara Malaysia, Kuala Lumpur

British Military Administration Administrative, 1945–6: BMA/ADM
British Military Administration Departmental, 1945–6: BMA/DEPT
Malayan Union Secretariat: MU
Perak State Secretariat: Pk Sec

# National Archives of Singapore

British Military Administration Headquarters, Singapore, 1945–6: BMA/
HQ
British Military Administration Chinese Affairs, Singapore, 1945–6: BMA/
CA

*Microfilm collection:*
Files from National Archives of Australia (NAA)
From series: CRS, DEF, FAR

Files from National Archives and Records Administration, United States (NARA)
From series: XL

## NEWSPAPERS AND PERIODICALS

*Amrita Bazaar Patrika* (Calcutta)
*Eastern Times* (Lahore)
*Far Eastern Survey*
*Greater Asia* (Rangoon)
*Leader* (Allahabad)
*Rangoon Times*
*Singapore Herald*
*Statesman* (Calcutta)
*Syonan Times/Syonan Shimbun* (Singapore)
*Times of Burma* (Rangoon)

## BOOKS, ARTICLES AND OFFICIAL PUBLICATIONS

Abu Bakar Hamzah, *Al-Imam: its role in Malay society, 1906–1908* (Kuala Lumpur, 1991)

Abu Talib Ahmad, 'The impact of the Japanese occupation on the Malay-Muslim population', in Paul H. Kratoska (ed.), *Malaya and Singapore during the Japanese occupation* (Singapore 1995), pp. 1–36

Abu Talib Ahmad, 'Japanese policy towards Islam in Malaya during the occupation: a reassessment', *Journal of Southeast Asian Studies*, 33, 1 (2002), pp. 107–22

Ahmad Boestamam, *Lambaian dari puncak* (Kuala Lumpur, 1983)

Aisha Akbar, *Aishabee at war: a very frank memoir* (Singapore, 1990)

Akashi, Yoji, 'Japanese Military Administration in Malaya – its formation and evolution in reference to sultans, the Islamic religion, and the Moslem-Malays, 1941–1945', *Asian Studies*, 7, 1 (1969), pp. 81–110

Akashi, Yoji, 'Japanese policy towards the Malayan Chinese, 1941–1945', *Journal of Southeast Asian Studies*, 1, 2 (1970), pp. 61–89

Akashi, Yoji, 'The Koa Kunrenjo and Nampo Tokubetsu Ryugakusei: a study of cultural propagation and conflict in Japanese occupied Malaya (1942–45)', *Shakai Kagaku Tokyo*, 23, 3 (1978), pp. 39–66

Akashi, Yoji, 'Lai Teck, Secretary General of the Malayan Communist Party, 1939–1947', *Journal of the South Seas Society*, 49 (1994), pp. 57–103

Akashi, Yoji, 'The Anti-Japanese movement in Perak during the Japanese occupation, 1941–45', in Paul H. Kratoska (ed.), *Malaya and Singapore during the Japanese occupation* (Singapore, 1995), pp. 83–118

Akashi, Yoji, 'General Yamashita Tomoyuki: Commander of the Twenty-fifth Army', in Brian Farrell and Sandy Hunter (eds), *Sixty years on: the fall of Singapore revisited* (Singapore, 2002), pp. 185–207

Akashi, Yoji, 'Watanabe Wataru: the architect of the Malaya Military Administration, December, 1941–March 1943', in Mohd. Hazim Shah, Jomo K. S. and Phua Kai Lit (eds), *New perspectives in Malaysian studies* (Kuala Lumpur, 2002)

Aldrich, Richard, *Intelligence and the war against Japan. Britain, America and the politics of secret service* (Cambridge, 2000)

Allan, Sheila, *Diary of a girl in Changi, 1941–45* (2nd edn, Roseville, NSW, 1999)

Allen, Louis, *Burma: the longest war* (London, 1984)

Allen, Louis, *Singapore, 1941–42* (2nd edn, London, 1993)

Amherst, Jeffery, *Wandering aloud: the autobiography of Jeffery Amherst* (London, 1976)

Andrew, E. L. J., *Indian labour in Rangoon* (Oxford, 1933)

Anon., *Two years of war: being a summary of important matters connected with the Indian Defence Services with special reference to the year 1940–1* (Delhi, 1941)

Anwar Abdullah, *Dato Onn* (Petaling Jaya, 1971)

Arasaratnam, S., *Indians in Malaya and Singapore* (London, 1970)

Arena Wati, *Cerpen Zaman Jepun* (Kuala Lumpur, 1980)

Arseculeratne, S. N., *Sinhalese immigrants in Malaysia and Singapore 1860–1990: history through recollections* (Columbo, 1991)

Atkins, David, *The reluctant major* (Pulborough, 1986)

Aw Yue Pak, 'The Singapore Overseas Chinese Salvation movement', in Foong Choon Hon (ed.), *The price of peace: true accounts of the Japanese occupation* (Singapore, 1991)

Ayer, S.A., *Unto him a witness: the story of Netaji Subhas Chandra Bose in East Asia* (Bombay, 1951)

Ba Maw, *Breakthrough in Burma: memoirs of a revolution, 1939–1946* (New Haven, 1968)

Ba Than, U, *The roots of the revolution* (Rangoon, 1962)

Baker, Maurice, *A time of fireflies and wild guavas* (Singapore, 1999)

Ban Kah Choon, *Absent history: the untold story of Special Branch operations in Singapore, 1915–1942* (Singapore, 2001)

Ban Kah Choon and Yap Hong Kuan, *Rehearsal for war: resistance and *underground war against the Japanese and the Kempeitai, 1942–45* (Singapore, 2002)

Bannerjee, Mukulika, *The Pathan unarmed* (London, 2000)

Bayley, Victor, *Is India impregnable?* (London, 1941)

Belden, Jack, *Retreat with Stilwell* (London, 1943)

Bhargava, Motilal, and Americk Singh Gill, *Indian National Army, secret service* (New Delhi, 1988)

Bilainkin, George, *Hail Penang!* (London, 1933)

Bix, Herbert P., *Hirohito and the making of modern Japan* (London, 2000)

Bjorge, Gary J., *Merrill's Marauders: combined operations in Northern Burma in 1944* (US Army Center of Military History, Washington, DC, 1996)

Blackburn, Kevin, and Edmund Lim, 'The Japanese war memorials of Singapore: monuments of commemoration and symbols of Japanese imperial ideology', *South East Asia Research*, 7, 3 (2001), pp. 321–40

Bose, S. K., and Sugata Bose (eds), *Subhas Chandra Bose, Azad Hind: writings and speeches 1941–1943*, Netaji Collected Works, vol. 11 (Calcutta, 2001)

Bower, Ursula Graham, *Naga path* (London, 1950)

Braddon, Russell, *The naked island* (London, 1952)

Brett-James, Anthony, *Balls of fire: the Fifth Indian Division in the Second World War* (Aldershot, 1951)

Brooke, Alan [Viscount Alanbrooke], *War diaries 1939–45*, ed. Alex Danchev and Daniel Todman (London, 1999)

Brookes, Stephen, *Through the jungle of death: a boy's escape from wartime Burma* (London, 2002)

Brown, J. M., *Gandhi: prisoner of hope* (New Haven, 1989)

Burchett, W. G., *Bombs over Burma* (Melbourne, 1942)

Burma Frontier Areas Committee of Enquiry. Cmd. 7138 (1947)

Callahan, Raymond, *The worst disaster: the fall of Singapore* (Singapore, 1991)

Chambert-Loir, Henri, 'Les Nationalistes Indonesiens vus par un romancier Malais: Shamsuddin Saleh', *Archipel*, 12 (1976), pp. 147–74

Chapman, F. Spencer, *The jungle is neutral* (London, 1949)

Chapman, F. Spencer, *Living dangerously* (London, 1953)

Charmley, John, *Duff Cooper: the authorised biography* (London, 1986)

Cheah Boon Kheng, 'The Japanese occupation of Malaya, 1941–45: Ibrahim Yaacob and the struggle for Indonesia Raya', *Indonesia*, 28 (1979), pp. 85–120

Cheah Boon Kheng, 'Sino-Malay conflicts in Malaya, 1945–1946: Communist vendetta and Islamic resistance', *Journal of Southeast Asian Studies*, 12, 1 (1981), pp. 108–17

Cheah Boon Kheng, *Red star over Malaya: resistance and social conflict during and after the Japanese occupation of Malaya, 1941–1946* (Singapore, 1983)

Cheah Boon Kheng, 'Japanese army policy towards the Chinese and Malay-Chinese relations in wartime Malaya', in Paul H. Kratoska (ed.), *Southeast Asian minorities in the wartime Japanese empire* (London, 2002)

Chelvasingham-MacIntyre, S., *Through memory lane* (Singapore, 1973)

Chin, Christina B. N., *In service and servitude: foreign female domestic workers and the Malaysian modernity project* (New York, 1998)

Chin Kee Onn, *Malaya upside down* (Singapore, 1946)

Chin Peng, *My side of history* (Singapore, 2003)

Clarke, Peter, *The Cripps version: the life of Sir Stafford Cripps* (London, 2002)

Cocteau, Jean, *Around the world again in 80 days (Mon premier voyage)* ([1936] London, 2000)

Collis, Maurice, *Last and first in Burma 1941–48* (London, 1956)

Connell, John, *Auchinleck: a biography of Field Marshal Sir Claude Auchinleck* (London, 1959)

Cook, Haruko Taya, and Theodore F. Cook (eds), *Japan at war: an oral history* (New York, 1992)

Cooper, Lady Diana, *Trumpets from the steep* (London, 1984)

Corner, E. J. H., *The Marquis: a tale of Syonan-to* (Singapore, 1982)

Crasta, John Baptist, *Eaten by the Japanese: the memoir of an unknown Indian prisoner of war* (Singapore, 1999)

Cunyngham-Brown, Sjovald, *Crowded hour* (London, 1975)

Danaraj, T. J., *Japanese invasion of Malaya and Singapore, memoirs of a doctor* (Kuala Lumpur, 1990)

Das, S. A., and K. B. Subbaiah, *Chalo Delhi! An historical account of the Indian independence movement in East Asia* (Kuala Lumpur, 1946)

Dawson, Thomas R. P., *Amusing sidelights on Japanese occupation (Malaya: January, 1942–August, 1945)* (n.p. 1946)

Donahue, Arthur Gerald, *Last flight from Singapore* (London, 1944)

Edwards, Jack, *Banzai, you bastards!* (London, 1990)

Elphick, Peter, *Singapore: the pregnable fortress* (London, 1995)

Elsbree, Willard H., *Japan's role in Southeast Asian nationalist movements, 1940–1945* (Cambridge, Mass., 1953)

Falconer, Jean, *Woodsmoke and temple flowers: memories of Malaya* (Edinburgh, 1992)

Falconnier, Henri, *The soul of Malaya* ([1931] Singapore, 1985)

Farrell, Brian, and Sandy Hunter (eds), *Sixty years on: the fall of Singapore revisited* (Singapore, 2002)

Fay, Peter Ward, *The forgotten army: India's armed struggle for independence, 1942–45* (Ann Arbor, 1992)

Fergusson, Bernard, *Beyond the Chindwin: behind the Japanese lines in Burma* (London, 1945)

*Financial and Economic Annual of Burma July 1943* (Rangoon, 1943)

Foong Choon Hon (ed.), *The price of peace: true accounts of the Japanese occupation* (Singapore, 1991)

Frei, Henry P., 'The island battle: Japanese soldiers remember the conquest of Singapore', in Brian Farrell and Sandy Hunter (eds), *Sixty years on: the fall of Singapore revisited* (Singapore, 2002), pp. 218–39

Fujita, Frank, *Foo: A Japanese American prisoner of the Rising Sun: the secret prison diary of Frank 'Foo' Fujita* (Penton, Tx, 1993)

Furnivall, John S., *Colonial policy and practice* (Cambridge, 1948)

Ghosh, K. K., *The Indian National Army: second front of the Indian national movement* (Meerut, 1969)

Gibney, Frank (ed.), *Senso: the Japanese remember the Pacific War: letters to the editor of Asahi Shimbun* (London, 1995)

Gilmour, O. W., *Singapore to freedom* (London, 1943)

Gilmour, O. W., *To Singapore with freedom* (London, 1950)

Goh Eck Kheng (ed.), *Life and death in Changi: the war and internment diary of Thomas Kitching (1942–1944)* (Singapore, 2002)

Gordon, Leonard A., *Brothers against the Raj. A biography of Indian nationalists Sarat and Subhas Chandra Bose* (New York, 1990)

Gough, Richard, *SOE Singapore, 1941–42* (London, 1985)

Gough, Richard, *Jungle was red: SOE's Force 136 Sumatra and Malaya* (Singapore, 2003)

Gould, Tony, *Imperial warriors: Britain and the Gurkhas* (London, 1999)

Grant, Ian Lyall, *Burma – the turning point: the seven battles on the Tiddim road which turned the tide of the Burma War* (Chichester, 1993)

Greenough, Paul, *Prosperity and misery in modern Bengal: the famine of 1943–1944* (New Delhi, 1982)

Greenwood, Alexander, *Field-Marshal Auchinleck* (Brockerscliffe, Durham, c. 1981)

Gupta, Partha Sarathi (ed.), *Towards freedom: documents on the movement for independence in India, 1943–1944*, Part I (Delhi, 1997)

Hamzah, Abu Bakar, *Al-Imam: its role in Malay society, 1906–1908* (Kuala Lumpur, 1991)

Harrison, Kenneth, *The brave Japanese* (London, 1967)

Havers, Robert, 'The Changi POW camp and the Burma–Thailand railway', in Philip Towle, Margaret Kosuge and Yoichi Kibata (eds), *Japanese prisoners of war* (London, 2000), pp. 17–36

Hino, Iwao, and S. Durai Rajasingam, *Stray notes on Nippon–Malaysian historical connections* (Kuala Lumpur, 2004)

Ho, Ruth, *Rainbow around my shoulder* (Singapore, 1975)

Ho Thean Fook, *Tainted glory* (Kuala Lumpur, 2000)

Hodgson, Barbara (ed.), *Letters from Harry: Malaya, 1941–42* (Durham, 1995)

Holman, Dennis, *Noone of the Ulu* (London, 1958)

Holman, Dennis, *The green torture: the ordeal of Robert Chrystal* (London, 1962)

Hsü, Marco C. F. (trans. Lai Chee Kien), *A brief history of Malayan art* (Singapore, 1999)

Hudson, Lionel, *The rats of Rangoon: the inside story of the fiasco that took place at the end of the war in Burma* (London, 1987)

Huxtable, Charles, *From the Somme to Singapore* (London, 1987)

Hwang Lian, 'Film distribution services for the last three years in Malaya', *Allied Screen Review*, 1, 1 (January, 1946)

*INA heroes: the autobiographies of Maj.-General Shahnawaz, Col. Prem K. Saghal and Col. Gurbax Singh Dhillon of the Azad Hind Fauj* (Lahore, 1946)

Indian Tea Association, *Indian Tea Association report on the evacuation of troops and civilians from Burma via the Pangsan route, Namyang River to Lekhpani, May to July, 1942* (Calcutta, 1944)

Insun, Mustapha (ed.), *Memoir Mustapha Hussain: kebangkitan nasionalisme Melayu sebelum UMNO* (Kuala Lumpur, 1999)

Iwaichi, Fujiwari, *F. Kikan: Japanese intelligence operations in Southeast Asia during World War II* (Singapore, 1983)

Jackson, E. L. J., *Indian labour in Rangoon* (Oxford, 1933)

Jain, Ravindra K., 'Leadership and authority in a plantation: a case study of Indians in Malaya (*c.* 1900–42)', in G. Wijeyewardene (ed.), *Leadership and authority: a symposium* (Singapore, 1968), pp. 163–73

Japanese Association in Singapore, *Prewar Japanese community in Singapore: picture and record* (Singapore, 1998)

Jeffrey, Betty, *White coolies* ([1954] London, 1971)

Jones, David H., *The rise and fall of the Japanese empire* (London, 1952)

Kamtekar, Indivar, 'The shiver of 1942', *Studies in History* (Delhi), 18, 1, n.s. (2002), pp. 81–102

Kathigasu, Sybil, *No dram of mercy* (Singapore, 1983)

Kazuo Tamayama and John Nunneley (eds), *Tales by Japanese soldiers of the Burma campaign 1942–5* (London, 2000)

Kennedy, Joseph, *British civilians and the Japanese war in Malaya and Singapore, 1941–45* (London, 1987)

Khan, Shah Nawaz, *The INA and its Netaji* (Delhi, 1946)

Kibata, Yoichi, 'Japanese treatment of British prisoners of war: the historical context', in Philip Towle, Margaret Kosuge and Yoichi Kibata (eds), *Japanese prisoners of war* (London, 2000)

Kinvig, Clifford, *Scapegoat: General Percival of Singapore* (London, 1996)

Kratoska, Paul H., *The Japanese occupation of Malaya, 1941–45* (London, 1998)

Kudaisya, Medha M., *The life and times of G. D. Birla* (Delhi, 2003)

Lau, Albert, *The Malayan Union controversy, 1942–48* (Singapore, 1991)

Leach, Edmund, *Current Anthropology*, 27, 1986, 4, pp. 376–8.

Lee, Cecil, *Sunset of the Raj: fall of Singapore, 1942* (Durham, 1994)

Lee Hock Chye, *Comfort homes and earlier years* (Kuala Lumpur, n.d.)

Lee Kam Hing and Chow Mun Seong, *Biographical dictionary of the Chinese in Malaysia* (Kuala Lumpur, 1997)

Lee Kip Lee, *On amber sands: a childhood memoir* (Singapore, 1995)

Lee Kuan Yew, *The Singapore story* (Singapore, 1998)

Legge, J. D., *Sukarno: a political biography* (Harmondsworth, 1972)

Leong, Stephen, 'The Kuomintang–Communist United Front in Malaya during the National Salvation period, 1937–1941', *Journal of Southeast Asian Studies*, 8, 1 (1977), pp. 31–47

Li Dun Jen, *British Malaya: an economic analysis* ([1955] Kuala Lumpur, 1982)

Lim Boon Keng, *The Great War from a Confucian point of view* (Singapore, 1917)

Lim Heng Kow, *The evolution of the urban system in Malaya* (Kuala Lumpur, 1978)

Lim, Janet, *Sold for silver* (London, 1958)

Lim Kay Tong, *Cathay: 55 years of cinema* (Singapore, 1991)

Lim Kean Siew, *Blood on golden sands: the memoirs of a Penang family* (Kuala Lumpur, 1999)

Lim Pui Huen, Patricia, and Diana Wong (eds), *War and memory in Malaysia and Singapore* (Singapore, 2000)

Lindsey, Timothy, *The romance of K'tut Tantri and Indonesia: text and scripts, history and identity* (Kuala Lumpur, 1997)

Lockhart, R. H. Bruce, *Return to Malaya* (London, 1936)

Low, N. I. and H. M. Cheng, *This Singapore (our city of dreadful night)* (Singapore, 1946)

McCall, A. G., *Lushai chrysalis* (London, 1949)

Macfarlane, Iris and Alan Macfarlane, *Green gold: the empire of tea* (London, 2003)

McHugh, J. N., 'Psychological warfare in Malaya, 1942–46', *Journal of the History Society of the University of Malaya*, 4 (1965/66), pp. 48–64

McHugh, J. N., *Words and phrases related to political organizations and procedure at meetings* (Kuala Lumpur, 1948)

McKie, R., *This was Singapore* (London, 1952)

MacNulty, Sir Arthur Salisbury (ed.), *The civil health and medical services, Vol II: The colonies, the medical services of the Ministry of Pensions, public health in Scotland, public health in Northern Ireland* (London, 1955)

Mahmud bin Mat, *Tinggal kenangan: the memoirs of Dato' Sir Mahmud bin Mat* (Kuala Lumpur, 1997)

Malaka, Tan, *From jail to jail*. trans. and intro. Helen Jarvis, vol II ([1946] Athens, Ohio, 1991)

Mansergh, Nicholas (ed.), *Constitutional relations between Britain and India. The transfer of power 1942–7*, vol. II: *Quit India 30 April–21 September 1942* (London, 1971)

Mant, Gilbert, *The Singapore surrender* (Kuala Lumpur, n.d. [1992])

Masters, John, *The road past Mandalay* (London, 1962)

Maung Maung, *To a soldier son* (Rangoon, 1974)

Maybury, Maurice, *The heaven-born in Burma* (Castle Cary, 1985)

Menon, K. R., *East Asia in turmoil: letters to my son* (Singapore, 1981)

Michiko, Nakahara, 'Labour recruitment in Malaya under the Japanese occupation: the case of the Burma Siam railway', in Jomo K. S. (ed.), *Rethinking Malaysia* (Kuala Lumpur, 1997), pp. 215–45

Michiko, Nakahara, 'Comfort women in Malaysia', *Critical Asian Studies*, 33, 4 (2001), pp. 581–9

Milner, A. C., *The invention of politics in colonial Malaya: contesting nationalism and the expansion of the bourgeois public sphere* (Cambridge, 1995)

Mitter, Rana, *The Manchurian myth: nationalism, resistance and collaboration in modern China* (Berkeley, 2000)

Montgomery, Brian, *Shenton of Singapore: governor and prisoner of war* (Singapore, 1984)

Moore, Michael, *Battalion at war: Singapore, 1942* (Norwich, 1988)

Morenweiser, Konrad, *British Empire civil censorship devices – World War II: British Asia* (London, 1997)

Mrazek, Rudolf, *Engineers of happy land: technology and nationalism in a colony* (Princeton, NJ, 2003)

Murfett, M. H., J. N. Miksic, B. P. Farrell and M. S. Chiang, *Between two oceans: a military history of Singapore from first settlement to final British withdrawal* (Singapore, 1999)

Murphy, H. B. M., 'The mental health of Singapore: part one – suicide', *Medical Journal of Malaya*, 9, 1 (1954), pp. 1–45

Nair, A. M., *An Indian freedom fighter in Japan: memoirs of A. M. Nair* (New Delhi, 1985)

Narayan, R. K., *My days* (Delhi, 1974)

Naw, Angelene, *Aung San and the struggle for Burmese independence* (Copenhagen, 2001)

Netaji Centre, Kuala Lumpur, *Netaji Subhas Chandra Bose: a Malaysian perspective* (Kuala Lumpur, 1992)

Nicolson, Harold, *Diaries and letters, 1930–67* (London, 1980)

Noone, Richard, *Rape of the dream people* (London, 1972)

Nu, U (Thakin), *Burma under the Japanese: pictures and portraits* (ed. and trans. J. S. Furnivall) (London, 1954)

Nu, U (Thakin), *Saturday's son* (Bombay, 1976)

Nunneley, John, *Tales from the King's African Rifles* (London, 2000)

Oatts, Balfour, *The jungle in arms* (London, 1962)

Oba, Sadao, *The 'Japanese' war: London University's World War Two secret teaching programme and the experts sent to beat Japan* (Sandgate, 1995)

O'Brien, Terence, *The moonlight war: the story of clandestine operators in Southeast Asia, 1944–45* (London, 1987)

Ong Chit Chung, *Operation Matador: World War II – Britain's attempt to foil the Japanese invasion of Malaya and Singapore* (Singapore, 2002)

Ong Siew Im, Pamela, *One man's will: a portrait of Dato' Sir Onn bin Ja'afar* (Penang, 1998)

Overy, Richard, *Why the Allies won* (London, 1995)

Palit, D. K., *Major General A. A. Rudra: his services in three armies and two world wars* (Delhi, 1997)

Pearn, B. R., *The Indian in Burma* (Ledbury, Herts., 1946)

Percival, A. E., *The war in Malaya* (London, 1949)

Pereira, Desmond, *The sun rises, the sun sets* (Singapore, 1993)

Pilcher, A. H., *Navvies to the Fourteenth Army* (Delhi, 1945)

Playfair, Giles, *Singapore goes off the air* (London, 1944)

Potter, John Dean, *A soldier must die: the biography of an oriental general* (London, 1963)

Prasad, B., *Official history of the Indian armed forces in the Second World War*, 4 vols. (Delhi, 1954–65), vol. I, *The reconquest of Burma*

Purcell, Victor, *Memoirs of a Malayan official* (London, 1965)

Purton, Ann, *The safest place* (Wells-next-the-Sea, 1982)

Reid, Caroline, *Malayan climax: experiences of an Australian girl in Malaya: 1940–1942* (Hobart, 1943)

Reisz, E. G., 'City as garden: shared space in the urban botanic gardens of Singapore and Malaysia, 1786–2000', in R. Bishop, J. Phillips and W.-W. Yeo (eds), *Postcolonial urbanism: Southeast Asian cities and global processes* (New York, 2003), pp. 123–48

Roff, William R., *The origins of Malay nationalism* (New Haven, 1967)

Rudolph, Jurgen, 'Amusements in the three "worlds"', in S. Krishnan et al. (eds), *Looking at culture* (Singapore, 1996)

Ruff-O'Herne, Jan, *50 years of silence* (Sydney, 1994)

Russell, Ralph, *Findings keepings: life, communism and everything* (London, 2001)

Russell-Roberts, Denis, *Spotlight on Singapore* (Douglas, 1965)

Sareen, T. R. (ed.), *Select documents on the Indian National Army* (Delhi, 1988)

Scott-Ross, Alice, *Tun Dato Sir Cheng Lock Tan: a personal profile* (Singapore, 1990)

Sein, Kenneth, and J. A. Withey, *A chronicle of the Burmese theatre: the great Po Sein* (Indiana, 1965)

Sen, M., *Rural Bengal in ruins*, trans. Chakravarty (Calcutta, 1945)

Shaw, William, *Tun Razak: his life and times* (Kuala Lumpur, 1976)

'A.J.S.T.' [A. J. Shelly-Thompson], *By-laws and history of the Lodge Johore Royal, No. 3946 E. C.* (Johore Bahru, 1922)

Sheppard, Mubin, *Tunku: his life and times* (Kuala Lumpur, 1995)

Shinozaki, Mamoru, *Syonan – my story: the Japanese occupation of Singapore* (Singapore, 1979)

Shwe Mra, U, 'Japanese interlude', *The Guardian: Burma's National Magazine*, vol. 13, no. 11 (Rangoon), November 1966, pp. 9–19

Silverstein, Joseph (ed.), *The political legacy of Aung San* (Ithaca, 1976)

Sim, Katherine, *Malayan landscape* (London, 1946)

Sim, Victor (ed.), *Biographies of prominent Chinese in Singapore* (Singapore, n.d. [1950])

Slater, Robert, *Guns through arcady: Burma and the Burma Road* (Madras, 1943)

Slim, Sir William, *Defeat into victory* (London, 1955).

Smith Dun, *Memoirs of the four-foot colonel: General Dun Smith, first commander-in-chief of the independent Burmese armed forces* (Ithaca, 1980)

Smith, Felix, *China pilot: flying for Chiang and Chennault* (London, 1995)

Smyth, Sir John, *The will to live: the story of Dame Margot Turner* (London, 1978)

Stilwell, Joseph W., *The Stilwell papers*, ed. Theodore H. Wright (London, 1949)

Stockwell, A. J., *British policy and Malay politics during the Malayan Union experiment, 1945–1948* (Kuala Lumpur, 1979)

Syed Naguib al-Attas, *Some aspects of sufism as understood and practised by the Malays* (Singapore, 1963)

Tai Yuen, *Labour unrest in Malaya, 1934–41: the rise of the workers' movement* (Kuala Lumpur, 2000)

Tan Chong Tee, *Force 136: story of a resistance fighter* (2nd edn, Singapore, 2001)

Tan Sooi Beng, *Bangsawan: a social and stylistic history of popular Malay opera* (Singapore, 1993)

Tan Thoon Lip, *Kempeitai kindness* (Singapore, 1946)

Tan, Y. S., 'History of the formation of the Overseas Chinese Association and the extortion by the J.M.A. of $50,000,000 military contribution from the Chinese in Malaya', *Journal of the South Seas Society*, 3, 1 (1946), pp. 1–12

Tanaki, Yuki, *Japan's comfort women: sexual slavery and prostitution during World War Two and the United States' occupation* (London, 2002)

Tarling, Nicholas, *A sudden rampage: the Japanese occupation of Southeast Asia, 1941–1945* (Singapore, 2001)

Tatsuro, Izumiya, *The Minami Organ* (Rangoon, 1981)

Telt, David, *A postal history of the prisoners of war and civilian internees in East Asia during the Second World War*, vol. I: *Singapore and Malaya, 1942–45 – the Changi connection* (Bristol, 2002)

Tewari, K. K., *A soldier's voyage of self-discovery* (Auroville, 1995)

Thein Pe Myint, *Wartime traveller* (Athens, Ohio, 1984); reproduced in R. H. Taylor, *Marxism and resistance in Burma 1942–5* (London, 1993)

Thivy, J. A. *The struggle in East Asia* (n.p., n.d.)

Thompson, Virginia, 'Malayan iron ore for Japan', *Far Eastern Survey*, 10, 11 (1941), pp. 130–1

Thumboo, Edwin (ed.), *The second tongue: an anthology of poetry from Malaysia and Singapore* (Singapore, 1976)

Tierney, Jane, *Tōbō: one woman's escape* (London, 1985)

Tinker, Hugh, 'The Indian exodus from Burma 1942', *Journal of Southeast Asian Studies*, 6, 1, 1975, pp. 1–22

Tinker, Hugh (ed.), *Burma: the struggle for independence 1944–1948*, vol. I: *From military occupation to civil government: 1 January 1944 to 31 August 1946* (London, 1983)

Toye, Hugh, *The springing tiger: a study of a revolutionary* (London, 1959)

Trager, Frank N., *Burma: Japanese Military Administration, selected documents 1941–5* (Philadelphia, 1971)

*Trained Nurses Association of India 50th anniversary volume, 1908–58* (Delhi, 1958)

Tsuji, Masanobu, *Singapore: the Japanese version* (London, 1962)

Tyson, Geoffrey, *India arms for victory* (Allahabad, 1943)

Uhr, Janet, *Against the sun: the AIF in Malaya, 1941–42* (St Leonards, NSW, 1998)

van de Ven, Hans J., *War and nationalism in China, 1925–45* (London, 2003)

Van Thean Kee, 'Cultivation of Taiwanese padi in Perak during the Japanese occupation', *Malayan Agricultural Journal*, 21, 1 (1948), pp. 119–22

Vickers, Adrian, *Bali: a paradise created* (Singapore, 1996)

Ward, A. H. C., Raymond W. Chu and Janet Salaff (eds), *The memoirs of Tan Kah Kee* (Singapore, 1994)

Ward, Ian, *The killer they called a god* (Singapore, 1992)

Ward, Ian, *Snaring the other tiger* (Singapore, 1996)

Warner, P., *Auchinleck: the lonely soldier* (London, 1981)

Warren, Alan, *Singapore, 1942* (London, 2002)

Warren, James Francis, *Ah Ku and karayuki-san: prostitution in Singapore, 1870–1940* (Singapore, 1993)

Williams-Hunt, P. D. R., *An introduction to the Malayan aborigines* (Kuala Lumpur, 1952)

Wilson, Harold E., *Educational policy and performance in Singapore 1942–1945* (ISEAS, Occasional Paper No. 16, Singapore, 1973)

Wong Yoon Wah, 'Yu Dafu in exile: his last days in Sumatra', in *Postcolonial Chinese literatures in Singapore and Malaysia* (Singapore, 2002), pp. 83–100

Wood, Maye, *Malay for mems* (Singapore, 1927)

Yamazaki, Tomoko, 'Sandakan No. 8 Brothel', *Bulletin of Concerned Asian Scholars*, 7, 4 (1975), pp. 52–62

Yap Pheng Geck, *Scholar, banker, gentleman scholar: the reminiscences of Dr Yap Pheng Geck* (Singapore, 1983)

Yeats-Brown, F., *Martial India* (London, 1945)

Yeo Song Nian and Ng Siew Ai, 'The Japanese occupation as reflected in Singapore-Malayan Chinese literary works after the Japanese occupation (1945–49)', in Patricia Lim Pui Huen and Diana Wong (eds), *War and memory in Malaysia and Singapore* (Singapore, 2000), pp. 106–22

Yong, C. F., *Tan Kah-Kee: the making of an Overseas Chinese legend* (Singapore, 1989)

Yong, C. F., *The origins of Malayan communism* (Singapore, 1997)
Ziegler, Philip, *Diana Cooper* (London, 1981)
Ziegler, Philip, *Mountbatten: the official Biography* (paperback edn, London, 2001)

## UNPUBLISHED STUDIES AND SOURCES

Fisher, Oscar Elliot, Diary of Japanese Invasion of Malaya, 11 and 12 December, 1941, http://freespace.virgin.net/sam.campbell/grandpa 1a.html

Grey, C. S., 'Johore 1910–1941: studies in the colonial process' (PhD, Yale University, 1978)

Halinah Bamadhaj, 'The impact of the Japanese occupation of Malaya on Malay society and politics, 1941–45' (MA thesis, University of Auckland, 1975)

Hewitt, A. R., Transactions of the Quatuor Coronati Lodge – craftsmen in captivity. Masonic activities of prisoners-of-war by Bro. A. R. Hewitt', dated 1 May, 1964, http://users.libero.it/fjit.bvg/prisoner.html

Lee, Karen and Li Yeng, 'Japanese occupation in Selangor, 1942–45' (BA Hons, Graduation Exercise, University of Malaya, 1973)

Liang, Clement, 'The Japanese in Penang 1880–1940', *The Penang File*, 28, http://thepenangfileb.bravepages.com/may-2003/histr282.htm

Lim Cheng Ean memoirs, *The Penang File*, http://thepenangfileb.bravepages.com

Mustapha Hussain, 'Malay nationalism before Umno: the memoirs of Mustapha Hussain, 1910–1957', translated by Insun Mustapha and edited by Jomo K. S.

Tan Meng Kiat, 'The evolution of the Nanyang art style: a study in the search for an artistic identity in Singapore, 1930–60' (M Phil. Hong Kong University of Science and Technology, 1997)

# Index

# FORGOTTEN ARMIES

*The Fall of British Asia, 1941 – 1945*

## CHRISTOPHER BAYLY AND TIM HARPER

In the early stages of the Second World War, the vast crescent of British-ruled territories stretching from India to Singapore appeared as a massive Allied asset. It provided scores of soldiers and great quantities of raw materials and helped present a seemingly impregnable global defense against the Axis. Yet, within a few weeks in 1941–42, a Japanese invasion destroyed all this, sweeping suddenly and decisively through south and southeast Asia to the Indian frontier, and provoking the extraordinary revolutionary struggles which would mark the beginning of the end of British dominion in the East and the rise of today's Asian world.

More than a military history, this gripping account of groundbreaking battles and guerrilla campaigns creates a panoramic view of British Asia as it was ravaged by warfare, nationalist insurgency, disease, and famine. It breathes life into the armies of soldiers, civilians, laborers, businessmen, comfort women, doctors, and nurses who confronted the daily brutalities of a combat zone which extended from metropolitan cities to remote jungles, from tropical plantations to the Himalayas. Drawing upon a vast range of Indian, Burmese, Chinese, and Malay, as well as British, American, and Japanese voices, the authors make vivid one of the central dramas of the twentieth century: the birth of modern south and southeast Asia and the death of British rule.

7299